Encyclopedia of Garden Ferns

Encyclopedia
of Garden Ferns

SUE OLSEN

TIMBER PRESS

Part title page illustration of *Asplenium trichomanes* by John E. Sowerby from *The Ferns of Great Britain* by John E. Sowerby and Charles Johnson, London, 1855.

Frontispiece: *Adiantum venustum* in the Bradner garden.

All photos by author unless otherwise stated.

Published in 2007 by
Timber Press, Inc.
The Haseltine Building
133 S.W. Second Avenue, Suite 450
Portland, Oregon 97204-3527, U.S.A.

www.timberpress.com

For contact information regarding editorial, marketing, sales, and distribution in the United Kingdom, see www.timberpress.co.uk.

Printed in China

Library of Congress Cataloging-in-Publication Data

Olsen, Sue (Suzanne)
Encyclopedia of garden ferns / Sue Olsen.
p. cm.
Includes bibliographical references and index.
ISBN-13: 978-0-88192-819-8
1. Ferns, Ornamental—Pictorial works. 2. Ferns—Pictorial works. I. Title.
SB429.O47 2007
635.9'373—dc22

2006013494

A catalog record for this book is also available from the British Library.

To my family—

My late husband, Harry,
Our three children, Greg, Kris, and Tamra,
Her husband, Karl,
And my sister, Jeanne

Adiantum aleuticum 'Subpumilum' in the Olsen garden.

Contents

Nature made ferns
for pure leaves, to show
what she could do in that line.
—Thoreau, unpublished

Polystichum polyblepharum

Foreword

What is there to see in a book of fern portraits? First of all there is the buoyant greenness of ferns, a refreshment for our eyes. And then there is the appeal of ferns to the artist in each of us, as endlessly varying sculptures of life. In a third sighting, ferns invite us to venture with them into the pre-human world they've come from, mighty time travelers that they are, arriving this morning as fresh and feisty as on the morning they have just now left—three hundred forty-five million years ago. It may be the presence of the Paleozoic that provides ferns their ultimate fascination. One can look at a fern as at a coelacanth, fastening on the anachronisms in its form (a little repellent in the fish, piquant in the fern), and see it as a life form of our time and yet eons distant.

Those are several of the qualities to be looked for in this book. There are, of course, others to be found by your own eyes and mind. The more than seven hundred fern portraits herein have been selected as the most telling from a collection of some twelve thousand images taken by Sue Olsen over decades—her best shots plus a few more that others of us have taken and given to the author, our friend.

Sue Olsen has been with ferns so long in so many ways—as a fern photographer, fern gardener, fern nurserywoman, and I daresay as a fern philosopher—I wouldn't be surprised if she were by now sprouting fronds at the shoulders where angels are known to sprout wings. There is undoubtedly a touch of the heavenly in a life with ferns.

George Schenk

George Schenk is a gardener by jet plane and has written books based on his international experience as a grower of a collection of plant species including many ferns. Aside from his gardening he operates a museum devoted to the tribal sculptures of northern Luzon in the Philippines.

Preface

Many years ago while querying me as a potential juror, an attorney asked about my nursery, Foliage Gardens. I told him that I was a fern grower and he responded, somewhat dismissively, "Ah, houseplants."

"No," I replied, "outdoor ferns."

"Oh!" said he, as my respect for his powers of observation plummeted, "I didn't know that ferns grew outdoors."

Ferns do indeed grow outdoors. There are approximately twelve thousand species worldwide and technically they all grow outdoors somewhere. They are presently found on every continent except Antarctica, and fossil evidence shows that two hundred million years ago they were growing there as well. Most are native to the tropics, where they thrive in lush abundance in warmth and humidity, but I have seen them in the wild (tree ferns at that) basking at the forward edges of imposing glaciers in New Zealand and settled in the protection of rocks in forbidding alpine terrains worldwide. Temperate ferns, which are the primary focus of this book, sweep in native magnificence across the Northern Hemisphere including North America, Eurasia, Japan, China, Korea, and the Himalayas. They are also well represented in the floristically rich Southern Hemisphere, especially New Zealand, South Africa, and Australia as well as at high altitudes along the spine of the Andes in Chile and Argentina.

In cultivation, ferns enjoyed a fashionable period in Victorian Britain before being replaced by another trend du jour. Horticulturally, they were then out of favor until an awakening of enthusiasm, accompanied by a renewal of literary attention, in the 1960s. International explorations and exchanges which provide an ever-increasing variety and availability have helped to establish a firm place for ferns in horticulture and gardens throughout the world today. The benevolent maritime climatic conditions, lacking extremes of temperatures (usually), that characterize the coastal U.S. Pacific Northwest and most of Britain are especially conducive to temperate fern cultivation. However, enthusiastic growers everywhere are establishing collections that are appropriate for their habitats, rewarding for their interest, and educational for all.

More than seven hundred of these ferns are illustrated and close to one thousand are described herein. My goal has been to present the ferns by illustration, information, and example so that they bring to you what I have sought for myself in doing research over the past forty years, and that is explicit help on identification along with cultivation guidelines, enriched where possible with anecdotal insights. The photos are all from 35-mm slides—no digital enhancement here! I use Fujichrome ASA 400 speed film and an Olympus OM4T camera with assorted lenses. By choice I never use a flash (it gives the subjects an artificial sheen) but do occasionally use a tripod.

As an editor I have read reviews over the years stating emphatically, "This is not a coffee table book," the implication being that such a work is somehow lacking substance. I would be happy to have this be a coffee table book, so long, that is, as you read it. And may it serve on the research shelf as well. Happy growing!

Acknowledgments

I am indebted to many talented and special friends and family members who have contributed advice and observations from their considerable knowledge, who have patiently offered welcome encouragement, and, for some, devoted many hours of time to the making of this book. Thank you does not begin to express my gratitude but I am indeed grateful to you all.

Very special thanks go to long-time friend George Schenk, who has kindly offered invaluable support, encouragement, and welcome advice throughout the entire process from writing to publishing. In addition he has contributed a delightful foreword and enriched the text with photos and his ever-lively written observations, presenting fresh information on tropicals that I could not have gotten from anyone else.

The line drawings are the work of multitalented Richie Steffen of the Elisabeth Miller Botanical Garden, who combines his artistic skills with his extensive knowledge of all plants, not just ferns. His contribution of slides includes selections from those taken around the world as well as diagnostic close-ups taken through the lens of a microscope.

Xeric specialist David Schwartz provided welcome observations and photos to expand the coverage of those challenging ferns. Pictures from Nils Sundquist of Sundquist Nursery, Poulsbo, Washington, give the reader a look at successful professional growing, and those from Naud Burnett and Kent Kratz of Casa Flora in Dallas, Texas, illustrate stages in tissue culture. Jim Baggett of Corvallis, Oregon, provided the detailed black-and-white photographs of rock garden ferns. Willanna Bradner offered her special art and computer skills to scan the two hand-colored prints. Thanks too to Graham Ackers, Joan Eiger Gottlieb, Richard Lighty, and Alan Ogden, all of whom donated photos.

I have been pursuing ferns and fern knowledge for decades and photographing them for almost as long. Many friends have welcomed me to their gardens where we have shared knowledge and good times. I am pleased to include pictures from some of these gardens including those of the late Don Armstrong, Jan and Jim Baggett, the late Mrs. Hugh Baird, the late Roy Davidson, Joyce and Fred Descloux, Joan and Milton Gottlieb, Yvonne and Russ Graham, Doris and Wayne Guymon, Joan and Jerry Hudgens, Sally and Richard Lighty, Carol and John Mickel, Marietta and Ernest O'Byrne, Milton Piedra, Rose Marie and Jack Schieber, Margaret and John Scott, Tom Stuart, Eve and Per Thyrum, and John van den Meerendonk and Karen Klein from the United States; Doreen and Clive Brotherton, Rita and the late Ray Coughlin, the late Reginald Kaye, Martin Rickard, and Jackie and Alastair Wardlaw of Great Britain; Erika and Ingo Carstensen, Ilse and Siegfried Förster, Wolfram Gassner, Ilona and Stefan Jessen, Margit and Christian Kohout, Sabine and Dietrich Nittritz, Berndt Peters, Eva and Helmuth Schmick, and Erika and Günter Stobbe all of Germany. And finally enthusiastic and warm thanks go to my special local supporters, Willanna Bradner, Sylvia Duryee, Jocelyn Horder, and Pat and the late Marilyn Kennar, whose beautiful gardens are always open and where I have always been welcome.

Botanical gardens and nurseries with their varied displays offer wonderful learning opportunities. I thank the following for permission to print photos from their gardens (and I also recommend a visit): Bellevue Botanical Garden, Bellevue, Washington; Birmingham Botanical Garden, Birmingham, Alabama; Bloedel Reserve, Bainbridge Island, Washington; Cornell Plantations, Ithaca, New York; Noel Crump Nursery, near Auckland, New Zealand; Dallas Arboretum, Dallas, Texas; Elandan Gardens, Bremerton, Washington; Elisabeth Miller Botanical Garden, Seattle, Washington; Elk Rock at the Bishop's Close, Portland, Oregon; the Flora and Botanical Gardens of Cologne, Germany; Hamburg Botanical Garden, Hamburg, Germany; Henry's Plant Farm, Snohomish, Washington; Institute of Ecosystem Studies, Millbrook, New York; Lakewold Gardens, near Tacoma, Washington; Longwood Gardens, Kennett Square, Pennsylvania; Lyndhurst (estate), Tarrytown, New York; Morris Arboretum, Philadelphia, Pennsylvania; Mount Cuba Center, Greenville, Delaware; New York Botanical Garden, Bronx, New York; Olbrich Botanical Garden, Madison, Wisconsin; Rhododendron Species Botanical Garden, Federal Way, Washington; University of California Botanical Garden at Berkeley, California; Washington Park Arboretum, Seattle, Washington; Wells Medina Nursery, Medina, Washington.

Many experts have generously assisted with information and I extend my sincere thanks to the following specialists for their notes and observations: Tony Avent, collection details on new introductions; Julie Barcelona, tropical identification; Dave Barrington, polystichums; Christopher Fraser-Jenkins, dryopteris and Asian species; Wolfram Gassner, Chad Husby, and Jürgen Schieb, for their pursuit of the correct identification on *Equisetum myriochaetum*; Chris Haufler, polypodiums and definitions of sporangiasters and nothospecies; Jim Horrocks, for years of research and helpful contributions with details on individual species for the *Hardy Fern Foundation Quarterly*; Richard Lighty for enlightenment on *Deparia*; David Johnson, matteuccias; Alan Ogden, for some philosophical additions; Martin Rickard, for guidance on tree ferns and *Pyrrosia*, and for carefully reading and making suggestions on the entire *Polypodium* entry; Keith Rogers for information on Australian gardens; Robert Stamps for commercial details on *Rumohra*; Tom Stuart for alerting me to newly published research, for checking herbarium material, and for providing information on apogamous ferns; Michael Sundue, for comments on distinguishing *Blechnum chilense* from *B. cordatum*; Alan Smith for a ready supply of help on assorted issues; and Alastair Wardlaw for in-depth descriptions of preserving tree ferns throughout the winter and for general information on *Pyrrosia*. Grateful thanks go to my German colleagues, especially Wolfram Gassner, Margit and Christian Kohout, and Berndt Peters, who have provided detailed information and helped with research on the extensive collections of plants they cultivate, many of which are rarely seen elsewhere and totally unavailable for study in the United States.

The appendices include recommendations for appropriate fern selections for various habitats across the climatic spectrum of North America, plus some from Britain, Germany, and Australia. I thank the colleagues who responded to the challenge of selecting "only twenty" of their favorite ferns. (For enthusiasts, this assignment is not nearly as easy as it sounds.) However, it is intended to be helpful for both the beginner and expert, and so I welcome the selections of Ralph Archer, Louisville, Kentucky; Tony Avent, Raleigh, North Carolina; Naud Burnett, Dallas, Texas; Joan Eiger Gottlieb, Pittsburgh, Pennsylvania; Catharine Guiles, New Brunswick, Maine; Robert and Robin Halley, San Diego, California; Sue Hollis, Kansas City, Missouri; James Horrocks, Salt

Lake City, Utah; Karen and Dan Jones, Birmingham, Alabama; Margit and Christian Kohout, Dresden area, Germany; Jean and Scott Lundquist, Niles, Michigan; Alan Ogden, Birmingham area, Britain; Berndt Peters, northern Germany; Martin Rickard, central England; Keith Rogers, Australia; Jack Schieber, Otto Heck, and John DeMarrais, mid-Atlantic states; David Schwartz, xerics in Bakersfield, California; Alan Smith, Berkeley, California.

I thank the board members of the Hardy Fern Foundation who have been enthusiastic and generous with their support, and especially Michelle Bundy who has given welcome help in many ways. I especially appreciate her work in compiling the lists of fern sources and sites.

Three very special friends have devoted a great deal of time and thought to the accuracy and progress of the book. I cannot begin to thank Ralph Archer of Louisville, Kentucky; Joan Eiger Gottlieb of Pittsburgh, Pennsylvania; and Tom Stuart of Croton Falls, New York, for the hours they devoted to reading the entire manuscript, in some cases several times, and for their valuable suggestions for improvement. In addition to their contributions of knowledge and encouragement, they went well beyond traditional proofreading expectations in many ways, including providing source material for practical help and verifying identification from herbarium and field sites (which sometimes involved quite a bit of travel). Each brought their special talents, with Ralph keeping a practiced eye on cultural requirements, Joan utilizing her keen skills on scientific and grammatical exactitude, and Tom applying his research interests and scientific capabilities in mining and sharing the resources of the Web and in giving logic to derivations. His Website, www.hardyfernlibrary.com, offers a wealth of comprehensive information and illustrates ferns hardy in USDA Zones 6 to 8 or 9.

I would like to respectfully recognize several friends who are no longer with us, but whose support over the course of many years, and especially during those of my early learning stages, encouraged me to continue the pursuit of all aspects of fern growing and knowledge and to make it an important part of my life. Dorothy Brauss, Neill Hall, Mareen Kruckeberg, Betty Miller, and Harriet Shorts, thank you for your mentoring and confidence.

Finally, my wonderful family members have been boosters for as long as I can remember. Son Greg and daughters Kris and Tamra have been my support team with their enthusiasm and positive feedback. In addition to their truly welcome encouragement, they have given tech support in keeping the computer on good behavior (even when the computer was not interested) and offering hours of editing, proofing, and secretarial relief with organizational tasks including compiling and recording information and creating assorted indices. To you I give my loving thanks. (And do not forget your first encounters with "*Asplenium dryopteris*"!)

Bellevue, Washington

Highlights of *Polystichum munitum*, from the Pacific Northwest, viewed and enjoyed for its reliable décor throughout the year: (from left to right) spring, summer, fall, and winter.

Portraits of Ferns
Through the Seasons

There is no season such delight can bring,
As summer, autumn, winter, and the spring.
—William Browne
"Variety," 17th century

Polystichum setiferum cultivar

Matteuccia struthiopteris in the Kennar garden.

Dryopteris erythrosora

Spring

The first call of Spring awakens the ferns. Before the last snow-banks have vanished from the shady hollows and while meadows are still bare and the woods deserted, the impatient young crosiers begin to stir the dead leaves.

—Willard Clute
Our Ferns in their Haunts, 1901

Adiantum venustum in the Kennar garden.

Dryopteris ×complexa 'Robust'

Dryopteris sieboldii

17

Summer green of *Dryopteris erythrosora* in the Horder garden.

The fern collection in summer in the Kennar garden.

Colorful fresh fronds of *Dryopteris lepidopoda* emerge throughout the season.

Summer

You will never learn to know the ferns if you expect to make their
acquaintance from a carriage, along the highway, or in the interval
between two meals. For their sakes you must renounce indolent habits.
You must be willing to tramp tirelessly through woods and across fields,
to climb mountains and to scramble down gorges.

—Frances T. Parsons
How to Know Ferns, 1899

New fronds of *Polypodium glycyrrhiza*
unfurling in summer in the Hoh Rain
Forest in western Washington's Olympic
National Park.

Woodwardia areolata at the Rhododendron Species Botanical Garden.

Autumn leaves settle on *Salvinia* in a pond in the Gottlieb garden.

Osmunda regalis 'Undulatifolia'

Autumn

There is no season when such pleasant and sunny spots may be lighted on, and produce so pleasant an effect on the feelings, as now in October.

—Nathaniel Hawthorne
American Notebooks, vol. 2

Athyrium filix-femina subsp. *angustum* forma *rubellum* 'Lady in Red' turns yellow for autumn.

Pteridium aquilinum along Snow Lake Trail, Cascade Mountains, Washington.

Matteuccia struthiopteris

Frosted *Blechnum penna-marina*.

Early snow catches *Gymnocarpium oyamense*.

Winter

When frost has clad the dripping cliffs
With fluted columns, crystal clear,
And million-flaked the feather snow
Has shrouded close the dying year;
Beside the rock, where'er we turn,
Behold, there waves the Christmas fern.
　　　—Willard N. Clute
　　　　Our Ferns in Their Haunts, 1901

Adiantum aleuticum 'Subpumilum'

Polypodium glycyrrhiza 'Malahatense'

Osmunda regalis 'Undulatifolia'

Polystichum acrostichoides (Christmas fern)

23

Spring fronds of *Osmunda regalis*, an ancient species.

Ferns Through the Ages

*F*erns grew in full sun three hundred forty-five million years ago when they were among the dominant plants on the planet. There were no trees to provide shade, and flowering plants were not to provide competition until two hundred million years later. Three hundred forty-five million years is quite a figure to contemplate, and adjusting to and surviving the earth's intervening vicissitudes is an incredible accomplishment that much of the flora and even the dinosaurs could not manage. According to fossil records and geological theory, the impact from an asteroid led to the extinction that doomed the dinosaurs sixty-five million years ago between the Cretaceous and Tertiary eras. It also led to a temporary (geologically speaking) fern spike as the fern flora rapidly filled the barren landscape and once again became the world's dominant plants.

Even as they apparently did historically, ferns today willingly colonize disturbed or burned areas. The reforestation on the 1980 volcanically destroyed flanks of Mount Saint Helens serves as a contemporary example. (Not surprisingly, *Equisetum* [horsetail] was among the leaders.) So it was that the ferns prospered and survive in variety today. Some, such as *Osmunda claytoniana*, believed to be the oldest continuously living fern species, can trace a family tree back two hundred million years. Others are, of course, younger (say two or three million years old, or about the same as humans). However, many of our most-familiar ferns are, at seventy-five million years old, truly juveniles, and one imagines that "new" ferns via hybridization or mutations are yet to come.

Ferns were once fairly uniformly distributed throughout the world, as evidenced by remnants of botanical relationships with prehistoric connections still in existence. On the land masses of the Southern Hemisphere, united before being separated by continental drift, South American blechnums have much in common with those of New Zealand. Eastern North American flora, including the ferns, has Japanese counterparts that were transported via ancient land bridges. Then as now, spores wafted on the air currents and were particularly significant in establishing island populations.

The uniformity of the world's floral distribution reached its zenith fifty million years ago when the earth was significantly warmer than today (envision tropicals in Greenland). It was interrupted as the ice ages developed. Plants migrated along with the warmth to the south and away from the glaciation. However, the upheavals of volcanic activity and the resultant creation of mountain ranges were influential here as well. In North America the uplifted mountains run north to south and consequently never presented a barrier to the southward floral shift or the forward movement and retreat of glaciers. In Europe the mountains run east to west, and the ice flows and plant survival were blocked resulting in a greater degree of plant extinction. As a direct effect the numbers of natives are far fewer in Europe than in the rest of the world.

Onoclea sensibilis once covered great areas of the earth.

Fern motif on a tombstone in Chudleigh, England.

In the social world, fern motifs appeared early in primitive artwork and have long been used in architectural ornamentation as well. By the mid 1800s, hand in hand with the fashionable interest in the live plants themselves, enthusiasm for ferns as art spilled into every opportune and marketable manifestation from decorating chamber pots to fine china. While not as extensive, their decorative uses continue to be popular today.

Scientifically, with their non-traditional reproductive system, ferns were very poorly understood botanically. Where were the flowers? And seeds? Speculation led to some fanciful theories, the most common being that the seeds, though there, were invisible. In turn this brought forth some magical connotations. Per the Doctrine of Signatures that gave life's issues and medical complaints a relationship with cures that were based on the visual attributes of plants, ferns with their "invisible seeds" offered, as oft quoted from Shakespeare (*Henry IV*, act 2, scene 1), the power to "walk invisible." First, however, one had to catch the elusive seeds or "fairy dust." Various theories, and one suspects a fair amount of revelry, surrounded the chase which was to be carried out on Midsummer Night's Eve with the sprinkling of the invisible seed powers showering and ready to be caught precisely at midnight.

Eventually, science caught up with the ferns. Their "dust" had long been noticed and sometimes confusedly considered as being pollen, but not otherwise related to

Ripe fern spores on the underside of a *Dryopteris* frond.

propagation. And, as accidents will happen (and someone must be alert enough to appreciate the significance), in 1794 John Lindsay, a British surgeon stationed in Jamaica, noticed that after rains quantities of ferns emerged from freshly disturbed soil (the best incubation sites in the wild for ferns today as well). Curious, he sprinkled some fern "dust" in a flower pot and soon discovered the development of the young plants', liverwort-like, small heart-shaped fertile structures, known scientifically as the gametophyte (sexual) generation. In time, these produced fronds, convincing Lindsay that he had found the "fern seed." He sent "dust" home to England along with sowing instructions, and fern propagation began in earnest at the Royal Botanic Gardens Kew as well as in horticultural and botanical circles throughout the country. Nurseryman Conrad Loddiges is credited with being an early proponent of carrying on propagation for commercial purposes and was the first to experiment with and recognize the value of shipping plants in Wardian cases some years later.

Although the discovery of the "seeds" answered some questions, true knowledge of the fern life cycle was yet several research stages later. In 1844 Karl von Nägeli, a Swiss botanist, observed and described the presence of sperms in the intermediate generation. The egg-producing female structure was in turn discovered in 1848 (and rather impressively, hybridization shortly thereafter in 1853). Thus the alternation of generations, as we know it today, became science.

The Wardian case, an unbelievably significant contribution to science, agriculture, and commerce, was probably as equivalent in importance to growers as the discovery of the life cycle was to botanists. Again its origins were accidental, this time the result of an entomology experiment by Britain's Nathaniel Ward in 1830. He had placed a moth chrysalis in a covered jar and some time later discovered two plants growing in mold in the jar. One was *Dryopteris filix-mas*, which, we are told, he kept alive without additional water for nineteen years. Although it is noted again and again in horticultural literature that Ward was not the first to experiment with an enclosure for growing plants, his promotion of the discovery must be credited as being the most consequential.

Glass enclosures were immediately recognized as beneficial protectors of plants from the ever-present smog of London, preparing the way for the ensuing fern craze. An industry of case-making, with some taking on elegant designs and proportions, followed. Meanwhile, their life-sustaining properties soon became of obvious commercial value enabling the transportation of plants around the world. (Prior import attempts, including the collections by Captain Bligh, yielded very poor survival rates, although Bligh actually brought back some live ferns.) Thus it was that the Wardian case carried tea plants from China to India establishing the huge tea industry there. Rubber plants were transported from South America to Malaya. In short, all manner of plants, including ferns, were protected on their long voyages from port to port enabling new and profitable agricultural industries to flourish. The system continued in its practicality until relatively recently when it was replaced by the ubiquitous plastic bag and derivations thereof.

A fancy British cultivar of *Polystichum setiferum* at Lakewold Gardens.

Britain's well-documented Victorian fern craze followed and brought ferns to widespread public attention. Collecting parties were the vogue, and unusual fern forms with various aspects of the foliage departing from the norm were especially prized. Hundreds made their way to the market, and an entire vocabulary developed to describe the abnormalities. Although many were subsequently lost to cultivation, cultivars in their assorted manifestations are popular and available to gardeners today.

In time the fern craze faded, perhaps from overexposure, and became subservient to other horticultural fancies. Happily, beginning in the 1960s, a balanced rejuvenation of horticultural interest in ferns returned and continues today, enriched by an ever-increasing body of knowledge, the support of enthusiasts along with their dedicated societies, and the ongoing introduction of varied plant selections from around the world. Long may it endure.

North American native ferns growing adjacent to a waterfall in a lightly shaded wild setting.

2

Cultivating Ferns

*F*erns today are the garden's graceful greenery. They are flowerless plants, reproducing by spores (which incidentally do not cause hay fever) rather than seeds.
(The asparagus fern with its little white flowers and red berries is actually a member of
the lily family.) So we grow them for their elegant foliage of varying heights, shapes,
and textures with an ornamental foliar structure that varies from the simple strap-
shaped fronds of the Hart's tongue fern (*Phyllitis scolopendrium*) to the plumose froth
of the finely divided British *Polystichum setiferum* cultivars. While newly planted ferns
must be kept moist, established ferns are a low-maintenance delight and, despite their
delicate appearance, are tough. Look for rhododendrons to curl and the grass to brown
before your ferns will signal trouble. They bring as their gift to the garden the serenity
of forest woodlands, peace in a shady nook, and the ability to give a unifying green
calm to a colorful garden palette.

There are ferns for every landscape situation from the
solitary pot on a patio to an aggressor for romping
through an abandoned meadow. Choose from diminutive charmers, evergreen and deciduous, through those
of intermediate heights to the dominant special effects of
several of the Goliath dryopteris and woodwardias (or
for warmer climates the tree ferns).

Woodland Gardens

In the woodland garden, ferns enjoy a site with filtered
light shade and soil[1] (not to be called dirt) enriched with
compost, humus, or the well-draining leaf mold associated with the undisturbed forest floor. Most species appreciate and thrive in acid soil that fortuitously occurs
naturally under a canopy of conifers with their annual
top-dressing droppings of lightweight needles.

A clay soil, while nutritionally dense, is problematic.
For most gardeners, it is easier to establish plants in

The evergreen *Polystichum neolobatum* is a reliable and
ornamental addition to temperate gardens.

---

[1] "Don't Treat Your Soil Like Dirt—'Free dirt'. Signs proclaim availability, but have you ever seen a sign offering 'Free Soil'? Of course
dirt is free. Anyone who's ever cleaned a house or tidied an old garage
knows that dirt costs nothing and arrives unbidden. . . . Dirt may be
composed of intriguing components such as old spider webs, insect
detritus, dog hair, and sweater lint, but it is never desired. Gardeners
crave and covet soil. The fragrance of a turned-over shovelful of soil in
early spring thrills the winter-bound soul. Soil-complex . . . has mineral, organic, and living elements combined. . . . [and] for gardeners
and lovers of tame and wild nature, it is soil not dirt in which all terrestrial life is ultimately rooted" (Kruckeberg and Robson 1999).

Native ferns offer serenity in the woodlands of the Bloedel Reserve.

Blechnum discolor along a woodland track in New Zealand.

Woodland planting in filtered shade in the van den Meerendonk-Klein garden.

raised beds (while not burying trunks of trees or shrubs) than to try to conquer the clay. The outmoded recommendation to dig a hole and fill it with good soil cost many plants their lives. Roots are unable to expand into the clay from such a planting site which will, however, attract all of the drainage from the surrounding clay and quickly turn to suffocating muck.

Mulch is one of the best gifts a gardener can give to ferns. I am often asked what fertilizer to apply to the fern bed and my answer is always that the best food is mulch. (If you do use chemicals, the application should be an evenly balanced 14–14–14, 20–20–20, for example, at half the manufacturer's recommended strength, and to prevent burning keep granular or slow-release material off the foliage, especially the fern's crown.) With mulching there are multiple benefits. Unlike chemicals, organic material helps to maintain a good loose soil texture while slowly decomposing and replenishing nourishment. With their low concentration of nutrition, mulches do not encourage excessive or weak growth that can invite problems including a feeding call to the neighborhood aphid population or a tendency for frond collapse in hot weather. In winter the soft carpet moderates

Mother Nature provides an ideal setting with a natural mulch under conifers in the Olympic National Park, Washington.

the temperature by adding a blanket of protection to the plants, increasing their cold tolerance. By contrast, in the summer it keeps the bed cool, reducing evaporation and the need for supplemental water.

Aged compost is an ideal additive, but leaves do splendidly as well. Oak leaves (shredded if need be) are excellent as they are acid in content, do not form an impervious mat, and break down slowly. In my garden, Japanese maples dominate the landscape and annually fill the garden with their fall litter. Before the emergence of spring growth I remove their deposits from the crowns of the ferns, but otherwise the leaves are left to compost at will. Conifer needles are another outstanding lightweight acid-yielding top dressing. Bark, meanwhile, is best left as a surface material for paths rather than mulch, unless it is obtained as aged compost.

Then regarding mulch, there is the "Olsen compromise" which is related to fern grooming. I have always preferred to leave the fronds on ferns for the purpose of replenishing the underlying soil. However, my late husband preferred the tidy look of groomed plants so we trimmed the fronds, ran them through a shredder, and returned them as mulch.

Trimming and grooming have both scientific and aesthetic considerations. Deciduous ferns are self-grooming, but the evergreens are not so inclined. Their fronds not only decorate the garden throughout the winter but also continue to produce food for the plant and protect the crown from the ravages of winter cold. Any shearing should be done in the spring. The least backbreaking and least labor-intensive system is to take the fronds off in bunches before the new foliage unfurls. For the maximum health benefit to the plant the best option is to leave fronds on until after the new growth has expanded. The extra boost of nutrition will create larger plants (which, however, if they are to be trimmed will need to be done individually, frond by frond . . . a great project for restless children). Much of the decision is determined by the number of ferns in the garden.

What we are able to cultivate is decidedly influenced by our climatic zone, usually governed by low winter temperatures, but many plants will grow in some parts of a hardiness zone but not in another part of the same zone. The explanation is an ongoing science, but several factors need to be considered. One is the length and temperature of the growing season. Short and/or cool growing seasons will not allow a plant to produce as much life-sustaining sugar as longer and warmer seasons. The more sugar, the better prepared a fern is to withstand winter cold.

Another contributing factor is the timing of late frosts in the spring. There is always an "exceptionally" late or early year, but repeated late frosts will in time take a toll on early emerging plants, reducing their vigor and sometimes killing them. Some garden centers sell a lightweight gauze that can be draped over sensitive plants when freezing temperatures are predicted. I have found this useful even in the middle of winter when exceptional cold is expected. Impromptu solutions include tossing a pillowcase over vulnerable plants (not just ferns). One year when we had a severe and extended cold spell my entire neighborhood had plants covered with all manner of sheets and assorted coverings. It looked as if we were having a huge winter white sale.

Hot summer weather presents its own set of challenges—drought, in a word, being one. Dry plants are more vulnerable to damage and foliar loss. Again mulch is extremely beneficial, but watering is also necessary, and once the soil is dry it takes longer to rehydrate. I do stress my plants, however, forcing them to reach their roots down for water and reduce the need for supplemental sprinkling. Some areas of my garden, never get watered and have adapted to the neglect. Of course, that is not where I locate my prize specimens. Watering early in the morning cools the soil surface at least temporarily and more water reaches the roots rather than evaporating in the heat. Water infrequently but deeply and try to keep water off the foliage during daylight hours so that the magnified sun's rays do not scorch the plant.

Deciduous trees such as oaks, dogwoods, Japanese maples, birches, and shagbark hickories all provide a lightweight canopy that encourages good health in the fern community. Those with creeping surface roots such as cherries are manageable but will greedily absorb moisture and nourishment. Beware also of beeches, native maples, walnuts, and all trees with invasive roots. While conifers clearly offer shade (which can sometimes be too dense) and beauty and create their own light mulch, beware of their ever-thirsty roots. Supplemental watering keeps both tree and fern happy, although with cedar trees even extra water will not be of much help.

Preferences for planting times vary. Fall is recommended in the Pacific Northwest and spring is preferred by many East Coast gardeners. However, ferns can be planted whenever the garden soil is workable, meaning soft but not soggy. Warm soil temperatures at any time encourage root growth thus giving the plant a head start. However, with spring or summer planting the first summer requires extra attention to watering while the plant gets established.

Another increasingly common transplanting issue involves polystichums that over the years may form pseudo-trunklike bases. This problem occurs with a number of the Japanese species that are ornamental but are not to be confused with tree ferns. As the old fronds drop, the new growth emerges from above the stipe stubs so that eventually the crown is well above the soil. These ferns are weakened and for optimum health should be replanted so the crowns are reestablished at soil level. Or, while less aesthetic, soil can be mounded up to protect the frond base. Otherwise, the plant gradually loses vigor and is likely to be short-lived.

Fern Colors

Ferns may be without flowers, but in their own special way many of them do have color. Lives there a gardener who does not find joy and inspiration as the garden awakens in springtime? Hepaticas, daffodils, primroses, and rhodies, usually in that order, bring life to the garden as well as the gardener. Foliage, while more subtle, enriches the springtime composition as well. And what are ferns but foliage? Fern lovers take delight in the unfurling new fronds that invite inspection and appreciation. Sturdy *Polystichum* crosiers emerge cloaked in coats of silver scales offering the garden design an especially striking duet in combined plantings with the matching whitish new foliage on indumentum-clad rhododendrons.

Dryopteris decorate their fiddleheads with scales in blackish, rust, and bronze hues, elegant with backlighting. Many species (although strangely none from Europe) unfurl with colorful new growth. These include the statuesque *Dryopteris wallichiana* (Wallich's wood

Decorative silvery spring crosiers of *Polystichum*.

Rosy spring color on the autumn fern, *Dryopteris erythrosora*.

fern) with vibrant yellow to orange fronds accented by dark scales. The lower-growing, 2-ft. (60-cm) *D. lepidopoda* (sunset fern) displays satiny, warm coral-colored spring foliage, while *D. erythrosora*, the popular autumn fern and its cultivars, unfurl in a rosy copper frost that in time fades to rich green. *Dryopteris koidzumiana*, new in cultivation, has saturated, velvety russet new growth.

The sturdy little *Blechnum penna-marina*, an 8-in. (20-cm) creeper, has red new growth as well. It is especially pronounced when planted in the sun where it will display the compact fronds typically seen in its alpine homelands of Chile and New Zealand. For this species, shade encourages rangy growth.

On a larger scale new growth on several woodwardias and a number of the taller New Zealand blechnums is suffused with blood-red vibrancy. The best of the woodwardias (*Woodwardia unigemmata* and *W. orientalis* var. *formosana*) may be on the tender side but are unfailingly ornamental. Give them affectionate care which includes protective attention in the depths of the bleak midwinter. All of the above are evergreens and join with other colorful individuals described in the text.

Several common deciduous Japanese athyriums offer distinctive color that lasts throughout the season. *Athyrium niponicum* 'Pictum', the popular and variable Japanese painted fern, is indeed painted in pastel shades of gray, pink, pale green, some blue, and wine. It is extremely hardy and gives life to somber shade. Names are being given to an ever-increasing, and probably excessive, number of cultivars including, among others, 'Silver Falls', 'Burgundy Lace', 'Ursula's Red', and a crested form, 'Apple Court'. In addition, 'Ghost' and 'Branford Beauty', two presumed hybrids with the American lady fern, add a soft gray contrast to dark green compositions. All make a stunning

The red-saturated new growth of *Woodwardia unigemmata* in complimentary tandem with the polished green of *Beesia deltophylla* in the Duryee garden.

statement when grouped together. (For additional impact add a plant or two of *Brunnera macrophylla* 'Looking Glass' or 'Jack Frost' to the composition.) While less flamboyant, the matte fronds on *Athyrium otophorum* (eared lady fern) bring a refreshing combination of lime foliage suffused with plum highlights. *Athyrium yokoscense* with its understated silver foliage adds a welcome quiet touch when centered among brilliant companions.

Silvers and pinks enhance the frond of *Athyrium niponicum* 'Pictum'.

Fern Pests

In general, pests are not a threat to ferns. Slugs and snails, never ones to miss a treat, occasionally chainsaw new spring growth, so precautions should be out early in the season. Bait should be broadcast about rather than positioned as a dinner bell adjacent to a vulnerable plant. Improved baits include several that remain potent after being wet and do not affect bird populations. Traps with assorted lures, including beer and coffee grounds, are efficient, but not particularly attractive to clean.

Aphids will land periodically and are more dangerous for their tendency to spread diseases than for eating foliage. Leafhoppers (arriving in 1998 in Washington State) appear on selected species and cultivars and can disfigure foliage, especially of the assorted and plentiful *Dryopteris* cultivars. These pests can be restrained, but so far not controlled, with the judicious application of a systemic insecticide. Oil-based sprays suffocate ferns and should never be used near them. I have also had poor luck with soap-based remedies. Light applications of other commercial products, especially those containing resmethrin have not harmed my ferns. All chemicals should be used with caution and tested on a nonvaluable plant (bracken perhaps) before applying them to anything special. Finally, I recommend limiting the application to the infected plant rather than spraying the entire garden to clean a few plants of their bugs, but then I am one who would rather not spray at all.

Deer populations, especially on the U.S. East Coast, are a serious garden and personal (Lyme and other disease carrying) menace, although unless really starving will generally leave ferns alone. (They tend to prefer roses and other ornamentals.) How-

A moat, the ultimate weapon against the ever-present threat of slugs, protects select plantings in the Gassner garden. Photo by Richie Steffen, Miller Botanical Garden.

ever they will eat whatever necessary to stay alive and, in spite of many imaginative repellent concoctions, will only avoid gardens when fenced out by a barrier at least 6 ft. (2 m) tall. Rabbits, meanwhile, consider the fern garden their personal salad bar and can and will demolish a collection over night.

Given these basics, most of the temperate ferns described in this book should provide years of beauty in the woodland. An exception must be made for ornate cultivars, however. I am talking about varieties with epithets such as cristatum (crested), capitatum (with a head or large crest), ramosum (branched), ramo-cristatum, and grandiceps (with a large terminal crest). These are the soloists of the crowd. Far be it from them to harmonize in the woodland chorus. Treat them as specimen plants, placing them center stage if you choose or in a featured pot somewhere.

Fern Companions

Once upon a time, a very long time ago, I considered my ferns to be companion plants for my rhododendrons. Now, of course, the rhododendrons are the companion plants for my ferns. With their similar cultural requirements, they do indeed complement each other. There are many other options for the woodland floor, however, and here are some of my favorites. *Helleborus niger* and *H. orientalis* and their hybrids contrast splendidly with ferny foliage and in my garden offer a floral bouquet from early winter through spring. *Helleborus orientalis* hybrids come in many colors and new strains, including some with double flowers that are the focus of current breeding programs. They need an annual grooming but are evergreen and easy.

Varied colors of hybrid hellebore floral offerings liven the winter garden.

Hosta sieboldiana 'Elegans' offers a bold contrast to the lacy architecture of ferns.

Both deciduous and evergreen epimediums are becoming available in an increasing assortment of foliar and floral colors. They too benefit from an annual shearing, but are extremely durable and desirable ground covers and, once established, will tolerate difficult areas of dry shade. I happen to be partial to those that produce red-tinged new leaves and find them particularly attractive with the rosy new fronds of *Dryopteris erythrosora*. (Back this up with a red-flowering or red-leafed rhododendron for a splendid spring picture.)

Hostas with their varied and sometimes bold leaves are favorites and make outstanding foils for the delicate tracery of fern foliage. They have compatible soil, shade, and moisture requirements and range in size from miniatures to giants. Unfortunately they have a tendency to attract slugs (so do not plant them near your aspleniums), but new strains are likely to be more resistant.

Heucheras, available in ever-increasing abundance, attract hummingbirds with their flowers while providing interesting foliar patterns. Unusual color combinations feature silvers and burgundies with assorted shades of green. Most heucheras require strong light for a healthy appearance. *Athyrium niponicum* 'Pictum' (Japanese painted fern) is stunning when planted with some of the shiny deep black-red cultivars, such as *Heuchera obsidian*.

Arisaemas, the Jacks-in-the-pulpit and friends with their unique habit and definitely unique "flowers," give

A bouquet of *Adiantum venustum* and *Cyclamen hederifolium* in the fall garden.

an added interest in the shade and do not challenge ferns for territory. They look best when embraced in foliage, however. A solitary plant is a lonely plant indeed. Regardless of how and how often they are planted, many of mine have a disconcerting tendency to turn their backs on their audience the following spring. *Arisaema sikokianum*, one of my favorites, consistently hides its loveliness in this manner. I now have mine planted in pots which I can locate so that their features face the footpath rather than the backside of the carport.

Asarums, likewise not common but increasing in popularity and surely attractive, have rather weird flowers bashfully concealed under the foliage and make excellent foliar and noncompetitive contributions to the woodland. Some of the best are *Asarum canadensis*, *A. europeanum*, *A. speciosum* (synonym *Hexastylis speciosa*), and *A. splendens*. Newly imported material, especially from Japan, has tremendous horticultural potential. Hardy cyclamen are durable and doable for late-summer and winter interest. Specifically, *Cyclamen hederifolium* will bloom for months and provide ground covering interest throughout the winter. It deserves and receives much praise.

Primroses and ethereal spring wildflowers, especially hepaticas, are immensely suitable as companions. Beware of that charmer the violet, however, which once acquired, while beloved, is yours forever. Finally, but not conclusively, I recommend the low-growing gaultherias,

Arisaema sikokianum adds variety to the woodland composition.

The welcome faces of diminutive hepaticas bring the promise of spring.

A woodland fern community, including *Lycopodium*, and its charming companion creeping dogwood (*Cornus canadensis*) on a mountain slope in Canada.

all of which are evergreen with many prostrate (or nearly so) and very choice. Choose, depending on your climate, from *Gaultheria procumbens*, *G. nummularioides*, *G. sinensis*, and *G. shallon* among others. Most of the above, with the exception of the last three gaultherias are suitable for Zone 5 and up.

I hope the reader has noticed that several well-known garden plants are missing from this list (deliberately). Among them the worst offender is ivy, *Hedera*, in its many invasive manifestations. English ivy (*H. helix*) will choke trees, not to mention overrun the choicest ferns, and is listed as an invasive weed in many regions. *Euonymus fortunei*, especially var. *coloratus*, can be just as overpowering, taking years of labor to eradicate once established. Popular ground covers including *Pachysandra*, *Ajuga*, *Vinca*, and *Oxalis* can smother delicate fern plantings. Unpopular ground covers also cause problems and some such as the western U.S. native *Maianthemum dilatatum* take on a life of their own, even when challenged by herbicides. Make your life easy and keep these out of the garden in the first place.

Containers

There are many excellent reasons for planting ferns in containers. With the current trend toward living in apartments and condos, gardening on decks, patios, and indoor sites becomes the only opportunity for foliar enrichment and the attendant nur-

Tree ferns and fuchsias in a large container collection at Longwood Gardens.

Equisetum hyemale, restrained (as it should be) in a container, grows in wet soil in the company of sarracenias.

turing instincts of plantfolks. Options for planting vary widely and include entire landscapes complete with trees and shrubs down to that favorite specimen plant which is frequently displayed at its best when containerized

Choose container culture for a myriad of special situations: close-up viewing of unique or rare specimens (and for a bit of horticultural braggadocio here), for species that have special soil requirements, for hobbies such as bonsai, for containing aggressive but, depending on one's taste, interesting collector's plants (*Equisetum* comes to mind), for portability of questionably hardy treasures that need to be moved for winter protection, or just for the joy of displaying and admiring a collection of plants that one would like to rearrange for seasonal decoration.

Recorded flower pot culture goes back to Good Queen Hatshepsut of Egypt who ruled from 1503 to 1480 B.C. and sent, in 1495 B.C., information gatherers, including designated plant collectors, rowing and sailing for the Land of Punt (now Somalia) in what is believed to be the world's first oceanographic expedition. The explorers returned with an eclectic collection including, among other things, assorted fish (that based on temple drawings at Deir el Bahri can be identified down to the species level today), as well as ebony, ivory, frankincense, AND, in clay pots, plants of the myrrh-producing incense tree. Pots, clay and otherwise, have carried treasures and introductions from afar ever since.

Wheelbarrow as a container for a refreshing mixed planting. Photo and planting by George Schenk.

Modern containers come in all sizes and designs, limited only by the imagination. The clay pots of yore, however, molting by inclination in winter frosts, have in many areas been supplanted by glazed ornamentals. Hypertufa troughs constructed with peat and cement, and carefully cured, are widely used to give a rustic appearance for the optimal display of alpine plants. Potential candidates for tufa culture should be chosen with care and caution, however, as the pot will leach small amounts of lime. Concrete pots, with the exposed aggregate styles being especially handsome, also slowly release lime into the soil. Wooden containers including the popular half whiskey barrels serve handsomely where a less formal effect is desired. They have a shorter life span but can be sealed with a wood preservative to prolong their usefulness. (Be sure to let it cure for at least a week before adding soil and plants.) For the specialist, little pots are appropriate for bonsai. (And yes, ferns of all sizes will reduce proportionately in pot culture.) In the whimsy class almost anything can pose as a container. I have seen old rowboats, boots, and retired wheelbarrows all carrying the gardener's treasures.

Baskets too are containers of sorts and popular for the ever-present Boston fern types. Many rhizomatous ferns display well in basket culture, the rhizomes themselves adding interest to the composition. In addition to the numerous nephrolepis cultivars, pyrrosias, davallias, certain lycopodiums, and especially polypodiums, and their near relatives are strongly recommended for both indoor and outdoor features.

Lycopodium trails from a basket perch at Longwood Gardens.

Ferns and a rhododendron grow under *Acer palmatum* 'Chishio' in a containerized landscape.

The baskets are usually lined with sphagnum moss, but the newly available coconut by-products marketed variously as coir or coco-fiber inserts literally help the baskets and their contents to hang together. (I do not like coir as a soil additive or substitute, but it has no apparent ill effects as a basket liner.) A plastic saucer installed at the basket's bottom and used with the coir allows for more leeway between watering sessions. Traditionally, the basket's skeleton has been wire that, although many plastic shapes are now available, is still eminently suitable.

With good horticultural husbandry, basket specimens will in time need to be extracted from their confinement. Short of major surgery, it is far easier and clearly kinder to the basket resident to take the cutting shears to the container rather than the plant, hence wire is preferred. Plastic baskets with their resplendent durability serve admirably well until this point of required expansion.

Choose the container size with care, however, as ferns do not like to be overpotted. Without root penetration, surrounding soil will sour and eventually so will the fern. Give them companions or a root-ball appropriate-sized container and, when potting on, gradually move them up to larger sizes. For dryland ferns and those that require excellent drainage, tall narrow pots improve drainage.

Aside from those mixes selected for specific soil requirements, normal, good draining, rich fern compost, with an emphasis on compost, will keep the container and contents in good health for many years. If you do not already have a favorite mix, try one part peat, one part washed pumice, a sprinkling of bark for drainage, and four parts compost or commercial soil mix. It is important to give the pumice a fierce hosing to wash away the talclike "fines" that will otherwise bind the soil and rob the container of life-giving oxygen pockets. Beware of an excess of peat, too, as once dry it is incredibly difficult to rehydrate. More than once I have seen pots soaking in improvised bathtubs for rehab.

A saucer placed under the container for the summer serves as a potential reservoir and drought preventative, especially since a dry pot will drain water down the edges without ever watering the planting. A top dressing will aid in keeping a pot moist and can be soil specific, such as marble chips for lime lovers. Meanwhile, keep your ferns watered. Watering in the wintertime is redundant unless dealing, such as we sometimes do by choice, with xerics deliberately placed out of the path of winter wet.

Attention to feeding is also a requirement in container culture. Good soil preparation enhanced occasionally with mulch will give garden-sited ferns years of contented vigor. By contrast, a container planting, including those sitting around in nursery pots waiting to be planted, will deplete nourishment and display displeasure with attendant poor growth and color unless periodically enriched. As with any feeding, my recommendation is for an evenly balanced, complete fertilizer applied at half the manufacturer's recommended strength. A spring infusion with a water-based fertilizer spray helps to get fronds up and about in vigorous health. Coated slow-release fertilizers that are blessedly easy to apply and last for months, but are heat-based for release, are best used as a supplement in early summer depending on your climate. Do keep granular, including slow-release, fertilizers off of the ferns' crowns and foliage to prevent burning or disfiguring. And as another precaution avoid late-summer applications of any fertilizers for garden or container as they encourage late growth that is vulnerable to the vagaries of fall and winter weather.

Finally, for the sake of drainage and for the health of the understory, pots of any type that will sit on a wooden surface are best raised with small tiles or those funny little feet sold in garden centers to save the wooden surface from the trouble of rotting.

Mounted Ferns

By George Schenk

Shingles (also known as slabs or plaques) cut from tree fern trunks and usually sold as mounts for epiphytic orchids serve equally well as supports for epiphytic ferns and fern relatives including *Drynaria, Lycopodium, Belvisia, Pyrrosia, Asplenium nidus, Polypodium,* and *Davallia.*

The makers of tree fern shingles saw their product into rectangular or irregular shapes and sizes. Shingles about 7 or 8 inches (18 or 20 cm) wide and 10 or 11 inches (25 or 28 cm) long are serviceable for most ferns growable as mounts. A shingle thickness of ¾ inch (19 mm) is typical; avoid thinner shingles. Tree fern shingles resist decay, even with the constant watering of the plants they hold, and usually remain sound for many years.

Press the fern's roots cushioned with moss and packed with humus to the shingle and attach with slim galvanized wire (about number 10 caliper). The texture of a tree fern shingle is meshed and porous, like that of shredded wheat breakfast cereal or of a steel wool scouring pad, and in any case easily pushed through with the ends of a short length of the wire, which are then to be twisted together at the back side of the mount to hold the fern securely. Before cinching the wire at back, stuff a couple of handfuls of leaf mold or of some other fibrous humus between the fern's root mass and the shingle at front. An additional short length of wire pushed through the shingle near its top will serve as a means of hanging the mounted fern on a shaded fence, wall, or door. The bare wire is a little unsightly and can be concealed by tucking moss around it. For a good-looking picture frame effect, use rattan, rawhide, or twine rather than wire.

Shingled ferns growing outdoors appreciate daily watering with a garden hose, or a splash from a bucket-and-dipper. Here in the Philippines, I also grow a number of shingle-mounted ferns as houseplants hung on walls of pine boards; these ferns receive water from a spray bottle. My houseplant ferns on shingles (*Asplenium, Drynaria,* and others) are actually part-timers—two weeks indoors, two weeks out—in rotation with others of their kind. All of the mounted ferns are fertilized every several weeks (I am not at all exacting about the schedule, although maybe I should be) with a complete fertilizer containing trace elements; the kind I use comes as a wettable powder.

Rock Gardens

Rock gardening began in China and Japan where the focus was on rocks and their formations rather than plants. The definition and style changed and eventually spread especially and initially to horticulturally enlightened Britain (as with so much of our horticulture, we are indebted to Britain). The first large-scale rock garden was constructed there at the Chelsea Physic Garden in 1772–73 with 40 tons of Portland limestone left over from the rebuilding of the Tower of London "combined with chalk flints and some basaltic lava brought back from Iceland by Sir Joseph Banks" (Cabot 1984). Eventually, the style migrated to America. The Brooklyn Botanic Garden built the first public rock garden in 1916 with another completed shortly thereafter at the New York Botanical Garden. Interestingly, in the Pacific Northwest one of the first to embrace the movement was Else Frye, whose husband, a botanist at the University of Washington wrote, in 1934, the first popular book on regional ferns, *Ferns of the Northwest.*

Potential candidates for planting include many of our alpine ferns, especially those of European origin as well as those of the upper mountainous elevations in the United States. Adjusting the generally unforgiving cultural requirements of many of these

Assorted ferns and companions growing in an alpine rock garden in Switzerland.

high-altitude plants to the comfort of lowland gardens presents a challenge. Here we have species that are accustomed to snow protection, which provides attendant winter warmth; short summer reproductive seasons with high light levels; and, as often as not, very specialized soil preferences. I do not recommend or approve of collecting these ferns, choice as they may be. Rather, the best chance for adaptation comes from plants grown from spores and introduced at infancy into lowland culture. There are no guarantees here either, but it is hoped that having originated away from the rigors of high-alpine stress a few given sporelings will adjust to an essentially foreign habitat. My successes with these introductions have been limited, but there have been just enough to encourage further experimentation.

A gentle slope offering both sunny and shady exposures, and encouraging good drainage is an ideal site. In

Ferns and alpines thrive in raised beds at the Kaye garden.

order to look appropriately stable, rocks need to be "planted" leaving only a small portion above the soil's surface. The soil and site can be designed for the peculiarities of the specific plant and may be as specialized as a limestone cobble (a rocky hill or knoll) or as casual as a bed amended by fast-draining granite grit. A miniaturized version can also be created in a container, and in drainage-stressed soil areas, a raised bed services both plants and gardener.

All rock garden ferns appreciate good light, rocks to protect and cool the roots, gritty soil with attendant sharp drainage, and good air circulation. Furthermore a top dressing of pebbles, volcanic rock, or dark chips adds both aesthetically and practically in keeping soil from splashing on, and perhaps disfiguring, the often procumbent foliage.

Aspleniums are especially suited to life among the rocks and display well in their company. The low-growing *Blechnum penna-marina* freely colonizes temperate gardens as it does its alpine homelands and may for some be too much of a good thing. While it is at home in full sun, it is not comfortable unless somewhat moist. *Adiantum aleuticum* 'Subpumilum' is a prize miniature. The finest planting I have ever seen of this somewhat slow-to-establish, graceful diminutive is in the alpine garden at the Rhododendron Species Botanical Garden in Federal Way, Washington (see photo). The characteristically dwarf, deciduous woodsias thrive in rocky rubble and are welcome as among the first to unfurl in the springtime.

Most all ferns in this sampling will take a rather unfernlike dose of sunshine, although I prefer not to let them bake in hot midday sun. Experimenting helps to determine not only the best site but also the most attractive combinations.

Ferns on Walls

Growing ferns on walls is a step more specialized and challenging than rock gardening but may include a number of species suited for both habitats. It appears to be the only situation that will support the lifestyle of that wretchedly difficult (but beautifully photogenic) *Ceterach officinarum*.

Wall dwellers tend to prefer grit rather than soil and are frequently seen peering from crevices in venerable old buildings in Britain and Europe. And what a wondrous sight they are.

It is possible, however, to build a habitat for these muralists. I find it best to start with very small plants and

Asplenium fontanum and *A. pinnatifidum* in the Baggett rock garden. Photo by Jim Baggett.

Adiantum aleuticum 'Subpumilum' flows around the rocks at the Rhododendron Species Botanical Garden.

Ceterach officinarum and *Erinus alpinus* happily established in a wall at the Baird garden.

Asplenium ruta-muraria, the wall rue, colonizes in mortared fissures of an old building in Wales.

Polypodium cambricum in a castle wall in Wales.

insert them, along with some moss for temporary support, into crannies, or better yet add them as the wall is constructed. Brick complements the fern foliage admirably, but stones are more easily managed and offer a handsome foil.

The mortared joints (now crumbling) where the European sporelings settled is of an ancient type and neither available nor practical now. Instead, use a lean organic mix incorporating pumice or granite grit (tempered for lime lovers with granules of broken concrete). Until established the ferns must not be allowed to dry out, but once thriving (says she optimistically) they need only a minimum of attention. Again, the aspleniums are adaptable candidates. *Ceterach*, if you can find a living plant, is outstanding when established in a sunny site, while *Phyllitis* and numerous polypodiums are eminently suitable and attractive additions to shady walls. Good luck!

Xeric Ferns

The ferns of the world's drylands offer a total contrast to the stereotypical concept of fern. Seeing them growing in the wild is an amazing sight indeed. One of my earliest exposures was at a remote place called Bumblebee 4 (no, I do not know why), Arizona. In a dry gulch that would serve as a site for a cowboy's last gasp in a western movie were assorted ferns nestled up against boulders. Here their roots reached deeply down for the minimal water source with the boulder providing a cool root run, a touch of shade, and a drop or two of morning dew. These xerics are your cheilanthes and pellaeas and their near relatives. Many are cloaked in hairs and scales to help prevent water loss. Others have an undercoat of white or yellow farinose wax. To the xeric enthusiast these protective traits add immensely to the ferns' beauty and charm.

Not surprisingly these citizens of the desert do not settle down with ease in cultivation (which may help explain why we all want to have them to display). Soil with excellent drainage is essential and the mix must be coarse. I use lots of well-washed pumice, bark, and granite grit, with just enough loamy compost to hold it all together.

Xeric habitat, Bumblebee 4, Arizona.

Heavy fur coats cloak xeric *Notholaena lanuginosa* in the Brotherton garden.

Author's half whiskey barrel filled with cheilanthes, showing the new planting in 1997 (center) and the resultant growth in 1999 (left).

Dryland garden at the
University of California
Botanical Garden at Berkeley.

In addition, these ferns need good air circulation and, more critically, protection from winter wet. I have mine planted in half whiskey barrels under the eaves on the south side of the house. They get full sun in the winter and light shade in the heat of the summer. They do need watering, however, especially in their new growth. Cheilanthes will let you know by curling up when dry. Fortunately, unlike some of their shade-land counterparts—maidenhairs and osmundas come to mind—they will revive with a gentle shot from the hose.

In California and southwestern gardens the xerics can be treated like ordinary rock garden plants without concern for winter wet. The University of California Botanical Garden at Berkeley, a must-see garden for all fern lovers, has a remarkable display. Look for the ferns in among the cactus.

Stumperies

Stumperies date back to Victorian times and are to the woodland landscape what a rock garden is to the sunny site—an effective foil for displaying plants. Essentially, ferns and companions are tucked into pockets of soil in downed trees, their stumps, or snags. Ecologically appropriate with a rustic appearance, stumperies offer a balance between nature and foliage contrasting texturally for a pleasing, natural, woodland effect. They are perfectly designed for ferns and can be as simple as a planting on a log or stump left in the woodland garden. Lacking such good fortune, logs, snags and freshwater drift-wood can be imported and stacked or artistically scattered along shady hummocks and trails to provide a backdrop for a fern collection. In other arrangements, large stumps are upended and the cavities where their roots exposed are filled and planted. On a smaller scale, weathered wood of all types can be used as individual frames where, with their silvery patina, they offer an accent and pleasing contrast.

Stumperies are becoming quite fashionable with the most famous being in the Highgrove garden of His Royal Highness Prince Charles, The Prince of Wales. Two of the Hardy Fern Foundation's display gardens, Whitehall in Louisville, Kentucky, and the Stephen Austin Arboretum in Nacogdoches, Texas, have incorporated stumperies

Natural bog in the
New Jersey Pinelands.

in their woodland design and plans are underway to create a stumpery at the Foundation's primary garden, the Rhododendron Species Botanical Garden in Federal Way, Washington.

Bogs

Certain ferns are at their lush and robust best in spongy to boggy soil. These include the osmundas, *Onoclea sensibilis*, a number of woodwardias, and some dryopteris and thelypteris. Most can be and are admired in their wild habitats especially from the midwestern to the eastern United States.

Private gardens usually do not come with pre-existing bogs, however, but bogs can be created artificially. First bury a plastic liner in the desired spot (lowland please). The liner should be punched with a few holes judiciously located at the low ends so that there is some drainage and the final product is indeed a bog rather than a lake. Use peaty soil with a good percentage of humus to fill the hollow and establish contour. Allow the whole to settle for a week or two. Then plant thirsty ferns and their companions. Sarracenias are especially ornamental. Certain irises add interest and contrast and the list goes on depending on locale and personal design preferences.

Once established the bog should be self-sustaining, but cannot go forever without water. Even bogs can dry out in summer heat leaving a collapsed composition. *Osmunda* fronds, once wilted, for example, will not recover. (Be of good cheer; the plant will.)

Bog area at Lakewold Gardens.

Sarracenias, *Dryopteris cristata*, and companions share the bog area in the Stuart garden.

Equisetum telmateia joins the iris in a swampy area at the Bloedel Reserve.

Worldwide, botanical garden bog displays are most likely to feature *Osmunda regalis*, which is regularly planted in wetlands and is often accompanied by massive stands of *Gunnera*. They can reach huge proportions, and the combination makes a most imposing sight. Equisetums, by contrast, willingly colonize in bogs whether invited or not, and can be attractive in the right setting.

Tree Ferns

Tree ferns are magnificent specimens native to the moist forests of the Caribbean, Mexico, Central America, and across the entire Southern Hemisphere where they stand tall and dignified. They are indeed treelike and range in height from 3 to 60 ft. (90 cm to 18 m) with members of the Cyatheaceae being the tallest. The arching fronds, among the largest "leaves" of any plant, flush from the top of the trunk and can reach 20 ft. (6 m). Like most ferns they are ancient plants, predating the dinosaur days and surviving the calamity that destroyed them. Look for tree ferns (or their replicas) as evocative features in those primeval movie scenes where the plot calls for a pre-historic atmosphere.

While widely admired, tree ferns are not extensively cultivated in temperate gardens, being best suited to humid pockets in Zones 9 to 11. Dedicated optimists coax *Dicksonia antarctica*, the cold-hardiest of the lot, into focal point displays in sheltered locations in Zone 8, where they do indeed make a dramatic fashion statement. However,

Dicksonia antarctica at the University of California Botanical Garden at Berkeley.

because their roots run down the outsides of the trunk, they are cold-vulnerable, high-maintenance plants requiring special winter protection. Larger, well-rooted specimens are better able to withstand some cold and should be sited in warm pockets away from winds. Otherwise, outside of Zones 9 to 11, they must be winter-protected. Attention ranges from a hastily applied skirt of bubble wrap or a quick toss of a gauze throw to secure burlap bundling or elaborate coffinlike structures that encase almost the entire tree.

So aided dicksonias have survived in some remarkably challenging areas including the garden of British Pteridological Society past president and tree fern specialist, Alastair Wardlaw, in Glasgow, Scotland. After years of experimenting he has developed an elaborate system for promoting winter survival. Basically (but greatly oversimplified) it is this: tree ferns without trunks and still in pots are overwintered in an insulated cold frame which does not go below 28°F (-2°C). Trunks

An annual burlap wrap protects *Dicksonia antarctica* at the Bellevue Botanical Garden.

Chicken wire encases a protective straw blanket for *Dicksonia*. Photo by George Schenk.

Tree fern air layer at the Hamburg Botanical Garden.

Lines of tree fern trunks at a New Zealand nursery.

on ferns planted in the ground are wrapped in a single layer of aluminum foil, which is then enclosed in a double layer of large bubble wrap. The top of the trunk is covered with 6 in. (15 cm) of horticultural fleece which is tucked into the crown and capped by aluminum foil. The whole is then protected by a transparent umbrella-like structure positioned above the fronds and designed to protect as much of the frond area as possible. The winter minimum air temperature in Glasgow is generally around 24°F (-5°C). Thanks to this care, *Cyathea australis*, *C. dealbata*, *C. smithii*, *Dicksonia antarctica*, *D. fibrosa*, and *D. squarrosa* not only survive but also have trunks of between 5 and 7 ft. (1.5 to 2.1 m). The purpose of the various systems is to keep the crown frost-free and dry, the trunks warm, and also, if possible, to avoid browning of the fronds.

Cultural requirements are similar to those of most ferns. Water is the exception. As water must be transported some distance from soil to frond, tree ferns need extra moisture, including an occasional hosing of the trunk, as well as wind protection. When will they form trunks? Essentially trunk formation is an ongoing process that begins as soon as there are fronds (although it may not always be obvious). Like humans, when well nourished they grow most measurably as youngsters and slow down with age. Dicksonias are rather slow with trunks, gaining about an inch (2.5 cm) a year. Cyatheas may increase by a foot (30 cm) or more. All rates are, of course, affected by the cultural conditions.

Propagation techniques include the traditional spore method, at its best with very fresh spores. Large-scale commercial production for some species, which enables shipment worldwide, is done from logs cut from the fern's "trunk." With the roots coming down from the fern's apex, the fern is "topped" and the resultant log reset in soil to form a new plant.

One of the most interesting operations I have ever seen was an air layer on a *Cyathea* that was literally threatening to raise the roof of the conservatory at the Hamburg Botanical Garden in Germany. As with woody plants a cut was made into the trunk and the wound wrapped in an envelope of sphagnum-stuffed plastic wrap. The newly rooted tree was then cut back and reduced, at least temporarily, to a more manageable size.

For gardeners whose tree ferns have not survived and who have an unadorned lonely trunk standing as a testament to the loss, George Schneider (1890, 1: 166) suggests playfully that they be decorated with young sporelings of hardy ferns to create a personalized "hardy tree fern."

Growing Ferns Indoors

As with garden ferns, the three major areas of concern when growing ferns indoors are soil, light, and water. In addition, attention to temperature is more critical and must be determined by the preferences of the individual species or cultivars.

Sacks of fern-specific soil, usually containing various combinations of peat, sterilized compost, and perhaps sand, pumice, and/or perlite, are easily purchased from most garden centers and are in general ready to use. I find many somewhat heavy, however, and prefer to cut them with a gritty amendment, so as to improve drainage. Well-washed pumice is always excellent, but perlite (which I find unaesthetic) and other inorganic additives may be used as well. Some growers amend with an orchid media.

As with outdoor containers, indoor containers require a drainage hole and the pot size should be just a bit larger than the plant's root ball. Most of the offerings need good but indirect light. East or north windows are usually the best, but south and west, when the light is tempered by gossamer curtains, work well. For most ferns direct sun is a killer. Air circulation keeps the fronds fresh. However, drafts, especially those from forced air heat or doors open to cold winter breezes, can be lethal, or at least damaging.

Watering is usually the biggest problem with indoor material. More house ferns die from drowning than from thirst. They should be well-watered, allowed to drain, and then watered again when the soil surface is dry. If the plant dries out quickly, it may be getting pot bound and ready for a new container approximately 1 in. (2.5 cm) larger in all of its dimensions.

Many ferns, such as adiantums (maidenhairs), have high humidity requirements, and these give indoor ferns a reputation as being temperamental. The easiest way to maintain them is in a cozy greenhouse. In the average home the most popular accommodation is to sit the pot on a tray of pebbles and water. Another option is to group plants in close proximity so that they offer humidity to each other. Do not mist them. Contrary to the recommendations of some authorities, I do not mist any indoor ferns as the moisture can remain on the foliage and eventually lead to mold and rot. This is especially a concern with maidenhairs or the dense ruffled *Nephrolepis* types where exposure to air is minimal and consequently evaporation takes place slowly.

Lacking the predators naturally present in outdoor gardens, indoor ferns will on occasion be visited by uninvited guests who help themselves to whatever edibles are to

The Fernery at the Morris Arboretum.

The Conservatory at Birmingham Botanical Garden.

their liking. Aphids, multiplying like rabbits, will suck the juices from the foliage and spread viruses, but can be washed away with a sink bath.

Other pests are either common or nonexistent depending on your locale. Beware of scale, however, which is universal and, once-present, difficult to bring under control. Small infestations can be treated by hand with dabbed applications of alcohol. If the entire plant is overrun with marching (and propagating) crowds, it should probably be discarded or at least quarantined and treated with chemicals. Chemical controls vary, however, and should be used with extreme caution. Oil-based sprays should never be used.

Periodic feeding of a very mild fertilizer at half the manufacturer's recommended strength should keep the plant happy. This is best applied when the fern is in active new growth, which brings me to the subject of grooming. Old fronds need to be removed and this can be a monster chore when the subject is naturally dense. With maidenhairs, I give them a complete haircut in the spring. They will be unsightly for a period, but the other option is to remove the fronds individually, a procedure for folks who have far more free time than I do.

Nephrolepis exaltata (the basic Boston fern) and its many cultivars, both for basket and table, are the easiest, most readily available and highly recommended for beginners or experts. I have a customer whose *N. exaltata* 'Bostoniensis' has been passed from generation to generation since 1935. It is an heirloom that is appropriately regarded

Adiantum raddianum in a complementary planting with the vireya rhododendron 'Bob's Crowning Glory'. Photo by George Schenk.

Tender ferns volunteer on the trunk of a palm tree.

Assorted ferns share the stage with orchids at Longwood Gardens.

with passionate pride. Davallias and assorted "animal-footed" ferns are also easy, as well as forgiving, in bright light and occasional forgetfulness in the watering department. *Pellaea rotundifolia* (button fern) is one of my favorites, but unfortunately one of the first to succumb if over watered. The staghorns are popular and have a dedicated communal following, but require specialized conditions. (See the *Platycerium* entry for details.) Almost all of the ferns generally considered "indoor" types can be grown outdoors in California, Florida, and other warm climates.

3

Propagating Ferns

*I*n addition to the promise of quantities of new plants, propagating ferns especially from spores offers to me precious moments, hours and days actually, of relaxation (horticultural uppers), mixed with the joyous anticipation of creating new life and perhaps new-to-U.S.-cultivation species to enrich gardens and knowledge. My original propagating "facility" was a table in the basement with an overhead fluorescent light. That was rapidly outgrown and now all of my propagating is done in a 12-by-18-ft. (3.6-by-5.4-m) "plant room" housing shelves with pairs of 4-ft. (1.2-m), cool white, 40-watt fluorescent tubes. The room, which is attached to the house, is surrounded on three sides with windows that catch winter sun filtered by shade cloth (on rollers like regular window shades), but with the protective shade of an overstory of Japanese maple trees, not the intense rays of summer. The ceiling and walls are painted white for optimum light distribution and, only somewhat by design, the clothes dryer vents into the area giving it a periodic boost of humidity. A ceiling fan runs 24 hours a day.

Greenhouses, while extremely efficient as well as wonderfully ambient work sites, are more labor intensive, as seasonal adjustments are required for a proper light-to-shade balance and in cold winter areas precautions must be in place for snow loads. At the other extreme, a workspace as small and convenient as a north-facing kitchen window can handle several cultures and be under the watchful eye of the propagator. It is a practical and totally expense-free option for getting started. Whether you choose a minimum arrangement or a full-blown propagation facility, I hope you too can find the special pleasure and reward in being up to your elbows in soil, watching and tending your progeny, and eventually bringing new ferns into your life and garden.

To create large numbers of young ferns, spore propagation is generally the option of choice. To duplicate existing ferns, building up numbers somewhat slowly but surely, vegetative methods are practical, faster, and definitely more consistent and reliable.

Vegetative Propagation

The two main types of vegetative propagation are quite different. On the one hand, some ferns will produce bulbils

Shelves with fluorescent lighting house the propagating activities in the author's "plant room."

or buds on their fronds which may reproduce with or without intervention by the gardener. Propagation by division, on the other hand, is totally dependent on assistance from the grower.

Bulbils

I once saw a program where a "professional," who should have known better, described how to grow ferns from cuttings. This was especially interesting (and disconcerting) since ferns do not grow from cuttings. (And folks wonder why they have little luck with fern propagating.) Growing from bulbils, or bulblets (little nodules along the fern's rachis, the stemlike section of the leafy portion of the frond), comes close, but is not the same.

Cystopteris bulbifera has bulbils the color and size of peas loosely distributed on the undersides of the fronds. These will drop, roll about, and reproduce without human assistance. Others, most commonly on assorted polystichums and especially *Polystichum setiferum* cultivars, remain fixed on the frond and benefit from some judicious midwifery. When there are just one or two bulbils at the tip of the frond such as with *P. andersonii* and *P. lentum*, I peg the tip down on surrounding soil in the fall and let nature take its course. I do, however, pamper the rare bulbiferous sterile hybrids, such as *P. ×dycei*. On these I remove the bulbils from the frond and pin them individually on the moist surface of light compost in a 4-in. (10-cm) pot, invert a clear plastic cup on top, creating a personalized greenhouse, and bring the whole into the plant room. Generally I do this in the fall, but one spring I happened upon an unexpected cache of similar bulbils. I picked them and put them in a bowl of water, promising that I would be back. Well, I did get back, actually several months later, and there they were sprouting away. So much for coddling.

I use a different procedure with *Polystichum setiferum* cultivars. Here we have masses of would-be plantlets lining the rachis. I pin the entire frond down on friable soil, sometimes leaving it attached to the parent plant and sometimes, for greater speed, in a flat of light compost, under the banks of fluorescent lights in the humid

Bulbils along the rachis on a *Polystichum setiferum* cultivar.

warmth of my plant room. Thus incubated, the babies will root and be ready for separation in a few months. I snip them apart and move them up to 4-in. (10-cm) pots. It will be a year, however, before they are ready to truly leave the nest. With more than 365 cultivars of *Polystichum setiferum*, it should be noted that not all of them produce bulbils, and not all of the bulbil producers will have them annually. The reason for this is not known but it is certainly a research project waiting for attention.

A rarely used variation of bulbil propagation was discovered by a Mr. Jackson in 1856 for growing leaf base bulbils. This specialized system is usually applied to the sterile cultivars of *Phyllitis scolopendrium*. In this method the desired fern is dug and thoroughly washed of soil. From the bottom of the clump, where the stipe bases are attached to the rhizome (underground stem), old frond stubs are peeled away. Although looking rather dead, they should show green tissue and possibly a few roots at the point of detachment. These are placed in a flat of the familiar light compost or sand. Dyce (1991) recommends sticking the top rather than the lower ends into the rooting medium but both ends work. The entire tray should be packaged in a clear plastic bag or placed in a mini greenhouse structure and stored under indirect or artificial light. In time and with luck, bulbils will form at the base and, once this is achieved, sporophytes will follow. From that point on they should be treated like any young plantlet. Unfortunately the parent plant can be sacrificed in this process. Therefore, I recommend reserving this strategy for the special sterile few, stripping only a minimum number of fronds and replanting a significant portion of the parent plant in a well-tended pot until it recovers from the surgery. Or, as a safer option, do not dig the plant but rather take a few of the outermost, dead-looking fronds and "plant" them.

Plantlets crowd the fronds on *Woodwardia orientalis* var. *formosana* at the Miller Botanical Garden.

Finally, for yet another vegetative propagation situation, there are the mother fern types where the babelets actually grow on the fronds. *Asplenium bulbiferum*, *Woodwardia orientalis*, and *Dryopteris erythrosora* 'Prolifica' all have such buds looking like miniature winged darts on their foliage. Prick them off and line them up closely in good soil in flats (or as described above in pots capped with inverted plastic cups), and nurture them in greenhouse or pseudo-greenhouse conditions. Rooting and new growth follow very quickly.

With any successful propagating procedure carried out in an enclosed system, it is very important to gradually harden off the progeny by slowly exposing them to increasing amounts of nonincubating fresh air with reduced humidity. Do not rush the procedure. Instead, gradually lift the lid and/or open the container in increments, keeping a watchful eye out for wilting.

Division

Division is a reasonable and practical option for increasing two types of ferns: ferns with a creeping and/or branching rhizome or those with multiple crowns. Many ferns have long-creeping rhizomes, those "feet" that circle the basket or roam about in the garden. These can be judiciously cut apart, taking care to take a growing tip and roots, and potted up in humusy soil or, if of substantial size, set directly into the garden. Try for 4-in. (10-cm) or even larger clumps, as many species, such as *Adiantum venustum*, do not like to be pried into small bits. I prefer to do this with a seriously sharp knife in the fall, but others use assorted utensils including a sharp spade and operate in the spring. The latter option is preferred for areas with harsh winters so that the foliage and roots can reestablish during mild weather. Among others, polypodiums, nephrolepis, davallias, gymnocarpiums, thelypteris, some woodwardias, and those masters of long

Multiple crowns suitable for dividing.

Stock plants for commercial production, Sundquist Nursery, Poulsbo, Washington. Clockwise from bottom, *Blechnum chilense, Adiantum venustum, Blechnum penna-marina, Polypodium scouleri,* and *Polystichum setiferum* 'Plumoso-multilobum'. These ferns all lend themselves to vegetative increase. Photo by Nils Sundquist, Sundquist Nursery.

rhizomes, dennstaedtias, are all easily multiplied in this manner.

Ferns with short-creeping and branching rhizomes with multiple growing tips are also candidates for division. These are your clump-forming rather than crown-forming types and include such gardenworthy specimens as *Athyrium niponicum* 'Pictum', *Adiantum pedatum, Adiantum aleuticum,* most cystopteris and cheilanthes, and a number of dryopteris. Cut these apart by taking a portion of the live growing tip(s) with roots and some fronds. To ease the transition cut back some of the foliage, or do the dividing in the fall or before the appearance of new fronds in the spring.

Stoloniferous ferns with rhizomes on steroids, such as *Matteuccia struthiopteris* (ostrich fern), will happily go forth and colonize, with new plants appearing at some distance from the parent. These can be dug as individuals and easily reestablished (or graciously given away to a friend in need of instant landscaping). I bought one *Matteuccia* some 20 years ago, and left it in its pot over the winter. It eventually found a home but not before the stolons escaped from the pot and made their way into the surrounding garden. Every spring two or three babies still doggedly appear at the original site and every spring I still doggedly dig them up.

Surgery of another sort is used to divide ferns with multiple crowns. Some dryopteris frequently develop offsets most easily observed when the fronds are removed. These are complete circles of coiled crosiers and each can be separated from the parent to produce a new plant. Taking half a circle will produce half a plant and a dreadful visual effect. As these divisions can be quite substantial in size, a good sharp spade or machete-sized blade is the recommended weapon. A kinder way is to place two strong forks back to back and then pry. I usually just carve away offsets from the plant's perimeter. Some growers find it more efficient to work with and divide a young fern as soon as it develops one or two offsets. When these are readily distinguished, they dig the entire

"Before"—mature plant dug in preparation for division. Photo by George Schenk.

"After"—resultant passel of offsets ready for planting. Photo by George Schenk.

clump, clean it, and cut off the new crowns with an appropriate portion of root material to support the offspring (Archer 2005).

In areas with mild winters, fall is an ideal time to divide, but my friends in colder areas prefer to operate in early spring. With either time line, the foliage should be thinned to reduce stress on the roots. Incidentally, left undivided, these same, multi-crowned plants can form massive specimens that are incredibly handsome, so choose wisely before taking knife in hand.

Spores

Although the average gardener looking for a few new ferns is rightfully happy with the season's crop at the local or mail-order nursery, the truly addicted eventually turn to growing their ferns from spores. Success will reinforce the addiction, causing it to grow exponentially, and can yield hundreds of plants, rapidly filling the garden (and on occasion leading to the establishment of a fern nursery). Despite its reputation, spore propagation is not particularly difficult, but it does take time to produce a mature plant.

Spores are dustlike and waft about like smoke. "Do you have an indoor fern that won't drop dust on my piano?" queried a customer. The spores are gathered in cases called sporangia, which in turn are in clusters called sori (singular, sorus) and are usually, but not always, on the underside of the fern frond. "I hate to tell you but you have

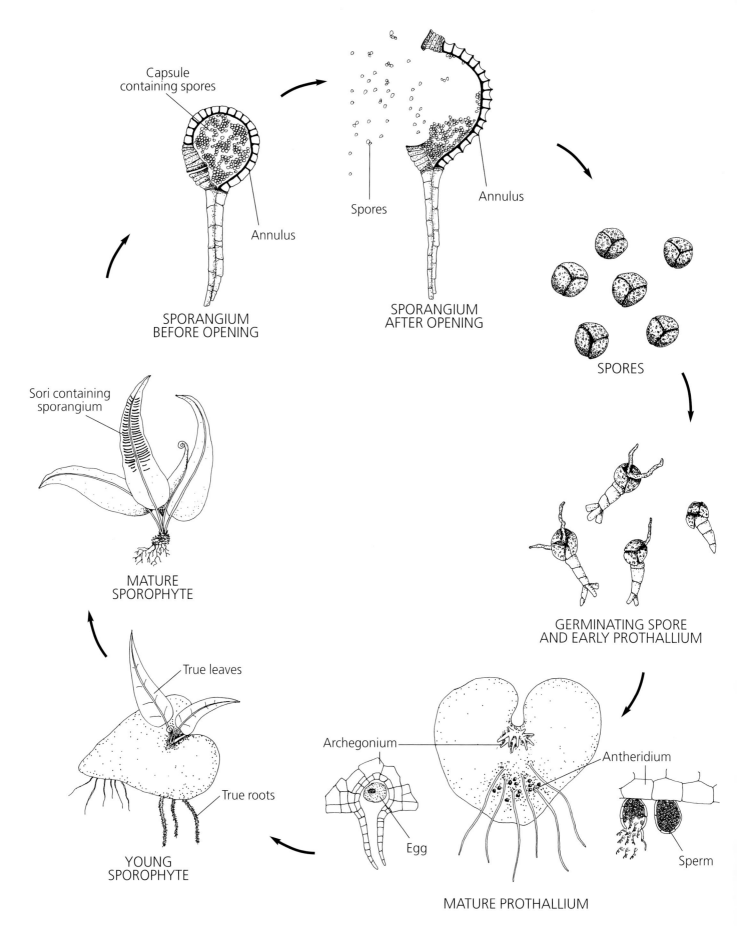

Capsule
containing spores

Annulus

**SPORANGIUM
BEFORE OPENING**

Spores

Annulus

**SPORANGIUM
AFTER OPENING**

SPORES

**GERMINATING SPORE
AND EARLY PROTHALLIUM**

Sori containing
sporangium

**MATURE
SPOROPHYTE**

True leaves

True roots

**YOUNG
SPOROPHYTE**

Archegonium

Egg

Antheridium

Sperm

MATURE PROTHALLIUM

The life cycle of ferns. Drawings by Richie Steffen, Miller Botanical Garden.

bugs all over the undersides of your ferns," observed another. Ah, yes, these are the sori with their spores, the fern's natural reproductive system.

With no flowers, and consequently no seeds, ferns have a unique life cycle consisting of alternating generations, the sporophyte and gametophyte. The familiar foliar form is the sporophyte, which when mature produces millions of spores. (Do the math. A single sporangium usually contains 64 spores. Multiply this by several dozen sporangia per sorus and dozens of sori per frond and we are talking serious numbers of spores. Moran [2004] calculated that a single 25-in. [63-cm] frond of *Dryopteris carthusiana* produces 7,305,216 spores. Large and Braggins [2004] reported that a large specimen of *Cyathea medularis* may release up to one pound [2 kg] of spores per year.)

When spores germinate they create the gametophyte generation with small, sexual, usually cordate, tissue-thin structures known as prothalli (singular, prothallus), which are about ¼ in. (6 mm) across. These contain an archegonium sheltering a single egg and antheridia housing the sperms. When mature and assisted by moisture, the sperms swim toward the egg and fertilization takes place. Shortly thereafter the "true" fern, or sporophyte, emerges, completing the cycle.

An odd bit of botanical magic takes place with some species, especially those from dry areas where fertilization is challenging, and this is a process called apogamy. Essentially the prothalli develop as described but with a nonfunctioning archegonium, the female egg receptacle. (Sperms perform normally and consequently are free to roam). In these juveniles a bud forms on the prothallus and develops directly into a sporophyte (frond-bearing generation) saving the propagator (and fern) lots of time and trouble. Approximately 5 to 10 percent of the world's ferns are apogamous, although research indicates that 13 percent of the Japanese natives are so inclined. Apogamous species are noted in the individual plant descriptions.

Spores can be yellow, green, brown, or black and the soral arrangement is of easily observed, botanical significance in determining differences among fern genera. Primitive ferns, such as the osmundas, carry their (green) spores in specialized structures separated from the foliage. When ripe they are dispersed practically simultaneously. Over the millennia, as competition increased in the plant kingdom, ferns had to be more circumspect and the sori moved to the frond's underside for some protection, although still distributing spores immediately upon ripening. As they became more sophisticated the sori developed a fine membrane, known as an indusium (plural, indusia), which covers the sori and lifts up when the spores are ripe. Thus protected, these evolutionary sophisticates gradually release their spores from the pinnae at the bottom of the frond to those at the apex and from the rachis outwards, efficiently dispersing the spores over a longer period of time and optimizing their potential for finding a suitable site for germination. To accomplish this, these featherweights sometimes travel long distances. Research indicates, for example, that *Asplenium adiantum-nigrum*, a nonnative, arrived and survived in the Hawaiian Islands on at least three, and possibly as many as 17, separate occasions.

Growing Your Own

Every grower has slight to significant variations in approach. These range from sowing spores on expanded peat pellets which are pretreated with boiling water, a popular method especially for limited production, to dusting spores on moist clay pots, to assorted modifications of the method described below. If you are successfully propagating, skip on to the next chapter.

Stages in the development of *Dryopteris erythrosora* spores: (left to right), immature, ripe, and past maturity.

A close look at developing spores ripening from the lower portion of the frond upwards and from the rachis towards the outer edges. Spores are past maturity in the brown areas and ripe for picking in the black.

The whole process starts with the spores. These can be gathered from the garden, solicited from a friend's garden, wild collected (with permission), or for really exotic, and perhaps lusted-after types, obtained from a spore exchange. (Caution: these are administered by conscientious and dedicated curators who spend hours sorting and filling orders, but are dependent on the donors for accuracy of identification. I have, however, obtained some of my most unusual plants from assorted exchanges as well as from correspondents throughout the world.)

Most garden spores mature, depending on your climate and the species, between late spring and midautumn, with the adiantums being among the last. (*Onoclea sensibilis*, matteuccias, and some woodwardias are among the exceptions. They produce their spores in fall and release them the following spring.) With practice, sometimes painful, the grower can chose a frond at the optimum time for collection. If an indusium is present, it will lift and expose the shiny spores. If the indusium is firmly attached, the spores are immature. If the indusium is shaggy-looking, the spores may be past maturity and already dispersed. It will then be best to wait for a freshly fertile frond—perhaps even from a future year's crop. (For live action, place a pinna with the presumed ripe spores under the light of a microscope. If they are indeed mature and ready for dispersal, the heat from the lamp will induce the spores to be jettisoned about in nature's way of distribution.) Otherwise, for collecting purposes, pick a promising pinna, cleanse it with a quick wash and dry, and place it between a folded sheet of white paper. If ripe the spores should drop within 24 hours and will leave a signature pattern on the paper.

Frequently chaff (sporangial detritus) will drop as well, and this must be removed before sowing. To get rid of the chaff, which frequently carries seeds of trouble in the form of fungus, algae, or mold spores, tilt the paper slightly and tap gently. The chaff will fall away while the spores remain behind. This can be disconcerting on the first try (especially if the sample is made up entirely of chaff), so practice with noncritical ferns to gain confidence.

Once cleaned the spores are now ready for sowing. I find it best to sow the spores when fresh. With osmundas and other species that have short-lived, green spores, it is essential to sow immediately. They are viable for about three weeks, although freezer storage prolongs their viability. (Spores of any ferns that will not be used immediately benefit from refrigeration.) Blechnums, while most are not of the green variety, can be temperamental sub-jects and are most likely to produce a successful crop when promptly sown. For beginners and those eager for instant gratification, I recommend starting with almost any *Dry-opteris* as they consistently germinate with ease. I do make a seasonally induced exception for deciduous material. Ideally they are best sown in a time frame that enables them to mature and progress to the out-of-doors (and dormancy) by mid to late summer. This takes trial and quite a bit of error to determine the ideal timing.

I use rigid, clear plastic containers, approximately 4 by 5 by 2-½ in. high (10 by 13 by 6 cm), which I recycle and sterilize by running through the dishwasher, on the top shelf away from the heating element. Containers that can be firmly sealed, such as from the salad bar of the local grocery store, are an inexpensive option, but are not to be treated to a meltdown in the dishwasher. For a medium, and here is where there are multitudes of op-tions, I use a commercially packaged earthworm com-post that is primarily a mixture of humus with some peat and a little perlite. I place this in a lasagna-type pan and pasteurize it by lightly moistening but not soaking the soil. It should not be muddy. I cover it, but do not seal it, with foil and bake at 175°F (64°C) for three hours. Hotter temperatures destroy the good as well as the bad in the soil mix. Be advised that the heated medium gives off an earthy fragrance and can scare off dinner guests. Other growers use their microwaves for sterilization; however, since there are so many variables, I cannot safely give a formula. Finally, for a simpler procedure, pour boiling water through the soil, being certain to "cook" the entire batch and noting that it may take some stirring and several immersions to sterilize thoroughly.

Spore and chaff drop from *Arachniodes aristata* 'Okoze'.

Dark spores are separated from under a blanket of tan chaff.

Once the medium has cooled, I place a ¾-in. (2-cm) layer of moist soil in clean containers and proceed to dust the spores on the surface. To prevent contamination when doing more than one culture, I start with the packets that have the least amount of material and I also do each sowing in a different room in the house. I put a label both inside the container and on the outside as well. I place the containers on the shelves in the plant room approximately 12 in. (30 cm) under cool white, 40-watt fluorescent lights that are turned on for 14 hours a day. Fancy or expensive light tubes are not re-quired. Throughout the entire procedure the cultures must be out of direct sunlight, although indirect light such as from a north window is fine.

Commercial growers leave lights on longer, sometimes up to 24 hours a day, and re-place bulbs frequently to produce a maximum output of consistent light. In addition, their controlled temperatures maintained at 65 to 70°F (18 to 20°C) are clearly beneficial but not necessarily practical for the home grower, especially those of us who keep our thermostats at or below 62°F (17°C). I must confess, however, that the pro-fessionals routinely produce an admirably uniform and attractive finished product far more efficiently than any of the amateur growers.

In time, perhaps as soon as several weeks, a thin green haze will form on the culture. This will expand into a carpet of prothalli (looking like miniature liverworts). When prothalli approach ¼ in. (6 mm) approximately, they should be lightly misted to encourage fertilization. Beware of overcrowding as the sperms, but not the eggs, will develop and fertilization will consequently not be possible. If this appears to be a problem, thin the population by lifting tidbits of prothalli and transplanting them into another container.

Meanwhile, if no little sporelings appear after several additional weeks, and the culture has a uniform distribution of prothalli, spritz again. Some growers recommend using distilled water, but I have found normal tap water, which has settled overnight to release the chlorine, to be just fine. An exception would be if the local water is naturally limey in which case it could kill or at least curtail growth on acid-loving species, especially blechnums.

I then move small clumps, not individuals, of prothalli-sporelings to 72-celled trays in a covered mini greenhouse in a mix of peat, vermiculite, washed grit, and composted potting soil. These too are under fluorescent lighting where they are grown on until they are above 1 in. (2.5 cm) tall. At that time I harden them off by gradually lifting the lid of the pseudo-greenhouse.

Wholesale commercial production of spore-grown ferns at Henry's Plant Farm.

The sporelings are then transplanted into pots with a soil mix of compost, peat, and well-washed pumice (extremely important for removing the fines that are chalklike and can plug the vital oxygen pockets in the soil). Do not be tempted to overpot as the soil that is not quickly penetrated with roots will drain poorly and sour in short order, a potentially devastating threat to the ongoing health of the young fern. A 4-in. (10-cm) pot provides ideal room for rooting without the danger of over potting.

When the fronds reach 4 to 6 in. (10 to 15 cm), the pots are ready to be transferred out to a cool lath or shade house, depending, of course, on the season. Elapsed time can be from 8 to 12 to 24 months or longer. Temperate polypodiums, pyrrosias, and their close relatives can take several years of nurturing before they develop and fill a small pot. Once beyond their prolonged infancy, however, all will behave and grow with the vigor associated with their hardy brethren.

Young sporelings of *Dryopteris sieboldii* in 72-cell trays.

Ferns in the finishing stages of production at Sundquist Nursery, Poulsbo, Washington. Alternating blocks of ferns and companions helps maintain varietal separation as well as helping to control pests. Irrigation is by overhead sprinklers. The large door opening and fan promote good airflow. Excellent floor drainage and overall cleanliness promote plant health. Photo by Nils Sundquist, Sundquist Nursery.

Time frames vary, of course, depending on the propagation situation, but all apogamous (growing without the sexual generation) species develop with speed. Many dryopteris, cheilanthes, and cyrtomiums are included in this group and even their nonapogamous species are among the best for hurried rewards. Arachniodes, athyriums, aspleniums, and certainly doodias and pteris are a sampling of reliable choices for reaching respectability in 12 to 18 months. Polystichums are erratic, ranging from prompt to reliable but long-term, and blechnums are slow.

As with any system, there are, of course, potential problems. In spite of precautions, algae or molds may develop on the surface of the culture, especially when there are only a few prothalli rather than a solid covering. A light application of diluted fungicide (the old standby captan is fine) can bring this under control. Fungus gnats are obnoxious, but not fatal. They can be recognized by their flight pattern, which generally centers around your eyes and nose, not unlike the nighttime mosquito that finds your ear. A light spray with an insecticide keeps them under control. As mentioned earlier, oil-based sprays are not appropriate for ferns, and I have also had disasters with soap-based formulas. Resmethrin, which is a component of many commonly available commercial products, is a safe and effective option that will also control aphids and a number of other pests.

Cultivars

Cultivars are deviations from the type species and present assorted variations in frond and/or pinnae shape, degrees of dissection, as well as assorted flourishes on the frond tips. They are especially common on athyriums, phyllitis, and some dryopteris, and perhaps best known on *Polystichum setiferum*. In the Victorian collecting heyday, hundreds of these were given descriptive names and many are displayed with pride by specialists today. Some come true from spores, but many others produce inferior imitations. Occasionally an abnormal feature may show up unexpectedly in spore cultures. I have seen some that are extremely worthy and others that are just temporarily "different."

Hybrids

Hybrids are possible between two closely related species and are common in some genera, for example, dryopteris in the eastern United States (where they are avidly pursued for educational purposes on field excursions and prized by gardeners for their unique contribution to collections) and aspleniums worldwide. In appearance hybrids usually reflect the influence of both parents, one or both of which are frequently found in close proximity. Some, however, can be quite challenging to identify and need microscopic examination. (Among other attributes, look for spores that are misshapen or shriveled.) Traditionally hybrids are quite vigorous, often outperforming their parents. While those in the wild are accidents of nature, some hybrids have been purposefully and successfully created in laboratories with specific scientific goals in mind. The techniques can be demanding and are usually beyond the abilities of the home propagator. Due to their chromosome composition, hybrids are almost always sterile and must be reproduced by division or, as is becoming increasingly common, tissue culture.

Tissue Culture

A number of commercial growers have developed a laboratory technique for producing great numbers of progeny via a vegetative reproduction system. The process involves selecting a meticulously cleaned and sterilized growing portion of the fern or spores and putting it (them) in a customized nutrient solution. This results in a multitude of plantlets that are rapidly grown on in test tubes until they are strong enough to survive as individuals. There are several advantages for the professional in that one plant can produce huge numbers of young in a short time. It also is a promising and successful way to reproduce sterile hybrids, cultivars, and other ferns that are difficult to impossible to raise from spores. It has not yet developed into a practical system for the homeowner, however, as the equipment required is very specialized and the antiseptic conditions are extremely difficult to duplicate.

Curiosity and lack of availability led to my first spore venture, back in the 1960s, with a sowing of the then-uncommon *Dryopteris erythrosora*. Fortuitously I ended up with some three hundred plants and have been immersed in the love of ferns, their cultivation, and propagation ever since. I wish all would-be growers the same good fortune.

Prothalli on agar in tissue culture at Casa Flora Nursery. Photo by Naud Burnett, Casa Flora.

Young tissue-culture plants at Casa Flora Nursery. Photo by Kent Kratz.

Evaluation of clones in tissue culture at Casa Flora Nursery. Photo by Naud Burnett, Casa Flora.

4

Fern Structure and Basic Diagnostics

*F*or many gardeners a pretty plant is an end in itself, but for others knowing more about the plant (including its name) is a natural part of the joy of growing. Current botanical research has advanced tremendously using sophisticated chemical and analytical techniques leading to important new insights. However, field characteristics rather than those determined in the lab remain the gardener's primary resource for identification and determining distinctions among their plants.

Watch a fern group on a garden tour and notice the penchant for looking at the undersides of fronds where, when fertile, the sori, which enclose the sporangia and hence the spores, are usually located. Their configurations are a significant aid in determining the genus of the fern. This can be muddied or impossible when the material is old and sori withered, so the following, which deals with the most common genera, is based on optimal conditions, usually of the midsummer. (Note too that those touring enthusiasts usually hang a hand lens around their neck to help observe these details.)

Terminology
Dimorphic having two different types of fronds, sterile and fertile
Spores the fern's reproductive unit
Sporangium (plural, **sporangia**) the case containing the spores
Sorus (plural, **sori**) clusters of sporangia
Indusium (plural, **indusia**) a membranelike covering over the sori

The following distinctions are intended to be very simple guidelines which barely scratch the botanical complexities that separate one fern from another. However with experience and a bit of practice, you should be able to identify the correct genus. The features described here apply to commonly encountered ferns.

Plants dimorphic.
Fertile material not attached to the underside of the foliage, maturing early in the season, may extend from the tips of the fronds, arise on a separate stalk, or be located midway between upper and lower leafy portions.

Osmunda: Plants tall, moisture loving, deciduous.

Fertile material on a separate stalk rising in late summer from the center of the fern and not maturing until the following spring.

Matteuccia: Plants very tall, spreading energetically, deciduous.

Onoclea: Plants spreading, fronds triangular, midsized, deciduous.

Fertile material maturing in autumn and attached to the underside of narrow pinnae.

Some *Woodwardia*: Plants creeping in boggy habitats, sori in linear segments on separate, upright fertile fronds, deciduous.

Blechnum: Plants forming rosettes in acidic but not boggy soil, sori in linear segments on upright deciduous fertile fronds that originate from the center of the rosette of sterile fronds.

Plants not dimorphic.

Fertile material attached to the frond's underside, but without an indusium.

Gymnocarpium: Plants widely creeping, deciduous, fronds triangular and delicate.

Polypodium: Plants short-creeping, forming dense clumps, often on trees, deciduous or evergreen, fronds lance-shaped, pinnatifid to once-pinnate.

Phegopteris: Plants widely creeping, deciduous, fronds bipinnate to tripinnate.

Fertile material on the frond's underside, indusia present.

Asplenium: Plants usually evergreen, hardy material often small, sori in a herringbone pattern. A few species are dimorphic.

Athyrium: Plants usually deciduous and large, sori J-shaped or half-moon-shaped but occasionally linear.

Cyrtomium: Plants usually evergreen with sickle or holly-like foliage, indusium peltate (round and centrally attached like an umbrella) on sori randomly scattered on the frond's underside.

Cystopteris: Plants deciduous, sometimes with bulbils, fronds lance-shaped, sori covered by a hooded indusium.

Dryopteris: Plants evergreen or deciduous, varied shapes, frequently scaly, indusium kidney-shaped.

Polystichum: Plants evergreen, scaly with spiny foliage with a pinnule thumb, indusium peltate, sori usually edge the margins of the fronds.

Thelypteris: Plants deciduous, spreading, soft-textured, hairy but not scaly, indusium when present kidney-shaped or occasionally round, on veins.

Woodsia: Plants deciduous, small, rock loving, indusium under the sori opening in starlike fashion.

Some *Woodwardia*: Plants tall and vigorous, evergreen, sori in sausagelike chains.

Fertile material with a false indusium of an inrolled pinna margin.

Adiantum: Fronds often fan-shaped, delicate, temperate species usually deciduous with wedge-shaped pinnae.

Cheilanthes: Plants hairy or scaly, upright growing in exposed sites, usually evergreen.

Pellaea: Plants not hairy, frequently with bluish foliage, growing in exposed sites, usually evergreen.

Once the genus of a plant is determined, details of the frond architecture and pinnae outlines (see the accompanying drawings) help to identify the species. Besides frond division look in the descriptions for notes on the patterns of the veins, which can be free or "netted" (joined), as well as details of scales, hairs, vascular bundles (those tubes that carry nourishment to the foliage) and other visual botanical clues. Knowing the native habitat, or country of origin, of the fern is immensely helpful as well, especially given an extensive library. For the pure pleasure of enjoying ferns for their ornamental addition to the garden composition, all of this may be superfluous. My advice? Enjoy.

Cystopteris montana by John E. Sowerby from *The Ferns of Great Britain* by John E. Sowerby and Charles Johnson, London, 1855.

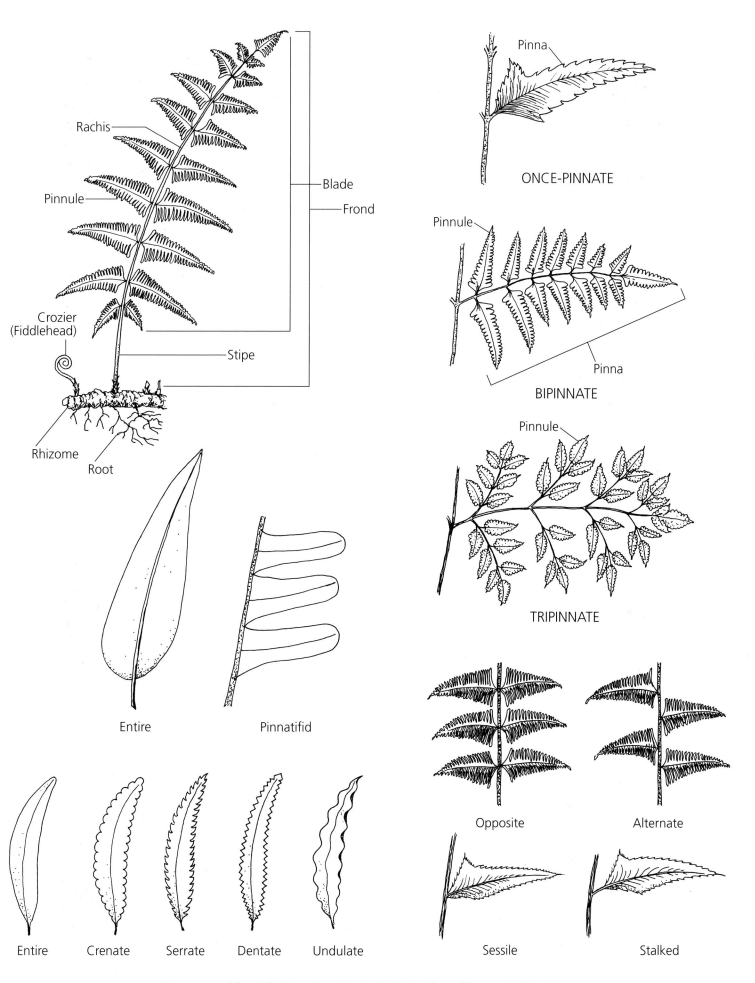

Rachis

Pinnule

Crozier
(Fiddlehead)

Rhizome

Root

Blade

Frond

Stipe

Pinna

ONCE-PINNATE

Pinnule

Pinna

BIPINNATE

Pinnule

TRIPINNATE

Entire

Pinnatifid

Opposite

Alternate

Entire   Crenate   Serrate   Dentate   Undulate

Sessile

Stalked

Fern parts and frond divisions. Drawings by Richie Steffen, Miller Botanical Garden.

Ferns on an indoor stumpery display at the Flora and Botanical Gardens, Cologne, Germany.

5

Ferns from Around the World

Fertile frond on *Acrostichum aureum* showing acrostichoid sori.

Acrostichum aureum near the Kennedy Space Center.

*H*ere are photos and descriptions of some of the crown jewels of the fern world. Most of these are suitable for cultivation as designated in the text, but a few are "for admiration only" and these too are noted. The majority of the photos were taken by me, with many from my garden where the opportunities, often with a brief window of interesting or dramatic light or special seasonal situations, lend themselves to an instant response with camera in hand. Others were taken in native habitats or gardens throughout the world. A number of friends (see acknowledgments) have kindly contributed photos as well, expanding on the scope and variety of the illustrations. Both the sites and photographers are credited.

> The bright colors of flowers are admired by the least intellectual, but the beauty of form and textures of ferns requires a higher degree of mental perception and more intellect for its proper appreciations.
>
> —Abraham Stansfield, in a nursery catalog, 1858

Acrostichum

Acrostichum (with sori covering the entire back of the fertile pinnae) is a genus with more synonyms than species. The three species are once-pinnate with netted veins. They grow in brackish water and muck in many of the warmer areas of the world and are more likely to be surrounded by alligators than the lovely floral abundance usually associated with a visit to a subtropical paradise.

Acrostichum aureum (golden) is included here for its functional contribution to gardens in difficult and wet areas of Florida or comparable climates. It will tolerate and welcome wet feet (fresh water is fine), and with large bursts of 3- to 6-ft. (90- to 180-cm) tall fronds is quite dramatic in structure. Look for it in mangrove swamps, on margins of canals or, along with eagles' nests, in the coastal backwaters near the Kennedy Space Center at Cape Canaveral, Florida.

Acrostichum danaeifolium (for Italian botanist J. P. M. Dana, 1734–1801) is from mangrove swamps and not often cultivated. It is of interest because the larvae of an unknown moth burrow into the foliage, creating homes for colonies of ants, apparently without benefit or harm to the plant (Mehltreter et al. 2003).

Actiniopteris

Actiniopteris (radiating, from the Greek *aktis*, ray, and *pteris*, fern) has but four or five species concentrated in nature on the African continent. They are small plants and look like miniature umbrellas with exposed spokes.

Actiniopteris semiflabellata (half-fan-shaped), essentially a collector's plant, is cultivated by knowledgeable xeric collectors in Southern California. It requires gritty, well-draining soil and careful attention to watering. Too little water and it will wilt, too much water and the crown will rot. This is a novelty to be admired and offers pride of ownership when well grown. It is best in Zone 9 or warmer.

Acystopteris

Acystopteris (away from *Cystopteris*), a genus closely related to *Cystopteris*, is comprised of a few deciduous species that are not heavily in demand. Two are occasionally found in cultivation.

Acystopteris japonica (from Japan) is a thin-textured creeper with fronds of 1 to 2 ft. (30 to 60 cm). The stipes are dark and the bright green, triangular blades are tripinnate and not hairy. This fern will spread in loose, moist woodland soil in Zones 8 and 9.

Acystopteris tenuisecta (slender, cut to the base) at 1 to 2 ft. (30 to 60 cm) is similar to *A. japonica* in height as well as structure. The stipes, however, are a translucent green and the blades are pubescent on both surfaces. This fern grows in friable soil in Zones 6 to 8.

Adiantopsis

Adiantopsis (sorus looking like *Adiantum*) is a genus of 12 to 14 species from the American tropics. With shiny stipes and finely divided blades they are similar to *Cheilanthes* but are separated based on their stipes usually being smooth or only slightly hairy and having non-continuous sori.

Adiantopsis chlorophylla (with yellow-green leaves) from South America is a deciduous species. Two-foot (60-cm) fronds have glossy mahogany stipes bearing a few minute silver hairs and bipinnate-pinnatifid to tripinnate, triangular blades shaped very much like *Cheilanthes*. Elongate sori with matching indusia are marginal. Introduced to North American horticulture by Plant Delights Nursery in 2005, it was found in moist ditches and is recommended for sun to partial sun in Zones 7b to 10.

Adiantum
Maidenhair ferns

The maidenhairs are popular and beautifully irresistible, delicate-appearing plants that evoke the traditional image of fern in the mind's eye of the gardening public. "The maidenhair fern . . . is one of the few species with which those who make no pretense to botanical knowledge are usually acquainted" (Clute 1901). There are some 150 to 200 species scattered over the world's various fern habitats with a rich assortment of natives populating favored sites in the American tropics.

Given their widespread distribution and range of habitats, there is truly a maidenhair ready to adapt to a garden or household niche. Old favorites and exciting new imports offer gardeners in temperate zones increasingly broad options for light and refreshing additions under the woodland canopy. And for indoor décor or outdoor enrichment in frost-free gardens, there's an even wider selection of varied and exotic decorative material.

The genus *Adiantum* is easily recognized by its fronds with glossy, brittle stipes in shades of black, blue, and chestnut, and tissue-thin wedge to rectangular sculptures of green pinnae. Fan-shaped, horizontal blades are familiar hallmarks, but variations on triangular foliage, while less recognized as a signature trademark, are common for both outdoor and greenhouse or houseplant choices. The veins are free and forking and there are one or two vascular bundles. Spores are produced marginally in sori protected under an inrolled false indusium. Unlike the sori of closely related genera, *Adiantum* sori are attached to the indusial segments rather than to the pinnule.

Most maidenhairs are easily propagated. Those that scamper about on creeping rhizomes can be divided in spring or fall with spring being the option of choice in the midwestern and eastern United States, and either season being appropriate for western gardeners. Most are easily grown from spores,

A cultivar of *Adiantum raddianum* with *Pyrrosia lingua* in the Fernery at the Morris Arboretum.

Sori of (left to right) *Adiantum chilense*, *A. capillus-veneris*, *A. venustum*, and *A. monochlamys*.

which, in the Pacific Northwest at least, mature very late in the season, usually September. The exception, unfortunately, is the beautiful and highly in-demand *Adiantum venustum.* In spite of many experiments and studious trials involving variations in timing, soils, and light by many seriously dedicated propagators, it defiantly resists spore culture. Some theorize that because the species can spread and maintain itself by creeping rhizomes, there has been little adaptive advantage to creating new generations from spores. This supposition applies to numerous species (besides the *Adiantum* of our attention, but including the bracken fern) with extensive and expanding rhizomes. Meanwhile, in the long term for a given number of species, such as our subject, *A. venustum,* lack of viability could easily be a genetic dead end. No need for horticultural gloom, however, as tissue culture is providing material for eager growers to distribute.

Adiantum comes from the Greek *adiantos,* which means "to shed water" or "unwettable" and refers to the inferred water-repellent characteristic of maidenhair foliage. (There are exceptions, of course, but the Greeks of A.D. 100 or so should not be held responsible for the undiscovered maidenhair cousins in as-yet-unexplored habitats.) The common name has a more fanciful collection of legends ranging from the mundane (the resemblance of the stipes and roots to lady's tresses) to a folkloric account of a German maiden whose lover turned into a wolf. In flight she tumbled over a precipice catching her black hair in the bushes where the hair took root and sprouted into our familiar fern. Today the "maiden's hair" surrounds a spring, called the Wolf's Spring, at the spot where she landed.

Historically the genus contributes to a plethora of purported herbal cures, potions that offered protection from less-than-kind magical spells, and assorted practical uses. To this day Native Americans use dark black-mahogany accents of locally available maidenhair stipes to create contrasting elements to the tan reeds in their beautiful basketry. In earlier times the highly alkaline fern ashes were used in making lye and, in combination with oil and fat, soap and shampoo. The concoction was also a treatment for skin diseases (and dandruff?). Traditional herbal recommendations are varied and imaginative with a range of treatments for ailments that include asthma, "stones," and snakebites. The most famous maidenhair "cure," however, is the mother of all cough medicines, the Syrup of Capillaire from France. The recipe:

> Maidenhair leaves 5 oz. [142 g]
> Licorice root, peeled 2 oz. [57 g]
> Boiling water 5 pints [2.5 l]
> Let stand six hours and then add
> Loaf sugar 13 lbs. [6 kg]
> Orange water 1 pint [0.5 l]

(And stir!) I do not know what this did for a sore throat, but the sugar high must have been absolutely amazing. (By the way, do not try this at home.) In time, it was decided that the maidenhair foliage was superfluous so the syrup became licorice/orange-flavored sugar, with various alcohol related additives replacing the attributes of the fern. Anything for a sore throat.

Today the maidenhairs are prized for their decorative properties indoors or out. In the temperate garden they add a cheerful lightness-of-being complement in filtered shade and moist compost. Their airy grace gives a buoyant visual relief to the somber elegance of broadleaved evergreens, those structural midlevel garden elements that offer a flowing continuity

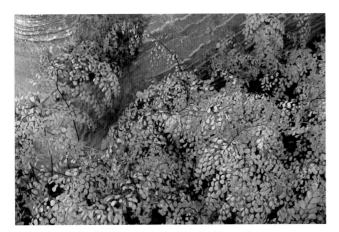

Feathery froth of *Adiantum venustum* in the spring.

Adiantum raddianum 'Gracillimum' with begonia leaves. Photo by George Schenk.

of design from the overstory of deciduous trees or the even larger coniferous patriarchs of garden shade to the woodland floor. Give them the company of wildflowers, fellow ferns, and carefully selected ground covers, and space to display their welcome wands of soft sylvan charm.

Those maidenhairs that add elegance outdoors are beloved by gardeners, but houseplant enthusiasts often bemoan the performance of indoor offerings. With their ephemeral and delicate structure, the plants entice and seduce from the shelves of the grocery store to favorite garden centers and all too often collapse as soon as they arrive in the home environment. Their airy appeal does indeed require customized care, and the more humidity the better.

Grouping like-minded plants so that they share their evaporation with each other helps to provide the required humidity. Another popular option is to stand the pot(s) on, but not in, a tray with pebbles and water so that the constant source of wispy vapors keeps the plant(s) appropriately comforted in a pseudo-greenhouse environment. It is tempting as well as disastrous to mist the foliage. The droplets can linger on and rot the leaves. (This applies to many other indoor ferns especially those with congested foliage. The dense fronds of assorted nephrolepis are particularly vulnerable.)

Give indoor maidenhairs good light, but not direct sunshine. The lightly shaded window is ideal, but mind you not too close to hot or cold glass panes. Brightly lit bathrooms where steam from showers regularly boosts humidity levels are select sites. Like most plants, however, even shade lovers, maidenhair ferns tend to direct their new growth towards light, so give pots a 90° turn periodically. Finally they should be protected from the drafts released by doors open to outdoor cold or, by contrast, the dehydrating breezes of forced air heat.

Plant your collections, indoors or out, in a healthy potting mix consisting of light composty soil and enough of a gritty additive to ensure good drainage. Containerized maidenhairs do not like to be overpotted, so choose a container just larger than the root ball. When it is time to transplant, move to the next larger sized pot with no more than 1 in. (2.5 cm) of fresh soil around the perimeter.

Feeding of plants in pots is not optional as nutrition is rapidly consumed. There are several choices, with the most popular recommendation being a light meal of a very strongly diluted, evenly balanced (10–10–10, 14–14–14, 20–20–20) fertilizer applied regularly throughout the growing season. Other growers use the same evenly balanced formula, at one-half strength and sparingly, with the arrival of new growth, once a year and let that application supply nourishment throughout the season. Both methods work. However, with either option let the fern rest when it is not producing new foliage. Caution! Do not use a slow-release fertilizer on indoor ferns. And be warned: if you have cats or kittens, stay away from fish-based formulas which will invite the "curiosity of the cat."

More indoor ferns are killed by kindness in the form of overwatering than any other complication. Maidenhairs lead the list. Stagnant water at the roots sours the soil and the plant. Wait until the surface of the soil is dry or the pot feels especially light when lifted. (However, do not wait until the fronds wilt. Though adiantums will recover and produce new fronds, they will not rehydrate.) Then give the pot a good soak with WARM water. Maidenhairs do not like a cold shower any more than I do, and furthermore it takes a full day for the soil to reheat and revert to its preferred room temperature. I am frequently asked, "Well how often?" This of course depends on the soil, room temperature, and exposure and must be individually determined. For a controlled supply of moisture, an excellent option is to double pot. Place your prize in a clay pot and sink that pot into a slightly larger container surrounded by a 1-in. (2.5-cm) buffer of sand or sandy soil that can be watered as necessary. The clay pot will wick the water and keep the maidenhair happy with an even supply of moisture. (This system works well with the whole spectrum of indoor ferns and friends.)

For grooming, which if neglected turns into quite a chore, give the plants a complete haircut just as the new fronds are emerging. In northern climates this is normally as daylight increases in springtime. In Southern California and Florida, it can be almost any time. A missed opportunity means removing fronds one by one, which can keep you out of trouble for quite awhile.

All said, your garden maidenhair population should provide years of decoration, and it is possible (truly) to keep your indoor maidenhairs in good health even away from their preferred greenhouse conditions. A little experimenting (along with a steady plant supply) helps.

Adiantum aleuticum
Western maidenhair
Epithet means "Aleutian."
Deciduous, 1½ to 2½ ft. (45 to 75 cm). Zones 3 to 8.

DESCRIPTION: The rhizome is short-creeping, producing bushels of bright green foliar fans on upright, iridescent blackish, grooved stipes. Unlike the extremely closely related (and former namesake) *A. pedatum*, *A. aleuticum* produces green, not cherry red, new growth. The stipes are one-half or more of the total frond structure and fork at their tips into two radiating and continuous branches. A close look may reveal a single fan-shaped pinnule on the rachis between the fork and the first pinnae. This is frequently present on *A. aleuticum* (and will be very close to the first pinnae) but is infrequent on *A. pedatum* (see upper left photo on page 85).

Six to eight outward-fanning pinnae per branch form pedate foliar blades. The pinnae extend horizontally to 1 ft. (30 cm) with the entire fan measuring up to 18 in. (45 cm) across. In this species, the rounded outer blade outline does not form a continuous semicircle, as with *A. pedatum*, but rather is interrupted by an extended middle pinna which may be as much as 25 percent longer than adjacent pinnae. Thirty or more pairs of pinnules with semicircular, incised leading edges are shaped like the wings of eagles. Fertile pinnules have sori on six to eight oblong, fringed, outer marginal segments protected by small curtains of inrolled false indusia. Pinnules on my plants are ¾ in. (2 cm) long by ½ in. (13 mm) wide. Propagate (and share) by division. (See also comments at *A. pedatum*.)

RANGE AND HABITAT: Western maidenhair prefers light shade in moist, rich woodland duff. While the serpentine form is disjunct in eastern North America, the typical species is scattered about with a curious and spotted distribution in western states. Home for most populations, however, is in coastal areas from Alaska to California. The species thrives in humid ravines, will occasionally colonize shady road banks, and may settle on vertical cliffs. Look for magnificent colonies on the walls above Willaby Creek along the nature trail at Lake Quin-

ault on Washington State's Olympic Peninsula. Farther south one of nature's most spectacular temperate fern displays is in "Fern Canyon" in northern California's Prairie Creek Redwoods State Park. Trails from a visitor's center wander towards the Pacific Ocean with a flourishing finale in a narrow half-mile (0.8-km) stretch of a gorgeous gorge. Here flowing sheets of maidenhairs cascade down 50-ft. (15-m) plus walls impressing even the least fern inclined or informed visitor. Companion plants include big trees and huge specimens of *Woodwardia fimbriata* luxuriating in the coastal comfort of their optimal habitat. Look too for the Roosevelt elk that graze the beach at the canyon's outflow. Bring your camera.

CULTURE AND COMMENTS: This is easily grown in western U.S. gardens and takes time to establish in eastern U.S. habitats. Give it light shade, compost, and a reliable source of water. New growth is a week or two later than the eastern counterpart, *Adiantum pedatum*, and by balance, the species remains green for several weeks longer into the fall. In the occasionally mild western winter, when temperatures dip only modestly and infrequently below freezing, it may surprise, tease, and confuse by maintaining a wintergreen complement of foliage.

There have been many nomenclatural "adjustments" and "realignments" since the 1980s. I find that the original segregates provide the horticulturist manageable guidelines for de-

Rogue pinnule on *Adiantum aleuticum.*

Adiantum aleuticum in a perennial display at Wells Medina Nursery.

Maidenhairs drape from the walls of California's Fern Canyon.

Upright serpentine form of *Adiantum aleuticum* growing with *Polystichum lemmonii* and *Aspidotis densa* on serpentine soil in the Wenatchee Mountains of Washington State.

A form of *Adiantum aleuticum* 'Imbricatum' in the Lyndhurst garden.

A different form of *Adiantum aleuticum* 'Imbricatum' in the Olsen garden.

termining differences. They include the "serpentine form" (the erstwhile *Adiantum pedatum* subsp. *calderi*), a distinctively upright, sun- and bog-loving type found in western mountain sites, especially Washington State's Wenatchee Mountains and similar habitats and occasionally in East Coast sites.

'Imbricatum' (overlapping) is a beautiful and variable low umbrella with overlapping pinnules on the typical radiating foliar fan. It comes true from spores and will tolerate brighter light than the species, but definitely not full or especially midday sun.

'Laciniatum' (jagged) is a 1- to 2-ft. (30- to 60-cm) cultivar with slender, irregular shreds of pinnules. Short-stalked, some pinnae have threadlike pinnules while others are broad and fringed-tipped. This form is rare in the United States, but grown by collectors in Britain and Germany.

'Subpumilum' (usually very small) was discovered in the 1960s by the late Seattle horticulturist-botanist Carl English, on sea cliffs on the west coast of Vancouver Island, British Columbia. He held this information carefully to protect the native site from collectors. It can even be hinted that by being studiously vague he carefully misled would be collectors. As a consequence many potential sites from northern Oregon to southeastern Alaska came under close scrutiny, all without a "sighting." He did, however, generously share spores so that this highly desirable little plant could be distributed to enthusiasts throughout the country and, in time, abroad. With various and varying designations in the nomenclature, it has been a bit of an orphan botanically. For years, I found it easier, by default, to just call it "dwarf maidenhair." And truly dwarf it is. Having spore propagated hundreds of plants, all of which consistently matured at less than 8 in. (20 cm), I agree with the late Herb Wagner in preferring to recognize it as a separate entity. While suitable for Zones 6 to 8, it is not the easiest to introduce. My most contented plants are in rich soil with good drainage and light shade. This cultivar does not tolerate heavy soil. Once established, however, 'Subpumilum' is an immensely ornamental foreground feature or functional ground cover in a mixed container planting. The pale green fronds offer a stunning contrast when planted in combination with black mondo grass, *Ophiopogon planiscapus* 'Arabicus'. Prematurely early growth should be protected from late frosts.

'Tasseled Form' has crested tips and, when available, is a handsome variant. It is not consistent from spores.

Adiantum capillus-veneris
Southern maidenhair, Venus-hair fern
Epithet means "Venus hair."
Deciduous, 1 ft. (30 cm). Zones 7 (with protection) to 10.

DESCRIPTION: The rhizome is short-creeping. Plum-black stipes are grooved and usually one-third of the frond length. The triangular blade is bipinnate with dark-stalked, wedge-shaped, drooping pinnules. A touch of the dark stem color radiates into the base of the foliage. Forked veins extend to the minute marginal teeth. Sori are elongate bars and marginal on the inrolled segments of the false indusia. This species reproduces with ease (and at random) from spores and willingly from divisions.

Adiantum aleuticum 'Subpumilum'

Adiantum aleuticum 'Tasseled Form' in the Rickard garden.

Adiantum capillus-veneris.

RANGE AND HABITAT: One of the world's most widely distributed maidenhairs, *Adiantum capillus-veneris* is native to tropical and warm-temperate zones as well as sites where cool to cold winters are balanced by hot summers. Sites reported in the seriously cold zones of South Dakota and British Columbia are associated with hot springs. Plants are partial to limestone where they especially delight in moist seeps. This species is often seen on walls, such as in Zion National Park, as pendulous curtains of green lace.

CULTURE AND COMMENTS: Descriptions note that nearly every frond is fertile and my nursery would testify to that. For me this is a "weed" (or at least a "volunteer") in the comfort of my humid greenhouse. By contrast, it is rather short-lived in my naturally acidic garden where accommodations need to

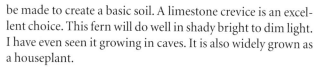

Adiantum capillus-veneris in summer at Zion National Park.

Adiantum capillus-veneris in winter at Zion National Park.

be made to create a basic soil. A limestone crevice is an excellent choice. This fern will do well in shady bright to dim light. I have even seen it growing in caves. It is also widely grown as a houseplant.

Adiantum capillus-veneris has a long and illustrious history of medicinal and magical applications and properties in fables and herbals. Apuleius who expanded on the herbal and medicinal observations and contributions of Dioscorides gave the plant its name in the fourth or fifth century. See the introduction for various interesting applications that were employed through the ages.

'**Fimbriatum**' (fringed) is a beautiful, vertical cultivar to 18 in. (45 cm). Lustrous ebony stipes are over one-half of the frond length. The broad pinnules are deeply fringed and shaggy. The plant dies down at the first frost, but adapts to neutral soils and is consequently easier to cultivate than the type, indoors or out. It comes true from spores.

'**Imbricatum**' (overlapping), known in the trade as 'Green Petticoats', is a magnificent cultivar with layers of cascading bright green shingles of foliage. Spores breed true for this strictly indoor plant, which is at its best as a coveted décor in humid greenhouses. It is a challenging beauty. For best results, water the pot and not the fronds.

'**Scintilla**' (sparkling) is infrequently cultivated as spores are rarely available. It is an interesting and attractive novelty, similar to, but more demanding than 'Fimbriatum'. The deeply cut pinnules look like mini shredded kites that lost the battle with the wind. The plant needs consistently high humidity but does not tolerate water on the foliage.

Adiantum chilense
Epithet means "from Chile."
Deciduous, 1 to 1½ ft. (30 to 45 cm). Zones 6 (with protection) to 9.

DESCRIPTION: The rhizome is short-creeping. The slightly grooved, luminous, black stipe is up to half of the frond length. Triangular blades are bipinnate with the small, fan-shaped pinnules looking like lollipops on black stalks. The sori are marginal on the 8 to 10 inrolled, scalloped segments of false indusia.

RANGE AND HABITAT: This is a species of temperate South American woodlands and mossy rocks in Bolivia, Chile, and Argentina.

CULTURE AND COMMENTS: Extremely attractive, this fern is cultivated in Zone 6 Germany but covered with extra protection in winter. It enjoys shade and moist but not wet soil.

Adiantum capillus-veneris 'Fimbriatum' in the Duryee garden.

Adiantum capillus-veneris 'Imbricatum' in the greenhouse at the Brotherton garden.

Adiantum hispidulum

Rosy maidenhair, rough maidenhair

Epithet means "with stiff hairs, bristly."

Deciduous, 1 to 2 ft. (30 to 60 cm). Zones 8 (in mild winters and with lots of protection) to 10. Apogamous.

DESCRIPTION: The rhizome is short-creeping. Charcoal stipes are up to one-half of the frond length and are whiskered with stiff hairs. (A quick rub between the thumb and a finger easily exposes the fern's "hispid" properties and aids identification.) Blades are pedate with pointed pinnae and crowded, dark green pinnules that as an ornamental bonus are red in new growth. Sori are marginal under rounded indusia segments.

RANGE AND HABITAT: This species has a sweeping range from Australia, New Zealand, and the Pacific Islands including Hawaii, to India, China, Africa, and the Atlantic Islands. In addition, it has naturalized in the southern United States and curiously is also reported to have escaped in Connecticut. In nature it is quite undemanding and grows in forests, on road banks, and in partially sunny open bush country.

CULTURE AND COMMENTS: The rosy maidenhair is widely available as an attractive houseplant and one of the easiest adiantums to introduce to long-term indoor culture. It should be given good light, a humidity-enriched site, and protection

Adiantum chilense in the Kohout garden.

Rosy new growth on *Adiantum hispidulum.*

New growth on *Adiantum monochlamys.*

from drafts. Do not overpot or overwater, but water sparingly when the soil surface is dry to the touch or the pot feels light. Outdoors in Zones 9 and 10 it is easily introduced into the shade garden, but has not survived most winters in Seattle's Zone 8. (So I am still wondering about that "escape" in Connecticut.) It is easily propagated by division or from spores.

'Whitei', with white hairs, is from Australia and is more upright than the species.

Adiantum jordanii
California maidenhair
Epithet possibly honors Rudolf Jordan (1818–1910), who reportedly discovered the species.
Wintergreen (summer dormant), 1 to 1½ ft. (30 to 45 cm). Zones 8 and 9.

DESCRIPTION: The rhizome is short-creeping, producing clusters of triangular, bipinnate fronds on chestnut stipes of one-third to one-half of the frond length. The pinnules are short-stalked, broad fans with a sweep of four or more linear, false-indusia-protected sori along the ultimate edges.

RANGE AND HABITAT: This is a species of drier sites in Oregon and California, and ranges down to Baja California. It prefers ravines and crumbly rocky habitats with efficient drainage and partial shade.

CULTURE AND COMMENTS: I have seen this in gardens on occasion, but not for long. It is for the expert grower for whom it offers frustration and an occasional frond (plus a certain temporary pride of ownership). It must be given sandy soil, light shade, and minimal summer water. It is not easily reproduced from spores. Admire it while on spring walks in the specialized semialpine, slightly arid habitats that are central between the Pacific Ocean and inland mountain ranges.

Adiantum monochlamys
Epithet means "one cloak" or "cover."
Evergreen, 8 to 18 in. (20 to 45 cm). Zones 6 to 9.

DESCRIPTION: The rhizome is very short-creeping. Smooth stipes are a polished chestnut and one-third of the frond length. Narrowly triangular blades, produced in upright tufts, are bipinnate to tripinnate with dark-stalked, cone-shaped pinnules. The free veins fan from a dark basal spot on the pinnule and terminate in the tips of the minute marginal teeth. Fertile pinnule tips are deeply indented with a lone medial cleft that bears a species-specific (for temperate maidenhairs), single (mono) indusial flap that encloses and protects the sori.

RANGE AND HABITAT: Of rocky slopes and dryish woodlands, this lovely species is found in China, Taiwan, Korea, and Japan.

CULTURE AND COMMENTS: It is quite reasonable to confuse this species with *Adiantum venustum* when fertile material is not present. The latter has a similar silhouette but creeps about and carries dual sori rather than a single sorus on the fertile pinnules. It is also easier to cultivate. Both are enhanced by salmon-tinged fresh spring foliage. Once established *Adiantum monochlamys* is a unique and rare addition to the collector's garden, so give it a prime location. Pot or foreground culture with attentive vigilance, gritty soil, and medium shade is appropriate.

Adiantum pedatum
Northern maidenhair, five finger fern
Epithet means "palmate" or "pedate," as in a bird's foot.
Deciduous, 1½ to 2 ft. (45 to 60 cm). Zones 3 to 8.

DESCRIPTION: The rhizome is short-creeping. Brittle stipes are purple-black and usually one-half the length of the frond.

Adiantum pedatum in the wild.

Adiantum pedatum 'Miss Sharples' with *Acer palmatum* HO 19.

They fork into two major branches that curl in an indeterminate recurved circular pattern. The six to eight pinnae per branch become progressively smaller, eventually forming a small curlicue. Note that, unlike *Adiantum aleuticum*, there is rarely a single fan-shaped pinnule between pinnae segments on the rachis. Another feature of importance in separating these species is the continuous semicircular outline of the horizontal blade, which has only a slightly extended middle pinna compared to the significantly longer comparable pinna typically present on *A. aleuticum*. Thirty or more pairs of pinnules on very short stalks are rectangular with serrate upper edges, but smooth margins on the remaining borders. Oblong sori with inrolled indusia are contained in four or five marginal segments. (See also comments at *A. aleuticum*.)

RANGE AND HABITAT: This North American native is found in moist deciduous woods from midwestern regions to the Atlantic Coast. Not surprisingly, alert British colonists, recognizing a good thing, sent plants home. It was one of the first North American fern exports, although not so profitable as those "funny" leaves (tobacco) exported from Virginia.

CULTURE AND COMMENTS: At one time the *Adiantum pedatum* classification included most of the fan-fronded material native to North America. (*Adiantum aleuticum*, the western native, is now considered a separate species, although quite difficult to distinguish from *A. pedatum*.) Woodland compost is an ideal provision along with regular water, good drainage, and light shade. Observant growers on both coasts have found that *A. pedatum* emerges a week or two before *A. aleuticum* and correspondingly disappears earlier in the fall. *Adiantum pedatum* is also shorter. Western slugs, with their ever-present fondness for choice plants, find the new growth attractive and must be lured away. This species is easily grown from spores and readily propagated from divisions.

'**Miss Sharples**' is a deciduous cultivar that unfurls quite early in the season in warm tones of lime-green. The fronds that mature at 8 to 15 in. (20 to 38 cm) are broad fans of soft billowy, slightly overlapping ¾- to 1-in. (2- to 2.5-cm) long pinnules. This form stands out in the garden's maidenhair glen as a fluffy contrast to the traditional structure of both the U.S. native species. Protect it from sunshine and keep it moist, but not wet. The original selection was given to Britain's charming, expert fern nurseryman-author, the late Reginald Kaye, by the Sharples family and tagged "Miss Sharples" for reference purposes by Reg. Some spores disappeared from the nursery, however, and the name along with them. The progeny subsequently appeared commercially and have been widely distributed ever since as 'Miss Sharples'. (Since *Adiantum aleuticum* was not known to be present in Britain at the time, it is presumed that the Sharples gal was a variant of *A. pedatum*.) The happy ending is that her legacy carries on across the continents along with her namesake cultivar.

Adiantum poiretii
Mexican maidenhair

Epithet is after French naturalist Jean Poiret (1755–1834).
Deciduous, 8 to 24 in. (20 to 60 cm). Zones 8 and 9.

DESCRIPTION: The rhizome is short- to long-creeping. Deep cranberry-black, smooth stipes are one-fourth to one-half of the frond length. Oval to narrowly triangular blades are bipinnate to tripinnate and carry the stipe color into the base of the stalked, softly scalloped pinnules. Marginal sori are oblong beneath the false indusia and infused with an unusual (for the genus) yellow farina.

Scalloped foliage of *Adiantum poiretii*.

RANGE AND HABITAT: The native range for this species extends from Mexico to South America and across the oceans to Africa in the east and China in the west. Mexican maidenhair grows in various habitats from rain forests, to pine and oak woods, to dryish rocky slopes.

CULTURE AND COMMENTS: This interesting species is in cultivation in the gardens of dedicated specialists in England and should establish in comparable maritime climates of the U.S. Pacific Coast. Hopefully it can be successfully introduced to the somewhat less accommodating but warm eastern sections of the country as well. Until passing the gardenworthy-hardiness test, it should be protected from extremes of heat and cold with appropriate precautions extended as necessary for long-term maintenance.

Adiantum raddianum
Delta maidenhair
Synonym *Adiantum cuneatum*
Epithet means "radiating outwards."
Evergreen as indoor plants, 1 to 2 ft. (30 to 60 cm). Zones 9 to 11.

DESCRIPTION: The rhizomes are short-creeping. Stipes are bright black and about one-fourth the length of the frond. Blades are usually narrowly triangular and bipinnate to tripinnate. Sori are enclosed in marginal pairs of false indusia. That said, the cultivars, and there are upwards of 70 currently named, rather than the type, are the exceptional offerings associated with this species. As in *Adiantum capillus-veneris* the inky black of the rachis or subrachis of this species carries forth into the veins on the leafy portion of the pinnae. In *A. tenerum* the color ends abruptly at the base of the pinnae. Unlike *A. capillus-veneris* the sori are kidney-shaped, rather than elongate, and usually only two, rather than many, per lobe.

RANGE AND HABITAT: The species and its various cultivars are found throughout tropical and semi-tropical areas primarily in the Southern Hemisphere.

CULTURE AND COMMENTS: These are the most commonly available of the assorted indoor maidenhairs. See the chapter introduction for cultural recommendations and note that misting the foliage is not appropriate. There are many cultivars and the list of the sometimes confused but multiple and attractive variations that come true from spores is a long one. The following are generally available commercially.

'Cluster Glory' is an exceptionally beautiful, five times or more pinnate, haze of minute green raindrops supported by a black structure. The total frond mass is less than 1 ft. (30 cm). There is also a crested form.

'Fragrans' (fragrant) is popular in the houseplant trade and also known as 'Fragrantissimum'. Goudey (1985) suggests that it may be a hybrid between *Adiantum raddianum* and *A. capillus-veneris*. It grows as a bushy, mophead fountain to 2 ft. (60 cm) with an equal drop. The pinnules are large wedges. One of the easier cultivars for indoor use, it is sometimes potted as a contrasting holiday companion with poinsettias.

'Fritz Luth' (often in the trade as 'Fritz Luthii') is an old cultivar with elongate triangular, tripinnate upright fronds of just under 2 ft. (60 cm). The stipes are one-half of the frond length. Overlapping, horizontal pinnae are also elongate with one to two fertile segmental sori per pinnule.

'Gracillimum' (slender, graceful) is a feathery mist of quadripinnate to quinquipinnate foliage. With drooping fronds, it is especially suited to basket culture. It is an excellent choice for humid conservatories where it is easier to cultivate than in the average home or garden. There is also a crested variety.

'Ocean Spray' is a popular cultivar, somewhat similar to 'Fritz Luth', but smaller with fanning fronds and dark foliage.

'Pacific Maid' has a dense mass of overlapping foliage on fronds that usually mature at 18 in. (45 cm). It is especially attractive when combined with floral companions in a pot or basket, but will not survive for very long away from humidity.

'Pacottii' (after Pacotto of Montreuil, France, who raised the plant in the 1880s) is an old-time cultivar of 1 to 2 ft. (30 to 60 cm). The fronds are irregular elliptical triangles with a wide pair of lower pinnae. The showy, congested foliage is up to four times pinnate. Give it a humid setting.

'Variegated Tessellate' is densely foliaged with both variegated and crested pinnae. It is a remarkable sight in the comfort of warmth and humidity. Hot tub environments come to mind.

'Variegatum' (variegated) has small splotches of cream streaks on the compact 1-ft. (30-cm) foliage.

Adiantum venustum
Himalayan maidenhair
Epithet means "graceful" or "beautiful."
Evergreen (wintergreen in Zones 5 and 6), 12 to 18 in. (30 to 45 cm). Zones 5 (with protection) to 9.

DESCRIPTION: The branching rhizome is creeping, eventually supporting a colony of elegant evergreen fronds. The black stipes, with a token cluster of tan basal scales, glisten and are one-half of the frond length. The broadly triangular, tripinnate blades greet the gardener in early spring with a flush of

Adiantum raddianum 'Fritz Luth' at Henry's Plant Farm.

Adiantum raddianum 'Gracillimum' at Henry's Plant Farm.

Adiantum raddianum 'Pacific Maid' at Henry's Plant Farm.

Adiantum raddianum 'Variegatum' at Henry's Plant Farm.

salmon-colored frothy feathers. The pinnae, likewise triangular, are staggered alternately along the slightly zigzag rachis. Pinnules on thin, dark stalks are somewhat asymmetrical and conical with short straight edges and a flared, rounded finish on the outer edge. The whole reminds me of a mitten with small, terminal fingers providing notches for the two fertile segments that protect the sori.

RANGE AND HABITAT: This fern is from the forested mountains of Asia, bringing its hardiness and ornamental appeal to woodland gardens throughout the world.

CULTURE AND COMMENTS: Although somewhat slow to establish, this species is one of the most desirable additions to any temperate garden. (Gardeners in Zones 5 and 6, however, as a fall ritual, should give it a generous protective skirt of chipped leaves.) It is a beautiful and easy ground cover that is an especially welcome and buoyant contrast under the heavier foliage of rhododendrons, kalmias, and spreading broadleaved evergreen shrubs. Give it a good diet of moist humus and a home in light shade. Strangely, and regrettably, it does not reproduce willingly from spores, perhaps because it is comfortable as a creeper and has no adaptive need for further reproductive efforts. In time, and with good husbandry, most plantings will expand and easily succumb to the serrated knife for divisions (and impressive gifts). Divisions of an ample size re-establish readily. Small pieces may struggle. Indoors the mature fronds do unexpectedly well in cut flower arrangements often lasting for two weeks or more.

Shorter Notes

Adiantum aethiopicum (from Ethiopia, which is questionable), common maidenhair, is native from Africa to New Zealand and Australia. It brings a typical maidenhair tracery of triangular sprays of pinnules on fronds that range from 1 to 2 ft. (30 to 60 cm) in height. In nature it wanders about, is readily established, and endures with ease in moist to dryish, lightly shaded sites. It is occasionally recommended for gardens in Zone 8, but will not tolerate, or survive, winter temperatures much below freezing (and certainly not for long.) This is, however, one of the easier maidenhairs for outdoor gardens in Zones 9 to 11. Elsewhere, for budding maidenhair enthusiasts, it is an excellent option for testing growers and their indoor sites for maidenhair compatibility.

Adiantum capillus-junonis (Juno's hair fern) is a tip-rooting, once-pinnate, hardy, but difficult-to-cultivate species that walks about on limestone in Japan, Korea, and China. The 1-ft. (30-cm) fronds are evergreen with polished plum-colored stipes and rachises, and rounded, smooth-edged pinnules. The species should be cold tolerant in Zones 6 and up, but I have yet to meet a plant that has found a happy home outside of its native habitat. (Draperies on rock wall sites in Beijing are stunning.)

Adiantum caudatum (tailed), the trailing maidenhair, offers a shower of cascading, once-pinnate, 12-in. (30-cm) fronds that tip-root, producing a fountain of delicate, walking foliage. The new growth is a warm orange-vermilion eventu-

Adiantum venustum in the Bradner garden.

ally fading to soft green. This tropical species is best displayed in warm and humid ferneries (but is happily established outdoors in Southern California) and is especially impressive when the rooting plantlets are encouraged to encircle hanging baskets. A recent introduction from the mountains of China is reputed to be more cold tolerant, offering potential for gardeners in Zones 7b and 8. Apogamous.

Adiantum davidii (after Father Armand David, 1826–1900) from China (where web searches translate the common name as "pig long neck hair grass") and Tibet has triangular, 6- to 12-in. (15- to 30-cm) bipinnate fronds on a

Adiantum caudatum in the Southern California garden of David Schwartz. Photo by David Schwartz.

New growth on *Adiantum japonicum*.

blue-black wiry structure. The pinnules are undulate wedges of soft green with spine-tipped terminal margins. Sori with inrolled, kidney-shaped false indusia are connected in pairs at the apex of each pinnule. The species, evergreen in warmer areas and deciduous in cold regions, is similar to *A. venustum* and distinguished by the more incised pinnule margins. It is cultivated in Zone 6 gardens in Germany as well as warmer gardens in England. When available, it should be an instant success with fern growers in the United States, especially the dedicated specialists looking to expand their hardy maidenhair collections in Zones 6 to 9.

Adiantum formosum (beautiful), plumed maidenhair or giant maidenhair, is from Down Under, especially Australia. It offers an unusual outline with broadly triangular fronds with pinnae that are tripinnate to quadripinnate at their basal attachment to the rachis, but narrow abruptly to whips of extended once-pinnate wings at mid pinnae. In nature the rhizomes are deeply buried (aiding hardiness and possibly fire resistance), creeping, and branched, producing majestic fronds of 3 ft. (90 cm) or more. In gardens they acclimate and spread, sometimes with abandon, in moist humusy soil in the warmth of Zones 9 and 10. (Description by George Schenk.)

Adiantum japonicum (from Japan), a name used in horticulture, has with good reason been listed as a variety of both *A. pedatum* and *A. aleuticum*. *Flora of Japan* (Iwatsuki et al. 1995)

Adiantum formosum and *Collospermum hastatum* with its 1-ft. (30-cm) racemes. Photo by George Schenk.

Adiantum macrophyllum at Henry's Plant Farm.

Adiantum macrophyllum 'Variegatum' in the Piedra garden.

classifies it as *A. pedatum* but notes that the Asian material is different from that of North America. The fan-shaped frond is similar to both species. Like *A. pedatum*, however, the new growth is colorful although a much warmer reddish orange. With a height of 1 ft. (30 cm), it is shorter than both near relatives. The lower hardiness range is Zone 6. By whatever moniker, it is a beautiful addition to a shade garden.

Adiantum macrophyllum (large leaved) is indeed large leaved with impressive, once-pinnate, 2-ft. (60-cm) fronds bearing tissue-thin bursts of rosy red, 2-in. (5-cm) triangular pinnae. The species is noted for the uninterrupted, elongate linear sori that trim the upper and lower pinnae edges but do not extend to the apices. It prefers basic, well-drained soil in tropical surroundings. Encourage it with warmth and kindness, but do not overwater or overpot. '**Variegatum**', a variegated form with soft pastel tones of rose, green, and ivory, is occasionally available and deserves to be a cherished addition to the displays of the skilled grower.

Adiantum ×*mairisii* (after Mairis of the British nursery Mairis and Company), Mairis's hybrid maidenhair, is an old-timer having been named before 1885. One parent is presumed to be *A. capillus-veneris* while the other is variously listed as *A. raddianum* (synonym *A. cuneatum*) or *A. aethiopicum* (Rush 1984). It is a rarely available, bipinnate, deciduous, sterile hybrid that reaches 15 in. (38 cm) and resembles an erect *A. capillus-veneris*. Given the parentage, it is surprisingly hardy and spreads about energetically amid the shelter and warmth of rocks in British gardens. It should be suitable in sites in Zone 8 and certainly at ease, and possibly evergreen, in Zone 9. Mickel (1994) notes that it can be coaxed into cultivation in colder climates when nestled against a damp shady wall. Propagation is by division.

Adiantum ogasawarense (from Ogasawara Island, Japan) is very similar in outline to *A. capillus-veneris* but far more difficult to cultivate. It has rounded rather than fan-shaped pinnules. The bipinnate, evergreen, foot-long (30-cm) fronds are ovate with soft green, imbricate pinnae on a blackish skeletal structure. The plant prefers exposed rocky sites and is an endangered species in its homeland. Having briefly made an unsuccessful appearance in the U.S. trade, it is also "endangered" in cultivation. Give it lean rocky soil with excellent drainage and bright filtered light in Zones 8 (heavily protected) to 10.

Adiantum peruvianum (of Peru), the silver dollar fern, is a native of tropical South American rain forests where it is reputed to be a bit of a weed. (We should be so lucky.) In the comfort of its natural surroundings, the bipinnate to tripinnate fronds can reach 3 ft. (90 cm) with asymmetrical diamond-shaped, 2-in. (5-cm) pinnules that are "silvery" in appearance, and a metallic rose in new growth. The pinnules are edged on two sides with multiple scallops of sori enclosed by inrolled marginal segments. When grown indoors this extremely appealing species must have consistently humid conditions for optimal health, impact, and long-term survival, but it survives surprisingly well outdoors in the dryish regions of Southern California. A well-grown specimen is truly a visual delight.

Adiantum reniforme (kidney-shaped) is a marvel of overlapping kelly-green pinnae looking like miniature, leather lily pads, and completely distinct from the stereotypical feathery appearance traditionally associated with maidenhairs. The 2-in. (5-cm) pinnae are totally bordered by fertile marginal segments and supported by hairy wires of dark brown stipes. The whole mass matures at a flat-topped 6 to 12 in. (15 to 30 cm). It is native to surprisingly exposed sites. My late husband, Harry, and I were amazed and delighted to discover cascades of fronds perched high above the waterfall at trail's end on the popular Canary Island hike into the Baranco del Infierno (less poetically, Hell's Gorge) on Tenerife. The substrate is lime and that is the recommended planting medium, along with porous soil, for keeping this conversation piece in good health. It is for dedicated specialists in Zones 9 and 10 or tempered indoor sites elsewhere. Goudey (1985) recommends cultivating it in terra cotta pots to encourage good drainage and aeration of the root system. *Adiantum asarifolium* (synonym *A. reniforme* var. *asarifolium*) is a bizarre hairy version with thick black margins, larger sori, and recurved lower frond portions that sometimes overlap the stipe. It is definitely a plant of interest.

Adiantum tenerum (delicate, tender), brittle maidenhair, is native to New World tropics from Florida and the Caribbean south to Brazil along with an unexplained presence in Hawaii.

Like *A. raddianum*, it shares a preference for humid sites in homes, greenhouses, and conservatories, as well as a propensity to produce exciting and exotic deviations from the type. Most of the commonly available cultivars (including offerings from the local supermarket to elite collector's nurseries) are derived from one or the other of these species. The differences between them are botanically slight, with one being that the color of the rachis or subrachis does not extend into the veins on the *A. tenerum* foliage whereas it does in *A. raddianum* and *A. capillus-veneris*. The differences between their desired cultivation requirements are none; good indirect light, humidity but no misting of foliage, protection from drafts especially from forced air heat, uniformly moist but not wet soil, and a pot proportionately sized to contain the root ball without excess surrounding soil. **'Farleyense'** (after Farley Hill) was discovered in the wild in Barbados in 1865. It caused an immediate stir among horticulturally enlightened British enthusiasts, and material was promptly exported. In optimal maidenhair

Adiantum reniforme in the Brotherton garden.

Adiantum tenerum 'Farleyense' at Henry's Plant Farm.

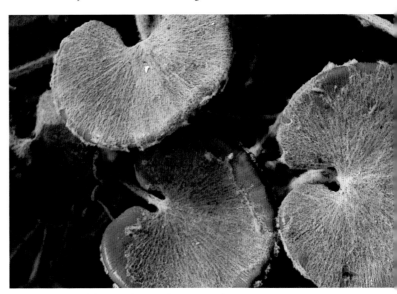

Adiantum asarifolium in the Brotherton garden.

conditions, it can reach 3 ft. (90 cm), but is more likely to form a 2-ft. (60-cm), shrubby fountain of arching and drooping foliage. **'Sleeping Beauty'** is periodically available in the florist or indoor fern trade and has "sleeping," lax pinnules. The fronds, however, are more erect in habit than many of the other tender cultivars. The 2-ft. (60-cm), triangular fronds are bipinnate to quadripinnate, with substantial rather than feathery pinnules. New growth can be an attractive warm rosy red.

Adiantum thalictroides

Adiantum thalictroides (like *Thalictrum*, meadow rue) is an attractive new introduction to North American horticulture from higher elevations above Buenos Aires. The drooping 2-ft. (60-cm) fronds have the traditional dark stems and are slightly dusted with a whitish/yellowish powder. The dainty pinnules look like miniature baseball mitts. This species is suitable for Zones 8 and 9, and with caution 7b, in light woodland soil.

Adiantum ×*tracyi* (after Joseph Tracy who collected a specimen in California in 1924) is the rare sterile hybrid between *A. aleuticum* and *A. jordanii* found in Oregon and California where the parental ranges overlap. It has a loosely triangular, evergreen 1-ft. (30-cm) frond with divided basal pinnae tapering to a once-divided tip. A handsome novelty, it is much easier to cultivate and more vigorous than *A. jordanii*. Grow it in Zones 7 to 9 in moist soil and light shade.

Adiantum trapeziforme (four-sided) is a tall-growing tropical that can reach 6 ft. (2 m) in the wild and must be quite a sight. The shallowly lobed, papery pinnules terminate in an elongated point and carry a pair of oblong sori on each lobe. The species needs warm and humid conditions.

Adiantum viridemontanum (Green Mountain) is derived from the hybrid between *A. pedatum* and *A. aleuticum* and found on serpentine substrates in the Green Mountains of Vermont. It is described in *Flora of North America* (1993) as

Adiantum ×*tracyi*

Adiantum trapeziforme in the conservatory at the Hamburg Botanical Garden.

having arching to erect fronds of 1½ to 2½ ft. (45 to 75 cm) and fan-shaped to funnel-shaped blades. East Coast growers, however, report that once away from serpentine the structure is like that of a small *A. pedatum*.

Aglaomorpha

Aglaomorpha (Greek *aglaios*, splendid, and *morphe*, shape) is a genus of large epiphytes that consequently like basket culture and good drainage. The tall fronds grow from large and broad bases designed to catch litter. Bases often turn a papery brown in maturity. Leathery fronds are pinnatifid and are striking in conservatory or greenhouse settings, but can grow as houseplants where space is not limiting.

Two of the most popular species are **Aglaomorpha coronans** (crowned) from the Far East, which can reach 6 ft. (2 m), but usually displays more modestly. The bottom of the frond is a parchment paper brown with upright, contrasting brilliant emerald-green foliage.

The other is **Aglaomorpha meyeniana** (after German botanist Franz Meyen, 1804–1840), a very attractive curiosity with dark green 3-ft. (90-cm) arching fronds. Tips of fertile fronds are reduced to foliar threads with beadlike nodules along their length. Both of these species are suitable for outdoor berths in Zones 10 and 11.

Arachniodes

Synonyms *Leptorumohra*, *Polystichopsis*

The arachniodes are an elegant and tidy collection of 50 to more than 100 species (depending, per Hassler and Swale [2002], on the status of the Chinese nomenclature) of well-mannered, primarily evergreen contributions to horticulture. Along with *Cyrtomium* and *Polystichum*, they were once classified as *Aspidium*. They share the botanical characteristic of kidney-shaped indusia with *Dryopteris* and the polished, frequently bristle-tipped pinnae and pinnules with *Polystichum*.

The rhizomes are short- to long-creeping, supporting a random production of clustered to widely spaced singular fronds that do not form a stereotypical arching vase of foliage. The stipes are long, often one-half or more of the frond length, and the blades are usually broadly ovate-triangular or pentagonal. Most species are noted for their spectacular luster and all described have a characteristically elongate lower inner pinnule (basiscopic in botanese) on the basal pinnae. The veins are free and forking. Four or more vascular bundles circle the inner walls of the stipe. (On my *Arachniodes standishii* the stipe is grooved with a dominant interior bundle on either side of the cleft, and a horseshoe of three smaller bundles on the rounded opposite edge.)

Most arachniodes come to us from Asia, especially China and Japan, and many more potentially temperate ornamentals should be forthcoming (sought out) from these regions as well as the Himalayas. Two species are from the New World. Grow this five-star group of ferns in partial sun to shade in light but moist compost where they offer 12 months of brightness with a minimum amount of maintenance.

Arachniodes translates from Greek *arachnion*, spider's web, and *odes*, having the form of a spider web, or "spiderlike." Leg-

end has it that the herbarium material studied by Carl Blume (1796–1862), the botanical author, was well wrapped in cobwebs, hence the name. A more mundane explanation indicates that it was named for the spidery appearance of *A. aristata*, the type plant.

Arachniodes aristata

Prickly shield fern

Epithet means "bearded," "with a hairlike tip," or "bristlelike." Evergreen, 1½ to 2½ ft. (45 to 75 cm). Zones 6 to 9.

DESCRIPTION: The rhizome is short- to long-creeping. Hay-colored stipes, heavily tan scaled basally are one-half or often more of the frond length. The rachis is grooved, but significantly, the stipes are not. Ovate to pentagonal blades,

Aglaomorpha meyeniana growing in the Fernery at the Morris Arboretum. Note the reduced fertile fronds.

contracting abruptly to an upward thrusting dagger at the apex, sport a brilliant, bright forest-green sheen and are tripinnate to quadripinnate with 5 to 10 pairs of spine-tipped pinnae. The innermost pinnules on the lowest pinnae aim their swordlike foliage in downward extensions well exceeding the length of the adjacent pinnules. Smaller upward-thrusting pinnules on the same pinnae are longer than their neighbors, but the characteristic is not as pronounced as with the downward pair. Sori are medial with kidney-shaped indusia. The species hybridizes with *Arachniodes simplicior* and *A. standishii*.

RANGE AND HABITAT: The extensive native range includes the traditional fern-rich Asian areas of Japan, China, and Korea as well as India, the South Pacific Islands, New Zealand, and Australia. The species grows in dryish montane forests.

Arachniodes aristata combines with *Hosta* 'June' and a silvery stump.

CULTURE AND COMMENTS: Easily established, *Arachniodes aristata* will quietly enhance the lightly shaded bed in woodland duff. Although the rhizome does creep (in theory), it produces only a few fronds annually. Those few fronds are spectacularly electric with their green brilliance. Use it for glassy green contrast among the subdued soft greens and blues of hosta foliage.

'Okoze', a 6- to 10-in. (15- to 25-cm) dwarf and imbricate Japanese cultivar introduced in the United States by Asiatica Nursery of Pennsylvania, is so incredibly shiny it could easily be mistaken for a plastic fake fern. Not so, however, and with its compact habit, it has great potential for container culture and collector's pride. It is recommended for Zones 7 to 10.

'Variegata', the handsome variegated *Arachniodes*, frequently listed as a cultivar of *A. aristata*, is now classified as *A. simplicior*.

Arachniodes cavalerii

Epithet is after Julien Cavalerie, a collector who was murdered near Kunming, China.
Evergreen, 2 to 3 ft. (60 to 90 cm), usually lower in cultivation. Zones 6 to 8.

DESCRIPTION: The rhizome is erect or very short-creeping. The dark plum-colored stipes are sparsely scaly at the base and one-half of the frond length. Thin-textured but luminous bipinnate to tripinnate blades are broadly triangular with tapered tips and five or more pairs of spine-tipped pinnae. The sori with kidney-shaped indusia are scattered along veins.

RANGE AND HABITAT: This species grows in dry woods in China, Taiwan, Japan, and Thailand.

CULTURE AND COMMENTS: Although perhaps a creeper in its native conditions, in cultivation this species is more likely to be a fern of very few fronds. Handsomely shiny, however, it does well without pampering and adds gloss to shady plantings with contrasting matte foliage. The new growth is late, just after the plant has been forgotten or dismissed. Rather than lose sight of it, I do not cut back the old growth (of three or four fronds) until the new are up and about.

Arachniodes denticulata

Epithet means "slightly toothed."
Deciduous to semievergreen, 1 to 1½ ft. (30 to 45 cm). Zones 8 and 9.

DESCRIPTION: The rhizome is ascending. Reddish-brown stipes with a few linear scales are one-third to one-half of the frond length. Triangular blades are deep green and finely divided into tripinnate to quadripinnate airy foliage with five to eight hair-tipped pairs of pinnae. As is typical with *Arachniodes*, the lower innermost pinnules on the lowest pinnae are significantly longer than adjacent pinnules. Sori with kidney-shaped indusia are medial.

RANGE AND HABITAT: *Arachniodes denticulata* is one of only a handful of neotropical arachniodes. With widespread distribution, it is found in wet montane forests from Mexico to Brazil with outlying populations in the Caribbean Islands.

CULTURE AND COMMENTS: Gloriously lacy, this potentially hardy species comes highly recommended by both Mickel (1994) and Rickard (2000). Beginning fern gardeners, testing their skills (and luck), should try other ferns first, however, as this clearly needs protection and with "iffy" hardiness is not likely to be a confidence builder. As yet, it is not common in cultivation.

Arachniodes miqueliana

Epithet is after Dutch botanist Friedrich Miquel (1811–1871). Deciduous, 2 to 3 ft. (60 to 90 cm). Zones 5 to 8.

DESCRIPTION: The rhizome is long-creeping, but with restrained frond production. Chestnut-colored stipes with scattered brown scales are especially dark basally and one-half of the frond length. The triangular tripinnate to quadripinnate blades are umbrellas of soft green pinnae with markedly elongate, signature lower pinnules on the basal pinnae. Frond apices are contracted. Unlike the polished, waxy foliar surface of its relatives, this species has a light dusting of hairs on both sides of the fronds, with a significant concentration in the pinnae axis, giving the fronds a soft downy appearance. The sori with kidney-shaped indusia are medial on the lobes or segments and reputed to be briefly reddish in the center when young. The species grows readily from spores and the creeping rhizomes are easily cut apart for divisions.

RANGE AND HABITAT: *Arachniodes miqueliana* is a native of forested areas in China, Japan, and Korea as well as significantly chilled habitats of Siberia and Amur.

CULTURE AND COMMENTS: This species offers great promise as a quiet community of green lace in the company of darker, shade-loving robust companions. Once established it is quite accepting of dryish conditions (within reason), but does need filtered shade and will rejoice in humus-rich soil.

Arachniodes simplicior

East Indian holly fern

Epithet means "simpler," referring to the fronds which are less finely divided than those of *A. aristata*.

Evergreen, 1 to 2 ft. (30 to 60 cm). Zones 7 to 9.

DESCRIPTION: The rhizome is long-creeping, producing fronds periodically. The plant is not bushy in the Pacific Northwest. The tannish-green stipes with dark basal scales are upwards of one-half of the frond length. Thick radiant blades are bipinnate daggers with expansive two to five lower pairs of pinnae sweeping out well beyond the ultimate, contracted upper pinnae. Greatly extended lower innermost basal pinnules and slightly expanded upward-facing pinnules make the fern look ready to take flight. They also simplify the identification process. In cultivated material, the rachis and pinnae midribs are highlighted with a creamy stripe, one of the few temperate ferns to be variegated. The sori with kidney-shaped indusia are medial.

RANGE AND HABITAT: This species is native to the woodlands of China and Japan and has escaped in South Carolina in the United States. It is definitely not an invasive threat to the surrounding environment.

CULTURE AND COMMENTS: With its variegation, solid texture, and sparkle, this species adds a distinctive elegance in partial shade or high light (minus midday sunshine, however). The one unfortunate negative is that the young growth is surprisingly

Arachniodes simplicior with its leathery foliage and creamy medial stripe at the Rhododendron Species Botanical Garden.

Triangular fronds of *Arachniodes miqueliana* in the Mickel garden.

popular with slugs. The tough, mature foliage is quite resistant, however. It is also a stress-free indoor plant. Give it good light and a bit of room to roam. It is occasionally offered under the name *Arachniodes aristata* 'Variegata'.

'**Major**', with more pairs of pinnae, shares the sheen of the species but not the variegation. This variety provides an attractive glow in the company of soft pale greens.

Frond of *Arachniodes simplicior* with a silhouette typical of the genus.

Long plumes of *Arachniodes standishii* reach into the landscape in the garden of the late Roy Davidson.

Arachniodes standishii
Upside down fern

Epithet is perhaps after John Standish (1814–1875), a British nurseryman who imported from Japan.

Evergreen, 2 to 3 ft. (60 to 90 cm). Zones 5 to 9.

DESCRIPTION: The rhizome creeps slowly. Grooved pea-green stipes are one-third of the frond length. The stipe scales are a dark russet and especially prevalent on new growth. Broadly ovate blades, produced in a more vaselike arrangement than other arachniodes, are tripinnate-pinnatifid to, rarely, quadripinnate with 10 to 18 pairs of borderline glassy, matte green pinnae. As is typical for the genus, the innermost lower pinnules on the basal pinnae are enlarged although not so exaggerated as in related species. The sori with kidney-shaped indusia are medial and, when spores are produced at all, ripen annoyingly late in the season.

RANGE AND HABITAT: *Arachniodes standishii* grows in mountainous forests in Korea, possibly China, and in Japan, where it is common in *Cryptomeria* forests (Iwatsuki et al. 1995). The Korean material, which tends to be larger, was introduced to cultivation in the United States by Richard Lighty of Pennsylvania.

CULTURE AND COMMENTS: This species is easier to grow than it is to obtain. The long evergreen fronds arch gracefully over companions in lightly shaded, slightly moist woodlands. Upside down fern? There are a number explanations as to the why of the common name, including having veins and/or sori prominently visible on the upper surface of the frond as opposed to the underside or "down" side of the frond, not a dreadfully unusual occurrence.

The late ripening spores can be fooled into dropping. My late husband, noting my frustration one December, suggested picking a fertile pinna, wrapping it securely in white paper and heating it under the gentle warmth of an incandescent bulb. Not only did I have spores to sow the next morning, I had an unusually good crop of progeny. In general, only a small percentage of the spores germinate, although growers in the eastern United States have a higher rate of success. Until it comes from tissue culture, this species is not likely to flood the market.

Shorter Notes

Arachniodes mutica (blunt) is a 2-ft. (60-cm) evergreen with black-scaled stipes and rachises. The broadly ovate, tripinnate blades are kelly-green above and paler beneath. While the lower innermost pinnules are extended as is typical for this genus, they are not so prominent as in other arachniodes. The species is native to eastern Russia and Korea, and is common in the humus-rich understories of beech and conifer forests in Japan. Zone 6 German gardeners have successfully added it to their collections. Given its native distribution, it should be hardy in shade in at least Zones 6 to 8.

Arachniodes webbianum (after Philip Barker Webb, 1793–1854, a collector in Portugal) is from Madeira and surviving nicely in Zone 9 central England. Shiny, open-growing, triangular 2-ft. (60-cm) fronds are evergreen and bipinnate to tripinnate. This species should do well in coastal California and possibly along the seaside in the Gulf states.

Araiostegia

Araiostegia (Greek *araios*, thin, and *stege*, roof, in reference to the indusium) is a genus of five to seven species typically bearing finely divided fronds and furry creeping rhizomes. They are native to the tropics with outposts in the Himalayas.

The tender *Araiostegia hymenophylloides* (thin or membranous leaf), giant carrot fern, grows to 3 ft. (90 cm) from a fleshy rhizome and is cultivated with winter protection in Zone 6 German gardens.

Araiostegia pseudocystopteris (false *Cystopteris*), synonym *A. pulchra*, is a soft green, deciduous species from China and the Himalayas and a near relative of *Davallia*. Silver-edged pale tan scales press against the creeping rhizome seemingly waiting to be named after some sort of animal foot. The stipe is greenish brown, and the foot-long (30-cm), shiny green, triangular blades are tripinnate to quadripinnate. Sori are on the veins and held by a broad cuplike indusium. My plant grows in a glazed pot that has assorted geometric designs cut away from the sides. The rhizomes escape via the holes making for a novel departure from basket culture. I keep the plant in an unheated greenhouse for the winter (2005 low was 28°F, -2°C) but it should weather outdoors in Zones 7b to 10.

Argyrochosma

Synonyms *Cheilanthes, Notholaena, Pellaea*

Argyrochosma gathers together some 20 intriguing xeric species that until 1987 (Windham) were classified under one or another of the above synonyms. The appropriately descriptive genus name *Argyrochosma*, from the Greek *argyros*, silver, and *chosma*, powder, references the waxy, white protective foliar undercoat that decorates many of the species. Others are included by virtue of the stalks and cordate bases on the minute ultimate segments. These are plants, frequently with bluish pinnae, of the New World drylands and grow efficiently on or among rocks. In times of stress and dehydration, they will fold their pinnae to expose the waxy undersides, which will offer a bit of protection from heat and deter water loss.

Argyrochosma dealbata (whitened), synonyms *Cheilanthes dealbata, Notholaena dealbata*, and *Pellaea dealbata*, bears the consistent common name, powdery cloak fern. This miniature lime lover, native to the north-south corridor of the central United States, manages to split its 3- to 4-in. (7.5- to 10-cm) triangular blades into quadripinnate to quinquipinnate divisions of delicate finery. The undersides carry the signature coating of white farina, while the upper blade surface is dull and lacking in ornamentation. All of this diminutive foliar display is crowded atop proportionately tall, wiry stipes that are equal in length to the blade and grow from short-creeping rhizomes. This, like other members of the genus, is a plant for the grower who enjoys a challenge. It is cold tolerant in Zones 6 to 9, but needs a basic soil and is touchy about exposure (requires bright light) and drainage (must be immediate and efficient). It is so closely related to the equally difficult and beautiful border cloak fern, *A. limitanea* (bounded, limited) of the U.S. Southwest and Mexico, that they can be treated as equals in their specialized demands and garden requirements. The latter is apogamous.

A frond of *Araiostegia pseudocystopteris* retiring for the winter.

Argyrochosma dealbata nestles in rocks at the Roaring River State Park in Missouri.

Argyrochosma limitanea in the University of California Botanical Garden at Berkeley.

Argyrochosma fendleri (for August Fendler, 1813–1883, a German naturalist who plant collected in the U.S. Southwest and Central America), the zigzag cliff break or latticework cloak-fern, synonyms *Notholaena fendleri*, *Cheilanthes cancellata*, and *Pellaea fendleri*, has an open "latticework" structure of up to 12 in. (30 cm), carrying minute starry sprays of pinnules on zigzag stems. The under surfaces are protected from the elements with a white waxy coating. This is the only *Argyrochosma* with a preference for acid soil and can be admired on the trails in New Mexico and Colorado. While it is not generally in cultivation, for potential garden use in Zones 5 to 8 give it good drainage in rough compost preferably amended with small, 1/2 in. (13 mm) or less, bark chips. Protection from winter wet is mandatory.

Argyrochosma jonesii (after Jones), Jones' cloak fern, is a rarely cultivated delicacy from limestone sites in the U.S. Southwest and adjacent regions in Mexico. The stipes are dark and the lanceolate blades are bipinnate to tripinnate with pinnae and pinnules supported by dark stalks. It does not share the characteristic white waxy undercoat that typifies the genus. It can be cultivated with the utmost care by California xeric specialists in coarse, well-drained but moist limestone grit. It will survive in Zones 8 and 9 cold, but prefers a summer rather than winter rainy season.

Argyrochosma microphylla (small leaves, a name that could be applied to the entire genus) lacks a white petticoat, but shares the typical display of minute dusky pinnae. Tripinnate to quadripinnate ovate blades are carried on dark stipes with the whole ranging from 5 to 10 in. (13 to 25 cm) in height. This native of limited limestone sites on both sides of the U.S.–Mexican border is an attractive addition to pot culture collections or, for the truly committed, a customized site in desertlike Zone 8 to 9 garden surroundings. Wet winter habitats are not suitable.

Aspidotis
Lace ferns

Aspidotis is a small genus with four species, three in western North America and one in Mexico. It prefers an exposed life among rocks, frequently serpentine, often in alpine settings. The elongate, glossy, pinnae segments are needlelike with a groove down the center. Sori with inrolled, papery, false indusia are submarginal, trimming the sides in either a linear (*A. densa*) or segmental (*A. californica* and *A. carlotta-halliae*) pattern. They have a singular vascular bundle and free veins. The genus name is derived from the Greek *aspidotes*, shield bearing, in reference to the false indusia.

Aspidotis has circulated among assorted classifications typically applied to dryland genera, including *Pellaea*, *Cryptogramma*, and more recently *Cheilanthes*. Among other characteristics, its shiny pinnae distinguish it from the dusky pellaeas and hairy cheilanthes. Splitting it from *Cryptogramma* is more challenging. Unlike *Aspidotis*, the latter is strongly dimorphic (having different sterile and fertile fronds) and lacks a linear groove on the surface of the pinnae segments. Both, however, present a united front with a stead-

fast resistance to domestication ("cultivated with difficulty" [Lellinger 1985]).

Aspidotis californica (of California), California lace fern, synonym *Cheilanthes californica*, is a low-growing, to 1 ft. (30 cm), species from granitic, not serpentine, rocky outcrops in lower to mid elevations in the coastal California mountains and Sierra Nevada. The reddish brown stipes are twice as long as the triangular blade. Five to seven pairs of pinnae carry sprays of finely divided quadripinnate to quinquipinnate foliage. The round sori are submarginal in disconnected segments with an overlay of papery indusia. It is a teasingly lovely Zone 8 species but not for the comforts of gardens.

Aspidotis carlotta-halliae (after Carlotta Hall) is a fertile hybrid between *A. californica* and *A. densa* midway in appearance between the two. Like *A. densa* it prefers serpentine habitats. Like *A. californica* it is quadripinnate with separated soral segments. Like them both, it is garden resistant. It is native to Zone 7 California.

Aspidotis densa (dense, crowded), Indian's dream, synonyms *Cheilanthes siliquosa*, *Cryptogramma densa*, and *Pellaea densa*, is a compact 4- to 8-in. (10- to 20-cm) evergreen with shiny, russet, strongly vertical, flagpolelike stipes bearing compact triangular, essentially monomorphic bipinnate to tripinnate blades. The five to seven pairs of congested pinnae terminate in linear, pointed, striated segments, pseudoconiferous in appearance. The sori are confined to the margins, but not the apex of the fertile pinnule, and are shielded with an inrolled, dryish false indusium. The species is native to craggy, usually serpentine, dryish outcrops where it snuggles against the rocks and extends its roots under their cover for both protection and a touch of cool moisture. It can be visually confused with its montane neighbor, *Cryptogramma acrostichoides*, especially when the latter has not produced its dimorphic foliage. Look for *Cryptogramma* on neutral or granitic substrates where the sterile, parsleylike, soft foliage is low and spreading and the fertile fronds are upright. It is not always easily or clearly differentiated especially since sunshine will modify the habit. *Aspidotis densa* is sometimes cultivated, but not for long. It is a plant of Zones 5 to 9 and away from its natural native setting needs very specialized intensive care, with customized soil, winter rain protection, superb drainage, and bright light. Rather than use it in the rock garden, treat it as a fern to admire, along with the views, on treks in the mid-to-upper regions of the mountains from British Columbia south to California, east to Wyoming and Utah and, as a rarity, in occasional soil-specific sites in Quebec. In addition to a cultivation challenge, *A. densa* brings us a curious common name, Indian's dream, whose origin in spite of extensive research efforts remains a mystery with a dimension of intrigue.

Asplenium

Aspleniums offer a wonderful assortment of fascinating and decorative ferns ranging from elfin and temperamental miniatures to willing rock plants and finally to mammoth tropicals that perch in treetops and adorn living rooms. The name is

Aspidotis densa in the mountains of Washington State.

Asplenium trichomanes and *A. ruta-muraria* at home on a church wall in Wales.

derived from the Greek *a*, without, and *splen*, spleen, and was named by Pliny and Dioscorides, the father of pharmacy, around A.D. 60 because of the fern's reputed ability to cure disorders of the spleen and liver. (Boil the "leaves" in wine and drink for 40 days was Dioscorides' recommendation.) There are approximately 700 species and more than 100 hybrids in this sprawling genus. They are largely denizens of tropical comforts. The temperate species, by contrast, prefer challenging rocky substrates, cliff faces, and associated inhospitable and frequently inaccessible sites.

Many authors include *Camptosorus*, *Ceterach*, *Phyllitis*, and *Schaffneria* in the *Asplenium* classification due to the ability of these genera to interbreed. However, there are botanical differences that can warrant maintaining them as separate genera. I follow the lead here of popular works by Chris Page (1982), John Mickel (1994), and Barbara Hoshizaki and Robbin Moran (2001).

The usually erect rhizomes of this genus have unique translucent clathrate (latticelike) scales. The stipes of varying heights are dark or may be a rather peculiar two-toned combination of dark on the outer side and green inward. This contrasting feature frequently continues up into the rachis. Characteristic back-to-back C-shaped vascular bundles merge into an X in the frond's upper portions. Blades are evergreen and range from simple to finely dissected tripinnate to quadripinnate laciness. Distinctive sori are linear and arranged in a herringbone fashion along veins. A single indusial flap of tissue opens in the direction of the pinna midrib (thus differentiating this genus from *Phyllitis* with its two-sided double opening sori). The veins are free.

Most temperate species tend to be alpines that cling tenaciously to their preferred rock strata and adjust reluctantly to an exiled life away from such habitats. It can be done, however, with geological wisdom tempered by a great deal of patience and testing (of both the fern and grower). While some specimens are willing in cultivation, others are difficult, and still others are very difficult and downright ungrateful. Customized container culture offers the best promise for initial trials. With many of the alpine- and rock garden–inclined species being dwarf at maturity, containers offer the added advantage of revisiting details in "up close and personal" viewing, portability to find the ideal site, and a measure of isolation from the ever-present threatening army of slugs. Regardless of the selected planting site, *Asplenium* crowns with their "delicate constitution" should be protected from rain or sprinkler-induced splattering soil. A top dressing of moss or pebbles and, in specific instances, limestone chips serves admirably to deflect superfluous moisture and give the planting a tidy presentation. (This is true with all dwarf ferns.)

Many of these species are lime lovers, but I have had disastrous results when adding lime especially that which is traditionally used to sweeten lawns. Gypsum, though periodically recommended, has been deadly. What is needed is a handy limestone quarry as a source for rocks and chips. Barring that, I add eggshells, which may or may not help the ferns, but at least makes me feel as if I am being accommodating. I have

also had success by lining the larger species along the concrete foundation of the house and/or adding chunks of broken concrete to the planting hole.

The tropical species, primarily for indoor use, like good humidity, small pots, filtered light, and minimal watering. More indoor fern furnishings are lost to drowning than they are to drought.

Aspleniums rarely produce offshoots for division. They compensate by coming readily and rapidly from spores. I sow mine on my traditional earthworm compost mix and, when transplanting, I add grit.

Historically, aspleniums have contributed to concoctions of herbal cures. In addition to healing the spleen, they have been used as a poultice for wounds, tea tonic for curing baldness, and even as a salve for broken limbs.

Asplenium adiantum-nigrum
Black spleenwort
Asplenium cuneifolium × *A. onopteris*.
Epithet is derived from *adiantos*, unwetted, and *nigrum*, black. Evergreen, 6 to 12 in. (15 to 30 cm). Zones 6 to 8.

DESCRIPTION: The rhizome is erect to short-creeping. Brittle, round stipes are one-half the length of the frond and are a lustrous chestnut with black scales surrounding a slightly swollen base. The characteristic darkness transforms to green at or near the junction with the blade. Strongly triangular, lacquered green blades are a variable bipinnate to tripinnate with 5 to 12 pairs of pointed pinnae. Blades can be ascending or horizontal depending on exposure and the size of the frond. Sori are linear with a linear indusial flap.

RANGE AND HABITAT: The range for this species is erratic. It can be found in lower elevations in Scandinavia, where it is endangered because of overcollecting, rocky coastal or mortared wall sites in the British Isles, humid terrains in Central Europe, and North Africa, Kenya, and Iran. In addition, it frequents forested areas in the Himalayas, where it occurs in sites up to 9000 ft. (2700 m). Finally it is found in some very rare stations in the continental United States as well as lava and scrublands in Hawaii. Although primarily mildly basic, the substrates vary and include serpentine for subsp. *cornunense*. Chris Page (1982) warns that in Britain adders enjoy a mutual habitat.

CULTURE AND COMMENTS: In spite of its divergent distribution, this is not an easy plant to cultivate. Good drainage is essential. It will establish more readily in the fissures of a shaded rock wall than in the luxury of a garden bed. The whole plant is glowing and worth the experimentation to find it a happy home. And, in addition to being welcome in the garden, for those lucky enough to have an adequate supply the petite fronds serve admirably as a shiny foil in flower arrangements. There is considerable latitude in frond division and height with some 20 varieties ranging from incised to crested being described in the literature of the early 1900s. Many of these have been lost to cultivation, but I am nurturing and testing a congested 4-in. (10-cm) variety that came from spores gathered from a mortared wall in Britain. It is but one of the variables.

Asplenium adulterinum

Asplenium trichomanes × *A. viride.*
Epithet means "not pure."
Evergreen, 4 to 6 in. (10 to 15 cm). Zones 5 to 8.

DESCRIPTION: The rhizome is erect, bearing full rosettes of lax fronds. The stipes are dark reflecting the *Asplenium trichomanes* heritage but become *A. viride* green in the upper portions of the rachis, making it an easy task to identify this

Asplenium adiantum-nigrum in its preferred mural habitat in England.

The congested form of *Asplenium adiantum-nigrum* prefers a rocky limestone setting.

Asplenium adulterinum in container culture.

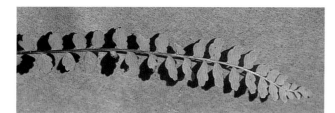

Rachis of *Asplenium adulterinum* progresses from black to green.

Asplenium ×*alternifolium* in a customized rocky habitat in the Jessen garden.

hybrid. Lanceolate, once-pinnate blades taper at both ends with 20 to 30 pairs of rounded pinnae. The sori are linear and covered with matching linear indusia. In spite of its hybrid origin, this fern reproduces readily from spores.

RANGE AND HABITAT: *Asplenium adulterinum* is rare in nature and grows in limestone crevices or, unlike its parents, on serpentine rocks in scattered sites in Scandinavia and Central Europe, where it is endangered. A very disjunct population occurs in British Columbia, Canada.

CULTURE AND COMMENTS: A charming dwarf, this hybrid adapts to rock garden culture (in pots or gardens) in a granular, well-draining, loose soil mixture. Specialized serpentine or limestone soil is, fortunately, not necessary for success. This fern prefers bright light with all but midday sun being acceptable.

Asplenium ×*alternifolium*
Alternate-leaved spleenwort
Asplenium septentrionale × *A. trichomanes* subsp. *trichomanes*.
Epithet means "alternate-leaved."
Evergreen, 2 to 6 in. (5 to 15 cm). Zones 6 to 8.

DESCRIPTION: The rhizome is erect. The plants are densely bushy with slender, dark stipes that are one-third to one-half of the length of the frond. The soft green blades are narrow with 6 to 12 stalked and alternate, mitten-shaped pinnae pointing towards the apex. Sori with abortive spores are few and linear.

Asplenium antiquum in a conservatory setting.

RANGE AND HABITAT: This extremely rare sterile hybrid is native to acid environments in the British Isles, Europe, Russia, and the Himalayas as well as a lonely site or two in the eastern United States.

CULTURE AND COMMENTS: Luxurious when well situated in acid rock garden pockets, this fetching little fern prefers partially sunny exposures.

Asplenium antiquum
Japanese bird's nest fern
Epithet means "ancient." Alternate spelling is *Asplenium antiguum.*
Evergreen, 2 to 3 ft. (60 to 90 cm). Zones 9 and 10.

DESCRIPTION: The rhizome is thick. Densely scaly stipes are very short to 2 in. (5 cm). Shiny, bright green blades are entire, gradually tapered at the base and pointed at the apex. The prominent midrib is rounded and succulent. Sori march in herringbone fashion on the upper portions of the frond and are covered with linear indusia.

RANGE AND HABITAT: This species is native to Korea, Hong Kong, Taiwan, and Japan, where it grows in dark forests on moist cliffs or more often on tree trunks.

CULTURE AND COMMENTS: Essentially for outdoor cultivation in Southern California, Florida, or comparable sites in greenhouses or living rooms elsewhere, this fern is easier to maintain than its cousin, *Asplenium nidus*. As with most epiphytes it should not be overpotted. It likes bright filtered light, porous soil, and a minimum of watering.

The attractive cultivar '**Victoria**' has wavy margins.

Asplenium bulbiferum
Mother fern
Epithet means "with bulbils."
Evergreen, 2 to 4 ft. (60 to 120 cm). Zones 9 and 10.

DESCRIPTION: The rhizome is erect. Stipes of two-toned green and brown are one-third the length of the frond. Ovate blades are variable bipinnate to tripinnate with families of ready-to-root babies on the upper frond surface. Sori with matching indusia are singular on the segments.

RANGE AND HABITAT: Mother fern grows in most of Asia as well as Australia and New Zealand. It prefers deeply shaded damp to evenly moist sites.

CULTURE AND COMMENTS: Outside of warmer areas, this species is popularly encountered as a houseplant with pots beckoning for adoption wherever ferns are offered for sale. It is easy to grow, and prefers low light and an evenly moist soil. The plentifully produced bulbils root themselves in moist compost and they keep on coming.

Asplenium csikii
Synonym *Asplenium trichomanes* subsp. *pachyrachis*
Epithet is after Ernö Csiki, a late nineteenth-century Hungarian beetle specialist.
Evergreen, 4 to 6 in. (10 to 15 cm). Zones 5 to 8.

DESCRIPTION: The rhizome is erect. Dark chocolate-black stipes are short to almost nonexistent and bear an occasional black scale or hair. Narrowly lanceolate blades are once-pinnate with 10 to 15 pairs of overlapping blue-green pinnae. Sori are in a linear herringbone pattern with matching indusia and are produced on very young plants.

RANGE AND HABITAT: This species is from limestone walls and overhangs in the British Isles and Europe. Given its

Bulbils crowd the fronds on *Asplenium bulbiferum.*

Asplenium csikii 'Trogyense' is a rock garden treasure.

similarity to *Asplenium trichomanes*, it likely goes unrecognized more often than not.

CULTURE AND COMMENTS: A charming miniature that splays like a starfish on rocky fissures, it is best in coarse, well-drained container culture. I have added very small bits of broken concrete to serve as slow-release lime.

The attractive '**Trogyense**' has deeply lobed pinnae.

Asplenium ebenoides
Scott's spleenwort, dragon tail fern
Synonyms *Asplenosorus ×ebenoides, Asplenium ×ebenoides*
Asplenium platyneuron × Camptosorus rhizophyllus.
Epithet means "like ebony."
Evergreen, 6 to 12 in. (15 to 30 cm). Zones 5 to 8.

DESCRIPTION: The rhizome is erect. Stipes of up to one-half the length of the frond are plum colored with dusky scales.

Fronds of *Asplenium ebenoides* arch in the familiar pattern of its parent, *Camptosorus rhizophyllus*.

A robust *Asplenium fontanum* in the Gassner garden.

Blades are lanceolate and irregularly divided from once-pinnate at the base to lobed, pinnatifid, or entire at the apex. Reflecting the influence of *Camptosorus rhizophyllus*, this hybrid will occasionally tip root. Sori are linear with linear indusia.

RANGE AND HABITAT: Dragon tail fern was first discovered on limestone cliffs along the Schuylkill River outside of Philadelphia, Pennsylvania, in 1866. It has since gained considerable status in scientific research as "the most famous hybrid fern" (*Flora of North America* 1993), and was one of the first to be recreated in a laboratory in 1902. Primarily of limestone and/or sandstone habitats in the eastern United States, it has been sterile in the wild except for one location in Hale County, Alabama. Spore-grown progeny from the fertile colony are now widely available commercially.

CULTURE AND COMMENTS: The dragon tail fern is a curiosity with its variable frond configurations even on the same plant. Slugs find it equally fascinating. I have had entire populations disappear overnight and now have mine planted in a hollow in a limestone rock which in turn is well off the ground on a display table. With its unusual, rather unfernlike dimensions, as well as its history, this fern is well worth special attention to its welfare. It is also the parent of the exceptionally unusual trigeneric hybrid with *Phyllitis scolopendrium*, which is worth even more attention for the fortunate few who may own this coveted rarity.

The dwarf form of *Asplenium fontanum* is an excellent selection for a trough or small, rock-protected setting.

Asplenium flabellifolium

Necklace fern, walking fern
Epithet means "fan-shaped," referring to the pinnules.
Evergreen, 6 to 15 in. (15 to 38 cm). Zone 9. Apogamous.

DESCRIPTION: The rhizome is erect, but fronds tend to be prostrate. Slender green stipes are one-third to one-half of the frond length. Blades are once-pinnate with 10 to 12 pairs of fan-shaped pinnae. The rachis extends well beyond the foliage and often bears a tip-rooting bulbil. Sori are linear with matching indusia.

RANGE AND HABITAT: Although delicate in appearance, this species colonizes in dry rocky sites in the company of *Cheilanthes* in New Zealand. In Australia it also naturalizes in damp forests as well as cliff faces, dry rocks, and scrublands.

CULTURE AND COMMENTS: With its cascading fronds, the necklace fern makes a wonderful basket display especially when the tips can be secured so that they root and walk about in the basket. The plant can be overwintered in Zone 8 in a cool, frost-free greenhouse. In all locations it needs to be out of the reach of roving slugs.

Asplenium fontanum

Fountain spleenwort, smooth rock spleenwort
Epithet means "growing near springs or streams."
Evergreen, 4 to 8 in. (10 to 20 cm). Zones 5 to 8.

DESCRIPTION: The rhizome is erect. Stipes transition from a dark base to green and are up to one-third of the frond length. Bright green blades are lacy, bipinnate-pinnatifid, lanceolate, and broadest in the lower midsection of the 10 to 20 pairs of pinnae. Sori are linear with linear indusia.

RANGE AND HABITAT: A denizen of dryish, alpine, limestone crevices and walls, this species grows in Europe and the Himalayas.

CULTURE AND COMMENTS: Truly a gem with petite green "fountains" of fronds, the fountain spleenwort is best planted in the controlled environment of a trough or alpine house. Loose soil, preferably with a touch of limestone, protection from overwatering, and precautions for slugs and snails will help to maintain this species at its ornamental best. A miniature replica that matures at 3 to 4 in. (7.5 to 10 cm) is in the trade in the United States and Britain and is a charming choice for a groundcover in bonsai plantings as well as the elite section of the rare plant collection.

Subsp. *pseudofontanum* is a geographical variant from Asia.

Asplenium foreziense

Synonym *Asplenium foresiense*
Epithet is after the Forez region in east-central France.
Evergreen, 3 to 8 in. (7.5 to 20 cm). Zones 5 to 8.

DESCRIPTION: The rhizome is erect. The stipes of one-fourth the frond length are bicolored, grooved, and shiny green on the inward side backed by an undercoat of glossy brown. Sparse hairs are color-coordinated respectively. Blades are narrowly lanceolate with 10 to 15 pairs of bright green bipinnate pinnae. Sori are linear with linear indusia.

RANGE AND HABITAT: This species is exclusively European and unlike many of the alpine aspleniums prefers hollows and fissures in vertical acid rather than limestone accommodations.

CULTURE AND COMMENTS: Like so many aspleniums this brings diminutive charms to partially shaded rock gardens, amended with coarse soil, but because of slug hazards is best displayed in containers well distanced from even the smallest of the marauders. There is also a very rare forked form.

Asplenium incisum

Epithet means "incised."
Evergreen, 6 to 12 in. (15 to 30 cm). Zones 6 to 9.

DESCRIPTION: The rhizome is erect. Stipes of one-fourth the frond length are green and slightly grooved. Narrowly lanceolate blades are once-pinnate or more commonly bipinnate with 10 to 20 pairs of pinnae. They are widest in the

The forked form of *Asplenium foreziense* in the Baggett garden. Photo by Jim Baggett.

The alpine *Asplenium foreziense* serves nobly in the chunky surrounds of a rock garden.

Asplenium marinum grows out from a retaining wall by a bathing beach along the Atlantic coast of southwestern England.

Fertile frond with single sori on *Asplenium monanthes*.

Asplenium monanthes in a grit-laden container on the protected and partially sunny side of the house.

upper midsection. The basal pinnae are greatly reduced. Sori are linear and, with the indusia, spread across the lower frond surface.

RANGE AND HABITAT: This species is native to Sakhalin, Siberia, Korea, China, and Taiwan, and is especially common in Japan where it inhabits rocky sites.

CULTURE AND COMMENTS: Once again vigilance for ever-ready slugfests is required. Test your plants in protected sites. Unfortunately, like many favorite aspleniums, these are vulnerable but worth a concerted effort to get them established. I have also found that juvenile plants are more appetizing so that older, and perhaps toughened, specimens are better prepared to withstand the hazards of assorted predators.

Asplenium marinum
Sea spleenwort
Epithet means "of the sea."
Evergreen, 4 to 10 in. (10 to 25 cm). Zones 8 (with appropriate pampering) and 9.

DESCRIPTION: The rhizome is erect. The marginally winged stipes are deep purple and usually up to one-third of the frond length. Once-pinnate kelly-green blades are succulent and lanceolate with 20 to 25 pairs of stalked pinnae. Sori are easily recognized by their herringbone, linear pattern with an indusial flap.

RANGE AND HABITAT: Native to coastal sites facing the Atlantic Ocean or Mediterranean Sea, sea spleenwort grows in frost-free pockets with perpetual humidity on rock walls or in the security of sea caves. In the British Isles "it occurs where the sea is warmer than the land in the coldest weather, and where fine spray carries this winter warmth on to suitable rock faces, minimizing frost" (Page 1982).

CULTURE AND COMMENTS: This beautiful, but somewhat temperamental, dwarf species is a magnificent ornamental when grown in its frost-free range or a frost-protected site. Otherwise, it is eminently suited to, and long-lived, in a traditional terrarium. Several specialists in the British Isles have created customized habitats to accommodate the plant's specific requirements, with the most successful being a modified pseudo-cave in the scientifically designed garden of Alastair Wardlaw of Glasgow, Scotland.

Asplenium monanthes
Single sorus spleenwort
Epithet means "one-flowered," referring to the single sorus.
Evergreen, 5 to 10 in. (13 to 25 cm). Zones 8 (with protection) and 9. Apogamous.

DESCRIPTION: The rhizome is erect. Dusky, shiny stipes are one-fifth the frond length, naked, and slightly grooved on the upper surface. Blades are linear with 20 or more pairs of irregularly shaped oblong to rectangular, rather than rounded, sea-green pinnae. The species is recognized by the single (rarely more) indusium-covered, linear sorus that runs parallel to the edge on the pinna's lower side.

RANGE AND HABITAT: This species grows in rocky sites as well as piney woods from South America up through Mexico and in rare stations across a southern swath of the United States. It is also found in Hawaii, the Caribbean, Africa, and the Atlantic Islands.

CULTURE AND COMMENTS: I have given this species the same specialized treatment as the xeric ferns in my collection. They are planted in fast-draining, loose soil in a container with a southern exposure well protected from cold winter north winds. They should certainly do in Zone 8 partially shaded rock gardens, in coarse compost, with an emergency covering when threatened by temperatures below 20°F (-7°C).

Asplenium montanum
Mountain spleenwort
Epithet means "of the mountains."
Evergreen, 3 to 6 in. (7.5 to 15 cm). Zones 4 to 8.

DESCRIPTION: The rhizome is erect. Stipes are one-half of the frond length, briefly dark at the base, and grade into green. Warm green, narrowly triangular blades are bipinnate in the lower pair or two of pinnae, and once-pinnate as the pairs of pinnae approach the frond's apex. Sori are linear with linear indusia.

RANGE AND HABITAT: The mountain spleenwort grows on sandstone and acidic rocks down the backbone of the eastern United States from Connecticut to Alabama with the greatest concentration in the Appalachian regions. Look for it also in crevices on the walls approaching Frank Lloyd Wright's Fallingwater in western Pennsylvania. *Flora of North America* (1993) calls this fern "an ecological specialist" because it tends to be a loner in its preferred habitats.

CULTURE AND COMMENTS: While many rock garden spleenworts prefer limestone, here is a miniature that acclimates, by choice, to acid substrates. Even so, it is not eager to be introduced to garden culture. Give it a niche in a shaded, crumbly rock wall.

Asplenium nidus
Bird's nest fern
Epithet means "nest."
Evergreen, 3 to 5 ft. (1 to 1.75 m) tall. Zones 10 and 11.

DESCRIPTION: The fronds with virtually no stipe are undivided and it is especially significant for fine tuning that the midrib on the underside of the frond is rounded rather than keeled.

RANGE AND HABITAT: This pantropical species usually perches in trees.

CULTURE AND COMMENTS: Although it is an epiphyte in wild habitats, this species will grow as a terrestrial when provided with airy, fast-draining soil (either basically mineral or basically humus) in filtered shade. It is an easy and especially rewarding big-guy plant in the tropical garden. (Description by George Schenk.)

There are several cultivars including *Asplenium nidus* var. *plicatum*, commonly called the lasagna fern.

Asplenium obovatum subsp. *billotii*
Lanceolate spleenwort
Synonyms *Asplenium obovatum* subsp. *lanceolatum*, *A. billotii*

Asplenium montanum on a cliff face in Pennsylvania.

Asplenium nidus at 10 or 12 years old is about 7 to 8 ft. (2.1 to 2.4 m) wide. It will go on to become a 12 footer (3.6 m). Photo by George Schenk.

Asplenium nidus var. *plicatum*, the lasagna fern, in an indoor fern corridor at Longwood Gardens.

Asplenium obtusatum surf side on a sandy beach on New Zealand's South Island.

Epithets derived from *obovatum*, inverted, and *billotii*, after Billot.

Evergreen, 4 to 10 in. (10 to 25 cm). Zones 8 and 9.

DESCRIPTION: The rhizome is short-creeping or ascending. Stipes are one-third the length of the frond and bicolored, predominantly green on the upper surface and brown on the basal portions of the lower surface. Ovate-lanceolate blades are bipinnate with 10 to 20 pairs of slightly shiny midgreen pinnae. The lower pair is significantly smaller than those above and is inclined downwards. The sori are linear but short and when ripe appear to be round. The indusia bulge.

RANGE AND HABITAT: This species is European including the British Isles and is found primarily in acid grit, cliff faces, and rocks in coastal regions.

CULTURE AND COMMENTS: An engaging little plant, lanceolate spleenwort is best in an alpine house away from the extremes of temperatures. Like many aspleniums it is admired by slugs and protection is an on-going requirement. New growth is early—another reason to tuck the plant in an alpine house.

Asplenium obtusatum
Shore spleenwort
Epithet means "blunt."
Evergreen, 6 to 18 in. (15 to 45 cm). Zones 8 (with protection) and 9.

DESCRIPTION: The rhizome is thick and ascending. Fleshy stipes with translucent, plum-colored scales are green above and darker at the base and up to one-half the length of the frond. Once-pinnate blades are lanceolate with 10 to 15 pairs of stalked, round-tipped toothy pinnae. Sori and indusia are linear along the veins.

RANGE AND HABITAT: This succulent New Zealand native grows just ashore from where the Hector's dolphins romp. It is also found in Australia and the Pacific Islands. Salt spray and sandy soils are standard habitat companions.

CULTURE AND COMMENTS: With dutiful attention to the slug watch, this is a beautiful fern for gardens in California, the coastal British Isles, and the collector's customized, protected sites in the temperate Pacific Northwest of the United States. Give it sandy humus and bright indirect light.

Asplenium platyneuron
Ebony spleenwort
Epithet means "broad-nerved, wide-veined."
Evergreen, 8 to 18 in. (20 to 45 cm). Zones 4 to 8. Dimorphic.

DESCRIPTION: The rhizome is erect. Short stipes are a polished, dark mahogany-brown and usually about one-fifth or less of the frond length. Lanceolate blades are once-pinnate with up to 40 pairs of auriculate pinnae without stalks. It is of diagnostic significance that the pinnae are alternate and the auricles overlap the rachis. The sterile fronds are lax and short; the fertile fronds, upright and taller. Sori and indusia are linear in a herringbone pattern. This species is very close in appearance to *Asplenium resiliens* but differs in having dark reddish-brown stipes rather than black and having alternate pinnae that usually overlap the rachis. It hybridizes with a

Asplenium platyneuron in the rock garden at the Mount Cuba Center.

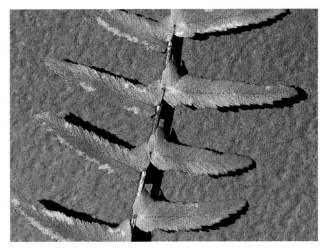

Detail of alternate pinnae overlapping the rachis on *Asplenium platyneuron.*

number of aspleniums, the best known being with *A. montanum* to form *A. bradleyi.* It also hybridizes with *Camptosorus rhizophyllus* to form *Asplenium ebenoides.*

RANGE AND HABITAT: This is primarily a midwestern and eastern U.S. native with a disjunct population in Arizona and another in South Africa. It grows in basic and slightly acid soils, on buildings, in woodlands, and in scrub. It prefers light shade.

CULTURE AND COMMENTS: I think the easiest way to acquire this fern is to buy property where it is already established. Pampering is more of a hindrance than help, and even in the wild, populations are unstable, appearing and disappearing seemingly at whim. Give it good drainage and good wishes. Ironically, this is one *Asplenium* that will persevere in spite of slug attacks. The long-ago former name for this plant was *A. ebeneum.* No fan of name changes, D. C. Eaton commented in 1878, "Although the Linnaean name for the present fern is unquestionably the oldest, it is scarcely probable that those authors who are disposed to insist upon an inflexible law of priority will attempt to replace the name which has been accepted by nearly all botanists for nearly a century by one so inappropriate as *A. platyneuron.*" He was 10 years too early. *Asplenium platyneuron* became official in 1888.

Asplenium resiliens
Black-stemmed spleenwort
Epithet means "resilient, springy."
Evergreen, 6 to 12 in. (15 to 30 cm). Zones 6 to 9. Apogamous.

DESCRIPTION: The rhizome is ascending. Short stipes are shiny black and one-fourth the length of the frond or usually shorter. Linear blades are once-pinnate with a sharp auricle that does not cross the rachis. Up to 40 pairs of opposite pinnae tend towards bluish green. Sori and indusia are two to five pairs per pinna.

RANGE AND HABITAT: The black-stemmed spleenwort is found on limestone rocks and in crevices from Delaware south and west to Texas in the United States, as well as the Caribbean, Mexico, and down into South America.

CULTURE AND COMMENTS: A challenging species for the determined collector, this fern will establish, albeit reluctantly, in limestone-improved garden sites and may even last a year or two. Give it a top dressing of marble chips. The opposite pinnae help to distinguish it from *Asplenium platyneuron.*

Asplenium ruta-muraria
Wall rue spleenwort
Epithet means "wall rue."
Evergreen, 2 to 6 in. (5 to 15 cm). Zones 4 to 8.

DESCRIPTION: The rhizome is short-creeping to erect. Stipes are plum-colored at the base, grading into green, and are usually one-half of the frond length. Small triangular blades with two to five pairs of pinnae are bipinnate with variable rounded to wedge-shaped pinnae. Sori and indusia are linear and abundant.

RANGE AND HABITAT: This species appears to grow everywhere except in your garden. It is native to North America, Europe, North Africa, the Middle East, and most of Asia. It colonizes in the mortared crevices of historic European and

Asplenium resiliens in the crags on a rocky slope in Missouri.

British buildings as well as the surrounding walls. It can also be found on limestone ledges, cliffs, and rocky sites. In the United States, however, it does not grow on the walls of buildings. Are ours too young? (Or perhaps a different, yet-to-be-determined species?)

CULTURE AND COMMENTS: The lush clusters of this deceptively sturdy wee plant peer from inhospitable alkaline niches and taunt the would-be grower. Wall rue does not transplant and is not long-lived from spores. This is in the classification of "to admire" rather than "to cultivate" for most gardeners. Historically, however, it was held in high esteem when functional and perceived herbal value were far more essential than ornamentation. In incipient efforts at animal husbandry European dairymaids, for example, fed their cattle daily doses of *Asplenium ruta-muraria* (an all-purpose cure-all) to prevent milk from souring and also to keep their cows from becoming bewitched.

Asplenium septentrionale
Forked spleenwort
Epithet means "northern."
Evergreen, 2 to 6 in. (5 to 15 cm). Zones 4 to 8.

DESCRIPTION: The rhizome is erect. The brownish-transitioning-to-green stipes split once or twice into forks at the tips and that is the extent of the frond. There are no pinnae. Sori and indusia are linear along the narrow ultimate segments.

RANGE AND HABITAT: This is a fern of acid habitats usually at high elevations in North America, Europe, including the British Isles where it is rare, Asia, China, and Taiwan.

CULTURE AND COMMENTS: Easily confused with a wispy tuft of bright green grass, *Asplenium septentrionale* does not readily adapt to domestication. It is charming and needs a niche in an acid pocket ("like those in old overalls" [Schenk, pers. comm.]). Pot culture with acidic grit and good drainage offers the best opportunity for success. For a similar visual I recommend *A.* ×*alternifolium*, the hybrid with *A. trichomanes*, which is far more vigorous and generous with frond output.

Slender fronds of *Asplenium septentrionale* sheltered by boulders in the Swiss alps.

Asplenium ruta-muraria in an alpine setting near the summit of Austria's Grossglockner Pass.

Upright fronds of *Asplenium trichomanes* in the alpine garden at the Rhododendron Species Botanical Garden.

Asplenium trichomanes subsp. *hastatum* in the garden of *Asplenium* specialist Stefan Jessen.

Sori on the fronds of *Asplenium trichomanes*

Asplenium trichomanes

Maidenhair spleenwort

Epithet means "soft or thin hair." Also from Theophrastus, "hair madness."

Evergreen, 4 to 8 in. (10 to 20 cm). Zones 3 to 9.

DESCRIPTION: The rhizome is ascending. Glossy reddish-brown stipes with a flattened groove are one-fourth to one-third of the frond length and barely visible under the foliage. Some are persistent for years with batons of upright, naked spikes. Narrow, once-pinnate blades are linear with 20 to 30 pairs of round to oblong, matte green pinnae. Sori and indusia are linear in a herringbone pattern.

Asplenium trichomanes is a botanically complex species with chromosome numbers, ecology, and to a certain extent morphology factoring in identification. Subspecies and proposed subspecies number 20 in 2005. The most recognized are **subsp. *trichomanes*** with a strong preference for acidic habitats. Distinguishing characteristics according to Øllgaard and Tind (1993) are, "Plants growing on rock walls tend to arch away and down from the substrate; petiole (stipe) red-brown; the pinnae are shed from the ageing leaves, leaving the persisting leafless midribs and petioles as a tuft for several years." **Subsp. *quadrivalens*** is the lime lover of the lot, adorning castle walls and decorating European antiquities. Again quoting Øllgaard and Tind (1993), "Plants growing on walls tend to have the leaves appressed to the substrate; the petiole (stipe) is dark blackish-brown; most pinnae persist on old leaves until the whole leaf is shed." Finer species splitting yields **subsp. *hastatum***, which grows on limestone rocks and has arrowhead-shaped pinnules, and **subsp. *inexpectans***, which has "the blade tapering abruptly at the apex, the pinnae closely set . . . and usually perpendicular throughout most of the blade . . . often

Asplenium trichomanes 'Cristatum' in the Baggett garden.

parallel-sided, convex and saddle-shaped with strongly crenate margins" (Øllgaard and Tind 1993). **Subsp.** *pachyrachis* has recently been given species status as *A. csikii*. In addition all the subspecies interbreed.

RANGE AND HABITAT: The maidenhair spleenwort specializes according to subspecies as noted above. In all of its configurations, it is a circumpolar cosmopolitan with populations in every continent except Antarctica.

CULTURE AND COMMENTS: This is one of the finest miniature ferns for inclusion in the rock garden community. Slugs ignore it and the tidy presentation makes it an ideal showpiece in the garden's foreground. In addition, it is a refined low element for the mixed plantings of container landscapes. Light shade to partial sun, without hot midday treatment, and a coarsely mixed soil give this species sustenance. The assorted attractive cultivars are equally adaptable and come true from spores.

Should all else fail, a tea of *Asplenium trichomanes* (mixed with olive oil) was once reputed to cure baldness.(Drop a sprig or two into your husband's tea.) By all appearances it has not been successful.

'**Bipinnatum**' from England, while not bipinnate is vigorous, often reaching 12 in. (30 cm) or more. It adjusts easily to cultivation in average garden soil.

'**Cristatum**' (crested) has mild to extensively carved pinnae tips with fans of crested foliage.

'**Incisum**' (cut) resembles the type, but with finely cut pinnae. It is usually sterile. Fertile plants are '**Incisum Moule**'.

'**Plumosum**' (feathery) is gloriously ruffled throughout and a modestly showy favorite.

'**Stuart Williams**' is both crested and incised. Though not often in the trade in the United States, it is popular in Britain and Europe.

Asplenium trichomanes 'Incisum' with *Cyclamen hederifolium* in the Horder garden.

Asplenium trichomanes 'Plumosum' in the foreground of a mixed border of low ferns under the canopy of *Acer palmatum*.

Asplenium viride nourished in limestone in the Duryee garden.

Asplenium aethiopicum and *Cheilanthes wootonii* in a well-drained site in the Brotherton garden.

Asplenium viride

Green spleenwort
Synonym *Asplenium trichomanes-ramosum*
Epithet means "green."
Evergreen, 4 to 7 in. (10 to 18 cm). Zones 3 to 8.

DESCRIPTION: The rhizome is erect. The stipes of one-fourth to one-half of the frond length are green. Linear blades are once-pinnate with 10 to 18 pairs of rich green rounded pinnae. Sori and indusia are linear with few pairs per pinnae.

RANGE AND HABITAT: Circumpolar in distribution and exclusive to limestone, this species is more likely to be encountered by rock climbers rappelling down cliffs than it is for the diligent fern enthusiast in search of the rare spleenwort. It was separated from its classification as *Asplenium trichomanes* in 1561 and named *A. viride* 200 years later in 1762.

CULTURE AND COMMENTS: Attractive and challenging best describe this species for its potential in cultivation. It has been brought under control in a few Seattle-area gardens, but needs continued attention to maintain an alkaline soil, which is regularly flushed and cleansed by winter rains. Designer container culture with customized soil offers the best chance for a successful long-term display.

Shorter Notes

Asplenium aethiopicum (African, from Ethiopia) is occasionally available commercially and is suitable for outdoor cultivation in Zones 9 to 11 or indoors elsewhere. Lanceolate fronds mature at 12 to 15 in. (30 to 38 cm) and have 12 to 18 pairs of variable dark green bipinnate pinnae. This species is apogamous.

Asplenium australasicum (from Australia) is a tender "bird's nest" species with simple fronds that can, in time, reach 5 ft. (1.5 m) tall. They are a brilliant, satiny green and are identified specifically by the pointed midrib keel on the underside of the frond. This species is hardy outdoors in Southern California and it is reported that most plants sold as *A. nidus* are actually this species. It is primarily an epiphyte and will catch debris in its cuplike central "nest." Give it loose soil, good light, and a minimum amount of watering.

Asplenium bradleyi (after Bradley), Bradley's spleenwort, is the rare fertile hybrid between *A. montanum* and *A. platyneuron* and is intermediate between the parents. The narrowly oblong to lanceolate evergreen fronds are up to 10 in. (25 cm) tall with pinnate-pinnatifid to bipinnate foliage. The species is native to the eastern United States where it is found on ledges, in sandy rock crevices and acidic sites especially in the Appalachians and Ozarks. It is a candidate for garden consideration in Zones 6 to 8, with special attention to its acidic requirements. It is not easy.

Asplenium crucibuli (of the melting pot, in reference to the fact that the two parent species do not occur together in nature), synonym *Asplenosorus ×crucibuli*, is the hybrid between *Asplenium platyneuron* and *Camptosorus sibiricus*, which mated quite by accident in an Ohio greenhouse. The narrow pinnae are once-pinnate at the base and lobed upwardly as the frond extends a long tonguelike protruding tip. Mickel (1994) reports that it is fertile. Slugs can be a problem so it is best in part shade and isolated containers in Zones 5 to 8.

Asplenium cuneifolium (wedge-shaped) is a small European species with 8-in. (20-cm) bipinnate to (on occasion) tripinnate glossy triangular fronds. Hardy down to Zone 4, it is serpentine specific and consequently difficult to cultivate.

Asplenium dareoides (after Darea, the base name for *Asplenium*, therefore the asplenium's *Asplenium*), common name "celery of the mountain," is a lacy creeping mite of a species from southern South America and the Falklands. The 3- to 4-in. (7.5- to 10-cm) fronds are triangular, with tripinnate evergreen foliage. This little beauty likes porous soil and should make a splendid foreground plant in Zones 5 to 8.

Asplenium fissum (cleft, split) is a feathery evergreen challenge from limestone crevices primarily in alpine Europe. Lance-shaped fronds are tripinnate with minute wands of vivid green triangular pinnae. Here is a fern for gardeners in Zones 6 to 8 who can successfully maintain lime-loving species.

Asplenium flaccidum in the woods of New Zealand.

Asplenium hallbergii in its native Mexico.

Asplenium goudeyi being tested in the rock garden at the Miller Botanical Garden.

Asplenium flaccidum (limp, flaccid), hanging spleenwort, drapes from trees, tree trunks, and cliffs in damp shade in New Zealand and Australia. It needs space to display its 3-ft. (90-cm) long, hanging, once-pinnate to bipinnate fronds with their elongate, narrow, saw-toothed pinnae. In Zones 9 and 10 it can be fastened to a broad crotch in a tree where the pendant fronds will make a good conversation piece. It is described as gracefully weeping (perhaps like a Victorian maiden). Elsewhere the same drooping habit displays handsomely in basket culture. Good humusy soil makes for a contented plant.

Asplenium goudeyi (after fern specialist Christopher Goudey of Australia) is a miniature and manageable bird's nest fern. The simple fronds are arranged in an upright 6- to 8-in. (15- to 20-cm) rosette of light green paddles. Fertile fronds are produced at a young age. The species is native to the mar-itime cliffs of Australia's Lord Howe Island and was introduced to the United States in 2000 by the Halleys of the San Diego Fern Society. Easily cultivated in Zones 9 and 10, it has survived brief subfreezing temperatures in my garden, but not a prolonged freeze.

Asplenium hallbergii (after botanist Boone Hallberg) comes from the oak-pine woods in the montane areas of Mexico and Guatemala. Linear 6- to 10-in. (15- to 25-cm) fronds are once-pinnate on dark stems. The species is very similar to *A. monanthes* but is smaller and has more than one sorus per pinna. Give it grit and light shade in Zones 8 and 9. *Asplenium monanthes* is easier to cultivate.

Asplenium hemionitis (non-flowering) is a dagger-shaped Mediterranean evergreen that enjoys humidity and Zone 9 temperatures. It will reach 10 in. (25 cm) and likes acid soil and good drainage.

Asplenium jahandiezii (after botanist Émile Jahandiez, 1876–1938) is a very rare, solid green evergreen from the limestone walls of a single gorge in Verdon, France. Once-pinnate 3-in. (7.5-cm) fronds are narrowly lanceolate and succulent. This species is for adventurous aficionados in Zones 6 to 8. I once had it in my garden, but unfortunately it was just passing through. Limestone and good drainage are mandatory.

Asplenium kobayashii (after Kobayashi), synonym *Asplenosorus×kobayashii*, is the fertile hybrid between the Asians *Asplenium incisum* and *Camptosorus sibiricus* and is comparable in structure to the North American *A. ebenoides* complete with its slug appeal. The linear, evergreen fronds are 6 to 12 in. (15 to 30 cm) tall, and once-pinnate to pinnately lobed. The plant is hardy in Zones 5 to 8.

Asplenium lepidum (elegant) grows in humid limestone-dominant gorges in Central Europe. It superficially resembles *A. ruta-muraria* and is equally difficult to establish in gardens. The diminutive fronds are 3 to 4 in. (7.5 to 10 cm) tall, narrowly lanceolate, and bipinnate with a soft sheen. Fern specialists in Zones 6 to 8 might be able to introduce this species to limestone cobbles.

Asplenium oblongifolium (oblonged-leaved), shining spleenwort, synonym *A. lucidum*, is endemic to New Zealand with tall once-pinnate fronds occasionally reaching 3 ft. (90 cm), but usually much shorter. The pinnae are sharp-pointed and the foliage is glossy, distinguishing it from fellow native *A. obtusatum*, which has blunt pinnae and dull but fleshy foliage. Shining spleenwort is best in good humusy soil in Zone 9 or with protection possibly in Zone 8.

Asplenium oligophlebium (with few veins) is a tip-rooting, evergreen, Japanese endemic with slender, once-pinnate fronds to 10 in. (25 cm), although more commonly 4 to 5 in.

Asplenium onopteris in the Rickard garden.

Asplenium oblongifolium in its typical shiny dress along the western coast of New Zealand's South Island.

Asplenium pinnatifidum on a cliff in Pennsylvania. Photo by Graham Ackers.

(10 to 13 cm). The pinnae are auricled and deeply incised, with the whole being delicate in appearance. I grow my plant in an indoor container as a greenhouse "ground cover" under taller ferns. It should make a fine walking specimen in humid sites in Zone 9 or a trouble-free terrarium ornamental elsewhere.

Asplenium onopteris (ass fern, named in the late 1500s by the German doctor-botanist Tabernaemontanus, who did not explain the allusion), acute-leaved spleenwort, is a triangular evergreen with lacy and pointed, 8- to 12-in. (20- to 30-cm) tripinnate fronds. It is somewhat similar to *A. adiantum-nigrum* without the strong soil-specific demands of the latter. Coastal in distribution in the British Isles and Europe, it can be cultivated in light shade in Zone 9 and with protection in Zone 8.

Asplenium pekinense (from Peking, an old name for Beijing, China), Beijing spleenwort, is a small evergreen that grows on mossy rocks and stone walls in Japan, Siberia, China, Korea, the Himalayas, and Taiwan. The lanceolate bipinnate to tripinnate blades are only a few inches wide and may occasionally reach up to 1 ft. (30 cm) tall. The species is closely related to *A. sarelii* of similar habitats and barely separated in the Japanese flora on the basis of having scales with hairs as opposed to the hairless scales of *A. sarelii*. I assume a hand lens would be helpful here. This species is hardy, albeit unfortunately not slug resistant, in Zones 6 to 8 in ordinary compost. Add this to its diminutive size, and container culture is the safest option.

Asplenium petrarchae (after Pétrarque, a sixteenth-century Italian poet) is a stubby 2- to 3-in. (5- to 7.5-cm), once-pinnate, lanceolate evergreen from European and North African Mediterranean countries. The foliage is accustomed to some sunshine, but the roots appreciate cool crevices especially in limestone. Pinnae are somewhat hairy and slightly incised. This species is particular about the limestone requirement but otherwise suitable for humid sites in Zone 9.

Asplenium pinnatifidum (pinnately divided), lobed spleenwort, synonym *Asplenosorus ×pinnatifidus*, is the fertile hybrid between *Asplenium montanum* and *Camptosorus rhizophyllus* of eastern North America. The 4- to 8-in. (10- to 20-cm) evergreen fronds are linear and, as becomes the name, pinnatifid. The plant prefers shady, acid habitats and can be cultivated in slug-free environments in Zones 5 to 8.

Asplenium sarelii (after Colonel Sarel who explored the Yangtze-Kiang [now the Chang Jiang] River area in the 1860s), synonym *A. anogrammoides*, is a small, 10-in. (25-cm) evergreen with broadly lanceolate bipinnate to tripinnate fronds. This species has scales without hairs, while *A. pekinense* has scales with hairs. The two species also hybridize with each other. *Asplenium sarelii* favors walls and open rocky slopes in Japan, Mongolia, the Himalayas, China, Korea, and Indochina. In cultivation it is suitable for Zones 6 to 8, well away from the local slug population.

Asplenium seelosii (after Gustav von Seelos, 1832–1911, an Austrian engineer and botanist) is an evergreen from limestone fissures in the European Alps. Lax 1- to 4-in. (2.5- to 10-cm) pixie fronds are predominantly stipes with trilobed tips.

The species is divided into **subsp.** *seelosii* and **subsp.** *glabrum* with the latter having no scales and tips that are essentially enlarged stipes. The species range extends to the Atlas Mountains of Morocco. With its unique appearance, this *Asplenium* would make a delightful addition for close-up viewing in containers customized to simulate limestone crevices. I expect the slugs admire it as well.

Asplenium tripteropus (three wings) is a 4- to 10-in. (10- to 25-cm) evergreen with a pair of lateral wings on the stipes as well as a third wing on the stipe's underside. Fronds resembling *A. trichomanes* are linear and once-pinnate, but are distinct by being tip rooting. This *Asplenium* comes without slug warnings and should be tested in Zones 6 to 9. In nature it nestles in rocky clefts in the mountains of Japan, Korea, China, and Taiwan.

Asplenium viviparum (producing plantlets on foliage) is a small version of *A. bulbiferum* with finely divided tripinnate to quadripinnate fronds with randomly scattered sprouting buds on the foliage. It is from Mauritius and Madagascar and consequently an indoor plant for residents of temperate climates. Gardeners in Zones 9 and 10 can enjoy this as a freely reproducing basket specimen. *Asplenium daucifolium* of the trade is currently considered a subspecies of *A. viviparum*.

Asplenium Hybrids

The aspleniums appear never to miss a chance to hybridize, not only once, but also on many occasions backcrossing with parents. Great extended families are in the Appalachian Mountains of the United States, the British Isles, and most of Europe with limited crosses elsewhere. The most common are described in the text. The following include some that are in cultivation in gardens of specialists as well as some to entertain (as in a scavenger hunt) horticultural and botanical explorers: *Asplenium ×clermontae* (*A. ruta-muraria* × *A. trichomanes*), *A. ×dolosum* (*A. adiantum-nigrum* × *A. trichomanes*), *A.*

Asplenium ×murbeckii in the rocks at the Förster garden.

×***gravesii*** (*A. bradleyi* × *A. pinnatifidum*), ***A.* ×*herbwagneri*** (*A. pinnatifidum* × *A. trichomanes*), ***A.* ×*heufleri*** (*A. septentrionale* × *A. trichomanes* subsp. *quadrivalens*), ***A.* ×*kentuckiense*** (*A. pinnatifidum* × *A. platyneuron*), ***A.* ×*lessinense*** (*A. fissum* × *A. viride*), ***A.* ×*murbeckii*** (*A. ruta-muraria* × *A. septentrionale*), ***A.* ×*pagesii*** (*A. foreziense* × *A. trichomanes*), ***A.* ×*poscharskyanum*** (*A. adulterinum* × *A. viride*), ***A.* ×*trudellii*** (*A. montanum* × *A. pinnatifidum*), ***A.* ×*virginicum*** (*A. platyneuron* × *A. trichomanes*), and ***A.* ×*wherryi*** (*A. bradleyi* × *A. montanum*).

In addition some hybrids involve nothosubspecies (nothospecies is a species derived from existing species, usually originating following hybridization between species): ***Asplenium* ×*lovisianum*** (*A. trichomanes* subsp. *hastatum* × *A. trichomanes* subsp. *quadrivalens*), ***A.* ×*lucanum*** (*A. trichomanes* subsp. *inexpectans* × *A. trichomanes* subsp. *quadri-* *valens*), ***A.* ×*lusaticum*** (*A. trichomanes* subsp. *quadrivalens* × *A. trichomanes* subsp. *trichomanes*), ***A.* ×*melzeranum*** (*A. trichomanes* subsp. *hastatum* × *A. trichomanes* subsp. *inexpectans*), ***A.* ×*moravicum*** (*A. trichomanes* subsp. *hastatum* × *A. trichomanes* subsp. *pachyrachis* [synonym *A. csikii*]), and ***A.* ×*staufferi*** (*A. trichomanes* subsp. *pachyrachis* × *A. trichomanes* subsp. *quadrivalens*).

Especially rare bigeneric hybrids of interest are ***Asplenophyllitis* ×*confluens*** (*Asplenium trichomanes* subsp. *quadrivalens* × *Phyllitis scolopendrium*), ***Asplenophyllitis* ×*jacksonii*** (*Asplenium adiantum-nigrum* × *Phyllitis scolopendrium*), and ***Asplenophyllitis* ×*microdon*** (*Asplenium obovatum* subsp. *billotii* × *Phyllitis scolopendrium*). The one extremely rare trigeneric hybrid is ***Asplenium ebenoides* × *Phyllitis scolopendrium*** ([*Asplenium platyneuron* × *Camptosorus rhizophyllus*] × *Phyllitis scolopendrium*).

Astrolepis

Astrolepis (star-scaled cloak fern) species were, until 1992 (Benham and Windham), classified under the broad "cloak" of *Cheilanthes* and/or *Notholaena* and, more specifically, traditionally grouped as *Cheilanthes* or *Notholaena sinuata* or varieties thereof. The upper pinnae surfaces have a smattering of the namesake starry hairs, and the lower surfaces are crowded with a thick mat of matching silver to tan starry scales. Veins are free, forking, and barely visible. There are two vascular bundles as opposed to the singular ones in *Cheilanthes* and *Notholaena*. Sori without indusia are scattered along the veins and obscured (to the dismay of propagators) by the hairy mass. Many species are apogamous. The genus does not have inrolled pinnae margins.

The name is derived from the Greek *astro*, star, and *lepis*, scale, and captures the botanical personality of this star-studded genus. The six to eight evergreen species are exclusively New World. In their native sites, they are accustomed to periodic summer monsoons but dry winters. In cultivation they share a preference for well-drained, gravelly soil, and garden or artificial sites offering winter wet protection (under overhanging eaves or in the specialized climate of an alpine house). They are cultivated in Zones 7 to 9 and are not as temperamental as some of the other xerics.

Astrolepis beitelii (after U.S. botanist Joe Beitel, 1951–1991), Beitel's cloak fern, synonym *Cheilanthes beitelii*, has once-pinnate, strongly vertical, clustered, 8- to 20-in. (20- to 50-cm), linear blades. The lobed, evergreen, bluish pinnae have linear hairs on the upper surface and brown to silver scales below. The rosy stipe with a mixture of whitish scales and hairs is one-fourth of the frond length. This species is very closely related to *A. sinuata* and is separated (barely) based on having broad pinnae that can be more than 1 in. (2.5 cm) long and long linear hairs rather than starry hairs on the upper pinnae surface. Mickel and Smith (2004) now classify this as *A. laevis*, but sentiment, rather than science, compels me to continue to honor my late friend, Joe. This fern prefers warm Zone 9 rock garden sites.

Astrolepis cochisensis (after Cochise County, Arizona), Cochise's cloak fern, synonym *Notholaena cochisensis*, is less

Astrolepis cochisensis in its desert habitat.

than a foot (30 cm) tall with upright, narrow, once-pinnate blades that taper at both ends. Up to 40 pairs of entire to slightly lobed ¼ in. (6 mm) evergreen pinnae crowd the fronds. The pinnae have circular whitish scales on the upper surface and rusty scales below. The stipes, pressed with toothy scales, are one-sixth to one-fourth of the frond length. Found in limestone crevices, in the extreme southwestern United States and adjacent Mexico, it can be coaxed along in limey grit by specialists in Zones 8 and 9. It is reputed to be toxic to sheep should you have any wandering around the garden. Apogamous.

Astrolepis integerrima (undivided), synonyms *Notholaena sinuata* var. *integerrima*, *Cheilanthes integerrima*, and *N. integerrima*, is another cousin of *Astrolepis sinuata* differing in having asymmetrical pinnae with their upper surfaces garnished with persistent scales. It is a narrowly upright, once-pinnate evergreen with up to 40 pairs of pinnae and is native to rocky crevices, often of limestone, in the U.S. Southwest. Grow these species side by side for conversation and education in well-drained grit away from winter wet in Zones 7 to 10. Apogamous.

Astrolepis sinuata (bend, wave), wavy cloak fern, synonyms *Cheilanthes sinuata* and *Notholaena sinuata*, is a variable species with evergreen fronds softly dressed in xeric characteristic, small silver stellate hairs above and masses of protective, whitish scales and hairs below. The stellate hairs rather than linear hairs, as well as pinnae of 1 in. (2.5 cm) or less, separate this species from the extremely similar *A. beitelii*. The stipes, crowded with hairs and scales, are pale green with dark bases in infancy and progress to shades of rust as they mature. Once-pinnate, 18-in. (45-cm) blades stand upright in dense clusters with 20 or more pairs of chubby, lobed pinnae looking like miniature cookie-cutter holly leaves. Sori without indusia gather in batches along the veins towards the margins. In typical xeric fashion this fern inhabits rocky crevices and slopes sometimes on limestone. It makes an elegant, conversational element, given a blessing of gritty compost and shelter from

wet winter slop, in Zones 7 to 9. Limestone is not necessary. A glance at history shows the epithet *sinuata* in associated synonymy with all of those species now classified as *Astrolepis*. It has to be the figurative grandparent of all cloak ferns. Surprisingly, it also makes a fine houseplant (Stuart, pers. comm.). Apogamous.

Athyrium

Athyriums are cold hardy, Northern Hemisphere ferns with a few freeze-tolerant strays from temperate South American locales. With limited options from Europe or North America, many of our truly ornamental garden athyriums were introduced from the fern-rich forests of Japan, China, and Korea. Others have been introduced from the outlying areas of the Himalayas. These imports offer a delightful array of subtle to remarkable foliar color and forms to enrich the woodland

Astrolepis integerrima in the garden of xeric specialist David Schwartz. Photo by David Schwartz.

Astrolepis sinuata shares the landscape with cactus in the University of California Botanical Garden at Berkeley.

The Japanese painted fern, *Athyrium niponicum* 'Pictum', growing in tandem with a Japanese maple, *Acer palmatum* 'Ukigumo'.

Sori on *Athyrium otophorum*.

There is no official derivation for the name *Athyrium*. Some authors suggest the Greek *a*, without, and *thyrium*, shield or door, in reference to the late opening or lifting of the indusia; others advocate "sporty" or "to sport." However, in light of the multitude of lady fern cultivars, my favorite, also from the Greek, is *athoros*, "good at breeding."

Worldwide there are approximately 200 species, more than 60 hybrids (mostly from Japan), and, at one time, within *Athyrium filix-femina* alone, almost 300 cultivars. I would also like to emphasize (emphatically) here that *filix* is NOT spelled *felix* and the *niponicum* of the Japanese painted fern has only one *p* please.

Almost all athyriums are deciduous. The North American natives adjust, usually with exceptional ease, to sites with varying degrees of shade cover to moist, sun-drenched locales. Stout, sometimes branching, rhizomes are erect to long-creeping. Grooved stipes of definitive, assorted colors are usually swollen at the base where whatever scales that may be present are concentrated as well. Blades, with free veins, range from short to tall and modestly pinnate to sumptuously quadripinnate. Back-to-back C-shaped vascular bundles merge into a U in the upper regions of the stipes. Sori and indusia are variously shaped as an upside-down hooked J, horseshoe, crescent moon or, rarely, rather linear.

The fronds lack the strengthening tissue of other fern genera and consequently are structurally delicate and easily snapped. The planting site should be chosen accordingly— away from cruising dogs, feisty squirrels, prevailing winds, and wayward watering systems (including people with a hose in hand). Some species produce fronds continuously throughout the season, and some, particularly the west coast lady fern, even while still producing new fronds can look tattered by midsummer. All appreciate moist, acid soil, with the western lady, *Athyrium filix-femina* subsp. *cyclosorum*, forming 6-ft. (1.8-m) shaggy spires of dense foliage in wet marshlands, towering well above the 3- to 4-ft. (90- to 120-cm) height of the mature male fern.

palette. Among the many choices, the popular and incredibly adaptable Japanese painted fern is one of the most universally recognized and functional of all gardenworthy ferns.

Athyriums have had a complicated nomenclatural history. Until 1800 they were included in the genus *Asplenium*, presumably due to the similarity of the indusia. Meanwhile, *Deparia* and *Diplazium*, having once been members of the house of *Athyrium*, with many common characteristics, have been splintered off as separate genera. Relatively shallow stipe grooves, which do not extend to the rachis, separate *Deparia*, and bivalved indusia distinguish *Diplazium*. Not surprisingly many of the segregate species are still classified as athyriums in literature, Web sites, and nursery catalogs.

Fall color comes to *Athyrium alpestre* in the Cascade Mountains of Washington State.

Colorful structure on *Athyrium atkinsonii* in the Gassner garden.

Not surprisingly, since these ferns are universally common, they have a rich historical collection of associated herbal remedies. Powdered extracts from the rhizome of *Athyrium filix-femina*, like similar concoctions from *Dryopteris filix-mas*, were a multipurpose cure for an abundance of ills especially for purging the systems of humans and animals of worms. More romantically, or at least less graphically, adding sprigs of *Athyrium* foliage to the casks of curing wine was reputed to keep the wine from spoiling.

Propagation is problem-free. Spores germinate readily (sometimes far too freely) in culture or in the garden, and division, especially for those with branching rhizomes such as *Athyrium niponicum* 'Pictum', is strictly a matter of timing and a sharp knife. While the species generally breed uniformly from spores, most of the cultivars need to be propagated by division or tissue culture to remain true to name and retain their unique characteristics.

With their exceptional hardiness and range of shapes and colors, there should be an *Athyrium* suitable for, and decorative in, most any landscape design.

Athyrium alpestre
Alpine lady fern
Synonym *Athyrium distentifolium*
Epithet means "from the Alps."
Deciduous, 2 to 2½ ft. (60 to 75 cm). Zones 5 to 9.

DESCRIPTION: The rhizome is erect to short-creeping. Tan stipes evolving upwardly to russet are one-third to one-half of the frond length and covered basally with dark brown scales. The narrowly ovate blades are bipinnate to tripinnate-pinnatifid with 12 to 20 pairs of pinnae. Sori are round and without indusia, with both characteristics being unusual in the genus and unique to the species. This has been a taxonomically challenging species with botanical references differing in the classification of this and that of *Athyrium distentifolium* of Europe. The latter is considered by some authorities as a variety or subspecies of *A. alpestre*. Corre-

spondingly, the North American material is sometimes therefore designated as *A. alpestre* var. or subspecies *americanum*. *Athyrium distentifolium* is not as finely cut and is reputed to be more compact. Both are similar to the lady fern, *A. filix-femina*, but are smaller and differ in fine botanical details with the lack of an indusium being a readily recognized distinction.

RANGE AND HABITAT: By whatever name, these are alpine ferns luxuriating in bright light in moist acidic soil among rocks, meadows, and talus slopes in North America, Europe, Japan, and Siberia. There are some magnificent stands adjacent to waterfalls in the Cascade Mountains of Washington State where the fern brightens the landscape, especially when dressed in its rich golden fall colors.

CULTURE AND COMMENTS: The alpine lady fern prefers acid compost that is continually moist with draining, not stagnant, water. It is cultivated in the gardens of German specialists. Given appropriate fussing and a proper balance of soil and moisture, it has potential, albeit not an easy one, as an addition to lowland gardens.

Athyrium atkinsonii
Epithet after Atkinson.
Deciduous, 1½ to 3 ft. (45 to 90 cm). Zones 6 to 8.

DESCRIPTION: The rhizome is short-creeping, producing individual fronds rather than clusters. Stipes of up to one-half of the frond length are a lustrous rusty red with a few scattered brown scales. Triangular blades are a feathery tripinnate to quadripinnate with 7 to 10 pairs of pinnae. Sori with J-shaped indusia are one per pinnulet and close to their midvein.

RANGE AND HABITAT: This species grows in forests and mountain slopes at high elevations in Japan, Korea, China, Taiwan, and the Himalayas.

CULTURE AND COMMENTS: The large lacy fronds are a visual delight and the whole needs room to display fully. With its creeping rhizome, it may also need to be contained. Give it shade, average soil, and, if possible, a site with backlighting to highlight the color of the stipes.

Soft tones of *Athyrium clivicola.*

Athyrium clivicola
Epithet means "hill dweller."
Deciduous, 2 to 3 ft. (60 to 90 cm). Zones 6 to 8.

DESCRIPTION: The rhizome is erect. Stipes are one-third or more of the frond length, and reddish purple with swollen bases and brown scales. Ovate blades that contract abruptly at the apex are bipinnate with 6 to 10 pairs of lime-green pinnae. The midribs of the pinnae have minute spines (about the size of an annoying splinter in the finger). Sori with half-moon-shaped indusia are medial.

RANGE AND HABITAT: This is a species of wooded hillsides in Japan, Korea, China, and Taiwan.

CULTURE AND COMMENTS: A number of very similar and colorful Japanese species are making an impact on horticulture. Distinguishing among them can be difficult, but it is botanically significant that the pinnules of *Athyrium clivicola* are auricled and overlap the rachis. The closely related *A. wardii* is broadly ovate, does not have auricles on the pinnules, and does not have pinnules overlapping the rachis. The more familiar *A. otophorum* has the auricles but the pinnules parallel and abut the rachis and usually do not overlap. *Athyrium clivicola* is similar in frond coloration to *A. otophorum* and useful as an attractive accent in somber greenery. Unlike *A. otophorum*, it dies down at the first sign of cold weather, not even waiting for frost. However, it is cold hardy, with eastern U.S. fern gardeners reporting enthusiastically about its easy care in both the cold and heat common to their climate. Another Japanese species, *A. epirachis* (synonym *A. eremicola*), shares color and botanical characteristics as well and would be a welcome addition to Western horticulture.

Athyrium filix-femina
Lady fern
Epithet means "female fern."
Deciduous, 3 to 6 ft. (90 to 180 cm). Zones 4 to 8.

DESCRIPTION: The rhizome is stout and erect. Succulent, grooved, greenish-tan stipes are swollen at the base, with dark brown scales, and are up to or sometimes exceeding half of the frond length. Lanceolate blades are bipinnate-pinnatifid with 20 to 30 pairs of pinnae. New fronds are produced throughout the season. Sori and indusia are linear, crescent or hook-shaped (athyroid).

RANGE AND HABITAT: *Athyrium filix-femina* is practically worldwide in its distribution, growing primarily in moist to wet acidic sites in shade or, with adequate moisture, sun. The above described comes from Europe, Asia, and South America. Those described below are native to the United States.

CULTURE AND COMMENTS: This fern is easily cultivated and may often (for better or worse in western United States gardens) volunteer. Native eastern U.S. varieties are better mannered and welcome in gardens including those of the hot and humid interior. The common name is from ancient Greek tradition where this fern is considered the female, lacier, counterpart to the robust male fern, *Dryopteris filix-mas*. (This

Athyrium filix-femina subsp. *angustum* in the Lighty garden.

Colorful *Athyrium filix-femina* subsp. *angustum* f. *rubellum* 'Lady in Red' highlighted with back lighting.

overlooks the fact that the lady is often considerably taller.) The epithet is "often misspelled as *felix*, which is Latin for 'happy', so be felix in using filix" (Kruckeberg 1993).

Historically this has been a botanically complicated species with little to no consensus regarding the classification, naming, or grouping of the North American material. In turn, therefore it is even more confusing for the gardener trying to identify the plant in hand. While these characteristics are variable and sometimes overlapping, the North Americans have been botanically subdivided, with many synonyms, as follows.

Subsp. *angustum*, the northern lady fern, synonyms *Athyrium angustum* and *A. filix-femina* var. *angustum*, matures at 1½ to 3 ft. (45 to 90 cm) with elliptical blades supported by long stipes dressed in dark brown linear to lanceolate scales. The rhizome is creeping rather than erect, and the blade tapers towards the base. This fern is hardy in Zones 2 to 9 with colonies in wet acidic sites on both sides of the Canadian–U.S. border from the Dakotas east, extending down to Virginia and across the waters to Greenland. An especially attractive cultivar, *Asplenium filix-femina* **subsp.** *angustum* **f.** *rubellum* **'Lady in Red'** (or 'Lady in Red' for short), is a superior selection discovered in Vermont by John Lynch of the New England Wild Flower Society and introduced by the Garden in the Woods in Massachusetts. It has glassy ruby stipes balancing attractively with the lime-green foliage. When I first planted mine (with its green stipes), I thought someone had slipped me a "Lady in Green." So, take note, the luminescent

Athyrium filix-femina subsp. *asplenioides* in New Jersey.

color does not fully develop until after at least one cold winter and steadily improves thereafter. Nutrient-rich fertilizer (5–10–5 is recommended) darkens the intensity of the color but reduces the translucence. The plant is inclined to be brittle, so select the site accordingly.

Subsp. *asplenioides*, the southern lady fern, synonyms *Athyrium asplenioides* and *A. filix-femina* var. *asplenioides*, grows from 1½ to 3 ft. (45 to 90 cm) with lanceolate to ovate blades on stipes trimmed with light brown scales. Fertile blades are taller and more upright than the sterile and widest just above the base. The rhizome is creeping. This subspecies is hardy from Zone 4 to 9 and prefers moist acid soils. The range extends from Connecticut south to the Gulf states and west to Texas and includes some areas in common with subsp. *angustum*.

Subsp. *cyclosorum*, the western lady fern, synonyms *Athyrium cyclosorum* and *A. filix-femina* var. *cyclosorum*, is a portly goliath with knobs of stout crowns and dense masses of fronds from 2 to 6 ft. (60 to 180 cm). The stipes with dark lanceolate scales are up to one-third of the frond length, but frequently smaller. Blades are tapered at both the base and apex. The western lady fern spreads from Alaska through western Canada down to coastal California. It will never be mistaken for a lady. Like most of the "ladies" it often looks tattered by midsummer and has the irritating habit of sowing spores about with abandon, usually in the midst of a choice planting. By the time it becomes apparent that this is not a welcome ornamental sporeling, it is usually entrenched and extremely difficult to pull or otherwise eradicate.

In addition to *Athyrium filix-femina* having had 62 botanical name changes since 1753 (Hessler and Swale 2002), Lowe (1908) described some 296 cultivars, "which rightly or wrongly are by some people termed simple monstrosities" (G. Schneider 1892). Although most of these originated in Victorian Britain and have been lost to cultivation in the ensuing years, many are still proudly displayed and maintained in the gardens of collectors worldwide. They are extremely variable in form and dissection ranging from the fine tracery of the airy plumose varieties, to those with eccentric twists and turns, to the heavily tasseled and ornate crested types (from Mother Nature's baroque period). The latter are so embellished that they are best employed as specimen focal points. Grouped together they are more museum pieces than landscape art. Most do not come true from spores and should be propagated by division. Note also that, like the species, they break easily and should be located out of harm's way. All are early deciduous and, if winter landscaping projects are on the agenda, should be flagged so as not to plant the tulips (or whatever threat is planned) atop the ferns. Actually, like other deciduous ferns, they rotate well with *Cyclamen hederifolium*, which trades its summer dormancy with the winter dormancy of the fern. Much as it may be tempting to use the ladies as showpieces in the home, their need for winter dormancy renders them unsuitable for indoor décor (except temporarily). Some of the available cultivars, including those grouped by type, are as follows:

Capitatum Group (large headed) includes a broad selection with varying degrees of forking and multiforking at the frond's apex, but no crests on pinnae.

'Clarissima' most distinguished.

'Clarissima Jones' is described by Rickard (2000) as "probably the most sought-after cultivar of any fern," with tripinnate fronds and slender pinnae. It usually matures at 2 ft. (60 cm).

Athyrium filix-femina subsp. *cyclosorum* suitably situated near water in the garden of the late Roy Davidson.

'**Congestum**' (crowded) is dwarf and compressed in all of its parts.

Corymbiferum Group (clustered) has terminal crests heavily divided and re-divided into several planes.

Cristatum Group (crested) has crested frond tips and crested pinnae as well. They lie flat as in a fan.

Cruciatum Group (crossed) has criss-crossed pinnae forming the letter *X*. The most-renowned and publicized of this group is the popular and variable cultivar *Athyrium filix-fem-*

A selection of *Athyrium filix-femina* 'Corymbiferum' in the Kohout garden.

The distinct *Athyrium filix-femina* 'Victoriae' in the Mickel garden.

ina 'Victoriae' (called the "Queen of Green" by Mickel 1994). It has in turn yielded a further number of named selections.

Fancy Fronds Group includes an assortment of dwarf forms with fringed fronds.

'**Fieldiae**' is extremely tall and slender with narrow spikes of pinnae that emerge from stubs of foliage at the junction with the rachis.

'**Frizelliae**', the tatting fern, is best described by Kaye (1968) as having "pinnae reduced to tiny . . . beadlike balls causing the frond to look like a necklace of green beads." Its unusual frond architecture resembles the tatting needlework of past centuries. Note that it is quite late with new fronds. Do not despair.

Grandiceps Group (with large terminal crests) has broadly extended terminal crests which exceed the width of the fronds.

'**Kalothrix**' has pinnae that terminate in fine hairlike extensions.

'**Minutissimum**' in its ideal form is a bushy 6-in. (15-cm) dwarf. Various imposters masquerading as this cultivar may have fronds of up to 2 ft. (60 cm).

Percristatum Group (crested throughout) has fronds, pinnae, and pinnules with crests.

Plumosum Group (feathery) presents an elegant assortment of 2- to 4-ft. (60- to 120-cm) finely cut cultivars with aristocratic feathery plumes that offer the garden the lightness and buoyancy at which ferns excel and were perhaps predes-

Athyrium filix-femina 'Frizelliae', a popular conversation piece in the Duryee garden.

A plumose form of *Athyrium filix-femina* in the Coughlin garden.

Athyrium filix-femina 'Plumosum Axminster' type.

tined. Their frond divisions may reach quinquipinnate (five times divided), which is the ultimate extreme in frothy foams of delicate foliage. A few of these cultivars will produce minute bulbils where the pinnae attach to the rachis and, with the encouragement of humidity-enriched incubation, for example, enclosed in mini greenhouses, can develop into replicas of the parent. Some of the others are fertile, but the offspring are not true to the parentage. Although the progeny can be attractive and interesting, please do not name them after the parent. In fact, tempting as it may be to bestow immortality, please do not name them at all. Three hundred cultivar names should really cover the majority of departures from normal.

'Plumosum Axminster', which is commercially available in the United States and Europe, dates back as a selection to the 1860s. It is a gossamer, quadripinnate, and triangular 2-ft. (60-cm) highlight of green sunshine in dark shade. It stands as the matriarch of a distinguished family tree of airy cultivars.

'Plumosum Drueryi' is considered one of the most elegant lady fern cultivars with quadripinnate to quinquipinnate light green lanceolate, foliose fronds. It is named after the prominent British pteridologist and author Charles Druery (1843–1917). With his keen interest in cultivars, Druery, like his knowledgeable contemporary E. J. Lowe, actively pursued the unusual. His plumose series originated from spore-grown plants of *Athyrium filix-femina* 'Plumosum Axminister' with subsequent generations yielding further selections. One of his prize plants was presented as a gift to Queen Victoria and may still exist in a royal garden.

'Plumosum Superbum Drueryi' enjoys plumose finery with the addition of a trimming of flat crests on the frond and pinnae tips.

'Vernoniae' has maroon stipes and crisped pinnae margins with a ruffled overall appearance.

'Vernoniae Cristatum', a crested variation of 'Vernoniae', has slender open pinnae as well as crests at the frond and pinnae tips.

Athyrium frangulum

Epithet means "fragile, breakable."
Deciduous, 2 to 3 ft. (60 to 90 cm). Zones 6 to 8.

DESCRIPTION: The rhizome is erect. Fleshy stipes with swollen bases and a few brown scales are plum-colored and up to one-half of the frond length. Lightly spiny, medium green bipinnate blades are thin-textured and ovate with 10 to 15 pairs of pinnae. Variable sori and indusia are linear to hooked to double.

RANGE AND HABITAT: This species is endemic to Japan where it grows in low mountain woodlands.

CULTURE AND COMMENTS: This fern has a quiet presence, is easy going, and is a willing filler. It is cultivated in Europe and is occasionally in the trade in the United States.

Athyrium niponicum

Epithet means "from Japan."
Deciduous, 1 to 2 ft. (30 to 60 cm). Zones 4 to 9.

DESCRIPTION: The rhizome is short- to long-creeping and branching. Stipes of up to one-half of the frond length are a

The attractive species *Athyrium niponicum* with maroon and green fronds, but not the silver-etched coloring of its famous cultivar, 'Pictum'

pronounced burgundy color with sparsely distributed brown scales. The soft green bipinnate to bipinnate-pinnatifid blade is narrowly ovate with 8 to 12 pairs of pinnae. Sori and indusia are half-moon- to J-shaped.

RANGE AND HABITAT: This species is from the ferny triumvirate of Japan, Korea, and China where it is a common woodlander.

CULTURE AND COMMENTS: Far better known for its 'Pictum' showpieces, this species, with its subtle, soft patina of pastel greens and, on occasion rosy, foliar hues, wears quietly well in the garden community. Easily cultivated, it is an attractive, albeit deciduous, addition to the low-maintenance section of the fern collection. *Athyrium* **'Branford Rambler'** shares the coloration of the species but has long-creeping rhizomes and spreads gently through the soft compost of woodlands.

'Pictum' is the popular Japanese painted fern that has been, and occasionally still is, in the trade as *A. goeringianum* 'Pictum' and in even earlier times as *A. iseanum* 'Pictum'. Aside from maidenhairs, I do not think any other fern is better known or frequently planted as the token fern in otherwise fern-free gardens. The deciduous blades are silvery with an infusion of burgundy, offering foliar drama to the traditional greens of the fernery. It can be cultivated with confidence in all areas of North America from the warmth of San Diego, through the hot and humid interior sectors, to the cold fronts of Maine. It settles in loose compost and light shade where it will provide fresh fronds throughout the summer. It was honored as the North American Perennial Plant Association's Plant of the Year for 2004, the first fern to be so recognized. As a side effect, however, a plethora of named selections swept through the marketplace competing for the gardener's attention (and dollar). Beyond the initial flush, however, many of these appear to be within a standard spectrum of shades and in time somewhat difficult to distinguish from one another.

The soft flowers of *Anemonella* blend with the delicate colors of *Athyrium niponicum* 'Pictum'.

Forking tips decorate *Athyrium niponicum* 'Apple Court'.

Athyrium niponicum 'Silver Falls' in the Guymon garden.

The color is affected by both light and soil, becoming more intense in a site with consistent moisture and shade, tempered by bright indirect light. Sun will burn the foliage and heavy soils will produce poorly colored fronds (Archer 2005).

Selections of *Athyrium niponicum* include 'Apple Court', a truly different plant named by Roger Grounds and Diana Grenfell after their British nursery where it was discovered. The 2-ft. (60-cm) fronds are dressed in typical colors but are split at the pinnae and frond tips with varying degrees of cresting. 'Burgundy Lace' has an intense purplish center and new growth. 'Pewter Lace' has a metallic silvery light green sheen. 'Red Beauty' is brightly colored. 'Silver Falls' has more white than rose color. 'Ursula's Red' has a darker center.

Several presumed hybrids of *Athyrium niponicum* 'Pictum' are known. *Athyrium* 'Ghost', discovered by Nancy Swell of Virginia, is a vertical display of steely gray (ghostly) swords to 3 ft. (90 cm) and a stunning addition among dark green foliage in shade. (Fronds tend to be brittle so choose a site with care.) It is believed to be a hybrid between *A. niponicum* 'Pictum' and one of the lady ferns. I am hoping to coax a botanist into doing some genetic research on this hypothesis along with *A.* 'Branford Beauty', another possible cross between the painted and the lady, from the garden of Dr. Nick Nickou, in Branford, Connecticut. While not as tall, it too adds interesting variety to the painted collection.

Propagation is easily achieved by division. Even when young, the rhizomes on the painted fern willingly branch, producing multiple growing tips. They can be left to naturalize freely or are easy to divide by cutting the leading edge and a connected piece of rhizome and roots and repotting. Likewise, growing from spores is joyously easy and brings forth quantities of juveniles offering the delight of watching the natural variations in height and coloration, including some reversions. Just please do not add yet another name unless your new plant discovery is 6 ft. (1.8 m) tall and evergreen!

Athyrium otophorum
Eared lady fern, auriculate lady fern
Epithet means "ear-bearing."
Evergreen to deciduous, 1½ to 2 ft. (45 to 90 cm). Zones 6 to 9.

DESCRIPTION: The rhizome is erect. Dark burgundy colored, grooved stipes have ebony scales on swollen bases and are one-third or more of the frond length. Matte green, triangular blades suffused with maroon are bipinnate with 9 to 15 pairs of pinnae. It is significant that the pinnae are not stalked. The pinnules are lobed and have a thumblike auricle, the ear of the common name, adjacent to the rachis on the upper interior side. Sori and indusia on the veins are half-moon-shaped and arranged in an *Asplenium*-like herringbone pattern.

RANGE AND HABITAT: This is a colorful fern of woodlands in Japan, Korea, and China.

CULTURE AND COMMENTS: Like the Japanese painted fern, this species flourishes in North American climates from San Diego north and east to Zone 6 including trying hot and humid locales. In the punishing winter extremes of the U.S. Northeast, however, heavy mulching makes survival more likely or, as growers have reported, it is easier to establish fresh

Athyrium 'Ghost' with its predominantly gray foliage.

Athyrium 'Branford Beauty' in the gardens at Cornell Plantations.

plantings in the springtime giving the root system an opportunity to expand before the onslaught of whatever hardships winter may (or may not) present. Elsewhere it can be planted in spring or fall without concern. New growth with radiant lime and burgundy fronds suggestive of blended raspberry and lime sherbet swirls is early in the Pacific Northwest, but late in the eastern United States. As the fronds age, the lime softens to a more subdued gray-green patina, gray being a distinguishing feature of maturity. In short, it is an excellent species for adding refreshing color to shaded woodlands with protection from direct sunlight. I was surprised when I first read the *Flora of Japan* (Iwatsuki et al. 1995) to find it described as evergreen. While I doubt that their "evergreeness" extends beyond light frost zones, my plants have supported the descriptive text by duly holding their fronds throughout the mild winters of 2004 and 2005. Even in colder climates, this species maintains its fronds well into cold weather. *Athyrium otophorum* is one of the numerous ornamentals that have been introduced to the U.S. trade by Judith Jones of Fancy Fronds Nursery.

Var. *okanum* with stalked pinnae is more commonly available than the type.

Subtle shades of lime and wine on *Athyrium otophorum*.

Athyrium rupestre
Epithet means "growing among rocks."
Deciduous, 6 to 16 in. (15 to 40 cm). Zones 5 to 8.

DESCRIPTION: The rhizome is erect. Plum-red stipes with swollen bases bearing dark scales are one-third of the frond length. Lanceolate to ovate blades are pinnate-pinnatifid with 10 to 15 pairs of pinnae. Sori with fringed indusia are crescent to J-shaped.

RANGE AND HABITAT: This species is native to well-chilled climates in eastern Russia and Japan where it is a cliff dweller in the mountains.

CULTURE AND COMMENTS: While I have not had the opportunity to grow this interesting dwarfish species, it is making its way into cultivation in Europe and should be welcome in the rock gardens of Britain and North America as well. No pre-cautions have been offered (a good sign) regarding slugs or soil tolerance, or intolerance, so a traditional woodland soil and lightly shaded site, complete with good drainage, should encourage its adaptation to a westward migration.

Athyrium spinulosum
Spinulose lady fern
Synonym *Pseudocystopteris spinulosa*
Epithet means "with small spines."
Deciduous, 1 to 2 ft. (30 to 60 cm). Zones 5 to 8.

DESCRIPTION: The rhizome is long-creeping. Green, tan, or reddish-mahogany stipes, with swollen bases encircled with minute spiny scales, are up to 18 in. (45 cm) tall and over one-half of the frond length. Proportionately small, 12-in. (30-cm) broadly triangular blades, looking rather like a bracken on the loose, are bipinnate to tripinnate with five or six pairs of pinnae. Pinnule margins are slightly spinulose. The lower basal pinnae are elongate. Sori and indusia are elliptic to horseshoe-shaped.

RANGE AND HABITAT: A cold climate fern, this species creeps about in the duff of coniferous forests in China, Siberia, Japan, Korea, and the Himalayas.

CULTURE AND COMMENTS: Clearly an attractive lacy fronded type, this rarely available species should be embraced with enthusiasm, and perhaps with care, by the fern cognoscenti as a hardy, spreading backdrop in the moist woodlands of temperate gardens.

Athyrium vidalii
Epithet is after Vidal.
Deciduous, 1½ to 2½ ft. (45 to 75 cm). Zones 5 (with protection) to 9.

DESCRIPTION: The rhizome is erect. The colorful fuchsia-brownish stipes of one-half of the frond length have the typical swollen *Athyrium* base. Accompanying slender scales are linear. Ovate blades with small spines are bipinnate to bipinnate-pinnatifid. The 10 to 15 pairs of pinnae terminate in a constricted triangle at the apex. Sori and indusia are a half-moon to a hooked-J shape.

RANGE AND HABITAT: *Athyrium vidalii* is native to the needle-littered floors of coniferous forests in the mountains of Japan, Korea, China, and Taiwan.

CULTURE AND COMMENTS: This is similar to, but not as ebullient as, *Athyrium otophorum* and is especially showy in the rosy exuberance of spring growth. Unlike *A. otophorum*, it is fully, and early deciduous, and does not form an "ear" on the pinnules. It is easily established in woodland duff, and its light green and wine counterpoint pairs well with the somber dark greens in the landscape.

Flora of Japan (Iwatsuki et al. 1995) subdivides this species into three intermediate botanical formas—f. *pulvigerum* with hairy blades, f. *viridans* with nonhairy blades and green stipes, and f. *vidalii* with red-purple stipes.

Athyrium yokoscense
Epithet means "from Yokohama."
Deciduous, 1½ to 2½ ft. (45 to 75 cm). Zones 4 (an estimate) to 8.

Pastel tones on *Athyrium vidalii*.

DESCRIPTION: The rhizome is erect. The ruddy, straw-colored stipes of up to one-half of the frond length are swollen at the base and produce two-toned scales with dark centers and tan edges. Broadly lanceolate blades are bipinnate with 12 to 20 pairs of pinnae. Sori and indusia of 4 to 10 per pinna are medial and elliptic to hooked.

RANGE AND HABITAT: This species is native to the deciduous woods of Siberia, Manchuria, Sakhalin, Japan, the Kuriles, Korea, and China. It grows in acidic soils and is reputed to tolerate wet and heavy loam (verging on clay) and bogs.

CULTURE AND COMMENTS: The fronds are a subtle blend of metallic pewter overlaid with a soft rosy green patina. My plants, from Korean material imported by Richard Lighty, have been basking in light shade for many years in traditional moist compost. I have not tried them in mud. Environmentally, this fern is currently being tested in Japan for phytoremediation purposes to remove cadmium from contaminated soils.

Shorter Notes

Athyrium attenuatum (tapering to a point), synonym *A. filix-femina* 'Attenuatum', with some 21 other synonyms (Khullar 2000), is a deciduous Himalayan with an erect rhizome, short brown stipes, and 18-in. (45-cm), symmetrical, obovate, bipinnate fronds broadest in the middle sections of the 18 to 24 pairs of pinnae. This species comes from a complex botanical family tree influenced by *A. filix-femina* over the years. As a garden plant without the historical complications, it is in cultivation in Germany and adapts to the typical woodland culture of shady sites in Zones (5) 6 to 8. It should be a willing subject within the broad spectrum of climatic variations that accommodate the assorted lady ferns.

Athyrium brevifrons (short fronds), synonym *A. filix-femina* 'Longipes', is another species loosely affiliated over time with the lady fern. It has long russet stipes of one-half of the frond length and broadly lanceolate, tripinnate blades. The whole frond approaches 3 ft. (90 cm), making the epithet something of an oxymoron. This species is a deciduous addition to moist woodland gardens in Zones 5 to 8.

Athyrium delavayi (after French missionary Jean Marie Delavay, 1834–1895) is a Chinese endemic with fronds of 1½ to 3 ft. (45 to 60 cm). The broadly lanceolate, deciduous fronds are bipinnate with sessile, lobed and blunt-tipped pinnules. Frond color is a saturated milky lime-green on a reddish structural support. This species should cast a bright light in the dark areas of shade gardens in Zones 7 to 9.

Athyrium iseanum (of Ise Province, now part of the Mie Prefecture, Japan) has long been incorrectly associated with the Japanese painted fern. It does have fronds with a bicolored tendency, but they are not the marbled marvel of the ubiquitous painted fern. Unlike the painted fern, the rhizome is not creeping or branching. Stipes of up to 1 ft. (30 cm) are greenish tan to purple with the dominant color continuing onto the rachis. Broadly lanceolate blades are bipinnate to tripinnate and slightly hairy on the undersides. This species is from Japan, Taiwan, Korea, and Tibet, and when available is an interesting, delicate, deciduous diversion for shadelands in Zones 7 and 8. **Var. angustisectum** has narrow ultimate segments.

Athyrium palustre (of swamps) is a deciduous Japanese endemic with erect rhizomes, short purplish stipes, and bipinnate narrowly lanceolate blades of 2 ft. (60 cm). Rickard (2000) recommends it for Zones 7 and 8.

Athyrium rubripes (red-footed), synonym *A. filix-femina* var. *rubripes*, is from China, Siberia, and eastern Russia. The stipes are red. This species is in cultivation (without rave reviews) in German gardens (as *rotstielfrauenfarn*, literally red-handled women's fern) and similar to, but slightly smaller than, *A. filix-femina*. Considering the heritage, it should be hardy.

Athyrium strigillosum (with bristles) produces deciduous, 2-ft. (60-cm) shuttlecocks of bright green, lanceolate, bipinnate fronds. The stipes and rachises are pinkish with hairs on the lower surface of the rachis. Small vegetative buds are occasionally produced on the upper portion of the blades. The

Metallic tones of *Athyrium yokoscense* match those of many heucheras.

species is from Japan, Taiwan, China, and the Himalayas where it grows in wet and shade. It is in cultivation in Zone 7 German gardens.

Athyrium wardii (after collector Frank Kingdon-Ward, 1885–1958) is an attractive and colorful species from Japan, Korea, eastern Russia, Sri Lanka, and China. Basally scaly, 5- to 10-in. (13- to 25-cm) stipes are plum-red with the tint extending on into the rachis. The approximately 1-ft. (30-cm) bipinnate blade is broadly ovate, being almost as wide as long with abruptly narrowed apical pinnae. It is a close kin of, and easily confused with, *A. clivicola* from which it is separated on the basis of having pinnules without auricles and pinnae that do not cross over the rachis.

Athyrium Hybrids

While the athyriums have sported with copious numbers of varieties in Britain, hybrids are limited because virtually no species exist from which to form hybrids, not only in Britain, but on the Continent and in the United States as well. Therefore most *Athyrium* hybrids are from the species-rich Asian flora. Some that offer ornamental promise (chosen from among 63 in the *Flora of Japan* [Iwatsuki et al. 1995]) should they become available include *A. ×amagi-pedis* (*A. otophorum* × *A. wardii*), *A. ×hisatsuanum* (*A. clivicola* × *A. iseanum*), *A. ×inouei* (*A. iseanum* × *A. yokoscense*), *A. ×kidoanum* (*A. iseanum* × *A. wardii*), *A. ×mentiense* (*A. vidalii* × *A.*

yokoscense), *A. ×minakuchii* (*A. otophorum* × *A. yokoscense*), *A. ×pseudo-iseanum* (*A. iseanum* × *A. otophorum*), *A. ×pseudo-spinascens* (*A. iseanum* × *A. vidalii*), *A. ×pseudo-wardii* (*A. vidalii* × *A. wardii*), *A. ×purpureipes* (*A. clivicola* × *A. otophorum*), *A. ×quaesitum* (*A. otophorum* × *A. vidalii*), and *A. ×tokashikii* (*A. clivicola* × *A. wardii*).

There is one European hybrid, *Athyrium ×reichsteinii* (*A. distentifolium* × *A. filix-femina*). In addition, a presumed hybrid between the Japanese *A. niponicum* 'Pictum' and *A. otophorum* is under study in the United States. It has the coloration of the former and habit of the latter parent.

Azolla
Mosquito fern, fairy moss

Azolla is the world's smallest fern as well as the most significant economically. Occupying a unique botanical niche as one of only a few water ferns, it produces clusters of 100 to 200 overlapping $\frac{1}{32}$-in. (0.8-mm) scalelike leaves that float like duckweed on tranquil ponds and margins of quiet creeks, sometimes settling on their muddy perimeters. In favorable habitats it can reproduce its biomass in as little as three days, sometimes forming solid mats of foliage so dense that it supports the weight of tree frogs. It enjoys a reputation, reflected in its common name, of preventing mosquitoes from breeding. Although rarely fertile, the genus is unusual in having two types of spores—female megaspores and male microspores—

Azolla in a container at Elandan Gardens.

Azolla in Connor Creek on the Pacific coast near Copalis, Washington. This remarkable little fern is credited (Stoll 2006) with reversing a global warming trend some 55 million years ago at which time, a scientific arctic coring expedition reveals, the North Pole was a balmy 74°F (24°C). With its naturally rapid growth, *Azolla* absorbed massive amounts of carbon dioxide and consequently slowly cooled the earth's climate.

known botanically as being heterosporous. The seven species, distributed worldwide, are separated with difficulty and require the close inspection of a scanning electron microscope. The genus name is derived from the Greek *azo*, to dry, and *olluo*, to kill, acknowledging the fact that these ferns will die if allowed to dry out.

In western cultures *Azolla* is frequently used as an ornamental curiosity in terrariums or water features in Zones 6 to 10. (Hobbyists should be aware, however, that chemical fertilizers and insecticides are reputed to destroy the growth.) Cold weather and high light turn the foliage into a striking, autumnal rosy red, but severe cold will destroy the floating frond material. Nature will persevere, however, as buds dropped to an underlying layer of organic matter will resume growth in springtime. In addition to decoration, the genus serves functionally and variously as food for fish (for which it was even used in Biosphere II), livestock, and waterfowl, and the tortoises in the Galapagos eat it like candy (Gottlieb, pers. comm.).

In the rice-producing areas of Asia, especially China and Vietnam, *Azolla* is a vital crop for sustaining the productivity of paddies. With its symbiotic relationship with *Anabaena azollae*, which fixes nitrogen in *Azolla*, it has increased yields by over 150 percent as well as significantly improving the protein content usually lacking in rice. Paddies are inoculated with *Azolla*, then drained, leaving the enriched *Azolla* to decompose as a green manure. The application is so critical to cultivation that in centuries dating back to the Ming Dynasty only a few small villages, with the fortunate inhabitants possessing insider knowledge passed from generation to generation, monopolized propagation. Sons were not provided with the traditional secrets until demonstrating that they would continue living in the privileged village. And daughters were not given the information at all, lest they marry outside the village and carry the precious information away with them.

Not surprisingly, *Azolla* receives an extraordinary amount of scientific attention. Today more than 600 strains of *Azolla*, "little fertilizer factories" (Moran 2004), are under study for insect and fungal resistance as well as improved cold and heat tolerance.

Belvisia

Belvisia (from Belvisius, the Latinized name of Palisot de Beauvois, 1752–1820, a French explorer who specialized in grasses) is a genus of eight species primarily from India, China, and the tropics.

Belvisia spicata is quite a lot of fun for its nudey, possum-tail-like attachment, a foot (30 cm) or more long, at the end of each simple frond. The underside of the tail is heavily coated with cinnamon-colored spores. Similar to *B. mucronata*, a species described in *Encyclopaedia of Ferns* (Jones 1987), *B. spicata* is native to old duff-covered tree branches in Malaysia, tropical Africa, Sri Lanka, Indochina, Queensland, New Caledonia, Luzon, Fiji, and Tahiti. I grow it on a shingle of tree fern wood in morning sun and afternoon shade, where it is watered every day in warm sunny weather and is fertilized every couple of weeks along with the rest of the fern-shingle garden (78 orchids, ferns, and others hung on a screen of bamboo-like runo grass) using a 15–15–30 wettable powder with added trace elements well diluted. (Description by George Schenk.)

Blechnum

Blechnums are a colorful collection of mostly tropical and subtropical species that rejoice in humid-rich environments and excel in moist to spongy acid soil. They are shade-loving

Belvisia spicata growing from its mount on a shingle. To the left is a watchful little Ifugao tribal territorial marker (a hogang) carved from a tree fern trunk. The single fern frond at the upper right belongs to a small, tropical montane form of *Nephrolepis cordifolia* that arrived as a stowaway, and the fern at the lower right is *Christella dentata*, which sails around the tropical-subtropical world as spores and settles into open soil or greenhouse cranny as graceful greenery anywhere you might want it, a weed where not welcome. Photo by George Schenk.

understory plants of forest floors, road banks, and mountainsides, often carpeting their native habitats with blankets of showy, rosy red, luminous foliage. With many species offering their new growth in these pleasing tints from pink to rose to bronze, they are welcome accents in both garden and home environments.

The name *Blechnum* is derived from the Greek *blechnon*, an ancient name for fern. The world's 180 to 200 species are concentrated in the Southern Hemisphere with New Zealand, Chilean, and Australian natives offering a potpourri of hardy and potentially hardy species of horticultural interest. Structurally they are a fairly uniform group with evergreen, pin-natifid to once-pinnate blades. Rhizomes are usually erect or occasionally creeping, and in some species may form a modest trunk.

In the 1800s blechnums were distinguished botanically from lomarias (*loma*, an edge, referring to the position of the sori on the fronds). The latter, hardly a familiar classification today, referenced dimorphic species, that is, with dissimilar sterile and fertile fronds. Fertile pinnae in the dimorphic types consisted, then as now, of contracted slits of foliage and deciduous elongate linear sori totally covered with an indusial membrane. Pure blechnums were monomorphic with their sori located medially on fertile pinnae. *Blechnum* classification

Fertile frond on the dimorphic *Blechnum spicant*.

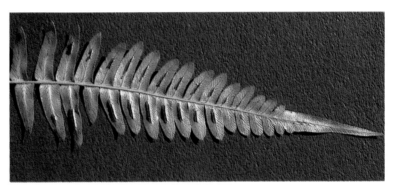

Fertile frond on the monomorphic *Blechnum appendiculatum*.

Brilliant new growth on *Blechnum chilense* in the Alerce Andino National Park in Chile. Photo by Richie Steffen, Miller Botanical Garden.

today includes both the dimorphic, producing fronds that are exclusively sterile or fertile, and the less common monomorphic types. Veins are free and the vascular bundles of various sizes are arranged in a circular manner looking (given some imagination) similar to an asymmetrical smiley face.

Propagation from spores is an inconsistent science. All species should be sown as soon as practicable after the spores mature. In general I find that monomorphic types tend to germinate more promptly and with greater vigor. Dimorphic species vary. Some such as *Blechnum discolor* have remarkably short-lived spores and unless sown immediately upon ripening deliver a minimal to nonexistent percentage of progeny. To add to the difficulty, there are intermediates that germinate (generating enthusiasm) and then fade when the budding sporelings are given their first transplant. *Blechnum niponicum* and even *B. spicant* come to mind. Division is an excellent option but, until more Southern Hemisphere species are in general cultivation, limited by the lack of ready material and the minimal numbers that produce creeping rhizomes. Known hybrids are few although they do mix it up a bit where habitats overlap in Mexico and occasionally in New Zealand.

Unlike many ferns, blechnums do not have an illustrious history of miraculous offerings of herbal cures. Britten (1881), in his delightfully informative and intellectually entertaining book, *European Ferns*, comments rather apologetically on the "hard fern" (the vernacular name for *B. spicant*, aka *Lomaria spicant* in those days): "in the good old times, when no plant was considered entirely destitute of 'virtues', it was not regarded as quite useless." He goes on to recommend a concoction of dried fronds and vinegar to dissolve hardness of the spleen.

Though only a few qualify as hardy, those blechnums that do are an elite addition to the moisture-nourished woodland garden. All offer a tidy year-round presence, and many are especially glamorous when unfurling their fronds in rainbow shades of red, pink, and rose before quieting to variations of green. I recommend them strongly for their refreshing indoor and outdoor visual enrichment.

Blechnum appendiculatum

Synonym *Blechnum occidentale* var. *minor*
Epithet means "appendaged."
Evergreen, 12 to 18 in. (30 to 45 cm). Zones 8 (with protection) and 9.

DESCRIPTION: The rhizome is erect with creeping stolons. Grooved greenish-brown stipes with a few scales are one-third to one-half of the frond length. Narrowly lanceolate blades are once-pinnate with 6 to 10 pairs of pinnae before becoming sessile and ultimately tapering to pinnatifid at the apex. Pinnules have a hint of a hump at their point of attachment to the rachis. The underside of the rachis is dusted with minute peach-fuzz-like hairs. Unlike many blechnums this species is monomorphic with the unreduced fertile pinnae similar to the sterile. Sori and indusial tissue are linear on the pinnae. Freshly collected spores germinate enthusiastically.

RANGE AND HABITAT: This species grows streamside in the southern United States and continues down through Mexico

Rosy new growth on *Blechnum appendiculatum*.

to Central and South America with disjunct populations in Hawaii.

CULTURE AND COMMENTS: Very similar to the less-hardy *Blechnum occidentale*, it unfurls with cheerful Christmas greens and reds. It survived outdoors in Bellevue, Washington, during the winter of 2005 with temperatures dipping, albeit briefly, to 25°F (-4°C) but not in a short 14°F (-10°C) February cold snap in winter 2006. It should be cultivated in friable acid soil in part shade and moist surroundings.

Blechnum brasiliense

Epithet means "from Brazil."
Evergreen, 2 to 4 ft. (60 to 120 cm). Zones 9 and 10, or greenhouse.

DESCRIPTION: The rhizome is erect, eventually lifting to form a stipe-stubbled trunk of 12 in. (30 cm) in circumference. Fronds form a dramatic upright shuttlecock of open foliage. The succulent, short, 2-in. (5-cm) stipes are dark with matching chocolate-colored linear scales. The obovate blade is widest above the midpoint and tapers strongly at the base.

Intense red temporarily colors the new fronds on *Blechnum brasiliense* 'Crispum'.

Blechnum brasiliense in the Fernery at the Morris Arboretum.

Twenty-five to 30 pairs of pinnae are long-pointed and sessile. The species is monomorphic with matching sterile and fertile fronds, the latter bearing linear slots of sori along the pinnae midribs. The trunk occasionally produces an offshoot that can be carefully amputated for propagation purposes.

RANGE AND HABITAT: Not surprisingly this species is native to humid sites in Brazil as well as elsewhere throughout South America. An extremely disjunct population is reported to exist in the Democratic Republic of Congo.

CULTURE AND COMMENTS: New growth is a striking, saturated vermilion, fading in time to shiny green. This fern is an Oscar-winning attraction in greenhouse luxury where it appreciates bright light, neutral loamy soil, and a humid atmosphere.

'*Crispum*' (curled) has wavy pinnae margins and is very attractive.

Blechnum chilense
Epithet means "from Chile."
Evergreen, 3 to 5 ft. (90 to 150 cm). Zones 7 (with protection) to 9. Dimorphic.

DESCRIPTION: The rhizome is long-creeping, tossing up sturdy erect fronds at random. Grooved stipes, with abundant basal scales, are the color of weak tea and are one-half of the frond length. The once-pinnate, narrowly oblong blades have 10 to 20 pairs of rubbery pinnae on a bit of a stalk. The extended apex resembles an elongated pinna. The lower edges of the pinnae overlap the rachis, and appear to be "holding hands," or at least thumbs. This characteristic is one of the few distinctions between this species and the extremely closely related and visually similar *Blechnum cordatum* (both ready, along with their growers, for taxonomic clarification). The fertile fronds are tall wands of narrow, linear pinnae that are solely composed of sori running out on the horizontal from the rachis.

RANGE AND HABITAT: *Blechnum chilense* is abundant in Chile and also grows in Argentina, Brazil, and Uruguay. In the lowlands the new growth is green, but at higher altitudes, the new fronds are a very attractive red. This species is a common and sensational ornamental in botanical gardens in the British Isles and, with its increasing availability, is immensely popular in the Pacific Northwest of the United States.

CULTURE AND COMMENTS: Rickard (2000) observes that "few popular garden plants can have been so frequently misnamed as this one." Most recently it has been distributed in the United States as *Blechnum cordatum*, but that has lost favor (and botanical authority). By whatever name, this is a fern for instant impact in moisture and part shade. It should not be allowed to dry out. The huge (by ferny standards) fronds are frequently enhanced by bright red to salmon-colored new growth, especially in nutrient-poor soils, and give an exuberant tropical magnificence to temperate gardens. Use it for height and boldness. New growth with colorful inrolled pinnae is a highlight among the many delights of assorted unfurling spring crosiers. Chileans call the unfurling frond *costillas de la vaca*, "ribs of the cow" (Ogden, pers. comm.). The

The unfurling fronds of *Blechnum chilense* looking like *costillas de la vaca*.

Mature fronds on a spreading clump of *Blechnum chilense*.

species comes readily from spores and the long rhizomes are tailor-made for division. Propagators and growers should take care, however, and not apply fertilizer to very young plants. They will reward your efforts by turning a sickly brown and attracting every slug in the vicinity. Sturdy, established plants are not effected by fertilizers, but with their natural vigor do not need any supplemental food.

Blechnum discolor
Crown fern
Epithet means "of two different colors."
Evergreen, 1½ to 3 ft. (45 to 90 cm). Zones 8 (with protection) to 10, or greenhouse. Dimorphic.

DESCRIPTION: The rhizome is erect, rather quickly forming a trunk of 6 to 12 in. (15 to 30 cm). The once-pinnate sterile fronds are elliptic with 30 to 40 pairs of sessile pinnae with prominent veins. They taper strongly at the base above short stipes that are about one-sixth of the frond length. The blades are a bright green with whitish undersides, an attractive duet. Fountains of fertile fronds flow forth from the center of the sterile rosettes and are quite vertical. The "fertile" stalks are an intriguing combination of sterile and fertile pinnae with the lower portions composed of zigzag stubs of sterile tissue and the upper portions sporting pointed darts of sori.

RANGE AND HABITAT: This species is endemic to New Zealand where it is abundant in damp to dry soil in beech forests especially at higher altitudes and on the North Island. In native habitats the stolons wander about producing magnificent colonies of foliage. "Such scenes are one of the great delights of the bush" (Metcalf 1993).

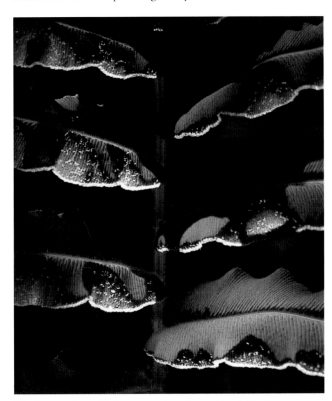

The lower edges of pinnae overlap the rachis of *Blechnum chilense*.

White undersides distinguish *Blechnum discolor* in the New Zealand woodlands.

CULTURE AND COMMENTS: *Blechnum discolor* is easily identified by the lightness of the frond underside, which makes it an ideal plant for hanging or posting up where the "discolor" can be admired. The Maoris use the fronds with their white undersides as trail markers. Crown fern enjoys rich soil and greenhouse culture but I, for one, would like to try it in protected microhabitats in Zone 8. British specialists are cultivating it successfully. The spores are very, very short lived and must be sown as soon as ripe. Stolons provide a better propagation option, producing plants that are willingly separated and reestablished in composty soil.

Blechnum fluviatile
Ray water fern, creek fern
Epithet means "of rivers and streams."
Evergreen, 12 to 18 in. (30 to 45 cm). Zones 8 and 9. Dimorphic. Apogamous.

DESCRIPTION: The rhizome is erect. Grooved, ebony stipes are one-sixth of the frond length and covered with bristly, translucent tan, linear scales that have a prominent black splotch at their point of attachment. These signature characteristics travel upward through the lower portions of the rachis. Ground-hugging sterile, medium green fronds radiate horizontally with 20 to 40 pairs of oval ⅜-in. (9-mm) pinnae trimmed in prominent stubbles of dark bristles and marked with a dark midrib vein. The distinctive, strongly upright, sori-bearing pinnae are parallel to and could almost graft with the rachis of the slender, vertical, fertile fronds.

RANGE AND HABITAT: This wonderful little specimen is native to New Zealand and Australia with a disjunct population in Borneo. It prefers dampish surroundings.

CULTURE AND COMMENTS: Grow *Blechnum fluviatile* in moist and protected shadelands in Zone 8 and with associated New Zealand natives in Zone 9. When my lone plant is threatened with sweeping arctic freezes, I cover it with horticultural gauze. My last carefully spread protective blanket for such nurturing was carried away by a presumably needy crow and found the following morning in the upper limbs of a neighbor's tree. The fern survived. Like many blechnums, this species is unpredictable and erratic in growth from spores and is more productive in its native habitats than in the persuasions of propagators from the Northern Hemisphere.

Blechnum montanum
Mountain kiokio
Synonyms *Blechnum* sp. #2, *B. capense*
Epithet means "of mountains."
Evergreen, 2 to 3 ft. (60 to 90 cm). Zones 7 to 9. Dimorphic.

DESCRIPTION: The rhizome is short-creeping. Stipes of up to one-half of the frond length have sparsely distributed tan

Blechnum fluviatile in the wild in New Zealand.

Blechnum fluviatile in cultivation with *Elatostema rugosum*. Photo by George Schenk.

scales with darker centers. Once-pinnate, ovate, upright, sterile fronds carry 10 to 12 pairs of pinnae with an upward swing at the pinnulc tips. The pairs of pinnae do not taper at the frond base. Erect fertile fronds have linear pinnae enclosing the sori.

RANGE AND HABITAT: Endemic to New Zealand, this species is a subalpine native in cool and damp mountainous areas. On the west coast of the South Island it is a dominant feature with elegant long fronds swooping down roadside banks. Look for it, complete with pink fronds, on New Zealand's $10.00 bank notes as well.

CULTURE AND COMMENTS: In the 1990s the former *Blechnum capense* of New Zealand was subdivided, and in anticipation of upcoming botanical research, designated as blechnums 1, 2, and 3. Here we have "Blechnum #2," which reflects its alpine preference versus #1 (*B. novae-zelandiae*) and #3 (*B. triangularifolium*). By whatever name, with its architectural strength, this fern is to be welcomed as an accent or encouraged as a hillside spreader where it offers a lustrous glow and adaptability in cool and humid temperate gardens. Like many *Blechnum* species from Down Under, it takes some patience to get a response from spores which, when available, should be sown as soon as ripe (or as soon as you can get your hands on them).

Blechnum niponicum
Japanese dccr fern
Epithet means "from Japan."
Evergreen, 1 to 1½ ft. (30 to 45 cm). Zones 6 to 9. Dimorphic.

DESCRIPTION: The rhizome is erect. This species balances prostrate 12- to 18-in. (30- to 45-cm) wide rosettes of ever-

Blechnum niponicum in the Hardy Fern Foundation's woodland planting at the Rhododendron Species Botanical Garden.

Blechnum montanum, a colorful New Zealand native found at higher altitudes.

green sterile, once-pinnate fronds and upright, deciduous, fertile spikes of equal length. The stipe is essentially nonexistent, but the frond base has a small complement of rusty scales. The blade is widest above the middle and tapers to the ground with 30 to 36 pairs of sessile pinnae. The lowest pinnules are ¼ in. (6 mm) long. Fertile pinnules are ½-in. (13-mm) linear segments with sori running the entire length.

RANGE AND HABITAT: This is a fern of mountainous forests in China, Japan, and Korea. A dwarf form is endemic to Japan.

CULTURE AND COMMENTS: Although temperamental as a juvenile, this tidy species displays with elegant restraint in the peat-enriched foreground of lightly shaded woodlands. New growth is an enhancing brilliant pink and fades to a matte green. The species does not take to being moved about, however, and is temperamental from spores. Approximately 10 percent of the sporelings survive until transplant time (which in turn destroys another 10 percent). Once settled, however, this ornamental fern requires minimal maintenance.

Blechnum novae-zelandiae
Palm leaf fern
Synonyms *Blechnum* sp. #1, *B. capense*
Epithet means "from New Zealand."
Evergreen, 2 to 5 ft. (60 to 150 cm). Zones 7 to 9. Dimorphic.

DESCRIPTION: The rhizome is short-creeping, producing dense clusters of frond bouquets. Stipes of one-fifth or more of the frond length are slightly tan scaled. Fronds with oval, once-pinnate sterile blades offer showers of 20 to 40 pairs of bright green pinnae with wavy margins. Fertile fronds are upright with feathery, linear pinnae approaching the apex and contrasting sterile pinnule nubs descending from the midpinnae downwards.

RANGE AND HABITAT: This species is a common fern in New Zealand, where it is found in moist, shady woodlands.

CULTURE AND COMMENTS: In its homeland, this species "is not particular about soil and can become a weed" (Brownsey and Smith-Dodsworth 2000). I would like to have such a problem. With long drapes of variously shaded glossy green-hued

foliage, this species offers showy enrichment as a hanging tapestry in Zones 8 and 9. Well-irrigated, wet loamy soil and light shade are the key components to successfully cultivating this species. It is frequently in the trade and literature as *Blechnum novae-zealandiae*. (Note the erroneous *a* in *zea*.)

Blechnum nudum
Fishbone water fern, black-stemmed water fern
Epithet means "naked."
Evergreen, 2 to 4 ft. (60 to 120 cm). Zones 8 (with protection) and 9. Dimorphic.

DESCRIPTION: The thick rhizome is erect, occasionally developing a trunk. Glossy black stipes with a slight groove and shiny basal scales are one-fourth of the frond length. Lanceolate, 2- to 3-ft. (60- to 90-cm), once-pinnate, sterile blades taper symmetrically from top to bottom. The erect fertile fronds are shorter than the sterile with linear spore-bearing pinnae.

RANGE AND HABITAT: This Australian endemic romps at will in acid soil in moisture-laden streamside or lowland sites as well as on forested slopes. With adequate moisture it is also sun tolerant, albeit with a corresponding loss of height and color saturation.

Blechnum novae-zelandiae in the Kohout garden.

Green foliage on *Blechnum nudum* in the Gassner garden.

CULTURE AND COMMENTS: A common fern in its home country, this is a handsome upright shuttlecock for light shade and rich dampish soil. It is successfully cultivated in the Seattle area, although the trunk needs winter cosseting. I like it in a container, which, should an arctic emergency threaten, can be moved to a temporary shelter. Spores of this species need to be sown as soon as ripe, but will then reward the propagator with prompt and vigorous growth.

Blechnum occidentale
Hammock fern
Epithet means "western."
Evergreen, 1 to 2 ft. (30 to 60 cm). Zones 9 to 11, or greenhouse.

DESCRIPTION: The rhizome is erect with an extensive network of stolons that produce dense stands of cascading, striking ruddy and glossy green foliage. The 6- to 10-in. (15- to 25-cm) stipes are scaly at the base and half of the frond length. Monomorphic, broadly lanceolate, once-pinnate blades taper to narrow points at the apices. Sori are linear on the midribs of the fertile pinnae.

RANGE AND HABITAT: This common fern is an unforgettable sight along roadsides in the West Indies, Mexico, and South America. It grows in the coarse duff of forest floors in shaded tropical woodlands.

CULTURE AND COMMENTS: Unlike the similar *Blechnum appendiculatum*, this species is glabrous along the rachis. It is a member of a complex group of Mexican blechnums all of which are receiving botanical scrutiny as of this writing. By whatever classification, it is a noteworthy addition to and showy attraction in frost-free, humid sites (as well as in flower arrangements). Light shade and moist to wet acid soil keep it at its optimum party-dressed best.

Blechnum penna-marina
Alpine water fern, little hard fern
Epithet means "sea feather" or "sea pen."
Evergreen, 4 to 8 in. (10 to 20 cm). Zones 6 to 8. Dimorphic.

DESCRIPTION: The rhizome is creeping, producing tight clusters of prostrate sterile fronds and upright spikes holding minute fertile pinnae. The stipes of one-fourth to one-third of the sterile frond length are grooved with small tufts of basal scales. The linear, once-pinnate, ½-in. (13 mm) wide sterile blades emerge in brilliant russet tones with 20 to 25 pairs of thick, sessile pinnae arranged in a zigzag fashion. Fertile fronds are vertical and taller with stipes of up to one-half of their length and tight inrolled hard knobs of fleshy pinnae with a firm grip on the sori. Spores are released in late summer to early autumn.

RANGE AND HABITAT: *Blechnum penna-marina* is as varied in its native habitats as it is accommodating in cultivation. Its range extends from wet lowlands to alpine talus in New Zealand and Australia with related colonies in South America. The South American material is generally larger in all of its proportions than the magnificent compact buns sometimes designated as var. *alpinum* from exposed upper montane habitats of New Zealand. Those from comparable areas in Chile are upright clusters of dwarf spikes. In addition to the traditional Southern Hemisphere sites for these common colonizers, there are unexpected (and inexplicable), extraordinarily disjunct populations in the Mexican highlands of Chihuahua and Durango (Mickel and Smith 2004).

CULTURE AND COMMENTS: This is a marvelous fern for ground covering with its small stature and adaptability. In the Pacific Northwest it is an excellent choice for sunny sites where it remains tidily compact and colorful throughout the seasons. In hot climates it needs protection from intense midday sunshine. By contrast, too much shade encourages it to become raggedy and a tad too rambunctious. A dwarf selection maturing at 5 in. (13 cm) in sunshine is especially attractive and popular for lining mixed container plantings. All prefer acidic, well-drained moist soils but are forgiving when watering requirements are treated casually. Like many creeping ferns, and blechnums in particular, it does not propagate readily from spores. (South American material is more responsive than that from New Zealand.) However, with its crawling rhizomes,

Lush tropical fronds on *Blechnum occidentale* in the warmth and humidity of Trinidad.

Blechnum penna-marina in an alpine scree in New Zealand.

Blechnum penna-marina in the higher elevations of the
Conguillio National Park in Chile. Photo by Richie Steffen,
Miller Botanical Garden.

Forked tips of *Blechnum penna-marina* 'Cristatum'.

Another view of *Blechnum penna-marina* in the higher elevations of the Conguillio National Park in Chile. Photo by Richie Steffen,
Miller Botanical Garden.

division is easy. All it takes is a sharp shovel and a handy pot of fresh soil.

'**Cristatum**' (crested) is a crested variety with split frond tips.

Blechnum spicant
Deer fern
Epithet means "spiked, tufted."
Evergreen, 1½ to 2½ ft. (45 to 75 cm). Zones 5 to 8. Dimorphic.

DESCRIPTION: The rhizome is erect. Horizontal whorls of evergreen, oblanceolate, sterile fronds are once-pinnate with 40 or more pairs of pinnae that are greatly reduced at the base. The purplish-brown grooved stipes are one-sixth or less of the frond length. Deciduous fertile fronds, with grooved shiny ebony stipes of up to one-half of the frond length, are taller and upright, waving to the breeze to insure the dispersal of their spores. Narrow, linear pinnae fully enclose the sori and indusia.

RANGE AND HABITAT: This jewel of the woodlands can be found in acid soil in deep to light shade in the coniferous forests of the Pacific Northwest and sweeping down gullies in wet acid seeps in Europe. In addition it is native to North Africa, the Canary Islands, and parts of Russia. The height is variable and dependent on moisture and depth of soil and shade. Moran (2004) observes that fern prothalli are most likely to be found on disturbed soils. For me the deer fern provides the archetypical example and is, in fact, the only species where I have seen prothalli in nature. They were clustered in the dark, on the remains of recently uprooted tree underbellies in a site clearly defined as disturbed in the Olympic National Park in Washington State.

CULTURE AND COMMENTS: The deer fern is totally intolerant of lime whether applied inadvertently in a general broadcast of an all-purpose fertilizer or as an inherent ingredient of native soils or water. Otherwise, it is an extremely well-mannered addition to soft, peat-enriched soil, in moist shade. To me it is synonymous with the serenity of unhurried woodland walks and forested mountain hikes where, in the Pacific Northwest, it

Blechnum penna-marina as typically seen in cultivation.

Blechnum spicant in the woodlands of the Olympic National Park in Washington State.

Blechnum spicant 'Crispum'

Unfurling fronds on *Blechnum spicant* 'Imbricatum'.

Blechnum spicant 'Rickard's Serrate'

associates naturally with such delights as bunchberry (*Cornus canadensis*), oak fern (*Gymnocarpium*), and twinflower, (*Linnaea borealis*). It is especially dominant around Lake Quinault in the Olympic National Park where the Roosevelt elk are reputed to prefer a diet of the deer fern's competitor and companion, *Polystichum munitum*, the sword fern. Thus relieved as a menu item, the deer fern dominates the forest understory, where it serves beautifully in 12-month splendor. In eastern and southwestern U.S. sites, away from its native habitats, it is not always easily established. Spring planting is recommended as well as dutiful respect for its spongy acid soil demands.

Just under a century ago British literature (Lowe 1908) described 83 *Blechnum spicant* cultivars. Most have not survived, but horticulture still enjoys a number. They include 'Crispum' with undulate pinnae margins; 'Cristatum' bearing fronds with crests at the apex; 'Imbricatum', a small form with overlapping pinnae; 'Incisum' with cut pinnae edges; and from a 1972 discovery, 'Rickard's Serrate', which has neatly scalloped pinnae margins. The latter two are almost identical.

While fern populations in the United States, especially in the west, are not prone to sport (produce cultivars), *Blechnum spicant* will surprise, or at least tease, the observant naturalist strolling along the trail with an occasional plant with bifid (forked-tipped) fronds.

Blechnum wattsii

Epithet is after William Watts (1856–1920), a collector in Australia.

Evergreen, 2 to 3 ft. (60 to 90 cm). Zones 8 (with caution and serious protection) and 9, or greenhouse. Dimorphic.

DESCRIPTION: The rhizome is creeping, producing numerous closely spaced upright fronds. Buff-colored, grooved stipes, with shiny dark brown scales at the base, are up to one-half of the frond length. Narrow, lanceolate blades are once-pinnate with 10 to 15 pairs of slightly stalked pinnae and a long terminal apex. Slender, upright, fertile fronds are taller than the sterile with the sori and their indusial wrap covering the entire undersides of the linear fertile pinnae.

RANGE AND HABITAT: This species is an endemic colonizer in moist woods, decorating waterfall environs and streambanks in Australia, where it grows in the company of the tree fern *Dicksonia antarctica*. It is very closely related to, and sometimes classified as synonymous with, the New Zealand native, *Blechnum procerum*.

CULTURE AND COMMENTS: Young fronds are lightly frosted with a rosy patina, contrasting in a comely fashion with the darker foliage of older growth. Although the species comes readily from spores, it tends to resent transplanting and will collapse unexpectedly with a change in scenery. The preferred planting site is in shaded, close humid confines with humusy soil and a consistent supply of moisture at the plant's root zone. A greenhouse setting serves nicely.

Shorter Notes

Blechnum amabile (lovely), with a short-creeping rhizome, produces 1- to 2-ft. (30- to 60-cm) once-pinnate, evergreen, dimorphic fronds approximately equal in length on short

Blechnum wattsii weather-shielded by a log in the Miller Botanical Garden.

stipes. The blades are frequently pinkish in new growth and taper at the base. Fertile fronds have constricted pinnae. This species is rarely available commercially, but is similar to *B. niponicum* differing in having a creeping rather than an erect rhizome and in the more obscure characteristic of ovate rather than linear stipe scales. A native of Japan, it grows in partial shade in cliff crevices and well-drained rocky sites in the mountains or forests. When available it should adapt in moist, crumbly soil in the shady sites of Zones 7 and 8.

Blechnum auriculatum (eared), classified by some authors as *B. australe* subsp. *auriculatum*, grows from 1 to 2 ft. (30 to 60 cm) and has once-pinnate fronds with the pinnae eared adjacent to the rachis. The sterile and fertile fronds are similar and subevergreen. Native to South America, this species creeps slowly, looking almost like a *Nephrolepis*. It is cultivated in Zone 8 central England.

Blechnum australe (of the south) is an evergreen with dimorphic 2-ft. (60-cm) fronds. Sterile fronds are once-pinnate and elliptic with reduced basal pinnae. Fertile fronds match the sterile in the lower portions and have narrow linear spore-bearing pinnae from the waist up. An African native, this species prefers filtered light and will spread with restraint in perpetually moist sites in Zones 8 and 9.

Blechnum blechnoides (like a *Blechnum*) from New Zealand and Chile is, like many blechnums from Down Under, brilliantly enhanced with red new foliage. It is dimorphic with 9-in. (23-cm) sterile, zigzagged fronds and smaller fertile

fronds with widely spaced narrow pinnae. Commonly called the salt spray fern, it grows in nature in coastal areas and is suited for comparable areas in Zones 9 and 10 along the U.S. west coast from the California redwoods south.

Blechnum cartilagineum (like cartilage), the gristle fern, is an Australian with outlying populations in the Philippines, New Guinea, and India. It colonizes in swamps and on marshy streambanks. Monomorphic, leathery 2- to 4-ft. (60- to 120-cm) fronds, with metallic, bronze to pinkish new growth, are once-pinnate with pointed pinnae. In spite of its native haunts, it is more accepting of dryish conditions than other blechnums and should acclimate in Zones 9 and 10 or in transitional greenhouse regions between the humid and "normal" atmosphere sections.

Blechnum chambersii (after Thomas Chambers, director of the Royal Botanic Gardens, Sydney, Australia), lance water fern, is native to damp and rather dark sites in New Zealand, Australia, Fiji, and Samoa. With its erect dimorphic fronds, it adds to decorative waterside options in Zones 9 and 10. Arching lanceolate swoops of 2- to 3-ft. (60- to 90-cm) rose-enhanced emerging foliage which gradually mature to a glossy dark green are comfortable in moist to wet shade.

Blechnum colensoi (after William Colenso, 1811–1899), Colenso's hard fern, or the waterfall fern, is a dimorphic New Zealand endemic with short-creeping rhizomes. Deep blackish-green, pendulous sterile fronds, all terminating in a needlelike "drip tip" point, are variable from undivided to

Blechnum colensoi in the wild in New Zealand.

Young pink fronds on *Blechnum cordatum* growing in Ecuador. Photo by Joan Eiger Gottlieb.

The fronds of *Blechnum filiforme* clamber up a tree in New Zealand.

broadly elliptical with the latter divided into several pinnate pinnae. The fertile fronds have a few long wispy threads of pinnae. This species is suitable for deep shade and wet soil in Zone 9 or as a sultry understory in the humid rainforest section of conservatories.

   Blechnum cordatum (heart-shaped), from the high-elevation, 5,000- to 10,000-ft. (1500- to 3000-m) cloud forests of Columbia, Peru, Venezuela, Bolivia, and Ecuador (note not from Chile), is a tall dimorphic species with ruby new growth. It is extremely closely allied botanically with *B. chilense* although the two species are separated in nature by hundreds of miles. The easiest observable difference is that *B. cordatum* pinnae do not have the lower lip of the pinnae overlapping the rachis. In addition, Mickel and Smith (2004) observe, "*B. cordatum*... widespread and common in South America and with many syn-

Small fronds of *Blechnum gayanum* colonize against a log in the Gassner garden.

A slender trunk supports the fronds of *Blechnum gibbum* in the Fernery at the Morris Arboretum.

onyms, is very closely related to *B. schiedeanum* [of Mexico] and perhaps not distinguishable. Monographic study is needed on this group of blechnums before names can be applied with confidence." To which my colleagues and I say, "Amen."

Blechnum filiforme (threadlike), the thread fern, is a climbing plant with miniature 2- to 6-in. (5- to 15-cm) juvenile fronds romping about indiscriminately, vinelike, in the bush country and on the forest floors in New Zealand. When it encounters a tree, the species continues its opportunistic viney inclination and spirals upward, gaining in girth as it gains in altitude eventually cloaking the entire host tree. The creeping young fronds are sterile. The mature fronds, festooning the treetops, sometimes reach 2 ft. (60 cm) in length. The adult population produces both fertile and sterile fronds with the slender fertile ones being the threads of the common name. This unconventional attraction for Zone 8 and 9 woodlands is a potential conversation piece for fern enthusiasts in the moisture-laden coastal gardens of the Pacific Northwest and even more so along the Gulf Stream–tempered Atlantic rim of the British Isles. The migrating juvenile stems prefer to be rooted in heavy soil, and the upwardly mobile fronds need an arboreal climbing gym for complete success. Basket culture is an excellent option. This species can be propagated by carefully executed division as well as by spores.

Blechnum gayanum (after French botanist Jacques Gay), synonym *B. microphyllum*, is a dense, dimorphic little bushlet of a fern from the mountains of southern Chile and Argentina. Crowded bunches of sterile fronds mature at 6 to 8 in. (15 to 20 cm) in the shadow of slightly taller fertile fronds. This species prefers bright light and dampish acid soil in Zones 7 to 9. Plant it in your favorite prominent site, be it rock garden, container, or woodland foreground. As with other miniatures it is especially appropriate for display at eye level.

Blechnum gibbum (humped, referring to the swollen stipe), the "dwarf tree fern" from the South Pacific Islands, is an appropriate fern for gardens, greenhouses, and conserva-

tories that provide the signature tropical humidity and warmth of its South Seas homeland. Bright green swirls of evergreen 2-ft. (60-cm) fronds are dimorphic and arise from a stout rhizome that may in time form a small trunk. For household use it needs well-aerated but consistently moist soil. 'Silver Lady' is a cultivar that has done well in California.

Blechnum magellanicum (from the Straits of Magellan) is a would-be tree fern from southern Chile and Argentina. Once-pinnate dimorphic fronds produce towers of cycadlike foliage. The rhizome can form a trunk of up to 4 ft. (1.2 m) in lowland habitats. At higher altitudes, the trunk is absent, presumably since the colder exposures render it vulnerable to the desiccation and vagaries of alpine weather (and there is no one there to tenderly apply a protective wrap). In the past this

Blechnum magellanicum in the bush in the Alerce Andino National Park in Chile. Photo by Richie Steffen, Miller Botanical Garden.

species has been confused with *B. chilense*, which does not have a trunk. In addition, the foliage of *B. magellanicum* is shiny and the pinnae are stalkless. Spores of this species are short-lived, but plants, by contrast, are statuesque additions to Zone 9 and protected Zone 8 gardens.

Blechnum minus (small) is a swamp-loving species, which comes in two manifestations and much nomenclatural confusion, from New Zealand and Australia. The New Zealander, which upon further study may be reclassified as *B. procerum*, is nurtured successfully in Britain whereas the Australian is reputed to be difficult to establish. Both are dimorphic with oval sterile fronds and spidery fertile fronds.

Blechnum orientale (of the East) grows in Japanese lowlands (as weeds according to Iwatsuki et al. 1995) and the tropics in huge 3- to 5-ft. (90- to 150-cm) bushels of rosy, once-pinnate fronds. It is a showstopper in the humidity of greenhouses, conservatories, and lanai sides in the lush banana belts of Zones 9 to 11. Think Hawaii—with colorful cascading fronds in hotel lobbies, elegant entryway approaches, and let loose the travel appetite.

Blechnum patersonii (for William Paterson, 1755–1810), the strap water fern, synonym *Stegania patersonii*, is from Australia, New Zealand, the Philippines, and South Pacific Islands. It has atypical (for a *Blechnum*) undivided, simple, 12- to 18-in. (30- to 45-cm) "straps" of sterile fronds. Fertile fronds with matching, straplike bases branch into several pairs of pinnae and finish with an extended tip. Often pendulous with bronzy new growth, this fern enjoys the streamside comforts of continually moist, rich soil in light to deep shade and should adapt accordingly in Zone 9 gardens or elsewhere in greenhouses. Once established, it does not like to be disturbed.

Blechnum procerum (extended, tall) is a dimorphic New Zealand native with a short-creeping rhizome. The oblong, sterile blades emerge in shades of bronze and have a long stipe and three to eight pairs of pinnae embracing an extended tonguelike apical tip. In its native haunts, ranging from subalpine scrub, where it is common, to bogs, where it is not, it reaches 2 to 3 ft. (60 to 90 cm). Unlike the drooping sterile fronds, the fertile fronds are upright and slightly taller. This species adapts to life in the open and comes recommended as a ground cover for Zones 8 (where it needs to be tested for prolonged cold tolerance) and 9.

Blechnum punctulatum (with small dots), the glossy hard fern, is a variable species from South Africa with dimorphic 2- to 3-ft. (60- to 90-cm) fronds widely spaced on a stoloniferous base. Linear to lanceolate sterile blades are once-pinnate with crowded unstalked pinnae. Fertile fronds have sori running the length of the linear pinnae. Red new growth adds elegance and interest to this species. It is cultivated in light shade and rich soil in Zone 7 German gardens. Commercially, it is popular in the cut flower trade.

Blechnum tabulare (from Table Mountain above Cape Town, South Africa) has for years been lumped into the confused horticultural kettle of assorted Southern Hemisphere blechnums. This is an upright, evergreen species with strongly vertical fertile fronds erupting from the center of leathery sterile fronds. It can form a small trunk, taller in high rainfall areas, and has pinnae, which are reduced in size on the fronds' lower portions. Pinnae bases are unique in being unequally shaped with a notch on the lower side. The undersides are embellished with tawny hairs. This species is recommended as a centerpiece for humid shade or container planting in Zones 9 and 10.

Blechnum vulcanicum (of volcanic soils), wedge water fern, is dimorphic with narrowly triangular, once-pinnate, somewhat hairy, sterile fronds pointing their basal pinnae downwards. Both sterile and fertile fronds, of up to 2 ft. (60 cm), have long stipes of one-half of the frond length. With bronzy new growth, this species is frequently seen as an attractive drapery on moist banks in the South Island of its native New Zealand. It is also found in Australia and the Pacific Islands and is a decorative addition in moist to wet Zone 9 gardens. Ideally (and perhaps optimistically) it is also a candidate for the sheltered niche in Zone 8.

Bommeria

Bommeria (after Joseph Bommer, 1829–1895, a Belgian pteridologist) is a small genus with only five species. They are all from inhospitable rock-crusted Zone 7 to 10 sites in the U.S. Southwest, Mexico, and Central America.

Bommeria hispida (hairy), the copper fern, is the most familiar species. Forest blue-green, pinnate-pinnatifid pentagonal blades, with long basal pinnules, are coated with a protective white cottony froth, which is beneficial to the fern and ornamentally appealing to the collector. Rhizomes are creeping and the tall stipes, of at least one-half of the 10-in. (25 cm) frond, are a rich copper brown. Sori without indusia trim the free veins, increasing in abundance toward the margins. Specialists in the Greater Seattle, Washington, area have attempted to acclimate this species in their customized xeric sites without lasting success. Assorted cheilanthes, by contrast, will succeed. Give it good drainage, air circulation, protection from winter wet, and your best wishes.

Stressed *Bommeria hispida* reacts to attempts at cultivation.

Botrychium
Grape ferns

Botrychiums (Greek *botrys*, cluster) are commonly called grape ferns because of the clustered arrangement of their rounded sporangia. These ferns are avidly pursued, but not collected, in the wild by aficionados who enjoy "the find." I have joined with fellow travelers to search along several miles of trail and rejoice in spotting a patch of a dozen or so 4-in. (10-cm) high fronds. (Grazing deer have been known to annually eat the reward.) Part of the challenge is the structure of the fern itself which has one, or occasionally two, sterile fronds usually accompanied by a single fertile spike that may originate as an extension from the stipe or from below ground where it would deceptively appear to be an independent stalk. Field populations are not obvious to the casual passerby, although I will confess to once finding *Botrychium multifidum* on a sandy ocean side lot strictly because of the timely appearance of bright yellow, spore-laden fertile stalks.

Worldwide there are approximately 60 species primarily in North America and eastern Asia. Fleeting and frequently rare in nature, they are widely admired but not considered ornamental in the traditional fern sense, nor for that matter are they willing in the landscape. (One of their best functions is to provide an excuse for a timely social fern foray.) They are characterized by fleshy underground stems, which are dependent on a mycorrhizal (fungal) relationship to survive. Sterile blades with free veins are once-pinnate to tripinnate or more, erect to horizontal, and often with overlapping pinnae. The vascular bundle is a broad, elongate letter *C*, resembling a slender crescent moon. Spores germinate underground, requiring darkness and the same fungal connection as the parent. In nature it can take as long as eight years to produce a plant. Obviously they are not a practical option for home gardening unless you buy property where they are already established. (And then beware of deer and slugs.)

Historically botrychiums have a rich association with herbal cures and magical powers. The moonwort, *Botrychium lunaria*, with its lunate (half-moon-shaped) pinnules and once-abundant nearly worldwide distribution, was a leader in mystical powers. (Harry Potter would love it.) Specific uses included boiling the leaves in red wine to produce a concoction that would curtail bleeding and vomiting, as well as heal both internal and external wounds. More fanciful attributes based on the double "key"-shaped pinnae gave it the ability to undo locks and unshoe horses. My favorite, however, is that the fairy folks used the leaflets as their wee horses.

Botrychium biternatum (two sets of three) is native to the U.S. Southeast. Ten-inch (25-cm) fronds are triangular with two to three pairs of pinnate-pinnatifid pinnae. Fronds emerge in summer with the fertile stalk extending well beyond the tip of the sterile and withering as soon as spores are dispersed. The sterile remains wintergreen. Look for it in swampy habitats.

Botrychium dissectum (cut into deep lobes), synonym *B. obliquum*, is an evergreen with finely divided triangular, shiny sterile blades growing to 8 in. (20 cm). Fronds appear in the summer and often are bronzy in the fall. The fertile stalk emerges from the base of the stipe or occasionally from below ground. Two botanical forms are recognized with f. *dissectum* bearing incised-pointed pinnae and f. *obliquum* carrying smooth-lobed pinnae. They join each other in the wild in the woodlands of eastern North America.

Botrychium lanceolatum (narrow and tapering at each end, lance-shaped) is widespread in nature with deciduous populations in North America, Europe, and Asia. New growth appears in the spring and the plant disappears at the end of summer. The frond is primarily composed of a single slender stipe, usually maturing at 6 to 12 in. (15 to 30 cm), topped with a proportionately small triangular sterile blade and matching slender fertile stalk, both of which branch from the tip of the stipe. In the United States it grows in wet meadows on the northern tiers of both coasts with disjunct populations in the Rocky Mountains.

Botrychium lunaria (lunate), like other botrychiums, cannot be introduced into cultivation, but with its unique silhouette is referenced here in deference to the challenge (and potential reward) of the field search. It is a fleshy dwarf, with an annual spring output of single 2- to 6-in. (5- to 15-cm) fronds and a tendency to be camouflaged in grassy sites making it an adventure to find. Both the fertile and sterile portions of the frond, which dies down in late summer, are rigidly erect, parting near the tip of its proportionately long stipe. The fertile extends beyond the sterile. A ladder of four to seven pairs of little, pale green, moonlike overlapping pinnules on the sterile portion gives the species its name as well as an appearance similar to a double-sided key. In nature this, the most widespread of the world's botrychiums, sweeps from Alaska across Canada and down through most of the Pacific Northwest as well as New England, Eurasia, South America, Australia, and New Zealand.

Botrychium matricariifolium (leaves like *Matricaria*) demands a sharp-eyed hands-and-knees search to detect the 3- to maybe 6-in. (7.5- to 15-cm) fronds of this little critter of a grape fern. It also requires a timely search as the short-lived fronds usually die down by midsummer. The lanceolate to oblong sterile blade is pinnate-pinnatifid and suspended under an upright fertile stalk. The species is common in the woodlands of Europe and the northern portions of midwestern to eastern North America, with spotty populations elsewhere on the continent.

Botrychium multifidum (much divided) is a stubby wintergreen species with succulent bipinnate to tripinnate, rounded sterile foliage reaching 6 to 8 in. (15 to 20 cm) with taller upright fertile stalks. It grows in exposed sandy and well-drained loamy sites in the fields of northern and upper midwestern areas of the United States and Canada with populations extending down the Rockies and the West Coast as well as New England. For assistance in the field, look for the brilliant yellow flags of fertile fronds, which appear in midsummer.

Botrychium oneidense (after the Oneida Nation, in New York) is a rare evergreen from woodlands and damp sites in eastern North America. New growth emerges in summer. The

Botrychium dissectum in the New Jersey woods.

sterile and fertile fronds part company just above the ground with the triangular bipinnate to tripinnate sterile blade extending on an outward plane and the fertile continuing upwards in the typical *Botrychium* structural configuration. The combined height is usually around 6 in. (15 cm).

Botrychium simplex (simple, undivided), the little grape fern, is unusual in occasionally having the sterile frond with tripartite lower pinnae. The 2- to 6-in. (5- to 15-cm) portions are fleshy, small, and once-pinnate with the lissome fertile stalk extending well beyond the sterile. This is a deciduous, circumpolar species with a quiet and sometimes seemingly hidden presence in moist woodlands. New growth occurs in early spring.

Botrychium virginianum (of Virginia), the rattlesnake fern, has an erect stipe. The horizontal sterile portion of the frond is pointed and tripinnate, or even more finely divided, with elongate lower pinnae. A solitary upright fertile stalk originates at the base of the sterile blade with the whole, sometimes reaching up to 18 in. (45 cm) tall. This is a deciduous species with new growth appearing in spring and dying in late summer. One of the most common botrychiums, it grows in moist woodlands in Canada and all but the most arid areas of the United

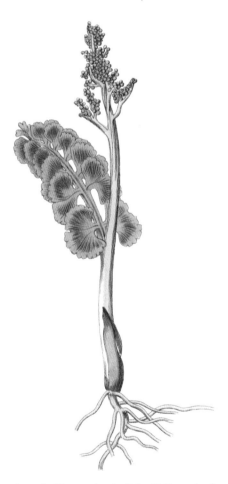

Botrychium lunaria. Illustration by John E. Sowerby from *The Ferns of Great Britain* by John E. Sowerby and Charles Johnson, London, 1855.

Fertile *Botrychium multifidum* stands out among the native scrub in sandy soil on the coast of Washington State.

States as well as Mexico, Central and South America, and Eurasia. Native Americans used mashed roots of the species to treat bites of poisonous snakes, hence the common name.

Camptosorus

Camptosorus is reputedly the only scientific name shared by both a plant and animal (Mattei 2002) (although one must fudge a little bit on the spelling). *Camptosaurus*, which means "bent lizard," was a 15-ft. (4.5-m) long dinosaur of the Jurassic period some 150 million years ago. The *Camptosorus* (which actually translates to curved sorus) of today's fern world has an extended, narrow-tipped frond that certainly resembles a lizard's bent tail. It is frequently classified as *Asplenium* because of the common shape of their vascular bundles as well as the ability to hybridize with species from that genus. However, some botanists separate it because of the namesake curved sori and presence of netted veins versus the herringbone linear sori and free veins of *Asplenium*.

Worldwide there are two species, one in eastern North America and a counterpart in eastern Asia. They come easily from spores if protected from devastation by slugs and, of course, by nature they are tip-rooting so they form new plants by "walking."

Camptosorus rhizophyllus
Walking fern
Synonym *Asplenium rhizophyllum*
Epithet means "rooting leaves."
Evergreen, 4 to 9 in. (10 to 23 cm). Zones 4 to 8.

DESCRIPTION: The rhizome is erect. Stipes are rusty at ground level and green on the upper portions. The length relative to the total frond is variable. Entire, rich green, arching blades have a heart-shaped base and are narrow with an extended tapering rooting tip. Sori with one-sided indusia point outwards like an upside down V.

RANGE AND HABITAT: The walking fern meanders about, rooting along the way, in moist to wet deep shade on moss-covered limestone rocks or occasionally on shale or sandstone. It spreads from the upper midwestern to eastern North America down to Tennessee, West Virginia, and northern Alabama, and is one of the most easily recognized of the East Coast natives.

CULTURE AND COMMENTS: This very unusual species is cultivated with difficulty because of the ever-present threat from slugs and snails. My plant was on a limestone rock, in a container high up on a table, and still it disappeared. The slugs apparently dropped out of the trees. Truly a conversation piece, this fern is not totally impossible. East Coast experts seem to have better luck with it.

Shorter Note

Camptosorus sibiricus (from Siberia), Asian walking fern, synonym *Asplenium ruprechtii*, is from Japan, Korea, Manchuria, China, and eastern Siberia and although smaller is extremely similar to its North American counterpart. The frond base is tapered rather than heart-shaped and it is widest at the mid frond. This species hybridized with *C. rhizophyllus* quite by accident in an Ohio greenhouse producing a fertile offspring, ***Asplenium crucibuli***. Both are hardy in Zones 4 to 8 but vulnerable to slug and snail damage.

Ceterach

Ceterach (from the Greek *sjetrak* or, prior to that, the Persian *chetrak*, both being ancient names for "fern") is a small genus often included with *Asplenium*; however, various authorities segregate it based on the scaly undersides and the reticulate (netted) venation. The species are compact, low swirls of dense pinnatifid masses of foliage. Traditionally the fronds carry a functional, protective undercoat of thick and showy scales that develop in silver and fade to rust. The succulent

Camptosorus rhizophyllus walks along the surface of a limestone outcrop in Massachusetts.

Dwarf forms of *Ceterach officinarum* selected from several batches of sporelings create an attractive patch in the Baggett garden.

fronds are attractively lobed and carry linear sori with a matching indusium along the veins.

These species have a strong preference for a challenging life in the limestone mortar of walls and a corresponding distinct disdain for luxury living in a traditional (even customized) garden situation. Spore sowings are usually quite promptly productive. Cultural problems do develop, however, usually in adolescence. The sporelings are difficult to cultivate and transitioning them from the propagation bed to the garden is very challenging indeed. For best results tend the plants in a scree of basic rubble or shoehorn them in between rocks and secure with moss on a vertical wall. Good drainage is mandatory, and watering should be kept to a minimum. Are they worth the effort? A good display (or even a living plant) can make for a proud gardener and bring forth the admiration of the cognoscenti.

In ancient Greece it was the original spleenwort, credited before the aspleniums we know today, with curing ailments of the spleen, even dissolving said spleens in animals (supposedly confirmed when the animals were sacrificed at ancient game rituals). Elsewhere it has historically been used to remedy a variety of ills. And in a rather unusual departure from medical miracles, the Reverend Hugh Davies reports, in his *Welsh Botanology* (1813), that *Ceterach officinarum* was collected almost to extinction in Anglesea where it was used as bait for rock cod fishing (apparently successfully).

Ceterach officinarum
Rusty back fern
Synonym *Asplenium ceterach*
Epithet means "medicinal."
Evergreen, 3 to 8 in. (7.5 to 20 cm). Zones 5 to 8.

DESCRIPTION: The rhizome is erect. Succulent tan-green stipes with a sparse smattering of brown scales are one-fourth the length of the frond or less. The rich green blades with zigzag lobes of pinnae are reminiscent in outline of the rickrack that adorned the dresses of little girls in my childhood. Young fronds emerge with a shimmering undercoat of translucent and protective silvery scales. In time these mature to the rust color of the common name. Sori in a herringbone pattern with linear indusia are along veins and often concealed by the abundant cloak of scales.

RANGE AND HABITAT: The rusty back fern, when happy, is a photogenic inhabitant of sunny walls and crumbly crevices throughout Britain, Europe, North Africa, the Caucasus, Russia, and the Himalayas. Even in good health the pinnae tend to roll ever so slightly inwards exposing the seasonally appropriate skirt of silver to rust-colored scales. It will, however, curl tightly when drought stressed fully exposing the protective and water-collecting scales of its undersides. When moisture re-enters the scales and consequently the pinnae, the fern rejuvenates as a fresh rosette.

Ceterach officinarum in the springtime, mingling eloquently with *Erinus alpinus* down a wall in the Baird garden.

Container planting of *Ceterach officinarum* 'Crenatum'.

Ceterach aureum in the Peters garden.

Ceterach dalhousiae shares a rock garden habitat with *Asplenium adiantum-nigrum* in the Peters garden.

CULTURE AND COMMENTS: This and *Asplenium ruta-muraria* are among the most difficult ferns to introduce to cultivation. Acclimated plants are a magnificent sight indeed. The hands-down best that I have ever seen were in the garden of the late Mr. and Mrs. Hugh Baird of Bellevue, Washington, where a few plants were tucked into the top of a west-facing wall in full sun. To the envy of Mrs. Baird's fellow pteridomaniacs, sporelings cascaded down the wall joining the equally successful planting of *Erinus alpinus*. Give this fern coarse grit, a limey additive such as broken concrete chunks the size of marbles or smaller, and a sunny exposure. Beware the lime of lawns and avoid the occasionally recommended gypsum altogether. Do not over-water. Troughs, which give the gardener the opportunity and mobility to test various exposures, are an excellent option.

Subsp. *bivalens* is smaller with spores proportionately reduced in size, and the attractive '**Crenatum**' has crenate (scalloped) margins.

Shorter Notes

Ceterach aureum (golden) is similar to *C. officinarum* but larger in all dimensions. Magnification reveals toothy rather than smooth scales. The species is from Madeira and the Canary Islands and best suited for Zone 7 and warmer sites.

Ceterach dalhousiae (after Countess Dalhousie, 1786–1839, of Scotland), synonyms *Asplenium dalhousiae* and *Ceterachopsis dalhousiae*, has the typically thick, deeply pinnatifid, evergreen fronds associated with *Ceterach*. They usually mature at 6 to 8 in. (15 to 20 cm), but lack the heavy, scaly trimmings of *C. officinarum*, hence the affiliation with and frequent classification as *Asplenium*. The distribution is downright bizarre, with scant populations in Arizona and Mexico, and abundant colonies in the Himalayas. Cultivation is difficult but possible in Zones 9 and 10.

Cheilanthes

Cheilanthes are dryland ferns and quite the opposite of the traditional, stereotypical and beautiful woodland shade lovers that evoke visions of greenery in the world's forests. We cherish and cultivate those for a myriad of reasons, but many avid gardeners also attempt the xerics, including cheilanthes, for their unique ornamental qualities as well as the challenge of establishing notoriously difficult species. And challenging they are. Cheilanthes like arid, desertlike habitats and have developed adaptive strategies for succeeding in sunshine and drought. Most noticeably the fronds and especially the pinnae and small pinnules produce diagnostic cottony hairs and/or woolly scales and occasionally waxy undercoatings that are ornamental to the viewer and functional for the plants. These adornments serve to moderate the ambient temperature around the fronds, to reflect heat and light, and to catch dew and whatever minimal moisture may be available.

In addition most species crowd together to reduce transpiration and snuggle their colonies against rocks to provide a modicum of shade as well as a cool shelter for the extensive, long-running moisture-seeking roots. In severe or prolonged drought the entire fern can curl without damaging cell structure and will rehydrate with the arrival of a good drink. This

Hairy upper surface of *Cheilanthes tomentosa* as viewed through the microscope. Photo by Richie Steffen, Miller Botanical Garden.

characteristic has earned some of them the epithet "resurrection ferns."

The name *Cheilanthes* comes from the Greek *cheilos*, lip, and *anthos*, flower, in reference to the curled pinnae margins that enclose the sori. They are consequently also commonly called "lip ferns."

There are 180 to 200 species worldwide with high concentrations in the U.S. Southwest and northern Mexico. Most, with their single vascular bundle, are short, usually around 12 in. (30 cm) more or less, and strongly vertical. The blades are often very finely divided, up to quadripinnate, with green, blue, or grayish evaporation-resistant, minute pinnules. Veins are free but usually obscured by the hairs and scales. Unlike most ferns, many cheilanthes are distinct by having noncircinate vernation, where the emerging bud is not at the center of a coil, as opposed to the traditional crosier pattern usually associated with unfurling fronds.

Taxonomists have been actively researching relationships among the cheilanthoids resulting in a number of reclassifications in recent years. This will be ongoing, I am sure, as botany is a living science. As of 2005, *Argyrochosma*, *Aspidotis*, *Astrolepis*, *Bommeria*, *Mildella*, *Notholaena*, *Pellaea*, *Pentagramma*, and *Pityrogramma* are all considered separate genera with a preference for xeric habitats. Not all of these classifications are new but some are rearrangements.

It is not necessary to be a geologist or chemist to cultivate these ferns, although it may help. Some species are very soil

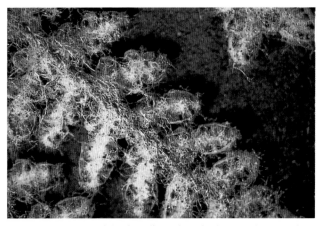

Microscopic view of the frond's underside showing hairs and spores on *Cheilanthes tomentosa*. Photo by Richie Steffen, Miller Botanical Garden.

specific; however, most will respond to some general guidelines. The soil composition must be loose to encourage free drainage whether for basic or acid-loving species. I have had my best successes with mixtures that include volcanic rock, pumice, and/or granite grit, which is sold as chicken scratch and comes in at least three different grades from fine through coarse. It is extremely important to give any of these inorganic additives a good hosing to flush away the siltlike "fines" that can clog oxygen circulation in the soil with devastating results. (Like vermiculite and perlite, these products produce dust that humans should take precautions against inhaling.) I add composted bark, charcoal, and humus to the basic mix. When growing plants in containers, tall narrow pots provide the best drainage.

Protection from overhead winter wet emulates the natural southwestern environment, which gets summer but not much winter rain. Water sitting on the fronds in the cool of winter does not readily evaporate and will slowly destroy the foliage. When watering is necessary, I direct it to the soil and not the foliage.

Plant surroundings need good air circulation. In addition they need bright light as opposed to the conventionally shaded ferny sites. In climates with high heat, light shade is appropriate. In cool, cloudy climates, full sun, at least in winter, is suitable. Experimentation and adjustments are necessary to determine the ideal location(s), and cultivating the lot in portable containers certainly simplifies the "educational" experience.

Theories vary regarding fertilizer with one being that none should be added and the other being that the xeric native habitats are high in mineral nutrients and fertilizer is welcome. I do not feed mine, mostly because of a lack of prioritized time rather than strong convictions, but some of the best xerics I have seen are in bonsai pots and regularly fed. (While these pots are not usually deep, they have extra large drain holes to facilitate the ferns' required good drainage needs.) Whichever course you chose, be sure that applied amounts are no more than one-half of the manufacturer's recommended strength. Feeding for any ferns, including xerics, is most effective when applied during active new growth.

Propagation can be accomplished by division. Established plants do not like to be disturbed, so I selectively remove a piece or two from the perimeter of the plant with a sharp knife. Spore culture is a rewarding option, however, as many species are apogamous, which efficiently compensates for the desert's lack of available water for fertilization. Spores will drop almost immediately when a ripe frond is removed from the parent plant and are so grateful to be sown on a moist medium that they germinate rapidly. (In nature it can be a long wait for suitably ideal conditions to successfully create new plants from spores. In Southern California, native cheilanthes are actively growing during the winter, ready to release their spores with the arrival of the favorable spring conditions.) I use my regular mix of pasteurized earthworm compost for starting the spores, but when transplanting I give them a lean mix enriched with pumice and/or granite grit to emulate their natural habitats. I do not add lime to mixes used with any young plants.

Cheilanthes have many charming species worthy of the extra care to keep them presentable (or at least alive). They are not for beginners. (It helps to live in the Southwest or Southern California.) I recommend them for the specialist's rock gardens and container plantings. And, I especially recommend a visit to the University of California Botanical Garden at Berkeley that has a magnificent and beautifully presented comprehensive collection of these fascinating species.

Far upward 'neath a shelving cliff
Where cool and deep the shadows fall,
The trembling fern its graceful fronds
Displays along the mossy wall.
The wildflowers shun these craggy heights
Their haunts are in the vale below;
But beauty ever clothes the rocks
Where Nature bids the ferns to grow.

—Unknown

Cheilanthes alabamensis
Alabama lip fern
Epithet means "from Alabama."
Evergreen, 1 ft. (30 cm). Zones 7 to 10. Apogamous.

DESCRIPTION: The rhizome is short-creeping. Rounded stipes are black, up to one-half of the frond length, and noted for lacking scales. The dull green blade is lanceolate, bipinnate-pinnatifid at the base although less divided toward the tip. Fifteen to twenty-five pairs of pinnae are very sparsely hairy and carry sori that are continuous along the margins covered by an inrolled false indusium.

RANGE AND HABITAT: *Cheilanthes alabamensis* spreads across the southern tier of the United States from Alabama west to Texas and north to Arkansas and Tennessee in rocky limestone habitats.

CULTURE AND COMMENTS: This attractive species is difficult to domesticate. It requires limestone, good drainage and air circulation, and bright light, and is best located under the gardener's watchful eye in an alpine house.

Cheilanthes argentea
Silver cloak fern
Epithet means "silver."
Evergreen, 8 in. (20 cm). Zones 5 to 8.

DESCRIPTION: The rhizome is short-creeping to erect. Stipes are shiny plum-colored with a few basal scales. They are up to

Cheilanthes alabamensis in the Schwartz garden. Photo by David Schwartz.

one-half of the frond length. Blades are matte green, broadly triangular with extended lower inner pinnae pinnules giving a pentagonal effect. The lower surface is coated with a white wax that is especially prominent when the frond curls in drought or stress. Sori are marginal and covered with an inrolled false indusium. When the spores are ripe, they give a black etch to the frond.

RANGE AND HABITAT: *Cheilanthes argentea* is widely distributed in limestone habitats in eastern Asia including Japan and China. A rock wall population adjacent to a hotel in Beijing, where just incidentally, a 1988 pteridophyte conference was headquartered, delighted the participants (and their cameras).

CULTURE AND COMMENTS: This irresistible species is difficult in cultivation but has been distributed to the trade and successfully maintained in gritty, limey mortar with good drainage, bright light, and a minimum of winter wet. New growth emerges in late winter.

Cheilanthes bonariensis
Golden cloak fern
Synonym *Notholaena aurea*
Epithet means "from Buenos Aires."
Evergreen, 1 ft. (30 cm). Zones 8 and 9. Apogamous.

DESCRIPTION: The rhizome is short-creeping to erect with dark chocolate-colored, slight stipes to one-fifth of the frond length. The narrow 1- to 1½-in. (2.5- to 3.8-cm) wide, linear once-pinnate blades have 30 to 40 pairs of many lobed pinnae. The blue-green upper surface is lightly dusted with an occa-

sional stubby hair. The undersides, however, are magnificently coated with mats of woolly, cream-colored to tan-tinted hairs.

RANGE AND HABITAT: This species is located among acidic rocks and is native to the U.S. Southwest–Mexico border with an extended range down through Central and South America.

CULTURE AND COMMENTS: My love affair with xeric ferns began when I first saw this fern as *Notholaena aurea* in the rock garden collection at Oregon's Siskiyou Rare Plant Nursery many, many years ago. Its preference for acid soil, versus lime, makes it somewhat easier to introduce to the rock gardens and alpine houses of devoted specialists. Its cultivation is not to be confused with being easy, but when encouraged by good drainage, comparable air circulation, and protection from overhead winter wet, it can be coaxed along.

Cheilanthes buchtienii
Buchtien's lip fern
Synonym *Notholaena buchtienii*
Epithet is after Otto Buchtien (1859–1946), a German plant collector in Bolivia.
Evergreen, 6 to 9 in. (15 to 23 cm). Zones (8) 9 and 10.

DESCRIPTION: The rhizome is short-creeping, producing upright tufts of 1-in. (2.5-cm) wide, linear fronds on short stipes that are one-fourth of the frond length. The blades are bipinnate in the basal portions and pinnate-pinnatifid upwards. The whole is coated in a decorative but functional creamy cocoa mass of protective scales. Sori border the frond's edge and are covered with an inward curled lip.

RANGE AND HABITAT: This species is native to rocky sites in Bolivia and Argentina.

Cheilanthes bonariensis in the desert garden at the University of California Botanical Garden at Berkeley.

Cheilanthes buchtienii with cactus at the University of California Botanical Garden at Berkeley.

CULTURE AND COMMENTS: For home gardeners container planting with good drainage is recommended. The container can then be moved at will away from damaging winter rain or cold. In the garden or container give the water-seeking roots the cool protection of a rock.

Cheilanthes covillei
Coville's lip fern
Epithet is after Frederick Coville (1867–1937), chief botanist for the U.S. Department of Agriculture.
Evergreen, 6 to 12 in. (15 to 30 cm). Zones 7 to 9.

DESCRIPTION: The rhizome is short-creeping. Coffee-brown, rounded stipes are up to one-half of the length of the frond. The lanceolate tripinnate blades have 10 to 12 pairs of pinnae with beady segments. The upper surface is glabrous, but the rachis and midveins of the pinnae undersides have small, overlapping, ovate scales with a heart-shaped base. Sori with false indusia are continuous around the margins.

RANGE AND HABITAT: Coville's lip fern is tucked in rocky cliffs or ledges usually on igneous rocks in desert areas of the U.S. Southwest, northern Mexico, and Baja California.

CULTURE AND COMMENTS: This species is especially suited to pot culture in bright light with a fast-draining mix. In nature it is accustomed to summer rains but not much winter wet. It should be situated according. This species resembles *Cheilanthes fendleri* but can be separated (with great difficulty) based on the underside scales, which in *C. covillei* are hair-tipped and strongly heart-shaped at the base. *Cheilanthes fendleri* has matching scales but no hairlike extensions and only a mildly heart-shaped base. In addition, the rhizome on *C. fendleri* is long-creeping.

Cheilanthes distans
Woolly cloak fern
Epithet means "similar parts distant."
Evergreen, 6 to 12 in. (15 to 30 cm). Zones 8 to 10. Apogamous.

DESCRIPTION: The rhizome is short-creeping. The erect stipes of up to one-half the frond length are rusty colored and heavily scaled. The bipinnate to tripinnate dark green blades are linear with silver hairs above and masses of tawny scales below. The sori edge the pinnae and are covered by false indusia.

RANGE AND HABITAT: This species is a native of poor soil sites among rocks from the lowlands to montane areas in New Zealand and Australia, usually in full sun.

CULTURE AND COMMENTS: *Cheilanthes distans*, like a number of other cheilanthes, has had some identification problems in the trade, but the true plant is easier in cultivation than many fellow xerics. It needs the required accommodations for good drainage, no winter wet, and a good dose of bright light. Pot culture is an ideal solution.

Cheilanthes eatonii
Eaton's lip fern
Epithet is after U.S. botany professor Daniel C. Eaton (1834–1895).
Evergreen, 6 to 18 in. (15 to 45 cm). Zones 6 to 9. Apogamous.

Cheilanthes distans growing at the base of rocks in the Schwartz garden. Photo by David Schwartz.

DESCRIPTION: The rhizome is short-creeping, producing deep brown slender stipes one-third of the frond length. Lanceolate blades are narrowly erect and tripinnate to tripinnate-pinnatifid with 15 to 20 pairs of pinnae enveloped in a fleece of curled silvery hairs above and a blend of cream to tannish hairs and scales below. While all are designed to protect the species from the woes of harsh environmental situations, they are also a visual wonder of Mother Nature at her ornamental adaptive best. Sori are marginal within the wrapping of a recurved marginal false indusia.

RANGE AND HABITAT: This species grows on a variety of substrates in the lower southwest of the United States with a disjunct population in Virginia.

CULTURE AND COMMENTS: Cheilanthes in all of their beautiful configurations do not readily adjust to civilized life away from the wild. This species is easier but still needs the attention of a devoted caretaker. Give it the ever-recommended well-drained, grit-enriched sunlit site away from winter rains. A protective cloche for a winter covering helps to encourage long-term health. The ornamental reward is well worth an extra effort.

Cheilanthes farinosa
Farinose lip fern
Epithet means "powdery."
Evergreen, 1 ft. (30 cm). Zones 9 and 10. Apogamous.

DESCRIPTION: The rhizome is erect carrying tall, chestnut, farinose stipes that are usually more than one-half the length of the frond. The matte green bipinnate blades are narrowly triangular with 10 pairs of pinnae. The innermost lower pinnae pinnules expand downwards beyond the adjacent pinnules. The blades are dressed with a white farinose protective wax on the undersides. (Viewed through a microscope this is a magnificent display of nature's artwork.) The upper surface has a minute smattering of farina, which is most visible on juvenile fronds. The sori are marginal with their dark spores exposed, when ripe, from under the recurved marginal segments.

RANGE AND HABITAT: *Cheilanthes farinosa* is native to Africa and Asia, but is primarily Mexican. Like most xerics it grows in and among rocks with igneous substrates being the rock of choice for this species.

CULTURE AND COMMENTS: The white waxy undercoating, typical of this species, is especially attractive and can best be enjoyed from below. Pot culture, good drainage, and winter dry horticultural husbandry are most likely to produce encouraging and long-lasting results. I annually transport my container-grown plants from a comfortable, winter-unheated, and freeze-resistant greenhouse to the full exposure of Pacific Northwest summer sunshine. I am rewarded with a healthy display of xerics in a winter greenhouse. My spores were a gift from San Diego specialists. And, it must be noted, the species is better adapted to the warmth and longer days of theirs and comparable climates.

Cheilanthes feei
Slender lip fern
Epithet is after French botanist Antoine Fée (1789–1874).
Evergreen, 6 to 10 in. (15 to 25 cm). Zones 5 to 8. Apogamous.

Upright fronds of *Cheilanthes eatonii* among rocks in the Horder garden.

The underside of a fertile frond on *Cheilanthes farinosa* showing the namesake white farina.

Cheilanthes fendleri silhouetted against a stump in the Carstensen garden.

A colony of *Cheilanthes feei* on the east side of the Ladronas Mountains, Soccoro County, New Mexico. Photo by David Schwartz.

The West Coast native *Cheilanthes gracillima* in customized soil in a container.

Cheilanthes gracillima var. *aberrans* in the Schwartz garden. Photo by David Schwartz.

DESCRIPTION: The rhizome is short-creeping with densely packed bundles of small 8-in. (20-cm) fronds. The stipes are one-half the length of the frond, blackish-brown with a hairy white trim. Lanceolate, bipinnate-pinnatifid, dull bluish-green blades with approximately eight pairs of pinnae are rather beady. The lower surface bears long creamy tan hairs that are sparsely present on the upper surface as well. Sori are continuous around the margins with an inrolled false indusium.

RANGE AND HABITAT: The slender lip fern spills on both sides of the Rocky Mountains from Mexico to Canada. It is a fern of limestone cliffs. (Look for it in crevices on the vertical walls of Montezuma's Well in Arizona.)

CULTURE AND COMMENTS: Here is a fern to admire as it clings tenaciously to cliffs and ledges. It is cold hardy, but not easily cultivated.

Cheilanthes fendleri
Fendler's lip fern

Epithet is after Augustus Fendler (1813–1883), a German naturalist who collected in the U.S. Southwest and Central America. Evergreen, 6 to 12 in. (15 to 30 cm). Zones 5 to 8.

DESCRIPTION: The rhizome is long-creeping, encouraging colonies of fronds that wander among rocks and rubble. Dark brown stipes have narrow scales and are one-half the length of the frond. The tripinnate blades are oblong-lanceolate with 10 to 15 pairs of pinnae with characteristic rounded segments. The lower surface is coated with white to rusty brown scales. It is of diagnostic significance that the scales are not hair-tipped. Sori are marginal with false indusia.

RANGE AND HABITAT: *Cheilanthes fendleri* grows from Colorado through the U.S. Southwest to northern Mexico. It is found in rocky fissures and ledges on assorted substrates from acid to slightly basic.

CULTURE AND COMMENTS: This *Cheilanthes* is easier than most, surviving handsomely in rock gardens in western Washington. It wants bright light, good drainage, and artificial protection from winter wet. An alpine house or location under eaves works well. In the garden try an old-fashioned glass cloche placed slightly off the ground to let air circulate, while keeping water off the foliage. In the event of a threatening arctic express the cloche can be lowered to the ground—just do not fry the plant in sunshine. *Cheilanthes fendleri* differs from *C. covillei* because of the scales, which in *C. covillei* are hair-tipped and strongly heart-shaped at the base. *Cheilanthes fendleri* is also separated from *C. tomentosa*, which has hairs on the upper surface of the ultimate frond segments; *C. fendleri* is glabrous.

Cheilanthes gracillima
Lace fern

Epithet means "very slender."
Evergreen, 4 to 8 in.(10 to 20 cm). Zones 6 to 8.

DESCRIPTION: The rhizome is very short-creeping, producing tidy rosettes of glistening blue-green, horizontal fronds. The shiny stipes of up to one-half of the frond length are burnt cinnamon with an occasional tan scale. The lanceolate blades are bipinnate with 10 to 12 pairs of pinnae. A thick blanket of tan and white scales and hairs protects the frond's lower surface.

Sori with a false indusium are continuous around the pinna margins.

RANGE AND HABITAT: This species is native to the mountains of western Washington as well as the surrounding states and Canada. It grows on rocky outcrops (with one very special floral-covered promontory, "Penstemon rock" in the Wenatchee Mountains of Washington State being a favorite of my children from the time they were able, as youngsters, to join in the delights of discovering plants in the wild). It is strictly an alpine, growing in full light for the summer and then retiring under the snow for winter. The substrate can vary, but most populations are on igneous rocks.

CULTURE AND COMMENTS: This *Cheilanthes* can be introduced to lowland gardens by paying careful attention to the requirements for good drainage and by providing soil that is not overly rich. My pride-and-joy specimen has been in a low 2-in. (5-cm) high bonsai pot with huge drainage holes for four years. No fertilizer, no mulch, and nothing other than filtered sunshine have been offered for encouragement. A container planting is recommended.

Var. *aberrans* is an apparent hybrid between *C. gracillima* and *C. intertexta*, which is believed to be a hybrid between *C. covillei* and *C gracillima*.

Cheilanthes lanosa
Hairy lip fern
Epithet means "woolly" or "softly hairy."
Evergreen, 6 to 12 in. (15 to 30 cm). Zones 5 to 8.

DESCRIPTION: The rhizome is short-creeping, producing stands of upright foliage. Rounded dusky stipes are one-fourth to one-third of the frond length and significantly have hairs but no scales. The lanceolate bipinnate blade is made up of 10 to 15 pairs of gray-green pinnae that are sparsely "woolly" with a reddish undercoat of hairs. (The derivation "woolly" is actually far more descriptive of other cheilanthes.) Sori are marginal and have false inrolled indusia.

RANGE AND HABITAT: *Cheilanthes lanosa* is a resident of rocky hillsides, ledges, and ankle-breaking terrain from the midwestern to eastern United States.

CULTURE AND COMMENTS: This species has been successfully established in the gardens of specialists in Britain and the United States. The traditional cautions, especially the need for good drainage, apply. For those anxious to include xeric ferns in the garden palette, this is a litmus plant. With good luck, proceed.

Cheilanthes lendigera
Beaded lip fern
Epithet means "with spikelets."
Evergreen, 6 to 15 in. (15 to 38 cm). Zones 8 to 10.

DESCRIPTION: The rhizome creeps. Stipes are one-third of the frond length and brown with white hairs that are also on the undersurface of the beadlike pinnae segments. Scales, if any, are very few and their absence is a feature in identification. The tripinnate blades are triangular with 10 to 18 pairs of pinnae. This species is noted for its sizeable indusia that cover most of the undersides of the pinnules.

Cheilanthes lanosa with *Rhodohypoxis* in the Horder garden.

RANGE AND HABITAT: *Cheilanthes lendigera* is found on igneous rocks in the U.S. Southwest as well as Mexico and Central and South America.

CULTURE AND COMMENTS: Xeric experts have maintained this species in dry, rocky sites with attentive consideration given to drainage, air circulation, and protection from winter wet.

Cheilanthes lindheimeri
Lindheimer's lip fern, fairy swords
Epithet is after Ferdinand Lindheimer (1801–1879), the first permanent-resident plant collector in Texas.
Evergreen, 8 to 12 in. (20 to 30 cm). Zones 7 to 9. Apogamous.

DESCRIPTION: The rhizome is long-creeping. Stipes are dark, woolly and one-half the length of the frond. Ten to fifteen

Cheilanthes lindheimeri with dryland companions at the University of California Botanical Garden at Berkeley.

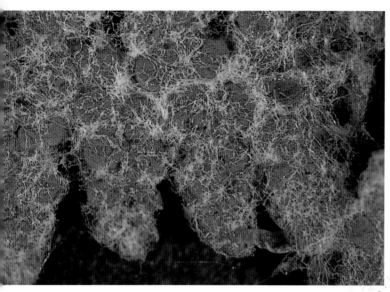

A microscopic view of the furry upper surface of *Cheilanthes lindheimeri*. Photo by Richie Steffen, Miller Botanical Garden.

pairs of pinnae are on the finely divided oblong-lanceolate blades which are up to four times pinnate. With a thick covering of white curly hairs on the upper surface, the fronds are pale blue in appearance. The lower surface presents a contrasting but equally thick coating of translucent tan slivers. Sori with false indusia are continuous along the margin.

RANGE AND HABITAT: This species colonizes along the edges of igneous rocks, sandstone, and granite in Arizona, New Mexico, and Texas in the United States as well as in northern Mexico.

CULTURE AND COMMENTS: I love the common name "fairy swords" for this species with its irresistibly attractive white-haired upright fronds. The good fairy of the desert must have waved a magic wand rewarding horticulture with an exquisite dryland species. It will survive in exposed rocks and rubble in traditional temperate gardens when sheltered from winter wet. My pot-cultured plant, growing in full winter sun but only partial summer exposure under the eaves of the house, has been an ornamental addition to my xeric collection for many years. New growth arrives in late winter in the Pacific Northwest but is not damaged by late surges of winter frost.

Cheilanthes newberryi
Newberry's cloak fern, cotton fern
Synonym *Notholaena newberryi*
Epithet is after John Newberry (1822–1892), a U.S. geologist-botanist.
Evergreen, 4 to 8 in. (10 to 20 cm). Zones 8 to 10.

DESCRIPTION: The rhizome is short-creeping. The dark brown stipe is rounded, with curly hairs. It is one-third to one-half the length of the frond. Ovate-lanceolate blades are bipinnate to tripinnate with up to 10 pairs of pinnae. "Cottony" and "woolly" are the appropriate descriptives for this species with its masses of long, curly white hairs on the frond's upper surface and tawny mats of curls on the undersides. Sori are not continuous around margins.

RANGE AND HABITAT: This species grows in sun in and around acidic boulders in Southern California and Mexico (Baja California). I would also like to remind readers that while these ferns love warm rocks, so do snakes. I am sure that the rattler I saw near San Diego just after taking the accompanying photograph was at least 15 ft. (4.5 m) long.

CULTURE AND COMMENTS: In typical *Cheilanthes* fashion the cotton fern is challenging to cultivate. The magic word is drainage. Give it chunky soil, good air circulation, bright light, and protection from winter rains.

Cheilanthes pteridioides
Synonyms *Cheilanthes fragrans, C. acrostica*
Epithet means "like *Pteris*," a strange derivation as the species is not likely to be confused with *Pteris*.
Evergreen, 6 to 12 in. (15 to 30 cm). Zones 8 and 9. This is a relatively new classification. In 1990 *Cheilanthes acrostica, C. guanchica, C. maderensis* (synonym *C. fragrans*), *C. pteridioides*, and *C. tinaei* were all reclassified as subspecies of *P. pteridioides*.

DESCRIPTION: This rhizome is erect to short-creeping. The stipes are up to one-half of the frond length and dark brown

Cheilanthes newberryi in Southern California's rattlesnake country.

with lighter brown scales. The triangular, tripinnate blade has 8 to 10 pairs of pinnae with the basal pair shaped very much like butterflies in flight. They are all mildly endowed with tan scales. Sori are marginal with discontinuous indusia.

RANGE AND HABITAT: This species and its collection of assorted subspecies grows on various substrates and is widespread throughout Europe, the Atlantic Islands, North Africa, the Middle East as well as India, the Himalayas, and adjacent Far Eastern countries.

CULTURE AND COMMENTS: A charming little fern, this adapts to well-drained, sunny garden sites. although I have only seen it once, as *Cheilanthes acrostica*, and that was in the garden of British expert, Clive Brotherton, who is a whiz with xerics.

Cheilanthes tomentosa
Woolly lip fern
Epithet means "woolly."
Evergreen, 8 to 15 in. (20 to 38 cm). Zones 6 to 8. Apogamous.

DESCRIPTION: The rhizome is short-creeping, producing dense colonies of gray green fronds. The stipes are russet with creamy hairs giving them a pinkish hue. They are one-third to one-half of the frond length. Blades are oblong-lanceolate, and tripinnate with 10 to 15 pairs of well-spaced pinnae. The upper surface is lightly trimmed with spiderlike white hairs, and the lower surface has a combination of whitish hairs and scales so narrow that at first glance they look like hairs. Sori are marginal with false indusia.

RANGE AND HABITAT: This is a species of the midwestern United States with populations from Kansas south and into Mexico and stations in Pennsylvania and West Virginia as well. It grows on rocks in dissimilar soil types from basic to acid.

CULTURE AND COMMENTS: The woolly lip fern is one of the easiest xerics to establish in gardens. Mine spread quite aggressively (for a *Cheilanthes*) from a solitary plant to a 30-in. (75-cm) colony in just over two years. It is happily established in a fast-draining soil mix of pumice, bark, charcoal, and humus with the whole being in a half whiskey barrel container under the eaves of the house. It faces south and gets full winter sun, such as it is in the Pacific Northwest, and light shade in the summer. I have even had to water it occasionally in the winter wet season, confounding and amusing my neighbors. Although *C. tomentosa* is more closely related to *C. eatonii*, it is sometimes visually confused with *C. fendleri*. The latter is glabrous while *C. tomentosa* has hairs on the ultimate segments of the upper frond surface. *Cheilanthes tomentosa* is separated from *C. eatonii* based on the latter being more densely hairy and also having lanceolate scales on the rachis as opposed to the narrow linear scales of *C. tomentosa*.

Cheilanthes wootonii
Bearded lip fern, Wooton's lip fern
Epithet is after Elmer Wooton (1865–1945), a botanist-chemist in New Mexico.
Evergreen, 6 to 15 in. (15 to 38 cm). Zones 8 to 9. Apogamous.

Cheilanthes tomentosa in the xeric section of the Kennar garden.

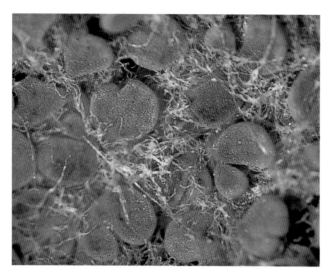

Upper frond surface of *Cheilanthes wootonii* viewed through a microscope, showing the hairs curling up and around from the lower surface giving it a "beard." Photo by Richie Steffen, Miller Botanical Garden.

DESCRIPTION: The rhizome is long-creeping. Stipes of over one-half of the frond length are chestnut brown and flatly trimmed with translucent, creamy mocha scales and hairs. Ovate-lanceolate blades are tripinnate with 10 to 15 pairs of pinnae. The upper surface is free of both hairs and scales (glabrous), but the scales and hairs on the lower surface extend well beyond the edges of the pinnules, giving it a fringed, "bearded" appearance. A hand lens is helpful here, and a microscopic enlargement is educational as well as truly beautiful. Sori with false indusia are continuous around the margins.

RANGE AND HABITAT: This species is native to igneous rocky outcrops and ledges in the U.S. Southwest and in northern Mexico.

CULTURE AND COMMENTS: Here is a xeric that will settle in the versatile container culture, with controlled soil and exposure. Recommendations include the required good drainage, air circulation, and protection from winter precipitation. This species is incredibly closely related to the newly separated species, *C. yavapensis*, with even the botanists noting that the differences are subtle and difficult to determine. New growth appears as early as late winter in Pacific Northwest gardens.

Cheilanthes wrightii
Wright's lip fern
Epithet is after one of the Wright botanists.
Evergreen, 3 to 10 in. (7.5 to 25 cm). Zones 8 and 9.

DESCRIPTION: The rhizome is short-creeping. Stipes are at least one-third to one-half of the frond length, grooved and brown without scales or hairs. The oblong-lanceolate blades are bipinnate with 8 to 10 pairs of pinnae. This species is remarkable for its lack of scales and hairs. Sori are discontinuous along the margins and protected by recurved toothy lobes of tissue.

RANGE AND HABITAT: Occurring primarily on igneous substrates, this species straddles the borders between the Arizona–

Cheilanthes wrightii in the Schwartz garden. Photo by David Schwartz.

New Mexico–Texas desert regions and those of adjacent Mexico.

CULTURE AND COMMENTS: Cultivated in the hot inlands of Southern California but reluctant in other locales, this species is a candidate for trials in areas where enthusiasts can create custom sites. Success is most likely in sunny, low humidity climates with attention to good drainage and no overhead winter wet.

Shorter Notes

Cheilanthes arizonica (Arizona lip fern) is apogamous with small 10-in. (25-cm) fronds open in structure with pentagonal blades up to four times pinnate. The innermost pinnules throughout the frond are conspicuously elongate. The species is rare in nature with but a few stations on igneous rocks on the border between Arizona–New Mexico and Mexico and southward to Central America. It is not in cultivation but would make a lacy companion to its more densely compact *Cheilanthes* cousins.

Cheilanthes austrotenuifolia (rock fern) is an apogamous Australian with triangular, emerald-green tripinnate fronds of up to 20 in. (50 cm). The silhouette resembles the more familiar oak fern (*Gymnocarpium dryopteris* and friends), but the cultural requirements are those of the xerics with special emphasis on rocky, well-drained acid substrates and consistently good light.

Cheilanthes bicolor (two colors) is an upright to 18-in. (45-cm) bipinnate species from the Far East including the Himalayas. The ebony stipe is typically longer than the blade and has bicolored scales concentrated at the base. The deltate-lanceolate blade is without scales or hairs on the upper surface, but covered on the lower with a white or greenish-white farina (waxlike coating). Rarely seen, it is in cultivation in Zone 9, in the Bakersfield, California, garden of xeric specialist David Schwartz and can be cultivated in soil with excellent drainage.

Cheilanthes clevelandii in the wild in northern California.

Cheilanthes pruinata at the University of California Botanical Garden at Berkeley.

Cheilanthes chusana (from Zhoushan, China) is a compact 1-ft. (30-cm) evergreen from the fern-rich Japanese, Korean, and Chinese floras. Bipinnate fronds are produced in upright tufts with shiny ebony stipes and, significantly, lack hairs or scales on the blades. The round-edged, false indusia segments are separated with each covering one sorus (or occasionally two sori). The species is probably cold hardy in Zones 8 and 9 (possibly 7) given the traditional precautions for maintaining xerics.

Cheilanthes clevelandii (after Cleveland), from rocky ledges in southernmost California and Mexico (Baja California), is a creeping 6- to 12-in. (15- to 30-cm) species with brown stipes and lanceolate tripinnate to quadripinnate blades. The lower surface carries an abundance of rusty brown hairy scales. The species is suitable for cultivation in Zones 9 to 11.

Cheilanthes coriacea (tough leathery) is a North African species that has been successfully cultivated in specialized garden sites in Britain. The triangular fronds are a minute 2 to 6 in. (5 to 15 cm) and pinnate-pinnatifid to bipinnate. This is a lovely little specimen in Zones 8 and 9 for close-up viewing in a container with customized xeric compost and the requisite good drainage.

Cheilanthes jamaicensis (of Jamaica) is an upright tripinnate evergreen to 12 in. (30 cm). It is a white-haired species for partial sun in Zone 9 or with protection in Zone 8. I grew it for several years, but it really did not take to non-Caribbean life in the Pacific Northwest.

Cheilanthes kaulfussii (after Kaulfuss), the glandular lip fern, is a lime-green evergreen with fronds to 16 in. (40 cm). The delicate, horizontal blade is tripinnate-pinnatifid with extended basal pinnae giving it a pentagonal silhouette. Glandular hairs make this easy to recognize by the gummy feel of the foliage. The species is native to acidic rocky habitats from Texas to South America and should be tested in Zones 8 and 9. Apogamous.

Cheilanthes myriophylla (many leaves), the beaded lip fern from Mexico and South America, is a triangular evergreen with emerald-green fronds up to 18 in. (45 cm). The blade is quadripinnate with beadlike pinnules and a lower surface resplendent with buff-colored scales. This delicately divided species grows in lightly shaded rocky sites and is suitable for Zone 8 and 9 gardens. It is similar in structure to *C. villosa* but does not have a hairy-scaly upper frond surface.

Cheilanthes parryi (after Parry) snuggles in crevices in assorted substrates in the hillsides and mountains of the southwestern states that border Mexico and indeed in Mexico as well. We first found it outside of Las Vegas, where the odds of finding the fern were about equal to the odds of winning in glitztown. (We were there for the botanizing.) This is a truly fleece-covered, cottony species that captures the eye of the xeric enthusiast with 8-in. (20-cm) puffballs of bipinnate, lanceolate blades. It has not been successfully maintained in the Greater Seattle area, but should be tried in an assortment of exposures in Zones 8 and 9 to introduce it into the civilized world of cultivated ferns.

Cheilanthes platychlamys (broad cloaked) is a promising Himalayan introduction that is barely referenced in literature but described in Rickard (2000) thus: "Fronds triangular, pinnate-pinnatifid, powdery white meal scattered on the upper surface, lower surface white all over. No conspicuous hairs or scales." It has ornamental potential as well as collector's appeal, but has not yet been thoroughly tested in the United States.

Cheilanthes pruinata (with a white powdery bloom) has extremely narrow, linear evergreen bipinnate to bipinnate-pinnatifid fronds growing in dense upright clumps to 12 in. (30 cm). The innermost pinnules are smaller than adjacent pinnules and the whole is enveloped in russet hairs and scales at maturity. This rare species of *altas montañas* grows in sheltered rock strata at 14,000 ft. (4200 m) in the Andes from Bolivia and Peru to Argentina and Chile. It should be cold tolerant in Zones 6 to 8, with the ever-present precaution of protection from winter wet.

Cheilanthes quadripinnata (with pinnae four times divided) is a promising species from the unmined riches of South Africa. Minute pinnules on broadly triangular blades adorn the deep ebony, wiry structure. In its native habitat at 11,000 ft. (3300 m) elevation, it grows to 10 in. (25 cm) in cool, rocky crevices and almost full sun. Give it protection from excessive wet in rock gardens in Zones 7 to 9.

Cheilanthes sieberi (after Franz Sieber, 1789–1849), synonyms *C. humilis* and *C. tenuifolia*, is native to sunny and rocky sites in New Zealand and Australia. By nature it is stiffly upright with bipinnate to tripinnate dark green foliage. It should be considered garden worthy in Zone 9 and, with appropriate cautions, in Zone 8. Apogamous.

Cheilanthes villosa (villous, shaggy) is an apogamous evergreen from southwestern North America with, as the name implies, a woolly pinnae undercoat of scales in addition to lightly scattered hairs on the frond's upper surface. It is finely divided into tripinnate to quadripinnate segments and worthy of admiration when displayed, with its needs successfully nourished and accommodated, in Zone 9 and, when well tended, in Zone 8.

Cheilanthes yavapensis (from Yava, Arizona) is an apogamous evergreen believed to be a hybrid between *C. lindheimeri* and *C. covillei*. It is similar in appearance to *C. wootonii* from which it was recently separated botanically. The differences are difficult to determine from field characteristics, but the upper blade surface on *C. yavapensis* is slightly hairy rather than smooth as in *C. wootonii*. Gardeners in Zones 8 to 10 can enjoy this fern in a site where it is protected from winter rain and provided with free-draining, gritty soil.

Cibotium

Tree ferns are immensely popular with specialists in Zones 9 to 11 as well as devotees who in colder zones are willing to take the extra precautions required to secure their health throughout the assorted vagaries of freeze-dry winter cold. Cibotiums, however, are confined to tropical climes. Look for them as an excuse to visit Hawaii, where 6 of the 11 species are native. Typically they form a small to large trunk carrying a spreading canopy of bipinnate to tripinnate fronds of up to 20 ft. (6 m) long. They have hairs rather than the scales of *Cyathea*. The name *Cibotium* is derived from the Greek *kibotos*, a box or casket, a not-so-cheerful reference to the shape of the indusia with one lobe enclosing another. (And ironically hairs from *Cibotium* are used for embalming in some cultures.) These lobes are, however, one means of distinguishing this genus from *Dicksonia*, which has sori in cuplike, two-valved dissimilar lobes. The species are from Asia, Mexico, Central America, and Hawaii.

Cibotium barometz (Tartar for "lamb"), the "vegetable lamb," is a fern of the medicine chest as well as the tourist trade. The "lamb" is widely recognized as an offspring of a Middle Age myth spread by John Mandeville, "the great travel liar of the time" (Moran 2004), about a half-plant, half-animal. Mandeville recounts visiting the Great Khan of Tartary where he supposedly found a tree that bore little lambs in pods. The myth grew, as myths will do, until finally it was determined that the little lamb was actually part of a tree fern stem. But, lo, further research pointed to the common cotton plant as the source of our little lamb and so it is today. Meanwhile, parts of *Cibotium*, configured as "little lambs," are sold

throughout Asia as charms to fend off evil. Medicinally the golden hairs from the stipes are currently used to stem bleeding, and material from the rhizomes is used for arthritis and joint problems. The plant itself has a prostrate trunk, stipes to 5 ft. (1.5 m), and lime green bipinnate to tripinnate fronds to 9 ft. (2.7 m). It is usually not cultivated outside of Asia, although plants may be found in Southern California.

Cibotium glaucum (white or grayish bloom) is an Hawaiian ornamental immediately recognizable by the silvery blue of the frond's undersides. The trunk may be prostrate or upright reaching 9 ft. (2.7 m). Stipes are covered with golden brown hairs (sometimes used in padding) and the 3- to 8-ft. (90- to 240 cm) fronds are bipinnate to tripinnate. The species can be propagated from small log-sized trunks or spores. On the islands it grows in forests and at elevations that are higher than those of the other native tree ferns. It is in the trade in warm areas of the United States, but cannot tolerate frost.

Cibotium schiedei (after Christian Schiede, 1798–1836, a German plant explorer in Mexico), the Mexican tree fern, has towering, glaucous undersided, 6- to 10-ft. (1.8- to 3-m) fronds produced from a 16-ft. (5-m) trunk. The stipes and young foliage are clothed in golden hairs. With its large proportions, this species is scaled for botanical garden exhibits in Zones 10 and 11.

Coniogramme
Bamboo ferns

Coniogramme is a little-known genus that includes a collection of species with a nontraditional profile. Rather than feathery plumes, these have strap-shaped pinnae resembling those from the more familiar genus *Pteris*. The common name says it all. There are upwards of 20 species worldwide primarily in Africa, eastern Asia, and the Pacific Rim including Japan and Hawaii. The typical species has a short-creeping rhizome and linear upright fronds. Stipes are grooved and have a V-shaped vascular bundle. Variable vein configurations are mostly free, but those free veins may extend from a netted chain of veins that run the length of the pinnae midrib. Sori without indusia are packed along the veins running from the pinnae midribs towards the margins. The genus name is derived from *conio*, dusky, and *gramme*, line, in reference to the soral pattern. Only a few species are temperate and currently in cultivation, and these are surrounded by taxonomic question marks. I am using *Flora of Japan* (Iwatsuki et al. 1995) as the nomenclatural authority for this genus.

Coniogramme gracilis
Narrow leaf bamboo fern
Synonym *Coniogramme japonica* var. *gracilis*
Epithet means "slender."
Evergreen, 1 to 1½ ft. (30 to 45 cm). Zones 7 to 9.

DESCRIPTION: The rhizome is creeping. Green-grooved stipes are up to one-half of the frond length. Basal pairs of pinnae are bipinnate with the remainder of the blade carrying narrow 10-in. (25-cm) pinnae that taper at both ends. The terminal pinna is the same as the lateral counterparts. Veins are netted at the midrib, forking freely towards the margins, and

Hairy coating on *Cibotium glaucum*.

are prominently visible on the upper frond surface. Sori without indusia parade in close formation along the veins.

RANGE AND HABITAT: This species is endemic to Japan where it grows in the shady perimeters of forests.

CULTURE AND COMMENTS: Tony Avent of Plant Delights Nursery first marketed this in North America and recommends planting it in a slightly moist woodland site where it will form a dense clump over time, looking rather like a very dwarf bamboo. It functions well as a contrasting element to lacier garden components.

Coniogramme intermedia

Intermediate bamboo fern
Synonym *Coniogramme fraxinea* var. *intermedia*
Epithet means "intermediate."
Semievergreen to evergreen, 2 to 4 ft. (60 to 120 cm). Zones 8 to 10.

DESCRIPTION: The rhizome is creeping. Long stipes toned purple and green are up to one-half of the frond length. Ovate blades are bipinnate at the base with long linear pinnae terminating in narrow tips on the 8 to 10 pairs of pinnae. The ultimate pinna matches the outline of the lateral pinnae. Significantly the veins are free and forked. They carry the sori from the midrib out towards the margins but do not reach the edge of the pinnae.

RANGE AND HABITAT: This species grows in deep forests in Japan, Sakhalin, the Kuriles, eastern Asia, and the Himalayas.

CULTURE AND COMMENTS: A tall diversion with long willowlike pinnae, this fern provides an interesting contrast among fine-feathered friends in the deep shade of moist woodlands. It does not like to dry out and needs vigilance against the slugs and snails that can come to feed on the foliage. Two unusual cultivars are **'Rasha'** (velvet), which grows to 8 in. (20 cm) and has a rippled frond surface, and **'Shishi'** (lion), a heavily crested 8-in. (20-cm) dwarf.

Coniogramme japonica

Japanese bamboo fern
Epithet means "from Japan."
Semievergreen to evergreen, 2 ft. (60 cm). Zones 7 to 9.

DESCRIPTION: The rhizome is creeping. The greenish stipes are one-third to one-half of the frond length. Lustrous dark green, ovate blades are basally bipinnate with the ultimate pinna the same as the lateral pinnae. Unlike *Coniogramme intermedia* the veins are netted at the midrib and freely forking towards the margins. Sori without indusia are carried on the veins.

RANGE AND HABITAT: Found on forest floors, this is native to Japan, Korea, China, Taiwan, and Indochina.

CULTURE AND COMMENTS: In moist woodlands, Japanese bamboo fern spreads much more gently than the namesake bamboo. It forms airy thickets spreading to 3 ft. (90 cm) in 10 years and is a nice upright counterpoint to wispy shade companions. Keep it moist and give it protection from slugs and snails.

Willowy foliage of *Coniogramme japonica* in the Peters garden.

Shorter Note

Coniogramme emeiensis (from Mount Emei [Omei], China), alternate spelling *C. omeiensis*, has recently been imported into the United States. The correct name for the material in the market may be *C. emeiensis* 'Variegata', as this is a prominently variegated plant. The deciduous fronds are 2 to 3 ft. (60 to 90 cm) tall with bipinnate willowy foliage. The free veins are cream-colored giving the pinnae an unusual striped appearance. The plant needs partial shade and is tentatively rated for Zones 8 to 10.

Cornopteris

Cornopteris is very similar to *Athyrium* but differs in having sori without indusia. The species are all deciduous natives of Japan, China, Korea, and the Himalayas. The genus name is derived from *corno*, horned, and *pteris*, fern.

Cornopteris crenulato-serrulata (edged with small teeth), often found filed under *Athyrium*, is a deciduous species native to the same countries and habitats as *C. decurrenti-alata*. The 2-ft. (60-cm) triangular fronds are approximately half stipe and half bipinnate-pinnatifid blade. The species is hardy in Zones 5 to 8 and recommended as a lacy woodland contribution in partial shade.

Cryptogramma acrostichoides in the rock garden at the Rhododendron Species Botanical Garden.

Cornopteris decurrenti-alata (*decurrenti*, running down the stem, *alata*, wings or ridges), alternate spelling *C. decurrentialata*, is in cultivation in the gardens of German specialists in Zones 6 to 8. The epithet is an apt description of this species, which has foliar tissue "running" down the rachis between the pinnae. The fronds of up to 3 ft. (90 cm) are bipinnate-pinnatifid and broadly lanceolate. Sori without indusia are linear or occasionally Y-shaped. The distinguishing feature, however, is a series of minute translucent spikes at the axis of the pinnae and the rachis on the upper frond surface. These would-be slivers are visible even on very young material. Give the species space and moisture in the back of the shady bed.

Cryptogramma
Parsley ferns

The parsley ferns (and parsley-looking they are) greet hikers at higher elevations along the trails in North America, Europe, the Andes, and parts of Asia. They snuggle with their roots protected at the bases of rocks or in crevices, sometimes in abundance, and bravely face the sunshine. Fronds are dimorphic with leafy sterile fronds responsible for the common name and taller, upright fertile fronds responsible for the botanical. The genus name comes from the Greek *kryptos*, hidden, and *gramme*, line, a description of the sori, which are "hidden lines" under the incurved margins of the fertile pinnae. Free veins likewise are obscure. Stipes are grooved and enclose a stubby Y-shaped vascular bundle. There are about 10 species, all of them difficult to cultivate.

Cryptogramma acrostichoides
Parsley fern, American rock brake

Epithet means "with the sori covering the entire underside of the pinnae."
Evergreen sterile fronds and deciduous fertile fronds, 4 to 10 in. (10 to 25 cm). Zones 2 to 8.

DESCRIPTION: The rhizome is short-creeping and branching, bearing the stubs of old stipe bases. Grooved stipes basally brown and becoming green are over one-half of the frond length. Tufted, ovate bipinnate to tripinnate, slightly hairy fronds vary with the short sterile blades evergreen, while the taller, upright fertile blades are deciduous. Sori are on narrow segments and covered by a false indusium of rolled leaf margins.

RANGE AND HABITAT: The American parsley fern grows among sunny rocks in mountains in acid to occasionally neutral soil. Its native range extends from Alaska to California and high elevations in Arizona and New Mexico as well as down from the Yukon through central Canada.

CULTURE AND COMMENTS: An attractive fern, this species, like so many alpines, is difficult in cultivation. Give it a rocky root run, good drainage, a handful of acidic or granitic soil, and a top dressing of pebbles. It is not for areas with hot summers. In nature it can easily be confused, especially when fertile material is lacking, with fellow mountaineer *Aspidotis densa*. Geology enlightened hikers will note that *Aspidotis* prefers serpentine substrates. The latter is also monomorphic and has dark wiry stipes rather than the pliant green ones of the dimorphic *Cryptogramma*.

Cryptogramma crispa
Parsley fern
Epithet means "wavy" or "curly margins."
Deciduous, 3 to 12 in. (7.5 to 30 cm). Zones 2 to 8.

DESCRIPTION: The rhizome is short-creeping and branching with tufts of old stipe bases. Tan to green stipes are one-half the length of the sterile frond and up to two-thirds of the fertile. Blades are tripinnate to quadripinnate. Sori are in linear segments and covered by the false indusia of marginal edges.

RANGE AND HABITAT: This fern is widely distributed in Europe, Asia, Japan, and the Andes where it can colonize sunny to partially shady rocky slopes at higher altitudes. It must have acid soil.

CULTURE AND COMMENTS: Almost impossible to cultivate even when spore grown (and should not be collected), this is a fern to be admired in the wild. One of my all-time favorite hikes was in England's Lake Country where in the fashion of Brigadoon, the parsley fern and the "heather on the hill" dominated an entire rocky mountainside. This species strongly resembles *C. acrostichoides*, which was at one time classified as *C. crispa*, but the latter is fully deciduous.

Var. *chilensis* is from Chile. Herbarium specimens of this variety differ in several characters from Northern Hemisphere material, in today's taxonomy usually sufficient to distinguish a species (Stuart, pers. comm.).

Cryptogramma stelleri
Slender rock brake
Epithet is after naturalist George Steller who accompanied the Bering expedition of 1741.
Deciduous, 3 to 7 in. (7.5 to 18 cm). Zones 2 to 5.

DESCRIPTION: Unlike many *Cryptogramma* species, the rhizome of this species is long-creeping and the fronds are not tufted. Straw to greenish stipes are one-half the length of the pinnate-pinnatifid sterile fronds and more on the taller, bipinnate fertile fronds. Sori are enclosed in a false indusium of recurved pinnae margins.

RANGE AND HABITAT: A fern of rocky, shaded limestone habitats, this species is native to higher elevations in Siberia, China, Japan, Taiwan, the Himalayas, Europe, and highlands of eastern and western North America. It dies back in early to mid summer.

CULTURE AND COMMENTS: Like its brethren, slender rock brake does not submit to domestication and would be especially uncomfortable in warm summer areas. Admire it in the wild (if you can find it).

Shorter Notes
Cryptogramma cascadensis (from the Cascade Mountains) grows in rocky, often igneous, crevices and talus, in a mountainous slice of the Pacific Northwest from British Columbia down to California. Unlike *C. acrostichoides* it is deciduous with the current year's fronds disintegrating totally. (Fronds of *C. acrostichoides* remain on or under the plant into the following season.) It also lacks the sparse covering of hairs on the foliage. This species is hardy in Zones 2 to 8 but not recommended for cultivation.

Cryptogramma sitchensis (from Sitka Island, Alaska), the Alaska parsley fern, resembles *C. acrostichoides* but has more finely divided quadripinnate fronds and lobed pinnae. It is from acidic sites in the Yukon and Alaska and not likely to adapt to gardens away from those of Mother Nature's wild wilderness homeland.

Cyathea
Tree ferns are marvels of the plant kingdom, having once been the dominant features of the world's landscape. Their fossil records go back 305 to 340 million years (easily written, but truly amazing to contemplate) with *Cyathea* at 144 million years give or take, being a relative newcomer on the scene. Currently the genus is either all encompassing or narrow in definition, with most of the discussion centering on overlapping characteristics involving technical details of the cellular structure of the scales on the stipes. The species herein, which are

Cryptogramma crispa in England's Lake Country.

Cryptogramma cascadensis near Coal Lake in Washington State.

Cyathea contaminans, still furled crosiers. Photo by George Schenk.

occasionally segregated as assorted splintered genera, are presented under the frond, so to speak, of *Cyathea*, and follow the definitions of Large and Braggins (2004).

The genus name is from the Greek *kyathos*, wine cup, referring to the indusia that circle the sori on the undersides of the fronds, but not on their margins as in *Dicksonia*. The approximately 600 species are majestic and solid members of the humid, mountainous, subtropical landscape with scaly (*Dicksonia* is hairy) trunks to 8 in. (20 cm) in diameter. Fronds with long stipes are up to 18 ft. (5.4 m) long, and trunks when young may grow as much as a foot (30 cm) a year. Sori are nestled in cups, like eggs in a bird's nest. Spores are short-lived.

A number of species are amenable to cultivation in temperate zones. Martin Rickard (2000) recommends planting them in a moist, wind- and lime-free site and watering the trunks, which house the roots externally, "copiously" until they are established. (And again in dry weather.) However, do not water the crowns during winter. Instead, Rickard recommends stuffing them with straw, thus protecting the growing tip from freezing and ice formation. He goes on to note that plants with a trunk of 2 ft. (60 cm) or more will be less susceptible to cold damage. In questionable climates, where these plants may be vulnerable, enthusiasts put them to bed in winter, well mulched and wrapped in assorted blankets for protection. Foam, bubble wrap, straw, aluminum foil, and fleece or combinations thereof are all used successfully. Alastair Wardlaw, a tree fern specialist, who maintains one of the world's best collections in the dark and cold winters of Glasgow, Scotland, has an elaborate system for maintaining his collection under winter stress. (See "Tree Ferns" in chapter 2.) In addition to protecting the trunk, some growers wrap the fronds for winter insulation. This can cause some breakage, but tends to keep them green. Another option is to toss a layer of horticultural gauze over the entire canopy in frosty weather.

Cyathea can be propagated from spores, but many species are rooted from loglike "cuttings," if you would, of the trunks, sunk in moist soil and surrounded by constant greenhouse humidity. It takes quite some time and they need to be supported and kept moist throughout the process. I have also seen them reduced in height in conservatories by an air layering system. The trunks are wounded and wrapped in a moisture-retentive moss or other sterile material and secured with a cloak of opaque plastic. When sprouts emerge, the total plant is beheaded, giving a lower canopy as well as a new plant.

George Schenk (pers. comm.) writes:

Tree fern crosiers offer the viewer some of the best fern-watching, which easily ranks with whale- or bird-watching as an absorbing, even an exciting, visual sharing of the life of a fellow species. Actually, the thrills of the ferner, if gathered at a more leisurely pace, are also far more sustained than any to be had in the sudden sightings of the birder or the ocular whaler. It takes but a little imagination. One may see fern crosiers as heads bowed in meditation. I find it easy to suppose in them an intelligence serene and yet aware, a gathering of will toward the coming season of the fern, the big push, the pteridotechnic explosion upward and outward. This promise, appreciable and ponderable in the furled crosiers of any fern, is enlarged and intensified, not at all surprisingly, in the huge crosiers of tree ferns. Those in the picture are as big as the head of some nonhuman critter or another. I am disinclined to anthropomorphize them. With their dense pelt of palest ochre-yellow hairlike scales, surely they [crosiers of *Cyathea contaminans*] belong to some furrier mammal, perhaps a sloth. In some other tree ferns the color of the crosier fur is exactly that of orangutans.

Cyathea cooperi

Australian tree fern, coin spot tree fern
Synonyms *Sphaeropteris cooperi, Alsophila cooperi*
Epithet is after British naturalist Daniel Cooper (1817–1842).
Evergreen, 40 ft. (12 m). Zones 8 (with heavy winter protection) to 10.

DESCRIPTION: The trunk, up to 6 in. (15 cm) in diameter, can quickly reach 40 ft. (12 m) and has "coin spots," oval scars where old fronds have broken away. Bipinnate-pinnatifid broadly lanceolate fronds on long stipes arch to 15 ft. (4.5 m) long. Stipes and trunk have white scales with brownish teeth. Sori without indusia are in nonmarginal rows.

RANGE AND HABITAT: This species is endemic to Australia, where it grows in subtropical to tropical rain forests up to 4500 ft. (1400 m). It has escaped in the Hawaiian Islands and is a serious environmental threat to their native tree fern populations.

CULTURE AND COMMENTS: The Australian tree fern is one of the most widely grown and popular tree ferns for cultivation in the continental United States, growing quickly in humid and moist sites. It will take a brief exposure to light frost, but must be enclosed in a protective wrap where winter cold is common. There are several cultivars.

Cyathea dealbata

Silver fern
Epithet means "with a white powdery covering."
Evergreen, 30 ft. (9 m). Zones 9 and 10.

DESCRIPTION: The trunk, with protruding persistent stipe bases, can be up to 8 in. (20 cm) in diameter and grows slowly to 30 ft. (9 m). Bipinnate-pinnatifid lanceolate fronds extend to 12 ft. (3.6 m). They are pale green on the upper surface and coated with showy silver powder on the undersides. Sori in cuplike indusia are on either side of the midveins.

RANGE AND HABITAT: This New Zealand endemic grows in well-drained soil at elevations up to 3000 ft. (900 m).

CULTURE AND COMMENTS: "Known in Kiwi English as silver fern and Maori as ponga, this is one of the slowest tree ferns to develop arboreally" (Schenk, pers. comm.). It is one of New Zealand's national emblems. Look for it as a symbol on the hull of the America's Cup 12-meter contenders as well as on the uniforms of national teams. It may someday grace their national flag having been proposed and supported by 100,000 petitioners in the summer of 2005 in response to a broad-based enthusiasm for a referendum that would redesign the flag. For practical purposes, with their silver lining, the fern fronds have been used as trail markers. The trunks are sometimes used in retaining walls and are particularly engaging when they start to sprout.

Cyathea medullaris

Black tree fern
Synonym *Sphaeropteris medullaris*
Epithet means "pithy."
Evergreen, 60 ft. (18 m). Zones 9 and 10.

DESCRIPTION: The black trunk, which is covered with scars from fallen fronds, grows rather quickly to 60 ft. (18 m) in the

Cyathea dealbata with its signature silver undercoat. Self-sown plants at the half-sunny entry of a shady pathway in a very dry Auckland garden have yet to develop any trunk at all after 16 years. Photo by George Schenk.

wild. At a slender 8 inches (20 cm) in diameter, the trunk supports bipinnate-pinnatifid to tripinnate masses of fronds 10 to 18 ft. (3 to 5.4 m) long on a black skeleton with black scales. Sori are in pairs and surrounded by an indusium.

RANGE AND HABITAT: This native of South Sea Islands including Fiji, Tahiti, and New Zealand grows in dark gullies at elevations up to 1500 ft. (450 m).

CULTURE AND COMMENTS: Although a striking tree fern to be admired by the traveler, it is not often in cultivation outside of its native range. It has, however, recently been imported into England where specialists have a tradition of success with tree ferns. Even there it does best in frost-free environs. The Maoris use the pith of the trunk as a food source which is quite slimy

A mature grove of *Cyathea medullaris* in the Waitakeri Range of North Island, New Zealand. The specimens in the picture have attained a height of about 35 ft. (10.5 m) trunk and crown at an age by which human beings usually retire. Photo by George Schenk.

until steamed. When dried, however, it is reputed to be a sweet. "With adequate moisture, black mamaku, as it is known in New Zealand, can become as quickly tall as *Cyathea contaminans*, yet it is long-lived" (Schenk, pers. comm.).

Cyathea smithii

Soft tree fern
Synonym *Alsophila smithii*
Epithet is after John Smith (1798–1888).
Evergreen, 25 ft. (7.5 m). Zones 9 and 10.

DESCRIPTION: The brown trunk reaches 25 ft. (7.5 m) and is surrounded just below the crown by skirts of dead frond

Crosier of *Cyathea medullaris* at the Noel Crump Nursery in New Zealand.

midribs that offer protective insulation from winter cold. Soft green, tripinnate fronds are 7 to 9 ft. (2.1 to 2.7 m) long and have abundant brown scales along the stipes. Sori with saucer-shaped indusia are on both sides of the pinnae midrib.

RANGE AND HABITAT: This species, the most southerly growing of the world's tree ferns, is native to high elevations in New Zealand and as far south as the Auckland Islands. It prefers wet cold forests and thrives right up to the snow line of the glaciers on New Zealand's South Island. As life insurance, it produces a chemical that when dispersed can inhibit the root growth of competing plants.

CULTURE AND COMMENTS: Like most tree ferns, it needs humusy soil and an overstory of protective trees, plus shelter from wind and prolonged frost. It would make a good trial plant for hardiness in the warmer regions of Zone 8 with, of course, the requisite winter protection.

Shorter Notes

Cyathea australis (of the south), the rough tree fern, synonym *Alsophila australis*, by virtue of its relative cold and slight frost tolerance, is one of the more practical tree ferns for probable success in U.S. gardens. In nature the trunk can reach 35 ft. (10.5 m) and supports bipinnate to tripinnate fronds of up to 15 ft. (4.5 m). New growth and old stipe bases are covered with spines. As this species shares habitats with the

Cyathea smithii and the rata tree (*Metrosideros*, which is endangered due to browsing possums) near the Fox Glacier on the South Island, New Zealand.

White spines on the stipes of *Cyathea australis* at Wells Medina Nursery.

Scaly fronds of *Cyathea tomentosissima*.

relatively cold hardy *Dicksonia antarctica*, there's optimism and hope for it as a potential ornamental in Zone 8 and certainly with confidence in Zones 9 and 10.

Cyathea contaminans is one of the speediest growing tree ferns if planted where it can get its roots down to constant moisture. Native to India, New Guinea, Indonesia, the Philippines, and Malaysia on sites at least several thousand feet above sea level, it does not take to gardens in tropical lowlands. The fur will flake away in gobs if the gardener bothers it with a stick (out of curiosity), or some other creature with its jaws (out of hunger). The detaching fur will be enough to clog the throat. And to counter any animal smart enough to claw away the fur before biting, the plant has a secondary defense: a thicket of spines hidden beneath its pelt. Yet there is an appetite that braves its way past all that armature to gather these crosiers as food (along with the fiddleheads and tender young

fronds of 31 other fern species—arboreal down to knee-high—in the Asian Pacific regions of the world alone): the hungry human. (Description by George Schenk.)

Cyathea dregei (after Johann Drège, 1794–1881, a German horticulturist who collected plants in South Africa), synonym *Alsophila dregei*, is native to the open grasslands at 6300 ft. (1900 m) in the Drakensberg Mountains of South Africa and disjunct sites throughout the African continent. The trunk is up to 15 ft. (4.5 m) tall with arching bipinnate to tripinnate fronds to 9 ft. (2.7 m). The plant regularly withstands grass fires and frosts, although it will lose fronds in severe cold. Considering its provenance, it has great promise as an ornamental in Zones 9 and 10 (and is a temptation for Zone 8 coddling). Plants with small trunks are growing outdoors in Scotland's coastal Logan Botanic Garden and with considerable protection in the Royal Botanic Garden in Edinburgh. The species would seem especially suited to Southern California.

Cyathea princeps (princely), reclassified in 2004 by Mickel and Smith as *Sphaeropteris horrida*, is a magnificent silhouette from wet montane habitats of Mexico and Central America where it grows with gusto to 60 ft. (18 m). Bipinnate to tripinnate fronds form a 15-ft. (4.5-m) canopy. Trunk, stipe, and rachis are covered with tawny scales that are especially showy on unfurling young crosiers. This fern has been tested with varying degrees of success in central England where the crown needs protection from winter wet and cold. It would

Cyathea contaminans in a Philippine garden, in a stone-retained bed of soil on a broad concrete sidewalk beside a pond fed by a brook. Planted when they were sporelings only two or three years old, with no trunk development at all, the two tree ferns found water and in five years went from trunkless to having trunks. The larger fern forms an overhead canopy 18 ft. (5.4 m) across on a trunk 8 ft. (2.4 m) tall. The smaller fern has a 6-ft. (1.8-m) trunk. Ultimate trunk height for both is expected to be about 20 ft. (6 m). Photo by George Schenk.

presumably be better suited to mellow southern England, coastal Scotland, Southern California, or Florida winters.

Cyathea tomentosissima (super hairy) bristles with burnt orange to rusty scales right down the midribs on the pinnules. For a tree fern it is modest in scale with a trunk of 6 to 10 ft. (1.8 to 3 m) and bipinnate to tripinnate fronds of up to 3 ft. (90 cm). More drought tolerant than most of its relatives, it is an easy choice for Zones 9 and 10 in sunny California and will tolerate the occasional frosty evening.

Cyrtomium
Holly ferns

Cyrtomiums are commonly called holly ferns due to the resemblance, given a little imagination, of the pinnae to holly leaves. Their numbers, of about 20 species, are extremely limited by fern standards. Distribution is equally restricted with all but one species native to Asia (although *Cyrtomium falcatum* and *C. fortunei* have naturalized in various areas of the United States and compatible habitats throughout the world). By contrast, options for ornamental applications and decorative uses from the garden to the shaded shelf by the kitchen window are far from confined. The distinctive, atypical fern foliage serves graciously as a contrast for delicate companions in the shaded woodland community. And, with their leathery constitution, a number adapt to less-than-fern-friendly indoor habitats.

The fronds are evergreen or (in stressfully cold climates) subevergreen. Many are finished in soft matte patinas of light yellow or gray-greens. The exception, of course, is the common *Cyrtomium falcatum*, which has polished dark sprigs of pseudo-holly foliage, and is welcomed indoors or out. *Cyrtomium* blades are once-pinnate with an abundance of sori scattered seemingly at random on the undersides. The sori are shielded with peltate (centrally attached umbrella-like) indusia. The stipes are proportionately short and usually carry a copious coating of scales. The broad pinnae have prominent midveins as well as netted (interlocking) veins, an impressive picture with backlighting. Three or four vascular bundles have no set pattern.

Cyrtomium comes from the Greek *kyrtoma*, arched or bulged, in reference to the archlike appearance of the netted veins that are one of the signature characteristics of the genus.

Cyrtomium sori.

Based on overlapping features, cyrtomiums were in the late 1800s and early 1900s lumped together with polystichums and arachniodes in the now obsolete genus *Aspidium*. Though now botanically separated, common features remain the same. *Cyrtomium* and *Polystichum* both have a peltate indusium protecting the sori on their fertile fronds. However, cyrtomiums are distinguished by having netted veins and a terminal pinna, which, while slightly smaller, is similar to the lateral pinnae. In some instances polystichums and cyrtomiums also share a characteristic auricle (thumb) at the base of each pinnae or pinnule. (Think "thumbs-up.") With the large pinnae on cyrtomiums, this feature is either especially obvious or clearly missing, while the "thumb" is a typical feature on polystichums.

Cyrtomiums are easily cultivated and are one of the best options for, but not confined to, deep shade where they will not only thrive but give foliar excitement to somber sites. They are primarily plants for Zones 6 (with considerable protection) to 10. While evergreen, they can, like people, look a little weary in winter. Plant them in the universally recommended fern mix of rich, but light composty duff with good drainage. Some species are from limestone habitats, but limey supplements are not necessary for plant vigor or health.

Spore propagation is very efficient as many species are apogamous (producing plants directly from prothalli) and are extremely fruitful, yielding crops quickly (sometimes even when not expected). Division is generally not an option as the species rarely produce the requisite multiple crowns.

Cyrtomium caryotideum

Epithet means "nutlike," from Greek *caryo* or *caryota*, referring to the leaves which are similar to those on nut trees. Evergreen, 2 ft. (60 cm). Zones 7 to 10. Apogamous.

DESCRIPTION: The rhizome is erect. Straw-colored stipes with dark basal scales are one-third to one-half of the frond length. Oblong, once-pinnate blades bear three to six pairs of pale green pinnae and a large terminal pinna. Slightly stalked 2-in. (5-cm) long triangular pinnae are auricled frequently on both sides of their base (biauriculate) and taper to a point. They have serrate margins and are noted for the inconspicuous nature of their veins. Sori with peltate indusia are on veinlets enclosed in areoles (the rounded outlines defined by the netted venation).

RANGE AND HABITAT: In many of its natural sites, this species grows in muddy limestone clefts, though neither mud nor lime is necessary, or for that matter even welcome, in garden situations. The native range extends from the mountainous regions of the Himalayas, Japan, China, and Vietnam to the Philippines and Hawaii.

CULTURE AND COMMENTS: Readily cultivated and welcomed as a visual contrast to more feathery garden material, this species is not fussy and can be sited in light shade and rich soil. Use it freely, with its trademark matte green fronds, as a design element to break the potential monotony of a continuous spread of forest-green foliage in the garden's woodlands.

The rare **variety *micropterum*** is native to South Africa, Uganda, Kenya, Tanzania, and Madagascar.

Cyrtomium falcatum
Japanese holly fern, Asian holly fern
Epithet means "falcate" or "sickle-shaped."
Evergreen, 1 to 2 ft. (30 to 60 cm). Zones 7 to 10. Apogamous.

DESCRIPTION: The rhizome is erect. Stipes are straw-colored, densely cloaked in russet scales and one-third or more of the frond length. Once-pinnate, oblong blades are bright beacons of lacquered forest-green. The 5 to 18 pairs of pointed, polished pinnae have entire, sometimes undulate, margins that are not toothed. Veins are netted. Plentiful sori with peltate indusia are distributed among the veins.

RANGE AND HABITAT: The species grows in lowland regions in Japan, China, Taiwan, Korea, India, and Vietnam. It has escaped and naturalized in Hawaii, the southern United States, the Atlantic Islands, Australia, New Zealand, and South America. Look for a population near you.

CULTURE AND COMMENTS: With its whorls of shiny green fronds, this makes an easy and outstanding accent plant, especially when surrounded by contrasting gossamer foliage. Give it average fern soil and light shade, as it will burn in too much sun. Its leathery texture and heat tolerance make it an ideal candidate, together with its varieties, for indoor use. Cut fronds provide long-lasting greenery in flower arrangements, usually remaining fresh and healthy longer than the flowers. The cultivars all come true from spores.

'**Butterfieldii**' is in the indoor trade and has serrate margins.

'**Eco Korean Jade**' is a dwarf form, usually less than 1 ft. (30 cm) tall, with five pairs more or less of shiny oblong pinnae. It was introduced by Don Jacobs of Georgia and has survived with mulch in a lime cobble in Pittsburgh's Zone 6 where *Cyrtomium falcatum* has failed.

'**Maritimum**' (by the sea) has been distributed as "Mini Holly" and is a shiny dwarf for Zone 8 or warmer gardens.

'**Mayi**', synonym 'Cristatum', has crested pinnae and frond tips.

Cyrtomium falcatum at the Birmingham Botanical Garden.

Shiny foliage on *Cyrtomium falcatum* 'Rochfordianum' in the Duryee garden.

Cyrtomium fortunei var. *intermedium* at the Bellevue Botanical Garden.

'**Rochfordianum**', Rochford's holly fern, is the stereotypical holly fern but with fringed glossy pinnae. It is hardy outdoors in Zones 7 to 10 and indoors just about anywhere.

Cyrtomium fortunei
Fortune's holly fern
Epithet is after Scottish plant collector Robert Fortune (1813–1880), who was responsible for spreading tea cultivation from China to India and Sri Lanka.
Evergreen, 2½ ft. (75 cm). Zones 5 to 10. Apogamous.

DESCRIPTION: The rhizome is erect. Short, 4-in. (10-cm) greenish stipes are barely visible under clouds of large tan scales. Fronds on the species are upright with lanceolate, once-pinnate, lightly luminous green blades. Twelve to twenty-five pairs of pinnae with a matching terminal pinna are oblong, and sometimes auricled. Pinna tips curve in a graceful upward sweep towards the frond's apex. Veins are netted, and sori with peltate indusia are in a series of rows parallel to the pinnae midrib.

RANGE AND HABITAT: This is a fern of Korea, China, Vietnam, and Thailand and is especially common in Japan where it grows from city walls to mountainous forest floors. Like *Cyrtomium falcatum* is has escaped in a disjunct assortment of habitats from Oregon and South Carolina in the United States to Italy.

CULTURE AND COMMENTS: This is the *Cyrtomium* for climates with cold winters such as in Zone 5 or 6. It successfully survives rigorous temperature extremes from Salt Lake City to southern Massachusetts. While lime tolerant it does not depend on supplements for good health. Normal woodland compost and light to deep shade will maintain its dependable display of soft green circles of fronds.

Var. *clivicola* from Japan and China has fewer (10 to 15) but larger pairs of pinnae. The pinnae are auricled and broader than the ½ in. (13 mm) typical pinnae width of the species. This variety prefers deep shade, has no sheen, and tends to be a pale yellowish green. It is visually similar to var. *intermedium*; however the latter has indusia with a central brown spot compared to uniformly grayish white indusia on this variety.

Var. *intermedium*, a Japanese endemic, presents a low rosette of striking, lime-green pinnae with prominent veins and blackish midribs. Six to ten pairs of 1-in. (2.5-cm) wide, broad-based pinnae are slightly auricled. Site it in the dark depths of the woodlands where it is guaranteed to attract attention and admiration as a relaxing visual for the gardener. Both varieties come true from spores.

Cyrtomium hookerianum
Hooker's holly fern
Epithet is after either Sir W. J. Hooker (1785–1865) or Sir Joseph D. Hooker (1817–1911), both of whom served as directors of the Royal Botanic Gardens, Kew.
Evergreen, 2 ft. (60 cm). Zones 6 (with protection) to 10.

DESCRIPTION: The rhizome is erect. Pea-green stipes with a smattering of brownish scales are half the length of the frond. Broadly lanceolate, once-pinnate blades have up to 15 pairs of

Broad foliage on *Cyrtomium hookerianum*.

pointed oblong pinnae without auricles. Polished dark green, the pinnae are 5 to 6 in. (13 to 15 cm) long by 2 in. (5 cm) wide, and swirl upwards at their tips. Veins are netted but not prominent. Peltate-protected sori are abundantly distributed on the fronds' undersides, and clearly visible as pimples on the fronds' upper surfaces. (In 1997 Christopher Fraser-Jenkins reassigned this species to *Phanerophlebiopsis caduca*, a genus intermediate between *Cyrtomium* and *Polystichum*.)

RANGE AND HABITAT: This Japanese native comes from the deep and moist woods of Kyushu.

CULTURE AND COMMENTS: German specialists have this in cultivation in protected Zone 6 gardens. My lone plant survived its first winter (as a youngster) in Zone 8. With its mid green radiance, it is a handsome complement to the pastel greens, hosta blues, and pale yellows in the garden design. Give it nutrient-rich compost, plenty of shade, and a site nestled among shrubby plants for protection from the extremes of heat and cold.

Cyrtomium lonchitoides
Epithet means "spear-shaped" or "lance-shaped."
Evergreen, 1 to 1½ ft. (30 to 45 cm). Zones 6 to 9.

DESCRIPTION: The rhizome is erect. Bright green stipes of one-fourth of the frond length emerge from dark chocolate bases and are sparsely trimmed with buff scales. Once-pinnate

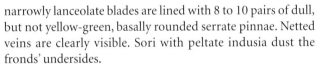
Slender fronds of *Cyrtomium lonchitoides* in the Gassner garden.

Bold large "leaves" on *Cyrtomium macrophyllum*.

narrowly lanceolate blades are lined with 8 to 10 pairs of dull, but not yellow-green, basally rounded serrate pinnae. Netted veins are clearly visible. Sori with peltate indusia dust the fronds' undersides.

RANGE AND HABITAT: No information is currently available about the natural site preferences of this interesting dwarf species. It is endemic to China.

CULTURE AND COMMENTS: This species adapts readily to woodland habitats and, with its small stature, is an attractive foreground feature mixed among perennials in shaded beds. Give it full shade and friable moist soil.

Cyrtomium macrophyllum
Large-leaved holly fern
Epithet means "large-leaved."
Evergreen, 1 to 2 ft. (30 to 60 cm). Zones 6 to 10. Apogamous.

DESCRIPTION: The rhizome is erect, producing a frugal rosette of unfernlike, portly pinnae on 1- to 2-ft. (30- to 60-cm) fronds. The grooved, green stipes, with translucent coffee-colored scales, are one-third to one-half the length of the frond. Lanceolate blades are once-pinnate with broad pinnae shaped more like tree leaves than fern trimmings. Four to eight pairs of pinnae surround a large (macro) terminal pinna that is twice-eared (biauriculate) with an outline that reminds me of the tulips I drew in elementary school (some time back). Pinnae are attached to the rachis as substantial, broad-based, 2-in. (5-cm) pads and remain rounded until terminating abruptly in a short, but noticeable pencil-thin whip tip. Foliage is a pale, matte green with netted and conspicuous veins. Sori with peltate indusia are distributed on the lower surface of the frond and appear as pinheads or minute dots on the upper surface.

RANGE AND HABITAT: *Flora of Japan* (Iwatsuki et al. 1995) reports that the species grows in "dense gloomy forests." With its pale green mats of foliar lightness, perhaps this is nature's way of brightening the gloom. It is also found in the Himalayas and China.

CULTURE AND COMMENTS: Other than in size, this species is somewhat similar to *C. caryotideum* but differs in having conspicuous venation, nonserrate margins, and large nonauricled lateral pinnae. Both settle comfortably into the shaded glens of woodland gardens and appropriate forest floor soil. With its nontraditional foliar outline and matte lettuce-green-colored fronds, it is a welcome evergreen contrast in beds of frilly and dark foliage.

Var. *tukusicola*, from Japan and China, though rarely available, has wedge- rather than round-based pinnae and indusia with a dark brown-black center rather than a uniformly gray-white indusia. This variety has made fleeting appearances in the catalogs of U.S. fern specialists, but no confirmed sightings yet. (As of this writing, it is being imported from China.) Like the species, from which it barely differs, it should be a welcome addition to collections in Zones 6 to 10.

Shorter Notes

Cyrtomium balansae (for Benjamin Balansa, 1825–1892, a French plant collector) is an evergreen Japanese species with auricled pinnae that is hardy in Zones 9 and 10. It is similar to *C. fortunei*. Material from the Ullong Island of Korea, distributed under this name, is beautiful and hardy, but likely to be *C. fortunei* rather than *C. balansae*.

Cyrtomium falcatum × *C. caryotideum* is an evergreen 18- to 24-in. (45- to 60-cm) hybrid with the outline of *C. caryotideum* and a subtle foliar gloss approaching, but not equal to, that of *C. falcatum*. It is hardier than either parent and can be reliably introduced to gardens in Zone 6, or Zone 5 when given an annual mulch, where neither parent would survive the cold winter stress. Full shade is appropriate and welcomed along with friable and moist soil.

Cystopteris
Bladder ferns

The cosmopolitan *Cystopteris* species spread broad bands of small, and sometimes inconspicuous, creeping colonies throughout cool sites in the mountainous areas of the world. They are typically modest in stature and deciduous. The delicate fronds are among the first, along with the woodsias, to unfurl in late winter, frequently in February in the Pacific Northwest. In consequence, their fertility is also precocious and the fronds often wither early in the summer, having accomplished a quick and efficient cycle of growth. When heat desiccates their soft foliage, they tend to replenish fronds throughout the season with smaller replicas. Although these often look tired and rusted, they are still functional. In all sites the stipe bases, like those of several other cold-climate natives (osmundas and select dryopteris, for example), are storage re-

ceptacles for starch, a nutritional insurance policy against the arctic chill associated with their cold-challenged habitats.

Fronds range in height from 8 to 24 in. (20 to 60 cm) or occasionally more on lustily happy plantings of *Cystopteris bulbifera*. Succulent and brittle stipes are grooved, enclosing two vascular bundles. Fronds are from once-pinnate to tripinnate, all with free veins. Sori are held on the veins, covered by an indusial hood that is the namesake bladder-like in appearance and genus indicative. The early deciduous indusium is soon gone, however, often making identification, especially in comparison with the closely allied woodsias, confusing. Spores, when ripe are black. Ripe *Woodsia* spores are brown.

Cystopteris comes from the Greek *kystis*, bladder, in reference to the appearance of the swollen indusium, and the universally applied *pteris*, fern. Worldwide, there are approximately 20 species, plus an ever-expanding collection of hybrids and backcrosses with varying degrees of distinctions, defining, and redefining differences. They are easily grown in moist to wet, often highly basic, friable soil or rock crevices in temperate gardens where, with their smallish stature, they are especially at ease in lightly shaded rock garden communities. Their deciduous cold winter rest is mandatory.

Propagation by either division or spores (which ripen very early in the summer) is easily accomplished. For *Cystopteris bulbifera* and its hybrid offspring with their abundant supplies of little green peas of rolling bulblets, reproduction frequently occurs without any attention, or even awareness, whatsoever from the grower. Pleasant surprises happen.

Cystopteris bulbifera
Bulblet bladder fern
Epithet means "bearing bulbils."
Deciduous, 1½ to 2½ ft. (45 to 75 cm). Zones 3 to 8.

DESCRIPTION: The rhizome is short-creeping, carrying starch-rich old stipe bases. Colored stipes are a refreshing spring tonic of a clear wine-red and range proportionately upwards from one-half to more of the frond length. Bipinnate

Cyrtomium falcatum × *C. caryotideum* reflects the influence of both parents.

Ready-to-roll bulblets on *Cystopteris bulbifera*.

Slender fronds of *Cystopteris bulbifera* in the garden of the late Don Armstrong.

Cystopteris fragilis

CULTURE AND COMMENTS: One of, if not the most handsome of, the cystopteris, this fern needs shade. A limestone substrate or supplement encourages good foliar health with an attendant natural beauty but is not necessary for survival. Do plant it in a consistently moist site especially on stonewalls (broken concrete is excellent), where it will produce a continuous fountain of handsome foliage and willingly populate surrounding garden sites with its bulblet cast offs.

There is a crested as well as a "crispa" variety.

Cystopteris fragilis
Fragile fern
Epithet means "fragile, brittle."
Deciduous, 8 to 16 in. (20 to 40 cm). Zones 2 to 9.

DESCRIPTION: The rhizome is short-creeping, bearing food-storing stubs of old stipes. Fresh green stipes are grooved and one-half of the frond length. Lanceolate blades are bipinnate with up to 15 pairs of thin-textured lax pinnae. Sori are bundled in bladderlike torch-shaped indusia. The new fronds unfurl early, somewhere between the welcome blossoms of snowdrops and crocuses, eagerly announcing, albeit precociously, the arrival of spring. The fronds are almost all abundantly fertile. On the downside, they often collapse (or at least look dark and weary) soon after dispersing their spores early in the summer.

RANGE AND HABITAT: This is one of the most common of the world's ferns with populations distributed in cool mountainous habitats from the Siberian cold to the high-altitude tropics. Plants prefer damp sites within the rocky chinks of a lime substrate. With its widespread distribution, *Cystopteris fragilis* appears to be taking on a life of its own, producing variants and hybrids along with backcrosses. It is reputed to be the most poorly understood of European ferns botanically, and the entire range of complex relationships is currently under study.

CULTURE AND COMMENTS: These ubiquitous harbingers of spring are easily cultivated. They like being cold and nestled into limestone crumble, although they will adapt almost anywhere. Unfortunately, they tend to be lacking in dynamics and, unless the landscape is severely restricted by winter cold, are best used as fillers for areas where other, more ornamental options have not been successful. Watch out for slugs.

blades, with an elegant counterpoint of lime foliage, are elongate, often downward draping, triangular spears of 18 to 25 pairs of pinnae. The foliage is soft and has a rachis bearing a solid undercoat of three or more ready-to-reproduce minute bulblets reminiscent in shape to the Pacmen of early video games. Unlike most fern bulbils these fall readily from the parent, spreading cascading colonies of plantlets. As they are easily plucked they are not an invasive threat. Sori are in cone-shaped bladders, but with the easy reproductive ability of the bulbils, verge on superfluous.

RANGE AND HABITAT: This species of midwestern and eastern North America ranges from Wisconsin, Texas, and Utah to all areas east including comparable sites in Canada. In nature, it is primarily located on limestone. Look (up) for it on ledges where bulbil-encouraged rivulets flow down in moisture-rich limestone crevices.

Cystopteris protrusa
Southern fragile fern, southern brittle fern, lowland brittle fern
Epithet means "protruding."
Deciduous, 12 to 18 in. (30 to 45 cm). Zones 5 to 9. Apogamous.

DESCRIPTION: The rhizome is creeping with, unique to the genus, golden hairs and also unique tips "protruding" beyond the current crop of fronds. Grooved green to straw-colored stipes are one-half of the frond length. Bipinnate blades are lanceolate with 6 to 12 pairs of pinnae. The species is slightly dimorphic with small and relatively coarse sterile fronds the first to emerge followed by the more delicate fertile fronds. Sori are marginal with an early deciduous hoodlike protective indusium. The species easily hybridizes with fellow locals and is one parent along with *Cystopteris bulbifera* of *C. tennesseensis*, and, along with an unknown ancestor, of *C. tenuis*.

Cystopteris protrusa in the Hudgens garden.

RANGE AND HABITAT: Unlike its relatives, this species prefers to settle into ordinary soil rather than limey crevices or their watery trickles. It is native to middle America (with a few disjunct sites in eastern Canada), in areas from Ohio, Minnesota, and Oklahoma eastward to the Mid-Atlantic States.

CULTURE AND COMMENTS: This species adapts and colonizes in a non-aggressive fashion in shade-protected neutral soil. It is an especially valuable choice for areas where stressful cold winters limit the available options for fern gardening, but it thrives in equally stressful hot summer climates as well.

Shorter Notes

Cystopteris alpina (alpine), synonym *C. regia*, is small and delicately beautiful with lacy tripinnate, slightly oval, deciduous fronds, and narrow pinnules. The stipes are up to one-half of the length of the frond, which is variable in size, though usually under 12 in. (30 cm) in height. It is similar in outline to *C. fragilis* but distinguished by an oval blade and finely divided, toothed pinnules. Should you be reading this in Lapland, here is a plant for your garden. The species not only wants, but also excels in alpine habitats "blessed" with nature's thermal blanket of long, snow-covered winters. "Belongs in snowbeds where no other ferns grow, often associated with

Cystopteris alpina. Photo by Jim Baggett.

Salix polaris" (Øllgaard and Tind 1993). It is found exclusively on limestone from northern Scandinavia to the Pyrenees. In cultivation, it is for Zones 2 and up to perhaps 7 or 8, but must be planted in an alkaline cobble or equivalent, where summers are reliably cool.

Cystopteris diaphana (transparent), synonym *C. fragilis* subsp. *diaphana*, is a deciduous native of Mexico, South America, and southern Europe. The small, usually under 1-ft. (30-cm), fronds are tripinnate with pointed tips and pinnules that sometimes overlap. In nature it grows among rocks and in ravines primarily in humid sites. German and British enthusiasts are cultivating it successfully in Zones 6 to 9.

Cystopteris dickeana (after Dr. George Dickie), Dickie's bladder fern, synonym *C. fragilis* var. *dickeana*, is rare in nature with the original find of the early 1800s, and perhaps the only true type, growing on dripping rocks in a coastal cave near Aberdeen, Scotland. Although its botanical status is insecure and under continued taxonomic scrutiny, it is also reported from assorted locales in Europe and, probably, the United States (opinions vary). Many botanists separate it from the spiny spored *C. fragilis* because of its wrinkled, warty spores (which we are not likely to notice in the garden). Horticulturally, the deciduous pinnae are set close together, frequently overlapping, with matching close-set pinnules. Note that the sori edge the pinnules. This species comes true from spores and is an attractive, 4- to 8-in. (10- to 20-cm) treasure for troughs and rubble-enriched rock gardens in Zones 3 to 8.

Cystopteris laurentiana (from the Saint Lawrence River area) is an upright, deciduous species with bipinnate, lanceolate fronds to 18 in. (45 cm). Bulblets are rare but when present are small with distorted shapes. The plant is best suited to moist limestone cliffs in cold-challenged northern areas of North America and Europe. As a fertile hybrid derived from some chromosome acrobatics between *C. bulbifera* and *C. fragilis*, it is difficult to distinguish from the latter. *Flora of North America* (1993) recommends looking for the occasional bulblets and unique glandular hairs that give the species a separate status from either parent.

Cystopteris montana (from mountains), mountain bladder fern, is a handsome, arctic-inclined elusive fern in nature (and even more so in cultivation). Years ago, my family was directed to a Colorado site where, it was promised, we would be immersed in masses of the desired fern. On arrival, I offered a bribe to my children; the first to find a fertile frond would be rewarded with $1.00 (money went farther in those days). After about 15 minutes, the stakes increased to $5.00 for the "first to find a fern." It was not to be. (I suspect we were too late in the season and that during a spring visit we would have seen the envisioned delight.) It is similar in outline to the more familiar gymnocarpiums with broad 18-in. (45-cm), triangular, deciduous fronds held horizontally or slanting downwards from pale green stipes. The long innermost pinnules on the lowest pinnae are significant and separate it from *C. sudetica*, which has correspondingly short interior pinnules. Though rarely cultivated, it is an attractive collector's choice for wet basic soil and cool to cold (even better) winter sites. It is recommended for Zones 2 to 5 but is known

in cultivation for up to cool Zone 8 gardens. Wherever grown, it must have shade and a guaranteed rest in winter. Fern trivia buffs, and we are many, should note that when bruised the fronds are reputed to smell like prussic acid, which all references compare to the fragrance of almonds in assorted stages of abuse.

Cystopteris moupinensis (from Mupin, China) is a small, deciduous charmer native to China and extending beyond into Asia. The stipes grow from creeping rhizomes and are over one-half of the 4- to maybe 6-in. (10- to 15-cm) long fronds. The delicate blades are bipinnate to tripinnate and triangular. This species is likely to be lost to view in the garden, but should elicit admiring oohs and aahs along with envious, "Who's that?" questions in shade-protected troughs and strategically located containers in Zones 5 to 8.

Cystopteris reevesiana (after U.S. botanist Timothy Reeves), southwestern brittle fern, synonym *C. fragilis* var. *tenuifolia*, grows on rocks and terrestrially in assorted substrates from Utah and Colorado south to Texas and Mexico. The rhizomes are creeping, producing long basally dark stipes and finely divided bipinnate to tripinnate blades. The pinnae are widely spaced giving the entire frond a feathery touch. It is easy and cold hardy in Zones 5 to 9.

Cystopteris sudetica (from the Sudetenland of the Czech Republic and Poland) is a rare species from Europe, Japan, China, Korea, and Siberia, so yes, cold hardy. The rhizome is long-creeping and the stipes are tall, usually better than one-half of the 18 in. (45 cm) frond length. The tripinnate blades are broadly ovate-triangular and lightly scaly. *Cystopteris sudetica* is visually similar to *C. montana* but is more robust and lacks the latter's elongate innermost lowest pinnule (basiscopic) on the basal pinnae. Like *C. montana* its habitat of choice is in humus on "limestone debris." It is cultivated in Europe and when available in North America should be incorporated into moist limestone, rocky crevices in shady sites from Zones 3 to 8.

Cystopteris tennesseensis (of Tennessee), Tennessee bladder fern, is the deciduous, fertile hybrid between *C. bulbifera* and *C. protrusa*. At a mature height of 18 in. (45 cm), it is smaller in all proportions, but otherwise similar in portraiture to *C. bulbifera*, including a complement of miniature ready-to-roll bulblets. It is locally common in the Ozarks where it occupies limestone shelves and moist crevices. Grow it in lime-enriched, semishaded cobbles in Zones 5 to 8. Long fronds are fresh light green furnishings and more narrowly triangular than the comparable foliage of either parent.

Cystopteris tenuis (slender), slender fragile fern, MacKay's brittle fern, synonym *C. fragilis* var. *mackayi*, is a candidate for determining successful or discouraging results on that last final exam in Botany 501 (note this is an advanced course) with an A awarded to the student who can define the differences between it and closely related fellow cystopteris. It differs from *C. protrusa* and *C. fragilis* in having pinnae that curve upwards and in having rounded margins as opposed to serrate. The 18-in. (45-cm) deciduous fronds are bipinnate on green to hay-colored stipes of just under one-half of the frond length. The species grows on rocks as well as soil and is especially abundant in the Great Lakes area of North America with an eastward spread and a few disjunct westward populations. It is easily cultivated, without a strong soil preference, and can be used with other cystopteris in a comparative educational exhibit for the cognoscenti in Zones 4 to 8.

Davallia

Members of this genus are characterized by furry rhizomes that creep along the surface of the soil, producing baskets of finely divided fronds and tangles of rhizomes. Their common names are often dedicated to various critters including squirrels, rabbits, hares, and even bears—epithets that tend to overlap in the literature and certainly in commerce. Basically they are Zone 9 to 11 plants but have a welcome ease of cultivation in households everywhere. Humidity is not critical, nor is the degree of shade/partial sun going to create a life-or-death experience.

The name *Davallia* honors the Swiss botanist Edmond Davall (1763–1798). There are 29 or more species ranging in nature from the tropical forests of Tahiti and Africa to the Himalayas, Japan, Korea, and Australia. Common characteristics include the creeping woolly rhizomes, long stipes, and finely divided, but sturdy triangular blades. The sori have cup-like indusia attached at the base as well as along the sides creating a pocket holding its contents like a cut away of a flat-bottomed ice cream cone.

Away from frost zones, plants are easily grown outdoors in ordinary soil and may clamber over rocks colonizing with a tolerance for a small amount of drought and neglect. Likewise, they are certainly one of the easiest choices for basket culture, indoors or out. The rhizome is an interesting feature so give them a wiry container with ample room for the rhizomes to circle about and produce a ball of finely divided, showy greenery. If so desired reduced watering will decrease frond production with no ill effects resulting in a better display of the characteristic furry creeping "foot" (rhizome). Propagation from division is easy and immediate. Propagation from spores is effective but definitely a longer term project.

Botanically we have yet another genus that is being redefined, and this is one area where the common names can be as confusing as the botanical. A small sampling of the commonly available species follows.

Davallia fejeensis (from the Fiji islands), synonym *D. solida* var. *fejeensis*, is popular in the houseplant trade and makes an attractive filling for a moss-lined basket. Thick creeping

A lush basket of *Davallia mariesii* decorates the entry area of the Coughlin home and garden.

rhizomes support five-parted evergreen fronds that may live for two to three years. This species is extremely variable in dissection and habit, and multiple cultivars have been named. All thrive in good light, regular potting soil, and frost-free sites from Zones 9 to 11.

Davallia mariesii (after British plant collector Charles Maries, 1850–1902) with a creeping foot named after several animals is, as distributed in the trade, a beautiful and easily established 6-in. tall (15-cm) deciduous selection. This cultivar is reputed to be the first Japanese fern grown in a pot having been thus given as a gift to a Japanese general in 1462. It is a resilient fern for good light and ordinary soil, outdoors in Zones 9 and 10, and indoors elsewhere. Give it a basket to effectively display the creeping fuzzy rhizome and finely divided tripinnate, triangular fronds. Pinnae sometimes overlap. In 2005 Plant Delights Nursery introduced the selection 'Korea Rocks' from the Wolchusan Mountain in Korea. It offers potential promise for cold tolerance for growers in temperate Zone 7 climates.

Davallia trichomanoides (hairy) is the nom du jour of the *Davallia* most commonly offered in the trade. It will circle a basket with fronds that are very briefly deciduous and rhizomes that are ornamentally hirsute. Triangular fronds are tripinnate and up to 8 in. (20 cm) tall. Pinnae do not overlap. Give it bright indirect light, an occasional good soak, and enjoy. It is slightly less cold tolerant than *D. fejeensis* or *D. mariesii*. Per Hoshizaki and Moran (2001), its correct name is *D. mariesii* var. *stenolepis*.

Davallia tyermannii (after Tyerman), synonym *D. griffithiana*, is probably better known by its popular former name of *Humata tyermannii* or by its common name white rabbit's foot. Pencil-sized silky "feet" follow the contours of a pot or basket and produce bushels of deep forest-green, tripinnate, 8- to 12-in. (20- to 30-cm) fronds. The species always presents a tidy display and is an excellent low-maintenance choice for an indoor decoration or, when protected from frost, an outdoor specimen.

Dennstaedtia

Here is a genus of strong, some might say strongly aggressive, species with soft, feathery deciduous fronds. Most of the approximately 55 species are native to the subtropics or tropics, but a few are temperate and useful in various ways. They have short to widely creeping rhizomes with brownish hairs but no scales. Stipes are usually also hairy and have a horseshoe-shaped vascular bundle. Pale yellow-green to gray fronds are broad at the base and pinnate-pinnatifid to tripinnate. Sori are in cups, looking like pinheads, created by marginal flaps and scattered on the edges of the pinnae. These plants are sometimes called "cup ferns" and are named after August Dennstaedt (1776–1826), a German botanist.

Dennstaedtia hirsuta
Epithet means "hairy."
Deciduous, 10 to 18 in. (25 to 45 cm). Zones 4 to 8.

DESCRIPTION: The rhizome is short-creeping. Yellow-green, pilose stipes are up to one-half of the frond length. Hairy, sterile, broadly lanceolate, pinnate-pinnatifid fronds are slightly smaller than the comparably divided and hairy taller upright fertile fronds. Sori with their cup-shaped, protective indusia are distributed along the pinnae margins.

RANGE AND HABITAT: This is native to sunny rocky crevices and cliffs in colder regions from Japan, China, Korea, and Manchuria to Siberia.

CULTURE AND COMMENTS: Given its provenance, it is not surprising that this species is successfully cultivated in Zone 6 German gardens. And, since it is not as aggressive as the American *Dennstaedtia punctilobula*, it is a promising prospect, albeit with a slightly less feathery profile, for cold-moderated North American gardens as well.

Dennstaedtia punctilobula
Hay scented fern
Epithet from *punctum*, spot, and *lobus*, lobe, in reference to the placement of the sori on the pinnae lobes.
Deciduous, 1½ to 2½ ft. (45 to 75 cm). Zones 3 to 8.

DESCRIPTION: Rhizomes are very long-creeping going from state to state on the U.S. East Coast. Stipes of one-fourth to one-third of the frond length are brown to fawn-colored with soft white hairs. Broad-based, lanceolate blades are bipinnate-pinnatifid with 10 to 24 pairs of feathery yellow-green to gray pinnae carried in an almost ladderlike fashion and bearing glandular-tipped hairs. The foliar glands give off a freshly mown grass fragrance, especially pronounced in dried fronds, earning the fern its common name. Sori in cuplike indusia are spotted on the pinnae margins.

RANGE AND HABITAT: This species grows eagerly in acid soil and is especially at home among the boulders of hillsides and roadsides in eastern Canada, the eastern Midwest, and particularly in New England south to Alabama. It is quite tolerant of sunny exposures and turns russet early in the fall before dying down for the winter.

CULTURE AND COMMENTS: Unless it is dutifully and regularly pruned, the hay scented fern is not suited for any garden other than as a scenic attraction in the widespread, open rock-strewn fields provided by Mother Nature or the untended wilds in the outlying acres of public or private gardens. There it is incredibly useful for its tolerance of the testing and difficult unfernlike conditions associated with drought and exposure. It was Thoreau's favorite fern and one must presume he saw quite a bit of it. He wrote that "[t]he very scent of it, if you have a decayed frond in your chamber, will take you far up country in a twinkling." But, Clute (19091) notes that since "[c]attle will not eat it and it is almost impossible to eradicate from stony soil . . . the farmer has no desire for its presence in his fields." In cultivation give it a site where the meandering rhizomes and attendant foliage will not be an inconvenience. They are, after all, quite pretty when examined as individual fronds or as fulsome summer displays along the highways and byways in their native haunts.

Dennstaedtia wilfordii
Synonym *Microlepia wilfordii*
Epithet is after Charles Wilford, who collected in China and Japan in the 1800s.

Dennstaedtia punctilobula wends its way through a mixed planting in the Kennar garden.

Dennstaedtia punctilobula sweeps around boulders along a roadside in New York.

Large arching fronds of *Dennstaedtia davallioides* in the Peters garden.

Deciduous, 6 to 16 in. (15 to 40 cm). Zones 4 to 8.

DESCRIPTION: The rhizome is long-creeping. Multitoned, shiny, black, green, and russet stipes are up to one-half of the frond length. Lanceolate blades are bipinnate to tripinnate and significantly without the hairy peach fuzz associated with others in the genus. Fertile fronds are slightly but not significantly taller than the sterile. Sori are carried in conical containers along the pinnae margins, the typical reproductive arrangement for the genus.

RANGE AND HABITAT: Rocky sites and mountain forests are the homelands of this species with a native range from Japan, Korea, China, and India to Manchuria.

CULTURE AND COMMENTS: Already established in European and British gardens, this should be an easy introduction to horticulture in temperate North American landscapes.

Shorter Note

Dennstaedtia davallioides (resembling *Davallia*), the lacy ground fern, is an Australian with tall "lacy" tripinnate, triangular semievergreen fronds and a creeping but manageable rhizome habit. It is recommended for partial shade in Zones 7 to 10.

Deparia

Until the late 1990s, most species assigned to *Deparia* were classified elsewhere, frequently as athyriums, but occasionally as diplaziums. Botanically they can be distinguished from both *Athyrium* and *Diplazium* because the grooves on the midrib of the *Deparia* pinnae do not join those of the rachis. In addition *Deparia* has multicellular hairs on the midribs, and as growers will notice, a long-creeping rhizome. *Diplazium*, with bivalved indusia, is segregated more easily. Taxonomic designations are extremely variable and currently more confusing than complete. Watch for *Athyriopsis*, also with long-creeping rhizomes and multicellular hairs, and linear single or double sori with matching indusia, plus some scales, to swallow some familiar species (Ching 1964).

Deparia is derived from the Greek *depas*, cup, and refers to the shape of the indusium in some species. There are about 40 species worldwide with a range from eastern Asia to Africa and a few, either native or naturalized, in North America and Europe. The deciduous blades are generally pinnate-pinnatifid and supported by shallowly grooved stipes with a pair of vascular bundles. Plants are easily propagated by division and come readily from spores, which are in sori covered by linear or hooked indusia.

Deparia acrostichoides

Silvery glade fern, silvery spleenwort
Synonyms *Athyrium thelypteroides*, *Diplazium acrostichoides*
Epithet means "like *Acrostichum*."
Deciduous, 2½ to 3½ ft. (75 to 105 cm). Zones 3 to 8.

DESCRIPTION: The rhizome is short-creeping. Stipes are russet basally and then green. They are lightly scaly, have two rows of teeth, and are one-third of the frond length. Blades, tapering at both ends, are pinnate-pinnatifid with 18 to 24 pairs of pinnae. They have hairy midribs and sori with a straight to

Deparia acrostichoides in the gardens at Cornell Plantations.

Deparia conilii as a ground cover in the Lighty garden. Photo by Richard Lighty.

A crested form of *Deparia acrostichoides*.

slightly curved indusium. Per the very apt common name, these are silvery and become increasingly so with age.

RANGE AND HABITAT: This extremely cold tolerant species ranges from Newfoundland south to Georgia and west to Minnesota. It can be found in moist glades, on damp slopes, and in shady woodlands.

CULTURE AND COMMENTS: This species is easily introduced to gardens where its bright, contrasting green-and-silver foliage makes a pleasant backdrop for darker greenery.

Deparia conilii
Synonyms *Diplazium conilii, Athyriopsis conilii, Asplenium japonicum, D. grammitoides* var. *conilii*
Epithet origin not known.
Deciduous, 1 to 2½ ft. (30 to 75 cm). Zones 5 to 8. Dimorphic.

DESCRIPTION: The rhizome is long-creeping. Stipes on fertile fronds are blackish and over one-half of the length of the frond. On the shorter sterile fronds the stipes are about one-third of the frond length. Narrowly lanceolate blades are bipinnatifid with 12 to 20 pairs of pinnae. The rachis and pinnae midribs bear multicellular hairs. Sori in a herringbone pattern are covered with a linear indusium and border both sides of the pinnae midribs.

RANGE AND HABITAT: This is a fern of moist woods in Japan and Korea. Richard Lighty, director emeritus of the Mount Cuba Center in Delaware, introduced the Korean material to North American culture in 1966.

CULTURE AND COMMENTS: An attractive creeper, this species rambles about among woodland plants where it serves as an easygoing ground cover. It is readily divided and makes for great gifts to fellow fern collectors.

Deparia japonica
Black lady fern
Synonyms *Athyrium japonicum, Diplazium japonicum, Lunathyrium japonicum, Athyriopsis japonica*
Epithet means "from Japan."
Deciduous, 1 to 2 ft. (30 to 60 cm). Zones 6 to 9. Dimorphic.

DESCRIPTION: The branching rhizome is short-creeping. Stipes are dark and scaly at the base with scales and hairs continuing upwards through the length of the frond. Bipinnatifid sterile blades are oblong and the taller, erect fertile blades are narrower with 12 to 16 pairs of pinnae. Sori with linear-inrolled indusia are arranged in a herringbone pattern along the veins adjacent to the pinnae midribs.

RANGE AND HABITAT: Widespread in nature from the Himalayas, China, Korea, Japan, and Malaysia, this species grows in moist woodlands.

CULTURE AND COMMENTS: Dark forest-green to black-green fronds are a striking feature and should be used to visual advantage by juxtaposing this fern with lighter colored and/or feathery textured companions. Give it shade and a consistent supply of moisture. It reputedly breaks dormancy late in spring but is a welcome guest whenever it joins the garden party. This species is extremely similar to *D. petersenii* and often considered synonymous. The botanical differences as noted in *Flora of Japan* (Iwatsuki et al. 1995) are minute: the inrolled indusia and the gradually tapering terminal portion of the frond distinguish this species from *D. petersenii*, which has a flat indusia and an abruptly tapering frond apex.

Shorter Notes

Deparia okuboana (after Saburo Okubo, a nineteenth-century Japanese botanist) is a tall, deciduous species from Japan, Korea, and China. The broadly ovate blades are tripinnatifid and unusual in having round rather than herringbone sori. A recent introduction to horticulture in the United States, it is growing successfully in Zone 6 and recommended for dampish shade where a tall and tolerant species is a welcome addition to the garden design.

Deparia petersenii (after Petersen) produces a colony of pea-green fronds less than 1 ft. (30 cm) high, extending on short stolons. In the wild this Philippine native seeks moist loamy soil alongside rivulets or in weeps, in sunny places. It adapts easily to garden life in open ground with average moisture or in containers where it does best with daily watering. The fern remains freshly green in all seasons year after year. Deserving of a place as a tidy small-area landscape plant in sunshine, it is one of relatively few ferns that will fill the bill. For cultivation in the Western world it may be grown outdoors in Zones 7 to 10. (Description by George Schenk.)

Dicksonia

This genus offers some marvelous options for tree fern enthusiasts, whether new to the experience or experts in the genre, gardening in Zones 9 and 10 as well as those with a dedication to enjoying and overwintering them in Zone 8. Named for James Dickson (1738–1822), the genus has 22 species from montane tropical sites in the South Pacific with temperate relatives native to New Zealand and Australia. The type species is from the island of Saint Helena, which is probably better known for its association with Napoleon's final exile than for its botanical wonders.

With spreading canopies of bipinnate-pinnatifid to quadripinnate, leathery, 6- to 8-ft. (1.8- to 2.4-m) fronds, dick-sonias are recognized by the hairy aspect of their skeletal support structure as well as a complete lack of scales. Trunks are slow growing and slender in their basic vascular structure, but are broadened significantly by the bundles of roots that extend in a linear cloak from the trunk's apex to water and nutrients in the ground below.

Spores are carried in miniature cups along the frond's margins, but are relatively short-lived and for best results should be sown as soon as practical after ripening. Logs from the trunks of *Dicksonia antarctica* are propagated much as one would root cuttings, albeit of a size well beyond the traditional concept of cutting material. Britain's Martin Rickard (2000), an experienced and successful tree fern propagator, recommends sinking

Deparia petersenii at three years old in a shallow container with *Neoregelia* 'Fireball', a dwarf bromeliad. Photo by George Schenk.

logs in moist soil (no deeper than necessary to keep them upright) and shade. Daily and thorough watering of the "trunks" is mandatory. Once they are rooted, they are ready for Zone 9 or 10 garden sites. Elsewhere they need winter protection, which can be provided by an insulated wrap. An easy option, when they are juveniles, is to cultivate them in pots. These can be carted for the winter into a cool greenhouse or sheltered garden location until such time as the tree and container outgrow and outweigh you, the gardener. By this stage, with a trunk of 2 ft. (60 cm) or more, they should be ready for a year-round garden site with a protective winter embalmment.

Dicksonia antarctica
Tasmanian tree fern

Epithet means "from Antarctic regions," a bit of a stretch. Evergreen, 15 to 20 ft. (4.5 to 6 m). Zones 8 (with an annual winter-insulating wrap) to 10.

DESCRIPTION: Trunks are dark brown and from 10 to 20 ft. (3 to 6 m) tall or occasionally more. Arching sprays of bipinnate to tripinnate, 6- to 12-ft. (1.8- to 3.6-m) fronds are on very short stipes which emerge with a fleeting fringe of long plum-colored hairs. Sori of two to six per pinnule are in cups under hooded edges of the margins.

RANGE AND HABITAT: This species is from Tasmania as well as mainland Australia where in some areas it has been collected to extinction. In nature it enjoys the encouragement of a ferny combination of humidity and soil moisture.

CULTURE AND COMMENTS: Of all the tree ferns, this is the one species most likely to succeed away from Zones 9 and 10. It is magnificent in the wind-sheltered environments of the cool coastal belts in Scotland, southern England, and California, as well as in true tree fern climates worldwide. In Zone 8 it needs a winter life-support system in the form of an insulating enclosure or at the minimum an umbrella of frost-resistant

Cross section of the trunk on _Dicksonia antarctica_.

Exuberant young frond of _Dicksonia antarctica_ at Wells Medina Nursery.

Slender new growth on *Dicksonia antarctica.*

Dicksonia fibrosa in New Zealand. Note the skirt of old fronds.

horticultural gauze. The easiest insurance is to grow it in a sizable but transportable pot. Some day, however, like children, it will outgrow its nest and need to be on its own. Plants with a trunk of at least 2 ft. (60 cm) are more cold resistant and better prepared for a year-round location in the garden. Do, however, safeguard the trunks from winter's extremes and give the crown a pillow of insulation. Some growers enclose the fronds in burlap or other loose clothing. The choice is unimportant so long as the fronds can "breathe." Do not use plastic or clear material that would magnify the sun's rays and scorch the fronds you are trying to protect.

Dicksonia fibrosa
Woolly tree fern
Epithet means "fibrous, matted roots."
Evergreen, 18 ft. (5.4 m). Zones 9 and 10.

DESCRIPTION: The fibrous, rusty colored trunk grows to 18 ft. (5.4 m). Erect fountains of tripinnate to quadripinnate narrow fronds with short stipes are mass produced and reach a length of 8 or 9 ft. (2.4 to 2.7 m). The species is readily recognized in the wild by the skirts of old fronds that droop and drape the trunk with blankets of cold-protective, dead fronds that even in their final stages still serve a purpose. The pinnae have upturned margins that give the fronds a coarse texture. Both the trunk and hairs on the rachis are a darker brown than those of *Dicksonia antarctica*. Sori are marginal with a circular indusium.

RANGE AND HABITAT: A New Zealand endemic, this is an interesting fern for moisture-rich soils where it can survive periods of frost. It is the most habitat-versatile of New Zealand's native ferns, accepting shade or somewhat exposed locales so long as the roots do not dry out.

CULTURE AND COMMENTS: In the landscape design this is a stout and solid element with a height somewhat more home-garden proportionate than the *Cyathea* giants. It should be an easy choice for Zone 9 and 10 gardens. Tidy gardeners need to adjust to the appearance of the "dead" skirts and resist the temptation to remove them, which, while possibly improving the fern's cosmetic appearance, would hinder their cold resistance.

Dicksonia squarrosa
Rough tree fern, harsh tree fern
Epithet means "rough, with sharp edges."
Evergreen, 12 to 20 ft. (3.6 to 6 m). Zones 9 and 10.

DESCRIPTION: This species is stoloniferous, sometimes forming multiple trunks. These narrow trunks are up to 20 ft. (6 m) tall and embedded with the upright stalks of old stipe bases as well as buds that can produce multiple crowns. Bristles of outstretched dark russet hairs surround the old and the new and are an ornamental feature on the trunks, stipes, and emerging crosiers. Deep green, shiny, tripinnate fronds with basal pinnae aimed downwards are harsh (or rough and sharp, if you would) to the touch. Significantly, old fronds do not surround the trunks. Sori are under circular to oval indusia.

RANGE AND HABITAT: One of the most common New Zealand endemics, this is abundant in forests from the coasts to moun-

tains throughout the country. It prefers shelter from wind and needs moist soil. The sturdy trunks are popularly used in construction. Look for sprouting walls in the landscape.

CULTURE AND COMMENTS: I grew this as a transient (indoors in winter, out in the summer) for a number of years until the logistics of transferring it exceeded my muscular capabilities and eventually those of my family. Now it is an accent in the plant propagation room, where it is restricted by pot size. Thus restrained it is a manageable 4-ft. (120-cm) specimen, $2\frac{1}{2}$ ft. (75 cm) of which is trunk. Watering requirements of plants in confinement need special vigilance however. Neglect will lead to collapsed fronds and a dormancy period of approximately six months. The fern recovers just in time to escape a trip to the compost heap.

Diphasiastrum
Formerly considered fern allies but now having their own independent lineage (see comments under *Selaginella*), these clubmosses or running pines were also classified, and often still are, as lycopodiums. They differ in having flat, scalelike leaves rather than the bristles of the latter. The genus name means "false but incomplete resemblance to *Diphasium*." They are trailing creepers with upright shoots and are without

Furry new frond on *Dicksonia squarrosa* looks as though it is ready to be petted.

gemmae (leafy propagules that detach and grow into new plants). Fertile cones are either single without a stalk or multiple on individual or branched stalks. The species hybridize freely. In general they are not cultivated, but instead are admired novelties in the woodland understory and sometimes gathered for use in holiday wreaths and decorations.

Diphasiastrum alpinum (alpine), the alpine clubmoss, synonym *Lycopodium alpinum*, has a horizontal network of creeping stems with clusters of evergreen, upright 4- to 6-in. (10- to 15-cm) branching shoots. The branchlets are square and have prominent winter bud constrictions. Single cones are carried without stems at the apex of the shoots. The species is native to Zone 2 dryish coniferous forest sites and mountainous areas in western North America, extreme northeastern Canada, Greenland, Europe, Asia, and Japan.

Diphasiastrum complanatum (flattened), the evergreen running pine, synonym *Lycopodium complanatum*, sends up multitiered fountains of green shoots to 16 in. (40 cm) from spreading horizontal stems. The branchlets are flat with conspicuous annual bud constrictions and compressed, scalelike leaves. Fertile cones are upright centerpieces on branching stalks. This species is a Zone 2 circumboreal alpine resident of forests and open mountain slopes.

Diphasiastrum digitatum (handlike, fingered), the southern running pine, synonym *Lycopodium digitatum*, has horizontal shoots running on the soil surface or buried shallowly in the woodland litter, and 18-in. (45-cm) evergreen upright shoots with many-fingered rays of outstretched flat branches. They are usually without annual bud constrictions. Candelabras of fertile cones stand upright on slender stalks. This species is a common Zone 3 to 6 North American endemic, native to mixed forests from New England south to the Carolinas and west to Minnesota.

Diphasiastrum sitchense (from Sitka, Alaska), the Sitka clubmoss, synonym *Lycopodium sitchense*, presents dense evergreen clusters of upright 4- to 6-in. (10- to 15-cm)

branching spikes arising from compact-spreading horizontal stems. The branchlets differ from fellow *Diphasiastrum* colleagues in being round instead of flat. Vertical cones are without stalks and gathered at the tips of the shoots. Yet another Zone 2 or possibly Zone 1 alpine, this circumboreal species relishes a home in meadows, rocky woodlands, and above the treeline in the forbidding cold areas of northern Canada, Kamchatka, Japan, and parts of Asia.

Diphasiastrum tristachyum (dull spikes), the blue ground cedar, synonyms *Diphasium tristachyum* and *Lycopodium tristachyum*, has widely spreading buried horizontal stems. The upright, flat-topped, 12-in. (30-cm) evergreen shoots are blue-green with fanlike lower branches. The fertile stalks look like upright dinner forks extending in a slender fashion 3 in. (7.5 cm) above the sterile. This is a common fern in the forests, frequently with oak and pine, of eastern North America and is involved in more hybrid combinations than any other North American *Diphasiastrum*.

Diplazium
Twin-sorus ferns

The genus name *Diplazium* comes from the Greek *diplazios* or *diplazein*, to double, in reference to the two-valved indusium that splits open on both sides of a vein. The definition "duplicate" is also applied, as the two sides are indeed mirror images. More than 400 species grow worldwide essentially in damp tropical jungles and forests. They are deciduous or, on occasion, evergreen, with upright rhizomes, once-pinnate to tripinnate blades on deeply grooved stipes with two curved vascular bundles and back-to-back paired sori. The grooves on the pinnae midribs connect continuously into those of the rachis like a merge at a highway interchange, thus separating the genus from *Deparia*. The over-40 crowd may find some familiar sounding names but recognize them as the athyriums (from which they are now separated based on the *Diplazium* sori which are usually bivalved rather than hooked or crescent-shaped as in *Athyrium*) of years past where indeed some may still be found. With their many variables, expect *Diplazium* to be split yet again in the future. All are easily propagated by division and/or spores.

Diplazium pycnocarpon

Narrow-leaved glade fern, narrow-leaved spleenwort
Synonyms *Athyrium pycnocarpon*, *Asplenium angustifolium*
Epithet from *pycnos*, close, and *carpos*, fruit.
Deciduous, 2½ to 3½ ft. (75 to 105 cm). Zones 4 to 8. Slightly dimorphic.

DESCRIPTION: The rhizome is short-creeping, producing clumps of upright, narrow, delicate foliage. Stipes with deep grooves are russet at their base and green above with the whole equaling one-third of the frond length. Lanceolate, once-pinnate blades that taper at the base are statements of simplicity with 20 to 30 pairs of outstretched, linear, ½-in. (13-mm) wide pinnae. Fertile fronds with narrower pinnae emerge later in the season, and are slightly taller than the sterile. Sori, crowded

Diplazium pycnocarpon in the Schieber garden.

in a herringbone fashion, are covered by linear indusia opening on one side. This species is similar to many athyriums, but not so finely divided.

RANGE AND HABITAT: The glade fern sweeps across eastern North America from the Great Plains to the Atlantic Coast with a few excursions into eastern Canada. In nature it creeps about modestly in rich, neutral to slightly alkaline, moisture-retentive soil.

CULTURE AND COMMENTS: A favorite in East Coast gardens, this slender upright offers ease of cultivation as well as vertical diversion in woodlands crowded with spreading foliage. Keep it moist to prevent premature dieback in late summer.

Diplazium sibericum

Synonym *Athyrium crenatum*
Epithet means "from Siberia."
Deciduous, 1 to 3 ft. (30 to 90 cm). Zones 5 to 8.

DESCRIPTION: The rhizome is long-creeping. Grooved stipes are scaly and ebony at the base and green above. They are one-half of the frond length. Triangular blades taper strongly at the tip and are bipinnate-pinnatifid with 10 to 15 pairs of pinnae that are somewhat hairy on the undersides. Sori with matching indusia are linear along the veins and may be back to back on the lowest pinnules.

RANGE AND HABITAT: This species is native to Russia, Siberia, Manchuria, China, the Himalayas, and Japan. The taller material is disjunct in Scandinavia where, "[s]teep rocky and narrow, forested river gorges, rich with the atmosphere of fairy tales and wood spirits, are the preferred habitats" (Øllgaard and Tind 1993).

CULTURE AND COMMENTS: Illustrations of this species (from Øllgaard and Tind 1993) show a lovely bright green upright creeper. Given its provenance, it should easily adjust to cultivation in cold temperate gardens in light but moist acid soil, with partial shade. Its adaptability is questionable for long-term survival in muggy warm and humid summer sites.

Shorter Notes

Diplazium australe (of the south) is a large 3- to 4-ft. (90- to 120-cm) deciduous fern from New Zealand and Australia, where with its creeping tendencies it can become somewhat weedy. Like others in the genus the rhizome roams about, creating a colony of tufted foliage. The ovate bipinnate to tripinnate fronds are thin-textured and not resistant to prolonged frosts. This species is easily established as background filler in part shade and moist ordinary soil in Zones 9 and 10.

Diplazium esculentum (fit to eat, vegetable fern), from Africa, parts of Asia, and Polynesia, has an upright rhizome, which in time forms a small trunk. It colonizes from root buds. Tall, straggly fronds, which may reach 4 ft. (1.2 m) or more, are ovate and bipinnate-pinnatifid at maturity. This tropical species has naturalized in Hawaii, Florida, and Louisiana, growing in wet soils in Zones 9 to 11. Young crosiers are eaten cooked or raw in Asia.

Diplazium subsinuatum (nearly wavy margined), synonym *D. lanceum*, is from Japan, Korea, China, eastern Asia,

and nearby islands from the Philippines to Borneo. It produces upright narrow and entire, evergreen fronds from branching creeping rhizomes. With a height of 6 to 18 in. (15 to 45 cm), it is recommended for use as a ground cover in light shade and composty soil in Zones 9 and 10.

Diplazium tomitaroanum (cut) is very similar to *D. subsinuatum* but with lobed frond margins. I have grown this handsome species indoors for 20 years. It is well behaved and totally undemanding of anything but regular watering. Outdoors it is suitable for Zones 9 and 10.

Dipteris

Dipteris (two-winged) is a genus of 6 to 8 species from India, China, and the South Pacific.

Dipteris conjugata is exactly as described by Jones (1987), "a fern which colonizes clearings, embankments, road verges, etc. . . . Plants can be somewhat tricky to establish and once growing are best left undisturbed." The species prefers full sun or light shade in mineral soil. It produces a long ropy rhizome and is not easy to move, needing a year or so to settle in after being transplanted. (Description by George Schenk.)

Tall, to 6-ft. (1.8-m), striking, palmate foliage of *Dipteris conjugata* towers over its companion, *Dicranopteris linearis*. Photo by George Schenk.

Doodia
Rasp ferns, hacksaw ferns

With only 12 to 15 species this is a very small genus but it includes several marvelous options for those tough sunny and even dryish spots in the garden. The species are native from Sri Lanka to Polynesia and Hawaii; however, those with garden potential are from Australia and New Zealand. With overlapping characteristics, some tend to look alike (with distinctions varying from reference to reference but garden values constant). Called rasp or hacksaw ferns, the plants have pinnae edged with marginal teeth terminating in minute spines. A little stroking will find them rough to the touch. Blades are upright and once-pinnate with netted veins. Unfurling fronds are frequently tinted from pink to a rich red maturing to deep green. The intensity of the color varies with exposure (and possibly soil types). For enhanced and prolonged color grow them in slightly moist and well-drained sunny sites. (They bring the same buoyant coloration indoors as trouble-free houseplants.) Stipes have a hint of a groove and enclose two vascular bundles that are shaped like teardrops. Sori are lined like rows of dashes along both sides of the pinnae midrib and have an indusium opening away from the margins. With soral similarities these species are closely related to *Blechnum* and *Woodwardia*. The name *Doodia* honors Samuel Doody (1656–1706), curator of the Chelsea Physic Garden in London, and Britain's first cryptogamic botanist.

Doodia aspera
Prickly rasp fern
Epithet means "rough."
Evergreen, 8 to 18 in. (20 to 45 cm). Zones 9 to 10.

DESCRIPTION: The rhizome is short and erect and has underground runners. At one-fifth of the frond length, black stipes with a smattering of glistening dark scales are likewise short. Narrowly elliptical, dentate, dark green shiny blades are once-pinnate with an elongate tip and 30 to 40 pairs of pinnae that are reduced to nubbins at the frond base. Significantly, with the exception of the basal pair, they are broadly attached to the rachis. Sori are in broken lines running parallel to the pinnae midveins.

Upper surface of *Doodia media* with the linear soral pattern embossed as ridges.

RANGE AND HABITAT: This species is native to India, Sri Lanka, and Australia and has been introduced but not well established in New Zealand. It colonizes readily in light shade by forested stream banks as well as in drier rocky sites where it forms compact clumps.

CULTURE AND COMMENTS: With its sassy pink to ruby new fronds, prickly rasp fern is a delightful refreshment among the traditional green foliage of ferns and companions. It is best in partial sun with rich soil, but good drainage, in Zones 9 and 10 where it excels in rock garden crannies. Zone 8 gardeners should give it a trial site in the side of the garden that receives winter sun or better yet where the house protects the planting from polar wind and cold.

Doodia media
Common rasp fern
Epithet means "middle, intermediate."
Evergreen, 8 to 18 in. (20 to 45 cm). Zones 7 (with abundant protection) to 10.

DESCRIPTION: The rhizome is erect and produces runners. Grooved, short, almost nonexistent, stipes are a lustrous two-toned striped blend of dark brown and muddy green. Stiff, upright fronds are once-pinnate, forest-green swords with upwards of 30 pairs of pinnae and an extenuated tip that bears sori to the very edge of the apex. In sunny sites the new growth is a vivid coppery scarlet. The lowest six to eight pairs of pinnae are severely reduced in size and stalked, but the majority are broadly attached with a barely connected small lower lip-like foliar extension. They are bristly to the touch. Sori run the length of the pinnae midribs in dual rows of broken linear tracks that are clearly visible on the upper frond surface. The Maori name *pukupuku*, gooseflesh, is a magnificent and appropriate descriptive.

RANGE AND HABITAT: Common rasp fern is primarily a species of New Zealand and Australia with outlying populations in Fiji and New Guinea. In nature it spreads about in damp but well-drained sunny habitats, often among rocks, but in forested areas as well.

CULTURE AND COMMENTS: With rough-textured and weather-resistant leathery fronds, this plucky species is both handsome and trouble-free in sunny rock gardens or a well-drained pocket in a front-row site. A mass planting with unfurling red trimmings is a stunning display. Although evergreen, this new growth is extremely late. In the Pacific Northwest the first tentative red crosiers come calling in early summer, the penultimate fern to emerge, just one step ahead of the season's finale, *Lygodium japonicum*.

Shorter Note
Doodia caudata (tailed) is a dimorphic evergreen with a lax rosette of soft (for the genus), short, sterile fronds and upright clusters of fertile fronds reaching 10 in. (25 cm). It is once-pinnate with the lower pinnae stalked and a long tail-like whip at the apex. New growth is an attractive rose color. While I have never had the opportunity to grow this native of New Zealand and Australia, it is recommended for Zones 8 to 10 shade in seeps or sites with a consistent moisture supply.

Drynaria

Drynaria includes a handsome assortment of epiphytes that are usually quite large. Visually they resemble *Aglaomorpha* but differ in having lobed, small fertile fronds rather than the reduced threadlike structures of *Aglaomorpha*. They are quite a tolerant crew and recommended as low-maintenance house plants.

Drynaria quercifolia, with a common name that fits the plant neatly—oak leaf fern, bears, in addition to coarsely feathery leaves, leaflike bracts that are quite oaklike in their scalloped outline. These turn from green to a rich brown very like that of fallen oak leaves, but persist for years and channel rain to the fern's base. Widespread in the Pacific tropics, this is an especially easy and adaptable species. In nature it is a clinger on trees and fertile rocks. In cultivation it grows readily as a terrestrial and is useful as a ground cover. Set out at 1-ft. (30-cm) intervals, oak leaf fern is well worth several feet or yards of soil. When planting, cover only the lower half of the fern's rhizomes. It can be grown in shade or half sun in any reasonably fertile, well-drained soil, and it tolerates dryness. In sun with periodic drought it reaches about 18 in. (45 cm) tall, becoming twice that height in shade and rich, moist soil. It can also be grown as a houseplant or in a greenhouse, in a container about 10 in. (25 cm) or more in diameter. Shingle culture also suits the oak leaf fern. (Description by George Schenk.)

Dryopteris

Wood ferns, buckler ferns

Within the fern community, *Dryopteris* is a proportionately huge genus with more than 225 species and 77 hybrids at last count. They include vast numbers of elegant and functional species and cultivars ranging in size from dwarfs for rock gardens to dramatic and majestic behemoths that are the sentinels of the landscape. Most prefer rich, acid soils and once established are quite low maintenance, drought tolerant, and accepting of dry soils (with my companion plants, including shrubs, wilting before dryopteris show signs of stress). The typical *Dryopteris* display features a shuttlecock of arching deciduous or evergreen fronds originating from erect or branching rhizomes. Plants may produce a single foliar rosette from an unbranched rhizome or a collection of crowns from a branching rhizome. Many species are very challenging to identify, and continuing research leads all too frequently to the name changes that beleaguer and bedevil gardeners.

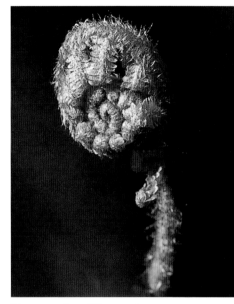

Young crosier of *Dryopteris* ×*complexa* 'Robust' greets the early spring.

The emergence of signature scaly fiddleheads and stipes, with exceptional ornamental value, bring buoyancy to the joy and promise of springtime. The sturdy stipes are grooved with three to nine

Vibrant color on the fresh fronds of *Doodia aspera* in the University of California Botanical Garden at Berkeley.

Sturdy and leathery low fronds of *Doodia media*.

Drynaria quercifolia with its oaklike brown lower foliage. Photo by George Schenk.

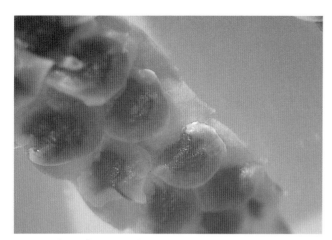

Dryopteris erythrosora sori.

Dryopteris filix-mas 'Linearis Polydactyla', an old British cultivar, remains popular today. Kennar garden.

vascular bundles arranged in variations on an open C pattern (with large bundles at the end points). Blades range from once-pinnate, simple structures to finely divided feathers of greenery. The spores are medium brown to dark brownish-black. The sori are round and, with very few exceptions (*Dryopteris scottii* and *D. gymnosora*, for example), are covered when fresh with a kidney-shaped indusium. With time and weather these can disintegrate and appear deceptively round.

When multiple crowns develop, dryopteris are easy to divide with a judicious slice of a sharp spade or sturdy knife. They are also easily propagated from spores. Harvesting will bring copious amounts of chaff along with the spore drop, so extracting the spores from the chaff, with its potential for contamination, is especially important for success. Many species are apogamous (reproducing asexually directly from the prothallus) and, with prompt spore germination, all are excellent and encouraging options for those first tentative ventures into propagation or the continuing education of the addicted.

The name *Dryopteris* is from the Greek *drys*, oak or forest, and *pteris*, fern, in reference to its once common occurrence in oak woods. (To carry the thread back farther, the dryads of Greek mythology were the nymphs that inhabited oaks.) Common names are wood fern in North America and, more imaginatively, buckler fern (in deference to the shape of the indusium) in Britain and Europe. In earlier times it was classified under *Aspidium* or *Lastrea*.

These are primarily ferns of worldwide temperate regions, with a concentration of natives in the moist woodlands of eastern North America, Europe, Japan, and Asia. Some of the most desirable imports from Japan and Asia unfurl in fashionably warm rainbow shades with pigments ranging from coppery red through amber. Not surprisingly, many of these glamorous options are supplanting the North American natives in commerce; however, the natives are reliable options and excellent selections for those embarking on their first cautious ventures into the marvelous world of fern gardening. Meanwhile, further botanical expeditions continue to introduce exciting new-to-horticulture temptations regularly, guaranteeing interesting selections well into the future. Unfortunately, not all of these adapt to garden settings in por-

tions of Middle America where the summers are either too hot or too humid, or both. Natives of high Himalayan elevations are especially likely to find the transition challenging. However, with microclimates varying from area to area and with the imaginative efforts of individual gardeners no species should be automatically excluded from consideration without a creative trial. "I consider every plant hardy until I have killed it myself . . . at least three times" (Tony Avent, Plant Delights Nursery).

European species, especially *Dryopteris affinis*, *D. dilatata*, and the circumboreal *D. filix-mas*, are noted for their tendency to produce a variety of sports (that is, genetic variations). These were prized introductions reaching the zenith of their popularity as well as great monetary value in the British Victorian fern heyday. Lowe (1908) lists some 52 varieties of *D. filix-mas* alone. They still inspire a passionate following especially for the collector wanting something "different." It has been reported, however, that "the stronger the genetic variation from a normal appearing plant, the poorer the fern's performance" in hot and humid summer climates (Archer 2005).

With their cosmopolitan distribution, dryopteris have a history of applications in folk medicine as well as practical uses born of functional necessity. The latter ranged from using

Dryopteris affinis 'Crispa' in the Bradner garden.

Chubby unfurling fronds of *Dryopteris affinis* 'Crispa Gracilis'.

tinctures of burned fern ashes for green coloring in wine glasses (viva la France) to dyes for fabrics. Medicinal uses, especially for the universally available *D. filix-mas* were varied and plentiful, ranging from unappetizing to those with potentially terminal effects.

Dryopteris aemula
Hay-scented wood fern, hay-scented buckler fern
Epithet means "imitating or rivaling other ferns."
Semievergreen, 2 ft. (60 cm). Zones 6 to 8.

DESCRIPTION: The rhizome is erect. The frond is half purple-brown stipe, with scattered brown scales, and half medium green, triangular-ovate blades bearing minute glands. The 10 to 20 pairs of tripinnate pinnae curve gracefully towards the drooping frond apex. The sori are medial (between the midrib and margin), and the indusium is kidney-shaped.

RANGE AND HABITAT: This species is primarily restricted to acidic, humid, oceanic coastal regions of Europe plus the Atlantic Islands and Turkey.

CULTURE AND COMMENTS: In cultivation this species needs year-round humidity and deep, humus-rich soil in moist shade. Try it near your waterfall. It prefers a long growing season and is susceptible to early frosts. Though popular in Britain, it is not widely grown in the United States. The fronds,

with their tiny glands, smell like new mown hay when crushed, hence the common name. Botanical details separate this from the similar *Dryopteris dilatata*, which has stipe scales that are brown with dark centers rather than the uniformly brown stipe scales of *D. aemula*.

Dryopteris affinis
Golden-scaled male fern
Synonyms *Dryopteris borreri, D. pseudomas*
Epithet means "similar to."
Evergreen to subevergreen, 3 to 4 ft. (90 to 120 cm). Zones 4 to 8. Apogamous.

DESCRIPTION: The stout rhizome produces a thick crown, flush with sturdy sprays of lush foliage. The soft green new growth is handsomely dressed in translucent russet scales. The stipe is up to one-fourth the length of the frond and the lanceolate blade is pinnate-pinnatifid to bipinnate. It is "similar" in structure to *Dryopteris filix-mas*. Of diagnostic significance, it differs in having a small black dot at the base of the 30 to 35 pairs of pinnae where they join the rachis. (It helps to have magnification and sometimes a stretch of the imagination to see this.) In addition the stipe scales, being more abundant, are much more prominent than in *D. filix-mas*. The sori are medial with kidney-shaped indusia.

Dryopteris affinis 'Crispa Gracilis' with its dwarf proportions in the foreground in the Kennar garden.

RANGE AND HABITAT: This woodlander grows throughout Europe including the British Isles, western Russia, and Turkey, and extends its range to North Africa.

CULTURE AND COMMENTS: *Dryopteris affinis* is easily grown and handsome in almost any spacious garden situation—partial sun, shade, acid, and even lime—it takes them all. Once established in the garden, it is drought tolerant. Although it can be deciduous in colder areas it is fully evergreen in milder zones. The spring growth, covered in lustrous golden scales, is a truly elegant display especially when backlit with early morning or late afternoon sunshine. With its inclination to clump, this species and its offspring can be readily propagated by division or for a bountiful crop, they all offer a great opportunity for learning via "Introductory Spore Propagation 101."

Botanists have divided this species into several subspecies although with no universal agreement. (For several opinions on the subject, see the British Pteridological Society's publication, *Pteridologist* 3 (1) 1996: 23–28.) Taxonomy notwithstanding, there is an extensive range of variation with an attendant yield of named cultivars. (Unfortunately, many of these interesting derivations are subject to disfiguring attacks by leafhoppers and thrips where these are present in the garden community.) Most of these varieties of the type and subspecies are commonly available and come true from spores.

'**Congesta Cristata**' is low growing, to 9 in. (23 cm), with congested fronds and crests at the apex.

Dryopteris affinis 'Cristata Angustata' with its frilly edges in the Kennar garden.

'**Crispa**' (curled) is a magnificent specimen with wavy margined pinnae and spring bright growth of yellow-green. At 3 to 4 ft. (90 to 120 cm) tall, it is a lively contrast in dark plantings.

'**Crispa Gracilis**' is a fastigiated forest-green 12-in. (30-cm) dwarf suggestive of a miniature conifer. It is a favorite for foreground plantings.

'**Cristata**' (crested), also known as 'Cristata the King', is im-

Dryopteris affinis 'Stableri Crisped' with its upright narrow architecture is one of the most popular cultivars commercially and ornamentally. Kennar garden.

Dryopteris affinis 'Revolvens' with its turned-under margins in the Schieber garden.

mensely popular with its 2- to 4-ft. (60- to 120-cm) arching fronds displaying crests at the apex as well as at the tips of the pinnae. Use it as a focal point.

'**Cristata Angustata**' (crested and narrow) with nicely proportioned slender and short fronds is an alternate choice, instead of 'Cristata', for decorating small spaces.

'**Grandiceps**' (with large terminal crests) is so overly crested that it appears to be covered with cheerleader pom-poms.

'**Polydactyla Mapplebeck**' has tapering fronds and pinnae that split into dangling fingers.

'**Revolvens**' has pinnae edges rolled inwards.

'**Stableri**', synonym *Dryopteris* ×*complexa* 'Stableri', is a tall upright cultivar to 4 ft. (1.2 m) presenting parsimonious 3- to 4-in. (7.5- to 10-cm) wide fronds.

'**Stableri Crisped**', synonym *Dryopteris* ×*complexa* 'Stableri Crisped', like 'Stableri', has narrow, upright, slightly arching fronds. It is adorned with and admired for its crisped and ruffled pinnae. Neither cultivar is likely to be confused with others with the possible exception of *Dryopteris filix-mas* 'Barnesii' which is also stiffly erect.

Dryopteris amurensis
Amur wood fern
Synonym *Leptorumohra amurensis*
Epithet means "from the Amur River" in Siberia.
Evergreen, 1 to 2 ft. (30 to 60 cm). Zones 4 to 8.

DESCRIPTION: The rhizome is short-creeping and the major portion of the frond is a tall stipe. Blades are broadly triangular, tripinnate at the base with elongate lower pinnules resulting in basal pinnae resembling lopsided triangles. The whole could masquerade as a *Gymnocarpium*. Sori are medial with a kidney-shaped indusium.

RANGE AND HABITAT: *Dryopteris amurensis* colonizes in high-elevation coniferous forests in Siberia, China, Japan, and Korea.

CULTURE AND COMMENTS: Although described in many reference works, this feather-topped species is not often seen in cultivation. When available it should be extremely cold tolerant and acclimate in a shaded, moist woodland garden where it should not be allowed to dry out. It is not likely to be a suitable choice for areas with hot summer days and nights.

Dryopteris arguta
Coastal wood fern, western wood fern
Epithet means "sharply toothed."
Evergreen, 2 to 3 ft. (60 to 90 cm). Zones 7 to 9.

DESCRIPTION: The rhizome is slowly short-creeping and produces dense clusters of fronds. The short green stipe is edged with brown scales and is about one-fifth of the frond length. The dark green pinnate-pinnatifid blade is lanceolate

Dryopteris arguta is a dependable evergreen Pacific Northwest native for acidic woodlands.

with 17 to 18 pairs of pointed pinnae. The sori with kidney-shaped indusia are medial.

RANGE AND HABITAT: *Dryopteris arguta* grows in open woods from British Columbia to Baja California with a disjunct population in Arizona. It is especially common under the native oak trees in Oregon's Willamette Valley.

CULTURE AND COMMENTS: The species is easily grown in moist acid soil in light shade and is welcome in maritime climates wherever a medium-sized evergreen is appropriate.

Dryopteris ×australis
Dixie wood fern
Dryopteris celsa × D. ludoviciana.
Epithet means "southern."
Semievergreen, 4 to 5 ft. (1.2 to 1.5 m). Zones (4) 5 to 9.

DESCRIPTION: The rhizome is short-creeping and branches modestly. The stipe is one-third of the frond length, and the creamy green, lanceolate blades are pinnate-pinnatifid. There are 16 to 20 pairs of pinnae with the "fertile" upper portions reduced in size and bearing abortive spores.

RANGE AND HABITAT: Like its parents, this fern is native to dampish areas of the southeastern swath of the United States.

The tall *Dryopteris ×australis* in a garden setting. Notice that the upper frond, which houses the abortive spores, narrows abruptly towards the apex.

CULTURE AND COMMENTS: This is a popular, easy, and desirable garden plant that is especially useful as a vertical component in the moist woodland bed. The planting site should be protected from prevailing winds. The foliage reclines but remains green well into winter. Although southern in origin, it is quite hardy in cold regions and adapts to high summer heat locales as well. Young fronds are considered a consumable by untended slug populations, but subsequent growth is more durable and defiant. Until recently this sterile hybrid was propagated only by division, which is still the practical choice for sharing a robust garden specimen with fellow enthusiasts. Since the early 2000s, however, successful tissue culture has brought it to the mass market where it is welcome indeed.

Dryopteris bissetiana
Beaded wood fern
Synonym *Dryopteris varia* var. *setosa*
Epithet is after botanist James Bisset (1843–1911).
Evergreen, 1 to 2 ft. (30 to 60 cm). Zones 5 to 9. Apogamous.

DESCRIPTION: The rhizome is short-creeping and produces a vase of ornamental fronds that are one-third stipe and two-thirds deep green, ovate, bipinnate to tripinnate blades. There are 15 or more pairs of pinnae with the pinnules closest to the rachis on the lowest pair (basiscopic) disproportionately longer than surrounding pinnules. The new growth is lightly and briefly flushed silver and emerges late (sometimes very late) in the spring. The pinnule segments are small and beady. Sori are evenly distributed and covered with kidney-shaped indusia.

RANGE AND HABITAT: Like so many of the truly ornamental dryopteris, this species is from the woodlands of Korea, China, and Japan where it is commonly found from forests to roadsides.

CULTURE AND COMMENTS: While sturdy, this very attractive fern offers lightness to the fern bed. It is easily established in any shaded situation. Over the years it has been confused with closely and not so closely related Japanese species, sometimes *Dryopteris erythrosora* but more often with *D. varia*. Botanists separate them based on two characteristics, one being the color of the stipe scales, which are reddish brown on *D. varia* and black to blackish-brown on *D. bissetiana*. The other distinction is that the upper frond portions of *D. varia* narrow suddenly, whereas those of *D. bissetiana* narrow gradually. Both species are quite handsome.

Dryopteris blanfordii
Blanford's wood fern
Epithet is after British geologist Henry Blanford (1834–1893), who worked in India.
Deciduous, 2 to 2½ ft. (60 to 75 cm). Zones 5 to 8. Apogamous.

DESCRIPTION: The rhizome is ascending and covered with dark scales. The short tan to dark brown, 4-in. (10-cm) stipes bear ovate, brownish black scales decreasing in numbers up into the grooved rachis. The bipinnate blade is lanceolate, tapering to the base with the lowest pinnae about 2 in. (5 cm) long. The sori are on the upper third of the frond's 20 to 30 pairs of pinnae and covered with a kidney-shaped indusium.

RANGE AND HABITAT: This Asian native is found in China, Afghanistan, Pakistan, Tibet, India, and Kashmir in oak forests and ranges up into lower alpine elevations.

CULTURE AND COMMENTS: Blanford's wood fern is quite variable in nature and in the botanical literature. For the gardener, however, it is a handsome, rounded, flat, pale green fern with fronds becoming prostrate with the arrival of frost. Although not fussy, it is best in filtered light and friable compost. Visitors consider the Hardy Fern Foundation's planting at the Rhododendron Species Botanical Garden exceptionally attractive.

Dryopteris bissetiana with its beaded appearance in the Gassner garden.

Relaxed rosette of soft *Dryopteris blanfordii* foliage joins a rhododendron floral display for a spring show.

Dryopteris ×*boottii* in the Lighty garden.

Diagnostically significant basal pinnae with the pinnule gap on *Dryopteris campyloptera*.

"*Dryopteris kashmiriana*" (from Kashmir), synonym *D. cashmiriana*, is a semievergreen, 2 to 3 ft. (60 to 90 cm) from the Himalayan forests. The erect rhizome supports a sturdy crown with fronds radiating in a broad horizontal pinwheel. The stipe, which is one-fourth of the frond length, is tan with contrasting ebony scales that extend well up into the rachis. The blade is lanceolate and bipinnate with 20 to 24 pairs of pinnae tapering towards the base. The sori are close to the midribs and the indusium is kidney-shaped. Christopher Fraser-Jenkins examined a frond from my garden and considers it to be within the normal variation range of *D. blanfordii*. German specialists introduced this to horticulture in the 1990s as a then-undescribed species. This variant accommodates readily in fern-friendly habitats in Zones 6 to 8 and is particularly attractive when the semihorizontal circular fronds are festooned over the silvery contrast of rocks or driftwood.

Dryopteris ×*boottii*
Boott's wood fern
Dryopteris cristata × *D. intermedia.*
Epithet is after William Boott (1805–1887).
Deciduous, 1½ to 2½ ft. (45 to 75 cm). Zones 3 to 8.

DESCRIPTION: The rhizome is short-creeping. The frond's blades are lanceolate and bipinnate on a stipe that is one-quarter to one-third of the frond length. The pinnae are held horizontally as with *D. cristata* and have glandular hairs that resemble minute hatpins, similar to those on the fronds of *D. intermedia.*

RANGE AND HABITAT: For a hybrid, this is relatively common where the two parents grow in tandem in the northeastern and Great Lakes areas of the United States and Canada.

CULTURE AND COMMENTS: This sterile fern is propagated by division and is occasionally available commercially. It is not fussy about soils but is best suited to cold winter climates.

Dryopteris campyloptera
Mountain wood fern
Dryopteris expansa × *D. intermedia.*
Epithet means "curved wing."
Deciduous, 2 ft. (60 cm). Zones 4 to 7 (8).

DESCRIPTION: The rhizome is erect. Stipes with pale scales are usually one-third of the frond length. The blades are thin-textured, triangular, and up to four times gracefully divided with significantly elongated lower pinnules. There is a measurable and significant gap, easily mistaken as missing pinnules, between the rachis and the first lower pinnule on the bottom pinnae. They are fewer in number and much larger than their counterparts on the same pinnae (see photo at left). Sori are medial with a kidney-shaped indusium.

RANGE AND HABITAT: This fertile hybrid is native and common in moist woods from New England to the lower Appalachian Mountains where the range extends predominantly to higher altitudes.

CULTURE AND COMMENTS: With a strong preference for woodlands and cold winters, mountain wood fern is easily established in partial sun or shade. Influenced by its *D. expansa* parent, it will wilt and perform poorly in areas with hot humid summers. It bears a strong resemblance to *D. expansa* but the latter is more upright in habit. It is similar as well to the European *D. dilatata*, which, however, has tan stipe scales with a dark center rather than a monochrome brown.

Dryopteris carthusiana
Spinulose wood fern, toothed wood fern
Synonym *Dryopteris spinulosa*
Epithet is after botanist Johan Cartheuser (1704–1777).
Deciduous, 1½ to 2½ ft. (45 to 75 cm). Zones 2 to 7 (8).

DESCRIPTION: The rhizome is ascending and produces clumps of airy triangular blades on stipes that make up one-third of the frond. The smooth foliage, with 12 to 14 pairs of triangular pinnae, is bipinnate-pinnatifid and lacks glandular hairs. Early deciduous, it colors the Indian summer landscape with an autumnal butter-yellow warmth. Sori with kidney-shaped indusia are evenly distributed on the upper pinnae but sparsely produced on lower pinnae.

RANGE AND HABITAT: This species is cosmopolitan and circumboreal in distribution with populations in the moist mountainous areas of northern North America, the Pyrenees, and the Himalayas. In the eastern United States it is notably promiscuous and produces assorted hybrids that fascinate serious collectors and provide good entertainment and challenging excursions for the "weekend fern warrior."

CULTURE AND COMMENTS: *Dryopteris carthusiana* is one easy-to-grow, adaptable fern although care should be taken to protect its somewhat brittle fronds from wind. Plant it in shade and loamy soil and forget it. It can be confused with *D. dilatata* but the stipe scales are uniformly tan as opposed to the bicolored scales of *D. dilatata*. Field characteristics are also somewhat similar to *D. intermedia*, but the latter bears minute glandular hairs, is evergreen, and has more uniform-sized basal pinnae. A crested form is in cultivation in Europe and may soon be available from fern specialists in the United States.

Dryopteris caucasica
Epithet means "from the Caucasus."
Deciduous, 2 to 3 ft. (60 to 90 cm). Zones 5 to 8.

DESCRIPTION: The rhizome is erect and the fronds are up to 3 ft. (90 cm) with one-third stipe and two-thirds lanceolate bipinnate blades. The 20 to 25 pairs of pinnae are a flat green with double-toothed margins giving a serrate appearance. It is one of the parents of *Dryopteris filix-mas*. Sori are medial with kidney-shaped indusia.

RANGE AND HABITAT: A native of Turkey, Iran, and the Caucasus mountains, this fern appears to be better represented in the literature than in gardens. Don Hackenberry of the Appalachian Wildflower Nursery in Reedsville, Pennsylvania, introduced it to the U.S. trade.

CULTURE AND COMMENTS: This species should be easy in traditional moist woodland settings wherever *D. filix-mas* is grown, although it needs more protection and more moisture during hot weather. It resents transplanting and tends to die down earlier than *D. filix-mas*. In addition it differs in having the indusium remain white until shedding. The dissimilari-

Comparison of lower pinnae on (left to right) *Dryopteris campyloptera*, *D. carthusiana*, and *D. intermedia*, all eastern U.S. natives.

Dryopteris carthusiana in the gardens at the Mount Cuba Center.

ties between the two species are relative and separated by adjectives such as *paler* and *more serrate* and complicated by the fact that *D. filix-mas* is extremely variable. Distinctions are hard to determine without having both in hand.

Dryopteris celsa
Log fern
Dryopteris goldiana × *D. ludoviciana*.
Epithet means "tall, lofty."
Deciduous to semievergreen, 3 to 4½ ft. (90 to 135 cm). Zones 5 to 9.

DESCRIPTION: This hybrid exhibits the shine of *Dryopteris ludoviciana* and the shape, albeit narrower, and cold hardiness of *D. goldiana*. The rhizome is short-creeping and the fronds are one-third stipe and two-thirds ovate-lanceolate pinnate-pinnatifid to almost bipinnate blades. The 15 to 20 pairs of pinnae have medial sori that are covered with kidney-shaped indusia. The fertile pinnae are not contracted.

RANGE AND HABITAT: This fern grows on logs as the common name implies. It is a swamp lover and thrives just above bog line in moist acidic soils from New England to the Gulf states. I find it interesting that the two parents do not currently share a common range. Moran (2004) reports that *D. goldiana* was forced southward by glaciation some 18,000 years ago and hybridization took place at that time. Like the glacier, *D. goldiana* retreated leaving behind the fertile hybrid.

CULTURE AND COMMENTS: This attractive upright fern prefers a site with rich, moist loamy soil (although a swamp is not necessary). It is smaller than its hybrid offspring, *D.* ×*australis*, but offers a comparable upright visual. *Dryopteris celsa* is recommended for its ease of cultivation in both cold and warm climates; however, the equally nondiscriminating slugs find its tender new foliage delicious. Once discouraged they will leave for better feeding grounds, ignoring the sturdier later fronds. The fronds are technically not evergreen but become procumbent and persist photosynthetically well into the arrival and early duration of cold weather. Like many east-

Dryopteris celsa in the Thyrum garden. Note the gradual taper of the frond tips.

ern North American native dryopteris, it hybridizes with its genetic companions.

Dryopteris championii
Champion's wood fern
Synonym *Dryopteris championi*
Epithet is after British botanist John George Champion (1815–1854), who brought samples of 500 to 600 plant species from Hong Kong to England, thus putting an end to the myth that Hong Kong was a barren rock island.
Evergreen, 2 to 3 ft. (60 to 90 cm). Zones 5 to 9. Apogamous.

DESCRIPTION: The rhizome is erect and supports sparsely produced, airy, ovate, brilliant green bipinnate blades. The 12 to 14 pairs of pinnae are widely separated with the lowest pair thrusting sharply downwards. The greenish stipes with reddish brown scales are one-half of the frond length. The sori are at the ends of veins near the margins and covered with a kidney-shaped indusium.

RANGE AND HABITAT: In nature this species grows in forests in China, Japan, and Korea.

CULTURE AND COMMENTS: With its lacquered upright wintergreen foliage, this fern is truly a highly recommended champion. Look for fronds that persist and sparkle through snowy or dreary gray days of winter as well as the contrasting sultry days of summer. The showy young crosiers are tem-

Dryopteris championii presents its elegant display of late-emerging but superb foliage.

porarily fleeced with juvenile silver hairs, and, be very aware, are among the very last to appear late in the spring. Give it light shade and humus in the section of the garden that can be admired through frosted winter windows and summer garden strolls.

Dryopteris chinensis
Synonym *Dryopteris subtripinnata*
Epithet means "from China."
Deciduous, 1 to 1½ ft. (30 to 45 cm). Zones 5 to 8. Apogamous.

DESCRIPTION: The rhizome is short-creeping to ascending, holding small fronds that are one-half scaly, green stipes and one-half triangular, basally tripinnate blades. The stalked lower pinnae are ovate while the remainder, also stalked, are lanceolate. The sori are small, submarginal, and covered with a kidney-shaped indusium.

RANGE AND HABITAT: This species grows on the forest floor as well as on walls in Manchuria, Korea, China, and Japan.

CULTURE AND COMMENTS: While cultivated in European gardens, this delicate fern is rarely available commercially in the United States. It should make an airy underplanting for weighty, evergreen broadleaved shrubs.

Dryopteris clintoniana
Clinton's wood fern
Dryopteris cristata × *D. goldiana.*
Epithet is after George William Clinton (1807–1885).
Deciduous to semievergreen, 2½ to 3½ ft. (75 to 105 cm). Zones 3 to 8. Dimorphic.

DESCRIPTION: This hybrid leans towards *Dryopteris cristata* in appearance with broadly triangular lower pinnae but without the strongly horizontal pinnae habit. The deciduous fertile fronds are narrowly lanceolate, pinnate-pinnatifid to 3 ft. (90 cm), and the sterile fronds, with 14 to 16 pairs of pinnae, are evergreen and smaller. The rhizome is short-creeping and the stipes are one-third to one-half of the frond length. The sori are medial and the indusium kidney-shaped.

RANGE AND HABITAT: Clinton's wood fern is endemic to North America, sweeping across the wetlands of the northeastern United States and Canada. It is one of the most promiscuous of the so-inclined native dryopteris and is involved in the parentage of six hybrids.

CULTURE AND COMMENTS: Here is a comely fern that performs reliably in cold winter sites as well as warm summer habitats. The upright fronds are stiff and brittle, however, so protect them from wind as well as the peregrinations of local squirrels and your neighbors' dogs.

Dryopteris ×*complexa*
Dryopteris affinis × *D. filix-mas.*
Epithet means "circled, encircled."
Evergreen, 2 to 4 ft. (60 to 120 cm). Zones 4 to 8. Apogamous.

DESCRIPTION: This fertile hybrid has an ascending rhizome and massive upright fronds. The heavily scaled stipes of one-fourth of the frond length are topped with lanceolate, pinnate-pinnatifid to bipinnate blades. The sori are close to the midribs and covered with kidney-shaped indusia.

RANGE AND HABITAT: This is a woodlander from Europe and Asia.

CULTURE AND COMMENTS: The rusty-scaled new crosiers provide a dramatic springtime show, and the massive mature massif adds reliable year-round substance to the garden design. Its bushy habit makes this useful for screening as well as a statuesque single specimen. It is not particular about soil or site and once established is quite drought tolerant. There are several widely distributed cultivars. All are exceptionally cold tolerant and all come true from spores.

'Robust' is, as the name implies, very vigorous indeed and at 5 ft. (1.5 m) high and up to 7 ft. (2.1 m) across is a majestic display. It has been in the trade as 'Robusta' and 'Undulata Robusta'. By whatever name, this exuberant fern is one of the all-time bests for the landscape; a year-round reliable centerpiece.

Dryopteris clintoniana is a dependable upright especially for gardens in cold climates.

Dryopteris ×*complexa* 'Robust' with its magnificent height and spread is one of the most outstanding and dependable evergreens for gardens everywhere.

Dryopteris conjugata

Epithet means "joined together in pairs."
Evergreen, 2 to 3 ft. (60 to 90 cm). Zones 6 to 8.

DESCRIPTION: The rhizome is erect. The stipes are one-quarter of the frond length and are splashed with dark russet scales that extend up the rachis. The blades are lanceolate and once-pinnate with up to 40 pairs of narrowly lobed pinnae. The sori hug the midribs and are covered with kidney-shaped indusia.

RANGE AND HABITAT: This species has been introduced to cultivation from the Himalayas and China where it grows in dark forests and on wooded slopes.

CULTURE AND COMMENTS: Although grown for some time in Europe and Britain, this dark and quietly refined species is just now (2003–05) being introduced in the United States. It is easily nurtured in the Pacific Northwest and I definitely recommend it for testing and display in areas with greater variances in weather. It and a number of other Asian garden ornamentals are very similar. It is botanically significant that the lowest pair of pinnae do not point downwards (see photo below).

Dryopteris corleyi

Dryopteris aemula × *D. oreades* (the latter is also a parent of *D. filix-mas*).
Epithet is after British botanist Hugh Corley.
Semievergreen, 2 ft. (60 cm). Zones 8 and 9.

DESCRIPTION: The rhizome is ascending with fronds that are equal parts slightly scaly, tan to green stipe and lanceolate to narrowly triangular blade. The blade is bipinnate with 20 to 24 pairs of pinnae. The sori are medial and covered with kidney-shaped indusia. The overlapping genetic influence of *D. oreades* is displayed in the pinnae which are similar to those of *D. filix-mas*. The blade shape, however, differs from *D. filix-mas*, which narrows at the base while *D. corleyi* does not taper.

RANGE AND HABITAT: Only described in 1982, this species is exclusively Spanish and prefers acid soil in humid areas near the Atlantic Coast.

CULTURE AND COMMENTS: I have grown this for a number of years and do not find it particularly distinctive. It is, however, a problem-free selection and useful for those keeping a run-ning tally of numbers of ferns in the garden's collection. Tuck it under a shrub.

Dryopteris crassirhizoma

Thick-stemmed wood fern
Synonym *Dryopteris buschiana*
Epithet means "thick rhizome."
Evergreen, 2 to 3 ft. (60 to 90 cm). Zones 4 to 8.

DESCRIPTION: The rhizome is stout and erect. "Massive" is the universal buzzword for the crown, which will produce an occasional offshoot. At 4 in. (10 cm), the stipes are short with margins and undersides decorated with ¾ in. (2-cm) scales of polished tan. The elongate, pinnate-pinnatifid to bipinnate blades are lanceolate with 20 to 30 pairs of pinnae. Pinnules have crenate margins. The entire mass becomes winter procumbent with the arrival of early frosts. The sori with kidney-shaped indusia are medial on the upper portions of the blade.

RANGE AND HABITAT: Widespread in Northeast Asia including Siberia and Japan, it colonizes in humusy forestlands.

CULTURE AND COMMENTS: With circles of stately glowing foliage, this is an exceptional and highly recommended choice for fern furnishings in light shade and average loamy soil. The new growth puts in an early spring appearance and may need

Dryopteris conjugata

Comparison of the lower pinnae on the very similar fronds of (left to right) *Dryopteris conjugata, D. cycadina, D. namegatae, D. pycnopteroides,* and *D. stenolepis.*

emergency protection in the event of late frosts. Growers in warm summer areas will be pleased to know that this species adjusts to heat as well as cold.

Dryopteris crispifolia

Epithet means "wavy foliage."

Evergreen, 1½ to 2½ ft. (45 to 75 cm). Zones 6 (with protection) to 9.

DESCRIPTION: The rhizome is short-creeping and over a long period of time will produce a number of modest crowns. The green stipe with an occasional tan scale is one-third to one-half the length of the frond. The beauty of this species is in the triangular blades with their sparkling spun-glass-green tripinnate to quadripinnate crispy foliage. There are about a dozen pairs of pinnae with the lower ones elongate lopsided triangles. In cultivation the spores are produced only reluctantly on sori that are medial and covered with a kidney-shaped indusium.

RANGE AND HABITAT: This species is endemic to the Azores and has demonstrated remarkable hardiness in the temperate Pacific Northwest through 10°F (-12°C) winters and rare (and unwelcome) 90°F (32°C) droughty summers.

CULTURE AND COMMENTS: With bright green fronds born on a procumbent plane, this is a cheerful accent for the mixed

Dryopteris crassirhizoma unfurling in early spring.

Imposing mature specimen of *Dryopteris crassirhizoma.*

Dryopteris corleyi

Late afternoon light highlights the dense foliage on *Dryopteris crassirhizoma.*

shady fern and floral bed. It is similar in dissection to *Dryopteris dilatata* 'Crispa Whiteside' but without the attendant attraction to leaf hoppers. Easy of cultivation, give it the typical fern blend of light shade and humusy soil.

Dryopteris cristata
Crested wood fern
Epithet means "crested," a totally incorrect description.
Deciduous to evergreen, 2 ft. (60 cm). Zones 3 to 8.

DESCRIPTION: Contrary to the name bestowed by Carl Linnaeus (1707–1778), this is not a crested fern. The erect fronds, which emerge from a short-creeping rhizome, are about one-third lightly scaly stipe and two-thirds pinnate-pinnatifid, bluish green, narrowly lanceolate blades. The slightly triangular pinnae, which are held parallel to the ground in an open venetian blind fashion, give this species a unique profile (and the photographer a challenge). Fertile fronds are erect and deciduous, while the low sterile fronds are arching and usually evergreen. The sori are medial and have a kidney-shaped indusium.

RANGE AND HABITAT: This species is native across northern, midwestern, and eastern North America as well as Britain (where it is extremely rare), Central and Northern Europe, including Russia extending eastward to Siberia. It grows naturally in wetlands, meadows, and moist forested areas.

CULTURE AND COMMENTS: Commonly and easily cultivated in the eastern United States and comparable climates in British and continental gardens, this fern prefers consistently damp sites and rich soil. With its unusual profile, it is a worthy and welcome addition wherever visual variation is desired. The young fronds are subject to breakage, however, and benefit from respectful protection. The plant does not do well in Louisville, Kentucky, style heated summers, wilting even when well watered. Likewise, it shuns attempts at cultivation in coastal gardens in the U.S. West, gradually diminishing in size until it is no more. There are a number of hybrids which can confuse matters in the field.

Dryopteris cycadina
Shaggy shield fern, shaggy wood fern
Epithet means "like a cycad."
Evergreen, 2 to 3 ft. (60 to 90 cm). Zones 5 to 8. Apogamous.

DESCRIPTION: The rhizome is short-creeping. The green stipes are about one-third of the frond length and are covered

Rotund epimediums provide a foil for the "crispy" foliage of *Dryopteris crispifolia*.

Bogside planting of *Dryopteris cristata* in the Stuart garden.

with dark scales that are especially prominent on the young crosiers. The once-pinnate blades are lanceolate with 20 to 30 pairs of pinnae universally described as leathery and serrate. It is of diagnostic significance that the lower pinnae point strongly downwards and backwards (see photo at left on page 220). The midrib on each pinna is grooved and appears as a contrasting black stripe. The sori are adjacent to the midribs and covered with a kidney-shaped indusium.

RANGE AND HABITAT: The shaggy wood fern grows in dark forests, often streamside, from 5000 to 8000 ft. (1500 to 2400 m) in Japan, southeastern China, and Taiwan.

CULTURE AND COMMENTS: Growing as a symmetrical fountain of fronds, this two-toned bright-green-and-black duet is a natural beauty in shade and normal, humus-rich fern soil. I find that the blackish new growth provides a welcome visual

Dryopteris cycadina and azaleas—a spring portrait.

contrast as a backdrop for pastel spring flowers. The species is accommodating and readily available throughout the United States and Europe. For many years it has been frequently, and incorrectly, marketed as _Dryopteris atrata_, a tender native of southern India and lower altitudes in the East Himalayas. There are, however, a number of closely allied Asian species that share a similar skeletal structure and offer ornamental promise to woodland gardeners.

Dryopteris cystolepidota

Synonyms _Dryopteris nipponensis, D. erythrosora_ var. _dilatata_
Epithet means "pouched scales."
Evergreen, 2 ft. (60 cm). Zones 6 to 8. Apogamous.

DESCRIPTION: The rhizome is short-creeping and the fronds tapering at their tips are usually up to 2 ft. (60 cm) tall. The broadly triangular, shiny, basally tripinnate blades can be briefly red tinged in new growth and are supported by foot-long (30-cm) stipes. The 8 to 12 pairs of pinnae have medial sori covered by a kidney-shaped indusium. For technical confirmation check the lowest pinnae, which has a short pinnule next to the rachis and a longer second pinnule.

RANGE AND HABITAT: This species is from Japan and Korea where it grows in the composting duff of the forest floor.

CULTURE AND COMMENTS: Easily grown in light shade to partial sun and strangely overlooked in nurseries, this is a reliable and sturdily dependable selection for gardens wherever its colleague _Dryopteris erythrosora_ succeeds. The fronds fan in lax upward arches. My plants have been faithfully drought tolerant and evergreen. There is, and has been, confusion regarding the botanical placement of this species with some authorities preferring the designation _D. nipponensis_.

Dryopteris decipiens

Epithet means "deceptive."
Deciduous to evergreen (winter cold dependent), 1 to 1½ ft. (30 to 45 cm). Zones 5 to 8. Apogamous.

DESCRIPTION: The rhizome forms an erect crown. Spare rosettes of blunt-tipped, pinnate-pinnatifid fronds, with a silky opalescent pink glow, grow shyly. The short, grooved stipes are usually less than one-fourth of the frond length. There are 15 to 20 pairs of pinnae with the lower pair flaring forward and downwards. Spores are produced reluctantly on medial sori.

RANGE AND HABITAT: A fern of lowland forests, this species is found in Japan, China, and Taiwan.

CULTURE AND COMMENTS: _Dryopteris decipiens_ is a lovely and very choice low-growing selection for the woodland foreground where it will tolerate drought, but prefers enriched, moist acid compost. The unfurling fronds are a soft satin rose with a unique silvery patina, giving the species a subdued elegance that persists throughout the season. It grows slowly in the garden, and even more slowly from spores, making it unprofitable for mass marketers. Look for it instead in the catalogs of specialized nurseries devoted to providing gardens and gardeners with temperate, ornamental ferns.

Dryopteris cystolepidota at the Rhododendron Species Botanical Garden.

A *Dryopteris decipiens* frond with its characteristic soft silvery patina.

Dryopteris dickinsii in the Nittritz garden.

Dryopteris dickinsii

Epithet is after Frederick V. Dickins (1838–1915).

Evergreen, 1½ to 2 ft. (45 to 60 cm). Zones 6 to 8. Apogamous.

DESCRIPTION: The rhizome is short and erect. The grooved stipes are one-quarter of the frond length with small scales, usually brownish. The once-pinnate narrow blades are a refreshing light green and have shallowly scalloped pinnae. The lowest pinnae pair is shorter and inclined slightly downwards. The sori are submarginal and covered with a kidney-shaped indusium.

RANGE AND HABITAT: *Dryopteris dickinsii* grows in the moist forestlands of Japan, China, Taiwan, and India where it is rare.

CULTURE AND COMMENTS: Here is a pleasant small to medium-sized fern that adapts easily to and brightens the average woodland habitat.

Dryopteris dickinsii 'Crispa' with the airy flowers of *Brunnera macrophylla* 'Langtrees'.

'**Crispa**' (curled) is smaller and even more attractive with flowing wavy margins and a more horizontal presentation.

'**Incisum**' (cut) has pinnae cut ¼ in. (6 mm) or more. It is occasionally referenced as *Dryopteris kiyotensis* and is a welcome variant for the enrichment of a collection.

Dryopteris dilatata
Broad wood fern, broad buckler fern
Synonym *Dryopteris austriaca*
Epithet means "dilated, expanded."
Deciduous to subevergreen, 2½ to 4 ft. (75 to 120 cm). Zones 4 to 8.

DESCRIPTION: The rhizome is erect and produces an occasional offshoot. The frond blades are broadly triangular and tripinnate with the lower pinnules, adjacent to the rachis, greatly enlarged on the lowest pinnae. The stipes are one-third of the frond, grooved and distinguished from many other dryopteris by their scales that are bicolored with dark centers framed by light brown borders. The 12 to 15 pairs of triangular pinnae bear sori that are medial and covered with a kidney-shaped indusium.

RANGE AND HABITAT: This variable species is quite cosmopolitan in Europe and areas of Asia. Once upon a time the nomenclatural botanical umbrella encompassed the North American *Dryopteris expansa* as well. In nature D. *dilatata* has a strong preference for acidic sites.

CULTURE AND COMMENTS: This vigorous addition to the low-maintenance cool woodland will return faithfully in the ignored corner especially when encouraged by acidic conditions. It grows poorly in areas with extended hot humid summers. There are passels of varieties, many of which are far more handsome than the type. All, however, are susceptible to the disfiguration of leaf hopper and/or thrip damage.

'**Crispa Whiteside**' is an especially ornamental selection with crisped pinnae on a broadly based elongated pyramid of foliage.

'**Cristata**' is, as the name implies, crested at the tips of the frond and pinnae.

'**Grandiceps**' (with large terminal crests) has a "grand head" of heavily divided terminal and pinnae crests.

'**Jimmy Dyce**' is a low-growing 1 to 1½ ft. (30 to 45 cm) blue-green, ornamental evergreen, triangular cultivar.

Dryopteris dickinsii 'Incisum' in the Gassner garden.

Dryopteris dilatata surrounded by *Alchemilla*.

Dryopteris dilatata 'Crispa Whiteside'

Dryopteris dilatata 'Jimmy Dyce'

'Lepidota' is a finely divided filigree of medium height (2 ft. [60 cm]). The pinnae are a refreshing bright emerald-green and the stipes with their brown scales make this a highly recommended companion for russet indumentum-clad rhodies. 'Lepidota Cristata' is minutely crested.

'Recurved Form', also known as 'Recurvata', is unusual in having the pinnae rolled inwards. The fronds arc forest-green.

'Stansfieldii' is an extremely rare cultivar that was part of the collection brought from Britain to British Columbia, Canada, by British fern expert F. Wiper in the late 1800s. Following his passing, it was subsequently rescued from extinction by the alert attention of the late British Columbia plant expert, Don Armstrong. It is beautiful as is its close cousin *Dryopteris dilatata* 'Lepidota' from which it can be distinguished by its thickened wavy pinnae.

Dryopteris erythrosora
Autumn fern
Epithet means "red sori."

Evergreen, 2 to 3 ft. (60 to 90 cm). Zones (5) 6 to 9. Apogamous.

DESCRIPTION: The rhizome is short-creeping and produces a bountiful spring crop of remarkable red-stemmed and red-foliaged fronds. The frond is one-half stipe with an equal portion of broad, shiny, bipinnate, triangular blades with upwards of 10 pairs of pinnae. In time they fade from their coppery-red spring glory to a most acceptable glossy summer green, interrupted pleasantly on occasion by the arrival of a contrasting rosy autumn-colored new frond. The sori, of the botanical *erythro* (red), *sora* (sori), are indeed covered by bright red indusia, which yields to a traditional brown as the spores mature and depart.

RANGE AND HABITAT: A native of Japan, China, Korea and the Philippines, autumn fern is common in their temperate forests.

CULTURE AND COMMENTS: This is THE species that inspired my interest in cultivation, propagation, and immersion in the wonderful world of ferns. (That was close to 40 years ago when, amazingly by today's market standards, it was unavailable commercially.) My admiration endures and I still hold it in my highest esteem for its universal adaptability and brilliant contribution to the garden's panorama. It is a top-10 recommendation for beginners and experts alike. Once established, the plant is drought tolerant. The evergreen winter

Dryopteris dilatata 'Lepidota Cristata'

Dryopteris dilatata 'Recurved Form' in the Kennar garden.

fronds remain cheerful and upright and put on a spectacular show when reaching above winter snows.

Autumn fern is variable, and specialty nurseries occasionally offer a number of equally attractive options. These include a dwarf form that has all of the appealing characteristics of the parent but matures at 18 in. (45 cm) at best.

'**Brilliance**' is a selection with especially bright, orange-toned, longer lasting color, and white to pale green rather than red indusia.

'**Gracilis**' (slender) is grown in Europe and is similar in structure to 'Prolifica' but without any inclination to produce bulbils. It does, however, come true from spores.

'**Prolifica**' is a finely cut, smaller version of the parent with propagable bulbils appearing sporadically along the rachis. The bulbils are more likely to be produced when the plant is slightly stressed (inducing survival?). To propagate simply and reliably, prick off the bulbils and incubate them in the comfort of a moist greenhouse enclosure or, as previously described, in pots capped with inverted clear plastic cups. Sporelings are consistently attractive, but not always bulbiferous.

'**Prolifica Whirly Top**' is a dwarf, 6- to 12-in. (15- to 30-cm) extremely congested sport which does bear bulbils.

Dryopteris expansa
Northern wood fern, alpine buckler fern
Synonyms *Dryopteris assimilis, D. dilatata* var. *alpina*
Epithet means "expanded."
Deciduous, 1½ to 2½ ft. (45 to 75 cm). Zones 3 to 8.

DESCRIPTION: The rhizome is erect, supporting upwardly tending sprays of fronds with one-third being grooved stipes. The scattered basal scales are brown with a darker stripe. The blade is broadly triangular-ovate, tripinnate-pinnatifid, and a pale, thin-textured green. There are 12 or more pairs of trian-

Ripe spores with their red characteristic on *Dryopteris erythrosora*.

Coppery red "autumn" spring fronds on *Dryopteris erythrosora* in the Kennar garden.

gular pinnae with the lower pinnules on the lower pinnae "expanded" to twice the size of the corresponding upper pinnules. The characteristic is repeated in its offspring, *Dryopteris campyloptera*. The sori are medial and enclosed in a kidney-shaped indusium.

RANGE AND HABITAT: The northern wood fern has a strong preference for moist acidic soils and grows throughout the north temperate areas of North America, Europe, and Asia.

CULTURE AND COMMENTS: This species, along with *Dryopteris intermedia*, is a parent of *D. campyloptera* and is difficult, at best, to distinguish in the field where their range overlaps. (*Flora of North America* [1993] recommends counting chromosomes.) It is also challenging to the patience of the casual observer to differentiate it from *D. dilatata* with the latter being tripinnate rather than tripinnate-pinnatifid at the base. It is an easy garden plant for moist cool climates but does not do well in warmer areas, wilting even when well watered. Although deciduous, the fronds persist well into the frost season. I have always dismissed it as acceptable woodland filler until I met the stunning, black-stemmed Norwegian cultivar (and Scandinavia's only endemic) **D. expansa var. willeana** in several German gardens. Here is a showpiece ready to be prominently displayed among the best of the best. Like the type the leafage is airy but a chartreuse green perched in elegant contrast on shining black stems that in turn are decorated with pale brown scales.

The select *Dryopteris erythrosora* 'Brilliance'.

A comparison of *Dryopteris erythrosora* 'Prolifica' wth its typical skeletal form (left) and *D. erythrosora* with its substantial contours (right).

The native woodlander *Dryopteris expansa* in a coastal Washington habitat.

Dryopteris filix-mas in Pennsylvania.

Dryopteris filix-mas 'Barnesii' gives a ruffled show.

Ornate foliage of *Dryopteris filix-mas* 'Crispa Cristata' in the Schieber garden.

Dryopteris filix-mas
Male fern

Dryopteris caucasica × *D. oreades*.

Epithet means "male fern," a name applied by the Greeks because of the fern's robust masculine character. (We ladies get the supposedly delicate *Athyrium filix-femina*.)

Deciduous, 2 to 4 ft. (60 to 120 cm). Zones 4 to 8.

DESCRIPTION: Stout erect rhizomes support bouquets of fronds with dull green pinnate-pinnatifid blades and tan grooved stipes that are one-quarter to occasionally one-third of the frond length. They are sparsely trimmed with a unique mixture of light to reddish brown scales and hairs. The pinnate-pinnatifid lanceolate blades with 15 to 30 pairs of pinnae taper at the base. The sori are medial and covered by a kidney-shaped indusium. This fertile hybrid is easily confused with *D. affinis*, with the most obvious difference being that *D. affinis* is evergreen to semievergreen and *D. filix-mas* is deciduous. A less obvious difference is that *D. affinis* has a small black dot on the pinnae underpinnings at the juncture with the rachis and *D. filix-mas* does not.

RANGE AND HABITAT: This is a hugely common fern in Europe where it grows at will in assorted habitats. In North America there are two distinct types with natives from western areas resembling the Europeans and the rare eastern plants choosing a limestone habitat instead. Its range extends to parts of Africa as well as most of Asia.

CULTURE AND COMMENTS: The common form can be planted and neglected and will faithfully reappear year after year. Fern author Martin Rickard (2000) suggests using it in dark difficult sites such as "perhaps near the compost heap or site of the dust bin." I hasten to add that he likes the fern. Being readily available, this fern has a long association with herbal medicine. (It is the only fern ever included in U.S. Pharmacopoeia.) Although recommended for a plethora of ailments, the most popular application, dating back to 300 B.C., was to use an extract from the rhizome as a vermifuge specifically for tapeworm (an act of faith as an incorrect dosage was likely to be fatal). Like many of its European colleagues, it has a large number of popular varieties. As with other *Dryopteris* cultivars, these require precautions in sites that are subject to invasions from leafhoppers and thrips.

'Barnesii' is a strongly vertical, very narrow, 3- to 4-ft. (90- to 120-cm) drought-tolerant, distinctive specimen plant.

'Crispa Cristata' (curled, crested) is a 2-footer (60 cm) with linear, crested, wavy pinnae and a mop of fringed green tassels atop the frond apices.

'Crispatissima' (much curled), a crumpled 1-ft. (30-cm), bushy, upright dwarf with pinnae margins twisted and scrunched, is best used as a specimen in a formal planting.

Cristata Group includes cultivars with varying degrees of cresting throughout the fronds. 'Cristata Jackson' is a solid 2- to 3-footer (60 to 90 cm) with flattened, one-dimensional crests on both pinnae and frond apices. 'Cristata Martindale' has upward-curving pinnae, long terminal tassels at the frond apices, and smaller crestings at the pinnae tips.

'Decomposita' (exceptionally divided) has fronds that are bipinnate-pinnatifid and structurally finer than the type.

'**Grandiceps**' (with large terminal crests) has weighty, branching terminal crests and smaller crests at the pinnae tips.

'**Linearis**' (linear), a 2- to 3-ft. (60- to 90-cm) tall delicacy with finely slender, narrow pinnae, gives grace to its heavily weighted crested compatriots and is every bit as sturdy a survivor in the landscape.

'**Linearis Congesta**', usually about 1 ft. (30 cm) tall, has compressed linear fronds and is a logical choice for the foreground in a formal garden setting.

'**Linearis Polydactyla**' is many fingered at the frond tips (as implied by the botanically descriptive "Polydactyla") and lightly crested on the narrow linear pinnae. It is one of the most commonly available cultivars.

'**Parsley**' is a newer and lower growing cultivar with a height of 18 to 24 in. (45 to 60 cm) and unusual variable but crested foliage.

Dryopteris formosana
Formosan wood fern
Epithet means "from Formosa."
Evergreen (or at least tardily deciduous in colder areas), 1½ to 2 ft. (45 to 60 cm). Zones 6 to 9. Apogamous.

DESCRIPTION: The rhizome is erect and supports a grooved, dark brown-scaled, long stipe equal to about one-half of the frond length. The markedly pentagonal, lustrous, tripinnate blades are displayed on a horizontal plane (unusual for a *Dryopteris*). They are noted for the exceptionally elongated first and second lower pinnules that point earthwards like downward daggers from the lowest pinnae. Pairs of pinnae are few, usually less than a dozen, and the sori are medial with a kidney-shaped indusium.

RANGE AND HABITAT: This species is a native of forested areas in Japan and Taiwan.

CULTURE AND COMMENTS: Often overlooked, this impressively drought-tolerant, easily cultivated fern offers a pleasant golden-green sheen in average soil and exposure in the woodland composition. The new growth usually emerges very late in the season, but when it appears your patience will be rewarded with bright and broad contrasts to darker shadelanders.

Dryopteris fragrans
Fragrant cliff fern
Epithet means "fragrant."
Evergreen, 6 to 10 in. (15 to 25 cm) tall by 2 in. (5 cm) wide. Zones 3 to 8.

Tassels on *Dryopteris filix-mas* 'Cristata Martindale' in the Bradner garden.

A frond of *Dryopteris formosana*. Note the extended lower pinnules.

Crisped and crested foliage of *Dryopteris filix-mas* 'Parsley' in the Schieber garden.

DESCRIPTION: The rhizome is noticeably stout in proportion to the size of this small plant, and the stubby bases of the spent fronds are persistent. The frond stipes are less than one-quarter of the frond length and densely clothed in brown scales. The narrow blade is pinnate-pinnatifid to bipinnate and glandular, giving off a fragrance consistently described in various floral terms ranging from violet to raspberry and less flatteringly as "distinctive." It is abundantly fertile with medial sori that are covered by a kidney-shaped indusium.

RANGE AND HABITAT: Here is a truly northern species with a native habitat spreading across the extremes from north temperate to arctic areas. It prefers well-drained rocky screes often enriched with, but not requiring, limestone.

CULTURE AND COMMENTS: This species is particular and fussy in adapting to a lowland habitat. Like many alpines it can be co-

The dwarf alpine *Dryopteris fragrans* in its preferred setting among rocks.

erced into cultivation in the cool garden community given a rocky niche and that magical ingredient, drainage. It will not do in warm or humid climates in spite of the best of efforts. Where acclimated, it is also a handsome upright sprig among the buns in the alpine-oriented trough or scree. It is used for making tea in Russia and Alaska, so if all else fails, steep a frond or two to impress your fern-minded friends. In overall appearance this species can easily be mistaken for one of the lower growing woodsias. Look for the tufted and persistent stipe bases, the kidney-shaped indusium, and the evergreen inclination as distinguishing features of *Dryopteris fragrans*. By contrast the deciduous woodsias with their embedded sori wrapped in an origami star-shaped indusium are early to bed and early to rise.

Var. *remotiuscula* is easier to grow and larger in all of its dimensions than the type. It is highly recommended horticulturally although not always acknowledged as botanically distinct.

Dryopteris gamblei
Synonym *Dryopteris darjeelingensis*
Epithet is after James Sykes Gamble of the United Kingdom and India.
Evergreen, 3 ft. (90 cm). Zones 7 to 9.

DESCRIPTION: The rhizome is erect. Stipes are one-third to one-half the length of the frond and darkened at the base with a mass of sooty scales. The blades are lanceolate and once-pinnate with 15 to 20 pairs of pointed, slightly lobed pinnae. The lowest pinnae are 4 in. (10 cm) long and veer slightly forward. The medial sori are covered with a kidney-shaped indusium.

RANGE AND HABITAT: This species is native to forested areas throughout Asia.

CULTURE AND COMMENTS: Visually and botanically *Dryopteris gamblei* is related to a large and interesting group of once-pinnate evergreens that are undemanding in the garden. Although tall, the fronds are produced sparingly with a crown of perhaps three to four annually. Use it as a backdrop in moist woodlands.

Dryopteris goldiana
Goldie's wood fern
Epithet is after Scottish botanist John Goldie (1793–1886), who discovered the fern while visiting America.
Deciduous, 3 to 4 ft. (90 to 120 cm). Zones 3 to 8.

DESCRIPTION: The ascending rhizome is stout and supports dark-scaled, grooved stipes one-third the length of the frond. The broadly ovate blades, in variable shades from bluish green to light pastel green tints, are bipinnate and abruptly contracted at the apex giving the frond a stubby tip. There are 15 to 20 pairs of long pinnae. The sori are close to the midvein and covered with a kidney-shaped indusium.

RANGE AND HABITAT: Goldie's fern grows in moist woods throughout eastern Canada and the United States although it is endangered in several states.

CULTURE AND COMMENTS: One of the tallest, broadest, and handsomest of East Coast North American natives, it is prized in eastern gardens and suitable for cultivation in a wide range of temperature variables. In the West our ever-alert slugs are attracted to the juvenile foliage of this foreigner so precautions must be in place by early spring. Otherwise it is a fine specimen for light shade and consistently moist soil. This species hybridizes freely (see *D. celsa* and *D. clintoniana*), with the fertile offspring being recognizable by their dark scales and large blades. It has a unique niche in fern genetics as one of the parents along with *Polystichum lonchitis* of the exceedingly rare bigeneric, *Dryostichum ×singulare*, discovered by Florence and the late Herb Wagner of Michigan.

Dryopteris hondoensis
Epithet means "from Hondo," a city in Japan.
Evergreen, 2 ft. (60 cm). Zones 4 to 8. Apogamous.

DESCRIPTION: The rhizome is ascending to short-creeping. The crown bears fronds that are one-third sparingly scaly stipes supporting ovate, bipinnate to bipinnate-pinnatifid lustrous blades with up to 15 pairs of pinnae. The sori are medial and covered with a kidney-shaped indusium.

RANGE AND HABITAT: This is native to moist forested areas in Japan, China, and Korea.

CULTURE AND COMMENTS: *Dryopteris hondoensis* is smaller but visually similar to a green *D. erythrosora* and readily confused in the trade as well as the garden. It can be distinguished (with great difficulty) by its stalked pinnae and pinnules (Hoshizaki and Moran 2001). It is easy to cultivate in typical woodland habitats and recommended for its cold tolerance.

Forma *rubisora* has reddish indusia.

Dryopteris indusiata
Synonym *Dryopteris labordei* var. *indusiata*
Epithet means "possessing indusium."
Evergreen, 2 ft. (60 cm). Zones 6 to 9. Apogamous.

DESCRIPTION: The rhizome is erect and the fronds are one-half stipe with a triangular bipinnate blade growing on a horizontal plane. The lowest of 12 to 18 pairs of pinnae point forward like swallow's tails. Sori are medial and covered by a kidney-shaped indusium.

Dryopteris goldiana with its abruptly contracted frond apices.

RANGE AND HABITAT: This fern grows in forests in the warm regions of Japan and Taiwan.

CULTURE AND COMMENTS: With bright polished apple-green foliage this adaptable species offers highlights in dusky, dark communities. It adjusts in lean soils and shines even with minimal watering and benign neglect.

Dryopteris intermedia
Fancy fern, evergreen wood fern, glandular wood fern
Synonym *Dryopteris spinulosa* var. *intermedia*
Epithet means "intermediate," presumably between *D. carthusiana* and *D. campyloptera*.
Evergreen, 1½ to 3 ft. (45 to 90 cm). Zones 3 to 8.

Crocus surround the evergreen fronds of *Dryopteris indusiata* in spring in the mild Pacific Northwest climate.

Dryopteris intermedia in the Scott garden.

Saturated rusty red foliage of *Dryopteris koidzumiana.*

DESCRIPTION: The erect rhizome sports a loose bundle of arching fronds with one-third grooved tan-scaled, green stipes and two-thirds thin-textured bipinnate to tripinnate ovate blades. The soft blue-green foliage with 12 to 14 pairs of pinnae is covered, especially on the undersides, with fine hairs tipped with round glands looking like Lilliputian hatpins. (A hand lens is helpful here.) Of additional diagnostic significance the lower, innermost pinnules on the lowest pinnae are smaller than their adjacent counterparts (see upper photo on page 217). The sori are medial and covered with a kidney-shaped indusium.

RANGE AND HABITAT: This species is abundant in acid to neutral soils from moist woods and sandstone substrates to rocky slopes in northern and eastern North America as well as the mountains of the Southeast. The range extends westward to Tennessee, Kentucky, and eastern Missouri. It is especially common in moist and rocky hardwood habitats.

CULTURE AND COMMENTS: Readily available, this lacy specimen is recommended as an easily grown all-purpose addition to cold temperate gardens where it fits with ease into the shady to somewhat sunny woodlands. Hikers and gardeners especially welcome the evergreen foliage during the drab days of endless East Coast winters. It is not for Zone 9 to 10 climates. This is one of the most promiscuous of the dryopteris and the progeny carry the characteristic glandular hairs.

Subsp. *maderensis*, a more delicate type from the Atlantic Islands, is cultivated in Europe.

Dryopteris juxtaposita

Epithet means "close together."
Deciduous, 2 to 3 ft. (60 to 90 cm). Zones 7 and 8. Apogamous.

DESCRIPTION: The rhizome is erect and bears fronds with lanceolate to triangular, bipinnate blades that are pale green above and whitish green beneath. The stipes are clothed in glossy, blackish scales and are one-fourth of the frond length. Up to 25 widely spaced pairs of pinnae are black at their point of attachment to the rachis. The medial sori are covered with a kidney-shaped indusium.

RANGE AND HABITAT: A common fern in the western Himalayas, this species extends to China, Burma (Myanmar), India, Thailand, and Vietnam.

CULTURE AND COMMENTS: This is a lax grower for average soil and shade with a flush of four to five fronds annually. Politely speaking, it does not stand out in a crowd.

Dryopteris koidzumiana

Synonym *Dryopteris erythrosora* var. *koidzumiana*
Epithet is after Japanese botanist Gen'ichi Koidzumi (1883–1953).
Evergreen, 2 ft. (60 cm). Zones (7) 8 to 10.

DESCRIPTION: The erect rhizome produces an annual crop of four to five upright fronds that are one-half barely scaled grooved green stipes. There are 8 to 10 pairs of pinnae on the ovate bipinnate blade that tapers to an extended narrow apex. The lowest pinnae incline slightly inwards. The glory of this species is in the sumptuous new growth that is an intensely saturated brick-red, later fading to russet-green. New growth is alarmingly late, sometimes not making an appearance until early summer in the Pacific Northwest. Sori are medial and covered with a matching deep red kidney-shaped indusium.

RANGE AND HABITAT: This species is endemic to lowland forests in Japan.

CULTURE AND COMMENTS: Where hardy, this fern is a magnificent soloist for the green symphony. It is not fussy about soils, but prefers the hospitable climate of areas without extremes of temperatures. Plantings in carefully established and tended microclimates have brought marginal results elsewhere. Try it at least once, as success brings beautiful rewards (and a bit of horticultural pride). Barbara Hoshizaki introduced this to North America from Yakushima Island in the early 1990s.

Dryopteris kuratae
Epithet is after Japanese botanist Satoru Kurata (1922–1978). Deciduous, 2 ft. (60 cm). Zones 7 to 9. Apogamous.

DESCRIPTION: The rhizome is erect. The stipes are a short one-fourth of the frond, with brownish scales. The lanceolate blade with 20 to 25 pairs of pinnae is pinnate-pinnatifid, tapering with reduced pinnae towards the base. The sori are close to the margin and covered with a kidney-shaped indusium.

RANGE AND HABITAT: This species grows in moist woods in eastern Asia.

CULTURE AND COMMENTS: Recently described, this fern has a superficial resemblance to a series of pinnate-pinnatifid dryopteris. As more material and knowledge becomes available from China, the entire complex is likely to be revised, especially the relationship to *Dryopteris pycnopteroides*. This fern can be grown without special requirements.

Dryopteris lacera
Epithet means "torn into a fringe."
Semievergreen to evergreen, 2 ft. (60 cm). Zones 5 to 8.

DESCRIPTION: The rhizome is erect and the rusty brown-scaled, grooved stipe is one-fourth of the frond length. The ovate blade is pinnate-pinnatifid to bipinnate with 10 to 20 pairs of pinnae. Noticeably reduced fertile pinnae are restricted to the terminal stretches of the spore-bearing fronds. The sori with kidney-shaped indusia cover the undersides of the fertile pinnae. Not only will the spores fall at maturity, but the pinnae may as well.

RANGE AND HABITAT: *Dryopteris lacera* grows in moist forests and streamsides in Japan, China, and Korea.

CULTURE AND COMMENTS: This species is easily and readily established in moist to dryish light shade and is evergreen in all but the colder lower limits of its hardiness range. Spring growth is early, and growers should be wary of potential damage from late frosts. The matte green, shapely fronds with their early emergence make a handsome foil for epimediums, primroses, and ephemeral wildflowers (or vice-versa depending on your priorities). The Japanese common name translates to

"bear bracken." *Dryopteris uniformis*, which also bears its spores on the upper frond tips, differs from *D. lacera* in not having deciduous fertile pinnae.

Dryopteris laeta
Bright wood fern
Synonym *Dryopteris goeringianum*
Epithet means "vivid, bright."
Deciduous to semievergreen, 2 ft. (60 cm). Zones 5 to 8.

DESCRIPTION: The rhizome is erect with arching fronds of one-half broadly triangular bipinnate-pinnatifid to tripinnate blades and one-half tan-scaled stipes. The sori are submarginal and covered with a kidney-shaped indusium. Mickel (1994) notes that the species resembles *Dryopteris dilatata* "but is less dissected and less toothed, and the basiscopic (lowermost) pinnules are not long."

Dryopteris lacera frond with its smaller fertile pinnae towards the apex. Gassner garden.

RANGE AND HABITAT: From the cold temperate regions of China, Japan, Manchuria, and Korea, this species prefers limestone areas.

CULTURE AND COMMENTS: Rarely available commercially, *Dryopteris laeta* is an upright, bushy, but not particularly showy addition to the garden.

Dryopteris lepidopoda
Sunset fern
Epithet means "scaly feet."
Evergreen, 2 to 2½ ft. (60 to 75 cm). Zones (5) 6 to 9. Apogamous.

DESCRIPTION: The erect rhizome and stipes are adorned with dark chocolate scales. The proportionately tall stipes are one-half of the frond length. The bipinnate, glossy blades, with an average of 20 pairs of pinnae, are broadly lanceolate. They emerge in richly decorative hues of salmon, orange, pink, and deep rose that subside into warm green tones. With the base of the blade squared and blunt (truncate), the frond looks like a glowing arrow. The sori are covered with kidney-shaped indusia and are carried on the upper portions of the blade.

RANGE AND HABITAT: The sunset fern grows in mountainous areas from the Himalayas to China and Taiwan.

CULTURE AND COMMENTS: Here is the jewel for average soil in the lightly shaded to the early morning–late afternoon sunny ambiance of the woodland showcase. Additional colorful new fronds are produced throughout the summer giving continued buoyancy to the display. The height may well vary depending on climate, but this fern can be quite ornamental as a height-challenged, cold-tempered miniature as well as the full-bodied mild temperate display. The common name is picture perfect and accurately imaginative for this beauty of an earthbound sunset. Enthusiastic reports from the full spectrum of North American and European garden experts reinforce my endorsement of this elegant garden showpiece. I recommend it strongly.

Dryopteris ludoviciana
Southern wood fern
Epithet means "from Louisiana."
Semievergreen, 2 to 4 ft. (60 to 120 cm). Zones 6 to 9.

DESCRIPTION: The rhizome is short-creeping to erect. The grooved stipes have brown scales at the base and are one-fourth to one-third the length of the frond. The lanceolate dark green, shiny blades are pinnate-pinnatifid, tapering to the base with triangular lower pinnae. There are 20 to 30 pairs of pinnae with reduced fertile pinnae confined to the upper portions of the frond. The sori are medial with kidney-shaped indusia.

RANGE AND HABITAT: Look for this fern in swamplands and borders of wet cypress woods, where it is frequently associated with limestone, in the very southeastern areas of the United States.

CULTURE AND COMMENTS: Here is a selection for the difficult-to-manage muddy margins of ponds or bogs. It does not require lime or a swamp, although without irrigation it will not reach its potential (or depending on your zone, even survive)

in drier uplands. Give it a seriously hefty mulch in cool gardens. Here in Zone 8, I have lost it on a regular basis whenever I neglected its thirsty tendencies, as like many plants it will winter kill if it goes into the season in a weakened condition. Unlike many eastern U.S. natives, it does well in Southern California and comparable areas lacking the stress of extreme temperatures. It is the parent, along with *Dryopteris celsa*, of *D. ×australis*, a better choice for gardens out of the southern wood fern's natural range. There is a crested variety that is occasionally available and also just as occasionally comes true from spores.

Dryopteris marginalis
Marginal wood fern
Epithet means "margined," in reference to the marginal sori.
Evergreen, 1½ to 2½ ft. (45 to 75 cm). Zones 2 to 8.

DESCRIPTION: The erect rhizome forms a single crown and a vase-shaped plant. The ovate, bipinnate blades with 12 to 16 pairs of pinnae are leathery and frequently bluish green. The grooved, brownish stipes are wrapped in matching scales. They are one-fourth to one-third of the frond length. This species is easily identified by the sori that outline the edges of the pinnules, hence the common name.

RANGE AND HABITAT: Look for this common fern in rocky communities in woodlands and ravines and on slopes and walls, including some stands on limestone and sandstone, in eastern North America. It is disjunct in Greenland.

CULTURE AND COMMENTS: This is a highly recommended species for growing in shaded, average soil with good drainage from the Rocky Mountains eastward, as well as Europe and Britain. For unexplained reasons it is reticent in the uniformly temperate areas of the Pacific Northwest and will not do at all in subtropical warmth.

Dryopteris mindshelkensis
Limestone wood fern, rigid buckler fern
Synonyms *Dryopteris submontana*, *D. villarii* subsp. *submontana*
Epithet is after a district in the Karatau mountains of southern Kazakhstan.
Deciduous, 1 to 2 ft. (30 to 60 cm). Zones 6 to 8.

DESCRIPTION: The rhizome is ascending to short-creeping. The pale grooved stipe is one-third of the stiffly upright frond length. Blades are lanceolate and bipinnate with 12 to 20 pairs of dull green pinnae. Fragrant creamy to yellow glands cover the surfaces and are reputed to smell like balsam when brushed. The sori, located on the upper portions of the frond, are also glandular, medial, and covered with a kidney-shaped indusium.

RANGE AND HABITAT: This species grows in limestone habitats from northern Britain, through mountainous Europe to North Africa as well as eastern Europe and the Caucasus (where presumably it was blessed with this tongue twisting name).

CULTURE AND COMMENTS: *Dryopteris mindshelkensis*, which is far better known as *D. submontana*, is a good candidate for cultivation in a rocky, large-scaled limestone cobble and is reported to be easily grown wherever abundant amounts of limestone are present. It is very cold tolerant and appreciates good drainage. I would not recommend it for hot summer gardens.

Dryopteris muenchii
Epithet is after Münch.
Semievergreen, 1½ to 2½ ft. (45 to 75 cm). Zones 6 (with protection) to 9.

DESCRIPTION: The rhizome is erect with narrowly triangular fronds fanning out from the crown. The stipes are one-fourth to one-third of the frond length, and the willowy blades are bipinnate-pinnatifid. There are 20 to 25 pairs of pinnae with medial sori covered with a kidney-shaped reddish brown indusium.

RANGE AND HABITAT: This surprisingly tolerant fern is from high-altitude forestlands in Mexico.

Warm sunset tones on the emerging fronds of *Dryopteris lepidopoda.*

Dryopteris ludoviciana frond with a characteristic constricted apex at Mount Cuba Center.

Dryopteris marginalis in the woods of Massachusetts.

Diagnostically significant marginal sori on *Dryopteris marginalis.*

CULTURE AND COMMENTS: Despite its heritage this species has wintered without a whimper for many years in the semi-shade in my Zone 8 garden. While not showy, the foliage is delicate and a light yellow-green. The plant is remarkably tolerant of wind, poor soil, and benign neglect.

Dryopteris namegatae

Synonym *Dryopteris dickinsii* var. *namegatae*
Epithet is after the Namegata region of Japan.
Evergreen, 2 to 3 ft. (60 to 90 cm). Zones 6 to 8. Apogamous.

DESCRIPTION: The erect rhizome produces a corpulent crown up to 4 in. (10 cm) in diameter. The green stipes are densely wrapped in glossy, blackish scales with the basal masses ½ to 1 in. (13 to 25 mm) long. The stipes are one-quarter to one-third of the narrowly lanceolate, once-pinnate fronds. There are 20 to 25 pairs of pinnae with the lower pinnae slightly smaller and pointing forward and downward (see photo at left on page 220). The sori are medial and covered with a kidney-shaped indusium.

RANGE AND HABITAT: This is a rare find in the forested mountains of Japan and China.

CULTURE AND COMMENTS: *Dryopteris namegatae* is one of my favorite species with its waves of light green foliage immersed in dark scales. It welcomes rich humusy soil in shade but will acclimatize in lesser luxury, producing proportionately smaller fronds. This species is another member of the decorative Asian-Japanese once-pinnate group. *Flora of Japan* (Iwatsuki et al. 1995) considers it intermediate between *D. cycadina* and *D. dickinsii* and possibly a hybrid of the two.

Dryopteris neorosthornii

Epithet is after A. von Rosthorn, who collected in China in the late 1890s, and *neo*, new.
Evergreen (as found in the trade), 2 to 3 ft. (60 to 90 cm). Zones (6) 7 and 8. Apogamous.

DESCRIPTION: The rhizome is erect. The stipes with prominent, luminous blackish-tan ¼-in. (6-mm) scales are one-fourth of the shower of golden fronds. The radiant, bipinnate blades are lanceolate with 20 to 24 pairs of pinnae. The sori are medial and protected by a kidney-shaped indusium.

RANGE AND HABITAT: This fern is rare in nature, occurring in high-elevation forest scrub in the Himalayas and China.

CULTURE AND COMMENTS: Like *Dryopteris wallichiana*, this species is a springtime beauty with its unfurling fiddleheads protectively wrapped in a profusion of blackish-brown scales. The show continues as the contrasting bright green foliage unfolds. It is a dynamite of a plant and certain to evoke a wow from even the least fern enlightened of your garden guests. It is shorter than *D. wallichiana* with stipes and scales that are dark brownish-black at maturity rather than green and reddish-brown respectively. It is slow to establish and likes evenly moist compost in dappled shade. Christopher Fraser-Jenkins (pers. comm.) reports that material in the trade as *D. neorosthornii* has been misnamed and should properly be classified as *D. xanthomelas*. He adds that true *D. neorosthornii* is now classified as *D. wallichiana* subsp. *nepalensis*.

Dryopteris oreades

Mountain male fern, dwarf male fern
Synonym *Dryopteris abbreviata*
Epithet is from Greek mythology and means "nymphs of mountains, male fern of mountains."
Early deciduous, 1½ to 2½ ft. (45 to 75 cm). Zones 4 to 8.

DESCRIPTION: The rhizome is short-creeping producing narrow upright fronds. Grooved gray-scaled stipes are one-fourth of the frond length. The pinnate-pinnatifid to almost bipinnate blades are lanceolate and dull green, and have crispy pinna margins. There are 15 to 25 pairs of pinnae. The species is one of the parents, along with *D. caucasica*, of *D. filix-mas*, and is a dwarf version of the latter. However, the lower pinnae curve forward and downwards aiding in identification. The sori are close to the pinna midribs of the upper third of the fertile fronds and covered with a kidney-shaped indusium.

RANGE AND HABITAT: This fern is native to Britain and Europe, including Scandinavia, and extends eastward to the Caucasus and Pakistan. It grows predominantly in well-drained talus in mountainous areas.

CULTURE AND COMMENTS: This universally adaptable species accepts a range of garden climates from cold winter zones to hot and humid summer punishment. It needs dappled shade and well-drained gritty soil.

'Crispa' (curled) is lower growing with a tightly undulate edging.

'Cristata' (crested) is crested at the tips.

'Incisa Crispa' (cut and curled) has narrow pinnae that are cut and crisped.

Dryopteris pacifica

Synonyms *Dryopteris varia* var. *hikonensis*, *D. hikonensis*
Epithet means "from Pacific Ocean areas."
Evergreen, 2½ ft. (75 cm). Zones 6 to 8. Apogamous.

DESCRIPTION: The rhizome is erect and the sprays of fronds have polished, triangular, basally tripinnate, rich green blades. The stipes are one-third of the frond, grooved and lightly dusted with dark scales. It is diagnostically noteworthy that the inner pinnules on the lowermost pinnae are longer than those adjacent to it. There are 10 to 20 pairs of pinnae with the upper portion strongly contracted. The sori are medial with kidney-shaped indusia.

RANGE AND HABITAT: This species is native to the temperate woodlands of Japan, China, and Korea.

CULTURE AND COMMENTS: Plant this among ferns and companions in filtered light shade and fluffy garden compost. Although not generally available in the U.S. trade as of 2005, it is gradually appearing in the catalogs of specialists and deserves greater attention. It is botanically related to and confused with an assortment of horticulturally welcomed, decorative Asian species. The contracted upper pinnae distinguish it from its close relative, *Dryopteris bissetiana*; the blackish-brown versus reddish-brown stipe scales separate it from *D. varia*; and the lower pinnule configuration separates it from *D. cystolepidota*.

Dryopteris polylepis

Scaly wood fern

Epithet means "many scales."

Evergreen, 2 ft. (60 cm). Zones 6 to 8.

DESCRIPTION: The rhizome is erect with fronds radiating in arching horizontal sprays from short stipes that are one-fifth of the total foliage. As the common name implies, these are massively and handsomely dressed in blackish-brown scales that extend well onto the rachis. The narrow oblanceolate blades are pinnate-pinnatifid and a warm kelly-green. The 20 to 28 pairs of pinnae taper gradually toward the frond's base with the lower pair aiming slightly downward. The sori are submarginal on upper pinnules and covered with a kidney-shaped indusium.

RANGE AND HABITAT: This is a woodland species from Japan, China, and Korea.

CULTURE AND COMMENTS: Grow this fern for the excitement the scaly new foliage brings to the springtime garden and the assured ornamental contribution of the foliar black and green highlights throughout the rest of the year. It is an undemanding citizen of the woodland garden with a preference for light shade. Once established it is quite drought tolerant. (I would also like to note that my plants and those in cultivation in the United States came from spores that were gifted by the late Roy Davidson, an extremely talented, many faceted horticul-

Dryopteris muenchii

New growth on the fern circulating in commerce as *Dryopteris neorosthornii*.

Dryopteris namegatae against a backdrop of *Helleborus* 'Ivory Prince'.

Light foliage of *Dryopteris pacifica* in the Peters garden.

turist whose knowledge and generosity spanned an amazing botanical and gardening spectrum and whose contributions greatly enriched the gardens and gardeners of North America and beyond.)

Dryopteris pseudofilix-mas
Mexican male fern
Epithet means "false male fern." Alternate spelling is *Dryopteris pseudo-filix-mas*.
Semievergreen, 3 to 4 ft. (90 to 120 cm). Zones 5 to 8. Apogamous.

DESCRIPTION: The rhizome forms a stout, erect crown supporting a strongly upright shuttlecock of fronds with small, lightly scaled stipes that are usually one-eighth of the frond length. The pinnate-pinnatifid, lanceolate blade is densely foliated and bipinnate at the base. Pairs of pinnae number 20 to 30 or more. The sori are medial and protected by a kidney-shaped indusium.

RANGE AND HABITAT: The Mexican male is, not surprisingly, from moist high elevations in Mexico with an extended range to Guatemala.

CULTURE AND COMMENTS: Since its U.S. introduction in the late 1900s by John Mickel of the New York Botanical Garden, it has been extremely successful in varied habitats and will withstand the rigors of hot and humid summers in the American heartland as well as the associated rigors of frigid winter extremes. In addition to a vigorous spring flush, it produces fronds throughout the season until early frost. Use it for vertical interest in the humusy background area of the lightly shaded bed or give it greater exposure in areas where a drought-tolerant fern would be welcomed. (Keep it well watered for a season until it is established.)

Dryopteris purpurella
Synonyms *Dryopteris erythrosora* var. *purpurascens, D. indusiata* var. *purpurascens*
Epithet means "purplish."
Evergreen, 2½ to 3 ft. (75 to 90 cm). Zones 6 to 9. Apogamous.

DESCRIPTION: The rhizome is erect and the open vase of fronds is one-third or more stipe, sparsely dressed in dark scales. The bipinnate blade with upwards of six pairs of pinnae is broadly triangular and narrows towards the apex. The new growth is fleetingly glossed in a metallic fuchsia-purple hue. (Leave town for a week and you may miss this distinction from *D. erythrosora*.) The sori are submarginal and covered with a kidney-shaped indusium.

RANGE AND HABITAT: Closely affiliated with *Dryopteris erythrosora*, this fern is a denizen of forested areas in Japan, China, and Korea.

CULTURE AND COMMENTS: It is seriously questionable whether the true species is cultivated in Western gardens. The material distributed in the United States is beautiful but barely distinct from the equally attractive *Dryopteris erythrosora*. Comprehensive lists from Europe and Britain do not include this species. I can, however, recommend whatever passes for *D. purpurella* as a handsome addition to garden collections from the warmth of California to the chilly realms of the Mid-Atlantic states as well as warmer and more southerly Midwest

Dense black scales trim the fronds of *Dryopteris polylepis*.

Massive structure of the landscape heavyweight *Dryopteris pseudofilix-mas*.

Fleeting metallic appearance on young fronds of *Dryopteris purpurella*.

and East Coast states. Light shade and garden compost provide for its basic needs.

Dryopteris pycnopteroides

Epithet means "close winged."

Evergreen, 1½ to 2½ ft. (45 to 75 cm). Zones 6 to 9. Apogamous.

DESCRIPTION: The rhizome is erect with a swirl of pinnate-pinnatifid, narrowly lanceolate foliage on stipes that are one-fourth the length of the frond. The 20 to 24 pairs of pinnae have distinct, deeply scalloped margins. The lower pinnae are reduced but point neither forward nor downward (see photo at left on page 220). Sori with kidney-shaped indusia are medial.

RANGE AND HABITAT: The true species is a native of forested areas in China. Japanese plants are now considered by some authors to be the deciduous *Dryopteris kuratae*.

CULTURE AND COMMENTS: With new growth that unfurls in a brilliant lime-green sheen, this fern is a welcome addition to somber areas of the shade garden. Within reason, it is not fussy about soil or moisture and readily makes the transition from its Asiatic homeland to comparable temperate climates in the West. Great doses of water and mulch help it to adapt to areas with extended hot and humid summers.

Dryopteris remota

Scaly buckler fern

Dryopteris affinis × *D. expansa*.

Epithet means "scattered."

Semievergreen, 2 to 3 ft. (60 to 90 cm). Zones 4 to 8. Apogamous.

DESCRIPTION: The rhizome is erect, as is the fern, with a bushy mop of warm green, bipinnate lanceolate blades bearing more or less 20 pairs of pinnae. The tan-scaled, grooved stipe is one-quarter of the frond length. The sori are medial and covered with kidney-shaped indusia.

RANGE AND HABITAT: In nature this is a rare plant found in scattered subalpine areas in Central Europe, rare stations in Great Britain (including the shores of Loch Lomond), and Asia.

CULTURE AND COMMENTS: With its vigorous early flush of bright green foliage emerging from fluffy brown fiddleheads, this fern reminds me every spring of why it is so widely admired. It will flourish in bright filtered light, average soil, and in time will be more drought tolerant than most garden plants. With its dense clusters of fronds, it is useful for low landscape screening. Offspring may appear periodically from its spores, but are not a problem. This fertile hybrid has the scaly crosiers of its *Dryopteris affinis* parent and the delicate pinnation and texture of its *D. expansa* parent.

Dryopteris sacrosancta

Synonym *Dryopteris varia* var. *sacrosancta*

Epithet means "of holy places." Common name computer translated from Japanese is "princess weasel sheep tooth."

Evergreen, 2 ft. (60 cm). Zones 7 and 8. Apogamous.

DESCRIPTION: The rhizome is erect. The stipes are one-third or more of the length of the frond, grooved, and tan with shiny black scales. The broadly triangular blades are bipinnate to tripinnate (especially adjacent to the rachis) with about 16 pairs of flat yellow-green pinnae. The sori are submarginal and covered with kidney-shaped indusia.

RANGE AND HABITAT: The species is common in the warmer forests of Japan, Korea, and China.

CULTURE AND COMMENTS: This undemanding fern will settle in light shade in average and even dryish soil. It is one of a closely related complex of species that were at one time considered subspecies of *Dryopteris varia*. It differs in that it has blackish-brown rather than reddish-brown stipe scales. Others of the extended "varia" family are rather more handsome.

Dryopteris saxifraga

Synonym *Dryopteris varia* var. *saxifraga*

Epithet means "breaking rocks, of rocky habitats."

Evergreen, 1½ to 2 ft. (45 to 60 cm). Zones 5 to 8. Apogamous.

DESCRIPTION: The rhizome is erect and the fronds are one-third tan stipe with chocolate-colored scales. The ovate blade is bipinnate-pinnatifid with 12 to 14 pairs of warm green triangular pinnae. The sori are medial and covered with kidney-shaped indusia.

Soft green fronds of *Dryopteris remota* in the Bellevue Botanical Garden.

Dryopteris saxifraga at the Rhododendron Species Botanical Garden.

Dryopteris scottii with its silhouette of broad pinnae in the Kennar garden.

RANGE AND HABITAT: *Dryopteris saxifraga* comes from rocky, mountainous habitats of Manchuria, Korea, and China and is especially common in Japan.

CULTURE AND COMMENTS: This species is relatively new in North American commerce and is an attractive addition to the partially shaded woodland from northern areas to Southern California. It appreciates good drainage but is not particular about soil types. The species is closely related botanically to *Dryopteris bissetiana* and differs in having light brown rather than brownish-black stipe scales and a flat green, more compact overall appearance.

Dryopteris scottii

Epithet is after John Scott (1838–1880).
Evergreen, 2 ft. (60 cm). Zones 8 and 9.

DESCRIPTION: The erect rhizome bears fronds that are equal parts stipe and blade. The stipes are mildly endowed with scattered black scales. The once-pinnate, lanceolate blade carries about a dozen pairs of chubby lobed, grass-green pinnae. Although the fronds are described as reaching 3 ft. (90 cm) in nature, those on cultivated plants rarely extend beyond 2 ft. (60 cm). The species is distinct, for a *Dryopteris*, in having sori that are not covered by an indusium.

RANGE AND HABITAT: *Dryopteris scottii* grows in dense forests from India eastward to Malaysia, China, Taiwan, and Japan.

CULTURE AND COMMENTS: I am very fond of this choice fern and unfortunately the slugs agree. With care and caution it can, however, be maintained, although common sense decrees that it is not appropriate for group plantings. I have discouraged foraging mollusks by planting this fern well off the ground in a mixed composition in an exposed aggregate concrete planter. It needs protection in severe winters; a good mulch, including snow, will do nicely. Despite its shortcomings, it is an attractive companion to feathery friends and worth cultivating in moist soil and partial shade. For complete slug protection it can be grown indoors.

Dryopteris sieboldii

Siebold's wood fern

Epithet is after Philipp von Siebold (1796–1866), a German botanist specializing in plants of Japan.
Evergreen, 1½ to 2½ ft. (45 to 75 cm). Zones 6 to 9.

DESCRIPTION: The rhizome is short-creeping. The grooved soft, light green stipes are up to one-half of the frond's mass. The unique open blades are leathery and ovate, looking like a *Pteris* on steroids, with two to five pairs of broad, linear bluish pinnae and a lengthy 6- to 12-in. (15- to 30-cm) terminal pinna. The sori are distributed randomly and covered with kidney-shaped indusia. The new growth is significantly late with only a few sterile fronds produced per season and even fewer fertile companions.

RANGE AND HABITAT: This species is found in the drier forests of Japan, China, and Taiwan.

CULTURE AND COMMENTS: *Dryopteris sieboldii* is not likely to be confused with any other members of the fern community (and with its "unfernlike" structure can raise an eyebrow or two when so displayed for visitors). Its bold fronds are a welcomed and admired contrasting feature in warm shade and especially attractive when highlighted with a backdrop of silver driftwood or a boulder. In the Pacific Northwest and comparable temperate climates it is frugal with frond production. An annual output of three or four fronds is considered a vigorous display. By contrast, it is very partial to summer heat and as such is an outstanding performer in the U.S. Southeast. The most genuinely lush specimen I have ever seen was in the Fernery at the Morris Arboretum in Philadelphia where it was a suffocating 90°F (32°C) inside and out, a definite confirmation of the plants' preference for heat. Regardless of your summer temperature extremes, this is a unique, drought-tolerant addition for the shade-protected garden.

Dryopteris stenolepis

Synonyms *Dryopteris atrata* var. *stenolepis*, *D. hirtipes* var. *stenolepis*
Epithet means "narrow-scaled."

Evergreen, 3 to 5 ft. (90 to 150 cm). Zone 8. Apogamous.

DESCRIPTION: The rhizome is erect, supporting stout light brown stipes with abundant scales shading from light brown in the basal portions through brownish-black in the upward expansion of the frond and rachis. The stipes can be up to one-half of the tall frond. The narrowly lanceolate blades are once-pinnate with 30 to 50 pairs of long and extremely slender pinnae with a bare suggestion of toothy margins (see photo at left on page 220). The sori are close to the midveins and covered with kidney-shaped indusia.

RANGE AND HABITAT: This species grows in the bush from the Himalayas and China to Taiwan, but is absent from Japan.

CULTURE AND COMMENTS: Here is a tall, statuesque, thinly structured species producing three to four fronds annually in rich soil and mild climates. It is highly desirable and an easily grown addition to shaded fernlands. With an exceptionally dense scaly foliar dressing, this species is admired and

Unique and bold foliage of *Dryopteris sieboldii* set off by sculptured driftwood in the Duryee garden.

Long wands of *Dryopteris stenolepis* fronds in the Duryee garden.

distinguished for its scaliness in a class of like ornamental Asian species. *Dryopteris* expert Christopher Fraser-Jenkins (1989), who has spent most of his adult life studying and classifying ferns in the far reaches of India and the Himalayas, separates *D. stenolepis* from its would-be sibling *D. gamblei* based on the toothed, extremely narrow pinnae on *D. stenolepis* versus the lobed pinnae on its counterpart. For horticultural and botanical interest, I certainly recommend this for its height and lightweight contribution to the garden's composition.

Dryopteris stewartii
Epithet is after John Stuart, Earl of Bute (1713–1782).
Deciduous, 2½ to 3 ft. (75 to 90 cm). Zones 6 to 8. Apogamous.

DESCRIPTION: The rhizome is erect. The stipes are one-fourth of the frond length, grooved and enriched with dark brown scales. Blades are lanceolate and bipinnate with 12 to 20 pairs of pinnae. The sori are medial and covered with kidney-shaped indusia.

RANGE AND HABITAT: This is a mountainous species from the Himalayas.

CULTURE AND COMMENTS: Grow this bushy, upright species in a mixed border where it will get support (literally) from companion plants. It is easy-going in moderate to deep shade and moist soil and is especially popular with East Coast gardeners.

Dryopteris sublacera
Epithet means "almost torn into fringelike segments."
Evergreen, 1 to 2 ft. (30 to 60 cm). Zones (5) 6 to 8. Apogamous.

DESCRIPTION: The erect rhizome supports leathery fronds that are one-fourth grooved stipe with deciduous russet scales. The thick-textured blade is ovate-lanceolate and bipinnate with about 20 pairs of subdued milky green pinnae, which aim their tips towards the frond's apex. The sori are medial and covered with kidney-shaped indusia.

RANGE AND HABITAT: This species is native to high-altitude forests in China, Taiwan, and the Himalayas.

CULTURE AND COMMENTS: *Dryopteris sublacera* is a substantial, medium-sized selection for the moist to drier compost-enriched areas of the lightly shaded woodland. The fronds are arching but with a tendency towards the horizontal. The glabrous upper surface has the color of a green apple and the undersides are a complementary silvery green.

Dryopteris tokyoensis
Tokyo wood fern
Epithet means "from Tokyo."
Deciduous, 1½ to 3 ft. (45 to 90 cm). Zones 5 to 8.

DESCRIPTION: The rhizome is erect, as is the structure of the fern. At one-sixth of the total length of the frond, the grooved stipes are significantly short. The lanceolate, light green blades

Dryopteris stewartii in the Kennar garden.

Light green fronds of *Dryopteris sublacera* growing in harmony with bold hosta leaves.

Strongly vertical fronds of *Dryopteris tokyoensis* at the Cornell Plantations gardens.

Red flowers of *Heuchera* surround the green fronds of *Dryopteris uniformis* in a mixed border.

Fertile frond with narrowed pinnae on *Dryopteris uniformis.*

Dryopteris varia in the Kohout garden.
Note the narrowed frond apex.

are narrow and once-pinnate with 25 to 35 pairs of narrowly triangular, auricled pinnae. The sori are adjacent to the midveins and have kidney-shaped indusia.

RANGE AND HABITAT: Not surprisingly, this is a Japanese native with populations in wet acidic soil sites in China and Korea as well.

CULTURE AND COMMENTS: Here is the visual garden equivalent of a willowy ballerina "en pointe" with the slender arching fronds extending gracefully in a vertical reach. The plant is best displayed with a supporting cast of sturdy background leafy perennials, preferably evergreens. It is early deciduous and should be sited accordingly. It is not comfortable in or recommended for hot inland summer areas, but displays well in gardens in the heat-enriched Atlantic Coast.

Dryopteris uniformis
Epithet means "one shape."
Evergreen, 1 to 2 ft. (30 to 60 cm). Zones 5 to 8.

DESCRIPTION: Fresh warm green fronds emerge in early spring from the erect rhizome. The grooved stipes are one-fourth of the frond length and unfurl from an effervescent bowl of persistent blackish-brown scales. The prominent ebony stipe scales are basally sheltered by green cloaks. Ovate-triangular blades are bipinnate with 12 to 18 pairs of lanceolate pinnae. Fertile pinnae are produced exclusively on the narrowed upper third of the blade and do not wither when the spores are dispersed. The medial sori are covered with kidney-shaped indusia.

RANGE AND HABITAT: *Dryopteris uniformis* is a native of forested mountain areas of Japan, Korea, and China.

CULTURE AND COMMENTS: Easily grown in shaded, moist woodlands, this fern unfurls in concert and harmony with the early spring emergence of epimediums and pulmonarias under canopies of forsythia, chimonanthus, and fellow harbingers of the season. Together they make welcome compositions for the traditionally much desired and anticipated arrival of winter's end.

'Cristata' (crested), with forked and crested foliar tips, was introduced to Western horticulture in the late 1990s and combines well with the type. Both adjust to cultivation in cold area gardens as well as the warmer settings of Southern California.

Dryopteris varia
Epithet means "differing."
Evergreen, 1½ to 2½ ft. (45 to 75 cm). Zones 5 to 8. Apogamous.

DESCRIPTION: The upright rhizome produces a tuft of stiff fronds equally proportioned between stipe and blade. The lower stipe is clothed in dark chocolate scales, which become lighter as they approach the rachis. The triangular to pentagonal leathery blade, with up to 20 pairs of deltoid pinnae, transitions from tripinnate to bipinnate upwards from the base towards an abruptly narrowed apex. New growth as illustrated in Iwatsuki (1992) is coppery red. The lower pinnules adjacent to the rachis are slightly elongate, like stubby little tails. The sori are submarginal and covered with kidney-shaped indusia.

RANGE AND HABITAT: This species has an extensive Pacific range from Taiwan, Japan, Korea, the Philippines, and China to parts of eastern and Southeast Asia. It is most often found in lowland forests.

CULTURE AND COMMENTS: Use this fern where its bright foliage can serve as an ornamental backdrop for shade-loving flowers in moist woodlands. It survives wild winters and enjoys mild ones. Summer heat tolerance varies, but reports from Pittsburgh, Pennsylvania, and comparable stressful zones endorse its versatility. Fraser-Jenkins (1989) suspects that this species may actually be a complex series and may be subdivided following further taxonomic examination. *Dryopteris bissetiana*, *D. pacifica*, *D. sacrosancta*, and *D. saxifraga* have at one time or another all been treated as varieties of *D. varia*. By whatever names, grow them anyway.

Dryopteris wallichiana
Wallich's wood fern
Epithet is after Danish botanist Nathaniel Wallich (1786–1854).
Evergreen, 2½ to 5 ft. (75 to 150 cm). Zones 6 to 8. Apogamous.

DESCRIPTION: Warm, butter-yellow, arching foliar plumes erupt in mid to late spring from an erect rhizome. The short stipe is liberally coated with reddish-black narrow scales that extend along the rachis. The pinnate-pinnatifid blade tapers gradually at both extremities bearing two to three dozen pairs of sessile, linear pinnae with blunt-edged pinnules. After the dramatic spring debut, the fronds gradually revert to a polished green with pale undersides. The sori are medial with kidney-shaped indusia.

RANGE AND HABITAT: In describing the allure of this fern's native habitat, Mickel (1994) waxes wistfully of "high mountains of southern Mexico, to dripping forests of moss-festooned oaks and lichen-laden pines . . . through the drifting, chilling mists." The range extends beyond the Mexican highlands to similar tropical mountaintop settings from South America to Hawaii. In addition, cold-hardy material is found in an amazing assortment of forested homelands that include Japan, China, and most of Asia. The Japanese site is described as "restricted to a particular cave side on Sakurajima; probably extinct from recent volcanic activity" (Iwatsuki et al. 1995).

CULTURE AND COMMENTS: Despite or perhaps because of the disparities of its native habitats, *Dryopteris wallichiana* responds erratically to domestication. In my garden and nursery, winter cold of 10°F (-12°C) has destroyed young plants in the ground, while unexpectedly sparing smaller plants exposed to greater freezing stress while growing in 4-in. (10-cm) pots sitting on the soil's surface. As one of the most handsome of ferns available, *D. wallichiana* must be given a trial by gardeners in protected shade. Like most plants it will increase in fortitude and cold resistance with age and size. For an optimal display (and photo-op), select a planting site against a contrasting rocky or stumpery background. The most impressive planting that I have ever seen anywhere is the stunning collection of robust specimens in the Hardy Fern

Foundation collection at the Rhododendron Species Botanical Garden in Federal Way, Washington.

Dryopteris wallichiana is a botanically complex species with definitions, research, and splitting a continuing "learning experience." Fraser-Jenkins (1989) describes several variations including **subsp.** *himaliaca* with scales streaked with dark stripes; **subsp.** *coriacea* from Iran and Turkey, considered intermediate between *D. wallichiana* and *D. affinis*; and **subsp.** *nepalensis* (synonym *D. neorosthornii*), which has dark scales with brown apices and narrower fronds of 8 in. (20 cm) at the broad midsection as opposed to 12 in. (30 cm) for the type. *Dryopteris wallichiana, D. lepidopoda, D. xanthomelas,* and *D. yigongensis* are among a closely related group that is part of an Asian classification defined by Fraser-Jenkins (1989) as Section *Fibrillosae*, or more comfortably the *D. wallichiana* Group.

Dryopteris yigongensis

Epithet is after Yigong, China.
Evergreen, 1 to 1½ (30 to 45 cm). Zones (6) 7 and 8. Apogamous.

DESCRIPTION: The rhizome is short and erect. The light brown stipe has dark, basal, ovate scales that diminish in numbers towards the rachis. The stipe is one-fourth to one-third of the length of the frond. The lanceolate blade flares in a graceful arch and tapers towards the base. The lower pinnae point slightly downwards. It is pinnate-pinnatifid to bipinnate with 15 to 20 pairs of lanceolate, pointed pinnae. The pinnules are stubby-edged with submedial sori covered with kidney-shaped indusia.

RANGE AND HABITAT: This species grows in high-altitude forests in the Himalayas and China.

CULTURE AND COMMENTS: Though rarely available commercially, here is a modest-sized fern to use as a landscaping substitute for *Dryopteris wallichiana*. With subdued peach-hued new growth, albeit missing the dominant sheath of sinister scales, it is ornamental and content in light shade and woodland soil. Once established, it is drought tolerant as well as better adapted to extremes of temperatures.

Shorter Notes

Dryopteris aitoniana (for William Aiton, 1759–1793, head gardener at the Royal Botanic Gardens, Kew) is a finely divided, 2-ft. (60-cm) evergreen from the Atlantic Islands. The triangular, somewhat glandular blades are borne on long stipes. This plant is cultivated in Zone 8 in Britain.

Dryopteris ardechensis (from the Ardèche region of France) grows to 2½ ft. (75 cm) on rocky cliffs in cold regions of Mediterranean Europe. It is visually similar to both *D. filix-mas* and *D. affinis* and likely a hybrid between the latter and *D. tyrrhena*. A subevergreen, it has been successfully cultivated in German gardens in Zone 7 and needs gritty soil with good drainage.

Dryopteris atrata (blackish, clothed in black) is a native of southern India and is not cold hardy. Unfortunately, the name has been misapplied to the visually similar temperate species *D. cycadina* and widely distributed as such in error. The trop-

ical *D. hirtipes* from southern and Southeast Asia is very closely related (Fraser-Jenkins, pers. comm.).

Dryopteris cochleata (twisted like a snail shell) is strongly dimorphic with upright, contracted fertile fronds and leafy, arching sterile ones. Both types of fronds reach 2½ to 3½ ft. (75 to 105 cm), have long stipes, and are subevergreen. An attractive, but rarely available, fern from China and eastern Asia, it should be tried in woodlands in Zones 7 and 8.

Dryopteris dracomontana (from the Drakensberg Mountains of South Africa) is from high rainfall, alpine areas where it is found nestled in the lee of rocks in partial sun. It is dimorphic with erect fertile fronds to 1½ ft. (45 cm) and semiprostrate bipinnate to tripinnate, smaller sterile fronds. Like many alpine species, it is challenging, handsome, and tempting. Give it good drainage and a rock garden setting in Zones 7 and 8.

Dryopteris fuscipes (dark footed) is an apogamous evergreen with ovate, pinnate-pinnatifid to bipinnate fronds. The spring foliage unfurls in shades of pinkish red before turning a glowing green. Borderline hardy in Zone 7, it is a radiant addition to lightly shaded gardens in Zones 8 and 9. It comes to us from Japan, China, Korea, and eastern Asia.

Dryopteris guanchica (diminutive of Guanches, a name given to the early peoples of the Canary Islands) is a small evergreen from humid, rocky, wooded ravines in the Iberian Peninsula and Canary Islands. The shiny fronds are triangular and tripinnate or even more finely segmented. This fern needs the humidity of its native habitats but should be tested in Zones 8 and 9.

Dryopteris gymnosora (naked sori) is included only because it is periodically available commercially. The new fronds are reddish but quickly become edged in brown. This fern has persisted in my greenhouse for many years and I admire it for a few weeks every spring. Otherwise, it has potential for moist gardens in Zones 9 and 10 where it will need supplemental humidity as well. It is apogamous and the sori are not covered by indusia.

Dryopteris hawaiiensis (of Hawaii) grows in wet forests on all the major Hawaiian islands except Lanai. Martin Rickard (2000), who has had this species thriving in his British garden for many years, describes it as triangular, tripinnate, and deciduous with fronds to 2 ft. (60 cm). It is recommended for use in shady areas of Zone 9 and possibly Zone 8.

Dryopteris labordei (after Father J. Laborde who collected in Guizhou, China, in the 1890s) is an evergreen from the botanically rich triumvirate of Japan, China, and Korea. It is a 2-ft. (60-cm) narrowly triangular fronded candidate for Zones 7 and 8.

Dryopteris marginata (with a distinct margin) is an extremely tall, to 5 ft. (1.5 m), species from the Himalayas, China, and eastern Asia and is not to be confused with the North American *D. marginalis*. The tall stipes are at least as long as the ovate, tripinnate, evergreen blades. This species is not widely available but should be content in moist soil and shade in Zones 7 and 8.

Dryopteris ×mickelii (after John Mickel, fern curator emeritus at the New York Botanical Garden) is an energetic,

A mature plant of *Dryopteris wallichiana* at the Bellevue Botanical Garden.

Stunning spring fronds of *Dryopteris wallichiana* framed by rockwork at the Bellevue Botanical Garden.

Warm tones of *Dryopteris yigongensis* foliage.

pinnate-pinnatifid to bipinnate, semievergreen, sterile cross between _D. clintoniana_ and _D. goldiana_. The parents get together on the borders of hardwood swamps in the eastern United States. The rhizome creeps and branches producing 4- to 5-ft. (1.2- to 1.5-m) fronds that are "taller and more robust than _D. clintoniana_ . . . and more slender, shinier and erect than _D. goldiana_" (Mickel 1994). This fern can be propagated by division, but it is hoped that tissue culture will further extend its range in the gardening community.

Dryopteris monticola (mountain loving) is cultivated as a separate species in Europe but considered by some to be a subspecies of _D. goldiana_. With a native range in the well-chilled climates of Siberia, Japan, and China, it is a remarkable beauty with all the elegance of its American relative. The deciduous, pastel green, broad fronds mature at 2 to 3 ft. (60 to 90 cm) and are pinnate-pinnatifid. It is an excellent plant for Zones 3 to 8.

Dryopteris monticola, a cold-climate Asian species very similar to the North American _D. goldiana_, in the Förster garden.

Dryopteris ×sjoegrenii in the Peters garden.

Dryopteris nigropaleacea (covered with dark scales), a common fern of Himalayan forests and roadsides, has evergreen, blue-green narrowly triangular, bipinnate fronds up to 3 ft. (90 cm) tall. It is named for the dark scales at the base of the long stipes and should be a serviceable background plant for Zones 7 and 8.

Dryopteris panda (after Pande) is a thickly herbaceous, pinnate-pinnatifid, 2-ft. (60-cm) species from China and the Himalayas. The narrow, lanceolate blades have 12 to 15 pairs of openly spaced, glabrous pinnae with sori on the midribs. The airy structure makes this a decorative addition to partially shaded open sites in Zones (6) 7 and 8.

Dryopteris pulcherrima (beautiful) is a distant cousin of _D. wallichiana_, sharing the densely dressed, scaly stipe and rachis characteristics that are so engaging. The stipe is short and the 2-ft. (60-cm) evergreen blade is pinnate-pinnatifid with up to 35 pairs of dark green, leathery pinnae. As this elegant fern comes from elevations of up to 12,000 ft. (3600 m) in the Himalayas, woodland gardeners in Zones 7, 8, and possibly 6 should succeed with it.

Dryopteris sichotensis (from the Sichote-Alin mountains of eastern Russia), synonym _D. coreano-montana_, is a semievergreen species that is described as looking similar to _D. oreades_ although, at 4 ft. (1.2 m), larger. It can be grown in Zones 6 to 8.

Dryopteris sparsa (sparsely scaly) is extremely widespread in its Pacific distribution and is the only _Dryopteris_ that is native to Australia. It is a medium-sized apogamous evergreen reported to be similar in outline to _D. erythrosora_. This fern is appropriate for use in Zone 9 or perhaps Zone 8.

Dryopteris tyrrhena (from the islands in the Tyrrhenian Sea) is a mid-montane Mediterranean species that grows to 1½ ft. (45 cm). The lanceolate fronds are pinnate-pinnatifid. It can be grown in Zones 6 to 8.

Dryopteris ×uliginosa (of swamps or marshes) mates _D. cristata_ and _D. carthusiana_ in their natural British, European, and North American habitats. The deciduous fronds are 2 ft. (60 cm) tall with pinnate-pinnatifid to bipinnate foliage. Look for it in acidic swamps and the mineral-rich mud of bogs. It is a sterile hybrid but like _D. carthusiana_ it creeps about and can be propagated by division.

Dryopteris villarii (after Dominique Villars, 1745–1814, of France) is a deciduous, upright, gray-green species that once was included with _D. submontana_ (now _D. mindshelkensis_). It is difficult to distinguish between the two species, but small basal pairs of pinnae on _D. villarii_ are one of the defining, albeit minute, differences. This fern is native to rocky limestone substrates in the mountains of Europe and can be established in matching garden situations in Zones 6 to 8.

Dryopteris Hybrids

With the plentiful worldwide distribution of temperate dryopteris comes a cornucopia of hybrids. By nature (and chromosomes) most are sterile. Some of the fertile and even fewer of the sterile hybrids will be found in the main text. Most are rare but the following are among the best known.

From eastern North America (Mickel 1979, Montgomery 1982, 1992) come *Dryopteris celsa* × *D. cristata*, *D. clintoniana* × *D. cristata*, *D.* ×*dowellii* (*D. clintoniana* × *D. intermedia*), *D.* ×*leedsii* (*D. celsa* × *D. marginalis*), *D.* ×*neo-wherryi* (*D. goldiana* × *D. marginalis*), *D.* ×*slossonae* (*D. cristata* × *D. marginalis*), and *D.* ×*triploidea* (*D. carthusiana* × *D. intermedia*).

From Europe (Page 1982, Hegi 1984) come *Dryopteris* ×*ambroseae* (*D. dilatata* × *D. expansa*), *D.* ×*brathaica* (*D. carthusiana* × *D. filix-mas*), *D.* ×*deweveri* (*D. carthusiana* × *D. dilatata*), *D.* ×*mantoniae* (*D. filix-mas* × *D. oreades*), *D.* ×*sardoa* (*D. abbreviata* × *D. tyrrhena*), *D.* ×*sarvelii* (*D. assimilis* × *D. carthusiana*), *D.* ×*sjoegrenii* (*D. azorica* × *D. dilatata*), and *D.* ×*tavelii* (*D. filix-mas* × *D. affinis* agg.).

In addition I have listed some exotic combinations from Asia. These were selected because I would personally choose them as potentially hardy and glamorous additions to the garden when and if they become available. There are, of course, many others that are deserving of recognition especially from the Himalayas. From Japan (Iwatsuki et al. 1995) come *Dryopteris* ×*fujipedis* (*D. crassirhizoma* × *D. lacera*), *D.* ×*gotenbaensis* (*D. hondoensis* × *D. uniformis*), *D.* ×*hakonecola* (*D. dickinsii* × *D. uniformis*), *D.* ×*kominatoensis* (*D. monticola* × *D. tokyoensis*), *D.* ×*mituii* (*D. lacera* × *D. uniformis*), *D.* ×*sugino-takaoi* (*D. lacera* × *D. polylepis*), *D.* ×*tetsu-yamanakae* (*D. commixta* × *D. sieboldii*), *D.* ×*tokudai* (*D. crassirhizoma* × *D. polylepis*), *D.* ×*wakui* (*D. tokyoensis* × *D. lacera*), *D.* ×*watanabei* (*D. crassirhizoma* × *D. uniformis*), *D.* ×*yasuhikoana* (*D.*

crassirhizoma × *D. dickinsii*), and *D.* ×*yuyamae* (*D. pycnopteroides* × *D. uniformis*).

Equisetum
Horsetails

Historically these curious, and sometimes invasive, plants have been considered fern allies. Based on sophisticated research, however, their status has been significantly altered (Moran 2004). They are, as it turns out, true ferns, even though to most observers their "leaves" do not look like those of ferns at all. By whatever classification, they always have been ancient plants, dating back to the Carboniferous era of 345 million to 280 million years ago. (At that time they were also huge by comparison. Imagine having them march into the landscape at 20 ft. [6 m] tall.) Fossil records indicate that their early relatives actually had what we consider "leaves" but they along with the plant height have been reduced in size over the millennia.

Structurally, equisetums are designed like stacks of vertical peashooters joined by sheaths and extending like tripods with each new emerging segment smaller than the last. Stems are hollow, green, and furrowed. The collarlike, branch-protecting sheaths of whorled leaf bases vary in size, color, and number of teeth (which are the remnants of the "leaves") all of which are factors in identification. When present, the branches are hairlike extensions of the sheaths. Rhizomes are long-creeping, forming networks that are often deeply buried. Species may be evergreen or deciduous and are frequently dimorphic.

Equisetum as frequently encountered in situ, with or without invitation.

Spores carried in cones are green and consequently short-lived (fortunately). They reproduce eagerly on moist soil and have two types of gametophytes, male and female, an unusual characteristic. Division works well so to propagate, divide and conquer. Multisheathed stem cuttings may also root when plunged into moist sand.

Equisetum comes from the Greek *equis*, horse, and *seta*, bristle, referring to the horsetail appearance and common name of those in the genus, such as *E. arvense*, that have tiers of threadlike branches in bushy whorls. Scouring rush is the popular epithet for the unbranched species. All have a high silica content and have been used over the centuries for scouring pots and pans, and for that matter floors. (As a last resort, I have used it on camping trips for cleaning pots.) It has also been highly valued for the demanding and delicate final precision polishing of specialized wood and metal products including cabinets, pewter, and bones and may still be used for violins today. In the medicine chest the same silica content was valued for its use in compresses to help stem the flow of blood from wounds and to hasten the cure of open sores.

The 15 species of *Equisetum* occur throughout the world, although primarily in temperate climates. In addition there are many hybrids. They are not particular about soil, but do prefer moisture and sunshine and are often found in abundance in gullies, roadside ditches, and boggy meadows. Tough creatures, they were among the pioneering plants on the flanks of Washington State's Mount Saint Helens following the volcanic eruption of 1980. Some are aggressive and are quite willing to "pioneer" in the garden as well. To prevent invasions, but to enjoy their unique architecture, grow them in containers, please.

Equisetum arvense
Common horsetail
Epithet means "of ploughed fields."
Deciduous, 1 to 2 ft. (30 to 60 cm). Zones 1 to 10. Dimorphic.

DESCRIPTION: The rhizome is very long-creeping. Short, naked, jointed, baby pink fertile stems are the first to appear in spring, surviving just long enough to shed spores. Grooved, taller sterile stems are a rich green with 12 to 18 bicolored sheaths made up of 14 or fewer white-tipped brown teeth. Lower sheaths are spaced at 1-in. (2.5-cm) intervals with the distance between the segments becoming smaller approaching the upper portions of the stem. Whorls of green and grooved branching branches extend from the sheaths.

RANGE AND HABITAT: Truly an international species, this is native to and naturalized in Europe, Asia, and North America as well as New Zealand.

CULTURE AND COMMENTS: Although feathery, this species is weedy and should not be introduced to gardens. Once established, it is very difficult to eradicate. The taller but otherwise similar *Equisetum telmateia* has more teeth, a key distinction according to the *Flora of North America* (1993).

Equisetum hyemale
Scouring rush, Dutch rush
Epithet from *hiems*, winter, referring to the evergreen stems.
Evergreen, 2 to 6 ft. (60 to 180 cm). Zones 2 to 10.

DESCRIPTION: Rhizomes are long-creeping. Hollow, upright, slender stalks are a flat green with multiple grooves and toothy sheaths grading in color bands from black through brown to cream. There are no branches, but young springtime stalks may produce temporary short offshoots from the sheath collars. The sheath and branch may be removed and rooted in wet sand. Spores are carried in small cones on the tips of the stems.

RANGE AND HABITAT: Like most equisetums, this covers a broad band of North America, including Canada and Mexico, as well as parts of Central America, Europe, and Asia and has naturalized elsewhere. It springs from seeps and moisture-rich sunny to partially shady habitats.

CULTURE AND COMMENTS: This interesting variable species will eagerly colonize given the opportunity. Keep it confined. I grow mine in a large container in wet soil surrounded by low sarracenias. It is 6 ft. (1.8 m) tall and definitely attracts attention. I pick off the fertile cones before they have the opportunity to spread their joy. With caution, as those rhizomes love to escape, pots can be used as sunken gardens in water features. Be sure to diligently lift the display with disciplined frequency so that the "display" does not become a water hazard.

Equisetum scirpoides
Dwarf scouring rush
Epithet means "rushlike."
Evergreen, 4 to 8 in. (10 to 20 cm). Zones 1 to 8.

DESCRIPTION: The rhizome is short-creeping. Twisting, wiry, ridged branches without a central cavity form a tangled mass of foliage with small sheaths of three teeth garnished with deciduous hairlike tips. It is diagnostically significant that the stems are not hollow. Fertile cones are partially enclosed in the ultimate sheath and may persist over winter. The three teeth trim six equal-sided ridges, helping to distinguish this species from the similarly compact, although slightly larger, *Equisetum variegatum* that has four or more teeth, a matching number of ridges, and nontwisting shoots.

Fertile cones laden with short-lived spores on *Equisetum* growing in a soggy highway ditch.

Equisetum hyemale growing in a wet lakeside site with the Japanese blood grass, *Imperata cylindrica.*

Dwarf upright but nontwisting stems of *Equisetum variegatum* surround a seedling *Acer palmatum* in a small pot displayed for close viewing.

RANGE AND HABITAT: This dwarf is native to cold northern zones up to and including the alpine areas around the world. It appreciates moisture and can be found in a variety of substrates.

CULTURE AND COMMENTS: With its diminutive stature, the miniature scouring rush makes a delightful conversation piece in a well-watered container. It would, in fact, be overwhelmed in anything but a Lilliputian garden but has been used effectively as an understory in bonsai or, when containerized, as a companion plant on the borders of bogs. While not as aggressive as its brethren, it can spread, given the opportunity, so confinement is strongly recommended.

Equisetum telmateia
Giant horsetail
Epithet means "of marshes and mud."
Deciduous, 1 to 5 ft. (30 to 150 cm). Zones 7 to 9. Dimorphic.

DESCRIPTION: The rhizome is long-creeping and can tunnel about the neighborhood at a depth of 4 ft. (120 cm). Upright grooved stems have layers of branches spreading outward from collarlike sheaths. This species is extremely similar to *Equisetum arvense* but is taller, and alert readers of keys will find that it has upwards of 14 teeth on each sheath rather than the lower number of *E. arvense*. The fertile fronds are early risers, significantly shorter than the sterile, pale peachy brown, and quickly deciduous.

RANGE AND HABITAT: The distribution is somewhat amazing with colonies extending down the west coast of North America, but including Europe, the Azores, and Canary Islands. Some botanists divide the North American and European material into separate subspecies.

CULTURE AND COMMENTS: This species is a common weed and not suitable for garden use.

Equisetum variegatum
Variegated scouring rush
Epithet means "variegated."
Evergreen, 4 to 12 in. (10 to 30 cm). Zones 1 to 8.

DESCRIPTION: The rhizome is creeping giving rise to dense tufts of upright, slender, ridged, green stems. Sheaths are two-toned, black and white, a condition responsible for the "variegatum" of the botanical name. Numbers of teeth and ridges vary, but significantly are more than three. Stems are hollow and unbranched. Fertile cones, which may be long-lived, are enclosed in sheaths at the tips of the stems. The ridge numbers, taller size, and nontwisty hollow stems separate it from fellow dwarf, *Equisetum scirpoides*.

RANGE AND HABITAT: This species is circumboreal, forming colonies in open wet sites especially at colder higher altitudes.

CULTURE AND COMMENTS: Like *Equisetum scirpoides*, the variegated scouring rush is an interesting plant for close-up viewing in a container. It makes an atypical bonsai and given sufficient watering may be used successfully as a houseplant.

Shorter Notes
Equisetum ×ferrissii (after Ferris), a cross between *E. hyemale* and *E. laevigatum*, is the most common of the many *Eq-*

uisetum hybrids. It is intermediate between the parents with the lower portion of the stems evergreen as in *E. hyemale* and the upper deciduous as in *E. laevigatum*. Lower stem and upper stem sheath configurations and colorations respectively tend to match the parents as well. This *Equisetum* is found throughout Canada and the United States except for the consistently hot and humid lower southeastern states.

Equisetum fluviatile (of rivers and streams), the water horsetail or water pipes, is characterized by thick creeping rhizomes that wander about underwater or in muddy swamps. The deciduous aerial stems have small branches and mature at 2 to 3 ft. (60 to 90 cm). The species needs to be confined, but a container of "pipes" sunk into the border of a pond is certain to attract attention in Zones 1 to 8. It is not an appropriate choice for hot summer areas.

Tall spires of *Equisetum myriochaetum* offer a remarkable feathery display at the Hamburg Botanical Garden.

Equisetum laevigatum (smooth, polished), the smooth scouring rush, is a deciduous 2-ft. (60-cm) spreader and the only North American endemic. It is found in Zones 3 to 8 from mid-America westward. The ridges are smooth with black-trimmed green sheaths. Look for it in open, wet exposures.

Equisetum myriochaetum (numerous long hairs) offers a prehistoric experience with 15- to 24-ft. (4.5- to 8-m) tall spires carrying layers of feathery, horizontally drooping branches. While usually found in large conservatories, this species is reputedly hardy in Zones 9 to 11. Sopping wet soil, structural support, and wind protection would all be requirements.

Equisetum sylvaticum (of woods, sylvan), the woodland horsetail, is unusual in its preference for spreading throughout moist woods rather than the traditional inhospitable wet and exposed sites of other horsetails. Branches that subdivide (it is the only *Equisetum* to do this) extend in rather graceful whorls from square-cut rust-colored sheaths. In North America this 2-footer (60 cm) is native to Canada, dipping occasionally into the northern tier of the United States. Worldwide it is native to Europe, Asia, and Japan. Interested growers should give it a container, moisture, and shade in Zones 2 through cool summer 8.

Goniophlebium

Goniophlebium (angled vein, in reference to the arrangement of the veins) is a genus of 17 species, classified until relatively recently as *Polypodium* from which they are separated based on several characteristics including their venation pattern. In nature they are found in the Pacific Islands and Asia.

Goniophlebium persicifolium is similar to *G. subauriculatum* in form and garden value. Both plants are widely distributed as natives in the tropical world.

Goniophlebium subauriculatum, described as "one of the best basket ferns available" (Jones 1987), is a stunning plant with pendant, simply pinnate fronds nearly 6 ft. (1.8 m) long, hanging almost straight down. In the wild it drapes cliffs in shade, while in the garden it will form comforting drapery on a stone wall. It is an easy garden plant, a clump-former capable of staying for many years just where it is put. (Description by George Schenk.) **'Knightiae'**, an especially ornamental form mentioned in Jones (1987), has deeply incised pinnae.

Equisetum sylvaticum stands as a sentinel in the Jessen garden.

Goniophlebium subauriculatum growing on top of a wall, in nearly full sun, keeps its rich green color. Photo by George Schenk.

Gymnocarpium

These cheery dwarf delights are the elfin sprites of the fern world. Most are associated with moist, open, coniferous woodlands and the pleasures of leisurely strolls among wildflowers and ferns. They feature triangular to pentagonal, deciduous, moss green fronds waving, like delicate wands, on a horizontal plane from brittle upright stipes. Rhizomes are small and shallow growing. They travel in friable duff creating a loose woodland carpet of velvety fronds. Stipes are grooved with two vascular bundles. Veins are free, and sori without indusia are round to oval and carried between the midrib and margin. Plants are readily increased by division and easily propagated from spores.

Gymnocarpium comes from the Greek *gymno*, naked, and *karpos*, fruit, referring to the absence of an indusium. Worldwide there are eight species. Primarily they are from north temperate areas. They are all wonderful gardenworthy ferns charming even the undedicated. Several, however, are difficult to positively identify. The attachment and size of the second pinnae from the bottom are referenced as diagnostically significant botanical indicators.

Gymnocarpium disjunctum
Western oak fern
Epithet means "disjunct."

Deciduous, 9 to 18 in. (23 to 45 cm). Zones 4 to (cool summer) 8.

DESCRIPTION: In appropriately humusy soil, the rhizomes creep easily and widely. Smooth, brittle stipes are straw-colored and up to one-half of the frond length. Soft green triangular to pentagonal horizontal blades are tripinnate-pinnatifid. Six to ten pairs of pinnae have extended lower pinnules. Significantly for this species the innermost lower pinnules of the second pinnae pair are equal in size or longer than adjacent pinnules. The matching mate on the upper side is smaller. Round naked sori line up between the midrib and margin.

RANGE AND HABITAT: Look for this species in acid soil in moist coniferous woods, on streambanks and shaded rocky slopes along the Pacific coast of North America from Alaska south to Oregon and slightly inland to Montana and Wyoming. Across the sea it can be found in parts of Russia, Sakhalin, and Kamchatka.

CULTURE AND COMMENTS: This species gladly adapts to cultivation so long as it is in shade, the soil is loose, and the moisture constant. While it is a feathery attraction in cool temperate gardens, it does not perform well in hot summer areas. It is extremely similar to *Gymnocarpium dryopteris* but is larger, has tripinnate rather than bipinnate foliage as well as those telltale long and short pinnules. The natives *Blechnum spicant*

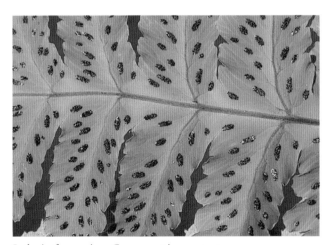
Indusia-free sori on *Gymnocarpium oyamense*.

Goniophlebium subauriculatum 'Knightiae' in the Fernery at the Morris Arboretum.

The pinnules and pinnae that are often used to make technical botanical distinctions between species of *Gymnocarpium*.

and *Linnaea borealis* share cultural requirements and are handsome companions.

Gymnocarpium dryopteris
Oak fern
Epithet from *drys*, oak, and *pteris*, fern.
Deciduous, 9 to 12 in. (23 to 30 cm). Zones 2 to (cool summer) 8.

DESCRIPTION: The rhizome is long-creeping especially in moist leaf mold. Grooved, delicate stipes are dark at the base and straw to green above and up to one-half of the frond length. Horizontal, rich green blades are triangular to pentagonal and bipinnate-pinnatifid with 6 to 10 pairs of pinnae. The second from the base has lower inner pinnules that are somewhat longer than the adjacent, but the matching upper ones are the same size as their neighbors. Round indusia-free sori are in rows near the margin.

Gymnocarpium dryopteris in the native garden at the Institute of Ecosystem Studies, New York.

The leafy plumes of fronds on *Gymnocarpium dryopteris* 'Plumosum'.

RANGE AND HABITAT: Oak fern is found worldwide in shaded acidic soil, wet seeps, and varied woodlands in cool temperate zones.

CULTURE AND COMMENTS: In ancient times the revered oak tree had special status for its supposedly superb magical powers. This species, being the oak fern, was likewise favored and credited with many wonders including preventing bad "spells" or offering protection from thunder and lightning when planted on roofs. The species has done quite a bit of taxonomic touring. By whatever name, it is to be welcomed for its light airy effect in woodlands and ease of maintenance given the basics of shade and composty soil. It does not adjust to the hot summers of interior climates.

'Plumosum' (feathery), with richly foliose fronds, is even more ornamental than the type and naturalizes in loose, shaded, woodland duff with equal ease.

Gymnocarpium oyamense
Epithet is after the Oya region in Japan.
Deciduous, 8 to 18 in. (20 to 45 cm). Zones 7 to 9.

DESCRIPTION: The slender rhizomes are long-creeping. Grooved, dull to slightly shiny green stipes are up to two-thirds of the frond length. Creamy green, horizontal blades

Clusters of thin-textured, horizontal fronds of *Gymnocarpium oyamense* offer a soft component in the woodland garden.

are long triangular and pinnate-pinnatifid with crenate, squared pinnule margins. There are 10 to 15 pairs of soft pinnae with the lowest pair pointing like downward wings away from the apex. Sori are oval and in multiple rows close to the margins of the pinnules and along the midribs of the pinnae.

RANGE AND HABITAT: Originally reputed to prefer limestone habitats, I can find no documentation in either direction. (Unfortunately it is just as easy to repeat inaccurate information, as it is to confirm what is accurate.) I do know that my plants are happy in woodland soil, but based on the long-ago proffered advice are adjacent to a concrete foundation, which may or may not be significant. However, it implies that a little leaching lime will not be harmful. This species is native to Japan, China, Taiwan, Nepal, the Philippines, and New Guinea.

CULTURE AND COMMENTS: An incredibly lovely species with a flowing soft texture, this is a high-priority plant for cool temperate gardens. Give it shade, regular moisture, humusy soil, and your admiration. Unfortunately hot summer climates are not suitable.

Gymnocarpium robertianum
Limestone oak fern
Epithet is supposedly after this plant's resemblance to *Geranium robertianum* (an insult).
Deciduous, 8 to 18 in. (20 to 45 cm). Zones 2 to (cool summer) 8.

DESCRIPTION: The rhizome is long-creeping. Tall pale green, grooved stipes are up to one-half of the frond length but usually of smaller proportions. Bipinnate-pinnatifid blades are triangular with 9 to 12 pairs of pinnae; the lower pair are similar to those immediately above. The surfaces and structure are covered with minute pinhead glandular hairs so small that they would make a grain of salt look like an iceberg by comparison. Sori without indusia are round and close to the margins.

RANGE AND HABITAT: Here is a truly lime-loving species that is circumboreal wherever the proper habitat permits. It grows in partially shaded calcareous swamps, rocky limestone slopes, and even on walls.

CULTURE AND COMMENTS: An excellent choice for a limestone cobble, this species will tolerate some sunshine but not drought.

Shorter Notes
Gymnocarpium appalachianum (from Appalachia), the Appalachian oak fern, has those pinnules on the second-from-the-base pairs of pinnae stalked rather than sessile as in *G. disjunctum* and *G. dryopteris*. A deciduous Appalachian endemic with populations in a narrow range from North Carolina and West Virginia to Ohio, this species grows in moist sandstone in the woods at higher elevations along its range. It should adapt to gardens wherever it can be kept cool in the summer from Zones 2 to 8.

Gymnocarpium fedtschenkoanum (after Boris Fedtschenko, 1872–1947, of Russia) from central Asia, China, Tibet, and Nepal, is an attractive deciduous pale green species with finely cut tripinnate triangular blades and with lower pinnules on the second pinnae pair from the base smaller than those adjacent. Matching upper pinnules on the same pinnae are missing. This species is hardy from Zones 5 to 8 and likely even colder zones. Use it with collector's pride as a modest and handsome, nonaggressive carpet in woodland shade and moist compost or as a ground cover in large container designs. It is somewhat slow to establish.

Gymnocarpium jessoense (after the Japanese island, Yezo, Hokkaido) is a species with the typical triangular outline and with glandular hairs strictly along the upper pinnae midribs, distinguishing it from *G. robertianum*, which has glands distributed over most of the frond. This is a high-elevation species with a preference for lime substrates and should do well in the cobbles of gardens from Zone 4 to 8.

Gymnocarpium robertianum in the limestone of a European rock garden.

The rarely available *Gymnocarpium fedtschenkoanum* offers a refreshing presence in the company of late summer-flowering *Cyclamen* in the Kohout garden.

Huperzia

The fir mosses were until extremely recently (Moran 2004) believed to be fern allies. Sophisticated research has changed this classification. (See comments under *Selaginella*.) However, they are indeed without flowers and seeds, and while most are tropical, several form evergreen carpets of miniature, mosslike, upright spikes on forest floors or rocky ledges and are included here for enjoyment and education. They are frequently lumped together with *Lycopodium*, and enjoy similar shady and generally acidic habitats. Plants differ from most other lycophytes in lacking horizontal stems and in having branchlets with attached gemmae (leafy propagules that detach and grow into new plants). Curiously, the roots originate at the tips of the shoots and burrow through the stem, eventually emerging at the base (rather like some of the tree ferns).

Unlike ferns, huperzias bear spores in the leaf axils but these are not a practical option for propagation. (Lycopodiums carry their spores in cones.) They can be divided but with a dependence on associated fungi are not usually long-lived in or recommended for garden settings (unless they are already happily established on the property). In addition to the species, there are many hybrids. The genus name honors the German fern horticulturist, Johann Huperz.

Huperzia appalachiana (from Appalachia) is a compact species that has ¼-in. (6-mm) smooth, narrowly triangular leaves on upright 2½- to 4-in. (6- to 10-cm) shoots. They are without annual growth constrictions (a narrowed, pinched ring of foliage). Gemmae-bearing, mature upper leaves are markedly smaller than the lower juveniles. Unlike most fir mosses, *H. appalachiana* is not noticeably shiny and grows in

A colony of *Huperzia lucidula* successfully established in the decomposing leafy litter in the Hudgens garden brings visions of spring walks in the woodlands.

Pendulous *Huperzia varia* foliage hangs from the forest overstory along a trail on Mount Cook on New Zealand's South Island.

alpine zones on exposed cliffs and among acidic rocks rather than in shady woodlands. The native range extends from Zones 3 to 6 along the Atlantic coast from eastern Canada south to Tennessee and Virginia and inland to Michigan and Minnesota with disjunct populations in Greenland.

Huperzia lucidula (shining), synonym *Lycopodium lucidulum*, is a glistening green creeper that roots from underground rhizomes in Zones 2 to 6. The ³⁄₈-in. (9-mm) leaves are toothed and on 6-in. (15-cm) shoots that have winter growth constrictions. With age the shoots become brown and decumbent. Gemmae are tucked in the ultimate whorl of the current year's leaves. This species grows in rich soil in damp coniferous and hardwood forests from upper midwestern North America to the East Coast.

Huperzia selago (flashing), synonym *Lycopodium selago*, forms glowing dark green, miniature forests of evergreen, upright 4- to 6-in. (10- to 15-cm) stalks with a hint of annual constriction rings. The smooth to slightly toothy ¹⁄₈-in. (3-mm) leaves are lanceolate. Gemmae are produced annually in the terminal whorl of foliage. Once considered to be widespread, albeit variable, the species has been divided into a number of closely associated relatives. What for years in the Pacific Northwest has been called *H. selago* (or more precisely *Lycopodium selago*) is now *H. haleakalae* based on the distribution of gemmae throughout the mature portions of the foliage rather than just the terminal whorl. As a group, they are

circumboreal Zone 2 natives of damp woodlands or sometimes bogs and less frequently on shaded rocky strata.

Huperzia varia (varied), the hanging clubmoss, synonym *Lycopodium varium*, is from New Zealand and Australia. As the common name implies, this is a variable species that usually perches as an epiphyte and hangs its long tassels of up to 6 ft. (1.8 m) from the crowns of trees in forested areas. It may grow terrestrially but is more often found as an epiphytic treat along the many hiking tracks that are popular with visitors. Shorter forms are found on tree fern trunks. It is a basket candidate in Zones 4 to 8.

Hypolepis

Worldwide there are 50 to 60 of these bramble ferns native primarily to Southeast Asia and islands of the South Pacific. They have long-creeping, branching rhizomes that can become aggressive when too happy. The deciduous fronds are much divided and tall. Sori are marginal and under a recurved flap or toothlike indusium. In Southern California, they are popular for use as ground covers or container plantings. Multiply them by division or propagate from spores. The genus name means "under scale," in reference to the protected sori.

Hypolepis millefolium (thousand leaved) is an emerald green, furry tripinnate-pinnatifid deciduous species with triangular fronds and long-creeping rhizomes. At 2 ft. (60 cm) it is one of the shortest in the genus. Native to subalpine areas in

Hypolepis millefolium wanders willingly among rocks in New Zealand.

New Zealand, it is also one of the hardiest and useful in Zones 7 to 10. Provide good drainage, partial shade, moisture, and acid to neutral soil.

Hypolepis punctata (spotted), an import from Asia, Australia, and New Zealand as well as Chile, has deciduous bipinnate-pinnatifid to tripinnate-pinnatifid blades on fronds up to 4 ft. (1.2 m). It is for Zones 8 to 10 where it will tolerate some sun so long as it has wet feet. It can be invasive.

Hypolepis repens (creeping), the bramble fern, can bramble up to 6 ft. (1.8 m) from spreading rhizomes. It is deciduous with tripinnate to quadripinnate fronds and spines along the stipe and rachis. Found in Florida and tropical America it is the only *Hypolepis* native to the United States. Easily grown in damp to wet seeping soils or woodlands, it is best when controlled or containerized in Zones 9 and 10.

Hypolepis rugosula (with small wrinkles), the ruddy ground fern, from the Southern Hemisphere, forms thickets of deciduous 3- to 5-ft. (90- to 150-cm), coarse, triangular, tripinnate fronds in its preferred moist to wet habitats. The dark green foliage is supported by "ruddy" stipes and rachises. It can be cultivated in Zones 7 (with protection) to 10 but is best contained as, like most of the genus, the rhizomes can assertively expand the fern's dominance into surrounding territory.

Hypolepis tenuifolia (slender leaved), from the South Pacific and Asia, has deciduous bipinnate-pinnatifid to tripinnate-pinnatifid blades on fronds to 4 ft. (1.2 m). They are somewhat glandular and grow in colonies from creeping rhizomes in moist shade in Zones 9 and 10. Material in the trade may actually be a different species.

Lastreopsis

Lastreopsis (resembling *Lastrea*, an early botanical classification that included *Thelypteris* and *Dryopteris* and was once a subsection under the even broader umbrella of *Aspidium* which claimed *Polystichum* as one of its own as well) is an attractive genus with a limited number of species mostly native to the Southern Hemisphere, particularly Australia and New Zealand. They are a handsome lot with kidney-shaped indusia on evergreen, bipinnate to quadripinnate, triangular, frequently shiny foliage. All are elegant and noteworthy additions for deep shade and consistently moist soil in Zones 9 and 10.

Lastreopsis acuminata (with a long pointed tip) has shiny, narrowly triangular, bipinnate fronds growing in clusters of up to 2 ft. (60 cm). Stipes are rosy and the innermost lower pinnules on the lowest pinnae are exaggerated in length.

Lastreopsis glabella (smooth) has bipinnate fronds with a long stipe equaling the blade in length. It grows to 2 ft. (60 cm) or slightly more from an upright rhizome and is glabrous except for a significant garnish of russet hairs on the upper surface of the pinnae midribs. Genus-typical, triangular fronds have pinnae with serrate margins and innermost lower pinnules extending beyond adjacent pinnules.

Lastreopsis hispida (with stiff hairs) has creeping rhizomes which produce scattered fronds with 2-ft. (60-cm) stipes wrapped in long bristles of ebony scales intermixed with glandular hairs. Broadly triangular blades matching the stipe in length are tripinnate to quadripinnate with the innermost lower pinnules on the lower pinnae only modestly longer than adjoining pinnules.

Lemmaphyllum

Lemmaphyllum (*lemma*, scale, and *phyllum*, leaf) is a genus of 5 to 10 species that grow as small but sturdy epiphytes in Asia.

Lemmaphyllum microphyllum (*micro*, small, and *phyllum*, leaf) is a charming creeper from the Far East including Japan, the Philippines, Korea, China, India, and the Asiatic Islands. Rhizomes creep just below the soil's surface producing succulent masses of overlapping, kelly-green, oval pads of pinnae. Stipes are virtually nonexistent. Plants are dimorphic with upright sentinels of slender fertile fronds on a little stipe. Sori without indusia are crowded in single linear rows on either side of the midveins. With its prostrate growth, this is an attractive and manageable groundcovering container plant. In conservatories such as the stunning Fernery at Philadelphia's Morris Arboretum, the species wanders freely, coating the ground and an occasional tree trunk with brilliant greenery. Outdoors, with much protection in Zone 8, it is modest in its annual expansion, and when grown in a container can be snatched in from threatening cold and stored until the danger has passed. It establishes comfortably in Zones 9 and 10.

Lophosoria

Lophosoria (*lopho*, crested, and *soria*, sori) consists of a single species from the Caribbean, Mexico, Central and South America. It is closely related to *Dicksonia* but separated based on its large fronds, hairy rhizomes, and lack of soral indusia.

Lophosoria quadripinnata (*quadripinnata*, four pinnate), aptly described in *Flora de Chile* (1995) as "*plantas grandes*," is a tree-fern style species native to wet montane cloud forests from Mexico to southern Chile. The thick rhizome often forms a trunk up to 3 ft. (90 cm) or more and is draped in long brown tresses. Evergreen, triangular fronds to 12 ft. (3.6 m) are a magnificent sight with overstory arches of tripinnate to quadripinnate foliage. Sori are at the base of the pinna lobes and without indusia. British specialists have this species in cultivation. Gardeners with moist habitats in Zones 9 to 11 (8 with protection) should grow this with ease (on a space-available basis).

Lycopodiella
Bog clubmoss

The names "little lycopodiums" or "little wolf paws" are applied to this diminutive former "fern ally" (see *Selaginella* for comments), a recent segregate genus from *Lycopodium*. *Lycopodiella* is botanically distinct by having primitive vertical cones carried as broad extensions from the upright shoots, and having those same upright shoots unbranched. They are not really candidates for cultivation but can be enjoyed in their wild habitats where they hybridize at will.

Lycopodiella alopecuroides (fox tail), synonym *Lycopodium alopecuroides*, is an acid bog species with horizontal, sterile perennial stems distinguished by their arching habit. The tips root as they inch about in sandy peat. The fertile upright foottall (30-cm) "foxtails" are deciduous and topped with a

Large umbrellas of fronds on *Hypolepis rugosula* arch over surrounding plants in the Peters garden.

Lastreopsis glabella on display in New Zealand.

Minute twists of *Lemmaphyllum microphyllum* decorate a tree trunk in the Fernery at the Morris Arboretum.

A canopy of huge *Lophosoria quadripinnata* fronds dwarfs the creeping plants of *Gleichenia squamulosa* in the Alerce Andino National Park in Chile. Photo by Richie Steffen, Miller Botanical Garden.

Drapes of fertile fronds of *Lophosoria quadripinnata*. Photo by Richie Steffen, Miller Botanical Garden.

toothed 1- to 2-in. (2.5- to 5-cm) cone. Native populations extend from New England to the Gulf Coast.

Lycopodiella appressa (lying close together), synonym *Lycopodium appressum*, is a deciduous bog dweller with slender, rooting, creeping stems. The upright 6- to 15-in. (15- to 38-cm) shoots are pale green and carry the fertile cones as a continuation of the stalk. These are not showy plants, but the sharp-eyed enthusiast can spot and enjoy them on the muddy or sandy floor of such fascinating habitats as the Pinelands of New Jersey in the company of the extraordinary *Schizaea* and its array of unusual companions. Its native Zone 6 range extends down the Atlantic Coast of North America to an outlying population in Cuba.

Lycopodiella ×*copelandii* (after Joseph Copeland, 1907–1990, botany professor at the City College of New York) is a rare hybrid between *L. alopecuroides* and *L. appressa* that was discovered and described (as what was then *Lycopodium*) by my sharp-eyed friend Joan Eiger Gottlieb in 1956. It was the first reported hybrid, of the many now known, for the clubmoss complex. The 8-in. (20-cm), erect stalks support 2-in. (5-cm) cones and have upward-pointing leaves that are mostly without teeth. The creeping stems hug the substrate like *L. appressa* but occasionally arch, resembling *L. alopecuroides*. A partially evergreen Zone 4 to 7 bog dweller, it is native from Massachusetts to New Jersey. The type plant was found in Lakehurst, New Jersey.

Lycopodiella inundata (of marshes), synonym *Lycopodium inundatum*, is a small, deciduous bog clubmoss but comparable in physical aspects to *Lycopodiella appressa*. It differs in having horizontal segments that are exceptionally slender, producing one upright shoot rather than several. Its native range is in the cold, more northerly latitudes or high mountain areas southward from Zone 1 northern Canadian extremes to Pennsylvania and West Virginia on the North American East Coast and Montana and Washington on the West. The population range extends from wet habitats above the Arctic Circle in Europe across the polar zones of Russia to their eastern coast and down to Japan.

Lycopodium
Clubmosses

Clubmosses produce extended rooting swags of rounded stems dressed in needlelike leaves. They were formerly classified as fern allies but under the scrutiny of modern research techniques (Moran 2004) now have a family tree of their own. (See *Selaginella* for comments.) Sometimes called "ground pine" or "running pine," visually descriptive although botanically incorrect epithets, these spore-bearing plants are

Lycopodiella appressa inconspicuously shares the bog at Websmill in the Pinelands of New Jersey.

Challenging to cultivate, *Lycopodium annotinum* spreads like an upright stand of conifers in the Jessen garden.

included here because of their traditional association with the fern community.

Internationally there are 350 to 400 species with habitat preferences ranging from groundcovering colonies in temperate forests to long skirts of epiphytic draperies in humid temperate to tropical climates. The latter with their tassels of fertile cones (strobili) and frequently unfamiliar green garments offer a fascinating departure from traditional basket subjects especially in conservatories.

Botanically, lycopodiums (from the Greek *lykos*, wolf, and *podes*, foot, describing the somewhat imaginative resemblance of the branch tips to a wolf's paw) can be separated from *Huperzia* by the long-creeping stems as well as, when fertile, separate drooping or upright spore-bearing cones often carried on stalks. The irregular branching of the upright shoots distinguishes them from *Lycopodiella*, which has unbranched shoots, and from *Diphasiastrum*, which has regular and equal branching.

Lycopodiums are sometimes cultivated, but with attendant difficulties. The woodland species are frequently associated with specific soil fungi, and need excellent drainage but moisture and highly acid soil in partial shade. In baskets the epiphytic species are easier but need warmth, humidity, a crumbly soil mix for drainage, and good air circulation.

Propagation is by division. Be sure to take a growing tip. Spores are produced in great clouds, but I once read (a myth?) that they need to go through the digestive tract of an animal in order to germinate so have not explored that option. They germinate underground and even under ideal conditions can take from months to years to produce a plant.

The spores, especially of *Lycopodium clavatum*, can be fun, however, as with their oil content they are highly flammable (and were once called witch's flour in parts of Europe). Try tossing some on the campfire for mini fireworks. More practically, in the early days of photography they were used as flash powder. In addition because of their water-repellent properties, they have been used much as one would use talcum powder. Pharmacists used them for coating pills among other applications.

The foliage also had assorted uses. Medicinally a concoction made with dried leaves and wine was recommended as a cure for gout (which sounds like an oxymoron). Socially, garlands of the trailing stems were popular adornments for festive occasions and were prized not only for being ornamental, but also for purported aphrodisiacal effects.

Lycopodium annotinum (with distinct annual increments), the bristly clubmoss, is an extremely widespread evergreen species with populations throughout the world. Crawling stems are up to a yard (1 m) long and bear upright 6-in. (15-

cm) shoots of bristly foliage topped with a solitary fertile cone. The branches are pinched with annual bud constrictions. The species is a denizen of Zones 3 to 6 in acid soil in wet woods and bogs to grasslands and rocky alpine slopes. The structural composition of plants varies extensively depending on altitude and environment.

Lycopodium cernuum, a pantropical sprawler, spreads its stringy green branches into a yard-wide (meter-wide) patch on sunny road banks and in farm animal pastures (they will not eat it). From these prostrate branches, fir-treelike structures arise to 1 or 2 ft. (30 or 60 cm) in height, bearing pendant cones at the tips of the "tree's" boughs. In the Philippines, the conifer portions of *L. cernuum* are gathered commercially just before Christmas, taken to Manila, hung with miniature ornaments, and made into tabletop Christmas trees. I grow this clubmoss in a sunny rock garden but have found that this species is not always easy to establish: other transplants have lived for a year or two and then faded away. (Description by George Schenk.)

Lycopodium cernuum with its treelike tiers of branches near a miniature *Agave* species and minor form of *Ophiopogon japonicum* (mondo grass). It has grown and spread here for years, transplanted from a road bank as a tangle of rooted branches. Photo by George Schenk.

A silvery driftwood log serves as a perfect backdrop for the crawling shoots and fertile uprights of *Lycopodium clavatum* growing in the sand and salty spray in a surprising home on a Pacific Ocean spit along the Washington coast.

Little patches of *Lycopodium fastigiatum* greenery poke through a carpet of *Raoulia* in an alpine area of New Zealand's South Island.

Fertile summertime growth on *Lycopodium obscurum* carpets the woodland floor in New Jersey.

Lycopodium clavatum (club-shaped), common clubmoss or running pine, does indeed run to 3 ft. (90 cm) or more. Upright 4-in. (10-cm) shoots (not counting the strobili) with bright green, hair-tipped leaves branch and fork from a trunk-like base. One to five cream-colored fertile cones are held upright on a pale and sometimes branched narrow stalk (peduncle). The sight of groves of these minute yellow "clubs," when produced en masse and supported on sheets of glossy greenery, is a truly memorable woodland experience. This variable evergreen species in its assorted manifestations is one of the world's most common lycophytes and is native to Zones 3 to 8 on forest floors and open sites in acid soil. The hair-tipped leaves are diagnostically significant and unique to the species.

Lycopodium dendroideum (treelike), synonym *L. obscurum* var. *dendroideum*, is an upright 8- to 10-in. (20- to 25-cm) tall, multibranching, evergreen tree with minute 1/8 to 1/4 in. (3 to 6 mm) bright green leaves. Up to seven 1- to 2-in. (2.5- to 5-cm) cones are carried without a stalk at the tips of the shoots. The growth is without annual ring constrictions and is botanically and visually very similar to *L. obscurum*. Observable differences presented by *Flora of North America* (1993) are rounded lateral shoots with nontwisting leaves equal in size in *L. dendroideum* versus lateral shoots that are flat in cross section carrying twisting leaves that are unequal in size in *L. obscurum*. It is happy in and around bogs and wet woods in a broad continental sweep from Zone 2 Alaska to the Atlantic coast.

Lycopodium fastigiatum (erect), the alpine clubmoss, is an upright species that is common in the mountainous areas of New Zealand and Australia. The dense tufts of up to foot-tall (30-cm) compact bushlets are recognized and noted for their incurved leaves. The whole may turn a bright orange in exposed alpine areas.

Lycopodium obscurum (dark), tree clubmoss, spreads across the woods of eastern North America in shaded, light woodland duff giving the understory a carpet of miniature, shrubby "trees" looking like western red cedar (*Thuja plicata*) seedlings. Lax 8-in. (20-cm) tiers of deep green foliage are without annual bud constrictions and topped with one to four stalkless cones. The species is structurally similar to *L. dendroideum* and found in comparable moist woodland to boggy habitats as well as sites in slightly drier shade. It can be cultivated but takes an expert's hand and devotion to proper husbandry. Give it acid, humusy soil and a regular dose of light irrigation.

Lygodium

What a pleasure it is to write about these interesting ferns and what a contrast they offer to cultivation from continent to continent. Internationally there are approximately 40 species, mostly tropical, ranging from the almost-impossible-to-cultivate temperate *Lygodium palmatum* to the almost-impossible-to-eradicate *L. microphyllum*. *Lygodium* comes from the Greek *lygodes*, flexible or willow-like, in reference to the vine-forming habit of the fronds. And viney they are with sterile foliage capable of twining to 100 ft. (30 m). The rhizomes are short-creeping. Stipes with a singular vascular bundle extend into long, usually bipinnate blades. Fertile fronds are an extension of the sterile, and have smaller pinnae edged with beadlike sori holding two rows of sporangia. Spores are green (or sometimes translucent) and need to be sown immediately upon ripening. The entire structure ropes around whatever is available for support but is easily trained on uprights.

Lygodium japonicum
Japanese climbing fern
Epithet means "from Japan."
Deciduous to evergreen, to 20 ft. (6 m). Zones 6 (with huge amounts of protection) to 10.

DESCRIPTION: The rhizome is short-creeping. Eight-inch (20-cm) stipes, soft and apple green when unfurling, mature to brittle tan shoots. In indoor or warm situations the fronds grow just slightly slower than blackberry vines and, especially when given appropriate support, can twist and tower to 20 ft. (6 m). Outdoors in Zone 8, one or two fronds faithfully emerge in midsummer and, in a good year, will perhaps reach 2 ft. (60 cm). Six-parted leaflets are elongate triangles and have a long terminal lobe. Sori along the margins of the pinnules look like a series of minute thimbles. Green spores should be sown promptly upon maturing.

RANGE AND HABITAT: This species is widespread on the margins of forests from eastern Asia to Japan, Korea, China, and the Philippines. It has escaped in the southeastern United States and Hawaii.

CULTURE AND COMMENTS: The Japanese climbing fern is an easily cultivated conversation piece indoors where it will, however, need a supporting framework. Outdoors in cold zones it is self-maintaining, but in warmer areas needs the same attention as those growing indoors. To prevent an unsightly tangle of the old and the new it is essential to cut the old fronds back to the ground in late winter before the new growth takes off in the spring. Give it good composty soil and keep it moist. My plant has been in the same, albeit large, pot for over a dozen years with no fertilizer nor attention other than regular watering and an annual haircut. If the growth has been stunted it is not apparent.

Lygodium palmatum
Hartford fern
Epithet means "hand-shaped, palmate."
Evergreen, 3 ft. (90 cm). Zones 3 to 9.

DESCRIPTION: The rhizome is short-creeping. Dark stipes are dwarfs in comparison to the total expanse of the fern. Twining fronds have bipinnate blades with palmate 2- to 3-in. (5- to 7.5-cm), chubby, sterile pinnae. Smaller fertile pinnae grow on the ultimate portions of the frond. Sori are in small projectiles trimming the margins of the pinnules. They ripen in late autumn or early winter, if at all, and are unusual in

Lygodium japonicum eagerly and easily climbs whenever provided with a structural support which may include, but is not limited to, other plants.

A beautiful planting of the challenging *Lygodium palmatum* thrives in the Carstensen garden.

being translucent. For an outside chance at success, they need to be sown immediately.

RANGE AND HABITAT: This is the only temperate climbing fern and is confined to habitats on the U.S. East Coast. It is very rare in nature, but where present is inexplicably abundant, spreading like netting across acres. Acid soil is mandatory and water must be free of lime (if need be, dipped from the rain barrel).

CULTURE AND COMMENTS: In short, this fern is a challenge to cultivate, although it can be done. German specialist Wolfram Gassner, who has an array of interesting plant material in his garden north of Hamburg, grows his specimen in a deep 16- to 20-in. (40- to 50-cm) container with no bottom drainage. It is filled with peat and acid compost. He has drilled holes approximately 4 in. (10 cm) down from the pot's rim to drain excess water. The planting is not only alive and well but is a collector's showpiece. Gassner and Mother Nature water it with rainwater and it is not allowed to dry out. At one time in the United States, the foliage was collected extensively for decoration. The resultant decimation of natural populations prompted the passage in Connecticut in 1869 of the first U.S. plant protection conservation law.

Shorter Note

Lygodium microphyllum (small leaves) is a tropical species with pinnae looking like small fringed arrowheads and fronds that can reach 100 ft. (30 m). It has escaped in Florida where it is not only weedy but also downright dangerous. Aggressive fronds are roaming across the countryside shading out the native vegetation and climbing trees where, with their viney fronds serving as volatile uprights, they are a serious fire hazard.

Marattia

Marattia (after Giovanni Maratti, 1723–1777, a Benedictine abbot) is a genus of 50 to 55 species native across much of the Southern Hemisphere.

Marattia salicina (willowlike), while not a tree fern in structure, is a huge species from the South Sea Islands including New Zealand and Tahiti. The stipes alone are up to 3 ft. (90 cm) tall. They support 8- to 10-ft. (2.4- to 3-m) long, broad fans of glossy, bipinnate blades. Veins extend in symmetrical straight lines from the pinnae midribs to the margins where they are cinched by linear beads of fused sporangia which open in a lengthwise slit, rather like minute and stubby pea pods. The succulent and starchy rhizomes were once a popular food source for indigenous populations, but in New Zealand, at least, wild pigs have almost completely destroyed the native stands. The survivors are in nature preserves or on the slippery slopes of muddy hillsides. Wherever cultivated, and they are certainly recommended for imposing statements in Zones 9 and 10, they need a copious supply of water and protection from the wind to keep their extensive foliar structure hydrated and at its ornamental best. Give them deep shade and room for the roots to run in rich compost.

The author under an overstory of *Marattia* fronds in a New Zealand park. Photo by Harry Olsen.

Marsilea
Water clover ferns

The water clover ferns are most unfernlike in their four-leaf clover configuration as well as in their preference for floating atop still waters. Most of the world's 50 to 60 species are from tropical wetlands, but a few grace ponds and gather at water's edge in temperate zones. The rhizomes spread about in the muck of bottomlands sending up fronds with signature clover-shaped pinnae that decorate surface waters in light shade or preferably sun. Their complex reproductive cycle, arising from underwater sporocarps (hard podlike structures) enclosing microspores and megaspores, differs from the traditional pattern of land ferns. Furthermore, this fertility arrangement keeps most of the definitive distinctions among the species well hidden under the floating frond canopy.

The species are attractive aquatic features and can be planted directly into the underwater soil or cultivated in pots and plunged into permanently wet conditions such as pond margins. Propagation is best achieved by cutting apart rhizomes, but the scientifically inclined may want to try spores, which if kept dry in the protection of their sporocarps, remain viable for more than 100 years.

Historically, the practical uses of this species do not have a happy tradition, as the sporocarps of *Marsilea drummondii* are the "nardoo," that, because of incorrect cooking preparations, took the lives of the British explorers William Wills and Robert Burke while traversing Australia in 1861. Their deaths are now explained as being the result of beriberi, a disease resulting from a vitamin B1 thiamine deficiency. The "nardoo" containing the thiamine-destroying enzyme thiaminase was a principal and filling element in the explorer's diet and slowly killed them. Incidentally, this same enzyme is in bracken, *Pteridium aquilinum*, but in lower concentrations. Watch your diet.

The name *Marsilea* honors Count Luigi Marsigli (1656–1730), an Italian botanist.

Marsilea drummondii (after Drummond) is a small deciduous species which needs bright light to thrive. The hairy foliage is a drab green. Some forms grow in mud and water while others adapt on land. Distribution is widespread in Australia where the native populations have used the sporocarps for food. Improper preparation leads to death. See notation in the introduction.

Marsilea minuta (small) is a petite species growing to 3 in. (7.5 cm). It is widespread in its native Southern Hemisphere habitats, especially India and Africa, and can be cultivated in comparably warm sites.

Marsilea mutica (without a point, blunt) has 2- to 3-in. (5- to 7.5-cm) rounded, cloverlike leaves colored in two tones of green separated by a thin brown band and riddled with outstretching veins. This unusual variegated characteristic, vaguely hinting of various types of oxalis, easily identifies the species. It is native to Australia and New Caledonia, and accepts summer, but not winter, life in the cooler waters of Zones 6 to the warmer ones of Zone 10. In areas where freezing is an annual expectation, cultivate it in containers that can be transferred from summer ponds to winter shelter.

Marsilea and *Azolla* share a water feature in the O'Byrne garden.

Marsilea at the Dallas Arboretum.

Marsilea minuta

Matteuccia spreads freely in the wild in Wisconsin.

Matteuccia celebrated in statuary at the Olbrich Botanical Garden, Madison, Wisconsin.

Marsilea quadrifolia (divided into four) is the most commonly cultivated, recognized, and available *Marsilea* species in the U.S. trade. It is native to Europe and Asia and has escaped in the American Northeast. The small, glossy, deciduous "clovers" are up to an inch (2.5 cm) across and prefer to spread in still waters and sunshine. This ferns serves elegantly as a top dressing, providing a finishing touch on aquatic features from those of the home garden to the sumptuous displays of botanical gardens in Zones 6 to 9.

Marsilea vestita (covered) is an extremely hardy, deciduous species that populates streamsides, marshes, and riparian sites in the eastern United States. The rhizomes are long-creeping and the pinnae are $\frac{1}{4}$ to $\frac{1}{2}$ in. (6 to 13 mm) long and wide. It is easy to cultivate in aquatic sites or consistently wet soil in Zones 3 to 10.

Matteuccia
Ostrich ferns

The ostrich ferns, with their huge vases of plumy ostrich-feather-like fronds, are easily recognized, and in the proper situation easily found. The world's three species are among the most cold tolerant ferns, growing in the severe and forbidding climates of Newfoundland and Alaska with a comparable circumpolar distribution. However, their range extends to more accommodating regions including most of Europe, Japan, China, and Asia. They do not perform well in hot summer areas.

Characteristic long-creeping, branching stolons ramble about assertively just beneath the soil's surface and produce new plants at random intervals year after year. Deeply grooved stipes (like celery stalks) have a pair of mirror image S-shaped vascular bundles and the sterile pinnae have free veins. Strongly dimorphic fronds typify this rather primitive species.

Deciduous sterile fronds unfurl with spectacularly handsome, large fistlike green balls in early spring and are always a welcome showstopper. Fertile fronds, by contrast, are shorter, vertical, slender bottlebrush brooms that appear as greenery in late summer. Carrying beadlike sori, they overwinter as interesting brownish-black stems which to the uninitiated look rather like untidy dead stalks of flowering perennials. The green spores mature in spring and are short-lived. However, with the fern's penchant for colonizing, there is no great need to fuss with spores. Divisions taken in the fall will be replaced the following spring by multiple crops of youth corps.

These are robust ferns for areas where there is ample room for their exuberant colonizing. Excess numbers of progeny can always be dug and given away and will be remembered as the "gifts that keep on giving."

The name *Matteuccia* honors Carlo Matteucci (1811–1868), an Italian physicist.

Matteuccia orientalis
Oriental ostrich fern
Synonym *Onoclea orientalis*
Epithet means "from the East."
Deciduous, $1\frac{1}{2}$ to 4 ft. (45 to 120 cm). Zones 5 to 8.

DESCRIPTION: The rhizome creeps producing new plants from erect crowns. Straw-colored, stout stipes with brown scales are up to one-half of the frond length. Sterile once-pinnate blades are ovate with 8 to 20 pairs of lobed pinnae. Unlike *Matteuccia struthiopteris*, which is dressed to the ground in pinnae, the downward-pointing lower pinna pair on this species is broad and at mid frond. Sori are carried in small brown balls on upright fertile stalks.

RANGE AND HABITAT: This species is native to Russia, Korea, Japan, China, and the Himalayas and found in acid woodlands.

CULTURE AND COMMENTS: The oriental ostrich fern is rarely in commerce, but when available offers promise as a smaller and perhaps more manageable version of *Matteuccia struthiopteris*. It is perhaps best tested as a large container plant with shade and loamy soil before being released into the garden.

Matteuccia struthiopteris
Ostrich fern
Synonyms *Pteretis nodulosa*, *Struthiopteris pensylvanica*
Epithet is from *struthio*, ostrich, and *pteris*, fern.
Deciduous, 3 to 6 ft. (90 to 180 cm) or more. Zones 2 to (cool summer) 8.

DESCRIPTION: Runners from the rhizomes spread ambitiously. Deeply grooved, exceptionally short stipes are black with a green inner lining. The eagerly awaited pinnate-pinnatifid sterile fronds, which are among the first ferns to flush in spring, are a brilliant green show of fiddleheads. In time they reach 4, 5, or sometimes 6 ft. (120 to 180 cm) and are trimmed from base to apex with 40 to 60 pairs of pinnae. The basal pinnules on the pinna overlap the rachis. In outline the blade is broadest just above the middle, tapering with minute pinnae at both the base and the apex. Sori are in small beads on 18- to 24-in. (45- to 60-cm) upright fertile stalks.

The species is often subdivided into two varieties: **var. *pensylvanica*** from North America and **var. *struthiopteris*** from Europe and Asia. There is a history of confusion surrounding the differences between them, but various authors note that the stipe scales on the American variety are brown and make a brief appearance on spring fiddleheads. By contrast the stipe scales of the European are persistent and a dark centered brown. In addition, with sterile fronds at 5 ft. (1.5 m) or more, var. *pensylvanica* is taller than var. *struthiopteris*.

RANGE AND HABITAT: Both varieties grow with enthusiasm in partial sun to full shade and damp to wet loamy soil. A jumbo cultivar is popular in the trade in the United States and

Matteuccia struthiopteris in autumn dress.

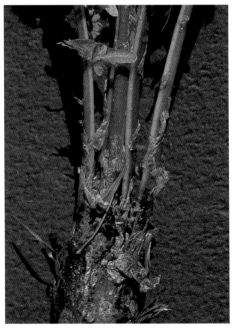

Brown scales make a fleeting spring appearance on *Matteuccia struthiopteris* var. *pensylvanica*.

New growth on *Matteuccia struthiopteris*.

Young green fertile fronds on *Matteuccia*.

Microsorum musifolium grows on stonework with other tropicals, including a poinsettia in flower. Photo by George Schenk.

Fleecy and pliant fronds of *Microlepia strigosa*.

Close-up of the venation on *Microsorum musifolium* in the Fernery at the Morris Arboretum.

has a trunk, which is at least 4 in. (10 cm) in diameter and, in my garden, 6 in. (15 cm) in height while yet still young.

CULTURE AND COMMENTS: Readily introduced, the ostrich ferns cover woodlands and roadsides in much of the cool temperate areas of the world, but do not succeed in climates with extended hot summers. Even in cool habitats if they go without steady irrigation they tend to look tattered and stressed by midsummer rather like a starlet who blossoms in youth and then fades in middle age. Plantings can become quite invasive but if you do not want them, you can always eat them. The new crosiers are the fiddleheads of the gourmet trade. Tons of freshly plucked young fronds are distributed during their brief spring flush. (Ostrich fern is the state vegetable of Vermont and largest export crop of New Brunswick, Canada.) Canned, fresh, or frozen, with the flavor of asparagus, they are best and nutritionally safest when cooked for at least 10 minutes. Sauté or bake them in butter and garlic and serve. Or as an alternative, how about a "cream of crosier" soup for the creative gourmet.

Matteuccia ×intermedia is a rare, presumed hybrid between *M. orientalis* and *M. struthiopteris*, however botanical confirmation is uncertain.

Microlepia

Microlepia (small scale, in reference to the indusia) is a genus of 50 to 70 species primarily native to Asia and Africa as well as Hawaii and New Zealand with scattered populations elsewhere.

Microlepia strigosa (with rigid hairs), the lace fern, is a downy, translucent green (similar to its relative *Dennstaedtia*), 2- to 3-ft. (60- to 90-cm) species from Asia, Japan, the Himalayas, Sri Lanka, Polynesia, and Hawaii (where it is sacred to Laka, goddess of the hula, and is widely used in lei making and hula decorations). It is popularly used as a spreading cover in Zone 9 to 11 gardens where it is evergreen and in Zone 7 and 8 where it dies down in late fall. Fronds are bipinnate to tripinnate and quite variable. **Forma *macfaddeniae*** has small narrow fronds.

Microsorum

Microsorum (small sori) is a tropical and subtropical genus with a worldwide collection of 50 or so primarily epiphytic species with straplike fronds or slight variations thereof. Some are quite willing candidates for cultivation in the consistently warm conditions of Southern California and Florida.

Microsorum musifolium is one of the more august of the strap-leaved polypods. Native to Malaysia, the Philippines, Indonesia, and New Guinea, it reaches 30 in. (75 cm) tall in my tropical highland garden and is taller in the lowland. It is colored pale green with a low gloss. This disheveled fern patch, fronds criss-crossing and torqued, with both upper and lower surfaces at once in view, displays simultaneously a mullioned windowlike pattern of black leaf veins at top and a copious stud pattern of orange-yellow spore dots underneath. This species is the biggest of four native polypod ferns that have shown up as surprises in my garden, arriving as wind-borne

The wild, parental form of *Microsorum punctatum* flanked by *Neoregelia* bromeliads and overseen by an Ifugao tribal idol. A frond of *Angiopteris palmiformis* brushes the idol's left shoulder, and water lettuce (*Pistia stratiotes*) floats in the bowl he embraces. Photo by George Schenk.

spores. Sporelings have established themselves mainly on moss-covered stonework from which—at times when inspiration or mayhem overwhelms the gardener's mind—they are easy to peel off, root system about 99 percent intact, clip into divisions, and replant in open ground, sun or shade, wherever the garden needs another fern. (Description by George Schenk.)

Microsorum punctatum. Practically pantropical and pansubtropical, save for its absence as a native of the Americas, this is another of the polypods that has come into my garden on its own. It forms a bright, light green spread of linear fronds to 2 ft. (60 cm) tall in my highland garden and stands as much as twice that in the lowland. The species has a number of named mutants. (Description by George Schenk.)

Mildella

Mildella (after Carl Milde, 1824–1871, of Germany) consists of 8 to 10 species often submerged in the genus *Cheilanthes*. They are found in rocky habitats in Haiti, Mexico, Central America, the Galapagos, India, and China.

Mildella intramarginalis is very similar to many cheilanthes, but differs in having false margins extending beyond the false indusia (which is easier said than imagined). An apogamous and dimorphic species, it spreads by creeping rhizomes and produces 12- to 18-in. (30- to 45-cm), bluish-green, bipinnate skeletal fronds. The basal pinnae are extended downwards, and the fertile fronds with their linear pinnae are taller than the sterile. This is a fern of rocky habitats in the piney

Mildella intramarginalis surrounded by rockwork at the University of California Botanical Garden at Berkeley.

Nephrolepis in a traditional setting as an outdoor decoration in the garden of a Mexican resort.

woods of Mexico, Central America, and the Galapagos. Xeric enthusiasts in Zones 9 and 10 can cultivate it in similar rocky exposures.

Nephrolepis

Although best known for the ubiquitous Boston ferns and their cultivars, there are some 30 to 40 *Nephrolepis* species worldwide. Two that are of most interest to horticulture and commerce are *N. cordifolia* and *N. exaltata*. As species, rather than their many cultivar manifestations, both have rows of the signature *Nephrolepis* (Greek *nephros*, kidney, and *lepis*, scale) sori with kidney-bean-shaped indusia. Their universally recognized once-pinnate fronds have ladders of many pairs of pinnae. Stringlike runners are common and generally meander in and around the foliar framework sending up periodic bursts of new fronds. They are easily clipped and rooted.

Use these readily available ferns for home décor or, where seasonally appropriate, as easily accommodated outdoor specimens protected from bright sun. For grooming, it is easier to give the entire plant a haircut, leaving it healthy but rather unsightly until the new fronds emerge. The other option is a labor-intensive removal of aging individual fronds which leaves the plant in a more presentable state but takes a considerable time commitment. (Occasionally a good yank will remove offending fronds, but caution is strongly advised.) As many of the cultivars do not produce spores they have the added advantage of not shedding their seasonal "dust" on the furniture, significantly contributing to their popularity and practicality as house plants.

Nephrolepis cordifolia
Tuberous sword fern
Epithet means "with heart-shaped leaves."
Evergreen, 18 to 30 in. (45 to 75 cm). Zones 9 to 11.

DESCRIPTION: The rhizome is wide creeping and forms unusual tuberous buds. Stipes are small and insignificant. Narrow upright blades taper at both base and apex and are crowded with 40 to 50 pairs of pinnae. Sori with kidney-shaped indusia are submarginal.

RANGE AND HABITAT: This species is native in a wide expanse of the tropics including the West Indies, Mexico, South America, the South Pacific, and Asia. It has naturalized in Florida and Hawaii. Soil is not as important as moisture, which should be a reliable constant.

CULTURE AND COMMENTS: Tough and justifiably popular, although sometimes invasive as a ground cover, this species colonizes with upright "swords" in the ornamental plantings that surround tourist facilities and home gardens in Zones 9 to 11. A disjunct and perhaps distinct variety adapts and submits to the fragrance of sulfurous fumes on the fringes of the thermal springs in Rotorua, New Zealand. Several easily domesticated varieties are available, although their names come with a certain amount of confusion.

'Duffii' is an upright sprite to 12 in. (30 cm) with proportionately minute pinnae all on a plant suitable for an indoor centerpiece.

Nephrolepis cordifolia in the thermal haze at the hot springs of Rotorua, New Zealand.

The lusty, colorful "ears" of elephant ears (*Caladium*) pose with the restful greens of *Nephrolepis cordifolia* 'Kimberly Queen'.

'**Kimberly Queen**' has dark green arching fronds to 3 ft. (90 cm) by 4 or 5 in. (10 to 13 cm) wide. It is an easy and energetic cultivar.

'**Lemon Button**' is a cute-as-a-button dwarf to 10 in. (25 cm) with minute round pinnae. It is an attractive choice for intimate small spaces indoors or as a table fern outdoors where it will take brief touches of frost. It has a hint of a lemon fragrance.

'**Timm's Petticoat**' from the Bill Timm family has twisted, forked, and congested upright foliage and is useful as a centerpiece.

Nephrolepis exaltata
Boston fern
Epithet means "tall."
Evergreen, variable. Zones 9 to 11.

DESCRIPTION: The rhizome is creeping and produces long threadlike scaly runners. Stipes are short and blades are once-pinnate with up to 50 pairs of pinnae. Sori are covered by kidney-shaped indusia.

RANGE AND HABITAT: The species and its cultivars are primarily plants of the New World with scattered populations elsewhere including South Africa, Australia, and India. Many are found as epiphytes as well as terrestrially or occasionally in rocky habitats.

CULTURE AND COMMENTS: The cultivars are the familiar and accommodating indoor ferns that hang with ease in hotel lob-

bies and dining rooms as well as being the token indoor ferns for the window décor of homeowners. The parent of the cultivars arrived in Boston as part of a shipment of *Nephrolepis exaltata* from Jamaica via Philadelphia. The distributor recognized it as different, thinking it to be *N. davallioides*. Some 50,000 sales later it was recognized as a cultivar and christened *N. exaltata* 'Bostoniensis'. That was in 1896 and they have been evolving and thriving ever since as indoor specimens as well as outdoor decorations in Southern California and Florida.

All cultivars are willing basket champions in bright indirect light and in moist potting soil with attendant good drainage. They thrive in frost-free and less-than-humid environments, but need regular watering. I do not recommend misting the foliage, even in hot weather, as the mist can settle in the midst of fronds without evaporating and encourage rot and mold. There are dozens of cultivars with suitable options for homes and gardens. Not surprisingly, with so much variety, there is some duplication and confusion regarding exact nomenclature. Many of the cultivars do not produce spores and to be true to name need to be propagated by division or tissue culture.

'**Bostoniensis**' is the mother cultivar of the entire lineage of genetic variations. It is the familiar once-pinnate, 3- to 4-ft. (90- to 120-cm) pendent basket offering suitable for display in the home if you have plenty of room. Otherwise chose from more-size-appropriate later mutations. A "junior" form matures at 2 ft. (60 cm). Do not overwater.

Nephrolepis exaltata 'Bostoniensis Bluebell' in a sales display with like-minded houseplants.

'Bostoniensis Bluebell' (synonym 'Blue Bells') is a mid-sized symmetrical ball that is manageable and suitable for 6- to 8-in. (15- to 20-cm) pots or baskets. Keep it warm.

'Boston Compacta' is more upright than trailing and proportionately smaller.

'Dallas' is an introduction from Casa Flora Nursery in, yes, Dallas, Texas. It is a tidy plant with dense ruffled foliage that is suitable for a table decoration. Casa Flora notes that this fern does not shed leaflets when transferred from the brightly lit production areas of greenhouses to average home conditions.

'Emerald Vase' ('Green Fantasy' in European markets) has foot-long (30-cm), bright lime-green, upright lacerated and forking fronds.

'Fluffy Ruffles' is one of the most commonly available cultivars and the name says it all. The 12-in. (30-cm) fronds are dark green with overlapping ruffled pinnae.

'Hillii' is another common, and in this case old (1930s), cultivar. At 4 ft. (1.2 m) it is rather out of reach for the average household (short of trading away a relative for some space). The wide fronds have wavy margins. It is an imposing basket plant.

'Mini Ruffles' is an even smaller version of 'Fluffy Ruffles' and at a diminutive 4 to 6 in. (10 to 15 cm) totally in scale for houseplant use.

'Norwoodii' is a finely cut, light green, feathery delicacy with layers of gossamer foliage worthy of centerpiece status. It is rarely taller than 12 to 15 in. (30 to 38 cm). Although it appreciates humidity, to keep it in show condition watering should be confined to the soil surface.

'Rooseveltii' is a traditional offering with 3-ft. (90-cm) fronds having curly margins.

'Sassy' is a short cultivar with fronds displaying varying degrees of laceration.

'Smithii' is the most finely divided of the dwarfs and a cloud of raindrop-sized pale green pinnules. It is best in a humid environment but avoid water or mist on the foliage.

'Tiger' is variegated with subtle stripes of yellow on lime-green. The fronds are low arches of 2 ft. (60 cm) or more.

Restrained variegation on *Nephrolepis exaltata* 'Tiger'.

'Wanamaka' is a compact, foot-tall (30-cm) vase of twisted linear pinnae wrapping around upright stalks.

'Whitmanii' is an old cultivar with drooping fronds and tripinnate, incised pinnae. It is still recommended for small baskets.

Shorter Notes

Nephrolepis falcata (sickle-shaped) spreads by creeping rhizomes and has pendulous foliage. Two popular cultivars are widely distributed; 'Furcans', the fishtail fern, has fork-tipped pinnae, and 'Macho' has massive broad bands of 5-in. (13-cm) wide and 4- to 6-ft. (1.2- to 1.8-m) long fronds. (It is sometimes classified as *N. biserrata*.)

Nephrolepis pendula (drooping) is a plant to hang from the ceiling in a conservatory or the top of the stairs on the three-story atrium entryways popular in new homes today. The fronds can drape downwards to 20 ft. (6 m) (and my inner child thinks of the hide-and-go-seek potential). Some authors propose classifying it under *N. cordifolia*.

Notholaena
Cloak ferns

Notholaena (Greek *notho*, false, and *chlaena*, cloak, referring to the hidden sori) species are intriguing xerics with hairs, scales, and/or frequently a waxy undercoat as requisite defenses against the angst of living in drylands. They are well traveled botanically. At present there are 20 to 25 species, a number recently reduced significantly. As the genus tends to be intermediate between *Cheilanthes* and *Pellaea*, many species have been transferred to those genera. Populations are found in rocky sites in the Americas, Europe, Asia, and Australia, although some botanists would restrict their definition and include only those that are waxy, thus limiting their scope to material exclusively from the Americas.

Cloak ferns are fascinating evergreens in situ and, on those rare instances when successfully coaxed into cultivation, are beauties to behold. Roots need to be tended by rocks to keep them cool and to collect life-sustaining moisture condensation. Good drainage and air circulation are required as is protection from winter wet. Sori are submarginal on veins often partially concealed by leaf margins or the dense presence of hairs, scales, or waxy undercoats.

Sadly these ferns do not linger in cultivation, but seriously dedicated growers can maintain them (or at least try to) in portable containers with lots of gritty soil and bright light. The site should be similar to the deserts of Arizona and New Mexico with cool, clear nights, warm sunny days, not much rain in winter, and steady heat and some rain in summer.

Notholaena grayi (after Gray) is an upright species from limestone or igneous rock talus slopes and crags of the U.S. Southwest and adjacent Mexico. Fronds are 12 to 18 in. (30 to 45 cm) tall, pinnate-pinnatifid to bipinnate-pinnatifid, and covered with a protective white waxy shield on the upper frond surface and more especially on the frond's underside. This species is consequently an ornamental jewel for the privileged and skilled specialist who can maintain it in the preferred xeric combination of well-drained, winter-wet-free, crumbly soil in Zones 9 and 10. Apogamous.

Notholaena lanuginosa (soft haired), synonyms *Cheilanthes vellea* and *Cosentinia vellea*, is a small, once-pinnate, upright species that I first saw in the most forbidding looking, rubbled slopes in the Canary Islands (although it is native as far away as the Himalayas). The 8- to 10-in. (20- to 25-cm) fronds with short, brown hairy stipes have 20 or more pairs of pinnae with undersides heavily protected by matted hairs. Outstanding and very skilled xeric specialist Clive Brotherton grows this in custom soil in his containerized central England collection. Elsewhere devoted enthusiasts will find that it germinates eagerly from spores that practically jump from the plant to the container, promptly producing quantities of plants for experimentation in different soils and exposures. In whatever site, from protected Zone 8 to exposed 9 and 10, it will require good bright light and excellent drainage and air circulation.

Notholaena lemmonii (after John G. Lemmon, 1832–1908), from southern Arizona and northern Mexico, grows to 1 ft. (30 cm) with short stipes and bipinnate blades. The pinnae, which look in pairs like butterflies, are decorated on the undersides with a white or yellow waxlike coating. Plants need the traditional good drainage and protection from winter wet and are garden potentials for Zones 9 and 10.

Notholaena marantae (after sixteenth-century Venetian botanist Bartolomea Maranti), synonyms *Cheilanthes marantae* and *Gymnopteris marantae*, is a lanceolate, bipinnate, 8-in. (20 cm) species with tall, dark stipes coated in scales and hairs. The 10 to 15 pairs of pinnae are decorated on their lower surface with an abundance of rich reddish scales. This species is widespread in Europe, the Middle East, China, and the Himalayas. German specialists are growing it in fast-draining rock garden pockets in Zones 6 to 9.

Notholaena standleyi (after Paul Standley, 1884–1963, who botanized in Central and North America) has glossy stipes of one-half to three-quarters of the 6-in. (15-cm) frond length. The blades are pentagonal with the basal pinna pair flaring like wings accentuated with lengthy innermost pinnules. Upper pinnae are pinnatifid. Deep butter-yellow to creamy white, waxy powder (farina) spreads across the undersides of the frond and etches the margins. For nature lovers the slowly creeping colonies are remarkable and rare discoveries nestled among rocks in the inhospitable dry gulches of the U.S. Southwest. These conditions must be mimicked in cultivation with the potential for success confined to Zones 8 to 10.

Onoclea

The name *Onoclea* is from the Greek *onos*, vessel, and *kleio*, to close or sheathe, in reference to the podlike pinnules enclosing the spores on the fertile fronds. Fossil records dating back 54 million years indicate that *Onoclea* was cosmopolitan in distribution until glaciation and the emergence of new mountain ranges subsequently restricted its range. Presently, there are only one to three species limited in native habitats to North America and Asia. The Asian material is sometimes designated as *O. interrupta* or *O. sensibilis* var. *interrupta*. Also, based on chromosome counts Kato (1991) places *Matteuccia* ×*intermedia* in the genus as *O. intermedia*.

Notholaena lanuginosa sunbathing with succulents on an exposed rocky slope in the Canary Islands.

Notholaena marantae in rocky compost in the Kohout garden.

Notholaena standleyi in the forbidding dryland surrounds of Bumblebee 4, Arizona.

Onoclea sensibilis as a ground cover in the perennial bed at the Bellevue Botanical Garden.

These are deciduous ferns with long-creeping rhizomes yielding a strong propensity to spread, especially in moist to wet areas. They are dimorphic with upright spikes of beadlike fertile fronds appearing in late summer and persisting until the following year. The green spores are released (rapidly in warmth) in winter or spring. Sterile fronds have two vascular bundles shaped like dog bones that join together in the upper portion of the frond. They have netted veins and are sometimes mistaken for those of *Woodwardia areolata*. The latter has minutely toothed rather than wavy margined pinnae, winged lower pinnae, and fertile fronds of narrow leafy tissue. When fertile fronds are present, the two are not likely be confused.

Onoclea sensibilis
Sensitive fern, bead fern
Epithet refers to the "sensitive" sterile fronds which turn yellow and die down at the first frost.
Deciduous, 2 to 3 ft. (60 to 90 cm). Zones 2 to 10. Dimorphic.

DESCRIPTION: The woody blackish-brown rhizome, partially submerged or skimming the soil's surface, is long-creeping and branching, producing fronds at frequent intervals. The stipe is one-half of the frond length. The triangular, papery-textured sterile blade is once-pinnate with a stalked basal pinnae pair and upper pinnae becoming variably lobed and pinnatifid toward the apex. The fertile fronds of about 15 in. (38 cm) appear in late summer and carry spores in a series of green beadlike attachments that turn dark brown and woody as they mature. The encased spores are released in late winter or spring (or when induced by an early harvest into a warm room). Like the spores of its close relative *Matteuccia*, *Onoclea* spores are green and should be sown promptly. *Onoclea* is impressively cold hardy although burdened by the name "sensitive fern."

RANGE AND HABITAT: This species is native to North America east of the Great Plains states and covers wide areas especially in wetlands, but also along roadsides and in woodlands. It was supposedly the first fern introduced to Britain from North America, in 1699. Not surprisingly it has escaped.

CULTURE AND COMMENTS: Sensitive fern is so ready-to-grow that eastern U.S. gardeners often reference it condescendingly. (When I first started studying ferns, my father, then a New Hampshire resident, offered to send me a trainload of plants [read weeds]. Since he did not know his ferns, I never did discover whether he meant *Onoclea* or *Dennstaedtia*.) In cultivation *Onoclea* should be kept watered but otherwise adjusts easily and happily to all soil types and exposures from cold to warm climates. The unfernlike "seed heads" of the fertile fronds are popular and welcomed as long-lasting additions for dried flower arrangements. (Let the spores shed first, before spreading joy on the table.)

A handsome form with transient but strikingly reddish new growth and persistent red stipes is a personal favorite and is a worthy addition to any garden's fernery. If need be both types adapt to container planting which will accomplish precisely what the name implies, containment.

Fresh spring fronds join the overwintering fertile fronds on *Onoclea sensibilis* in the Bellevue Botanical Garden.

The ephemeral rosy silver hues on the red-stemmed form of *Onoclea sensibilis*.

Onychium japonicum just above a clump of *Begonia heracleifolia* and just below tufts of that ridiculously skinny fern, *Nephrolepis cordifolia* 'Duffii', on steep terrain with a natural waterfall in the background. Photo by George Schenk.

European specialists are growing a charming but difficult dwarf selection, '**Nana**', which has diminutive fronds ranging from 2 to 5 in. (5 to 13 cm) and offers potential as a hardy and handsome petite ground cover. Like so many interesting and rare plants it was introduced to cultivation by the late Zdeněk Seibert of the Czech Republic.

The slightly different **var. *interrupta*** occurs in the colder areas of Japan, Korea, Manchuria, and eastern Russia.

Onychium

Onychium (Greek *onychion*, claw) comprises 8 to 10 species from Africa, India, China, and Japan.

Onychium japonicum (of Japan), in common with other of the world's ferns that are the most successful in terms of wide range and abundance, has adaptability as its life game. It can be found in shade on the forest floor, or in sun in loamy soil, or on fertile stone from India to Japan, to Java, to the highlands of Luzon in the Philippines. Finely lacy, none finer, with more sky than substance, the light green fronds grow as a clump about 16 in. (40 cm) high and then curve downward. It is an easy plant in the garden for Zones 8 to 10. (Description by George Schenk.)

Ophioglossum
Adder's tongue ferns

These weird, primitive novelties range from wee 3- to 6-in. (7.5- to 15-cm) temperate species, which are just as likely to be stepped on as recognized, to giant cascades of tropical epiphytes. The genus name comes from the Greek *ophis*, snake, and *glossa*, tongue, describing the fern's architecture, which for most species has a sterile, spoon-shaped blade surrounding a narrow upright fertile stalk suggesting a snake's tongue. These species have the highest numbers of chromosomes of any known vascular plant, a fact that trivia buffs might like to casually drop into ferny conversations.

The deciduous fronds grow from succulent rhizomes with roots that bud, and travel about producing new plants at random intervals. Temperate species prefer moist habitats, especially grassy sites, and have a special penchant for sprouting in cemeteries in the North American Gulf states. These are "belly plants" that are best viewed while on hands and knees ("botanists in a special kind of prayer meeting," Mickel 1994). Most do not accept domestication, but may spring up as surprises in untended wild flower lawns. Alan Ogden of England has such a lawn and notes that his plants rearrange their spontaneous appearances by as much as several feet each year, "more like a mole than an adder" (pers. comm.).

Ophioglossum pendulum is commonly known as ribbon fern. Those who garden nearby this plant's native forests in the South Pacific, Australia, or elsewhere in tropical Asia, where it clings to massive branches of old rain forest trees, may have an opportunity as I have had to grow this fern. Grow it with native leaf mold on the branch of a big, shady, broadleaf evergreen tree and keep it moist especially during any dry season. It is slow to adapt in garden conditions, yet within a year or two and with care and good luck, it will gain strength and grow on as heartily as it does in absolute wilderness. To grow

Onychium japonicum frond.

Long ribbons of handsome fronds drape from a high-up planting of *Ophioglossum pendulum*. Photo by George Schenk.

Less-than-showy but challenging to establish, *Ophioglossum vulgatum* mingles among grassy plants in the Wardlaw garden.

Immature green fertility on the tips of young *Osmunda* fronds.

a ribbon fern in a greenhouse or conservatory, poke its ribbony leaves down through the interspaces in a wire basket and then pack at least several inches (centimeters) of sphagnum moss around the fern's basal wad of roots and leaf mold. Hang it high. When ribbon fern gets going, it may well attain its wilderness length of 6 ft. (1.8 m) or even more. A well-grown plant of this species is easily one of the most dramatic of ferns. (Description by George Schenk.)

Ophioglossum pusillum (very small), northern adder's-tongue fern, and *O. vulgatum* (common), southern adder's-tongue fern, are such closely allied curiosities that some authorities consider *O. pusillum* to be a variety of *O. vulgatum*. Both are deciduous with small sterile sheaths that frame an upright taller fertile spike. Politely speaking they are inconspicuous, except for the avid fern hunter who knows what to look for, as well as when and where to look. On field trips this is often accompanied with a hint of competition and success makes for an interesting "find." The North American *O. pusillum* is hardy to Zone 2, while the internationally distributed *O. vulgatum* is hardy to Zone 6.

Oreopteris

Oreopteris (*oreos*, mountain, *pteron*, wing or fern) is a genus that has been under botanical scrutiny and revision. By current standards it includes three species from Asia and Europe.

Oreopteris limbosperma (*limbo*, marginal, and *spermum*, seed), the mountain or lemon-scented fern, is a deciduous species that graces the edges of mountain streams in acid soil in Britain and Europe (and if you are a fellow lumper) western North America. (See *Thelypteris quelpaertensis*.) Upright, pinnate-pinnatifid fronds are light green. The 2- to 4-ft. (60- to 120-cm) fronds are embellished with the translucent hairs traditionally associated with *Thelypteris*. Indusia-free sori are submarginal. Although not often in cultivation, this is an interesting choice for permanently moist, slightly spongy situations in shade, along with your osmundas in Zones 5 to 8. Not surprisingly there are several cultivars in Britain.

Osmunda

Osmundas are not ferny in the traditional sense of lacy green, frothy lightness that the word *fern* implies to so many. Look instead for sturdy upright whorls of foliage that serve as backdrops in perennial beds and borders as well as in the difficult-to-manage poorly drained garden lowlands.

They are among the patriarchs of the fern world and can trace their origins back through geological time to at least the disappearing dinosaur days. *Osmunda claytoniana* is one seriously old species with fossil records, found in the Antarctic, dating back 200 million years to the Triassic era, the longest continuous life span of any living fern.

Unlike more highly evolved ferns that bear their spores on the frond's undersides, *Osmunda* spores are borne on primitive, specialized, modified fertile stalks that extend the full length of the frond as in *O. cinnamomea* and *O. japonica* or are restricted to the frond's tips as in *O. regalis*, or midsections of the vegetative fronds as in *O. claytoniana*. The sporangia have no indusia. Spores mature in a matter of days, are green, and have a very short shelf life of about three weeks. Refrigeration extends their viability somewhat, and freezing (by simply wrapping the spores in a protective origami folded paper and stashing it atop the ice cream) improves their longevity significantly. While the spores germinate readily, the offspring are frustratingly slow to develop into mature plants.

There are approximately 10 to 16 species of these tall moisture-loving deciduous ferns. They are from acidic habitats and are extremely hardy and ornamental. Studies report that they, like so many ferns, are deer resistant. Winter-starved foraging slugs are attracted to the succulent, emerging stages of spring foliage on young plants, however, but comparable growth on mature plants is not particularly vulnerable. *Osmunda cinnamomea* and *O. regalis* have a strong preference for spongy soils where they can be admirably sun tolerant. All do well in traditional woodland mixes, although without acid soil and flooded feet, they will not reach the outstanding proportions for which they are widely admired.

Osmunda roots are black, fibrous, and wiry and are popularly shredded for use in specialized potting mixes designed for orchids and assorted epiphytes. They thread through the trunklike rhizomes that support the stubble of persistent old stipe bases. The stipe is frequently winged. The new growth is fleetingly downy, a down that is welcomed by hummingbirds for lining their nests. Fall color is yellow.

The name *Osmunda* is credited to Carl Linnaeus who reportedly named the genus after the Nordic god Thor, who was in turn the Saxon god Osmund. A more romantic interpretation credits the name to Osmund, a Saxon waterman on Loch Tyne, who upon hearing of an impending invasion from the Danes hid his wife and daughter in great stands of *Osmunda* (apparently successfully).

Osmunda regalis is referenced as far back as the late 1500s in British herbals as a treatment for a plethora of ailments. (*Osmunda cinnamomea* and *O. claytoniana* did not arrive in England until 1772.) Among other cures a poultice from the roots was popularly recommended for soothing burns and bruises and prescribed as a preventative for rickets. The Celts combined heather honey with the readily available, abundant supply of *O. regalis* spores to produce their mead. In North America various parts of the trio of native osmundas have been used by the Native Americans to cure an assortment of maladies. And today the young crosiers of *O. japonica* are offered in Japanese markets where they are considered a gourmet treat (although recent studies implicate the crosiers as potentially carcinogenic).

Osmunda cinnamomea
Cinnamon fern
Epithet means "cinnamon brown."
Deciduous, 3 to 5 ft. (90 to 150 cm). Zones 2 to 10. Dimorphic.

DESCRIPTION: The rhizome is upright, trunklike, and occasionally branching. The common name aptly describes the highly ornamental plumes of erect fertile fronds that are covered with cinnamon-colored shaggy sporangial cases following the shedding of their green spores in late spring. The light green lanceolate vegetative fronds, which encircle the fertile

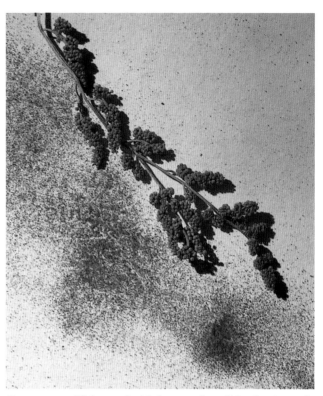

Green spores fall from a freshly harvested small fertile pinna of *Osmunda cinnamomea.*

Unfurling *Osmunda* crosiers with their temporary coating of silvery down.

Sterile frond of *Osmunda cinnamomea*. Note the small tufts of whitish hairs (which will fade to a rusty cinnamon) at the juncture of the pinnae and rachis.

Osmunda cinnamomea in a complementary planting with the russet-trunked *Acer griseum* at Elk Rock, the garden at the Bishop's Close in Portland, Oregon.

fronds, have tall tan stipes and tufts of whitish to rusty hairs at the base of the pinnate-pinnatifid pinnae.

RANGE AND HABITAT: This fern is common and locally abundant in wet acidic soils in northeastern Canada and the United States down to the Gulf states as well as the West Indies, Mexico, and South America.

CULTURE AND COMMENTS: The cinnamon fern is a very tolerant and willing garden subject that is especially handsome when combined with fellow color coordinates. The fertile fronds wither early in the summer and the sterile ones fade to a warm yellow-brown in autumn. The vegetative foliage can be confused with that of *Osmunda claytoniana*, however the cinnamon's pinnae hairs at the pinnae-stipe connection provide the distinction between the two. Spores should be harvested and sown as soon as ripe in early spring.

Var. *fokiensis* is the Asian counterpart of the cinnamon fern, differing in having black hairs as well as russet at the base of the sterile pinnae. It is native to Japan, Korea, and China and often botanically designated simply as *Osmunda cinnamomea*. Unfortunately the variety is rarely available in the trade.

Osmunda claytoniana
Interrupted fern
Synonym *Osmunda interrupta*
Epithet is after John Clayton (1686–1773), a British botanist in North America.
Deciduous, 2 to 3 ft. (60 to 90 cm). Zones 2 to 8. Dimorphic.

DESCRIPTION: The rhizome is thick and upright. The unique fertile fronds have leafy tissue at the bottoms and tops, with

Osmunda claytoniana showing fertile fronds interrupted with sporangia between top and bottom.

blackish sporangia in the middle, hence the common name, interrupted fern. (It also leads some customers to wonder whether the middle is diseased.) The sterile upright fronds are pinnate-pinnatifid and do not have tufts of hairs at the base of the pinnae, thus distinguishing them from comparable fronds on *Osmunda cinnamomea*.

RANGE AND HABITAT: Unlike some of its brethren this species does not grow naturally in marshes. It is native to parts of eastern Asia and northeastern United States where it is abundant in New England and the upper Midwest. Look for it on the grounds of Frank Lloyd Wright's Taliesin in Wisconsin. It does not grow as far south as *Osmunda cinnamomea* nor does it acclimate in more tropical areas. It hybridizes with *O. regalis* to form the very rare hybrid *O. ×ruggii*.

CULTURE AND COMMENTS: This fern is easily grown in moist acidic soil in the partially sunny to the lightly shaded garden bed. With its exceptional cold tolerance it is a welcome landscaping plant in nature's cold-challenged areas. *Osmunda claytoniana* was formerly known botanically and descriptively as *O. interrupta*.

Osmunda japonica

Epithet means "from Japan."
Deciduous, 1½ to 3 ft. (45 to 90 cm). Zones 6 to 9. Dimorphic.

DESCRIPTION: The rhizome is upright and supports slender fronds that are either entirely fertile or entirely sterile. The tall fertile fronds bear the sporangia on the upper portions. The lax sterile fronds are one-third stipe and two-thirds ovate, bipinnate blades with opposite pinnae. The new growth is fleetingly adorned with reddish brown hairs. The species is very similar to *Osmunda regalis*, differing in being lower growing and totally dimorphic, although late-summer *O. japonica* growth often thriftily combines sterile and fertile material on the same fronds.

RANGE AND HABITAT: The species grows in woods in eastern Asia from Sakhalin Island, Korea, China, the Himalayas, Taiwan, and Thailand to Indochina and Japan where it is especially common.

CULTURE AND COMMENTS: This fern is readily established in ordinary to moist soil and partial shade. The fronds remain green long after fellow osmundas have entered dormancy.

Osmunda lancea

Epithet means "spear-shaped."
Deciduous, 1 to 1½ ft. (30 to 45 cm). Zones 6 to 9. Dimorphic.

DESCRIPTION: The rhizome is ascending and the fronds completely dimorphic. The relaxed sterile fronds are the larger and have bipinnate blades. The stalked, narrow pinnules are lanceolate and pointed at both ends. The fertile fronds are smaller and early deciduous. New growth is russet.

RANGE AND HABITAT: This Japanese endemic grows at river's edge and in floodplains.

CULTURE AND COMMENTS: Cultivate this rarely available species in marshy sunny areas or moist shade. It is very similar to *Osmunda japonica* but smaller and less vigorous, and dies down in early fall.

Foliage-free, separate fertile stalks on *Osmunda japonica*.

The low-growing *Osmunda lancea* with its fronds tending towards horizontal in the Förster garden.

Osmunda regalis

Royal fern, flowering fern
Epithet means "royal."
Deciduous, 2 to 6 ft. (60 to 180 cm) or more. Zones 2 to 10.

DESCRIPTION: Here is the royal fern and regal it is with broadly ovate fronds occasionally up to 9 ft. (2.7 m) on trunklike rhizomes. One third is stipe and the remainder is made up of a bipinnate blade, with opposite pinnae suggestive of

Osmunda regalis in the springtime at the Miller Botanical Garden.

Fertile *Osmunda regalis* in the Bradner garden.

Osmunda regalis 'Cristata' in the Kennar garden.

Osmunda regalis 'Gracilis' in the Schmick garden.

Osmunda regalis 'Laurin'

Heavy forking on *Osmunda regalis* 'Grandiceps' in the Peters garden.

locust tree foliage. The fertile portion replaces the leafy tissue at the tips of the spore-bearing fronds, hence the "flowering" of the alternate common name. New growth is succulent and briefly trimmed with silver down. Some botanists classify the robust European with its stalked pinnae as var. *regalis* and the slender American with sessile pinnae as var. *spectabilis*.

RANGE AND HABITAT: This fern is truly international in distribution ranging from the extremes of snowy very northern latitudes to warm and humid semitropical habitats. In the wild it is naturally affiliated with swamps, marshes, and riparian sites where it will form wide colonies encouraged by boggy root areas.

CULTURE AND COMMENTS: Widely adaptable and cultivated, *Osmunda regalis* and its varieties are noble and trouble-free ornamental selections for the beginning fern gardener as well as the specialist. The tall bold sprays of foliage are statuesque as backdrops or as foreground focal points. All tolerate various exposures including full sun in wet sites and strongly prefer acid soils. In upland gardens supplemental water is a requirement. They are, however, deciduous so the garden design must allow for a winter visual void. Prior to the British Victorian fern-collecting heyday of the late nineteenth century, the species was very widespread in the British Isles including stands in central London. While diminishing the wild population, the collecting fever yielded some interesting cultivars that are still popular today.

Var. *brasiliensis* (of Brazil) is a borderline evergreen with red new growth. It is quasi hardy in Zone 8 and sometimes seen in conservatories.

'Cristata' (crested) has pinnae that are more angulated than crested. It is told that in the mid 1800s British pteridologist E. J. Lowe entered a specimen of this fern into a major, competitive garden exhibit. It reputedly had a rather remarkable circumference of 14 ft. (4.2 m) and went on to win Best of Show. Such exuberance is not to be found in gardens today, however, where the selection is usually a more modest 3 ft. (90 cm) high and perhaps (on a good day) 7 ft. (2.1 m) around. Like the type, it appreciates a constant supply of moisture.

'Decomposita' is more finely divided than the typical species. Discovered in 1901 in County Kerry, Ireland, it was subsequently lost to cultivation. British collector Martin Rickard, with his practiced eye, rediscovered it 90 years later.

'Gracilis' (slender) is a smaller cultivar with graceful and slim fertile spikes.

'Grandiceps' (with large terminal crests) has fronds that terminate in broad crests.

'Laurin' is an 18-in. (45-cm) dwarf introduction from Germany.

Robust new growth on *Osmunda regalis* 'Purpurascens' at Wells Medina Nursery.

Imposing plant of *Osmunda regalis* 'Undulatifolia' with its ruffled foliage.

Fertile fronds on *Osmunda regalis* 'Purpurascens' at Wells Medina Nursery.

Immature, green fertile frond of *Osmunda regalis* 'Undulatifolia'.

'**Philip Coke**' is a British cultivar that was selected for its red new growth.

'**Purpurascens**' (purple) produces a magnificent wine-purple fountain of spring fronds. These hues will eventually fade from the leafage but persist on the stipes. This fern is stunning in the company of complementary burgundy-leafed heucheras.

Var. *spectabilis* is the North American native which is thinner and more open in growth. It too has a "Purpurascens" variety.

'**Undulatifolia**' (wavy), synonym *Osmunda regalis* 'Crispa', is a wavy-margined showstopper with tall, full-bodied apple-green foliage.

Shorter Note

Osmunda vachellii (after George Vachell) is a Chinese and eastern Asian species occasionally in cultivation in the United States. It differs in having once-pinnate sterile pinnae and is best suited for Zones 9 and 10.

Paesia

Paesia (after Duke Fernando Diaz Paes Leme) is a genus of 12 species that are mostly natives of the South Pacific. Like its relatives, bracken for example, it can be weedy, producing an extensive network of long-branching rhizomes.

Paesia scaberula (rough) from New Zealand is the best known and is occasionally cultivated. It has hairy rhizomes, a ridged, zigzag rachis, and tripinnate to quadripinnate blades with sticky hairs on their undersides. The soral arrangement with a double indusium consisting of inrolled foliar margins covering an inner true indusium is unique. A Seattle-area nursery tried coddling this species for a few years, but eventually winter cold cost the plants their lives and the growers their enthusiasm. With its proclivity for territorial possession, it is best confined to basket culture in Zones 9 to 11.

Pellaea

Cliff brakes

Pellaeas, the cliff brakes, are those dusky blue charmers that enchant and taunt from cliff sides, mortared crevices, and other stressful and fern-forbidding sunny habitats with dry and lean, gritty soil. As such, those that are natives of the U.S. Southwest flourish in the challenging sites that delight passing tourists with periodic spring bursts of desert wildflowers but are not traditionally associated with our friends, the ferns. Their exquisitely adapted blue-toned fronds offer beauty to dryland landscapes extending from rocky gulches and tumbleweed countryside to the stunning panoramas of the brick "Red Rock" country around Sedona, Arizona (a favorite location with or without ferns). While these sites are associated with fern-desiccating sunshine, a closer examination will often find the fern's exposure tempered by the shade of a rocky companion that collects and funnels the minimal available desert moisture to a relatively cool ferny root run. Adaptive foliage color in the xeric species transitions, as light exposure increases, from frosted green to a sun-repellant blue. Ready-to-curl pinnae are an additional protective mechanism intended to reduce loss of moisture (and life). While these inrolled needlelike rods give the appearance of a fern struggling in terminal death throes, timely rains will usually rehydrate the fern for yet another season.

Of all the candidates for domestication in temperate gardens, the pellaeas in my opinion are the most difficult. It can be done, however, but it helps to live in California or the drylands of the U.S. Southwest or to artificially create an arid habitat. *Pellaea rotundifolia*, *P. falcata*, and other vivid green species associated with indoor cultivation rather than sunny exposures are the exceptions. (Look for them to be reclassified one of these days.) However, even they still prefer the well-drained sites that typify the natural settings for their xeric cousins.

The name *Pellaea* comes from the Greek *pellos*, dusky, in an apt description of the blue-gray foliage color on the xerics. Worldwide there are from 55 to 70 species primarily of rocky dryland sites in the Western Hemisphere.

The rhizomes are short- to long-creeping. Stipes are thin, ranging from blueberry through blackish in color, and brittle, indicative of its botanical relationship with cheilanthes and its comparable classification, but not cultural, relationship with the adiantums. (It is also closely allied botanically with *Argyrochosma* and *Astrolepis*.) The penetrating stalks, with a singular vascular bundle, are frequently toxic to grazing animals. Evergreen, naked blades are from once-pinnate to tripinnate with a terminal leaflet matching the lateral pinnae. Free, or in rare instances netted (*P. bridgesii* and *P. ternifolia*), veins are not prominent. Sori, protected by reflexed inrolled false indusial marginal tissue, line the pinnule perimeters.

Many of the species are apogamous, an efficient adaptive response to their native habitat's sparse supply of the water required for sexual reproduction. In the comfortable and uniform atmosphere provided by nursery propagation (vis-à-vis the uncertainties of natural sites with dodgy and inconsistent weather), they eagerly burst forth from spores. None like to be transplanted, however, so the native populations need to be left in situ and nursery products should be introduced with care to specialized soil and sites. The xeric species want bright airy exposures, but not quite full sun, and will turn weak and spindly in too much shade. Tuck their long-ranging roots in moist but well-drained crevices in rocky sites and give them a matching gritty top dressing. For most growers these are truly plants to be admired rather than cultivated.

Pellaea atropurpurea

Purple cliff brake

Epithet means "dark purple."
Evergreen, 8 to 18 in. (20 to 45 cm). Zones 4 to 9. Dimorphic. Apogamous.

DESCRIPTION: The rhizome is short-creeping. Shiny, rounded stipes with fawn-colored curly hairs are characteristically a midnight purple-black and one-third of the frond length. Lance-shaped blades are basally bipinnate grading to once-pinnate on the upper portions of the five to nine pairs of pinnae. Lower pinnae are stalked. Upper are sessile with a terminal pinna matching the shape of the lateral pinnae. The plants are mildly dimorphic with the sterile fronds shorter and less divided than the more upright fertile fronds. Sori are marginal, protected by inrolled margins of false indusia.

RANGE AND HABITAT: This species grows in limestone-enriched rocky crags across a broad expanse of midwestern and eastern North American habitats and extends its range down through Mexico and Central America. Look for it as well in the mortared crevices of old weathered buildings and the associated functional antiquities of bridges and highway abutments.

CULTURE AND COMMENTS: This species is not eager to grace average gardens, even of inspired enthusiasts. However, it is the "easiest" of all the xeric pellaeas. As is true for most dryland ferns, good drainage is critical and essential. A limestone substrate is also required and beyond that protection from excess winter wet (ironically snow cover serves here) all contribute to a potentially successful planting. Try growing it in limestone rubble, good light but not hot midday sunshine, and a well-drained vertical rock or simulated rock face. In cultivation in western North America it is usually short-lived. It is easily confused with the equally temperamental *Pellaea glabella*, a fellow limestone denizen of eastern U.S. habitats. The latter, however, with its essentially smooth stipes, is strictly monomorphic, displaying its diminutive fronds in arches over its preferred rocky habitats.

Pellaea glabella
Smooth cliff brake
Epithet means "smooth."
Evergreen, 4 to 14 in. (10 to 35 cm). Zones 3 to 8. Apogamous.

DESCRIPTION: The rhizome is short-creeping. Plum-brown stipes are one-half of the frond length and smooth with an insignificant and fleeting dusting of hairs. Blades are lanceolate with stalked bipinnate lower pinnae and sessile, once-pinnate upper pinnae on four to nine pairs of pinnae. Sori are enclosed in the inrolled false marginal indusia. Botanists have divided this species into four subspecies. See *Flora of North America* (1993) for technical details.

RANGE AND HABITAT: *Pellaea glabella* grows naturally in limestone crevices and mortared wall slices from midwestern to eastern areas of the United States. It also appears in random disjunct sites in the Rocky Mountains and western states. A limestone substrate is the common denominator.

CULTURE AND COMMENTS: Once established, and this is the challenge, this petite blue-green species will tolerate full sun in cloudy coastal haunts of the western United States and almost full sun elsewhere. I recommend a planting compost of two parts lava rock, one part light compost, and one part a mixed balance of bark, crushed concrete, and charcoal (or whatever gritty additives suit your personal preference). This has

Pellaea atropurpurea in nature's rock garden in Massachusetts.

Pellaea glabella on a bridge abutment in Pennsylvania.

worked for me in a half whiskey barrel, sheltered from winter rains under the eaves of the house. Chunks of rocks are added for a beneficial cool root run.

Pellaea rotundifolia
Button fern
Epithet means "rounded foliage."
Evergreen, 6 to 18 in. (15 to 45 cm). Zones 8 (with lots of protection) and 9.

DESCRIPTION: The rhizome is creeping. Coffee-colored stipes are bristled with rusty hairs and scales and usually one-third of the frond length. The linear blade is once-pinnate, bearing 30 or more pairs of glossy, widely spaced, short-stalked, round globes of pinnae. The fronds arch in horizontal layers of shiny green leaflets. Sori with inrolled false marginal indusia encircle the pinnae margins but significantly do not meet at the apices, which bear a small needlelike tip. Button fern can be propagated by both division and spores.

RANGE AND HABITAT: This species is a New Zealand endemic and one of its most welcomed ferny exports. It is found in light scrub, dry forests, and occasionally in moist rainforest habitats.

CULTURE AND COMMENTS: A healthy and well-grown button fern is an extremely attractive addition to the indoor fern collection or the patio pot displays and foreground focal points in temperate Zone 9 gardens. It requires an acid and well-drained grainy compost and, while it should not dry out, it is more likely to meet its demise by the overzealous attention of the eager guardian armed with a watering can. Give it good indirect light and occasional water, rather like the attention and site given to poinsettias.

Shorter Notes
Pellaea andromedifolia (foliage like *Andromeda*), the coffee fern, is a 1- to 2-ft. (30 to 60 cm) tall, evergreen, apogamous, wiry, open-faced tripinnate, triangular attraction in the niches of igneous rocks. In some populations the upper portions of the tan to grayish rachises are slightly zigzagged, but not as prominently so as in *P. ovata*. Small linear pinnules can be cof-

fee-colored in exposed sites with the whole looking like sprays of airy and delicate conifer branches. Growing natively from Oregon south through Baja California, it is, like most pellaeas, difficult in cultivation. Give it porous soil in the lee of nonbasic rocks or experiment with it as a container subject, testing mixtures of assorted soils combined with controlled exposures to a variety of sites. It is for Zones 8 and 9.

Pellaea brachyptera (with short wings), the Sierra cliff brake, is a 1-ft. (30-cm) evergreen native of Pacific Northwest igneous and, rarely, serpentine scree rubble. The linear blade is bipinnate with narrow, pointed, curled gray-green inrolled pinnules clustered in tight bristly bunches along the rachis, looking rather like a bottle brush. This fern is not easy to cul-

Sprays of blue pinnae on *Pellaea andromedifolia* in the upper Kern Canyon, Tulare County, California. Photo by David Schwartz.

Pellaea rotundifolia with cascades of green "buttons."

Pellaea brachyptera in a typically exposed montane site in northern California.

Pellaea bridgesii

tivate, but is easy to admire while trekking in the field. It challenges growers in Zones 7 to 9 where it should be offered a lean site with moist but well-draining soil and a daily dose of sunshine.

Pellaea breweri, Brewer's cliff brake, is named after William Brewer, a plant collector from California, who along with Sereno Watson and Asa Gray authored the first flora of California. His namesake *Pellaea* is a small 8-in. (20-cm) evergreen with shiny brown stipes and linear pinnate-pinnatifid blades. The species is unusual in the North American *Pellaea* population because of its prominent articulation lines breaking at the base of the stipes. The 6 to 10 pairs of bluish pinnae are sessile, looking like attached lopsided butterflies ready to take flight. These are Zone 5 to 9 plants of rocky cliffs from higher elevations in the Pacific Northwest and occasionally found eastward to Colorado. Like other pellaeas it resists cultivation and is most likely to last a season or two in well-drained crevices with a steady exposure to bright light.

Pellaea bridgesii (after Thomas Bridges), Bridge's cliff brake, is an evergreen, once-pinnate, 1-ft. (30-cm) cliff dweller with lustrous chestnut stipes and 6 to 12 pairs of stalked, blue-green, round to oblong pinnae. Look for the netted veins that are unusual for the genus (although also present in *P. ternifolia*). This species is not likely to be found in cultivation, but can be enjoyed in dryland, granitic sites high up in the Cascade Mountains of the Pacific Northwest and eastward to fern-stressed sites in Montana and Colorado. For the home gardener, the usual precautions apply—good drainage, high light, and restricted winter wet.

Pellaea cordifolia (heart-shaped leaves) is a Mexican native that barely reaches into a xeric nook or two in the southwesternmost arid areas of the United States. It is variously described as deciduous and as evergreen (or not defined at all). Basically, it is especially adapted to Zones 9 and 10. Fronds are usually 18 in. (45 cm) tall with stipes that are a dull wastewater-colored tan-gray. The lax ovate blades are bipinnate to tripinnate with stalked triangular pinnules looking like arrowheads ready to be launched. It is botanically significant that the rachis is not zigzagged, thus separating it from the similarly structured *P. ovata*. This species has been successfully introduced into the custom-designed eco-niche in the gardens of Southern California specialists and is reputed to be easier than most other pellaeas.

Pellaea falcata (sickle-shaped) is a 2-ft. (60-cm), rich leathery green species suitable for outdoor ornamentation in Zones 9 and 10 or for indoor décor elsewhere. It is native to India and even more common as a slow colonizer in Australia and New Zealand. The linear, once-pinnate fronds are upright with dark, scaly stipes and glowing oblong pinnae that taper to a point. The sori rim the margins but do not reach the pinnae apex. Old stipe bases are persistent and erect like upright straw sentinels, and new growth is occasionally fleetingly tinged with pink. Growers in San Diego, California, report that the species attracts thrips, which can be controlled with a carefully applied mild dose of a nonoil-based insecticide. Otherwise this species is an attractive foil for floral color from greenhouses to tropical gardens.

Pellaea mucronata (pointed), bird's foot fern, an apt description, is a spiny 18-in. (45-cm) evergreen with shiny ebony stipes and bipinnate blades with minute glaucous pinnules fanning forth in spreading sets of three. The blade is ovate with the lower pinnae noticeably smaller than the upper complements. All portions feature strongly pointed tips. Botanists have separated this into two subspecies. The species hybridizes with *P. bridgesii*. In all of its manifestations it is a fern of limestone-free terrain in the Sierra Nevada of California down to Mexico's Baja California. Away from its xeric habitat it is rarely cultivated successfully, but offers promise in gritty compost and brightly lit rock gardens from Zones 7 to 9.

Pellaea nitidula (with a shiny surface), synonyms *Cheilanthes nitidula* and *Mildella nitidula*, is a small foot-tall (30-cm) species with mildly hairy but glossy stipes up to two-thirds of the frond length. Lanceolate blades are bipinnate to tripinnate with four or five pairs of pointed pinnae with matching acute-tipped pinnules. The species is very closely related to and may in time be reclassified as *Mildella*. Populations are at mid to higher altitudes in the Himalayas and China and are candidates for specialized situations in Zones 7 (with luck and dedication) to 10.

Pellaea ovata (egg-shaped), flexuous cliff brake, is an amalgam of unfernlike characteristics from its rambling loosely lax fronds to the structurally significant zigzagged rachis. It is a tripinnate evergreen up to 2½ ft. (75 cm) tall with stalked deltas of yellow-green to gray-green pinnules. Soil preferences are on both geological sides of neutral. Widespread populations dot the rocky slopes and piney forests of its native Mexico and extend into Texas as well as South America. It can be introduced into temporarily successful displays, particularly in container culture, in the Zone 8 Greater Seattle, Washington, area, but is better suited to the natural drylands of Zones 9 and 10 in Southern California. Apogamous.

Pellaea ternifolia (three-parted foliage) is a typical xeric, growing in exposed drylands from assorted sites in the U.S. Southwest, Mexico, Central America, and the highlands of Hawaii. The 4 to 15 pairs of pinnae bear clusters of three short splayed sessile pinnules. The evergreen fronds are just under 1 ft. (30 cm) tall with glossy, plum-brown stipes and narrow, once-pinnate dull bluish blades. Like *P. bridgesii*, this species has netted (reticulate) veins—unusual for the genus. It has been in cultivation in sheltered sites in Britain and exposed sites in California, but remains a challenge. Good drainage with requisite porous soil and an alpinelike exposure help to maintain this species in cultivation. It is still not notoriously long-lived away from its preferred existence as a rock climber in igneous substrates. *Flora of North America* (1993) recognizes three subspecies: **subsp.** *villosa* (now designated as a species by some botanists), **subsp.** *ternifolia*, and **subsp.** *arizonica*. Horticulturally, however, all share the same cultural requirements with their attendant rewards and stresses.

Pellaea viridis (green), green cliff brake, is a bipinnate to tripinnate evergreen seen on occasion in conservatories, and less frequently in the warmth of Zone 9 to 10 gardens where its glossy presence is a welcome counterpoint to the vivacious exuberance of tropical flowers. Fronds with dark chocolate stipes

Pellaea mucronata in the University of California Botanical Garden at Berkeley.

Pellaea ternifolia. Photo by Jim Baggett

and glowing green foliage usually mature at 2 ft. (60 cm). Reported in Palmer (2003) and Burrows (1990) to be *Cheilanthes viridis*, it is by all accounts a variable species. A dryish site with superb drainage encourages successful cultivation. Apogamous.

Pellaea wrightiana (after Wright), Wright's cliff brake, is similar to and often classified under *P. ternifolia*. The foot-tall (30-cm) fronds with bipinnate blades grow in acid to slightly basic soil in the lower Rocky Mountain heartland of the United States from Oklahoma and Texas west and north to Utah, Colorado, New Mexico, and Arizona as well as northern Mexico.

Pentagramma

Pentagramma (*penta*, five, and *gramma*, line, in reference to the outline of the blade) includes two deciduous species, *P. pallida* and *P. triangularis*, recently split from *Pityrogramma*. The blades sit atop tall stipes, are pentagonal in outline, and have indusia-free sori carried along the veins.

Pentagramma triangularis in a typical setting with rocks and woodland duff.

Pentagramma pallida (pale) from the piney woods of California's Sierra Nevada foothills has dark, lusterless stipes dusted with white powder. Both surfaces of the blade are likewise decorated giving the upper a (sometimes temporary) distinctive, grayish tinge and the lower a waxy finish.

The more common *Pentagramma triangularis* (triangular), gold back fern, from the west coast of British Columbia down through Baja California, has slightly shiny, coffee-colored stipes. Blades are dark green on the upper surface and usually waxy yellow on the underside although occasionally creamy.

Both species, which appear to be so charming and innocent in the wild, are touchy in cultivation. Hardy in Zones 8 and 9, they have a strong preference for acid surroundings, free-draining soil littered with conifer needles or composting leaves, and bright light. As borderline xerics, and like so many of that type, they do not like excessive watering.

Phegopteris
Beech ferns

Depending on your age, the three *Phegopteris* species may be more familiar as members of the genus *Thelypteris* (and to many of us are recognizable under both classifications). They have many common characteristics including a fuzz of clear needlelike hairs, a pair of vascular bundles (looking remarkably, at their base, like peanuts in a shell), creeping rhizomes (or erect rhizomes with roots that produce creeping runners, a botanical distinction), and deciduous fronds. Currently *Phegopteris* is recognized as a separate genus based on a bipinnatifid frond structure, usually with sessile (stalkless) pinnae, especially in the upper portions. However, even farther back in history it was lumped with *Polypodium* because of its creeping rhizome as well as the lack of indusia. In the mid 1800s French botanist Antoine Fée determined that based on a number of botanical details, including having only two vascular bundles, *Phegopteris* was distinct. Under one name or another these ferns have been meandering around in gardens and botany ever since.

The species are all temperate and, like their *Thelypteris* counterparts, ready to colonize, sometimes needing restraint, in the woodlands of various zones from the chill of Zone 3 to the comforts of Zone 9. Rhizomes or runners creep, frequently in moss, just below the soil surface and, with an allotment of shade, moisture, and somewhat decent loam, beech ferns are an undemanding assortment of deciduous ground covers. I find them especially attractive in a natural setting enhanced by well-placed pieces of silvery driftwood accents. Or use them within the framework of a stumpery. They will wander about but can be trained for design and effect. Removing an offending or exuberant extension of rhizome-runner and foliage will give you, or your friends, a new plant and will not affect the health of the parent plant. These ferns are readily reproduced from spores that are carried in round to oblong bundles of sori without indusia. As noted, division is a reliable option and brings "instant gratification" with the ease of re-entry for the excised section of rhizome and fronds.

Phegopteris comes from the Greek *phegos*, beech, and *pteris*, fern, in reference to the plant's native origins of growing under

Phegopteris connectilis meanders around driftwood in the Horder garden.

Phegopteris hexagonoptera (left) and *P. connectilis* (right). Note significant pinna attachment on *P. hexagonoptera*.

beech trees. In cultivation, these ferns are indifferent to the type of shade tree overstory.

Phegopteris connectilis
Northern beech fern, narrow beech fern, long beech fern
Synonyms *Thelypteris phegopteris, Polypodium phegopteris*
Epithet means "joined."
Deciduous, 8 to 15 in. (20 to 38 cm). Zones 2 to 8. Apogamous.
DESCRIPTION: The rhizome is short- to long-creeping. Slender, rounded tan-green stipes are wrapped in hairs and narrow

scales and are one-half or more of the frond length. Pinnate-pinnatifid to bipinnatifid blades are triangular with 12 to 15 pairs of softly downy, thin-textured pinnae carried horizontally. Significantly the lowest pair is smaller, points downwards and forward, and is not fused to the rachis nor winged to the pinnae pair above. (Pinnae on *Phegopteris hexagonoptera* are connected by wings.) Upper pinnae are broadly attached to the rachis, however. Sori without indusia are submarginal.

RANGE AND HABITAT: The northern beech fern is very common in cold temperate zones, heavily populating mountain slopes, woodlands, and mossy rocks across northern and eastern North America and Eurasia. It prefers moist acid soil but is adaptable and, once established, amazingly drought tolerant.

CULTURE AND COMMENTS: Grow this low creeper in shaded rock gardens, to define foregrounds of borders, unify tangled stumperies, or wherever a mass of light greenery enhances the garden. New fronds emerge throughout the summer. Although slug precautions are advised, their threat should not discourage planting this cover. It is extremely cold tolerant, but does not adapt to heat such as that of the southern United States.

Phegopteris decursive-pinnata
Japanese beech fern, winged beech fern
Synonyms *Thelypteris decursive-pinnata, Lastrea decursive-pinnata*
Epithet means "wings running down the stem."
Deciduous, 1 to 2 ft. (30 to 60 cm). Zones 4 to 9.

Phegopteris decursive-pinnata in the Kennar garden.

A patch of *Phegopteris hexagonoptera* at the Mount Cuba Center.

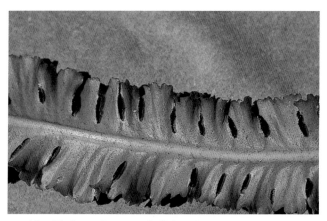

Double-sided openings on *Phyllitis* sori.

DESCRIPTION: The rhizome is erect with, depending on the friability of the soil, short- to long-creeping root runners. Short stipes, with fine hairs and scales, are the color of new mown hay and usually one-fourth of the frond length. Upright, pale green, narrowly elliptic blades, tapering at both ends, are pinnate-pinnatifid with 18 to 25 pairs of hairy pinnae. The pinnae are broadly attached to the rachis and connected to each other by wings of foliar tissue (a defining measure of the species). Round to oblong sori are without indusia and are medial on the pinnules.

RANGE AND HABITAT: This species is the Asian member of the genus with populations in mountains, woods, walls, and rock crevices from Japan, China, and Korea to Thailand, India, and the Himalayas.

CULTURE AND COMMENTS: Easily established in light shade and moist woodlands, this fern is suitable for gardens from the warmth of northern California to the testing winters and summers of eastern North America, Britain, and Europe. With its upright soft foliar swords, it is a welcome ground cover, easily providing a green summer understory lasting well beyond the first frosts.

Phegopteris hexagonoptera
Broad beech fern, southern beech fern
Synonym *Thelypteris hexagonoptera*
Epithet means "six-angled wing or fern."
Deciduous, 1½ to 2 ft. (45 to 60 cm). Zones 5 to 8.

DESCRIPTION: The rhizome is long-creeping, creating large stands of fern forests in moist woodlands. Tall stipes are buff-colored, hairy, and up to one-half of the frond length. Broadly triangular blades are bipinnatifid with 10 to 15 pairs of pinnae. Lower pinnae are the widest, extending in true triangular form from the base of the blade. All pinnae are broadly attached to the rachis and connected to each other by wings of foliage, a significant measure of identification. (*Phegopteris connectilis* has the lower pinnae pair distinctly "unconnected" to adjacent pinnae.) Sori without indusia, but occasionally with small unicellular hairs, are close to the pinnae margins.

RANGE AND HABITAT: The broad beech fern is endemic to eastern North America where it grows in acid soils in northern states, but more abundantly in the southern coastal tier down to Florida.

CULTURE AND COMMENTS: This species is easily introduced to shaded and moisture-rich gardens in Zones 5 to 8, where it can be slightly aggressive but is easily controlled by judicious "pruning." It is one of the last ferns to unfurl in the spring, but will produce fronds throughout the summer. Like its cousin *Phegopteris connectilis*, it too carries a slug alert, especially when tender and tempting young fronds are emerging. Plant it in moist sites. Poor soil will restrain its spread somewhat. Humusy soil will encourage more vigorous growth. Your choice.

Phyllitis

Hart's tongue ferns

With their kelly-green fronds in straplike or various configurations thereof, the hart's tongue ferns can be remarkable additions to the garden's fern portfolio. *Phyllitis* from Dioscorides' Greek means "simple frond." The common species, *P. scolopendrium*, as opposed to its multiple varieties, is an upright, unbranched (entire or simple) "tongue" growing from an erect rhizome. Short succulent stipes, with back-to-back vascular bundles, lift emerging fronds looking like budding Jacks in the pulpit (arisaemas) but expand instead into symmetrical rosettes of flared greenery. Their unfurling shape is credited as being the long-ago pattern for the scrolls (fiddleheads) on the tips of violin necks.

Sori line the fronds in a regimented herringbone series of buttonholes which, when enhanced by backlighting, are an elegant lesson in soral patterning. They are paired along the free veins and open, facing each other as mirror images, splitting longitudinally and exposing the sporangia like peas in a pod. Sori in the close relative *Asplenium* open as a single valve along a vein.

Phyllitis is frequently consolidated with *Asplenium*, however, and hybridizes with its species. (Furthermore, in a remarkable signature botanical event, *Phyllitis scolopendrium* crosses with the hybrid *Asplenium ebenoides* [*A. platyneuron* × *Camptosorus rhizophyllus*] to give the fern world its only trigeneric hybrid.) Based on the difference in soral structure and the classification presented in the works of respected authorities (Page 1982, Mickel 1994, Hoshizaki and Moran 2001), my personal classification preference is *Phyllitis*.

Worldwide the distribution is extensive and includes Europe, Asia, North Africa, the Middle East, and North America. Universally these ferns are primarily associated with limestone rocks and substrates. The rare North American native, *Phyllitis scolopendrium* var. *americana*, grows almost exclusively in shaded quarries and limestone-rich habitats frequently in hardwood forests. Alert visitors to Europe and Britain will find their native species, and an occasional variation, in mortared rubble on antiquities, faces of buildings, and in chinks on roadside walls (and can amuse the locals by taking close-up photographs of their "flora"). Garden specimens do acclimate in circumneutral soil as well but appreciate an amendment of ground oyster or eggshells, concrete pebbles, limestone chips, or other additives that offer a steady and slow release of lime. Powdered supplements of dolomite or lawn sweeteners are not recommended. However, fellow enthusiasts give an endorsement to pelleted dolomitic limestone.

Propagation from spores is an educational and horticultural adventure as the progeny often offer extremely irregular deviations in foliar architecture. These are, however, not your named varieties which in order to be correctly offered as a given cultivar usually need to be reproduced vegetatively by tissue culture or division. Or they can be propagated, in a most unusual fashion for ferns, as pseudo-cuttings from leaf stalks. To do so the fronds need to be stripped back from their base rather like peeling cloves from garlic (thus potentially destroying the parent plant incidentally, so chose with care), cleaned, and inserted into a propagation flat containing a receptive mix of moist sand and a token handful of basic compost. Another recommendation is to use old (dead or dead-looking) frond bases with whatever remnants of roots remain attached, without digging up the parent, and plunge them into moist sphagnum moss. With time and luck the basal buds will form new plants.

Phyllitis is surrounded by a rich history of mystical and medicinal properties. Based on the Doctrine of Signatures, which assigned medical cures to plants based on the similarities in their structure to the offending ailment, *Phyllitis* was consider a logical antidote to snakebites (thanks to their flickering and comparable "tongues"). Pharmacists and herbalists recommended mixing a mash of hart's tongue fern and wine for relief. (This assumed, however, that both the wine and fern were conveniently available at the time of the unfortunate encounter between the snake and the victim.)

The association of the heart-shaped frond base and romance offered some remarkable as well as opposing "signature" properties. A distilled drink infused with "essence of hart's tongue," for example, offered protection against the "passions of the heart," while wearing an amulet of the fronds was supposed to be effective in preventing conception. "Just how effective seems not to have been recorded" (Page 1988).

Phyllitis scolopendrium

Hart's tongue fern

Synonym *Asplenium scolopendrium*

Epithet means "with multiple legs like a centipede," in reference to the sori.

Evergreen, 1 to 2 ft. (30 to 60 cm). Zones 4 to 9.

DESCRIPTION: The rhizome is erect. Short stubby stipes are plum and green and when unfurling are trimmed in a suit of soft white downy hairs. Simple, undivided blades are erect with a heart-shaped base and pointed apex. The sori are in pairs along the veins and open as bivalves.

RANGE AND HABITAT: The European species, which is what we see, along with its varieties, in cultivation, grows with abandon in Britain, Europe, and beyond. I have seen it circling in concrete cracks under the protection of open lattice manhole covers, colonizing in limestone-enriched supports under wharfs as well as in the traditional sites that are blessed with a measure of damp mortar and partial shade. The temperamental, cultivation-resistant North American differs botanically by, among other traits, generally being smaller and having short sori strictly on the terminal portion of the frond rather than elongate sori that are distributed along the length of the frond. It is native to, and happy in, limestone habitats in upper state New York, Michigan, and the Bruce Peninsula in Ontario, Canada, with a few odd outlying crops in Alabama and Tennessee.

CULTURE AND COMMENTS: Hart's tongue selections are almost infinite, but whatever choice makes it to the garden should be cultivated, if possible, in basic soil, with a certain amount of lime enrichment and that magic ingredient, good drainage. My plants are prospering, with a minimum amount of coddling, as sentinels along the walled perimeters of a concrete foundation. I used to give them a cocktail of eggshells and water, but have not done so for quite some time. They do not appear to miss it. The bad news, at least in the Pacific Northwest, is that they do attract strawberry root weevils (black vine weevils) both as grubs and man-eating adults. Their nocturnal chewing begets frond edges that are severely notched. Try carefully timed early spring applications of beneficial nematodes as a control. Indoors, with their succulent fronds, they are also magnets for aphids, which in turn transmit viruses in greenhouses and propagation sites. These attacks are easy to manage with a method of your choice, although "soaps" often yield fatal results to the host as well as the offending insects. Once the plants are established in the garden, aphids, having found other gourmet options, are no longer a problem. While all of these threats to success may sound formidable, the plants are resilient and formally ornamental (and chewed foliage can just be given a varietal name). And varieties there are in Victorian abundance. Lowe (1908) lists 437 cultivars (and apologized for not listing them all) in 16 subdivisions.

The highest concentrations of commercially available forms, fondly called "Scollies," are in groups that are crested, crisped, or have variously altered frond margins as well as

Frond variations in a *Phyllitis* collection in the Graham garden.

Upright undivided fronds of *Phyllitis scolopendrium* in the Miller Botanical Garden. Note the buttonhole pattern of the sori.

A striking alteration on the apex of a *Phyllitis* frond in the Graham garden.

combinations thereof. Give them a place of honor in the garden's foreground. Crested varieties include a multiplicity of types listed under the umbrella of *Phyllitis scolopendrium* 'Cristata', which has forked tips on a single plane up to multidivided heads of cresting crests. Crisped and undulate cultivars have wavy, crinkled, and frilled margins. (This ornamentation has been described in literature since the early 1900s as resembling an Elizabethan ruff.) Beyond that the distinctions are more finely defined, ranging from crumpled and ridged margins to twirled spirals of fronds. A sampling of those available, often appropriately presented as "group" denominations, are listed here.

Crispa Group, a generic and very handsome group, includes undulate types with frilled and wavy margins as described above. **'Crispa Bolton's Nobile'** is a standout in British collections and a well-photographed specimen in the elegant rock and perennial garden displays at Britain's Sizergh Castle. Like many of the "undulate" and "crisped" types, the cultivar is sterile, but is marching out with a welcome band of fanfare from tissue-culture labs. It will hopefully soon be a staple in *Phyllitis* displays. Others in the group include **'Crispa Cristata'**, which is both wavy margined and forked; **'Crispa Fimbriata'**, an amalgamation of wavy margins with fringed edges; and **'Crispa Golden Queen'**, which is undulate and mildly variegated with horizontal lime striations (and not suited for sunny exposures).

Cristata Group has an array of cresting ranging from the simple forked apex in **'Cristata'** to multiple shredding, described by terms such as *digitata* (fingered) and *ramo* (branched). **'Ramo Marginata'**, for example, is divided into

many fingers extending from the base of the frond and looks like a ferny equivalent of escarole.

Heavily crested types such as **'Capitata'** (headed), **'Corymbifera'** (clustered), and **'Grandiceps'** (with large terminal crests) have fronds that are simple at their base, but are topped with ornate headdresses of dissected foliage. Do, however, protect these terminal embellishments from collecting excessive amounts of water, which is an invitation to breakage.

Two cultivars that are extremely popular and have fortunately been in commerce both in the United States and abroad

Fingers on the frond tips of *Phyllitis scolopendrium* 'Digitata'.

Variations on a variation, the *Phyllitis scolopendrium* Crispa Group. (Left) In the Stobbe garden. (Center) In the Kaye garden. (Right) In the Rickard garden.

are **'Kaye's Lacerate'**, a leaf lettuce of a fern with fringed edges, and **'Peraferens'**, which in an amazing display of foliar acrobatics has a curled frond apex enclosing a minute extended needle of foliar tissue. Both come true from spores.

Other variations in addition to the crisp, crested, and undulate include marginate in which the fronds are horizontally ribbed, muricate with rough surfaces, and sagittate in which the frond's lower portions extend like lateral arrowheads.

There are, of course, all sorts of combinations of these alterations in frond structure (remember Lowe with his 437

named cultivars) giving gardeners, and especially collectors, an abundant choice of individual selections with unique characteristics.

Phymatosorus

Phymatosorus (depressed sori) can be considered an umbrella genus for a number of species that have been variously classified as *Microsorum*, *Polypodium*, and *Lecanopteris*. The genus name itself may soon be obsolete pending further scientific examination of botanical details, but the creeping rhizome habit is common by whatever classification.

Phymatosorus diversifolius (leaves of different shapes) is native to New Zealand and Australia, where it forms extensive colonies on rough-barked trees, on tree fern trunks, or along the caps of old stone walls. It can be grown as a ground cover in shade, but is one of those ferns, the better enjoyment of which may be in contemplating it in the place that it has chosen for itself. (Description by George Schenk.)

Pityrogramma

Pityrogramma (*pityro*, scurf or loose scales, and *gramma*, line, in reference to the lines of sporangia under the powdery scales on the frond's lower surface) is a genus of 16 to 20 species (as currently revised) and is primarily distributed in the Americas.

Pityrogramma calomelanos (*calo*, beautiful, and *melano*, black or dark) is probably the greatest of those louche and contemptible, noble and indispensable species, the weed ferns of the world. There are only a few of these worldwide, and these few are mostly national or even more local in habitat.

Phyllitis scolopendrium 'Marginata' with stiffly ribbed frond margins in the Carstensen garden.

Rolled frond tips of *Phyllitis scolopendrium* 'Peraferens'.

Juvenile and adult stages of *Phymatosorus diversifolius* growing on the trunk of *Cyathea dealbata*. Photo by George Schenk.

A cloak of *Pityrogramma calomelanos* covers a dry stone wall. The fern fabric is made up of dozens of self-sown sporelings. Companion plants include *Alternanthera ficoidea* (at bottom), a red-leafed *Neoregelia* (lower right), *Iresine herbstii* (upper right), and white-flowered *Buddleia davidii* (center). Photo by George Schenk.

(The Pacific Northwest, for example, is the home of a big, pushy regional fern, *Athyrium filix-femina* subsp. *cyclosorum*, which gives fits to meticulous gardeners but is also of major value in casual shade gardening.) Quite the opposite of the regionalist weed ferns, *P. calomelanos* is a world-beater. From its original range in the New World (the West Indies to Florida to Central and South America) it has ridden the wind and settled into most of the world's tropics and subtropics. It adores the fresh dirt of road embankments and agricultural edges, and delights equally in stone walls, rock garden crevices, and sidewalk margins where feet do not go. It sneaks into flower pots and planters already planted with something the gardener treasures, and there it elbows out the rightful occupant as callously as any cuckoo chick. Yet there are places where its invasion is a betterment, places such as the stone wall which it dresses with fine, rich greenery at no cost to the gardener other than grooming the fern about once a year. This species is a tuft-maker not a stroller on stolons. A form of this variable species known as silver fern wears a coat of silvery white powder on its frond undersides; other forms are powdered yellow, orange, or even pink, or are not powdered at all. (Description by George Schenk.)

Platycerium
Staghorn ferns

With their unique outlines, the staghorn ferns are in a class all by themselves. Wherever available, and sometimes when not so available (making them all the more desirable), they have attracted an ardent support group devoted to their culture and definition. In nature they are epiphytes and in cultivation they hang from assorted structures as outdoor greenery in Southern California, Florida, and wherever else they can be protected from the elements. Indoors they are prized in homes and especially in conservatories where ancient specimens are dominant features, peering like trophies from walls and hanging their curious foliage from focal vantage points.

Structurally, platyceriums (Greek *platy*, broad, and *keras*, horned) are extremely dimorphic. They have two frond types, a "shield frond," which is essentially a spongy, usually nonshowy, but functional foot that provides ballast and attaches wherever appropriate, be it on trees in nature or, in cultivation, the grower's choice of background support. Youthfully, it is green, but in maturity can be a single or several times divided papery tan "shield." In areas of low rainfall these "shields" lean forward from their arboreal perches and act as receptacles for moisture and nutrients. In high-rainfall areas they close up to prevent damage from an over accumulation of water. From this foothold great wings of potentially fertile "antlerlike" fronds extend upwards, but more often drape downwards, in species-specific, multifingered configurations. Pale, star-shaped hairs coat the foliage like soft fuzz and, when fertile, the frond tips are cloaked in a spotty undercoat of brown sporangia patches looking like random smudges. The sori are without indusia. Plants can be grown, given time, from spores, but are best propagated by the careful removal of "pups," which are produced from buds on the roots of a number of species.

Culturally, the commonly available staghorns are regarded as somewhat finicky houseplants for the inexperienced or, for the specialists, incredibly easy. Rarely available species can be very demanding in their cultural needs and are best left for the skills of the seasoned expert. However, for both, watering is critical and not to be overdone. For an indicator, simply touch the shield frond. If it oozes, do not add to the accumulated hydraulics. Let the frond dry. I repeat here, as again and again throughout these chapters, that most indoor fern mortalities are due to excessive watering. Give these especially water-sensitive species bright light, an occasional drink (unless otherwise noted), and very lean soil. Attach them to a vertical mount. For efficient and thorough watering, when required, experts recommend a trip to and dip in the bathtub followed by drip-drying. Most staghorns are not frost tolerant but can be rotated without stress from indoors to out as a display of hanging ornamentals in the temperate summer garden or wherever benign weather gives them comfort.

Worldwide, there are 18 species with all but one, a South American, growing in the tropics of Africa and Asia. For assistance in identification, Hoshizaki and Moran (2001) divided them into three groups based on areas of origin and several distinguishing features including stipe design and root bud production. The Malayan-Asiatic species have a stipe cross section with a dark ring of tissue surrounding vascular bundles arranged in a circle, which include scattered bundles within the circle. *Platycerium coronarium*, *P. grande*, *P. holttumii*, *P. ridleyi*, *P. superbum*, *P. wallichii*, and *P. wandae* are in this group. They do not produce buds. African-American species have the same vascular bundle configuration without a dark ring of tissue. These include *P. alcicorne*, *P. andinum*, *P elephantotis*, *P. ellisii*, *P. madagascariense*, *P. quadridichotomum*, and *P. stemaria*. They do produce buds. Javan-Australian species do not have a dark ring or inner bundles. They also produce buds. *Platycerium bifurcatum*, *P. hillii*, *P. veitchii*, and *P. willinckii* are in this group.

Platycerium alcicorne (elk horned) has erect masses of linear fertile fronds, which split into numerous fingers. The sori are at the ultimate tips. It is one of the easier species for cultivation.

Platycerium alcicorne in production at Henry's Plant Farm. Note precautions against overwatering.

Platycerium andinum (from the Andes), the American staghorn, has bushy upright shield fronds and long, drooping fertile fronds that are broad at their base, then divided. It is difficult and especially sensitive to overwatering.

Platycerium bifurcatum (divided into equal parts) is the most commonly available and culturally adaptable staghorn. Although quite variable, it typically has forking fronds that are often both arching and pendant. Large plants form a spidery mass of foliage.

Platycerium coronarium (forming a crown) is a staghorn fern typical of the others in the genus in possessing, to my eyes, a horrific magnificence, the plant kingdom's equal of Louie the Sun King in his most hyacinthine portrait. Like other staghorns, this species grows as an epiphyte on primary forest trees. It ranges widely in tropical Asia, where it forms the usual upward-growing staghorn headdress (or "shield" as I read in more proper writing on ferns), and the usual beardlike drapery of narrow, curly green straps for fronds. These are said to grow to 9 ft. (2.7 m) in length, but I have yet to see them more than half that. (Description by George Schenk.)

Platycerium elephantotis (of the elephants), the Angola staghorn, has entire fronds ribbed with veins and looking to me (and perhaps the author of the name) like giant elephant ears. It needs an abundance of water while in new growth, but not while inactive in winter. It is cold sensitive.

Platycerium ellisii (after Ellis) is small (by *Platycerium* standards) with shiny shield fronds and upright V-tipped fronds looking like tulips in silhouette. It is considered challenging to grow.

Platycerium grande (large, showy) is, true to name, a huge beauty with a broad expanse of lacerated foliage. It is similar to, and often confused with, *P. superbum* but has two patches of sporangia per frond rather than one. In addition it is cold sensitive whereas *P. superbum* is one of the few that will tolerate a touch of frost.

Platycerium hillii (after Walter Hill, 1820–1904, superintendent of the Brisbane Botanic Gardens in Australia), the green staghorn, is an easily cultivated species with rounded rather than pointed tips on the fertile fronds.

Platycerium holttumii (after Richard Holttum, 1895–1990, an outstanding contributor to Malaysian botany and pteridology) is a difficult giant with upright shield fronds and claws of hanging fertile foliage. It is similar to *P. wandae* but without fringed trim around the base. Good air circulation is strongly advised.

Platycerium madagascariense (from Madagascar) is, according to *Platycerium* specialist Charles Alford (pers. comm.), the most difficult species to keep alive and presentable in cultivation. The plants, with corridors of veins patterned like waffles, are hosts to ants that in turn surround themselves with unfriendly insect pals. V-shaped slightly fringed fertile fronds hang with sporangia-trimmed lower margins. Plants need to be especially warm.

Platycerium quadridichotomum (forking four times) is a rarely available and challenging species in cultivation. The sterile shield fronds, looking like giant feet, are upright with pendant, forked, fertile fronds falling away from their heels. The plant reportedly appears dead if allowed to dry out and consequently curl during its dormant season, but does revive.

Platycerium ridleyi (after Sir Henry Ridley, 1855–1956, botanical explorer and director of the Botanic Gardens of Singapore) is another on the list of cultivation-resistant staghorns. More than most species, it is a victim of rot and is popular with insect pests, including colonies of ants that choose its structure for their nest building. The fertile fronds grow upright from helmet-style shield fronds and look like

Platycerium coronarium established on a stonewall, in morning sun and afternoon shade, where it is held by hidden wires attached to concrete nails driven into mortar between the stone. The wall is old and fertile, allowing other ferns such as *Christella dentata* (near the top of the scene) to have grown here from spores that found lodging in the built-up humus. Photo by George Schenk.

waving happy hands or the round-tipped antlers seen on stuffed toy animals.

Platycerium stemaria (an old name for staghorn) has triangularly lobed fertile fronds that spread like sails from base fronds that look like bedroom slippers. It is cold sensitive and needs extra heat as well as dry conditions for an optimal appearance.

Platycerium superbum (magnificent), the giant staghorn, is, for many reasons, one of the very best for both beginners and expert admirers. Handsome and bold shield fronds reach upwards in broad, outward-extending fans ready to collect moisture and nourishment for its fertile components. Swoops of fertile fronds arch and then drop hands and multiple fingers of foliage with, significantly, one fertile portion per frond (unlike the similar, but less cold hardy *P. grande*, which has two per frond). It is the most cold tolerant of the tribe, surviving freezing temperatures, albeit briefly. In turn it is also forgiving of extended periods of drought. Mind you, it is big, so place it accordingly or be prepared to accommodate its presence by moving some furniture.

Platycerium veitchii (for British nurseryman John Veitch, 1839–1870), silver staghorn, has upright torches of lovely soft gray fronds with slender stalks and poly-forked-tipped wands. They are vertical in bright light and will taper downwards in shade. The woolly surface protects the fronds in their unfernlike, native Australian habitats where they grow in full exposure on the faces of sunny cliffs. Cultivate them in comparable sites where they welcome bright light and minimum moisture and tolerate cold, but not freezing weather.

Platycerium wallichii (after Nathaniel Wallich, 1786–1854, a Danish physician-botanist who studied plants of India), Indian staghorn, is a giant fern with a reputation as a short-lived and difficult-to-cultivate species. Broad fertile fronds with upward and outward prongs spray from a circular base frond. It is the only species in the genus with green spores.

Platycerium wandae (after Wanda), the queen staghorn, with a foliar expanse of 6 to 7 ft. (about 2 m) across is the largest of a genus already crowded with super-sized species. Protective, outer, winglike fronds surround the pendant fertile fronds that hang like loose shrouds with tasseled tips. Sturdy, upright shield fronds have pups that are fringed at their edges, distinguishing this species from the rarer but somewhat similar *P. holttumii*. It is cold sensitive and needs water only when in active growth.

Platycerium willinckii, Java staghorn, has long outward-arching fountains of straplike fertile fronds that split into multiple cattails midway down their descent. Emerging fertile fronds extend as uprights from their large shield fern support structure, but when weighted by maturity are carried gradually downwards with an outward flow. Some authors classify this as a cultivar of *P. bifurcatum* although it is not as cold tolerant.

Polypodium

Polypodiums, our many footed friends (Greek *poly*, many, and *podion*, foot, in reference to the creeping and branching rhizomes [feet]), spread about, usually willingly, in gardens and greenhouses. Worldwide there are approximately 150 species with the greatest native concentrations in the New World trop-

ics. Many are epiphytes, with some, such as the Pacific Coast *Polypodium scouleri*, fraternizing with a specific tree species, in this case the native spruce *Picea sitchensis*. Most of the temperate tree dwellers can be cultivated terrestrially without problems. Other cold-hardy species prefer to wander about among rocks and can be more challenging to domesticate (as well as to identify). The British-European natives *P. cambricum*, *P. interjectum*, and *P. vulgare* have produced generous numbers of cultivars with crests and lacerations that are prized for their unique configurations and, in many cases, their rarity. Ornamental tropicals, some also with variations in structure, abound in the luxury of conservatories and can be decorative in slightly humid home environs.

The roving rhizomes should be maintained on the soil's surface and not buried. The monomorphic fronds, which are scattered along the length of the rhizome, are pinnatifid to once-pinnate (with the exception of the cultivars which can be more finely divided). Pinnae are not stalked but rather are united to the rachis along their width, a characteristic known botanically as adnate. Veins can be free or netted, sometimes enclosing a single veinlet. A microscopic examination of stipe slices from my garden collection shows vascular bundles ranging in number from three to seven basally, but often merging into one as the stipe approaches the rachis.

Most species are leathery and evergreen although some, such as *Polypodium glycyrrhiza* and *P. cambricum*, are wintergreen and summer dormant. Old fronds freely drop off the rhizome, a blessing for gardeners who are eager to keep their fern beds tidy. Sori are round to oblong and, in keeping with being a genus lower on the evolutionary family tree, without indusia. As a consequence the spores, which are yellow when freshly ripe, are dispersed simultaneously rather than over a period of time such as that of those released from under the protection of an indusium. The latter with its extended distribution is a reproductively more efficient stratagem.

The classification of the polypodies has been quite fluid in recent years as the complex genus is under study and revision. Formerly a very large genus, it has been divided into many smaller genera including *Goniophlebium*, *Phlebodium*, and *Pleopeltis*. Enthusiasts who once grew *Polypodium subauriculatum* 'Knightiae', for example, may have to stretch their research a bit before finding it as *Goniophlebium subauriculatum*

Rotund sori on *Polypodium scouleri*.

'Knightiae', the current designation. The list goes on, but synonyms are given in the text to help with the transitions. In addition, many of the North American species are differentiated botanically by the presence, absence, or condition of "sporangiasters" (a modified sporangium which protects the true sporangium). This is not exactly an everyday term nor are the sporangiasters readily apparent in the field, especially when fertile material is unavailable. Therefore, they are not in my descriptions, but serious students may want to investigate the *Flora of North America* (1993) for further details.

Rhizome taste-testing is popularly recommended in some floras for distinguishing among some of the North American species. They are not my favorite hors d'oeuvre, however. In addition, common sense suggests that tasting should be approached with caution as well as a jaundiced eye for the soil and surroundings of the source material.

I recommend that cultivation of the polypodiums be guided by the conditions of the natural habitat of the species in hand. The epiphytes, however, can adapt with ease in loose, leafy, shaded compost where they can be left happily untended. Or, given their natural drooping tendencies, display them in moss-lined hanging baskets with or without the company of flowering plants. They are also especially appropriate and ornamental as meandering plantings in stumperies. Polypodiums from rock strata prefer a comparable gravelly garden position with efficient drainage and bright indirect light. Many take some time to become established and then proceed to colonize.

Spore propagation is tediously and annoyingly slow, sometimes taking years. Division, however, is easy and practical. Cut off a rhizome section that includes a growing tip and some roots, and pot it in species-appropriate soil. The surgery is best accomplished in dormancy just prior to the arrival of new growth. The new offshoots will then quickly reestablish.

Historically, this has been a multiuse genus recommended for a conglomeration of herbal and practical purposes. Like other ferns, specifically bracken, with a high concentration of potash, it was used in glassmaking. Locally, the Native Americans have long used the rhizome of *Polypodium glycyrrhiza* for licorice flavoring (although it will never sell in a candy shop). Øllgaard and Tind (1993) report that in times of crop failure the Norwegians turned to *Polypodium* rhizomes for survival, using them raw or cooking them as porridge. Because of the association of polypodiums with the highly esteemed oak, especially in Britain and Europe, their curative powers were considered superior. Concoctions were used for such assorted maladies as whooping cough, tuberculosis, melancholy, and bad dreams. A special brew was, and still is in some areas, used to cure arthritis. (No, I do not have the formula.) In a more esoteric application, oil of polypody mixed with turpentine and honey was recommended as a coating for fish bait. It is not clear whether it was intended to catch the fish or poison them. It is far better to use these species as garden or greenhouse ornamentals than as functionals in the medicine chest.

Polypodium amorphum in a crevice on the flanks of Mount Rainier in Washington State.

It is very pleasant and cheerful nowadays, when the brown and withered leaves strew the ground and almost every plant is fallen, to come upon a patch of Polypody . . . on some rocky hillside in the woods, where in the midst of dry and rustling leaves, defying frost, it stands so freshly green and full of life.

—Thoreau, unpublished, 2 November 1857

Polypodium amorphum
Mountain polypody
Synonym *Polypodium montense*
Epithet means "shapeless" or "deformed."
Evergreen, 4 to 12 in. (10 to 30 cm). Zones 6 to 8.

DESCRIPTION: The rhizome is creeping and acrid. Pale stipes are one-third of the frond length. Pinnatifid, lanceolate fronds, which are slightly wider at midpoint, bear 6 to 12 pairs of ½-in. (13-mm) plump oblong or obovate segments. They are usually rounded at the tips. Sori are round (a diagnostic feature), lack indusia, and are closer to the margins than the midrib.

RANGE AND HABITAT: In nature, this species ranges from sea level to montane regions extending from British Columbia south to Oregon with disjunct populations in Wyoming and Colorado. It can be found leaning from rocky crevices to drape cliff faces and tucked among layers of ledges usually on igneous substrates.

CULTURE AND COMMENTS: This species is almost as difficult to cultivate as it is to identify. Like its alpine companions, it is very specific in the need for good drainage, air circulation, and moist but lean soil. It does best in gritty rubble slightly enriched with humus, with good light, but no direct hot sunshine. *Polypodium amorphum* is easily confused and difficult to differentiate, based on field characteristics, from its hybrid offspring *P. hesperium*. The latter has oblong sori, which unfortunately for field study may become round with age. It also is taller and the rounded pinnae segments terminate in a minute point (mucronate). By contrast *P. amorphum* is more leathery and stiff with a rounded segment tip and round sori.

Polypodium appalachianum
Appalachian polypody, rock cap fern
Epithet means "from Appalachia."
Evergreen, 4 to 12 in. (10 to 30 cm). Zones 3 to 8.

DESCRIPTION: The rhizome creeps and branches. Stipes are one-half of the frond length and tannish green, with sparse, diagnostically significant, uniformly light brown scales. The pinnatifid blades are elongate-triangular and widest at the base. The 10 to 15 pairs of pinnae are closely spaced with slightly pointed segment apices. Sori are without indusia, round, and midway between the margin and midrib.

RANGE AND HABITAT: This species grows on assorted substrates of shaded boulders (rock cap), cliff faces, and rarely arboreally in moist woods extending from the eastern coast of Canada down through the United States to South Carolina and Tennessee. (Sturdy students, however, participating in a Central Missouri State University tree canopy biodiversity study in 2000–01 found this species growing in a 4- to 5-in.

[10- to 13-cm] thick mossy mat on a horizontal branch of *Liriodendron tulipifera* [yellow tulip popular], some 125 ft. [36 m] above ground. The survey was part of a life forms mapping program in the Great Smoky Mountains National Park.)

CULTURE AND COMMENTS: Until recent close taxonomic examination, this species was classified as *Polypodium virginianum*. The two are segregated based on spore size and sporangiaster characteristics well beyond the scope of this book. As a generalization, however, the broader based blade, more closely set segments, and tan rather than bicolored stipe scales distinguish *P. appalachianum* from *P. virginianum*. Both share a common habitat in overlapping ranges and, adding to identification angst, hybridize with each other. The species and hybrid are cultivated with difficulty, "requiring shade, a rocky perch that is humus-rich but nutrient-poor, with

Polypodium appalachianum along the native fern walk at the Institute of Ecosystem Studies in New York.

excellent drainage and consistent moisture" (Gottlieb quoted in Olsen 2005). They are not for typically and consistently warm Mediterranean climates and have failed with regularity in Pacific Northwest gardens.

Polypodium californicum
California polypody
Epithet means "from California."
Wintergreen (summer dormant), 6 to 16 in. (15 to 40 cm). Zone 8.

DESCRIPTION: The rhizome is creeping and noted for not tasting like licorice. Dull green slender stipes are one-third of the frond length. Pinnatifid blades are ovate-lanceolate and broadest at the base with 8 to 12 pairs of serrated pinnae. Sori without indusia are oval and closer to the midrib than the margin.

RANGE AND HABITAT: No surprise here, this grows in California south to Baja California where it can be found in partial shade among rocks or on soil from sea level to 4500 ft. (1400 m).

CULTURE AND COMMENTS: This species is occasionally cultivated but not as easily introduced as *Polypodium glycyrrhiza* from which it differs by the broad frond outline and serrated margins, as well as scales on the rachis that are lanceolate rather than hairlike as in the latter. The adventurous may also want to give it a taste test. "Yuk" indicates that it may be *P. californicum*. For best results in a garden setting, nestle it among rocks in lean, moist soil and light shade.

'Sarah Lyman' is one of only a few North American cultivars and, although not as thin-textured as the other truly plumose cultivars in this genus, has the ornamental structure of lacerated, bipinnate pinnae supported by widely attached pinnae bases. It is a sterile cultivar.

Polypodium calirhiza
Polypodium californicum × *P. glycyrrhiza*.
Epithet from *cali*, short for *P. californicum*, and *rhiza*, short for *P. glycyrrhiza*, in reference to the parental ancestry of this hybrid.
Wintergreen (summer dormant), 6 to 16 in. (15 to 40 cm). Zone 8.

DESCRIPTION: The creeping rhizome is reputed to have an acrid to slightly sweet flavor. The slender, light green stipes are up to one-half of the frond length. Pinnatifid blades with 8 to 16 pairs of serrate pinnae are lanceolate and, of significance, wider just above the base. Sori are closer to the midrib than the margin, oval, and without indusia. *Polypodium calirhiza* has the serrate margins of *P. californicum* and the tapered segment tips of *P. glycyrrhiza*.

RANGE AND HABITAT: This fertile hybrid prefers the coastal habitats of northern California and southern Oregon where it is found on rock faces, but only very rarely as an epiphyte.

CULTURE AND COMMENTS: *Polypodium calirhiza* is not particular about soil types and is more easily established in gardens than *P. californicum* (with which it is readily, and quite

Emerging fronds of *Polypodium californicum*. Photo by Harry Olsen.

reasonably, confused). It needs light duff, good light, and drainage rather than rich and/or heavy compost.

Polypodium cambricum
Southern polypody
Synonym *Polypodium australe*
Epithet means "from Cambria," an old name for Wales. Wintergreen (summer dormant), 4 to 24 in. (10 to 60 cm). Zones 6 (when heavily winter mulched) to 9.

DESCRIPTION: The rhizome is short- to long-creeping. Stipes are one-half of the frond length, and the apple-green pinnate blades are ovate with the second from the bottom pair of pinnae the longest. The 12 to 18 pairs of pinnae are frequently serrate. Sori without indusia are round and pregnant with bright yellow spores when ripe. The species and all cultivars are summer dormant (perhaps reflecting an adaptive response to its developmental years in summer hot and winter wet Mediterranean climates), producing a flush of fronds in late summer to fall. They offer dependable sprays of fresh greenery throughout the winter and die back in early to late spring.

RANGE AND HABITAT: In its native southern European and British habitats it is found in mortared walls, especially on antiquities, as well as occasionally in well-drained limestone soil and even on oak trees.

CULTURE AND COMMENTS: Linnaeus gave the name *Polypodium cambricum* to what is now known to be a fringed form of *P. australe*. However, as the original botanical epithet has precedence, the species and all of its cultivars are currently considered correctly classified as *P. cambricum* rather than *P. australe*. Confusing, yes, but by whatever name they include some of the most desirable and interesting polypodium variations. Although they tend to prefer limey sites ("that difficult corner in the garden where the builders left all their rubble" [Rickard 2000]), the species and most all of the available cultivars will happily acclimate in traditional moist, ferny loam. I like to display the most unusual types in hanging baskets where they can be shifted about seasonally depending on whether or not they are dressed in foliage.

British collectors have selected and named a portfolio of varieties, some having been formerly classified under *Polypodium vulgare*. These cultivars yield visual delights and ease of maintenance to the gardener, although all selections will be without their greenery in the summer months. Many are sterile and not reproductively available except by division. Ah, but tissue culture is on the horizon and ideally will enrich our commercial options. While many cultivars are featured in British and European gardens, only a few of the most easily propagated selections are in circulation in the United States.

Barrowii Section (after T. Barrow) has exceptionally thick ovate foliage with some forms having twisted pinnae. It is a member of the Cambricum Group.

Cambricum Group (from Cambria [Wales]) includes a selection of sterile cultivars. All are old, having been discovered

Polypodium cambricum among the boulders of a wall in Wales.

prior to 1894. Typically the fronds are thin-textured and have varying degrees of laceration. Some also have twisted foliage.

'**Cristatum**' (crested) has pinnatifid fronds with the segments and apex crested. The terminal crest is narrower than the blade.

'**Grandiceps Fox**' (large-headed, discovered by Mrs. Fox in 1868) is heavily crested at frond and pinnae tips, wherever a fern could possibly be crested.

'**Omnilacerum Superbum**' (superbly torn) arches gracefully from a basket or the top of a wall with 18-in. (45-cm) fronds that have lacerated pinnae along their length. It is a fertile cultivar.

'**Prestonii**' (after Preston, who discovered it) has slightly twisted, ovate, thin-textured foot-long (30-cm) fronds and a delightfully entertaining tale of its discovery. "Found in . . . north Lancashire in 1871 . . . . It was growing in a block of limestone pavement and Preston could not extricate it, so he took the whole block home and gradually grew the fern out of its crevice" (Rickard 2000). It is a sterile, elegantly lacerated cultivar. It is in the Cambricum Group.

Pulcherrimum Group (beautiful) includes an assortment of thick-textured cultivars with ruffled, shredded pinnae supported by narrow, simple stipes on bipinnatifid or tripinnatifid fronds. These are occasionally fertile and, unlike the similarly structured *Polypodium* ×*mantoniae* 'Cornubiense', do not randomly produce reverted fronds.

'**Richard Kayse**' (after Kayse, who discovered this fern) was found in 1668 on a limestone cliff where it still grows today in Wales. It was the type plant named *Polypodium cambricum* by Linnaeus, and many would hope that it could be revised giving *P. australe* as a proper designation. However, this cultivar is one of the most beautiful of the many cultivars and also one of the most difficult to describe. The 18-in. (45-cm) blade is bipinnate with the pinnae simple at the point of attachment to the rachis and then blossoming into fringed pointed tips. They overlap giving a stunning layered effect.

'**Semilacerum Falcatum O'Kelly**' (half lacerated and falcate, discovered by O'Kelly) is a departure from the heavily cut types. The foot-long (30-cm), slightly incised, sickle-shaped pinnae curve strongly toward the apex of the frond.

'**Wilharris**' (after Wilharris or perhaps William Harris, curator of the Bristol Zoological Gardens) has narrow, leathery, foot-long (30-cm) fronds with lacerated pinnae. It is easily confused with 'Prestonii' when young or poorly grown. Old plants are more robust than similarly senior plants of 'Prestonii'. 'Wilharris' belongs to the Cambricum Group.

Polypodium formosanum
Caterpillar fern
Synonym *Goniophlebium formosanum*
Epithet means "from Formosa."
Wintergreen, 18 to 24 in. (45 to 60 cm). Zones 9 and 10.

DESCRIPTION: The striking creeping rhizome, crisscrossing itself freely in a tangle, is thick and a chalky pale green. It has small black scales as well as minute black craters (technically known as phyllopodia) that are the scarred stumps left after the fronds are shed. The chocolate-colored stipes are one-half

Yellow sori add interest to the fertile frond of *Polypodium cambricum* 'Semilacerum Falcatum O'Kelly', which is displayed to advantage in a hanging basket.

Appearing like the caterpillars of the common name, the rhizomes of *Polypodium formosanum* form a web of pale green succulent creepers.

Warm green fronds of *Polypodium formosanum* glow in the early morning filtered sunlight.

Fertile *Polypodium glycyrrhiza* with the red-berried *Arctostaphylos* on an exposed sand spit well away from the traditional shade of maple and alder forests.

of the frond length, and the color extends to the rachis. Pinnatifid, lanceolate blades have 18 to 24 pairs of light green, matte pinnae. Round, indusia-free sori are closest to the midribs and are visible as small bumpkins on the upper frond surface. New fronds appear in early fall and drop in late spring to midsummer.

RANGE AND HABITAT: This creeper grows as an epiphyte, where it must be quite a sight, on mossy tree trunks as well as on rock faces in Japan, China, and Taiwan.

CULTURE AND COMMENTS: Gardeners in Southern California and comparably warm climates can easily introduce this to their collections. It is best displayed as a basket specimen, however, where the crawling collection of greenish caterpillar rhizomes is as interesting as the plant itself. Elsewhere, use it as a cool greenhouse or, on a space-available basis, indoor conversation piece. It is not fussy about soil types and blessedly tolerant of benign neglect.

Polypodium glycyrrhiza
Licorice fern
Epithet means "sweet root."
Wintergreen (summer dormant), 1 to 2 ft. (30 to 60 cm).
Zones 5 to 8.

DESCRIPTION: The rhizome is long-creeping with a pseudo-licorice flavor. Stipes are tan, often maturing to a greenish brown, and one-third of the frond length. Blades are lanceolate and pinnatifid with 10 to 20 or more pairs of pointed linear, dull green, smooth-margined pinnae. The rachis is unusual in having a smattering of hairs on the upper surface matching a mild distribution of hairs on the pinnae midribs. The small, round, indusia-free sori are positioned midway between the pinnae midribs and margins. The species is summer dormant with new fronds emerging from midsummer onward into fall. It hybridizes with fellow natives.

RANGE AND HABITAT: This Pacific Northwest native is a common epiphyte on the mossy trunks and branches of big leaf maples (*Acer macrophyllum*). The fall foliage combination of freshly emerging brilliant green fronds with the platters of butter-yellow falling maple leaves is a magnificent sight indeed, particularly in the mountain passes. The species is also found on alders (*Alnus rubra*), especially in the rainforest areas of the Olympic Peninsula, and, furthermore, occasionally sprawls over exposed rocks. An unexpected surprise to me, however, was the discovery, years ago, of a thriving population on a sand spit, within the prevailing salt-water spray distance of the Pacific Ocean.

CULTURE AND COMMENTS: Here, at last, is a species that is easily identified and readily makes the transition into a home landscape. It will roam around in light soil without being invasive and is especially welcome as a winter cover in sites where other plants are dormant. Conversely, it does leave a blank in the summer garden design until new foliage unfurls from midsummer to early autumn. For year-round mobility, it can be grown in a basket and displayed or hidden as the seasons and foliar compositions demand. The rhizomes are used by Native Americans for licorice flavoring.

Shrouds of *Polypodium glycyrrhiza* on its preferred host (to which it does no harm), *Acer macrophyllum*, the large-leafed maple.

Polypodium glycyrrhiza growing terrestrially in the company of reindeer lichen on the coast of Washington State.

The tasseled tips of *Polypodium glycyrrhiza* 'Grandiceps' in the Peters garden.

Several cultivars are available. The most common are as follows:

'**Bifid Form**' (forked-tipped), or *P. ×coughlinii*, which is noted by Rickard (2000) as a possible new hybrid between *P. glycyrrhiza* 'Longicaudatum' and *P. vulgare* 'Bifido-cristatum', has terminally forked pinnae and fronds.

'**Grandiceps**' (with large terminal crests) has tasseled terminal tips.

'**Longicaudatum**' (long-tailed) is a creeper with an extended tonguelike apex.

'**Malahatense**' is an attractive, usually sterile cultivar discovered on the downside slope of Malahat Drive on Vancouver Island, British Columbia, by the late plant specialist Ed Lohbrunner. Had he not been alert and plant savvy, while accidentally tumbling down said slope, we probably would not have this handsome, slowly spreading, finely fringed fern with pointed pinnae to enrich our late summer, fall, and winter garden palette. There is an as-yet-undescribed fertile form.

Polypodium hesperium
Western polypody
Polypodium glycyrrhiza × *P. amorphum.*
Epithet means "western" or "evening."
Evergreen, 4 to 14 in. (15 to 35 cm). Zones 5 to 8.

DESCRIPTION: *Polypodium hesperium* is a fertile hybrid intermediate between its two parents. It is taller than *P. amorphum* and shorter than *P. glycyrrhiza*. The slender rhizome creeps and branches, and reputedly is acrid to sweet-tasting. Beige stipes, occasionally bearing pale brown scales, are one-third of the frond length. Pinnatifid blades that are generally barely wider at midfrond have 12 to 18 pairs of chubby pinnae with rounded tips that abruptly terminate in a very small point (mucronate). For botanical significance it is important to note that the rachis is without hairs on the upper surface, distinguishing this fern from *P. glycyrrhiza*. It is far more difficult to separate it from the *P. amorphum* parent. Both, of course, have indusia-free sori, with those of *P. hesperium* oblong and those of *P. amorphum* round. This tidy distinction becomes blurred when the sori of *P. hesperium* become rounded with age. (And all is for naught when sori are not present.) With its glabrous blades it is also closely related to *P. californicum*.

RANGE AND HABITAT: *Polypodium hesperium* is a Pacific Northwest native stringing along both sides of the Cascade Mountains from British Columbia south through the Sierras to Mexico. It prefers the partially shaded, lime-free sites of nature's mountainous rock gardens.

CULTURE AND COMMENTS: Here is a plant to admire (and carry on a running debate about its identification) while hiking in the hills and along rocky, alpine trails. It does not do very well in garden situations, much as one would like to capture its charm. Please do not collect these plants or those of the closely allied *P. amorphum*.

Polypodium interjectum
Intermediate polypody
Polypodium cambricum × *P. vulgare.*
Epithet means "intermediate," referring to the plant's form.
Evergreen, 12 to 18 in. (30 to 45 cm). Zones 5 to 8.

DESCRIPTION: Intermediate between its two parents, this *Polypodium* is more robust than either parent. The rhizome is

Polypodium hesperium among rocks in the Cascade Mountains of Washington State.

The very attractive, nonreverting, fringed fronds of *Polypodium glycyrrhiza* 'Malahatense' emerge in late summer and remain cheerfully green throughout the winter.

Polypodium interjectum volunteering on a hedgerow in Wales.

creeping, branching, and covered with tan scales. Pale brown stipes with scattered rusty scales are one-third of the frond length. Unlike the blades of many polypodiums, the pinnatifid blades of this species tend to be somewhat oval. Eighteen to twenty-four pairs of bluish green to moss-green pinnae bear oval to circular, indusia-free imbedded sori, which appear as minute bubbles on the upper frond surface. New fronds unfurl in mid and/or late summer to fall, earlier than *Polypodium cambricum* and later than *P. vulgare*.

RANGE AND HABITAT: Look for this common species on walls and among rocks in Britain and Europe. It prefers humid and high rainfall sites with good drainage and slightly basic to neutral soil, rather than the acidic habitats of *Polypodium vulgare*.

CULTURE AND COMMENTS: This is an excellent candidate for crevices and nooks where the vivid greenery can relax the stark face of retaining walls, soften "functional rockeries," and add lively winter foliage to both. Keep newly planted vertical sites moist (a mossy dressing helps) until the fern roots reach the soil behind the structures. In general *Polypodium interjectum* differs from *P. cambricum* in having heavier textured, dull-surfaced, and narrower fronds. By contrast, it differs from *P. vulgare* by being larger, wider, and absent from acid soils. Martin Rickard (pers. comm.) suggests that a good basis for separating the three species is that *P. cambricum* is broadest near the base with the second pair of pinnae usually the longest giving the frond a narrow triangular outline; *P. interjectum* is broad-est at or around the sixth pair of pinnae from the base giving the frond an oval outline; and *P. vulgare* has most pinnae in the lower half of the frond pretty much the same length, giving the frond a linear shape.

Polypodium polypodioides
Resurrection fern
Synonym *Pleopeltis polypodioides*
Epithet means "looks like a polypodium."
Evergreen, 4 to 10 in. (10 to 25 cm). Zones 6 to 10

DESCRIPTION: The rhizome is long-creeping and branching. Stipes are a washed-out tan-green, grooved, and densely scaly as juveniles. They are just under one-half of the frond length. Pinnatifid blades are lanceolate to oblong-lanceolate with 10 to 15 pairs of blunt-tipped pinnae. The undersides are coated with gray peltate scales while, by contrast, the upper surfaces essentially have but a few. (*Flora of North America* [1993] transferred this species to *Pleopeltis polypodioides* based on these scales, and botanists in general agree that the entire genus needs further study.) Sunken sori without indusia are closer to the margins than midribs and are visible as minute nodules on the upper frond surface. There are six varieties.

RANGE AND HABITAT: In the southern United States, **var. michauxianum** coats host trees, especially live oak, *Quercus virginiana*, with massive swags of foliage forming canopies over the highways and woodlands looking like a primeval forest. In

Polypodium polypodioides gradually expands from an established foothold on the craggy bark of an oak tree in Florida. It will not harm the tree nor will the tree harm the fern.

Like many polypodiums, *Polypodium scouleri* grows naturally on native trees, in this example, the dead snag of the coastal spruce, *Picea sitchensis*. Populations in nature always hug the forests adjacent to the Pacific Ocean.

the northern portion of its range it is often found on rocks. The other varieties are natives of Mexico and Central America.

CULTURE AND COMMENTS: For years conventional wisdom presumed that these fern fronds curled in drought and heat to protect their upper surfaces from moisture loss and "resurrected" when watered. However, in his fascinating book, *A Natural History of Ferns*, Moran (2004) cites experiments performed in the 1920s by Louis Pessin demonstrating that in reality more water actually evaporates from the underside of the fern's fronds. So why expose them in times of stress? Using *Polypodium polypodioides* (which can lose up to 97 percent of its water without harm) as his subject, Pessin's experiments concluded that the protective scales actually absorbed moisture more rapidly during rehydration than the roots. Subsequently, researchers identified the process by which the water feeds back into the frond's cellular structure which becomes functional again in as little as 15 minutes. In the garden, away from its natural sites, the resurrection fern is not always so forgiving, but rather is challenging. Offer it lean acid soil and good drainage. Firm it into place with moss and hope for the best.

Polypodium scouleri
Leathery polypody
Epithet is after Dr. John Scouler who accompanied David Douglas, of Douglas fir fame, on his journey to the Pacific Northwest in 1825.
Evergreen, 6 to 20 in. (15 to 50 cm). Zones 8 and 9. Apogamous.

DESCRIPTION: The rhizome is wide-creeping and apparently without flavor. The pea-green, grooved stipes, of up to one-half of the frond length, are, like the entire frond, thick and succulent. Glistening, deep forest-green, pinnatifid blades are ovate with 4 to 12 pairs of chubby lobed pinnae. One-eighth-inch (3-mm) large, indusia-free sori house showy spores that are a warm harvest moon yellow when ripe. *Polypodium scouleri* hybridizes with *P. glycyrrhiza*.

RANGE AND HABITAT: This species is confined to the coastal regions, usually within a few hundred yards of the salty Pacific, from British Columbia, Washington, Oregon, and ocean fringes to Baja California with the greatest concentration in the Pacific Northwest. Here they settle in dark woods in the crotches of the native spruce, *Picea sitchensis*, dead or alive, and can easily be overlooked in nature as perhaps a casually constructed spacious eagle's nest. Visitors to the Washington coast can find excellent photo ops at the state beaches especially those that are imaginatively named Beach 1 and Beach 4.

CULTURE AND COMMENTS: Neither salt spray nor decomposing spruce are needed to encourage the growth of this showy polypod in gardens with mild winters and cool summers in Zones 8 and 9. It prefers deep shade and acid, friable soil (although I have seen it strapped to trees where it must have regular attention from a misting system, human or otherwise). An established colony will spread ever so slowly and offers an especially attractive vignette as an uphill visual where the colorful sori can be admired from below. A basket planting is

The glossy fronds of *Polypodium scouleri* are a welcome component in the dark and shade of moist woodland gardens.

equally decorative. In spite of its leathery texture, this fern wilts in summer sun unexpectedly faster than many of its more delicate fellow natives.

Polypodium virginianum
Rock polypody
Polypodium appalachianum × *P. sibericum*.
Epithet means "from Virginia."
Evergreen, 6 to 18 in. (15 to 45 cm). Zones 3 to 8.

DESCRIPTION: The rhizome is long-creeping with an acrid taste again being a definitive litmus test. Pale straw-colored stipes, which are usually one-third of the frond length, have weakly bicolored scales rather than the uniformly tan stipe scales of *Polypodium appalachianum*. Blades are pinnatifid and long linear without broad basal pinnae. Ten to eighteen pairs of pinnae narrow at their tips and bear indusia-free, round sori between the midrib and margins. New growth emerges in early summer as the old fronds wither.

RANGE AND HABITAT: The rocky compost of inhospitable sites is more of a common denominator than any particular soil preference. *Polypodium virginianum* spreads in nature with picturesque ease on and among rocks from eastern Canada to the lower eastern states of North Carolina and borderline central states from Wisconsin to Tennessee. Haufler et al. (1995) noted that *P. virginianum* was likely pushed south by glaciation from its northerly parent *P. sibericum*. Interim eons allowed it to evolve and adapt.

CULTURE AND COMMENTS: Logic would imply that a neutral cobble or an equivalent garden site would enable a replication of the beauty of the wild finds. Easy success with logic would probably also remove the challenges, mental and physical, that keep the gardening faithful devoted to pleasing their charges. *Polypodium virginianum* will do that. The first requirement is

Polypodium virginianum growing in the wild in New York State.

The well-mannered *Polypodium glycyrrhiza* × *P. scouleri* spreads slowly in the Peters garden.

good drainage, followed by lean but moist soil, and finished off with a balance between warmth and shade. It does not do well in the year-round warmth of Southern California and comparably agreeable climates. And, in spite of its natural beauty and the gardener's coddling, it is not easily introduced in its native East Coast. Pity.

Polypodium vulgare
Common polypody
Epithet means "common."
Evergreen, 6 to 12 in. (15 to 30 cm). Zones 5 to 8.

DESCRIPTION: The rhizome is wide creeping. Pale straw-colored stipes with small russet scales are one-third to one-half of the frond length. Pinnatifid blades are lanceolate with 10 to 20 pairs of smooth to slightly crenately margined pinnae. Significantly the lowest pair points downwards. The sori, without indusia, are medial and clearly visible as pimples on the upper frond surface. New fronds appear in late spring to early summer, well before those of the related *Polypodium interjectum* or *P. cambricum*.

RANGE AND HABITAT: The common polypody is common indeed with populations throughout Europe and Asia, extending eastward as far as Siberia and Japan and south to the southern tip of Africa. (Historically it may well be a descendent of the North American native now known as *P. virginianum*, but formerly *P. vulgare*.) It colonizes at will on trees but more frequently as a ground cover on acidic soils in moist shade. This is the easiest of the British-European natives for cultivating in traditional loose compost—the mental image of ferny soils.

CULTURE AND COMMENTS: Once upon a time, *Polypodium vulgare* was the common species in North America as well as Europe. It has since been banished from the descriptions of North American flora. One does not need to go back very far into botanical literature, however, to find North American species such as *P. glycyrrhiza* and *P. virginianum* included under the broad umbrella of *P. vulgare*. Early descriptions of British and European cultivars were also listed as botanical variations of *P. vulgare*. Many have since been transferred to affiliated *Polypodium* maternity sites. Currently, *P. vulgare* cultivars include the following:

'**Bifido-Cristatum**', or '**Grandiceps**', has forked pinnae and a branching fan-shaped crested apex with the crest broader than the frond.

'**Bifidum**' (forked-tipped) has forked pinnae.

'**Cornubiense Grandiceps**' is a heavily crested form of 'Elegantissimum'.

'**Elegantissimum**' has historically been known as 'Cornubiense' but differs from it by having three types of fronds—tripinnatifid, bipinnatifid, and pinnatifid—all on the same plant. 'Cornubiense' has only bipinnatifid and pinnatifid fronds. 'Elegantissimum' is much more attractive but rarer and slower to spread. 'Cornubiense' is now considered a cultivar of *P.* ×*mantoniae* with *P. vulgare* 'Elegantissimum' as a possible parent, along with *P. interjectum*.

'**Jean Taylor**' is a crested variety with tripinnate to quadripinnate fronds. It is variable from spores, however, but reliably forked at the frond apex. Over time, it can revert, producing unembellished fronds.

'Ullong Island Form' (after the Korean island where it was discovered) has 6-in. (15-cm) narrowly triangular fronds that are broadest at the base with 10 to 18 pairs of tapered, slightly pointed pinnae. It adds cheer to the winter garden.

Shorter Notes

Polypodium amoenum (charming, pleasing), synonym *Polypodiodes amoena*, has pinnatifid, large (for a *Polypodium*) fronds reaching to 2 ft. (60 cm). The tips of the pinnae and fronds are sharply pointed with the pinnae swirling upwards toward the frond tips. The foliage is dull but leathery, scaly on the undersides and mildly hairy on the upper. The species is an interesting departure from the North American look-alikes and should have potential in protected Zone 8 sites and settle with ease in Zone 9. It is native to the Himalayas, China, and Taiwan where it grows as an epiphyte or on shaded rocks.

Polypodium glycyrrhiza × *P. scouleri* is very rare in nature and even rarer in cultivation. (I, a native of the Pacific Northwest, home of both species, first met it in the gardens of German specialists.) The fronds are a succulent dark green, like the *P. scouleri* parent, but pointed at the tips, and not summer deciduous like *P. glycyrrhiza*. Like its parents, it settles willingly into the woodland duff of Zones 7 to 9.

Polypodium ×*mantoniae* (after Irene Manton, 1904–1988), a hybrid between *P. vulgare* and *P. interjectum*, is found throughout Europe and Britain. It is easily confused in shape and habit with *P. interjectum*; however, the spores are mostly, but not always, abortive. The elegant and popular *Polypodium* cultivar '**Cornubiense**' now occupies a place of pride under the mantle of *P.* ×*mantoniae* (Rickard 2000). 'Cornubiense' is a bipinnate to tripinnate attraction with broad pinnae that are deeply lacerated at the outer extremities. It has a tendency to revert as well as to send up indecisive fronds that are midway between the two. Readily available by division, it is one of only a few cultivars in commerce in the United States. Wintergreen and briefly summer deciduous, it serves well as a focal point in the winter garden in Zones 6 to 9.

"*Polypodium okiense*" (from the Oki region) is a Japanese species that is in cultivation in the gardens of German collectors. It has not been officially described but has lanceolate warm green fronds to 18 in. (45 cm) with opposite round-tipped pinnae on proportionately long stipes.

Polypodium sibericum (from Siberia) is a small, 4- to 8-in. (10- to 20-cm) circumboreal species that was once classified as *P. virginianum* and is now believed to be one of its parents along with *P. appalachianum*. It is native to northern latitude extremes and qualifies as a Zone 2 to 5 candidate where it appreciates a long, dark winter and welcomes a cloak of snow.

Polypodium thyssanolepis (fringe scaled), the scaly polypod, is a creeping, small evergreen that grows on rocks and in the ground from the lower southwestern United States through Mexico to northern South America. It is recommended for Zones 8 (cautiously) to 10 and noted for its densely scaly stipes and narrow, foot-long (30-cm) fronds bearing a heavy undercoat of scales. (This characteristic may

Polypodium ×*mantoniae* 'Cornubiense' as found in the U.S. trade with bipinnatifid fronds that will indeed produce pinnatifid reversions.

"*Polypodium okiense*" in the Jessen alpine garden.

some day earn it a transfer to the definitively scaly genus *Pleopeltis*.)

Polypodium vaccinifolium (foliage like *Vaccinium*) is included as a fun distraction for its usefulness in twining around trees in semitropical gardens or in warm and humid household and/or conservatory conditions. Small, ½-in. (13-mm) pinnae look much like the leaves of creeping figs and have the same visual impact. The plants need humidity, soft light, and a handy tree for climbing helps. This species has recently been reclassified by many botanists as *Microgramma vaccinifolia*.

Polystichum

Ah, polystichums, what a wonderful lot they are. I have never met one I did not like and there are plenty to chose from with more than 200 species and at least 60 hybrids. They are elegant, almost always evergreen, and offer well-mannered har-

Polypodium vaccinifolium spreads like a creeping fig on a tree trunk in Trinidad.

mony to the garden's summer and winter woodland composition. The fronds on these tidy plants are frequently shiny and usually have spiny pinnules with a prominent and easily recognized genus-significant auricle (thumb) on the innermost portion of the pinnule(s). On many species and their hybrids, new growth is beautifully trimmed in silvery scales and the crosiers often flip backwards before maturing into uprights.

The genus name, from the Greek *poly*, many, and *stichum*, stitches, means "many stitches" in reference to the pattern of the sori that "stitch" the edges of the pinnae. Botanically significant sori have a peltate indusium (round and centrally attached tissue) that opens like a wind-blown umbrella.

Polystichum species are closely related to both *Dryopteris* and *Cyrtomium* and were once in a combined classification in the botanical conglomerate *Aspidium*. Like *Dryopteris*, they are heavily decorated and botanically differentiated by stipe and rachis scales in assorted colors, shapes, and sizes. While they do not have independent hairs, some of the scales may have hairs (splitting hairs botanically here, if you would). When fertile fronds are present, polystichums can readily be differentiated by their peltate indusia rather than the kidney-shaped indusia of dryopteris. Cyrtomiums share the peltate indusial characteristic but have easily observed netted veins rather than the free veins of polystichums.

Most polystichums are considered horticulturally hardy (which means temperate rather than "easy" as in some interpretations). They range from temperamental alpines, requiring specialized site preparation and maintenance, to stately and reliable garden ornamentals. Eastern North America and Europe are poorly represented with limited numbers of species, although Britain contributes a significant complement of cultivars. For promising hardy introductions, Japan, China (the capital of the fern world for once-pinnate polystichums), and the Himalayas have provided Western gardens with an abundance of ornamental offerings with the potential for yet more discoveries to come. Some of these may be difficult to establish in hot and humid summer climates, but with so many options, all are worth introducing to gardens—at least once.

Unless otherwise noted all of the polystichums described here like light shade and a regularly watered, moist but not wet site. Most will adapt in friable acid to neutral soil. Although all three British species, *Polystichum aculeatum*, *P. lonchitis*, and *P. setiferum*, are native to basic soil sites, they do not require them. The challenging alpines require good air circulation, excellent drainage, and fresh as opposed to stagnant water. They are accustomed to wintering under snow and usually are not long-lived at lower elevations. Please do not try to collect them. Enjoy them instead in their mountain habitats where they delight the horticultural hiker and are in harmony with their surroundings.

A number of species and some hybrids produce bulbils on their frond tips or, as in the British *Polystichum setiferum* and many of its cultivars, along the entire proliferous rachis strip. Propagation is easily accomplished by pinning these down onto soft soil. In addition the proliferous buds can be surgically removed from the parent plant and encouraged in the

Young crosiers of polystichums are elegant with their silvery coats as seen here on a *Polystichum munitum* hybrid.

accommodating climate of a humid mini-greenhouse. An inverted clear plastic cup over a 4-in. (10-cm) pot works nicely. Firm the bud onto the surface of the soil and place it in good light but not direct sunshine.

Spores are in most cases the only propagation option for the exotics. Germination tends to be erratic and more study is needed to determine optimum conditions for producing reliable and consistent crops. I have found that spores sown promptly from late season rather than early summer fronds tend to reproduce in better percentages.

Finally, since these are evergreens, I am frequently asked whether or not to trim off the old fronds. It is certainly the tidy thing to do, but leaving them on enriches the soil naturally and produces larger plants in ensuing years. If fronds are to be removed, it is easiest to attack the old foliage with one whack before new growth emerges in the spring.

Polystichum acrostichoides
Christmas fern
Epithet means "spreading across the surface," in reference to the sori.
Evergreen, 1 to 2 ft. (30 to 60 cm). Zones 3 to 9.

DESCRIPTION: The rhizome is branched and creeps slowly forming multiple crowns. Emerging fronds are wrapped in silky-soft silver scales. They fade to tan as they mature on the

A collection of evergreen polystichums offers year-round formal elegance in an entryway woodland planting.

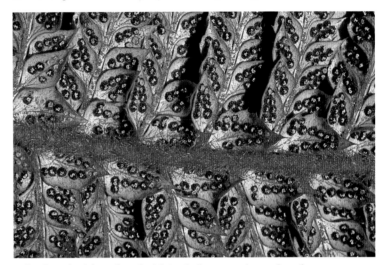

A fertile *Polystichum* frond with its dark spores ripe and ready to disperse from under a lifting peltate indusia. Note too that the rachis bears a significantly thick coating of scales.

Ready-to-root bulbil on the frond tip of *Polystichum setiferum* × *P. proliferum* in the Nittritz garden. Photo by Richie Steffen, Miller Botanical Garden.

green grooved stipes that are one-third of the frond length. The blades are polished green, lanceolate, very mildly spiny, and once-pinnate with an auricle where the pinnae attach to the rachis. There are 20 to 30 pairs of pinnae. The basal pinnae are small and point slightly downwards. Fertile fronds are taller than the sterile with the sporangia confined to con-stricted pinnae on the terminal third of the frond. These will wither when the spores are shed. The sori are covered with peltate indusia. Unlike most polystichums, with sori outlining the pinnae, the sori on this species are *acrostichoid*, covering the entire lower surface of the fertile pinnae.

RANGE AND HABITAT: The Christmas fern grows in Greenland and is abundant in eastern North America from Canada down the coast and inland to the Midwest. It adapts to most soil types, likes shade, and is especially common in rocky deciduous woods and on slopes where it is welcomed for erosion control.

CULTURE AND COMMENTS: This is the flagship fern of eastern North America where, with its easy-going and evergreen nature, it is cheerful in gardens and woodlands. It is especially conspicuous in the bleak winter months, rewarding those who venture from the warmth of the hearth to garden and countryside walks. New growth arrives early in the spring in the company of wildflowers, or, in cultivation, primroses and hepaticas. While this is a staple in the east, it has not been vigorous in West Coast gardens. Are we too mild or missing summer heat? I find the best chance for success in the Pacific Northwest is to start with a good-sized mature plant. While propagation by spores is easy, this is one of the few polystichums that are readily increased by division. Dig the plant and carefully tease apart and cut away the separate crowns. Treat the resulting progeny to a moist site in rich compost. Most eastern growers prefer to do this surgery in early spring.

There are several explanations for the descriptive common name, Christmas fern, ranging from the shape of the pinnae supposedly resembling Santa's boot or sleigh, to the more likely, and mundane, fact that the fronds are gathered for use as decorations at Christmastime.

Polystichum acrostichoides produces stable and unstable abnormalities in pinnae shapes as well as frond division and overall plant characteristics. (See Scott 2003a, 2003b, and 2003c for an illustrated discussion of variations in plant form including pinnae and frond shapes.) 'Crispum' (curled) has wavy pinnae margins; 'Cristatum' (crested) has crested frond tips; and 'Incisum' (cut) has deeply cut pinnae edges.

Polystichum aculeatum
Hard shield fern
Synonym *Polystichum lobatum*
Epithet means "having sharp points."
Evergreen, 2 to 3 ft. (60 to 90 cm). Zones 4 to 8.

DESCRIPTION: The rhizome is erect, bearing vases of firm, dark green, arching fronds. At barely one-sixth the length of the frond, the stipes are significantly short, but fat and heavily dressed in translucent russet scales. The lanceolate, bipinnate blade tapers strongly at the base with lower pinnae less than 1 in. (2.5 cm) long. The 25 to 35 pairs of pinnae are pointed with spine-tipped pinnules that are hard and slightly prickly to the touch. The sori stitch the pinnules and have peltate indusia.

RANGE AND HABITAT: In nature, *Polystichum aculeatum* prefers moist, lime-rich soils and can be found in shaded glens, ravines, and seeps in Britain, Europe, North Africa, and east to Turkey and the Caucasus.

Polystichum acrostichoides with its constricted frond tips turning brown with fertility in the Descloux garden.

Polystichum acrostichoides 'Cristatum' in the Kohout garden.

CULTURE AND COMMENTS: This is a truly handsome addition to the garden, but for optimal display appreciates a basic compost. I have mine adjacent to a concrete foundation in the belief that slightly leaching lime will keep it in good humor. It will adjust to neutral soil, however, so long as Mother Nature or the hose handlers tend to its moisture requirements. Two summers of drought reduced my parent plant from a splendid 30-in. (75 cm) display to a 15-in. (38-cm) survivor of sorts. It can be confused with *Polystichum setiferum*, its fellow Brit and continental associate. Common names come to the rescue here as *P. setiferum* is the "soft shield fern" and, at the risk of annoying your garden hosts, can be distinguished by the soft "feel" of the latter versus the hard of *P. aculeatum*. More scientifically, the stipes on *P. setiferum* are proportionately longer in relation to the blade, and the lower pinnae are closer in size to those of the midsection. Cultivars previously assigned to this species have been transferred to *P. setiferum*. There are, however, some contemporary diversions including an extremely attractive crested **'Cristatum'** from Germany and an elegant plumose selection **'Zillertal'**. In addition *P. aculeatum* hybridizes with *P. lonchitis* forming the sterile intermediate *P. ×illyricum* (see description).

Low arches of firm "hard" fronds of *Polystichum aculeatum*.

Polystichum acutidens

Synonym *Polystichum deltodon* var. *acutidens*
Epithet means "distinctly sharply pointed."
Evergreen, 1 ft. (30 cm). Zones 6 to 8.

DESCRIPTION: The small rhizome is erect and the equally small four to five annually produced fronds lounge in a relaxed fashion. The grooved pea-green stipe has a deciduous allotment of a very few pale tan scales which leave a darker stub when shed. The lanceolate, matte green blade is once-

Forked frond apex of *Polystichum aculeatum* 'Cristatum' in the extensive and comprehensive Kohout collection.

Miniature swords of *Polystichum acutidens* fronds stand upright in the foreground of the garden.

pinnate with a prominent spiny thumb adjacent to the rachis. Fifteen to twenty pairs of pinnae are serrate with pinnules traced by the sori with peltate indusia. In short it looks like a miniature edition of _Polystichum munitum_.

RANGE AND HABITAT: _Polystichum acutidens_ grows in the Himalayas, China, Taiwan, and Vietnam. References do not indicate natural habitat preferences.

CULTURE AND COMMENTS: This dwarf is easily grown in average woodland soil. It has been successfully introduced with rave reviews from devoted gardeners in Zone 6 in New Jersey to fellow zealots from temperate northern California to British Columbia. It is extremely close to _Polystichum deltodon_ in botanical definitions with the minute distinction being that the _P. acutidens_ pinnae are widely spaced and falcate whereas those of _P. deltodon_ are squared and close to overlapping. In the garden, both are undemanding and welcome as year-round greenery and hardy elfin foreground companions for the fleeting, flowering bright lights of springtime perennial beds.

Polystichum andersonii
Anderson's holly fern
Epithet is after Anderson.
Evergreen, 2 to 4 ft. (60 to 120 cm). Zones 6 to 8.

DESCRIPTION: The rhizome is stout and erect and in time will lift the crown on a trunklike mass of stubble. The green stipes are usually about one-fifth of the frond length and are barely grooved and armored with needle-pointed silver-turned-tan persistent scales of up to ½ in. (13 mm). The once-pinnate to pinnate-pinnatifid blade has deeply cleft pinnae bordering on and blurring the distinction between pinnate-pinnatifid and bipinnate. Magnification also shows small bristles along the edges of the 30 to 40 pairs of pinnae. The blade apex is tipped with one or occasionally more bulbils that willingly reproduce when pinned down on moist humus in the fall. (The fronds will lean in that direction as a reminder.) Current botanical research indicates that this species may be a hybrid between _Polystichum munitum_ and a presumptive coastal northwestern ancestor, _P. kwakiutlii_, with the latter being bulbiferous. Spores borne on the medial to outer fringes of the pinnules are mostly abortive, frustrating those who would like to increase their collections. Bulbils will, of course, propagate, marching the species slowly across the landscape—a long-term option for creating a colony.

RANGE AND HABITAT: _Polystichum andersonii_ is native to temperate climates in coastal zones in the Pacific Northwest with a few spotty natural stands in Washington State and better, but still lean, representation in British Columbia. It grows in leaf litter and shade.

CULTURE AND COMMENTS: This species is easily cultivated and displayed in West Coast gardens, enjoying the naturally acidic compost of its native habitat. (When in its exuberance, it forms a small trunk, the whole should be lowered so that the crown is once again at the soil's surface.) Welcome it for reliable and admired upright, evergreen winter foliage as well as the spring décor of silvery cloaked young crosiers. It is unfortunate that it does not travel well and presents a challenge to growers and collectors on the far sides of the Cascade Moun-

tains. Microclimates may help, as it is successfully cultivated in the gardens of specialists throughout Germany. It has been crossed in the laboratory with _Polystichum acrostichoides_ as well as _P. braunii_. In addition a sterile, bulbil-bearing natural hybrid with _P. munitum_ is found in coastal sites from British Columbia north to Alaska. It resembles an incised version of _P. munitum_ but with a bulbil.

Polystichum braunii
Braun's holly fern
Epithet is after Alexander Braun (1805–1877), a German professor of botany.
Evergreen, 1½ to 2½ ft. (45 to 75 cm). Zones 3 to 8.

DESCRIPTION: The rhizome is erect. The shiny green fronds are dressed to the ground. The stipes on my plants are 2 to 4 in. (5 to 10 cm) long, or at best one-sixth of the frond length. The young fiddleheads are covered with ornamental whitish scales that turn tan with time. The lanceolate bipinnate blade is broadest in the middle and tapers symmetrically towards both ends. There are 30 to 40 pairs of pinnae with the lower being less than 1 in. (2.5 cm) long. Pinnules are trimmed with minute spines. The sori are medial and have peltate indusia. There are a number of hybrids.

RANGE AND HABITAT: Braun's holly fern is rare and strictly northern in distribution from the deciduous forests of North America to Europe and across Russia to Siberia and Japan. (The North American material is sometimes designated as var. _purshii_ based on a different chromosome composition from the Eurasian.) It prefers moist shade.

CULTURE AND COMMENTS: This boldly decorative species is strictly for shaded humus in cool or temperate gardens. It does not adjust to warm or humid southern exposures. Protect the new growth from late frosts and enjoy the stately elegance of this evergreen.

Polystichum californicum
California holly fern
Epithet means "from California."
Evergreen, 1 to 2 ft. (30 to 60 cm). Zones 8 and 9.

DESCRIPTION: The rhizome is erect. The stipe with brown scales is one-fourth of the frond length. The pinnate-pinnatifid to bipinnate blade is lanceolate with 15 to 30 pairs of toothy pinnae. Sori vary from medial to submarginal. This genus has a promiscuous background; _Flora of North America_ (1993) classifies it as a hybrid, with _P. dudleyi_ and _P. imbricans_ as ancestors in its northern range and _P. dudleyi_ and _P. munitum_ in its southerly home. (And having nothing better to do they backcross as well.) New names are no doubt forthcoming.

RANGE AND HABITAT: _Polystichum californicum_ is coastal and habitat-specific to the west side of the Cascade Mountains and Sierras from northern California to British Columbia. Influenced by its _P. imbricans_ parent, it is found in the northern area of its range on rocky sites and often on cliffs. (There is a wonderful stand on Mount Rainier for those who are not height-challenged.) The southern stations are in wooded areas. It is rare throughout its range.

Polystichum andersonii is a stately and elegant addition to the Pacific Northwest woodland design, here fashionably highlighted in front of a stump in the Horder garden.

An 18-year-old *Polystichum andersonii* with a 6-in. (15-cm) "trunk" which should be buried leaving the crown at soil level.

Glistening fronds of *Polystichum braunii* are dressed to the ground in foliage.

The rarely cultivated *Polystichum californicum* at the Rhododendron Species Botanical Garden.

The delightful miniature *Polystichum cystostegia* in nature's alpine rock garden in New Zealand.

The exceedingly rare hybrid *Polystichum cystostegia* × *P. vestitum* in the company of fellow New Zealand alpines in the Jessen garden.

CULTURE AND COMMENTS: These attractive midsized to small evergreens are difficult to obtain because they are usually sterile. All are a bit touchy and need partial shade with good drainage.

Polystichum craspedosorum

Epithet means "fringed sori."
Evergreen, 6 to 12 in. (15 to 30 cm). Zones 5 to 8.

DESCRIPTION: The rhizome is erect and the stipes, with warm-brown scales, proportionately small. The linear-lanceolate once-pinnate blades feature an extended whiplike rachis that will tip root, depositing progeny well away from the competition of its parent. To enhance the proliferous inclination, the fronds are held in horizontal whorls. Twenty to thirty pairs of stalked, auricled pinnae bear sori with peltate indusia along the margins.

RANGE AND HABITAT: This species prefers shaded rocky slopes and cliffs in the cold of Siberia, Korea, China, and Japan.

CULTURE AND COMMENTS: *Polystichum craspedosorum* likes lime and is a desirable little munchkin for pampering in rock garden situations in cool shade. Unfortunately, it is not readily available so it is time for all of those tip roots to walk their way into cultivation.

Polystichum cystostegia

Alpine shield fern
Epithet means "pouched roof," referring to the inflated indusium.

Evergreen, 6 to 12 in. (15 to 30 cm). Zones 6 to 8.

DESCRIPTION: The stout rhizome is erect, bearing soft green fronds with stipes and rachises cloaked in distinct orange-brown scales. The lanceolate-ovate blade is bipinnate-pinnatifid with 12 to 18 pairs of imbricate pinnae that are tilted on a plane parallel to the ground. The sori, looking like a series of minute donuts, are medial and covered with an inflated peltate indusium.

RANGE AND HABITAT: Truly an alpine, *Polystichum cystostegia* grows in fellfields, wet but well-drained screes, and rocky crags at high elevations in New Zealand, primarily on the South Island. Flowering alpine vistas are a personal favorite and the view of this fern surrounded by gentians, lycopods, and celmisias in the New Zealand mountains will forever be a cherished memory. The species hybridizes with *P. vestitum*.

CULTURE AND COMMENTS: Here is a species for a bit of rock gardeners' lust. It is charming and challenging and should be tucked among scattered rocks in good light and good-draining but damp soil. Or give it individual attention in an alpine house. It is strictly for colder areas and even in its native New Zealand does not grow in warm zones.

Polystichum deltodon

Epithet means "deltoid, triangular in outline."
Evergreen, 8 in. (20 cm). Zones 6 to 8.

DESCRIPTION: The rhizome is erect and the deeply grooved stipe, which is one-fourth of the frond length, has an occa-

The low-growing *Polystichum deltodon* serves as a reliable foreground evergreen with kindred shade lovers.

sional appressed tan scale. Blades are lanceolate, once-pinnate with 15 to 18 pairs of chubby, leathery pinnae. Sori with peltate indusia are marginal. This species can be confused with *Polystichum acutidens*.

RANGE AND HABITAT: *Polystichum deltodon* grows in the low mountain forests of Japan, Vietnam, China, Taiwan, and the Philippines, frequently on limestone.

CULTURE AND COMMENTS: Jim Horrocks of Salt Lake City, Utah, introduced this species to U.S. culture. It has been a stalwart favorite in his Zone 6 garden and been reliable in gardens across the United States from Seattle, Washington, to Pittsburgh, Pennsylvania. I have my plant in shade and soil that is not enriched with limestone. This fern produces an abundance of spores, but they do not germinate with great enthusiasm.

Polystichum dudleyi
Dudley's holly fern

Epithet is after U.S. botanist William Dudley (1849–1911).
Evergreen, 1½ to 3 ft. (45 to 90 cm). Zones 8 and 9.

DESCRIPTION: The rhizome is erect. Stipes are one-fourth to one-third of the frond length and densely sheathed in pale tan scales. The bipinnate blade is broadly lanceolate with 15 to 20 pairs of pinnae. They do not taper at the base. Sori with peltate indusia are marginal. *Polystichum dudleyi* is one of the parents of *P. californicum*.

RANGE AND HABITAT: This rare species is confined to moist woodlands in coastal areas of central California.

CULTURE AND COMMENTS: When available, *Polystichum dudleyi* is a temperamental candidate for cool, Western garden climates.

Polystichum ×dycei
Polystichum proliferum × P. braunii.

Epithet is after the late Jimmy Dyce, a leader of the British Pteridological Society and an enthusiastic researcher into the variations and classifications of *Polystichum* cultivars (as well as the subtle variations of a good highland malt).
Evergreen, 2½ to 3½ ft. (75 to 105 cm). Zones (6) 7 and 8.

DESCRIPTION: The rhizome is stout with an imposingly robust crown. The 2- to 3-in. (5- to 7.5-cm) succulent, green stipes are crowded with blackish-brown scales etched in tan. The bipinnate-pinnatifid blade is broadest approaching the terminal third with 20 to 30 pairs of pinnae. Like *Polystichum braunii* the blade tapers at the base and is in full foliar dress to the ground. One to three propagable bulbils are on the fronds' undersides, 2 to 4 inches (5 to 10 cm) from the apex. Beyond the bulbil site, the ultimate foliage is greatly reduced in girth. Sori with abortive spores trim the pinnules, closer to the margins than midribs.

RANGE AND HABITAT: This is one of several hybrids created under laboratory conditions by the late Anne Sleep of Leeds University in Britain. Many of them involved a parent with a bulbil. While the resultant hybrids are sterile, the bulbiferous character persisted in the progeny, thus enabling scientists as well as horticulturists to reproduce the hybrids without the assistance of a laboratory. They are endowed with hybrid vigor and establish readily in gardens.

Polystichum ×dycei fills the garden with hybrid exuberance and a broad expanse of evergreen foliage.

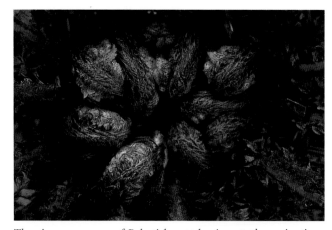

The vigorous crown of *Polystichum ×dycei* greets the springtime with its lusty unfurling crosiers.

CULTURE AND COMMENTS: This vigorous, sterile hybrid grows rapidly in light compost and dappled shade. It is an easy showpiece and choice focal point for a fern display garden and consistently brings admiring compliments from visitors. It is gradually being distributed in U.S. commerce and has been successful through the vagaries of many winters in British and

Fronds of *Polystichum falcinellum* enjoy the protection of an overhead log in the Gassner garden.

European gardens. The bulbils can be removed at any time from late summer on, or should you forget, in early spring and with real or simulated greenhouse encouragement will easily duplicate the plant.

Polystichum falcinellum
Epithet means "small falcate."
Evergreen, 1½ to 2 ft. (45 to 60 cm). Zones 7 and 8.

DESCRIPTION: The rhizome is erect with substantial rich green, once-pinnate fronds displaying each pinnae's signature auricle adjacent to its attachment to the rachis.

RANGE AND HABITAT: This species is endemic to the Madeira Islands and is successfully cultivated with protection in German and British gardens in Zone 7. It should be a welcome addition in comparable climates throughout Europe and North America.

CULTURE AND COMMENTS: Here is a diminutive edition, admired for its simplicity of structure, similar to both of the popular U.S. natives—the eastern Christmas fern and the western sword fern. Use it for strength rather than grace in lightly shaded sites with well-drained soil in bright Zone 7 and 8 microclimates.

Polystichum ×illyricum
Polystichum aculeatum × *P. lonchitis*.
Epithet means "from Ilyria."
Evergreen, 1 to 2 ft. (30 to 60 cm). Zones 4 to 8.

DESCRIPTION: The rhizome is erect. Reflecting the *Polystichum lonchitis* heritage, the very short stipes are about one-eighth of the frond length and thickly dressed in tan scales. The narrow, lanceolate blade tapers at the base and bears 30 to 40 pairs of glowing, deep green, falcate pinnae. Sori with abortive spores are abundant beneath the upper and outer portions of the pinnae.

RANGE AND HABITAT: This rare hybrid is found in a few limestone stations in Britain. It also occurs in the alpine screes of central Europe and a few sites in Scandinavia.

CULTURE AND COMMENTS: *Polystichum ×illyricum* offers the ornamental best of both parents to the fern garden palette. It combines the ease of cultivation of *P. aculeatum* with the lustrous sheen of *P. lonchitis*. Give it good light and coarse drainage. Unfortunately as a sterile hybrid, it is not readily available. Enlightened horticulturists should look to (and encourage) tissue-culture labs to duplicate and distribute this desirable hybrid.

Polystichum imbricans
Dwarf western sword fern
Synonym *Polystichum munitum* subsp. *imbricans*
Epithet means "imbricate."
Evergreen, 1 to 1½ ft. (30 to 45 cm). Zones 6 to 8.

DESCRIPTION: The rhizome is erect. The grooved stipe, with sparse patches of early deciduous, golden-brown scales, is about one-fourth of the frond length. The linear blade is

Polystichum imbricans in the mountains of Washington State. Note the overlapping pinnae.

once-pinnate with 20 to 25 pairs of strongly auricled, closely spaced pinnae. The sori with peltate indusia are submarginal.

RANGE AND HABITAT: Dwarf western sword fern is at home in rocky, often sunny sites from British Columbia south through the mountainous regions of western North America.

CULTURE AND COMMENTS: This attractive small evergreen is best suited for lean and coarse soils in rock garden culture. It looks like a congested *Polystichum munitum* and was once thought to be a form thereof, stunted by its exposed environment. The species hybridizes with *P. dudleyi* to create the northern form of *P. californicum*.

Subsp. *imbricans* has overlapping, "imbricate" pinnae that are held on the horizontal in a partially open, venetian blind fashion.

Subsp. *curtum* has narrow but not horizontal pinnae that are up to five times longer than wide.

Polystichum kruckebergii
Kruckeberg's holly fern
Polystichum lemmonii × *P. lonchitis*.
Epithet is after Arthur Kruckeberg, botany professor emeritus at the University of Washington.
Evergreen, 6 to 12 in. (15 to 30 cm). Zones 6 to 8.

DESCRIPTION: The small rhizome is erect. Pale brown scales trim the grooved stipe that is one-fifth or more frequently less of the stiffly upright frond. The once-pinnate blade with bright green, slightly imbricate, triangular pinnae is lanceolate. The 20 to 30 pairs of pinnae are reduced in size at the base. Sori with peltate indusia are submarginal on the terminal half of the frond. *Polystichum kruckebergii* is very close in structure to the look-alike *P. scopulinum* with which it shares

a parent. The former is so very rare in nature that, if confused, it is safe to assume you are looking at *P. scopulinum*. Botanically speaking, *P. kruckebergii* has spreading apical teeth whereas *P. scopulinum* has incurved apical teeth, an extraordinarily fine distinction.

RANGE AND HABITAT: This species grows in rocky crevices at high elevations in the mountains of western North America.

CULTURE AND COMMENTS: Here is an interesting plant to admire, photograph (to prove you found it), and leave behind on the mountain trail. It does not readily accept cultivation.

Polystichum lemmonii
Shasta fern
Epithet is after John G. Lemmon (1832–1908), who discovered the species on Mount Shasta in California.
Evergreen, 6 to 12 in. (15 to 30 cm). Zones 6 to 8.

DESCRIPTION: The rhizome is erect and creeping, covered with the stubble of old frond stipes. The stipe is one-fourth to one-third of the frond length and has russet scales. The very narrow linear-lanceolate blade is fully bipinnate to bipinnate-pinnatifid. The densely crowded 20 to 30 pairs of pinnae are twisted on a horizontal plane and are distinct in having pinnules that are not spine-tipped. The sori have peltate indusia. This species is very similar to *Polystichum plicatum* (formerly *P. mohroides*) of South America and has from time to time been botanically recognized as *P. mohroides*.

RANGE AND HABITAT: *Polystichum lemmonii* is a serpentine soil indicator in the high reaches of Pacific Northwest mountains. It can form extensive colonies as it crawls tenaciously at the bases of rocks to establish a cool root run. Contrary to fanciful rumors, the plant does not have a lemon fragrance. It hybridizes with both *P. scopulinum* and *P. munitum*.

Polystichum lemmonii shares the montane serpentine substrate with *Aspidotis densa* in the Wenatchee Mountains of Washington State.

CULTURE AND COMMENTS: I once-proudly had a spore-grown plant and tucked it in a container along with the requisite lump of green serpentine support. It lasted for three years becoming more of a miniature annually. It really is not for the garden, but if an attempt must be made, serpentine soil and protection from winter wet are requirements. Like all alpine ferns, it should not be collected from the wild.

Polystichum lentum
Himalayan holly fern
Epithet means "flexible."
Evergreen, 1 to 2 ft. (30 to 60 cm). Zones 8 and 9.

DESCRIPTION: The rhizome is erect. The stipe with dark brown or occasionally bicolored (dark brown with paler margins) scales varies in length from one-fourth to one-third of the frond. Blades are satin-green, once-pinnate linear to linear-lanceolate, with 20 to 25 pairs of pinnae that terminate in scalloped spine-tipped, blunt apices. Fronds are tipped with species-characteristic buds that willingly root when encouraged by being placed in a nest of garden humus or incubated in friendly, humid greenhouse conditions. The medial sori, produced on the upper half of the frond, have peltate indusia.

RANGE AND HABITAT: *Polystichum lentum* grows in damp forests in the Himalayas and China.

CULTURE AND COMMENTS: Although a Himalayan mountain native, this lovely species has not been reliably persistent in temperate western North American gardens. It may need longer and warmer summers to produce enough sugar for long-term survival. A customized microclimate should encourage good health in Zone 8 or with good husbandry possibly even Zone 7.

Polystichum lepidocaulon
Epithet means "thin stem."
Evergreen, 1 to 2 ft. (30 to 60 cm). Zones 8 and 9.

DESCRIPTION: The erect rhizome bears leggy stipes covered with brown scales and representing up to one-half of the frond. Arching fronds have lanceolate and once-pinnate blades with 10 to 12 pairs of shimmering forest-green elongate, stalked, and eared pinnae. This is a tip-rooting species walking about with an extended rachis tip readily rooting on contact with fern-friendly soil. Unlike typical polystichums, the sori with peltate indusia are in several rows on the sides of the midveins.

RANGE AND HABITAT: This species grows in humid, rocky and forested, frequently seaside, areas of Japan, China, Taiwan, and Korea.

CULTURE AND COMMENTS: An elegant species, it has not been hardy in temperate Zone 8 cultivation. I envision it thriving in the company of tree ferns in the coastal, morning fog areas of San Francisco Bay and northern California. With its handsome luster, it is well worth a prominent site in a select niche in cool greenhouses where the temperatures do not drop below freezing.

Polystichum lonchitis
Northern holly fern
Epithet means "narrow leafed."
Evergreen, usually 6 to 18 in. (15 to 45 cm). Zones 3 to 8.

DESCRIPTION: The erect rhizome produces an upright tuft of narrow, brilliant kelly-green foliage. The stipes, at one-eighth or less of the frond, are almost nonexistent and lightly dusted with pale straw-colored scales. The narrow, linear-lanceolate blade is once-pinnate with 25 to 30 or more pairs of

Polystichum lonchitis with its upright and jagged edged fronds is readily recognized and admired in woodland and alpine habitats.

Polystichum luctuosum

pinnae with reduced basal pinnae. The sori with peltate indusia stitch the edges of the upper pinnae pinnules in namesake *Polystichum* fashion. This species hybridizes with *P. braunii* to form *P. ×meyeri* and, in an exceptionally rare occurrence with *Dryopteris goldiana*, creating *Dryostichum ×singulare*.

RANGE AND HABITAT: *Polystichum lonchitis* populates alpine areas in the northern tier of the Northern Hemisphere. It is a remarkable sight in inhospitable rocky crevices from North America through Eurasia. Populations in the mountains of Utah can reach 3 ft. (90 cm) in height (Horrocks, pers. comm.).

CULTURE AND COMMENTS: It is very difficult to domesticate or propagate this deceptively sturdy-appearing alpine, although I have seen some remarkable plantings in German gardens. It needs crumbly, well-draining soil and a site preferably protected from overhead winter wet. Some growers recommend a limey soil, but that tends to give only transient success. Consequently, this species falls in the "to-admire" category of the introduction. However, many growers tend to respond to the challenge, attempting to succeed and display their "grand prize." All I ask is that the attempt not involve removing a plant from its home in the wild.

Polystichum luctuosum

Synonyms *Polystichum mayebarae, P. tsus-simense*
Epithet means "showing sorrow," in reference to the predominance of blackish scales.
Evergreen, 1 to 2 ft. (30 to 60 cm). Zones 6 (see precautions) to 9. Apogamous.

DESCRIPTION: The rhizome is short and erect. The stipe is one-fourth of the frond length and covered with dark brownish-black scales. Bipinnate blades are leathery, black and blue-green, and lanceolate. The 15 to 20 pairs of pinnae have a dominant ascending auricle. Sori are submarginal with peltate indusia.

RANGE AND HABITAT: This primarily South African species grows in limestone outcrops and is also reported from the Himalayas, Japan, Korea, Taiwan, and China. It is visually and easily confused with *Polystichum tsus-simense* as well as *P. mayebarae*. The latter is fully tripinnate and consequently does not have the prominent auricle adjacent to the rachis. In addition the stipe scales are brown rather than black. *Polystichum tsus-simense*, although more cold tolerant in cultivation and from neutral to acid rather than limestone habitats, is considered by some authors to be a synonym for *P. luctuosum*. They are indeed similar. The differences, if any, are likely to be chemically dependent and not easily determined by the layperson—a bit of horticultural quicksand here.

CULTURE AND COMMENTS: Depending on its provenance, this species can be successfully cultivated in Zones 6 to 8. In Zone 8, material originating from South Africa is borderline hardy and will need an emergency blanket when the temperatures dip below 20°F (-7°C). Himalayan material is hardy without precautions in Zones 6 to 9. This species is strikingly handsome and well worth the extra effort to give it comfort. I do not provide lime, but give it light shade and an extra portion of grit in the potting mix.

Polystichum makinoi
Makino's holly fern
Epithet is after Japanese botanist Tomitaro Makino (1861–1957).
Evergreen, 1½ to 2½ ft. (45 to 75 cm). Zones 5 to 9.

DESCRIPTION: The rhizome is erect with brown-scaled, grooved stipes that are straw-brown at the base transitioning to green approaching the foliage. The total stipe proportion is one-third of the frond. Forest-green, bipinnate, luminescent blades are lanceolate with 15 to 20 pairs of pinnae. The basal pair flares downwards. Sori are medial with peltate indusia.

RANGE AND HABITAT: This fern grows in humus-rich duff in the forests of Japan, China, Taiwan, and the Himalayas. It is the parent of numerous Japanese hybrids, all of which should be comparably magnificent additions to the collections of fern enthusiasts when and if propagation techniques bring them forth from their naturally sterile state.

CULTURE AND COMMENTS: Here is an outstanding beauty adapted to temperate gardens of all climatic persuasions. Give it compost, light shade, and the subtle company of matte foliage for a magnificent garden panorama. It also serves well in flower arrangements and is likely to outlast the flowers.

Polystichum mayebarae
Synonym *Polystichum tsus-simense* var. *mayebarae*
Epithet is after Kanjiro Maehara.
Evergreen, 1½ to 2 ft. (45 to 60 cm). Zones 6 (with protection) to 9. Apogamous.

DESCRIPTION: The rhizome is erect. The brown-scaled stipes are one-third of the frond length. The dark forest-green blades are tripinnate with 15 to 20 pairs of pinnae. The pinnules point their spiny tips towards the pinnae apices. Sori with peltate indusia are large and medial. Spores are produced from midsummer well into the fall (presenting a late option for those who have forgotten to collect spores for their favorite spore exchange).

RANGE AND HABITAT: This species grows in light shade in rocky but moist sites in Japan and China.

CULTURE AND COMMENTS: Here is a foliose feather for rich soil and shady habitats. It has a dark aura so contrasts well with light greens and bold companions. It has been considered a variety of *Polystichum tsus-simense* but differs in having brown rather than blackish stipe scales and in being tripinnate.

Polystichum munitum
Western sword fern
Epithet means "armed."
Evergreen, 3 to 5 ft. (90 to 150 cm). Zones 6 to 9.

DESCRIPTION: The rhizome is erect and supports bushels of swordlike lush foliage—sometimes up to 50 fronds per clump. The short, grooved stipe displays medium to dark brown scales and is one-fifth of the frond length. The linear-lanceolate blade is once-pinnate with 30 to 50 pairs of burnished, rich green pinnae prominently auricled. The sori with peltate indusia trace the margins of the pinnae including the auricle.

RANGE AND HABITAT: *Polystichum munitum* is the ubiquitous understory fern in the soft decomposing-needle compost of coniferous forests in the Pacific Northwest. It extends from

The handsome and reliable *Polystichum makinoi* with its lustrous fronds in the Gassner garden.

Polystichum mayebarae closely resembles *P. tsus-simense*.

Polystichum munitum in a natural setting at Elandan Gardens.

The sterile hybrid *Polystichum munitum* × *P. andersonii* is midway in structure between the parents and bears the typical *P. andersonii* bulbil on the tips of the fronds..

Alaska and British Columbia to California with an occasional disjunct station in Mexico (Guadalupe Islands) and South Dakota. Growing with evergreen upright fronds along forest walks and disturbed roadsides throughout the Northwest, it is a delight for the winter hiker and naturalist as well as for the foraging and hungry Roosevelt elk of the Olympic Peninsula, where this fern can reach 5 ft. (1.5 m) or more.

CULTURE AND COMMENTS: Were this species rare, there would be a tremendous demand (and price) for it. Adaptable, weather-resistant, and a multipurpose ornamental, the sword fern has "good bones" and settles with ease in maritime-moderated temperate climates. I have seen it in deep shade as well as full sun, although rather stressed in the latter sites and certainly not up to its potential proportions. It is highly recommended, as are most natives, as one of the best for beginning fern gardeners in the Pacific Northwest. Although unfazed when frequently snowbound in its native haunts, it suffers and declines in the typical summer heat and humidity in the eastern and southern United States (and is perhaps diminished by long freezing spells as well). Substitute *Polystichum acrostichoides*, *P. rigens*, *P. polyblepharum*, or others of the more heat-tolerant Asians. British and European gardeners grow it successfully. As expected with such densely massed

Backlighting highlights the sori on the margins of *Polystichum munitum*.

large populations, occasionally there are some variations in frond and pinnae structure including crested and crisped forms.

Polystichum neolobatum
Asian saber fern, long-eared holly fern
Epithet means "new lobed" or "new *Polystichum lobatum*."
Evergreen, 1½ to 2 ft. (45 to 60 cm). Zones 5 to 8. Apogamous.

DESCRIPTION: The rhizome is erect. The slightly grooved green stipes are barely visible under the lush coating of papery, reddish brown ½-in. (13-mm) prominent scales. These are reduced in size as they proceed up the frond, but are in such numbers that the viewer imagines the rachis to be ruddy. The succulent stipes are one-third of the frond length. The brilliantly polished blade, bipinnate at the base, is lanceolate. Twenty-five to thirty pairs of spiny pinnae produce severely spinulose pinnules so that the frond is noticeably and sometimes almost painfully sharp to the touch (hence the common name "Asian saber fern" given by Norio Sahashi). The innermost pinnules closest to the rachis are larger than adjacent pinnules. Sori with peltate indusia are medial.

This species is quite variable with two somewhat different forms in circulation as well as in illustrations. The type described here has been widely distributed and is representative of the material included in Japanese floras. Himalayan natives are more succulent in appearance, with a deeper, green gloss and, while still spiny, not as sharp to the touch. In addition both can be confused with *Polystichum squarrosum*, a fellow showpiece from the Himalayas that differs in having more widely spaced pinnae, very separate, well-spaced pinnules, a longer stipe that approaches one-half of the frond length, a waxy blackish green countenance, and narrower scales. Unfortunately these distinctions are difficult to determine without having material in hand for observation.

RANGE AND HABITAT: *Polystichum neolobatum* grows in and around forests from the Himalayas to Burma (Myanmar), China, Taiwan, and Japan. The late Zdeněk Seibert, a Czech specialist who generously shared enthusiasm, knowledge, and spores with colleagues throughout the world, introduced *P. neolobatum* to North America via Foliage Gardens. We are all richer for his contributions.

CULTURE AND COMMENTS: Here is a truly aristocratic jewel. It is well behaved, reliable, and beautiful throughout the year. Fronds remain upright in snowstorms, emerge in early spring with a flare of bright russet-trimmed fiddleheads, and continue to be decorative throughout the seasons. Its one drawback is that sun will scorch the foliage; however, when away from direct sun, it is very tolerant of hot and humid sites. Plant it in shade where it is a top choice for gardens and gardeners throughout temperate regions.

Polystichum nepalense
Nepal holly fern
Epithet means "from Nepal."
Evergreen, 1 to 2 ft. (30 to 60 cm). Zones 6 to 8.

DESCRIPTION: The rhizome is erect. The stipes with straw-brown-edged, dark-centered scales are up to one-half of the

Glowing fronds of *Polystichum neolobatum*.

Thick russet scales on the stipes of *Polystichum neolobatum*.

Unfurling spring fronds of *Polystichum polyblepharum*.

Glossy foliage of *Polystichum polyblepharum* adds luster to a woodland planting in the Bellevue Botanical Garden.

Polystichum proliferum in the Jessen garden.

frond length. Blades are narrowly lanceolate, firm-textured, and once-pinnate. The 15 to 25 pairs of toothed pinnae range from narrowly sickle-shaped with a hint of an auricle to chubby. The latter look like a series of wooden Dutch shoes stepping up and out from the rachis. The sori with peltate indusia are close to the midrib.

RANGE AND HABITAT: This species enjoys mossy shade and good drainage in the hills of the Himalayas, eastern Asia, Burma (Myanmar), Japan, and the Philippines.

CULTURE AND COMMENTS: Rarely found in cultivation, *Polystichum nepalense* challenges the spore propagator with its inconsistent and reluctant performances from sowings. So, I have had the opportunity to admire, but not to cultivate this species. I would consider it a prize for the collector's display in rocky woodland rubble and moist, humusy light shade.

The species has been compared in the literature with *Polystichum lentum* from which it is distinguished by the lack of a proliferous bud and a corresponding extended rachis, as well as having unlobed pinnae without the lower pair pointing downwards.

Polystichum polyblepharum
Tassel fern, bristle fern
Epithet means "many eyelashes."
Evergreen, 1½ to 3 ft. (45 to 90 cm). Zones 6 to 9.

DESCRIPTION: The rhizome is erect and can in time form a stout trunk that is 4 or 5 in. (10 to 13 cm) in both height and diameter. The rotund stipes with a hint of a groove are one-fifth to one-fourth of the frond length and emerge sheathed in silver scales. These will fade to a translucent warm brown. The young fiddleheads flip over in a backbend that typifies many polystichums but by common name (tassel) is associated with this species. The bipinnate, ovate-lanceolate blades bear 20 to 30 pairs of lustrous pinnae with the lowest sweeping broadly forward and downwards. The height varies with an average of 18 to 24 in. (45 to 60 cm), but there are several giants out there including a spectacular 4-ft. (1.2-m) tree fern wannabe from the Russell Graham nursery and garden in Oregon. Sori with peltate indusia are medial and shed their spores early in the season.

RANGE AND HABITAT: The tassel fern is another of the fine imports gracing our gardens and interior décor from China, Korea, and Japan where it is very common in deciduous forests and on hillsides.

CULTURE AND COMMENTS: *Polystichum polyblepharum* arrived in the gardens of North American hobbyists in the 1960s as a by-product of the indoor florist trade. It was an immediate success and enjoys tremendous popularity for its tidy, shiny presence in shady borders. The Miller Botanical Garden's Great Plant Picks Program chose this above all others as the first fern to be included in its recommendations. Plant it in rich soil in shade with a consistently and reliably moist root zone. So long as it is not allowed to dry out, it acclimates in hot summer areas as well as benign temperate regions. When a "trunk" develops, the plant should be lowered so that the crown is once again at soil level. New growth is early and needs shelter from late frosts.

Polystichum proliferum
Mother shield fern
Epithet means "bearing offspring," referring to the production of one or more buds at the frond's apex.
Evergreen, 2 to 4 ft. (60 to 120 cm). Zones (6) 7 to 9.

DESCRIPTION: The rhizome is erect, sometimes forming a small trunk and bearing remnants of old stipe bases. Short stipes of one-fifth to one-fourth of the frond length are grooved and decorated with a wrap of shiny dark-centered brown scales. Juvenile blades are bright, light, almost lime-green, maturing to rich, deep green coniferous hues. They are lanceolate and bipinnate with 18 to 20 pairs of pinnae. Sori with peltate indusia are medial with spores that mature early in the season.

RANGE AND HABITAT: *Polystichum proliferum* is endemic to Australia where it grows from sea level to snow level in the shade of moist forests or at high altitudes in sunny rocky sites. It has escaped in New Zealand.

CULTURE AND COMMENTS: This striking fern with glassy green foliage deserves wider distribution. It is easily cultivated in good woodland compost and light shade where, with bulbil assistance, it can form an elegant colony. (The readily rooting bulbils often form plantlets while still attached to the mother frond.) While recommended for the garden, it can also fill the living room as a specimen-sized houseplant. This species is the parent of some outstanding proliferous hybrids, including the handsome *Polystichum ×dycei*. Brownsey and Smith-Dodsworth (2000) note that it is similar to *P. vestitum* but the latter does not produce bulbils.

Polystichum retroso-paleaceum
Synonym *Polystichum aculeatum* var. *retroso-paleaceum*
Epithet means "twisted back scales."
Evergreen, 2 to 3 ft. (60 to 90 cm). Zones 5 to 8.

DESCRIPTION: The rhizome is erect. The grooved stipes are dark chocolate in color, one-fourth of the frond length, and trimmed on opposite outer sides with down- and forward-thrusting pale tan scales. The lanceolate blade with earthward-pointing basal pinnae is bipinnate with 20 or more pairs of pinnae. Sori are medial with peltate indusia.

RANGE AND HABITAT: Large populations grow in rich soil throughout forests in Korea and especially Japan.

CULTURE AND COMMENTS: An easily cultivated hardy fern, this species awakens in early spring chasing the crocuses and joining the daffodils and primroses. Protect it from late frosts and plant it where its beguiling early crosiers can be admired. It can be differentiated from the extremely similar *Polystichum ovato-paleaceum* by the scales that aim downwards rather than tending upwards as in the latter. In addition, new growth and spore maturation are earlier on *P. retroso-paleaceum*.

Polystichum richardii
Richard's holly fern, black shield fern
Epithet is after Richard.
Evergreen, 1 to 2 ft. (30 to 60 cm). Zones 8 (with protection) and 9.

DESCRIPTION: The rhizome is erect. The tall, slender stipes, covered with narrow, dark blackish scales, are up to one-half of the frond length. Blades are ovate-lanceolate and bipinnate with 15 to 20 pairs of pinnae. Sori are large with dark-centered peltate indusia.

The species hybridizes with *Polystichum vestitum*. In 2003 (see Perrie et al. 2003, Ackers 2005) taxonomists divided this variable species into four taxa as follows: *Polystichum neozelandicum* subsp. *neozelandicum*, *P. neozelandicum* subsp. *zerophyllum*, *P. oculatum*, and *P. wawranum*. Notice that the name *P. richardii* is nowhere in sight. The older name *P. neozelandicum* takes precedence sending *P. richardii* into botanical obscurity. For field characteristics, differences are based on scale size and shape, distance between pinnae, the size of the dark center in the indusia, and somewhat on geographical distribution. Naturally these all grade into each other. As a broad generalization *P. wawranum* has closely set pinnae, a very small dark center on the indusia, and is most prevalent on the North Island. *Polystichum neozelandicum* subsp. *neozelandicum* has less closely set pinnae, a large dark center, and is most common at the north end of New Zealand's North Island. *Polystichum neozelandicum* subsp. *zerophyllum* has more widely spaced pinnae, a medium-sized dark center, and is scattered on both islands. *Polystichum oculatum* has widely spaced

Polystichum retroso-paleaceum is one of the earliest ferns to unfurl in the spring.

Polystichum richardii whose name has changed but whose dark fronds remain enchanting by whatever designation.

Polystichum rigens in the Kennar garden.

pinnae, a small to medium dark center, and is concentrated on the southern half of the North Island and northern half of the South Island.

RANGE AND HABITAT: Endemic to New Zealand, these four are found in varied habitats.

CULTURE AND COMMENTS: In general the erstwhile *Polystichum richardii* with its magnificently dark and shiny, black-green foliage is readily recognizable and suggestive of early evening views of somber mountain lakes. In cultivation it grows in assorted soil types without complaint, but unfortunately, is only borderline hardy in Zone 8. For best results it needs serious protection or a life as an indoor plant.

Polystichum rigens

Epithet means "rigid."

Evergreen, 1½ ft. (45 cm). Zones 6 to 8. Apogamous.

DESCRIPTION: The rhizome is erect. Stipes are grooved and green with brown scales concentrated at the base. They are one-third or more of the frond length. Radiant, narrowly triangular, bipinnate blades are a rich deep green. Twelve to fifteen pairs of sickle-shaped pinnae are tipped with sharp spines. Sori with peltate indusia are medial.

RANGE AND HABITAT: *Polystichum rigens* is a rare species from the montane forests of China and Japan.

CULTURE AND COMMENTS: This species is slow growing and similar in effect to *Polystichum tsus-simense* with the latter having linear rather than the lanceolate scales. *Polystichum rigens* prefers a site enriched with compost in full shade and willingly tolerates the testing hot and humid summer climates of gardens in the eastern and central United States. When young this species gives off a slight "eau de skunk" which is not distracting in the garden but can attract circumspect comments when gathered in the greenhouse.

Polystichum scopulinum

Western holly fern

Polystichum imbricans × *P. lemmonii*.

Epithet means "of rocks."

Evergreen, 6 to 15 in. (15 to 38 cm). Zones 5 to 8.

DESCRIPTION: The rhizome is erect. The grooved stipes bear pale brown scales and are one-fourth to one-third of the frond length. Fleshy, stiffly upright blades are pinnate-pinnatifid with 20 to 35 pairs of closely packed, folded pinnae. Sori with peltate indusia are crowded in median rows.

RANGE AND HABITAT: This alpine from the western mountains of North America with disjunct populations in eastern Canada prefers a cool root run and nestles against boulders in bright light.

CULTURE AND COMMENTS: Western holly fern is essentially not for cultivation (although three brave survivors from one of my spore sowings show great promise and may lead to a better adapted second generation). Instead, admire it in among the Indian paintbrushes, gentians, and other colorful companions in its mountain habit. Here is a great excuse to go to the mountains for a day of botanizing. (The geology is not a bad study either.) *Polystichum scopulinum* is difficult to separate from *P. kruckebergii*. The latter has a much shorter stipe and spreading apical teeth compared to the longer stipe and larger numbers of incurved apical teeth of *P. scopulinum.*

Polystichum setiferum
Soft shield fern
Synonym *Polystichum angulare*
Epithet means "bristle bearing."
Evergreen, 2 to 3 ft. (60 to 90 cm). Zones 5 to 8.

DESCRIPTION: The rhizome is erect, supporting wide fans of soft, willowy fronds. The grooved stipes are coated with warm-brown scales that are a glittering silver on emerging fiddleheads. They are one-fifth of the frond length. The bipinnate, lanceolate blade is broadest in the middle with 30 to 40 pairs of pinnae with stalked, toothy spinulose pinnules. Sori with peltate indusia are medial.

RANGE AND HABITAT: Soft shield fern is common in its native Britain as well as Europe growing in hedgerows, and in deciduous woodlands along streambanks at low elevations. It is best in neutral soil, although it can be found in slightly basic or slightly acid compost.

CULTURE AND COMMENTS: Plant this species in a moist, but not wet, lightly shaded environment and give it room to let its lax fronds billow. I would have listed this as Zone 6 but was pleasantly surprised to learn that it does well in Binghamton, New York (Donnelly in Olsen 2005), which straddles the border between Zones 4 and 5. Folks in humid areas are not so lucky as it and its cultivars languish in summer heat.

Polystichum setiferum and its fellow British and continental species, *P. aculeatum,* can be difficult to tell apart. To add to

Polystichum setiferum in the Hardy Fern Foundation collection at the Rhododendron Species Botanical Garden.

Polystichum scopulinum in a rocky alpine setting in the Cascade Mountains of Washington State.

Silvery new growth on a *Polystichum setiferum* cultivar.

the confusion both are extremely variable. In addition, they hybridize with each other to form *P. ×bicknellii*. The easiest way to determine which is which is by feel. *Polystichum aculeatum*, the hard shield fern, is stiff and leathery. *Polystichum setiferum*, the soft shield fern, is lax and, yes, soft. In addition, the lower pinnae on *P. setiferum* are not severely reduced nor is the stipe as short as in *P. aculeatum*.

The development in the 1830s of the Wardian case, a simple to extravagantly elaborate terrarium-like structure, offered plants protection from the suffocating pollution of Victorian England and gave ferns a new and elevated status. Thus began the collecting epidemic know as the Victorian Fern Craze. In short, ferns were trendy and in high demand. Varieties with slight or major irregularities were especially prized, collected, and either proudly displayed or sold for a tidy sum. Thus *Polystichum setiferum*, the common native, yielded at one time some 366 of these varieties. I will not go into them all here! Some have persisted through time (although, regrettably, a private collection of prizes went unrecognized and was torch flamed at the end of World War II to make way for a vegetable garden). Cultivars have an ardent group of fans, especially in Britain and as this goes to press the British Pteridological Society has just published an excellent and helpful compilation, *Polystichum Cultivars: Variation in the British Shield Ferns* (Dyce et al. 2005), with a primary focus on *P. setiferum*. The book divides the variations into 32 manageable groups under the headings "Variation in Shape of Skeleton of Frond," "Variations in Shape or Dissection of Pinnules," and "Other" which includes a variegated group. With illustrations and descriptions it helps to bring order to some of the nomenclature (as well as the plants). Some of the cultivars come true from spores but many do not, although the progeny may be interesting or even, on occasion, an improvement. Frequently produced bulbils can duplicate the parents of sterile forms, and tissue culture has greatly expanded production and distribution. Some of the most decorative cultivars are mentioned here.

'**Acutilobum**' (acute lobed) is a leathery, 2- to 3-ft. (60- to 90-cm) cultivar similar to 'Divisilobum' but without bulbils.

'**Capitatum**' (headed) has a heavily crested terminal headdress, but no crests on the pinnae.

'**Congestum**' (crowded), an upright 10-in. (25-cm) dwarf, has tightly bunched overlapping pinnae and substantially thick foliage. It is suitable for the foreground in the fern bed.

'**Congestum Cristatum**', which is the same size as 'Congestum' and has the same dense structure, has mildly crested frond tips.

'**Cristato-pinnulum**', an old cultivar dating from the late 1800s but a very attractive one at that, grows to 2 ft. (60 cm). This slender lightweight has narrow pinnae stalks supporting open sprays of bright green fringe. It is basically sterile but reproduces easily from bulbils.

Cristatum Group encompasses cultivars with varying degrees of cresting at the pinnae and/or frond tips.

'**Dahlem**' (after the Dahlem Botanical Garden in Berlin, where it was discovered) grows in an upright cluster to 30 in.

Polystichum setiferum 'Congestum'

Polystichum setiferum 'Cristato-pinnulum'

Polystichum setiferum 'Dahlem' in the Schmick garden.

Polystichum setiferum 'Divisilobum'

(75 cm). There are true forms and there are confused forms all distributed under this name. The upright characteristic is deemed to be the genuine feature. Material cultivated in Germany is very attractive and can be reproduced from the abundant bulbils that line the rachis.

Divisilobum Group (divided lobes) includes the most readily available and signature cultivars from among the assorted and varied *Polystichum setiferum* offerings. Plants are typically finely cut, and often tripinnate, with a horizontal tendency for the relaxed and graceful 2-ft. (60-cm) fronds. Bulbils are produced along the rachis and root willingly when pinned down on inviting soil. However, a number of growers on both sides of the Atlantic have observed that the more "comfortable" a given cultivar is in the garden, the lower the bulbil production. Research is needed and would be welcome to deter-

Bulbils on *Polystichum setiferum* 'Divisilobum' in the Kennar garden.

Polystichum setiferum 'Foliosum Walton'

Polystichum setiferum 'Green Lace'

Polystichum setiferum 'Plumoso-divisilobum'

Polystichum setiferum 'Herrenhausen'

mine whether the tendencies and efforts to reproduce are affected by stress, the need to preserve the species, or some other cause. While I hate to perpetrate an incorrect name, it must be mentioned that this is the British fern known commercially in the United States as the "Alaska fern."

'**Foliosum Walton**' is a splendidly rich (foliose), spreading cultivar with lush, bright green shuttlecock foliage and bipinnate fronds approaching 2 ft. (60 cm). It has not produced bulbils in my garden, but does come true from spores.

'**Green Lace**' is the aptly named offspring of one of the rarely produced fertile fronds from the crown jewel of cultivars, *Polystichum setiferum* 'Plumosum Bevis' (whose status has just been elevated to Bevis Group). It is a finely dissected, 2-ft. (60-cm) bright green gem for special recognition in the fern collection. Unfortunately it is sterile, but tissue culture offers hope that it will someday grace more gardens.

'**Herrenhausen**', which comes from Germany, is highly recommended for the lacy effect of the 2- to 3-ft. (60- to 90-cm) finely divided dark green plumes of fronds. It has been as-signed to the Divisilobum Group.

'**Iveryanum**', a leathery "divisilobe" with dark green, finely divided fronds ranging from 2- to 3-ft. (60 to 90 cm), is bul-biferous and bears crests on the pinnae and frond tips.

'**Leinthall Starkes**' is an especially attractive cultivar that Martin Rickard raised in 1980 from the spores of a wild find in southern England's Devonshire. It is an airy tripinnate with dark green, bristle-tipped pinnae. The upper portion of the frond is fertile and narrowed.

'**Lineare**' (linear) is a 2-ft. (60-cm) cultivar with bipinnate skeletal fronds offering a wide open, spacious appearance.

'**Multilobum**' (multiple lobes), which can reach 3 ft. (90 cm), has tripinnate, bulbiferous fronds that are similar in out-line to the species but are separated by having one additional degree of division.

'**Percristatum**' (crested throughout) has fronds, pinnae, and pinnules with crests in a truly Victorian manner.

'**Plumoso-divisilobum**' (feathery, divided lobes) is one of the most beautiful and feathery fern cultivars ever discovered. Layers of gossamer green, quadripinnate (an ultimate in divi-sion) foliage dress its fronds in fine plumage. The fronds ex-tend in a sweeping horizontal whorl. This cultivar is appreci-ated and enjoyed whenever and wherever available, but rarely produces either spores or bulbils. A cultivar tentatively classified (by Sykes and Rickard in Dyce 2005) as a dwarf form has been admired in my garden by many visitors and offers great promise for the size-limited landscape.

'**Plumoso-multilobum**' (feathery, multiple lobes), syn-onym *P. setiferum* 'Plumosum-densum', is another magni-ficent quadripinnate cultivar that makes an impressive and buoyant understory evergreen. Pinnae and pinnules overlap, producing a dense froth of pale green. This form comes easily and rapidly from bulbils, especially when encouraged by greenhouse conditions.

'**Plumosum Bevis**', synonym *P. aculeatum* 'Pulcherrimum Bevis', now in its own distinguished Bevis Group, is the cher-ished treasure among *P. setiferum* cultivars. With its satin green, upright 2- to 3-ft. (60- to 90-cm), finely divided fronds, it is a stately evergreen presence and collector's pride in partial shade. Namesake, Mr. Bevis who was in charge of trimming hedgebanks in Devon, England, discovered this prize in 1876 and had the skill and presence of mind to recognize it as "dif-ferent." It has been a great gift to horticulture ever since. Al-though sterile it will, on occasion, produce a fertile frond that in turn consistently creates a new generation of unusual or-namentals. In addition, slowly but eventually, it will develop multiple crowns that can be divided. Meanwhile, tissue-cul-ture labs will soon make it a common and welcome commer-cial offering.

'**Plumosum Green**', an extremely rare sterile cultivar, was the first to be grown (by C. B. Green around 1900) from the in-frequently produced spores of *Polystichum setiferum* 'Plumo-sum Bevis'. Feathery lanceolate fronds are tripinnate to quadripinnate.

'**Ray Smith**' is a recent addition to ornamental cultivar op-tions. In the 1980s Ray Smith of Britain noticed a cruciate

A dwarf form of *Polystichum setiferum* 'Plumoso-divisilobum'.

Polystichum setiferum 'Plumosum Bevis' in the Rickard garden.

pinnae segment complete with a bulbil among his *Polystichum setiferum* cultivars. Propagation of his single bulbil produced this striking, narrowly upright selection.

'**Rotundatum**' (rounded) is a sturdy dark green 2-ft. (60-cm) form with rounded pinnules.

'**Rotundatum Cristatum**' (rounded and crested) has fronds, again with rounded pinnules, that fork at the apex and

Polystichum setiferum 'Plumosum Green' in the Rickard garden.

Polystichum setiferum 'Ray Smith' in the Nittritz garden.

Polystichum setiferum 'Rotundatum Cristatum' in the Horder garden.

carry a complement of ready-to-grow bulbils along their length.

Polystichum setigerum
Alaska sword fern
Polystichium braunii × *P. munitum.*
Epithet means "bristle bearing."
Evergreen, 2 to 3 ft. (60 to 90 cm). Zones 6 to 8.

DESCRIPTION: The rhizome is erect, producing grooved stipes dressed in light brown scales. They are short and one-eighth to one-fifth of the frond length. Blades are lanceolate and pinnate-pinnatifid to almost bipinnate with 25 to 30 pairs of bright green spiny pinnae. Sori with peltate indusia are medial. It is a presumptive fertile hybrid, exhibiting characteristics of both assumed parents.

RANGE AND HABITAT: *Polystichum setigerum* grows in cool coastal forests in British Columbia and Alaska with possible outlying stations in the Attu Islands.

CULTURE AND COMMENTS: This lovely warm-green species is quite content in cool compost and shady lowland gardens. It will not adjust to hot climates away from its natural homeland of perpetually and evenly moist habitats.

Polystichum silvaticum
Synonym *Polystichum sylvaticum*
Epithet means "of the woods."
Evergreen, 1 to 2 ft. (30 to 60 cm). Zones 8 and 9.

DESCRIPTION: The rhizome is erect. Stipes are one-third or more of the frond length with dark-centered, glossy brown scales. The lanceolate bipinnate-pinnatifid blades have 15 to 20 pairs of widely spaced pinnae with stretched-out pointed tips. Sori are noted for the absence of indusia.

RANGE AND HABITAT: Endemic to New Zealand, primarily on the North Island, this species prefers deep shade and damp woods.

CULTURE AND COMMENTS: Rarely, if ever, available, this fern is a candidate for cool, temperate coastal climates and protected gardens. With its open and delicate outline, it is a garden light-weight. This species hybridizes with *Polystichum vestitum*.

Polystichum squarrosum
Epithet means "with spreading parts."
Evergreen, 1½ to 2 ft. (45 to 60 cm). Zones 6 to 8.

DESCRIPTION: The rhizome is erect. Stipes are light straw-colored to deep brown with matching bright brown scales. They are one-third to one-half of the frond length. Blades are bipinnate and lanceolate with 25 or more pairs of leathery, forest-green pinnae. Pinnae and pinnules are spiny and widely spaced. The sori with peltate indusia are large and crowded onto the pinnules. New growth is briefly rosy colored.

RANGE AND HABITAT: *Polystichum squarrosum* grows on forest floors in the Himalayas and China. It is absent from Japan.

CULTURE AND COMMENTS: With its lustrous foliage and sturdy bearing, this fern is a very desirable addition to the garden. For educational as well as ornamental purposes, plant it adjacent to *Polystichum neolobatum*, with which it is easily and readily confused. The pinnae and pinnules of *P. squarrosum*

are more widely spaced, the stipe is longer, and the scales are narrower. It helps to be looking at them both at the same time. (See Khullar 2000.)

Polystichum stenophyllum
Narrow-leafed holly fern
Epithet means "narrow leaf."
Evergreen, 6 to 18 in. (15 to 45 cm). Zones 6 to 8.

DESCRIPTION: The rhizome is erect. The grooved green stipes are one-fourth of the frond length and trimmed with long-tailed tan scales. The once-pinnate linear blades are firm and very narrow, ranging from ½ to 1 in. (13 to 25 mm) wide. Frond tips can have a minute, proliferous bud, smaller than a pinhead, near the apex. (They are not obvious.) Fifteen to twenty pairs of serrate, auricled pinnae are rosy pink in new growth. Lower pinnae on my plants do not point downwards. Sori with peltate indusia trace the midsections and auricles of the pinnae.

Polystichum stenophyllum, a dwarf for the shady rock garden.

Polystichum tagawanum in the spring garden.

Polystichum tripteron with its "wings" on the lower portion of the frond.

RANGE AND HABITAT: This is a fern of higher mountain regions in the Himalayas, China, and Taiwan. It does not grow in Japan.

CULTURE AND COMMENTS: Grow this diminutive charmer in colonies in humus-enriched rocky sites in the shade. (Moisture and shade promote bulbil production.) It invites closer inspection and admiration in container plantings as well.

Polystichum tagawanum
Tagawa's holly fern
Epithet is after Japanese botanist Motozi Tagawa (1908–1977).
Evergreen, 1½ to 2 ft. (45 to 60 cm). Zones 4 to 8.

DESCRIPTION: The rhizome is erect. Green stipes are one-fourth to one-third of the frond length and framed with fringed, dull brown scales. Lanceolate blades are bipinnate and silky green with well-separated pinnae and pinnules. There are 18 to 25 pairs of pinnae with the lowest inclined slightly forward. Sori with peltate indusia are submarginal.

RANGE AND HABITAT: This Japanese endemic often appears in large colonies in mountain forests.

CULTURE AND COMMENTS: An attractive addition to the *Polystichum* collection, *P. tagawanum* at first glance superficially suggests *P. polyblepharum*. The fronds on the latter are glossier with a lacquered finish. They are also broader in midfrond with the lower downward-pointing pinnae almost parallel to the stipe/rachis. Use *P. tagawanum* where a soft finishing touch rather than a bright shine is desired.

Polystichum tripteron
Trifid holly fern
Epithet means "three wings."
Deciduous, 1 to 2 ft. (30 to 60 cm). Zones (4) 5 to 8.

DESCRIPTION: The rhizome is short-creeping, producing tufts of fronds among old stipe bases. The stipes are one-half of the frond length and pale green with straw-colored, early deciduous scales. The unique blades jut forth like daggers with an extended pair of bipinnate lower pinnae spreading like wings and supporting a central upward-pointing once-pinnate extended tongue (in keeping with the name "three wings"). Sori with peltate indusia are medial.

RANGE AND HABITAT: *Polystichum tripteron* is native to cool moist mountain locales in Siberia, Japan, Korea, China, and Manchuria.

CULTURE AND COMMENTS: The distinctive fronds provide an interesting diversion from traditional fern foliar silhouettes. The fern needs to be cool and planted in rich compost. Note, however, that unlike most polystichums, it is deciduous. (And what fern would want to keep its fronds above ground in Siberian and Manchurian winters?) Unfortunately, when it does appear, it is a magnet for slugs and will not survive without ample vigilance. I recommend a moat.

Polystichum tsus-simense
Tsus-sima holly fern, Korean rock fern
Epithet means "from Tsus-sima Island."
Evergreen, 1 to 1½ ft. (30 to 45 cm). Zones 6 to 9. Apogamous.

DESCRIPTION: The rhizome is erect. Grooved stipes with dark brownish black scales are between one-fourth and one-

Polystichum tsus-simense in the Duryee garden.

Golden-hued scales on the young fronds of *Polystichum vestitum*.

third of the frond length. Blades are lanceolate, bipinnate, and black-green with even darker veins. Fifteen to twenty pairs of pinnae support spine-tipped pinnules that are clearly separate and have a hint of a stalk. Sori with peltate indusia are medial.

RANGE AND HABITAT: Korea, China, Japan, Thailand, and Indochina are all homelands for this species which grows in forests and on rocky slopes.

CULTURE AND COMMENTS: *Polystichum tsus-simense* arrived in North America via the florist trade where it is a popular finishing touch for flowers in boutonnieres. Garden hardiness and worthiness came as an unexpected bonus. It is a tidy low-growing trimming for shady perennial beds as well as a very suitable low-maintenance choice for indoor culture. Current botanical research places this as a sister species or even as synonymous with *P. luctuosum*. However, the pinnules on the latter are partially attached to the pinnae (adnate) rather than separated. In addition *P. tsus-simense* is not indigenous to

limestone habitats whereas it is the location of choice for *P. luctuosum*. I have always been what is classified as a "lumper" as opposed to a "splitter" in separating or grouping species. (Age will do this.) In this instance, however, I will yield to the "splitters" in order to keep the traditional and familiar name *P. tsus-simense* from disappearing as the designated binomial for this species.

Polystichum vestitum
Prickly shield fern
Epithet means "clothed."
Evergreen, 1 to 3 ft. (30 to 90 cm). Zones (6) 7 and 8.

DESCRIPTION: The rhizome is erect. Stipes are one-third or more of the frond. Polystichums are noted for their heavy sheaves of stipe scales, like shingles protecting a roof, and this species is among the most decorated of all with broad and brilliant golden-brown dark-centered scales. The blades are

Polystichum vestitum in situ near Milford Sound, South Island, New Zealand.

lanceolate, glowing forest-green, and bipinnate with 20 to 30 pairs of pointed pinnae. Sori with peltate indusia are medial. This species hybridizes with all three fellow New Zealand polystichums.

RANGE AND HABITAT: This New Zealand native is common throughout the country and is especially plentiful on hillsides of the South Island. It has no particular soil preference and is reputedly the last of the shade lovers to survive in the sunshine created by the clear cutting of forests. Fern-enlightened tourists can delight in its presence near popular New Zealand destinations such as Queenstown and especially Milford Sound.

CULTURE AND COMMENTS: *Polystichum vestitum* is cultivated in Europe and needs to be brought to fern lovers in North America. It has been challenging to propagate because winter is summer and summer is winter when introducing material from Down Under. However, when this becomes available (and it will), grow it where the low rays of late afternoon or early morning sunshine can highlight the golden glow of the scale-wrapped stipes.

Polystichum xiphophyllum
Epithet means "swordlike leaves."
Evergreen, 1½ ft. (45 cm). Zones (6) 7 and 8. Apogamous.
DESCRIPTION: The rhizome is erect. Stipes are grooved, dark-scaled, and one-fourth of the frond length. The lanceolate

Bright fronds of *Polystichum xiphophyllum* shine in the woods in the Kennar garden.

once-pinnate blades with 20 to 25 pairs of pinnae have a silvery green patina. The detached auricle is prominent and gives the pinnae an upward-running tail adjacent to the rachis. Sori with peltate indusia are medial.

RANGE AND HABITAT: This is a rare species from China, Taiwan, and India. References do not define habitats, but based on successful introductions in Pacific Northwest gardens, I recommend light shade and humus.

CULTURE AND COMMENTS: *Polystichum xiphophyllum* is a lovely low-growing ornamental with a simple horizontal foliar presentation. Use it as a unifying ground cover under shade-loving floral uprights.

Shorter Notes
Many of the polystichums described here are already in cultivation and, though relatively unknown, all offer promise for gardens and inspired growers throughout temperate regions. In addition to the above, there are a number of currently unidentified species arriving from China, and specifically from Yunnan, including several ornamental prizes that are in cultivation in Europe.

Hybrids traditionally are vigorous and easy additions to the horticultural palette and the *Polystichum* progeny contribute a varied assortment. With many of the world's species growing in close proximity to each other and with contributions from science, including artificially created laboratory hybrids, they have produced an interesting range of intermediates. These mostly sterile offspring offer an intellectual challenge both in the field and in the garden in figuring out who's who among the hybrid generation. Simply stated, look for intermediate characteristics between the presumed parents. It is definitely not as easy as it might sound, but should keep the mind sharp and eye alert.

Polystichum acrostichoides × *P. andersonii* is a sterile, evergreen, bulbiferous hybrid from the research laboratory of Anne Sleep. It reaches 1½ to 2½ ft. (45 to 75 cm) tall and is suitable for Zones 6 to 8. It has the outline of *P. acrostichoides*

Polystichum acrostichoides × *P. proliferum* showing the bulbil sprouting on the frond in the Peters garden.

Polystichum andersonii × P. braunii.

Polystichum ×bicknellii in the Peters garden.

without the constricted terminal pinnae and with distinct rather than confluent sori. And, most fortunately, the fronds bear bulbils.

Polystichum acrostichoides × P. proliferum, also from the experimental breeding program of Anne Sleep, is evergreen, sterile, and bulbiferous. The fronds of 2 ft. (60 cm) or more are bipinnate. This is easily cultivated in shade in Zones 6 to 8 and very readily propagated from the single bulbil on frond tips.

Polystichum alticola (high dweller) is an evergreen alpine from the rocky heights of the Drakensberg Mountains of South Africa. Bipinnate, light green, and ranging in height from 1 to 2 ft. (30 to 60 cm), it has great potential for partially shady rock gardens in Zones 8 and 9.

Polystichum andersonii × P. braunii is a sterile, bulbiferous, evergreen hybrid that was produced by Anne Sleep. The lax 2-ft. (60-cm) fronds, like those of *P. braunii*, are bipinnate, broadest in the middle, and tapering at both ends. This fern brings good looks and collector's joy to cool shade gardens in Zones 6 to 8. One or occasionally more bulbils are produced on the tips of mature fronds and are easily rooted.

Polystichum andersonii × P. setiferum is an 18- to 24-in. (45- to 60-cm) sterile, evergreen hybrid from Anne Sleep's laboratory experiments. The fronds taper at both ends and pro-

duce bulbils sparingly. It is an attractive hybrid for shade in Zones 6 to 8.

Polystichum andinum (from the Andes) grows in woods in the subantarctic mountains of Chile and Argentina. Foot-tall (30-cm) fronds develop in tufts and are once-pinnate to pinnate-pinnatifid with pinnae that are often imbricate. Stipes have golden scales. This species is potentially challenging to cultivate and should be tested in Zones 6 to 8 with good drainage and gritty soil.

Polystichum ×bicknellii (after Clarence Bicknell, 1842–1918, of Britain) is a sterile hybrid between *P. aculeatum* and *P. setiferum*. It occurs in Europe and Britain in areas where both parents are present and can easily be confused with either. Its abortive spores separate it. Evergreen and variable, it conducts itself, when available, handsomely and with ease in gardens in Zones (5) 6 to 8.

Polystichum bonseyi (after Edwin Bonsey) is a 2- to 3-ft. (60- to 90-cm) evergreen from the higher elevations of Maui, Hawaii, where it grows in mesic wet forests and subalpine scrub. It has stipes densely clothed in red-brown scales and lanceolate bipinnate blades of flat green. Gardeners in Zones 8 and 9 should be able to cultivate this fern in moist shade, as it has been successfully grown in central England for many years.

Glossy sheen, similar to that of *Polystichum polyblepharum*, illuminates the fronds of *P. discretum* in the Kohout garden.

Young plant of *Polystichum dracomontanum* in the Jessen garden.

Polystichum chilense (of Chile), from southern Chile and Argentina, is evergreen and from 18 to 24 in. (45 to 60 cm) tall. Stipes are covered with large scales and the ovate-lanceolate blades are bipinnate to tripinnate. This is a candidate for cultivation in Zones 7 and 8.

Polystichum discretum (discrete, separate), synonym *P. nigropaleaceum*, is a leathery 2- to 4-ft. (60- to 120-cm) evergreen from Asia especially common in moist, humusy deep shade. The stipes have linear light brown to almost black scales rather than the broad scales that are so common on many polystichums. Shiny, lanceolate blades suggestive of *P. polyblepharum* are bipinnate with serrate and spinulose pinnules. New growth is early and needs protection from late frosts. Cultivate this in Zones 6 to 8.

Polystichum dracomontanum (of the Drakensberg Mountains) is an erect, colonizing evergreen up to 3 ft. (90 cm) tall. Stipes scales are straw-colored and blades are broadly lanceolate, leathery, and bipinnate. Cultivate it in compost and shade in Zones 6 to 8.

Polystichum drepanum (sickle-shaped) comes to us as a rarity from the Madeira Islands. It is a 2-ft. (60-cm) evergreen for trials in Zones 8 and 9, and has bipinnate, triangular foliage.

Polystichum drepanum in the Gassner garden.

Polystichum duthiei (after John F. Duthie, 1845–1922, who collected in India) is an exceptionally rare (and consequently greatly appealing) bushlet of an alpine from the higher elevations in the Himalayas and China. Stubby 6-in. (15-cm) once-pinnate fronds have bunched pinnae with the whole encased in varying degrees of pale brown scales. In addition, the upper frond surface bears small white glands. As of this writing this species is not available in the trade, but the illustrations and description are so attractive that I would like to encourage its distribution. The habitat parameters are defined as up to 21,000 ft. (6300 m) in damp sites and under rocks, so it should be hardy.

Polystichum fallax (false, deceptive) is an Australian native inhabiting rocky areas in open forests. Fronds are lanceolate to 2 ft. (60 cm) with glossy, evergreen, bipinnate to tripinnate foliage. The species should be hardy in Zone 9 and, with protection, possibly Zone 8 as well.

Polystichum formosanum (of Formosa) is a small, 1-ft. (30-cm) evergreen with slender, wiry stipes and once-pinnate narrow blades. It grows in dense, mossy duff in forests of China, Taiwan, and Japan and should adapt in Zone 8 and possibly Zone 7.

Polystichum haleakalense (after Mount Haleakala of Hawaii) has shiny, dark green, lanceolate, bipinnate to bipinnate-pinnatifid blades on short tan-scaled stipes. The fronds range from 8 to 18 in. (20 to 45 cm) tall. This high-mountain native has been successfully grown in England for over a decade and is worth trying in Zone 9 or well-mulched Zone 8.

Polystichum hancockii (after Hancock) is an evergreen with stipes one-half the length of the 2-ft. (60-cm) fronds. Blades are once-pinnate with an elongated pair of bipinnate basal pinnae rather like a reduced *P. tripteron*. This species grows in moist to wet areas in Japan, China, and Taiwan and is successful in European gardens in Zones 7 and 8.

Polystichum lachenense (milk-like), Aleutian holly fern, is a dwarf species with brownish-purple 2- to 4-in. (5- to 10-cm) stipes and 8-in. (20-cm) linear-lanceolate, once-pinnate to bipinnate blades. Old (dead) stipes and frond material are persistent and serve as indicators for identification purposes. This rare alpine has a native spread from the Himalayas, Burma (Myanmar), China, Taiwan, and Japan to the Aleutians. In all situations it prefers good drainage and rocky rubble and should be given comparable grit in gardens in Zones 6 to 8.

Polystichum ×*lonchitiforme* (long shape), a sterile hybrid, combines attractive features from both parents with its sheen from *P. lonchitis* and arching fronds from *P. setiferum*. The narrow 2-ft. (60-cm) fronds are evergreen with pinnatifid blades. The hybrid is easier to domesticate than *P. lonchitis* and grows in average well-drained loamy soil in partial shade from Zones 5 to 8. I look to tissue culture to introduce it to a broader (and eager) gardening public.

Polystichum ×*luerssenii* (after Christian Luerssen, 1843–1916, a botany professor at Leipzig) is a hybrid between *P. aculeatum* and *P. braunii*. Growing to more than 2 ft. (60 cm), this evergreen, bipinnate fern tapers in the manner of *P. braunii* and is very scaly. It is European in origin and hardy in shade in Zones 6 to 8.

Polystichum longipaleatum (long scales), synonym *P. setosum*, joins an illustrious group of shiny foliaged, showy evergreens that are garden worthy even as their botanical classification changes periodically. This Asian from China and the Himalayas has golden scaled, 6-in. (15-cm) stipes bearing bipinnate, broadly lanceolate, hairy 18-in. (45-cm) blades crowded with 40 pairs of linear pinnae. Introduce it to shade and rich soil in Zone 6 to 8 gardens, where it is well worthy of experimentation.

Polystichum manmeiense is a 3-ft. (90-cm) evergreen with equal parts brown-scaled stipes and lanceolate, bipinnate medium green blades. It is currently rare, and the material described is from Christopher Fraser-Jenkins's introductions to Britain. Gardeners in Zone 8 should find it hardy as it grows in the Himalayas as well as China, Taiwan, and the Philippines.

Polystichum mehrae (after Indian botanist P. N. Mehra, b. 1907), synonym *P. acanthophyllum*, is a charming low-growing spiral of 1- to 2-in. (2.5- to 5-cm) wide once-pinnate (rarely bipinnate) 1-ft. (30-cm) fronds with practically nonexistent light brown, heavily scaled stipes. The curved fronds that cling to rocks are the identifying and seducing feature of this high-altitude Himalayan, Chinese, and Burmese (Myanmarese) evergreen. It has tremendous potential for dedicated rock gardeners to introduce to shade and granular soil in the "rare plant section" of the garden, alpine house, or any area without high humidity. In Zone 6 it needs winter protection, but it should be willing in Zones 7 and 8. Remember to give it good drainage.

Polystichum ×*meyeri* (after Dieter Meyer, 1926–1982) is a hybrid between *P. braunii* and *P. lonchitis*. This narrow, bipinnate evergreen with fronds to 2 ft. (60 cm) tapers strongly at the base. It is easier to cultivate than its *P. lonchitis* parent and can be grown in partial shade in Zones 6 to 8.

Polystichum monotis (one ear) from China is an evergreen 1-ft. (30-cm) dwarf detailed in Rickard (2000) that will hopefully be available commercially. It is described as narrowly triangular, dark green, and once-pinnate with a detached auricle somewhat similar to a miniature *P. xiphophyllum*. There is good potential here for gardeners in Zone 8.

Polystichum monticola (mountain loving), the mountain shield fern from high-elevation exposed rocky mountainsides in South Africa, is a bipinnate to tripinnate evergreen with arching fronds of up to 30 in. (75 cm). The stipes are covered with rusty scales distinguishing it from *P. alticola*. Despite its provenance, it prefers light shade in Zones 8 and 9.

Polystichum multifidum (much divided) is an evergreen from South America with broadly lanceolate tripinnate to quadripinnate 2-ft. (60-cm) fronds. **Var. *multifidum*** is densely scaly and **var. *pearcei*** is sparsely scaly. The species and its hybrid with *P. chilense* are attractive shadelanders for Zones 7 to 9 or, with substantial mulch, Zone 6.

Polystichum ovato-paleaceum (ovate scales) is a close relative of *P. retroso-paleaceum* and similar to it except for having large upward-pointing ovate scales on the upper stipes and rachis that are not adpressed downwards. (Think standing ovation!) It is from Japan and Korea and has been successfully propagated and cultivated in Pacific Northwest gardens in Zone 8.

Polystichum piceopaleaceum (black scales) is a 2- to 3-ft. (60- to 90-cm) evergreen from the Himalayas, Japan, China, and eastern Asia with lanceolate bipinnate bright blue-green blades. The botanists distinguish it from the very similar *P. yunnanense* by the presence of three color types and sizes in the stipe scales of *P. piceopaleaceum* (Khullar 2000). In addi-tion, *P. yunnanense* has small but visible cavities above each sorus on the upper frond surface. (To add to the confusion they hybridize with each other.) Both are separated from *P. discretum* on the basis of having broad scales rather than nar-row, linear ones. All do well in light shade and good soil in Zones 6 to 8.

Polystichum ×*lonchitiforme* in the Jessen garden.

Polystichum ovato-paleaceum surrounded by the yellow spring flowers of *Epimedium* ×*versicolor* 'Sulphureum'.

Polystichum ×*meyeri* in the Kohout garden.

Polystichum piceopaleaceum

Polystichum plicatum (plaited), synonym *P. mohrioides*, comes from high elevations in the Andes. Fronds grow to 1 ft. (30 cm) tall with one-third being scaly stipes. Blades are ovate-lanceolate and bipinnate. Here is a species for rock garden type culture in partial shade, with good drainage, in Zones 7 to 9.

Polystichum ×potteri (after Potter), Potter's holly fern, is a sterile hybrid between *P. acrostichoides* and *P. braunii*. From North America, it brings with it the soft-textured influence of the *P. braunii* parent, albeit with longer stipes and a less tapered blade. With 2-ft. (60-cm) evergreen fronds, it is hardy and especially welcome in the colder regions upwards from Zone 3, although, like *P. braunii*, it is unsuitable for humid and hot gardens. It should acclimate wherever *P. braunii* flourishes.

Polystichum prescottianum (after Prescott), Prescott's holly fern, is a compressed soft green alpine about 1 ft. (30 cm) in height. The fronds grow in upright clusters in partially sunny high-altitude exposed rocky sites in the Himalayas, Taiwan, China, and Afghanistan. The blades are pinnate and the very short stipes are scaly. Although very rare in cultivation this would be a charming specimen for close viewing in a container or alpine trough in Zones 6 to 8.

Polystichum pseudo-makinoi (false *Polystichum makinoi*) is a 2- to 3-ft. (60- to 90-cm) evergreen from the mountain forests of Japan and China. The stipes are covered with dull brown scales. Blades are oblong-lanceolate and bipinnate. They are not shiny. German specialists have been successfully cultivating this in Zones 6 to 8. It hybridizes with *P. tagawanum* to form the stunning *P. ×kiyozumianum*.

Polystichum semifertile (half fertile) is a lowland Asian and Himalayan evergreen that has been grown successfully in England. The fronds are evergreen and up to 18 in. (45 cm) in height with the lower stipe portions covered with tan-trimmed black scales. The blades are lanceolate and bipinnate with unusual "fertile" fronds that are described by Christopher Fraser-Jenkins (1997b) as being one-third to one-half sterile. The species is growing in England and should do well in Zone 9 or protected Zone 8.

Polystichum stimulans (stinging), synonym *P. ilicifolium*, is a small, 1-ft. (30-cm) evergreen with very narrow 1-in. (2.5-cm) holly-like, leathery pinnae on once-pinnate blades. This alpine from eastern Asia and China but not Japan is recommended for lightly shaded rock gardens in crumbly soil. It is similar to *P. stenophyllum* but is copiously bristly. The lower pinnae do not aim downwards.

Polystichum thomsonii (after Thomson) has a lax rosette of fronds under 1 ft. (30 cm) tall and is a diminutive species for scree and lightly shaded rock habitats. The stipes are only sparsely scaly, and the narrow, once-pinnate blades have asymmetrical pinnae that are flat on the basal sides and lobed on the upper. The entire frond is fertile with large indusia. Coming from alpine territories in China, it should be tested in gardens in Zones 7 and 8.

Polystichum triangulum (triangular), synonym *P. echinatum*, is a small fern that is recommended for Zone 9 and possibly Zone 10. It is from South America and the West Indies and most attractive with shiny diamond to triangular-shaped pinnae. If it is not suitable for your garden, try it as a house-plant where, with fronds up to 18 in. (45 cm), it is showy, manageable, and unusual. It can be reproduced by small bulbils on the frond tips.

Polystichum wilsonii (after Wilson) is so densely scaly in new growth that some authors compare the crosiers to curled caterpillars. Evergreen fronds are 18 to 24 in. (45 to 60 cm) tall with scaly stipes and lanceolate, bipinnate blades. The species is native to rocky scrub in the Himalayas, China, Taiwan, and disjunct in South Africa. Gardeners in Zones 6 to 8 will find this adapts graciously to woodland cultivation. Toss in a rock or two to make it feel at home.

Polystichum ×wirtgenii (after German Ferdinand Wirtgen, 1848–1924) is a sterile hybrid between *P. braunii* and *P. setiferum*. It is open growing, bipinnate, and evergreen to 2 ft. (60 cm) or more with a slender stipe. From Europe, it is an interesting addition in the shade of Zones 6 to 8. (The European hybrids are well illustrated and described in detail [in German] in Hegi 1984.)

Polystichum woronowii (after botanist Georg Woronow, 1874–1931), from Turkey, the Caucasus, and Iran, is an evergreen that has pale tan-scaled, long stipes and lanceolate bipinnate blades. It is just making its first appearances in the United States where it is suitable for Zone 6 to 8 woodlands.

Polystichum pseudo-makinoi in the Kohout garden.

Compact and densely foliated *Polystichum triangulum* in the Peters garden.

Polystichum woronowii in the Gassner collection.

Polystichum yunnanense (from Yunnan) is one of the most common polystichums of the Himalayan flora, growing at mid-altitudes wherever moist soil beckons. Two-foot (60-cm) fronds are heavily black scaled at the base, but their presence decreases rapidly higher on the stipes. Blades are lanceolate and bipinnate, ranging from blue-green in deep shade to bright green when more exposed. The species is noted for dotted indentations on the upper frond surface above the position of the sori below, a feature that separates it from the genetically similar *P. piceopaleaceum*. It has been thriving in benign neglect and drought in my garden for a number of years and should succeed without fuss in the woodland shade of Zones 6 to 8.

Polystichum Hybrids

The following hybrids are cultivated primarily by German and British collectors in Zones 6 to 8. They would make wonderful additions to North American culture as well: *Polystichum aculeatum* × *P. munitum*, *P. aculeatum* × *P. proliferum*, *P. chilense* × *P. multifidum* (needs protection in Zone 6), *P. chilense* × *P. subintegerrimum* (needs protection in Zone 6), *P.* ×*kiyozumianum* (*P. pseudo-makinoi* × *P. tagawanum*), and *P. proliferum* × *P. setiferum*.

In addition Japanese combinations offer some tantalizing possibilities including, but not limited to the following selections from among 44 of their natural hybrids as listed in the *Flora of Japan* (Iwatsuki et al. 1995): *P.* ×*amboversum* (*P. ovato-paleaceum* × *P. retroso-paleaceum*), ***P. braunii* × *P. retroso-paleaceum***, *P.* ×*inadae* (*P. polyblepharum* × *P. retroso-paleaceum*), *P.* ×*izuense* (*P. makinoi* × *P. tagawanum*), *P.* ×*kasayamense* (*P. braunii* × *P. polyblepharum*), *P.* ×*kunioi* (*P. braunii* × *P. makinoi*), *P.* ×*kuratae* (*P. polyblepharum* × *P. pseudo-makinoi*), *P.* ×*kurokawae* (*P. makinoi* × *P. ovato-paleaceum*), *P.* ×*mashikoi* (*P. polyblepharum* × *P. tagawanum*), *P.* ×*microlepis* (*P. makinoi* × *P. retroso-paleaceum*), *P.* ×*okanum* (*P. retroso-paleaceum* × *P. tagawanum*), *P.* ×*ongataense* (*P. ovato-paleaceum* × *P. pseudo-makinoi*), *P.* ×*pseudo-ovato-paleaceum* (*P. ovato-paleaceum* × *P. tagawanum*), and *P.* ×*utsumii* (*P. pseudo-makinoi* × *P. retroso-paleaceum*).

Christopher Fraser-Jenkins (1997b) describes the following potentially hardy and interesting hybrids from the Himalayas: *Polystichum* ×*flemingii* (*P. discretum* × *P. yunnanense*), *P.* ×*inayattii* (*P. piceopaleaceum* × *P. yunnanense*), *P.* ×*jamunae* (*P. mehrae* × *P. squarrosum*), *P.* ×*stewartii* (*P. lonchitis* × *P. prescottianum*), and *P.* ×*tare-bjoremse* (*P. piceopaleaceum* agg. × *P. squarrosum*).

Psilotum

Psilotum (hairless) is a genus with only two species. In nature they spread across the South Pacific, Hawaii, and Africa, and in escaped colonies they are found in the U.S. Southeast and

Upper frond surface of *Polystichum yunnanense*. Note the puckered marks above the sori.

Polystichum aculeatum × *P. proliferum* in the Peters garden.

Polystichum aculeatum × *P. munitum* in the Förster garden. Photo by Richie Steffen, Miller Botanical Garden.

comparably inviting habitats. With their unusual "unfernlike" structure, they are not immediately recognized as ferns, but offer conversation-worthy additions to collections.

Psilotum nudum (hairless and naked, a bit redundant), the whisk fern, is an oddity that stretches the imagination when called a fern, but a fern it is. It features slender twigs of branching upright "whisks" without true roots or the traditional leafy adornment associated with fronds. Fertile portions are dotted with pinhead-sized triads of spore-bearing yellow pearls that are the fern's reproductive mechanism. They distribute the spores for a later, and frequently unexpected, emergence from underground incubation. This tropical species is abundant in various habitats both terrestrial and epiphytic (an unusual pairing). Visitors to Hawaii should look for it in the most unanticipated places from full sun near lava flows to elegant hotel gardens. In cultivation it is undemanding (and often inconspicuous) indoors, or, when it makes an appearance, outdoors in Zones 9 to 11. Japanese specialists have selected many cultivars.

Pteridium
Bracken ferns

Pteridium (from the Greek *pteridion*, small wing or, more often, small fern—which makes me seriously wonder about the plant author's powers of observation) is the universally recognized bracken fern. In various manifestations, all of them extremely weedy, it is worldwide in distribution, and has the honor of being the most widespread of vascular plants. Mickel (pers. comm.) jokes that they are all growing from a single creeping rhizome.

And creep the rhizome does, buried anywhere from several inches to 18 in. (45 cm) or more under ground. The deciduous fronds are usually between 3 and 6 ft. (90 and 180 cm) tall, but can be even taller. Slightly grooved stipes are the color of pea soup and up to one-half of the frond length. Blades are broadly triangular and usually tripinnate-pinnatifid with 10 to 12 pairs of very widely spaced pinnae. Sori are marginal and covered by a false indusium. Spore production, however, has decreased measurably in recent decades so many populations are sterile. Presumably they do not need to waste time reproducing from spores.

Chemically the fronds are infused with dangerous toxins. The fiddleheads, which are popular in Asian diets, are carcinogenic and responsible for much of the stomach cancer in those areas. Grazing animals are also vulnerable as the fronds are known to poison cattle, sheep, and pigs, making the bracken invasion in ranching areas, such as the hills of England and Scotland, a serious economic threat, and consequently the subject of much research. Bugs too pay a lethal price for nibbling on bracken foliage since the fronds release

Polystichum chilense × P. multifidum in the Kohout garden.

Polystichum ×kiyozumianum in the Kohout garden.

Fertile "fronds" of *Psilotum nudum* make a surprise appearance in a container planting and extend above the leafage of companion ferns.

cyanide when damaged. *Pteridium* asserts its dominance in the plant world as well. The toxins from decaying fronds repel competition from other plants by preventing the germination of seedlings. It even kills its own young. Technically this self-serving plant mechanism is known as allelopathy.

For informational balance, given its abundance (the original renewable resource?), bracken has a long and storied history of practical usages dating back to pre-Roman times. The applications were so critical that there were strict regulations regarding the timing of the frond harvest. A violation resulted in a fine and the loss of "cutting privileges." In Great Britain fronds were a portion of the required annual rent from peasants to their landlords. (Oh how wondrous it would be to take care of my tax burden by delivering a few truckloads of bracken fronds to the IRS.) In rural areas fronds were used as thatch. The insect-repellent chemical components rendered the cut foliage practical as bedding for stock and domestic animals (and in parts of the world is still used for help in controlling fleas) and, in desperation, as minimal mattresses for humans as well. It was used on the floors in the forts of Hadrian's Wall, for example.

Mold and insect damage control qualities made bracken an effective packaging preservative and their fronds were commonly used to wrap fruits, fish, and other perishables en route to market. High foliar concentrations of potash were returned to the soil as a top dressing for potato crops as well as an extremely important component in the production of glass, soap, and bleach, an "industry" that dates back to the 10th century.

This eclectic assortment of multiple uses doubtless kept the outward march of bracken colonies under control. Would that the ancient value of *Pteridium* could be put to an applied use today. Gardeners, farmers, and certainly the overseers of diminishing crop and grazing lands worldwide would joyously welcome an economic demand for their fern crop. (The one contemporary use, which I remember from my Camp Fire Girl days, is to apply the "juice" of bracken stipes to reduce the irritation from nettle stings. It works.)

As all of the above implies, uncontrolled bracken is not an ornamental addition to gardens. It does, however, often show up as an uninvited guest. Short of using a steam shovel, removing it by digging is not generally successful. Chemical sprays or diligent removal of emerging fronds eventually destroys the invasion.

Pteridium aquilinum (like an eagle, referring to the implied wing shape of the frond) is the familiar menace that establishes territorial rights throughout the world. Rhizomes circle about, producing tall fronds on long stipes with blades that are tripinnate-pinnatifid. (True to tradition, there are even crested cultivars in Britain.) The species has been subdivided into a number of varieties basically defined by the angle

Pteridium aquilinum var. *latiusculum* in Georgia.

Pteridium aquilinum var. *pubescens* in its typically weedy manifestation along the trail in the western mountains.

of attachment of the pinnae to the rachis as well as the ratio of pinnule length to width. Taxonomists are not in agreement as to their placement and the details are botanical rather than horticultural. Superficially **var. *latiusculum*** is from eastern North American and has a sparsely hairy undersurface. **Var. *pubescens*** is from the west and reputed to have a denser undercoat of hairs. Like *Equisetum*, **var. *pubescens*** was a pioneer plant on the devastated barrens of Washington State's Mount Saint Helens after the 1980 volcanic eruption. It is not a welcome addition anywhere and especially in forests, as the dried autumn fronds are a serious fire hazard.

Pteridium esculentum (fit to eat—while this is the official derivation, please be careful) is an Asian species with concentrations in New Zealand and Australia. Although tall and aggressive, it bears attractive tripinnate pinnae with atypical linear pinnules of such distinction from the western species that it is not immediately recognized as bracken. It is, however, still a weed.

Pteris
Brake ferns

The word *Pteris* is derived from *pteron*, which means "fern" in Greek as well as "wing," a definition that captures the essential silhouette of the pinnae. There are 300 or so species, cosmopolitan in distribution but mostly tropical, including, however, some that are cold tolerant. Many serve admirably as decorations in homes and offices. The rhizomes are generally erect but occasionally short-creeping. The common name refers to the resemblance of the proportionately long stipes of *Pteris* to the similarly long legs of the bracken. These stipes are ridged or prominently grooved and usually have one vascular bundle. Evergreen to deciduous blades have very few sets of widely separated long and narrow winglike pinnae with free veins. The sori surround the outer pinnae edges and are enclosed in recurved marginal tissue (making them botanical relatives of such visually and ecologically disparate species as *Adiantum* and *Pellaea*). Many brake ferns are dimorphic with slender upright fertile fronds. In addition many of the species are apogamous, reproducing directly from prothalli, which, with such proficiency, allows them to arrive unexpectedly (and not always as welcome guests) in greenhouse cultures. Growers looking for variegation will find many options among the cultivars. All are good choices for indoors, and as with most ferns they should have loose potting soil and good drainage, and not be over watered.

Pteridium esculentum spreading in the wild in New Zealand.

Low *Pteris cretica* fronds fan out in a garden setting.

Variegated foliage of *Pteris cretica* 'Albo-lineata' amid lush plantings in the Fernery at the Morris Arboretum.

Compact foliage characterizes *Pteris cretica* 'Ping Wu'.

Pteris multifida offers the garden or household light and airy slender foliage.

Pteris cretica
Ribbon fern, Cretan brake
Epithet means "from Crete."
Evergreen to deciduous, 1 to 2 ft. (30 to 60 cm). Zones 8 to 10. Dimorphic. Apogamous.

DESCRIPTION: The rhizome is short-creeping. Tall stipes of one-half the frond length emerge in green and blend to dark brown. Once-pinnate, ovate blades have two to four slightly spine-edged pairs of long linear pinnae. The lowest pair is branched with a minute stalk while the upper are sessile. The sterile fronds hover horizontally while fertile fronds are narrow and upright. Sori are under the false indusia of recurved margins.

RANGE AND HABITAT: This species grows worldwide in tropical and subtropical areas and has naturalized so extensively that the true native range is uncertain. It is found among boulders, in exposed rocky meadows, and on ledges in partial sun to shade. Although often on limestone, it does not need this association in cultivation.

CULTURE AND COMMENTS: Truly a willing plant for home and garden, ribbon fern is successful outdoors in Zones 8 to 10. Elsewhere it is one of the most popular and accommodating houseplants asking only for good indirect light, well-draining soil, and occasional, but not excessive, watering. Many cultivars acclimate with equally minimal attention.

'Albo-lineata' (white striped), synonym *Pteris nipponica*, offers bicolored green and cream contrast to the traditional monochrome of ferny green furnishings.

'Cristata Mayi' has white with green trimmed foliage and small crests at the tips of the pinnae.

'Parkeri' (after Parker) is larger than the species and a succulent, glowing, deep green.

'Ping Wu' (from near Ping Wu, China) forms a densely clustered 1-ft. (30-cm) dwarf with proportionately narrow pinnae. It is hardy outdoors in Zones 7b to 10.

'Rivertoniana' (after Riverton) has shags of fringed, irregularly cut pinnae.

'Western Hills', a vigorous 3-ft. (90-cm) cultivar from Yunnan, is hardy in Zone 7b.

'Wimsettii' (after Wimsett) has fronds divided into feathery pinnae with mild crests at the tips.

Pteris multifida
Spider brake, Chinese brake
Epithet means "many times divided."
Evergreen to deciduous, 1 to 2 ft. (30 to 60 cm). Zones 7 to 10. Dimorphic.

DESCRIPTION: The rhizome is short-creeping. Stipes are brown and one-third of the frond length. The once-pinnate sterile blade is long triangular with three to seven pairs of pinnae that have starlike forking on the basal pairs. Upright fertile fronds have narrow pinnae with sori under the false indusia of reflexed margins.

RANGE AND HABITAT: This species is native to China, Japan, Korea, and Vietnam where it grows in rocky and disturbed sites or in the ground in circumneutral soil. It has escaped in southeastern North America.

CULTURE AND COMMENTS: *Pteris multifida* is similar to *P. cretica* but has a winged rachis and very slender pinnae, while *P. cretica* is only slightly winged at the junction of the ultimate pinnae and rachis and has more substantial foliage. The two are difficult to distinguish especially as juveniles. Grow this as a houseplant or in the garden where the linear outline contrasts well with feathery foliage.

Pteris vittata
Ladder brake
Epithet means "longitudinally striped."
Evergreen to deciduous, 1 to 3 ft. (30 to 90 cm). Zones 9 and 10. Apogamous.

Pteris vittata and *Adiantum capillus-veneris* at home on the walls of the Castillo de San Marcos in Saint Augustine, Florida.

DESCRIPTION: The rhizome is compact. Heavily scaled stipes are greenish brown and one-sixth to one-fifth of the frond length. Once-pinnate blades are lanceolate, broadest above the middle, with 15 to 25 pairs of ladderlike horizontal pinnae. Marginal sori are enclosed in false indusia.

RANGE AND HABITAT: The species is native to Europe, Asia, and South America and has naturalized over a wide area of the southern and southwestern United States. It prefers limestone sites from masonry walls, such as those on historic Florida buildings, to basic rich understories in lightly forested areas.

CULTURE AND COMMENTS: The height is variable based on habitat, but this species is easily introduced to warm gardens where it can grow terrestrially or tucked into the mortar on walls. It is special for other than ornamental purposes, however, ever since it was discovered in the early 2000s that it absorbs arsenic from soil and water. It has received some well-de-

Red, white, and green blend in colorful harmony on *Pteris tricolor* at Henry's Plant Farm.

served press and wide distribution for recovery projects where it is efficiently removing toxins while remaining far more ornamental and environmentally peaceful than backhoes and steady processions of dump trucks.

'Benzilan' from China is 3 ft. (90 cm) tall and hardy in Zone 7b.

Shorter Notes

Pteris actiniopteris (sea anemone fern), synonym *P. henryi*, is an upright, semievergreen to deciduous unvariegated, 2-ft. (60-cm) species from Yunnan. The long stipes are topped with a fan of four or five slender pinnae somewhat similar in outline to *P. cretica*. With protection, this fern forms a bushy presence in the moist shade of Zones 7 and 8, adapts freely in the subtropical gardens of Zones 9 to 11, and succeeds indoors everywhere in bright indirect light.

Pteris aspericaulis var. *tricolor* (three-colored, rough-stemmed), the painted brake fern, is in the trade under assorted names from *P. quadriaurita* var. *tricolor* to plain *P. tricolor*. By whatever name, plants on the market produce 24- to 30-in. (60- to 75-cm) fronds decorated in a stunning swirl of silver, burgundy, and deep green. They mature to a less dramatic and more uniform green that retains silvery overtones looking like fronds of jade jewelry with veins of wine. Give this fern a prominent spot in the warm and humid gardens of Zones 9 to 11 or pamper it in greenhouses or the houseplant collection.

Pteris ensiformis (sword-shaped), the slender brake, is a deciduous strongly dimorphic 15-in. (38-cm) species for Zones 9 and 10 that is best known for its cultivars. 'Evergemiensis' enjoys well-deserved commercial popularity for the impact of the bipinnate to tripinnate fronds which display creamy streaks throughout the midsections of the foliage. 'Victoriae' (after Queen Victoria, 1819–1901) is more modestly colored with the variegation concentrated along the central axis.

Pteris gallinopes (chicken foot) from Yunnan is a low radiating spokelike span with masses of threadlike, dark, dull green pinnae suggestive of a horizontal Mondo grass. It is a fascinating addition as an understory in container plantings and popular as a distinctive alpine garden plant. Winter hardiness is unreliable in Zone 8 unless protected. Gritty soil with excellent drainage is as critical to success as temperature. Indoors it is a problem-free low mop-topped decoration that looks as if it should be walking around at night.

Pteris tremula (shaking), the trembling brake, is bushier than most of its more commonly available botanical brethren. It is a vigorous native of assorted borderline temperate to subtropical climates from Australia and New Zealand to the Atlantic Islands including the Azores and Canaries. This deciduous, tripinnate to tripinnate-pinnatifid, triangular species with 2- to 4-ft. (60- to 120-cm) fronds is cultivated with ease in woodland soil in Zones 9 and 10 and indoors elsewhere. It prefers more shade than most others of the genus.

Pteris wallichiana (after Danish botanist Nathaniel Wallich, 1786–1854) is a monster of a fern with fronds to 6 ft. (1.8 m) in the wild. The stipe is one-half of the frond and the blade is 3 ft. (90 cm) tall and equally broad. It is divided into three parts with an upright stalk and two lateral lower branches. Birmingham Botanical Garden's Fern Society in Alabama is testing this species outdoors (successfully as of fall 2005) in its beautiful Fern Glade in Zone 7b. Some variegated plants in the trade under this name are actually *Coniogramme*.

Pyrrosia
Felt ferns

Pyrrosias, with their unfernlike appearances, come to our temperate gardens, our contrasting subtropical comforts, and the luxury of greenhouses as felt ferns. The common name describes the coating of hairy silver stars that decorate the unfurling fronds. These will mature to a soft, felt-like, rusty blanket that persists on the fronds' undersides and protects the indusia-free developing spores.

Pyrrosia is a genus with short- to long-creeping rhizomes, with those of many species slender and wiry, while others are thick and stubby, all with matching stipes. Stipes are stiff and strong, often up to or more than half the length of the frond. Sentinels of round, elliptical or vertical tongues of simple, undivided, usually upright blades may be densely packed or widely separated as the rhizome creeps forward. The blades are clearly split by a prominent and succulent midrib, which in some species branches into linear subdivisions reaching to the margin of the frond. Netted veins, which may in turn enclose a singular veinlet (tail), are characteristic and are found between the linear veins or, when these are absent, independ-

ently. The vascular bundles are, well, presumably there given some imagination. My microscopic examination of stipe cross-sections, sacrificed from four different species, shows mostly pith. (Botanically speaking, the vascular bundles have to be present, but they are certainly not readily visible.)

As a rare occurrence, some species have what are technically known as hydathodes. These are specialized structures that secrete water, usually from the tip of a gland, and deposit a minute, telltale white speck on the upper frond surface. For identification purposes, and Botany 450 exams, look for crystals that give the frond the appearance of having been very lightly sprinkled with salt.

Sori without indusia are distributed on or between veins and often camouflaged under the protection of the stellate canopy. Spores are yellow. Most do not mature during the traditional summer harvest time, but cling to the parent until late winter. In the Pacific Northwest, droppings of yellow-gold, which could easily be mistaken for an erratic distribution of some mysterious alien pollen, are produced in late winter. Propagation is easily accomplished by division and not so promptly by spores. Spores of some species germinate readily and develop at a leisurely pace. Others germinate reluctantly and develop at an even more leisurely pace. Spores are best sown on sandy compost and the resulting plants, if any, need good drainage and partial shade.

With their distinctive, non-traditional, foliar structure these are plants to be featured in special sites. Give them a

Creamy variegation brightens the foliage of *Pteris ensiformis* 'Evergemiensis'.

coarse mix or whatever good-draining soil is at hand. I have never given mine any fertilizer. They are not demanding and, even when benign neglect leaves them in a frightening state of wilt and despair, will respond to a good drink, eagerly looking brand new.

There are from 50 to more than 70 species worldwide, depending on your botanical reference, with a native range spreading across a broad spectrum of homelands including Japan, China, the Indian subcontinent and the Himalayas, New Zealand, and Australia as well as Africa and islands of the South Seas. Explicit in this distribution description is the exclusion of North and South America. The genus name is derived from the Greek *pyrros*, meaning flame or fire in reference to the persistent, brilliant rusty hairs that decorate the fronds' undersides.

Historically, herbal remedies and medicinal properties associated with this genus date back some 5000 years and are remarkable and extensive in Asian cultures. They included multipurpose cures for many ailments. Compounds, especially from *Pyrrosia lingua* and *P. sheareri*, are still offered in contemporary Chinese medicine as remedies for assorted ills from bronchial infections and asthma to serious kidney and urinary tract disorders.

Away from the medicine chest, when used for garden enrichment, these are notable and distinguished ferns that are guaranteed to please the grower and surprise the uninitiated with their unusual silhouettes.

Pyrrosia eleagnifolia
Synonym *Pyrrosia serpens*
Epithet means "leaves like an olive tree."
Evergreen, 1 to 3 in. (2.5 to 7.5 cm). Zones 9 and 10. Dimorphic.

DESCRIPTION: The rhizome is long-creeping, producing masses of 1-in. (2.5-cm), fleshy, elliptic sterile fronds on very short stipes. Slightly taller narrow fertile fronds, say 2 or 3 in. (5 to 7.5 cm) tall, have two rows of indusia-free sori on either side of the midrib. The upper surface of the undivided pinnae is forest-green with a smattering of hairs. The undersides are coated with stellate hairs that are silver on the young fronds and fade to tan at maturity.

RANGE AND HABITAT: This extremely drought tolerant creeper comes from New Zealand. It covers rocks, walls, and trees with sheets of glorious foliage.

CULTURE AND COMMENTS: Unfortunately, in spite of its abundance, this species is difficult to establish. Fern fanciers in Zone 9 should offer it patience, dryish exposed conditions,

Dense crowds of sori under the frond of *Pyrrosia polydactyla* as seen through a microscope. Photo by Richie Steffen, Miller Botanical Garden.

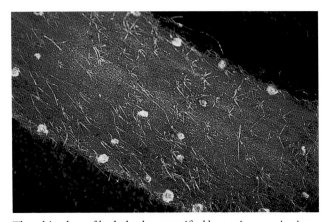

The white dots of hydathodes magnified by a microscopic view on the upper surface of *Pyrrosia hastata*. Photo by Richie Steffen, Miller Botanical Garden.

Close up of *Pyrrosia* on a *Dicksonia* trunk.

A host tree enveloped by *Pyrrosia eleagnifolia* in its native New Zealand.

and coddling. Rickard (2000) notes that it climbs about on the trunks of *Dicksonia antarctica* at Logan Botanic Gardens on the coast of Scotland.

Pyrrosia hastata

Synonym *Pyrrosia tricuspis*
Epithet means "arrowhead, three points."
Evergreen, 8 to 18 in. (20 to 45 cm). Zones 8 (with protection) to 10.

DESCRIPTION: The rhizome is short-creeping. Long fawn-colored stipes are more than one-half of the frond length and are crowded with buff scales. Both stipes and scales are a medium, misty green as juveniles. The blade is a semicircular expanse of velvet green, three- to five-lobed, palmate, foliar platters almost as wide as long. The central lobe extends well beyond the adjacent ones with the whole forming an upright, symmetrical *fleur-de-lis* pattern. Unfurling fronds are encased in silver slivers of floss, and mature fronds have an extensive undercoat of tawny stellate hairs. Look for minute deposits of "salt" that indicate the presence of hydathodes. Sori without indusia are distributed in mats on the undersurface of the frond. This species is similar in silhouette to *P. polydactyla* and can be distinguished by green stipes and midribs, whereas the latter has dark midribs especially at the point of transition from stipe to rachis.

RANGE AND HABITAT: This species clings to mossy rocks and tree trunks in the mountain forests of China, Korea, and Japan.

CULTURE AND COMMENTS: An unfernlike-looking plant, this will adapt to, and attract attention as, a large-scaled rock garden subject in warm climates. It creeps cautiously between stony crevices and needs lean soil and good drainage. It is an admirable pot plant and outstanding in basket culture. Winter protection is appropriate in exposed Zone 8 gardens.

Several cultivars, including '**Chejn Silver**', that offer visual variation and ornamental appeal are being introduced in increasing numbers by Asiatica Nursery of Pennsylvania.

Pyrrosia linearifolia

Epithet means "linear foliage."
Evergreen, 3 to 8 in. (7.5 to 20 cm). Zones 8 (with protection) to 10.

DESCRIPTION: The rhizome is creeping. Short pseudo-stipes merge gradually into the blades with the whole being shaped like a narrow paddle. The fronds are lax to procumbent and with their pubescent hairs look rather dull, but not uninteresting. Scattered hydathodes are visible on the upper frond surface. Sori without indusia are in rows of dots on either side of the midrib veering on an angle toward the fronds tips.

RANGE AND HABITAT: This small species perches on rocks and occasionally on trees in China, Korea, and Japan.

CULTURE AND COMMENTS: I have enjoyed my plant as a Zone 8 pot specimen for many years. The pot, with a modest circle of foliage, is displayed close to the basement door where, in an emergency, it can be snatched away from an impending exceptional cold spell. The plant is growing in lean, coarse soil and has spread very slowly. Small-scaled basket culture is an

Silver-frosted arrowheads of fronds of *Pyrrosia hastata* 'Chejn Silver'.

Layers of soft fronds of *Pyrrosia linearifolia* crowd together in container culture at the Miller Botanical Garden.

Bold foliage of *Pyrrosia lingua* meanders in the Fernery at the Morris Arboretum providing a handsome counterpoint for the more delicate ferns in the display.

The upright fertile fronds of *Pyrrosia lingua* in a garden setting.

attractive option but needs to be supplemented with other species in order to give a fully dressed display.

Pyrrosia lingua
Tongue fern, felt fern
Epithet means "tongue."
Evergreen, 8 to 12 in. (20 to 30 cm). Zones 7b (in warm summer areas) and 8 (with protection) to 10.

DESCRIPTION: The branching rhizome is long-creeping, often reaching and dangling well beyond the confines of a container and its attendant soil. It is rather brittle and forms a tangled web resembling an aboveground ferny cable network. The stipes are upright and distanced from one another giving the plant a spreading, open structure. However, when confined by pot or basket culture, the stipes circle and return to overlap and support a vigorous display of clustered leathery foliage. The stipes are up to one-half of the frond length, dark brown, and hairy when young. This dark characteristic continues into the midrib of the blades, but extended linear veins revert to bright green. The blades are simple and upright with a tapered, noncordate base. Indusia-free sori are crowded between the linear veins.

RANGE AND HABITAT: This species prefers a site among dryish rocks, as well as on tree trunks in China, Korea, Taiwan, and Japan.

CULTURE AND COMMENTS: I have maintained a sprawling plant, somewhat confined to a pot, but definitely accepting of benign neglect, for half a dozen years in Zone 8. It is casually nurtured in an unheated greenhouse during the winter, and the offspring, easily produced from rhizome cuttings, have survived, unprotected, the vagaries of winters with brief minimum temperatures of 18°F (-8°C). In severe situations, it can always be given a blanket for the evening lows.

Pyrrosia lingua has been generous in supplying horticulture with variations on its structural theme, producing unusual shapes that do not conform to the outlines of the species. Subtle to outlandish derivations of frond architecture include, among others, forked tips, fringed margins, and assorted combinations of both. Many of these selections come from Japan and are offered in the connoisseurs' trade under Japanese cultivar names. I might add that due to difficulties in propagation, pyrrosias in general are expensive and their novelties currently command a tidy price in the market place.

Pyrrosia polydactyla
Synonym *Pyrrosia polydactylis*
Epithet means "many fingered."
Evergreen, 8 to 12 in. (20 to 30 cm). Zone 8 (with protection) to 10.

DESCRIPTION: The rhizome is short-creeping. Upright stipes, which are pale green as juveniles and blackish in old age, support semicircles of palmate, three- to five-lobed, matte green, horizontal blades. New growth emerges cloaked in silvery, pussy foot fuzz and recedes in time with a modest sprinkling of residual hairy stars on the upper surface and an array of crowded stellate russet felt on the fronds' undersides. Linear veins extend from the midvein to the frond margin. Sori without indusia are packed in rows of dots between these outreaching veins. Visually similar to *Pyrrosia hastata*, it is segregated from that species by the dark, rather than light green, midveins that are especially prominent at the juncture of the stipe and rachis.

RANGE AND HABITAT: This delightful departure from the delicate skeletal structure traditionally associated with ferniness is an endemic species of Taiwan where it grows in habitats with lean soil and rocky supports.

CULTURE AND COMMENTS: Truly drought tolerant, this species is a novel addition to fern displays where it is a collector's prize. It must be sheltered from severe cold. In my Zone 8 garden I find it reasonable to maintain it in a decorative pot which can be offered a retreat in the safety of my unheated greenhouse during the stressful winter months. Lovers of the curious in Zones 9 and 10 can certainly cultivate this species without concern for the uncertainties of weather. It will, however, curl up with displeasure when severely underwatered but like its fellow pyrrosias, returns to life, with vigor, when rehydrated. In Zone 8, the spores do not ripen in fall, but drop like yellow dust in late winter or early spring. They are slow to germinate, but they will, and should be sown as soon as practicable after ripening. It will be many months that can easily extend into a two-year period of incubation before there will be a presentable plant to grace a 4-in. (10-cm) pot. Give it lots of grit.

Pyrrosia sheareri
Epithet is after Shearer.
Evergreen, 1½ to 2½ ft. (45 to 75 cm). Zones 7 to 10.

DESCRIPTION: The rhizome is short-creeping and not wiry. Succulent pea-green stipes are at least ¼ in. (6 mm) in diameter, covered with fawn-colored, downy stellate hairs and are one-third or more of the frond length. It is flat, but not grooved, on the upper surface. Simple blades unfurl in shimmering silver fleece and at maturity are leathery, dark green, and frequently cordate at the base. The contrasting, prominent midrib and parallel vein extensions are continuations of the green stipe color. Sori without indusia, but ringed with minute starry hairs, are abundant between the rows of veins.

RANGE AND HABITAT: In typical *Pyrrosia* fashion, this species grows on rocks and trees in Taiwan, China, and Vietnam.

CULTURE AND COMMENTS: I was given a plant in the 1980s. It was in an ornamental pot and remains so today, minus periodic divisions that have been shared as gifts. In spite of the

Starlike fingers of *Pyrrosia polydactyla* fan out horizontally in a gathering of ferns in containers.

An airy canopy of the linear leaves of *Acer palmatum* 'Koto No Ito' filters the light over the sturdy young fronds of *Pyrrosia sheareri*.

vulnerability of pot culture, this specimen has survived as a strapping plant through winter cold temperatures that plunged to below 10°F (-12°C). With its unconventional appearance, it is a center of attention for visitors, but kindly needs little in the way of attention from the gardener. Porous, humus-rich soil, an occasional nip from the hose, and an annual trimming of spent foliage keep it in good health and display-ready. The snowy dusted new growth is especially beautiful against the backdrop of the previous year's forest-green fronds. Wherever it is planted, be it a container or garden site, it will serve artfully, and with low maintenance, as a focal point and/or a counterpoint for more delicate companions. Spores mature here in late winter, casting billows of yellow powder on the surrounding foliage. They are best sown when fresh. Unfortunately, while they produce a nice layer of prothalli, very few of these develop into sporelings. And those few sporelings take their time, as in two years or so, to make a 6-in. (15-cm) plant. Although the plant spreads slowly, it can be divided. Expect a waiting list of interested friends.

Shorter Notes

Pyrrosia piloselloides is a miniature polypod fern with the outsize charm found in most small things that give us no harm or fright. Native to India, Malaysia, the Philippines, Indonesia, and New Guinea, it inhabits mossy tree bark in old-growth forests, spreading closely upon the moss, standing no taller than its co-epiphyte. Its sterile fronds are rounded, more or less ½ in. (13 mm) across, while its fertile fronds are of the oar shape typical of pyrrosias but in this species scaled small, suiting the plant. It is an easy grower in pots filled with horticultural granola (a coarse and crunchy mix) or as a mounted display. (Description by George Schenk.)

Pyrrosia rasamalae is native to Sumatra, Malaysia, Java, Borneo, and Luzon, where it inhabits outcrops, forest trees, road cuts, and trail banks, in part shade. The roots form a pad that fans out shallowly on stone, bark, or soil. The pad is easy to peel off its original place, together with the humus affixed to the roots, and is easy to re-establish by wiring it to a shingle cut from a harvested tree fern trunk. This species is engaging for its slim, foot-long (30-cm) leaves covered, while they grow out from the plant's base, with a down remindful of peach fuzz, a down softly yellow at first, then frost-gray. The maturing frond drops its fuzz, revealing a surface that is glabrous and olive-green. (Description by George Schenk.)

The miniature *Pyrrosia piloselloides* growing on a tree fern shingle hung on a door where it receives nearly day-long shade. Mounted four years previously, the fern colony now fairly covers the mossy 7-in. (18-cm) square shingle. Photo by George Schenk.

New and old fronds of *Pyrrosia rasamalae* displayed on a shingle mounting. Photo by George Schenk.

Quercifilix

Quercifilix (*querci*, oak, *filix*, fern) is a genus with but a single species.

Quercifilix zeylanica (from Ceylon) is a chubby ground-hugging evergreen species suitable for indoor pot culture or, with its creeping rhizomes, as flooring in the conservatory. The 6-in. (15-cm) sterile blades are three-parted. The extended oak-shaped undivided but lobed terminal pinnae is flanked like a dagger with a lower pair of outward-pointing matching pinnae. Fertile fronds are upright and slender, usually looking wilted. This species is appropriate outdoors in Zones 9 and 10 or in greenhouses and not overly humid terrariums elsewhere.

Rumohra

Rumohra was named in honor of Karl von Rumohr (1785–1843), an artist from Dresden, Germany. The species, numbering from one to eight, are Southern Hemisphere natives.

The recognized species of distinction, ***Rumohra adiantiformis*** (resembling maidenhair, a rather peculiar and in-appropriate comparison), is the leather leaf fern whose fronds are those familiar glossy, forest-green adornments that give the finishing touch to flower arrangements (and will long outlive the flowers). The lustrous and "leathery" variable evergreen foliage springs from creeping rhizomes. Grooved, shiny, rich green stipes with a smattering of pale russet scales are up to one-half of the frond length. The broad triangular blades are bipinnate to tripinnate and have pinnules with serrate margins. Sori, when present, are medial and have a peltate indusium. Height, from 1 to 3 ft. (30 to 90 cm), and configurations vary considerably and range from compact specimens in sunny high elevations in its native Chile to elongate wands in the deep shade of moisture-rich North American gardens.

The species is hardy in Zones 8 to 10, although it may lose foliage in cold winter areas. My Zone 8 plants have been thriving without protection ever since a long ago day when I became frustrated while trying to divide plants from a wooden flat overgrown with masses of rhizomes and fronds and in desperation "planted" the entire flat into the garden. Grow it in filtered shade and average compost and welcome the foliage

Quercifilix zeylanica in the Fernery at the Morris Arboretum.

Rumohra adiantiformis spreads gently with rich, low foliage in shades of deep green in the Duryee garden.

Truly leathery fronds of *Rumohra* growing in volcanic rubble in a fully exposed site in Chile. Photo by Richie Steffen, Miller Botanical Garden.

into the vase and boutonnière. Away from warmer climates, the species can be grown as a houseplant. It will need good light to keep from becoming leggy and space to stretch its lustrous foliage.

Economically, leather leaf fern fronds are of great commercial significance as a cut foliage crop with an epicenter in Apopka, Florida, as well as developing sites in Central America. Enthusiastically received by the public upon their introduction in the early 1900s, the long-lasting, glowing, dark green fronds replaced *Asparagus setaceous* (often referred to as *A. plumosus* or simply "plumosus") as Florida's leading foliar export well before midcentury. Sales reached their zenith in the 1980s with a 1984–85 wholesale value of $86,000,000. Subsequently, the devastating effects of assorted hurricanes reduced production so that the 2004 profit was $47,000,000. The industry's recovery is well under way, however, with artificial shade structures replacing the natural shade, and sun-loving substitutes, such as *Equisetum hyemale*, joining the cut foliage business.

Sadleria

Sadleria is named for Joseph Sadler (1791–1859), a physician and fern scholar from Hungary. There are six species, some common and some rare, but all endemic to the Hawaiian Islands. In the flowing, musical language of those islands, several species are known as 'ama'u, ma'u, ma'uma'u, and pua'a 'ehu 'ehu, some with religious significance.

The most familiar species is ***Sadleria cyatheoides*** (like *Cyathea*) with magnificent arching fronds that grace the islands' landscapes from moisture-laden skylines to the destitute, freshly distributed lava flows where it is an industrial strength pioneer (and considerably smaller in stature). Stunning, and apparently perpetually appearing, new growth emerges in brilliant red tones and becomes an equally attractive bright green with pale undersides at maturity.

The rhizomes creep and/or form small upright trunks. Straw-colored, grooved stipes have a complement of tapering, uniformly tan scales at their base. (Of the other more commonly encountered sadlerias, ***Sadleria pallida*** has scales with a dark center, and *S. souleyetiana* has a mass of papery scales that may or may not have a dark center. On all three species the scales are confined to the bases of the stipes.) The blades on the up to 5-ft. (1.5-m) fronds are pinnate-pinnatifid to occasionally bipinnate on larger lower pinnae, with 30 to 60 segments per pinna. Perished fronds droop around the trunks like discarded, silvery skirts. The genus is closely related to

Sweeps of *Sadleria* fronds and deep blue, clear tropical skies paint a memorable picture on a mountain top in Kauai.

Warm red unfurling *Sadleria* fronds are framed by their rich green mature foliage.

Blechnum as evidenced by the position of the linear sori, which extend with inward-opening indusia along the midribs of fertile pinna.

This marvelous and showy tropical can be cultivated in frost-free areas in fast-draining, mineral-rich, and especially volcanic soils. The species grows throughout Hawaii where wind-borne mists (and yes, rain), so typical in their island habitats, keep the large fronds brilliant and healthy. Even the stubby, tenacious invaders that emerge from volcanic cracks like grass in sidewalks appreciate the refreshing, cooling vapors that drop from passing or encompassing clouds.

Patient hobbyists in the Greater Seattle area have tried without success on many wishful occasions to introduce plants in comfortable and suitable microclimates. *Sadleria* produces spores erratically. Please do believe the tales that tell of sporelings, and potential sporelings, in promising production stages being resentful of any root disturbance. They collapse even when transferred from the highly encouraging initial cultural mass to matching conditions. An upgrade to a 4-in. (10-cm) pot plant is a major success, and often a fleeting one at that.

Salvinia

Salvinia (in honor of Antonio Salvini, 1633–1722, an Italian professor of botany) is a water fern genus, "water spangles" in the vernacular. The plants float in calm and warm, sunny waters. With their clusters of deciduous, rotund fronds, they look like water critters swept about and kept afloat by armies of submersed rootlike strands of foliar tissue (that are actually leaves in disguise). The upper frond surface has water-repellent hairs, and their configuration helps to define the differences between species. Some species are ornamental. Others are invasive. Cultivate the good ones in aquariums and, depending on the cold tolerance, in water features in Zones 6 to 10.

Salvinia minima (smallest) is semihardy in Zones 8 to 10. This small species has petite ¼- to ½-in. (6- to 13-mm) round leaves topped with freestanding hairs. It is from the U.S. Southeast and ranges down through Mexico to South America.

Salvinia individuals float in an ignored barrel behind a nursery.

Youthful plants of *Sadleria cyatheoides*, shown in this year 2000 photo, pioneer through the remains of a 1982 lava flow in Hawaii's Volcano National Park.

Salvinia natans crowds the surface of a water feature in the Stobbe garden.

Curlicues of *Schizaea pulsilla* in a botanically fascinating peat bog in the New Jersey Pinelands.

Salvinia molesta (annoying), which has closed "eggbeater" hairs, is, in keeping with its name, a serious threat to the health of many waterways in the world, with severe consequences for local populations. The spread has been partially brought under control by the appetite of a *S. molesta*–specific weevil. It is illegal to import or plant this in the United States and most countries of the world. *Salvinia auriculata* (ear-shaped) is somewhat similar to *S. molesta*. It is against the law to plant this as well.

Salvinia natans (floating) from Europe and Asia is the hardiest of the lot. Fronds are oblong and hairs are free. It is a novelty for pond and container surfaces in Zones 6 to 10.

Schizaea

Schizaea (cut fronds) is a genus of 20 species with native populations concentrated in the eastern U.S. pinelands and in boggy habitats in South America and the South Pacific including New Zealand and Australia.

Schizaea pusilla, the curly grass fern, is noteworthy not as a candidate for the landscape but as an exotic attraction for curious plantfolks and botanical tourists in the Pinelands of New Jersey, Long Island, and similar but more isolated sites on the eastern North American seaboard. Minute squiggles of curled threads, most certainly unrecognizable as fern fronds, swirl in wet peat bogs in the company of exotic orchids and assorted showy, carnivorous companions. The tiny 2- to 4-in. (5- to 10-cm) fertile heads, appearing in midsummer, stand upright and look like the closed petite jaws on a Venus fly trap (*Dionaea muscipula*). A good viewpoint for visitors is at the Websmill Bog site in southern New Jersey.

Selaginella

Selaginellas have traditionally been known as fern allies because, like ferns, they have a vascular structure and reproduce by spores in a life cycle similar to that of true ferns. Historically, the "true" ferns have been segregated because of their complex vascular systems that branch and form chains whereas the "fern allies" have a set of simple vascular ducts, one of which runs to each "leaf." Lacking the flowers and seeds of "higher" plants, they were, however, believed to be closely related. Meanwhile, research using sophisticated DNA techniques, fossil analysis, and computer algorithms is leading to some revolutionary revisions in evolutionary data and concepts (H. Schneider et al. 2002). The reorganization shows that the "allied" *Selaginella*, *Isoëtes*, and fellow lycophytes descended quite independently from traditional fern ancestors and are not relatives after all. They do, however, share some cultural characteristics and are included here as attractive diversions for garden and container highlights for fern lovers.

Worldwide there are 700 to 750 species (often called spikemoss because of their narrow, stalked structure) with many being native draperies of the tropics while others cling to exposed rocks or forest floors in temperate areas. The name comes from the combination of *ella*, little, with *selago*, a species now classified as *Huperzia selago*. The branching configurations of these species vary from creeping mosslike carpets and small brambles of wiry spikes to upright candelabras of leafage. Their leaves, often termed "microphylls," are composed of a single vein or midrib and are often scalelike and overlapping, forming densely woven threads of tiny foliage.

Technically, spores are of two types (heterosporous): megaspores that typically number only four per sporangium and microspores with 1000 to 2000 per sporangium. They are carried in separate sporangia in specialized cones tucked in the leaf axils at the branch ends of the small, simple fertile leaves. Consequently spore propagation is a laboratory process and not a practical option for the gardener. By contrast, division is an easy procedure. Creeping types, such as *Selaginella kraussiana*, have their forward tips followed immediately by an armada of fresh roots ready for separation. Others can be divided in the same manner as true ferns, by cutting away a portion of the plant that includes both a growing tip and some roots.

Successful cultivation depends on emulating the plant's natural habitat—terrariums for the tropicals, screes for the xerics, and moist compost for those from forest floors. Spreading ground covers can take hold in partially shaded woodlands; however, the noncreepers and xerics, with many growing extremely slowly, are best suited for close-up viewing and display in containers. I paid a king's ransom for a thumbnail-sized piece of a rare species back in 1997. Eight years later it is barely pushing a diameter of 4 in. (10 cm). Since these species can be very difficult to identify, handy opportunities for close inspection help.

German *Selaginella* expert George Hieronymus (1845–1921) listed an assortment of folk uses (1900) for the genus. They range from applications as a blood purifier on Reunion Island, as a cure for sick dogs in Mauritius, and as an aphrodisiac (*S. convoluta*, for the curious) in the East Indies. Currently Chinese medicine recommends *Selaginella* extracts for cirrhosis of the liver and hepatitis as well as for purported, overall antiviral properties.

Selaginella apoda
Meadow spikemoss
Epithet means "without a foot, stalkless."
Evergreen, creeping. Zones 6 to 9.

DESCRIPTION: The ground-hugging stems creep and branch, forming loose colonies of green mats. It is of significance in botanical keys that there are two types of flat leaves arranged in four ranks and not bristle-tipped.

RANGE AND HABITAT: This species is native from New England to the Gulf states. It enjoys the comforts of meadows and swamps, but has a predilection for showing up and spreading about in damp depressions in lawns.

CULTURE AND COMMENTS: Away from lawns, this species can be added as a ground cover in moisture-rich areas of gardens or as a finishing touch in container plantings.

Selaginella borealis
Epithet means "of the north."
Evergreen, 2 to 6 in. (5 to 15 cm). Zones 3 to 8.

DESCRIPTION: Small, tightly woven, thin threads of dark green braided foliage zigzag with airy twigs of scattering branches. The stalks are short and grow from slowly creeping wiry underground stems.

RANGE AND HABITAT: This is primarily a native of extremely cold habitats from China through Mongolia to Russia. There it grows on the exposed steppes adjacent to Lake Baikal, which at 5720 ft. (1720 m) is the world's deepest lake. In spite of this stressful northern location, and because of the moderating temperatures created by the lake, there is little or no winter snow cover. Therefore, the native plants of the surrounding areas are small and very tough weather-resistant cushions.

CULTURE AND COMMENTS: Here is a dwarf charmer for the foreground or focal point in a container. It would be lost in a garden setting. Surprisingly, it has behaved quite respectably in

The branching, wiry foliage of the creeping *Selaginella borealis* forms a small, expanding patch in the Jessen rock garden.

my humid greenhouse where I placed it to encourage new growth (both top and root). Horticulturally promising, it is equal to *Selaginella sanguinolenta* var. *compressa* in structure and ornamental appeal.

Selaginella braunii

Braun's spikemoss, Chinese lace fern, arborvitae fern
Epithet is after German professor Alexander Braun (1805–1877).
Subevergreen to evergreen, 6 to 18 in. (15 to 45 cm). Zones 6 to 10. Dimorphic.

DESCRIPTION: This upright arborvitae-type species has spreading, miniature, fernlike branches. The triangular, horizontal blades are somewhat hairy with scalelike, compact leaves. On the U.S. West Coast, plants could easily pass for young seedlings of western red cedar (*Thuja plicata*).

RANGE AND HABITAT: Frequently associated with southeastern U.S. habitats, this species is actually from China and India.

CULTURE AND COMMENTS: Braun's spikemoss offers a design counterpoint as a contrasting small understory in the company of bold shade lovers from hostas to pulmonarias, asarums, and even fellow fern types. Exceptional cold will take a toll, how-

The upright foliage of *Selaginella braunii* imitates that of a miniature or seedling conifer, in the Guymon garden.

ever, leaving brownish foliage until the arrival of new spring growth. Meanwhile, it is easily established in loose loam and maintained with the same attention to watering and shade as its companions. Among the nonxeric, nontropical selaginellas, this is one of the best for an all-purpose upright display and is quite capable of handling hot and humid summer stress.

Selaginella douglasii

Douglas's spikemoss
Epithet is after David Douglas (1798–1834).
Evergreen, creeping. Zones 6 to 8.

DESCRIPTION: Prostrate, branching stems form mats of shiny green carpets with papery, round-tipped lateral "leaves" that with age will turn brown and have a red spot at their base, and green median leaves with pointed tips.

RANGE AND HABITAT: Native populations are confined to partially shaded rocks, mossy crags, and riverbanks in Washington, Oregon, and Idaho. With its glossy foliage, this spikemoss is not likely to be confused with other native species.

CULTURE AND COMMENTS: This reserved creeper can join the refined complement of container garden displays as a showy ground cover. Keep it moist.

Selaginella involvens

Tree spikemoss
Synonym *Selaginella caulescens*
Epithet means "enveloping."
Evergreen, 6 to 12 in. (15 to 30 cm). Zones 6 to 9.

DESCRIPTION: The rhizome creeps, bearing upright "frondlike" spikes of dense, overlapping needlelike leaves that are more scaly than leafy. The lower portion of the mahogany-colored stem is without foliage for one-fourth to one-half of the "frond" length. Upper portions have widely spaced alternate branches.

RANGE AND HABITAT: This is native to tropical Asia, China, Japan, and Korea where *Flora of Japan* (Iwatsuki et al. 1995) reports that it grows in mud, on rocks, and in moss on tree trunks.

CULTURE AND COMMENTS: Material in commerce in the United States forms a small arboreal-like decoration in partial shade and loose soil. It is slightly more difficult to establish than the comparably upright *Selaginella braunii*.

Selaginella kraussiana

Epithet is after Christian Krauss (1812–1890), the German naturalist who collected the type plant in Africa.
Subevergreen to evergreen, creeping. Zones 7 to 10.

DESCRIPTION: Long-creeping, prostrate, branching stems are bright green with sprays of lighter green fanlike foliage leading the forward edges outward. The main stems and branches are trimmed with small foliar spikes of two different sizes. Translucent roots are promptly produced under the entire expanding carpet.

RANGE AND HABITAT: Originally from Africa, this species has spread from there to the far reaches of temperate zones including Europe, North America, and New Zealand. It has escaped from cultivation here and there along the way including New Zealand and the U.S. Southeast. It can become weedy and invasive.

CULTURE AND COMMENTS: This is an easily established walking ground cover in moist shady understories where it will spread under (and sometimes over) the companion ferns. In severe winters it turns a ghastly gray, but rejuvenates, like the rest of us, with the arrival of spring. In greenhouses, beware, as it can take control in moist pots and flats. Fortunately it is easily removed and transferred to a more appropriate location.

'Aurea' (golden-yellow) has lime-green rather than kelly-green foliage.

'Brownii' produces small round rosettes of green posies. It is extremely attractive, but not as hardy as the type and best in protected Zone 8 or better yet Zones 9 and 10.

'Gold Tips' has bright golden-tipped foliage producing an attractive two-toned mat.

Selaginella moellendorffii
Gemmiferous spikemoss
Epithet is after Otto von Möllendorf (1848–1903).
Evergreen, 6 to 15 in. (15 to 38 cm). Zones 6 to 10.

DESCRIPTION: This branching, lax upright creeps, with non-invasive good manners, in woodland litter where it forms a small colony of treelike triangular foliage. Approximately one-third to one-half of the reddish stem is naked. Above that the stem is green and 10 to 15 branches subdivide into small twigs of compressed linear leaves. In mature plants the ultimate branch tips produce gemmae (small conelike fertile structures), which drop and sprout in favorable conditions (especially in greenhouses). Foliage color varies from spring greens to the warm reds of fall in cooling weather.

RANGE AND HABITAT: From China, Taiwan, the Philippines, and Vietnam, this species inhabits partially shaded hillside slopes.

CULTURE AND COMMENTS: Loose, friable soil is the best choice for encouraging gemmiferous spikemoss to spread. It likes partial shade, is not drought tolerant, and will burn in too much sun. Mulch is necessary to preserve the evergreen character in the cold temperatures of Zone 6 gardens. Otherwise, it will die down for the winter, but rejoin the garden community in the spring.

Selaginella oregana
Oregon spikemoss
Epithet means "from Oregon."
Evergreen, hanging epiphyte. Zones 5 to 8.

DESCRIPTION: Oregon spikemoss drapes from trees and is often referred to as (and believed to be) a hanging moss, in the rain forests of Washington State's Olympic National Park. ("It is not likely that one in a hundred knows that it is not a moss" [Frye 1934].) Trailing, stringy foliage, sometimes reaching a length of 2 ft. (60 cm), readily extends along the trunks and branches of host trees shrouding them with curtains of greenery. The threadlike *Selaginella* branches are rounded with spiraled leaves all of one type.

The ground-hugging *Selaginella kraussiana* establishes quickly and spreads rapidly.

Shades of red and green vary with the seasons and weather on *Selaginella moellendorffii*.

Mosslike curtains of *Selaginella oregana* fall like garlands from the tree branches in the rain forest of the Hoh Valley in Washington State's Olympic National Park.

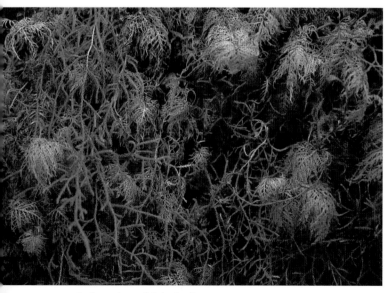

A close view of *Selaginella oregana*.

Selaginella uncinata dresses in unusual metallic-blue foliage.

RANGE AND HABITAT: This species is native to coastal British Columbia extending south to California, with concentrations in fog belts and high-rainfall areas. The Olympic National Park, for example, gets more than 140 in. (350 cm) of rain per year, which is pure luxury for encouraging the growth of the Oregon spikemoss. It thrives in the deep shade and, like *Polypodium glycyrrhiza*, it festoons the big leaf maple (*Acer macrophyllum*) and red alder (*Alnus rubra*). A journey up the park's Hoh River valley leads to a lush display of this pendant native, where joining with mosses, it wraps the visitor in a magical imitation of prehistoric forests.

CULTURE AND COMMENTS: Because of its demand for high and constant humidity, this species is not normally grown in an average garden. In addition, and with reason, it is rarely available commercially so is a plant to be observed and admired (and definitely photographed) in its native site. Meanwhile, please choose from other selaginellas for legitimate and potentially successful additions to the garden's rare plant collection.

Selaginella uncinata
Peacock fern
Epithet means "hooked, barbed."
Subevergreen to evergreen, prostrate. Zones 6 to 10.

DESCRIPTION: Creeping and branching stems create extended mats of stubby overlapping segments of iridescent electric-blue to blue-green foliage. The plant roots easily as it travels about.

RANGE AND HABITAT: Although native to China, this species has escaped in the southeastern tier of the United States. It needs moist shade.

CULTURE AND COMMENTS: While it is generally recommended for Zone 6 and up, peacock fern can be temperamental and regularly disintegrates in the wet winters of the Pacific Northwest or excessive heat elsewhere in the range. Let it skim the surface in light soil. A happy planting is a striking contribution

Shade-enhanced red foliage mingles with the green on *Selaginella erythropus*.

of blue foliage and well worth the pampering required for getting it established as a unique and eye-catching ground cover.

Selaginella wallacei
Wallace's spikemoss
Epithet is after Wallace.
Evergreen, prostrate to 3 in. (7.5 cm). Zones 6 to 9.

DESCRIPTION: Fleshy (in moist sites) monomorphic leaves in whorls of four are tightly compressed into twiggy creeping branches with pointed tips.

RANGE AND HABITAT: This species ambles about on exposed rocks or in moist moss in western Canada and the Pacific Northwest down to northern California.

CULTURE AND COMMENTS: A very variable plant, it is compact in exposed sites and more long ranging in moist shade. It will curl up in drought but recover when rehydrated. I have one happily planted in full sun as a container companion with the xeric *Cheilanthes gracillima*. In moist shade it is easily established as a slowly spreading ground cover and combines well with native ferns such as small polypodies.

Shorter Notes
Selaginella bigelovii (after physician-botanist John Milton Bigelow, 1804–1878), the bushy spikemoss, straddles the California-Mexico border where it clings to rocks on assorted substrates. Slender green fingers extend horizontally from tawny 3- to 4-in. (7.5- to 10-cm) stems. It is reputed to be hardy in Zones 8 to 10.

Selaginella densa (crowded) is an aptly named velvety green, furry creeper native from Canada down through the backbone of the Rocky Mountains to higher elevations in Arizona. The monomorphic leaves are tan on the undersides and curl to the same color in drought. This spikemoss grows on rocks and in meadows and can be introduced in exposed, winter-dry or snow-covered sites in Zones 6 to 9. Give it lean soil and good drainage.

Selaginella erythropus (red foot) is a tropical species from Central and South America that is a spectacular addition to conservatories or deserving of a terrarium of its own. Creeping, small, dark green foliar plumes have a brilliant ruby-red undercoat. The plant thrives in humidity and low light. It has outdoor potential in humid surroundings in Zones 10 and 11, possibly Zone 9.

Selaginella helvetica (from Switzerland) is cultivated in European and British gardens where it forms a low mat of evergreen sterile leaves that support upright, deciduous fertile stalks. In winter cold the sterile mats turn reddish. The species is native to Europe extending across the Caucasus, Russia, and Siberia to Japan and China. Cultivate this in moist acid shade in Zones 5 to 9.

Selaginella martensii (after Marten) is a tender species from Mexico and Central America with an escape in New Zealand. Creeping branches form a two-toned bramble of foliage, dark green above and pale green beneath. This is a good choice for terrariums or humidity-rich Zones 9 and 10. **Forma albovariegata** has elegant white variegation.

Creamy white tones blend into green on *Selaginella martensii* forma *albovariegata* in the collection at Longwood Gardens.

Selaginella wallichii in shade, at the base of *Philodendron* 'Red Emerald'. Photo by George Schenk.

Selaginella nipponica (from Japan) with its dimorphic structure is closely related to *S. helvetica*. Both have prostrate, evergreen sterile stems and deciduous, vertical fertile stalks. Likewise the sterile material may turn red in winter while the fertile branches wither. By contrast, however, it likes sunny slopes and rocky sites rather than a shady bedding. It is native to Japan, Korea, China, Taiwan, and Thailand and is an attractive candidate for landscapes in Zones 6 to 8.

Selaginella pallescens (becoming pale) has a loosely structured triangular outline of green foliage edged with hints of white. It is an interesting variation for conservatory culture as well as an attractive conversation piece in Zones 9 and 10 and elsewhere in terrariums.

Selaginella rupestris (of rocky places), the rock spikemoss, is a tough monomorphic species that spreads on an all-terrain radius from the U.S. Midwest and Canada down to Georgia with an outpost in Greenland. It is extremely variable but can be introduced and encouraged in rock garden crags and among fast-draining rubble in troughs from Zones 3 to 8.

Selaginella sanguinolenta (blood red) is native to Siberia and Siberian-like climates in China. While the species has not been in commerce in the United States, **var. *compressa*** has been in the trade for many years. It is an extremely attractive option for rock gardeners, but gives no indication of the red

designation of the name. The material in commerce is a handsome mass of wiry tangled thread like foliage with densely compact scaly leaves. The plant should adjust with ease in Zones 4 or 5 to 9. With its minute stature, it belongs in a container with coarse soil rather than in the landscape.

Selaginella siberica (from Siberia) pushes the extremes for cold hardiness with populations in Alaska and across the Straits into Siberia and down the Pacific to Japan. It is from dry alpine areas and grassy tundra where it grows as an exposed mat. Closely related to *S. rupestris*, it differs primarily in having an abundance of marginal hairs (cilia). German specialists are growing it in their Zone 6 and 7 gardens and it should be welcome elsewhere as well.

Selaginella stauntoniana (after either Sir George L. Staunton, 1737–1801, the first westerner to note orange flavor in tea while on assignment in China [leading to what we know today as Earl Gray tea], or his son Sir George T. Staunton likewise a botanist) is an upright Asian species with plumose triangular 6- to 8-in. (15- to 20-cm) foliage atop naked chestnut-colored stems. It is winter hardy in Zones 7 and 8 but slow to venture outward with its slender rhizomes. Plant it in light shade and compost.

Selaginella tamariscina (*Tamarix*-like) has twisted stems with tightly bunched leaves forming a spiral of 2- to 3-in. (5-

Selaginella wallichii in morning sun (with afternoon shade) responds to the direct ultraviolet by compacting itself and turning bronzy. Here it forms a leafy cover on the side of a fern basket attached to a stone wall. Photo by George Schenk.

to 7.5-cm) high evergreen foliage. It is incredibly slow growing and clearly should be featured in a container situation in Zones (6) 7 to 9. In Japan the species and its many varieties are prized as bonsai specimens. It is drought tolerant and will curl and rehydrate with the appropriate weather variations.

Selaginella wallichii (after Danish botanist Nathaniel Wallich, 1786–1854) is an airily open-textured ground cover within tropical forests and wooded home lots (having arrived there as spores) in New Guinea, the Philippines, Malaysia, and India. This species romps through leaf mold on long slim stems and sends up, to a foot (30 cm) or more in height, dark green glossy foliage, ample and frondlike. The many divisions of the leaves terminate in slender cones an inch long (2.5 cm) and, as a group, rather reptilian, suggesting the claws of a monitor lizard. Easy to transplant, *S. wallichii* makes an effective ferny contrast for tropicals with big, broad leaves. It takes on a strikingly different habit in a sunny location, compacting its growth and turning bronze-colored. (Description by George Schenk.)

Selaginella watsonii (after William Watson, 1858–1925, curator of the Royal Botanic Gardens, Kew) is a monomorphic evergreen from the Rocky Mountains where it forms mats in exposed rocky cliffs and crags to shady meadows and wetlands. In cultivation give it light shade as an understory in a container from Zone 6 to 9.

Selaginella willdenovii (after Karl Willdenow, 1765–1812, an early phytogeographer and curator of the Berlin Botanical Garden), the vine spikemoss, is a spectacular iridescent blue scrambler suited for the shade and humidity of terrariums, greenhouses, or moist gardens in Zone 9. The blue conifer-like leaves branch from long rambling stems. Plants need shade to develop good color. The species is from tropical Asia, Malaysia, the Philippines, Burma (Myanmar), and Indonesia and has naturalized in Florida, the West Indies, and Central America.

Selaginella willdenovii with its pastel blue foliage is an attraction in the controlled humid conditions of conservatories, terrariums, or greenhouses or in the comparably warm and close outdoor environments of perpetually subtropical to tropical habitats.

Sphenomeris

Sphenomeris (*sphen*, wedge, *meros*, parts, in reference to the form of the ultimate segments) is a genus of 18 tropical species that have been variously classified indicating their close botanical relationship to *Odontosoria* and *Lindsaea*.

Sphenomeris retusa, a species of wide range in the South Pacific, from the Philippines to New Guinea, to the Bismark and Louisiade Archipelagoes, to the Solomon Islands and New Caledonia, is one of the world's more graceful ferns: a tuft of weeping fronds finely divided into cuneiform pinnules that recall those of certain especially airy forms of the maidenhair *Adiantum raddianum*. In the wild the species colonizes steep or cliffy ground that is moist and of clayey composition with little or no humus, in sun or part shade. The fronds hang there as lacy shields in an open grouping that covers about 3 ft. (90 cm) top to bottom. Where the fern grows in full sun, its stems and newly unrolling foliage take on an ocher-red color; the fronds turn light green with maturity. As a garden companion this species adds leavening in plantings with weightier tropical leafage. (Description by George Schenk.)

Sphenomeris retusa flourishing in a post garden (a tree fern trunk hollowed at the top and then filled with humusy soil), together with *Medinilla pendula* in fruit, and the vine *Syngonium hoffmanii*, pale green, almost white, of leaf. Photo by George Schenk.

Thelypteris
Maiden ferns

The wide-ranging populations of *Thelypteris* are the ornamentally challenged orphans of the fern community. While they can be attractively functional in supporting miles of roadside banks in the eastern United States and elsewhere, it is hard to recommend many of them for decorative value. (It is especially difficult since the very best and most handsome of the lot have been reclassified as *Phegopteris*.) However, when found in nature, they occur in abundance and it is valuable to know who they are.

They are uniformly deciduous with pale to bright green thin-textured monomorphic, hairy foliage and definitely grow from creeping rhizomes. Vascular bundles are two, and the sori are often naked or briefly covered with a kidney-shaped indusium. They come all too readily from spores (often as a "bonus surprise" in the greenhouse) and are efficiently easy from divisions. Grow them in the moisture-laden "back forty" where a quick fill of greenery is desired but not a focal point.

There are as few as 30 to as many as 1000 types worldwide, depending on interpretations and delineations of current tax-

A mist system in the fern glen at the Dallas Arboretum cools the surroundings for *Thelypteris kunthii* and makes it possible to grow a varied assortment of other temperate ferns.

onomy. Most are tropical, while six or seven are of significance to gardeners in the Northern Hemisphere.

Thelypteris comes from the Greek *thelys*, female, and *pteris*, fern, hence the common name. I would like to think that the moniker is based on the supposed slender, delicate structure rather than the aggressive nature of the genus.

Thelypteris kunthii
Southern maiden fern
Synonym *Thelypteris normalis*
Epithet is after German botanist Charles Kunth (1788–1850).
Deciduous, 2 to 4 ft. (60 to 120 cm). Zones 8 to 10.

DESCRIPTION: The rhizome is short- to long-creeping. Stipes are straw-colored, with brown hairs and hairy scales, and are one-fourth to one-half of the frond length. Bushes of pinnate-pinnatifid blades are lanceolate to narrowly triangular, and truncate with 18 to 25 pairs of narrow, furry pinnae tapering gradually to the apices. Sori, also surrounded by hairs, are medial.

RANGE AND HABITAT: This species is native to a southern tier of the United States where it grows in roadside ditches and riparian habitats. Populations extend to the West Indies as well as rare stations south through Mexico, Central America, Colombia, Venezuela, and northern Brazil.

CULTURE AND COMMENTS: With its low maintenance and heat tolerance, this easily introduced species is popular in the southern U.S. nursery trade. Use it with care in moisture-rich sites where a quick cover is welcome.

Thelypteris nevadensis
Nevada wood fern, Sierra water fern
Synonym *Parathelypteris nevadensis*
Epithet means "from Nevada" (where it is not native!) or "from the Sierra Nevada."
Deciduous, 1½ to 2½ ft. (45 to 75 cm). Zones 6 to 8.

DESCRIPTION: The rhizome is short-creeping. Russet stipes fading in color upwardly to tan are one-fourth of the frond length or less. Pinnate-pinnatifid blades, with 18 to 25 pairs of pinnae, are tapered symmetrically at both extremities and have an undercoat of golden glands. Sori are medial with a horseshoe-shaped indusium.

RANGE AND HABITAT: Contrary to the descriptive name, this species is localized in the Pacific Northwest from British Columbia south to California. It is uncommon and universally described as native to woodlands, meadows, streambanks, and moist seeps.

CULTURE AND COMMENTS: Rarely available, *Thelypteris nevadensis* forms an attractive cover in exactly the same garden situations as in nature. Unlike its brethren, it is not aggressive but instead quietly spreads on moist rocks or in misty seeps and streambanks in mossy shade.

Thelypteris noveboracensis
Tapering fern, New York fern
Synonym *Parathelypteris noveboracensis*
Epithet means "from New York."
Deciduous, 1 to 2 ft. (30 to 60 cm). Zones 4 to 8.

DESCRIPTION: The rhizome creeps and creeps and creeps. Stipes colored straw, shading to avocado-green, are one-fourth of the frond length. Upright blades, with noticeably hairy but not glandular undersides, are apple-green, pinnate-pinnatifid, and per one of the common names taper gradually at the base and apex. There are 20 to 24 pairs of pinnae with the lowest barely ¼ in. (6 mm) long. Veins are usually not forked. Round sori with kidney-shaped indusia are near the margins and absent from the tips of the pinnules.

RANGE AND HABITAT: This fern colonizes down the eastern North American seaboard from Newfoundland to Georgia and extends inland brushing midwestern states from Michigan south to Oklahoma. Look for it in moist to wet woodlands, trickling seeps on roadside banks, and swampy muck usually in acid soil.

CULTURE AND COMMENTS: Frankly this is too aggressive for most home gardens; however, the light green colonies are re-

Thelypteris nevadensis in a moisture-rich seep at Lakewold Gardens.

Fall turns the foliage of *Thelypteris noveboracensis* from green to shades of gold and yellow along the roadways of the U.S. East Coast.

freshing when viewed as a woodland understory or bordering miles of highway margins. At 60 miles (almost 97 kilometers) per hour it is easily confused with another energetic eastern native, *Dennstaedtia punctilobula*, the hay scented fern. The dual taper of the frond distinguishes it from the latter as well as *Thelypteris palustris* and *T. simulata* whose fronds are widest at their base. The general absence of glands separates it from *T. nevadensis* as well as *T. simulata*.

Thelypteris palustris
Marsh fern
Synonym *Thelypteris thelypteroides*
Epithet means "swamp."
Deciduous, 1½ to 2½ ft. (45 to 75 cm). Zones 3 to 8.

DESCRIPTION: The rhizome is long- and wide-creeping, sending up fronds at sporadic intervals. Bronze-green stipes are up to one-half of the frond length. Lanceolate blades tending towards a soft blue-green are pinnate-pinnatifid with 12 to 18 pairs of widely separated pinnae. Veins are forked. Sori are medial with a slightly inrolled margin giving the fertile pinnae a narrow outline relative to the sterile pinnae.

RANGE AND HABITAT: Mainly found tangled among weeds along the margins of lakes and swamps, and in meadows and marshes, this species needs its moisture. It is native to Europe, the Middle East, and Asia.

CULTURE AND COMMENTS: This is not a particularly decorative nor, for that matter, unattractive fern for the garden and can be used effectively (on a space-available basis) to soften the contours adjacent to bogs where it will expand at will in sun or shade. The forking veins separate this species from *Thelypteris simulata*, which, significantly, has undivided veins but enjoys a similar swampy habitat.

The fleetingly hairy American native **var.** ***pubescens*** settles and spreads on the borders of wetlands in the eastern half of the continent.

Thelypteris quelpaertensis
Mountain fern, lemon scented fern
Synonyms *Thelypteris limbosperma, Oreopteris limbosperma, T. oreopteris*
Epithet means "from Quelpart," an old name for Cheju Island, Korea.
Deciduous, 1 to 3 ft. (30 to 90 cm). Zones 5 to 9.

DESCRIPTION: The rhizome is short-creeping. Tan stipes with matching scales are one-fourth of the frond length. Oblanceolate, pinnate-pinnatifid blades, which are widest just above the middle, taper at the base. The soft foliage is downy and carries small, fragrant glands on the undersurface. Round, submarginal sori are briefly covered with indusia. (See *Oreopteris* for the European counterpart.)

RANGE AND HABITAT: While once, under one or another of its former names, considered quite extensive in distribution including Europe and western North America, this has been split and is now exclusively assigned to the Pacific Rim coun-

Thelypteris palustris in its preferred habitat of moisture-saturated, boggy pond margins.

Fall color on *Thelypteris quelpaertensis* in the Cascade Mountains of Washington State.

Thelypteris simulata, among a grouping of ferns that prefer wet habitats, thrives on a log in a New Jersey swamp.

tries including China, Korea, Siberia, and the west coast of North America from Alaska on south. It prefers strictly acid soil and a constant source of moisture.

CULTURE AND COMMENTS: Though not often seen in cultivation, as plants are rarely, if ever, available, this is an attractive species, which I particularly enjoy in its autumnal golden colors. Give it an acidic site with a consistent supply of summer irrigation.

Thelypteris simulata
Massachusetts fern, bog fern
Epithet means "resembling lady fern."
Deciduous, 1½ to 2½ ft. (45 to 75 cm). Zones 4 to 6.
DESCRIPTION: The rhizome is long-creeping. Greenish stipes are one-third of the slightly shorter sterile fronds and one-half

of the somewhat longer fertile fronds. Lanceolate blades are pinnate-pinnatifid with an undercoating of burnt orange to golden glands and a sparse smattering of hairs. There are 14 to 18 pairs of pinnae with the lowest pair flaring downwards. The veins are unbranched. Sori are small, round, and medial with a kidney-shaped indusia.

RANGE AND HABITAT: The Massachusetts fern enjoys the typical *Thelypteris* surroundings of moist, boggy, and in this case, sphagnum, substrates. Its natural spread, however, is more localized than fellow native thelypteris with the range confined to eastern Canadian provinces, New England, and disjunct sites in Virginia and Wisconsin.

CULTURE AND COMMENTS: The simple, unforked veins are a readily observable difference between the pinnae composition of this species and *Thelypteris palustris*. It is also a better mannered garden subject without the inclination to dominate the landscape. Give it a wet, peaty, and winter chilly site where it will slowly establish and behave. While it can be tested in cultivation in Zones 7 and 8, it is best in colder zones.

Shorter Notes
Thelypteris beddomei (after Colonel Richard Beddome, 1830–1911, director of British gardens in Bangalore, India) is

Glassy green foliage of *Trichomanes reniforme* glows along the woodland trails of New Zealand.

Trismeria trifoliata with its nonfernlike foliage.

an 18-in. (45-cm) creeping, deciduous species from Korea that is the counterpart in habit and spread to *T. noveboracensis* in the United States. The darker green *T. beddomei* has 30 or more pairs of pinnae compared to 20 to 24 for *T. noveboracensis.* Use it as a ground cover that intermingles with ease in wet woodland conditions in Zones 7 to 9 and probably 6.

Thelypteris ovata (egg-shaped) is a tall deciduous species up to 4 ft. (1.2 m) that produces ovate fronds from creeping rhizomes. The apex narrows abruptly. The species is native to Mexico and the U.S. Southeast. **Var. *lindheimeri*,** from Texas, has a smattering of tan scales along the undersides of the midveins, whereas the eastern variety, **var. *ovata*,** usually lacks scales.

Todea

Todea (after German mycologist H. J. Tode, 1733–1797) is a genus of two species with one being ornamentally useful in mild climates.

Todea barbara (strange), a tall species related to *Osmunda*, is from Africa, New Zealand, and Australia. The rhizome is erect and forms a trunk, which in its native habitats can reach 3 ft. (90 cm). Deep green, substantial, bipinnate fronds are ovate and are often 4 ft. (1.2 m) tall, half of which is stipe. Sori are borne in a curious fashion next to the rachis on the innermost third of the basal pinnules. Spores are green and short-lived. This is a handsome species for cultivation in Zones 9 and 10 where it likes cool shade and damp soil. Devoted collectors have tried pushing and testing its cold resilience in customized Zone 8 locations, but even with protection the plant is almost always destroyed by the first severe winter (and if that does not do it in, a following cold winter will).

Trichomanes

Trichomanes (*tricho*, hair, and *manes*, thin) is a genus of approximately 180 species. They are "filmy ferns," representing an interesting segment of the fern community with foliage that is often translucent, usually only one cell thick, and sometimes only seen in a permanent state without sporophytes.

Trichomanes reniforme (kidney-shaped) is one of Mother Nature's gifts of elegance to New Zealand where it is an endemic filmy fern and as such only one cell thick. But what a filmy fern it is. The long-creeping rhizomes produce brilliant green, round to kidney-shaped, 3-in. (7.5-cm), translucent garlands of fronds. Sori held in distinctive tubular indusia stand shoulder to shoulder trimming the pinnae margins. Often in the company of native orchids, the species forms thick curtains on trees and floors of damp forests, and carpets rocks throughout the country. It seems tolerant of most every habitat except, regrettably, those of cultivated gardens. It is a "must see" for fern lovers traveling to New Zealand. Attempts at cultivation are attended with hopeful expectations, but, as with most filmy ferns, usually result in short-lived displays of struggling and straggling bits and pieces of the desired fern. Give it instead the attention of your camera along with your respectful admiration.

Trismeria

Trismeria (divided into three parts) is a genus that, based on the sori (but not appearance), is often placed under *Pityrogramma*.

Trismeria trifoliata (the epithet also means "divided into three parts"), the goldenrod fern, could easily pass for a tall herbaceous weed, although far more of an interesting conversation piece and "must have" species for fern buffs. For those (all too many) of you who like to pronounce that all ferns look alike, this fern is for you. Woody, burgundy stipes, almost pencil thick and lightly scaled at their base, are proportionately very short—4 in. (10 cm) of the 3-ft. (90-cm) frond on my new plant. In its preferred partially sunny, natural wetland habitat, the plant will produce fronds up to 5 ft. (1.5 m) long. Three-inch (7.5-cm) pinnae, looking essentially like triparted leaves, are attached to the rachis with a short stalk. White-powdered sori are carried in narrow linear pinnae on the upper third of the frond. Introduced to the U.S. trade by Tony Avent of Plant Delights Nursery, the parent material is from high elevations in Argentina. It does spread so is recommended for contained areas in the bizarre section of the garden from Zones 7b to 10. *Flora of North America* (1993) classifies it as *Pityrogramma trifoliata* (with *Trismeria* as an option), although it is highly unlikely to be recognized as a *Pityrogramma* while in the field.

Woodsia
Cliff ferns

Woodsias are those small charmers whose early emerging, cheerful green crosiers bring the promise of spring just when winter seems totally without end. In my Pacific Northwest garden the first green coils spring forth in late winter, leading a parade of unfurling fronds that continues until the Japanese climbing fern, *Lygodium japonicum*, finally, but faithfully releases a tentacle or two in midsummer. Woodsias are small, deciduous, and rugged with the majority of their 35 to 40 species native to temperate climates, frequently alpine, in the Northern Hemisphere. Four are from tropical montane sites and a few are from temperate climates in the Southern Hemisphere.

The genus is named for British architect Joseph Woods (1776–1864). Woodsias usually grow in densely foliated clumps from compact rhizomes. The stipes, with two vascular bundles, are sometimes jointed (a diagnostic) at their midsection with fronds falling off cleanly at the break. (Unjointed species break off at various lengths.) Significantly, old stipe bases are persistent. Blades tend to be lanceolate or linear and are once-pinnate to bipinnate. The lower pinnae are often reduced in size. Unlike genera with an indusial covering on the tops of the sori, woodsias are unusual in having a star-shaped "inferior" indusium that sits under the sori like a cup and wraps it with fingers looking, in some species, like the tentacles of a hydra. Mature spores are brown.

In spite of their soft, sometimes downy appearance, these ferns generally prefer exposed rocky habitats and are amazingly sun tolerant. Consequently, they are popular, both in scale and tolerance, for use in gritty niches and screes in rock gardens. Emerging fronds should be shielded from direct sun, however, when and if temperatures are expected to dip below freezing. Soil preferences vary from basic to acid, with good drainage a requisite. All the species benefit from a top dressing of rock crumbles to prevent mud and water from splashing on the foliage. In general they are not suited for warm summer

sites. They propagate readily from spores, and after several crowns have formed may easily be increased by division.

A number of woodsias are extremely closely related visually as well as botanically and a challenge to separate. Examine *Woodsia intermedia* versus *W. polystichoides* and *W. oregana* versus *W. scopulina* for details.

Some species, particularly *Woodsia obtusa*, are superficially similar in appearance to assorted species of *Cystopteris*. Both genera are deciduous and noted for breaking dormancy early in the spring. The indusia are different, however, with *Cystopteris* sori covered with a hooded indusia and *Woodsia* indusia looking "like a napkin drawn up around a bunch of grapes" (Mickel 1994). Mature *Woodsia* spores are brown whereas those of *Cystopteris* are black. In addition *Cystopteris* usually creeps whereas many woodsias tend to be clump forming. And finally, in the author's opinion the woodsias are far more ornamental and enhance their garden value by holding their fronds well into autumn without turning ragged.

Little is reported in the literature for historical herbal and practical uses of *Woodsia*. However, their quiet sites are associated with the Greek woodland and fertility god, Pan, who enjoyed napping in peaceful places (presumably ferny ones). He was known for his rage upon being disturbed (leading, according to legend, to the term *panic*). So, we are told, step quietly among the woodland woodsias so as not to disturb Pan. (Actually this is not bad advice for peaceful woodland experiences in any era.)

Woodsia alpina
Alpine woodsia

Woodsia glabella × *W. ilvensis*.
Epithet means "alpine."
Deciduous, 4 to 6 in. (10 to 15 cm). Zones 3 to (cool summer) 8.

DESCRIPTION: This is a fertile hybrid. The rhizome is erect and covered with the stubs of old fronds. Jointed stipes are dark and one-third of the frond length. Pinnate-pinnatifid, congested blades are lanceolate with 8 to 14 pairs of triangular, fanlike pinnae. Sori are closest to the margins and enclosed in fringed, cuplike indusia. This hybrid is taller (by a little) than its *Woodsia glabella* parent and, more scientifically, different in having hairs and scales which are lacking in *W. glabella*. To compare it with *W. ilvensis*, look for three pairs of pinnules on the largest *W. alpina* pinnae versus four to nine on *W. ilvensis*.

RANGE AND HABITAT: At home in the lands of perpetual cold, this true alpine is a circumboreal cliff dweller with native populations extending across the montane screes of Europe through Russia to Siberia, Japan, the Himalayas, and higher latitudes in North America. It is frequently associated with limestone.

CULTURE AND COMMENTS: Here is an ideal diminutive for the exposed crevices of rock gardens where devoted guardians welcome it for cold and lime tolerance (as well as its intrinsic ornamental value). Give it a coarse loam, bright indirect light, a rocky top dressing, and good drainage. Scree conditions are ideal. Consistently hot climates are not.

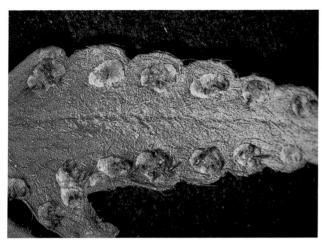

Woodsia sori as seen through a microscope. Photo by Richie Steffen, Miller Botanical Garden.

A trough with customized fast-draining, gritty soil provides an ideal home for (*left to right*) *Woodsia* sp., *Dryopteris fragrans* var. *remotiuscula*, *W. intermedia*, *W. fragilis*, and *Cystopteris dickeana*.

Woodsia fragilis
Fragile wood fern
Epithet means "fragile, brittle."
Deciduous, 6 to 12 in. (15 to 30 cm). Zones 5 to 8.

DESCRIPTION: The rhizome is short-creeping. Brittle stipes are colored a weak tea-brown grading into medium green. Pinnate-pinnatifid to bipinnate blades with wispy translucent hairs are lanceolate with 8 to 16 widely spaced, opposite pairs of pointed pinnae. The lower pairs are significantly reduced and separated from the next uppermost by at least 1 in. (2.5 cm). Bulbous sori with stellate indusia are marginal and tend to be close to the pinnae rachis.

RANGE AND HABITAT: In typical *Woodsia* fashion, this species is partial to chinks in rock faces in montane habitats, in this case specifically and exclusively the Caucasus. Unlike its relatives, its most vigorous populations are on wet limestone, which is neither required nor even welcome in the traditional fern garden.

CULTURE AND COMMENTS: My 10-year-old plants are growing, without coddling, in a deep, well-drained trough that receives late afternoon sun, water (since they are established) when convenient and necessary for surrounding plants, and little else. The jaunty, bright green, early spring fronds compete with snowdrops for rejuvenating the spirit of the garden as well as the gardener with the promise of springtime's pleasures. It is one of the easiest of these soft and leafy alpines to transfer to traditional garden sites.

Woodsia glabella
Smooth cliff fern
Epithet means "without hairs."
Deciduous, 4 in. (10 cm). Zones 3 to 6 (to 8 in coastal areas of consistently cool summers).

DESCRIPTION: The rhizome is erect and carries stubs of old stipes. The jointed, black-blending-to-straw-colored stipes are

A vigorous plant of *Woodsia fragilis* in the Jessen rock garden.

scaly and one-fourth to one-third of the frond length. The linear pinnate-pinnatifid blades, with 7 to 10 pairs of pinnae, are without hairs or scales (glabrous). Sori are in envelopes of upward wraps of indusial tissue.

RANGE AND HABITAT: This species is at home in the colder ranges of fern habitats and established circumboreally across the northern tiers of Europe, Asia, and North America as well as in their mountains. It prefers limestone-enriched crags.

CULTURE AND COMMENTS: While rarely available commercially, *Woodsia glabella* offers an attractive option for the rock garden or limestone scree and should be introduced with ease, but also with attention to the requisite partnership with good drainage and bright indirect light.

Handsome when well grown, *Woodsia ilvensis* is an excellent but sometimes challenging dwarf for a rock garden collection, shown here in the Peters garden.

Woodsia ilvensis
Rusty woodsia

Epithet means "from the Isle of Elba," of Napoleon fame.
Deciduous, 2 to 8 in. (5 to 20 cm). Zones 2 to (cool summer) 8.

DESCRIPTION: The rhizome is erect and covered with persistent stipe bases. Dark plum stipes are one-half of the frond and jointed at a node above the base. Dense clumps of lanceolate blades are pinnate-pinnatifid to bipinnate. Fourteen to twenty pairs of pinnae emerge in a cloud of silvery hairs and scales that later mature as a rusty coating. Sori are close to the margins and submerged in a tangle of hairy filaments.

RANGE AND HABITAT: Rusty woodsia is circumboreal in northern latitudes. It nests in cliff faces and rocky crevices primarily in acidic or occasionally in basic soils.

CULTURE AND COMMENTS: Like many woodsias, the rusty is a fetching option for a lightly exposed rock garden niche. However, it is also challenging. Wedge it between rocks in chunky soil. It loses its compact bushy demeanor in too much shade or wet and is not suited for climates with year-round warm temperatures. This species hybridizes with *Woodsia glabella* to form *W. alpina*, and with *W. alpina* to form *W. ×gracilis*.

Woodsia intermedia

Epithet means "intermediate."
Deciduous, 4 to 9 in. (10 to 23 cm). Zones 5 to 8.

DESCRIPTION: The rhizome is erect with bunches of old stipe bases. Slightly scaled chestnut stipes are jointed near their tops and are one-fourth to one-third of the frond length. Soft green, somewhat hairy, once-pinnate blades are narrowly lanceolate with 6 to 12 pairs of pinnae. Upper pinnae are without stalks, one of the features that distinguishes this species from *Woodsia polystichoides*. The pinnae, with shallowly lobed margins, have a prominent auricle and flare gently toward the frond apex. Sori are marginal and encased, when young, in opaque, creamy, cuplike segments.

RANGE AND HABITAT: This species is native to rocky crags in the mountainous regions of Japan, Korea, and China.

The miniature *Woodsia intermedia* showing its close visual and botanical relationship to *W. polystichoides* in the Stuart garden.

CULTURE AND COMMENTS: It is very challenging to distinguish this species from *Woodsia polystichoides* with their similar frond profile and habitat preferences. However, it is smaller in all of its parts and has fewer pairs of pinnae (6 to 12 compared to 15 to 25 for *W. polystichoides*). A perfect diminutive, *W. intermedia* prefers the gritty ground of rock garden surrounds and enjoys bright light and good drainage.

Woodsia manchuriensis
Manchurian woodsia
Epithet means "from Manchuria."
Deciduous, 4 to 15 in. (10 to 38 cm). Zones 4 to 8.

DESCRIPTION: The rhizome is erect. Russet stipes are not jointed and are very short, usually under 2 in. (5 cm). They are scaly at their base with few to no hairs or scales elsewhere. Lanceolate, pinnate-pinnatifid (and seriously close to bipinnate) blades are a pale chalky green on their undersides and bear 15 to 25 pairs of pinnae with the lowermost reduced to widely spaced stubs. Sori are close to the margins and are wrapped in a three-parted indusium.

RANGE AND HABITAT: Unlike many woodsias, this species prefers shade but upholds the *Woodsia* tradition of congregating in a cold rocky situ from Japan, China, and Korea to (of course) Manchuria.

CULTURE AND COMMENTS: Though not often available commercially in the United States, *Woodsia manchuriensis* should be introduced with ease into the shady side of the rock garden or the foreground of the woodlands.

Woodsia obtusa
Blunt-lobed woodsia
Epithet means "blunt, rounded."
Deciduous (sterile fronds may be wintergreen), 6 to 16 in. (15 to 40 cm). Zones 3 to 8.

DESCRIPTION: The rhizomes are erect as are the fronds. Tawny stipes are not jointed and are one-third of the frond. Bipinnate to bipinnate-pinnatifid blades are elliptic with whitish glands and hairs on both surfaces. There are 8 to 15 pairs of pinnae. Sori are midway between the margins and midribs and enclosed in a four-parted indusium.

RANGE AND HABITAT: Noted for its upright habit, *Woodsia obtusa* is equally at home as a vertical sentinel in mortared walls as in acidic rock ledges along the East Coast of North America from Canada to South Carolina extending westward to Oklahoma in the south and Wisconsin in the north.

CULTURE AND COMMENTS: While this species will never make a dramatic statement in the garden design, it is a dependable addition especially in the small-scaled, cold-temperate landscapes that would be overwhelmed by the towering presence of a 4-ft. (1.2-m) *Dryopteris*.

Woodsia oregana
Western cliff fern
Epithet means "from Oregon."
Deciduous, 8 to 12 in. (20 to 30 cm). Zones 4 to 8.

DESCRIPTION: The rhizome is erect. Reddish-brown stipes are darkest at their base, pliable, not jointed, and one-third to one-half of the frond length. Bipinnate blades are lanceolate with 8 to 10 pairs of pinnae. They can be naked to sparsely glandular and lack hairs along the midribs, testing the skills of the observer. Sori surrounded by threadlike filaments are medial between the midrib and margin.

RANGE AND HABITAT: While primarily a western U.S. species, populations of *Woodsia oregana*, or subspecies thereof, are reported from a disparate assortment of eastern and southwestern sites including the upper Midwest, New York, and Oklahoma. Limestone talus and screes are the common requirement.

CULTURE AND COMMENTS: Taxonomic surroundings for this species are a work in progress, which by implication means there will be some revisions sooner or later. At present it is dis-

Woodsia obtusa on the face of a stone wall in New Jersey.

tinguished from its fellow native, *Woodsia scopulina* (with difficulty), based on its lack of hairs on the midrib, a dull rather than shiny chestnut stipe, and pliable rather than brittle stipes. Meanwhile, garden attempts are short-lived. The species is offered here as an alpine to admire while on the trail. Plants should not be collected.

Woodsia polystichoides

Holly fern woodsia
Epithet means "like *Polystichum*."
Deciduous, 6 to 14 in. (30 to 35 cm). Zones 5 to 8.

DESCRIPTION: The rhizome is erect to creeping with tufts of old stipe bases. Mahogany stipes are jointed, breaking close to the rachis, and are typically one-third of the frond length. Narrow, once-pinnate, lax blades are linear with 15 to 25 pairs of

Woodsia polystichoides in the rock garden at the Bellevue Botanical Garden.

Furry foliage on the Kamchatka form of *Woodsia polystichoides* in the Peters garden.

auriculate (eared), dull green pinnae. The pinnae are stalked as opposed to *Woodsia intermedia* whose lower pinnae are stalked but grade into upper pinnae that are broadly attached to the rachis (adnate). Clear, glassy hairs are scattered on the stipes and both surfaces of the pinnae, with a noticeable trail lining the upper midribs. Sori outline the margins in a namesake *Polystichum* fashion and are encapsulated in hairy indusial cups.

RANGE AND HABITAT: This species is common among exposed rocks in the mountains of Japan, eastern Russia, Korea, China, and Taiwan. A heavily cloaked form from Kamchatka bears fronds that appear to be almost white under their protective polar fur coat of hairs and scales.

CULTURE AND COMMENTS: Easily introduced to the sunny, fern-forbidding sites of rock gardens, holly fern woodsia cheerfully cascades and meanders among the rocks and keeps company with alpine fellow travelers. My garden plants are in neutral to slightly acid grit, with slick drainage and exposure more critical than soil makeup.

Woodsia scopulina

Mountain cliff fern
Epithet means "of cliffs, twiggy."
Deciduous, 4 to 12 in. (10 to 30 cm). Zones 3 to 8.

DESCRIPTION: The rhizome is erect. Glossy chestnut-colored stipes are brittle but not jointed. They are one-third of the frond length. Bipinnate to bipinnate-pinnatifid blades, with 10 to 15 pairs of pinnae, are widest in the middle, tapering

Woodsia scopulina among mossy rocks in the mountains of British Columbia.

gradually towards the apex, but more abruptly, with reduced pinnae, towards the base. They are decorated with a smattering of white hairs and helpfully and hopefully identified by small glands. Sori are near the margins, protected by strands of underlying indusia.

RANGE AND HABITAT: *Woodsia scopulina* is quite variable and *Flora of North America* (1993) divides it into three subspecies. The primary range, however, is in the mountains of the Pacific Northwest with disjunct populations scattered through a radius of higher elevations in the south-central U.S. environs of Tennessee, Kentucky, and West Virginia and others in the Great Lakes area. All populations fancy crevices, but varied substrates.

CULTURE AND COMMENTS: Mountain cliff fern is not often cultivated and, in fact, difficult away from its alpine habitat of snow-protected cold winters and comparatively short summers. The species is a close cousin of *Woodsia oregana* and differs in very subtle variations, specifically in having shiny rather than dull stipes, which are brittle rather than flexible.

Var. *appalachiana*, which has bicolored scales, has occasionally been successfully introduced to gardens. Enjoy it while botanizing on scenic trips and trails where it shares the talus with an enchanting community of flowering alpine diminutives.

Shorter Notes

Woodsia elongata (lengthened) from China and above 7500 ft. (2200 m) in the Himalayas is short and narrow. The once-pinnate, 6- to 14-in. (15- to 35-cm) blades taper strongly at the base and have from 25 to 35 pairs of thick, hairy, lobed pinnae that are without stalks. Sori are marginal, covered with both indusia and tissue from the frond margin. While rarely available, this deciduous species is a featured candidate for the foreground among rocks in Zones 5 to 8.

Woodsia ×*gracilis* (slender), a hybrid between *W. alpina* and *W. ilvensis*, is intermediate between the two and not often in cultivation. It is from Canada and northern U.S. border states from New England to the upper Midwest. Imposters of unknown origin are occasionally in the trade under this name.

Woodsia montevidensis (from Montevideo, Uruguay) is a Southern Hemisphere deciduous charmer that deserves attention "north of the border." Sprays of elliptic foot-high (30-cm) bipinnatifid to bipinnate fronds have 10 to 12 pairs of pinnae. The pinnules hug each other, have toothy margins, and are sparsely coated with minute yellowish glands. Magnification is necessary here as, to the naked eye, the glands appear to be scales. Sori are in a three- to four-lobed cup. With populations at high elevations, to 13,000 ft. (3900 m) in South America as well as 9000 ft. (2700 m) in South Africa, this species should transition with delight to alpine gardens in North America and Europe. Plant it in the lee of a boulder in the soil of your choice.

Woodsia plummerae (after Plummer) is an upright, deciduous species usually maturing at 6 to 12 in. (15 to 30 cm). The bipinnate fronds are held on dark stipes with both stipes and blades covered with bulbous, stalked glandular hairs. The vivid green pinnae are lobed but without auricles. The species is native to California, the U.S. Southwest, and Mexico where it grows on granite or volcanic rocks. Populations in New Mexico and Arizona are difficult to distinguish from local colonies of *W. oregana*. However, unlike the latter, they transfer to rocky garden sites with only a minimum of difficulty.

Woodsia pseudopolystichoides (like *W. polystichoides*) is a stalwart Russian. Moss-green, 8- to 12-in. (20- to 30-cm) deciduous fronds are narrowly lanceolate. Ten to fifteen pairs of pinnae are almost bald with just a few scattered silver hairs. Pinnae are stalked, long triangular, and have lobes that separate into an auricle adjacent to the rachis. Sori with cream-colored, cuplike indusia trim the pinnae margins. Although this is fertile, scientists may someday determine that it is a hybrid between *W. intermedia* and *W. polystichoides*. Snuggle and treasure it among lightly shaded rocks in Zones 5 to 8.

Fronds of (*left to right*) *Woodsia intermedia*, *W. polystichoides*, and *W. pseudopolystichoides*.

Woodsia subcordata (nearly heart-shaped) is, like many of its *Woodsia* brethren, a wee mite of a deciduous fern that makes an exceptionally adaptable addition to the foreground of the woodland or partially shaded rock garden. The 6-in. (15-cm) lanceolate fronds that taper towards the base are pinnate-pinnatifid and hairy on the upper surface and both hairy and scaly beneath. With a native range that includes Japan, Korea, China, and eastern Russia, this species can be safely introduced into gardens in Zones 5 to 8.

Woodwardia
Chain ferns

The genus *Woodwardia*, while small, includes some remarkably ornamental ferns from stately giants to a pair of eastern U.S. natives adapted to inhospitable swamplands. The genus with 13 or 14 species as well as several hybrids was named in 1793 after British botanist Thomas Woodward. Native prima-

rily to north temperate zones, these species range from the United States to Costa Rica in North America, the Mediterranean area of Europe, and eastern Asia. The genus is characterized by foliage with partially netted veins and imbedded linear sori that on most species resemble links of chains or chains of sausages, earning them the common name "chain ferns." An indusial vegetative flap that folds over towards the center of the pinnae shelters the sori. All species have a preference for acid soil.

The two eastern U.S. natives, both deciduous, are noticeably different in appearance from the rest of their relatives as well as from one another. At one time they were botanically honored as members of distinct genera. The earlier names *Lorinseria areolata* for *Woodwardia areolata* and *Anchistea virginica* for *W. virginica* remain as synonyms, and, as research advances, may yet return as (so beloved by gardeners) name changes.

Woodwardia areolata
Netted chain fern
Synonym *Lorinseria areolata*
Epithet means "with distinct angular spaces."
Deciduous, 1 to 2 ft. (30 to 60 cm). Zones 3 to 9. Dimorphic.

DESCRIPTION: Slender long-creeping blackish rhizomes produce sterile fronds to 2 ft. (60 cm) tall and 6 in. (15 cm) wide with oval-triangular pinnatifid light green blades atop reddish brown stipes both approximately equal in height. The linear pinnae are mildly toothed and have netted veins. Narrower fertile fronds, which are taller and distinctively winged, follow later in the season. Slender, contracted corky pinnae enclose the sori. Indusia and spores may remain over winter. New growth is frequently reddish.

RANGE AND HABITAT: *Woodwardia areolata* is primarily a coastal species of eastern North America ranging from Nova Scotia down through Florida and sparingly west to Illinois, Indiana, and Oklahoma. It thrives in shady to partially sunny acidic boggy conditions from water's edge to drainage ditches and frequently shares the landscape with pines.

CULTURE AND COMMENTS: This extremely cold tolerant species is a natural choice for boggy areas of the garden where it will happily romp about. The Rhododendron Species Botanical Garden in Washington State has a particularly attractive pondside planting combining swampland ferns with pitcher plants (sarracenias). It does not require marshy soil, however, and will do nicely in the woodland garden albeit somewhat smaller and less exuberant with its wanderings. Although deciduous, the fronds persist well into autumn. Propagation is easy from division as well as spores. The species is sometimes confused with the superficially similar *Onoclea sensibilis*. However, the latter has wavy margined pinnae that are not toothed. Also the lowermost pinnae are not winged, and finally the fertile fronds consist of brown beadlike segments.

Chainlike sori on *Woodwardia fimbriata* in the University of California Botanical Garden at Berkeley.

Fall color on *Woodwardia areolata* in the pond area at the Rhododendron Species Botanical Garden.

Woodwardia fimbriata
Giant chain fern
Synonym *Woodwardia chamissoi*
Epithet means "fringed."
Evergreen, 4 to 8 ft. (1.2 to 2.4 m). Zones 8 to 10.

DESCRIPTION: This fern grows from a stout and ascending rhizome as a stately clump with tall arching fronds to 4 ft. (1.2 m) at the northern end of its range and closer to 8 ft. (2.4) in the mild temperatures of California's redwood forests. The greenish stipe is about one-third the length of the frond. The coarse dark green pinnate-pinnatifid blade is lanceolate and tapers slightly at the base. The pinnae with fine hairlike teeth are alternate and pointed. The chains of sori covered with a vegetative flap are parallel to the midvein and prominently visible on the upper surface of the frond. Note that the new growth is not red-toned nor does the frond sport a bulbil.

RANGE AND HABITAT: The giant chain fern is a coastal species located in moist coniferous woodlands from a few rare stations in British Columbia down through Southern California. It is especially common and impressive in the redwood forests of California.

CULTURE AND COMMENTS: Where suited this is an extremely showy specimen well deserving of a prominent place in the landscape. In cold winters it will need pampering when temperatures drop below 20°F (-7°C)—snow cover does very nicely, but conifer branches or, better yet, a cloche are more reliable. My plant is nestled in a wind-protected corner next to a brick chimney. Propagation is by spores and somewhat challenging and erratic. Spores harvested in spring or especially after a frost give better germination and even then usually produce only a lean crop.

Woodwardia martinezii
Epithet is after Martinez.
Evergreen, 18 to 24 in. (45 to 60 cm). Zones 8 (with protection) to 10.

DESCRIPTION: This species has a creeping rhizome, proportionately long green stipes, and arching pinnate-pinnatifid broadly triangular fronds. The pinnae are pointed and have minute teeth. The prominent sori are closely placed chains parallel to the mid veins.

RANGE AND HABITAT: This higher elevation native grows at 6000 ft. (1800 m) in Mexican woodlands.

CULTURE AND COMMENTS: At 2 ft. (60 cm) this is a manageable sized fern for the greenhouse, but it is worth testing outdoors in Zone 8 (if you have more than one plant) and should be reliable in Zones 9 and 10. It has not been available commercially in the United States, but is grown in Britain and Europe. Propagate it from spores.

Woodwardia orientalis
Oriental chain fern
Epithet means "from the East."
Evergreen, 3 to 5 ft. or more (90 to 150 cm). Zones 9 and 10.

DESCRIPTION: The scaly short ascending rhizome gives rise to a vase of bright green ovate fronds atop a thick green stipe that can be up to one-half the length of the frond. The blade, like those of so many woodwardias, is pinnate-pinnatifid with pointed toothy pinnae. A mature frond produces an astonishing number of little plantlets, suggestive of baby Japanese maple seeds (samaras), on the upper surface. These are directly above the soral location and will inhibit the growth of

Majestic fronds of *Woodwardia fimbriata* accented by a snag at Elandan Gardens.

A close look at a frond of the Mexican *Woodwardia martinezii* in the Peters garden in Germany.

Plantlets on the frond of *Woodwardia orientalis* var. *formosana* in the Kennar garden.

the sorus. Without these, the sori develop in the typical chain-like fashion. There may be hundreds of plantlets, the fern's re-forestation project, which will root readily when firmed onto moist soil in a humid environment.

RANGE AND HABITAT: In nature it grows in the forests of Japan, China, Taiwan, the Himalayas, and the Philippines.

CULTURE AND COMMENTS: I keep my plant in an unheated greenhouse during the winter, but this is an excellent candidate for warm areas including heated greenhouses. Fronds heavily dressed in buds tend to droop, so basket culture is ideal. Wherever grown, fertile plants are certain to be a conversation piece. Propagation is easily achieved with the buds. Give some away!

Var. *formosana* differs from the type in being slightly less cold hardy and having even larger fronds with matching ornamental plantlets that are rosy red in new growth. Use lean soil and withhold fertilizer to enhance color.

Woodwardia radicans
European chain fern
Epithet means "with rooting stems."
Evergreen, 2 to 6 ft. (60 to 180 cm). Zones 9 and 10.

DESCRIPTION: The stout ascending rhizome supports vigorously tall fronds approximately one-third of which is stipe

Rosy new growth on *Woodwardia orientalis* var. *formosana* in a container planting with *Leucothoe* at the Washington Park Arboretum.

Woodwardia radicans in the Schmick garden.

topped with a thick-textured, ovate-lanceolate, pinnate-pinnatifid blade. The pinnae, up to 20 in. (50 cm) across, are sharply pointed with small teeth. The sori with their indusial flap line the edges of the midribs, and the tips of the fronds sport one to several plantlets.

RANGE AND HABITAT: *Woodwardia radicans* grows in moist partial shade near streams and at the edges of woodlands in southern Europe. In the United States it has escaped in Florida and California.

CULTURE AND COMMENTS: This species with its imposing architectural fronds is frequently seen in conservatories where it enjoys the humidity and puts on a dramatic show often in large numbers. It can be grown from spores that are best sown as soon as ripe. The plantlets on the fronds' extremities root readily in moist soil.

Woodwardia unigemmata

Epithet means "single-jeweled," referring to the bulbil which forms at the tip of the frond.

Evergreen, 3 to 7 ft. (90 to 210 cm). Zones 8 to 10.

DESCRIPTION: A thick rhizome produces fountains of cascading fronds with a greenish stipe up to 30 in. (75 cm) and pinnate-pinnatifid blades up to 4 ft. (1.2 m) long and 2 ft. (60 cm) wide. Young fronds are a sumptuous sight of glossy red and fade in time to a deep green. The pinnae are alternate, very mildly toothed, and strongly acute at their tip and edges. The linear sori, covered with an indusial flap, follow the midribs, and their ridges are prominent on the upper surface of the blade. A bulbil (actually in some cases several) forms at the tip of the frond and will reproduce when pinned down on suitable soil.

RANGE AND HABITAT: This is a colonizer of mountain forests from Japan, China, and the Himalayas to the Philippines. An attractive undulate variety is being grown in Britain.

CULTURE AND COMMENTS: Here is the gem of the genus. As readers may have noticed I am more than slightly partial to ferns with colorful new growth and, by providing up to 6 ft. (1.8 m) of a rosy skirt, the new fronds on this species are remarkable indeed. My plant is sited in a protected niche at the top of a rustic wood retaining wall where the fronds flow downwards to the ground in a maternal effort to plant their bulbils. It has survived winter temperatures of 18°F (-8°C), but I do protect it when necessary with a blanket of light horticultural gauze. Future imports from China may prove even hardier than the Zone 8 designation. In colder areas it is a magnificent specimen for the greenhouse and is frequently seen in conservatories in Britain and Europe. Basket culture offers a handsome option. Propagation comes quite easily and

Woodwardia unigemmata in the Hardy Fern Foundation's Signature Bed planting at the Washington Park Arboretum in 2004.

Saturated, rich red new growth on *Woodwardia unigemmata*. Note also the intricate pattern of the veins.

The undulate form of *Woodwardia unigemmata* growing in the Ogden garden. Photo by Alan Ogden.

naturally with the bulbils; however, spores are reasonably willing (much more so than for *Woodwardia fimbriata*) for growers interested in a more plentiful crop. If the plant has a fault, it is that with its hanging habit it looks rather droopy on the sales shelf. Some researchers have proposed that the correct name should be *W. biserrata* reflecting differences in bulbil production between natives of eastern Asia and the Philippines.

Cascading frond of *Woodwardia unigemmata*.

Golden tones on the unfurling frond of *Woodwardia virginica*.

Woodwardia virginica mingles with other bog lovers at the Mount Cuba Center.

Woodwardia spinulosa in its native Mexican habitat.

Woodwardia virginica

Virginia chain fern
Synonym *Anchistea virginica*
Epithet means "from Virginia."
Deciduous, 1 to 3 ft. (30 to 90 cm). Zones 3 to 9.

DESCRIPTION: Erect fronds emerge from along a coarse, long-creeping and branching rhizome that frequently grows in mud or even under water. Up to one-half of the frond is a purple-black wiry, somewhat brittle stipe. The narrowly ovate blade is pinnate-pinnatifid. The pinnae, mustard-colored in new growth, are alternate and pointed at the tips but are rounded along the margins. The sori are chainlike in double rows along the midvein and can cover a large portion of the lower frond surface.

RANGE AND HABITAT: This is primarily a fern of partially shaded acidic swamps, bogs, and marshes in the coastal areas of Canada and the entire eastern seaboard of the United States as well as Bermuda. In wet areas it can take full sun.

CULTURE AND COMMENTS: Although handsome and garden worthy, *Woodwardia virginica* will migrate freely and somewhat aggressively in wet spongy areas. It is a logical choice where such a cover is welcome and useful. Conversely, with reports that rhizomes may be 10 ft. (3 m) long (or so), you may want to consider containing garden plantings. For your drier fern beds, chose another plant or water this one liberally. The species is quite unlike other chain ferns, but sterile fronds may sometimes be confused with those of *Osmunda cinnamomea*. Fronds arranged in a symmetrical crown rather than in randomly scattered growth easily distinguish the latter. Virginia chain fern also shares a habitat preference and perhaps mistaken identity with fellow aquatic *Thelypteris palustris*, which, however, does not have netted veins. It is easily grown from spores and even more easily propagated by division.

Shorter Note

Woodwardia spinulosa (with small spines), Mexican chain fern, is a large evergreen from the moist montane regions of Mexico and Central America. It is similar in structure to *W. fimbriata* and can be separated by its lax rather than upright growth plus the presence of fringed scales on areas of the lower frond surfaces as well as basal pinnae that may overlap the rachis. It is cultivated in Zones 9 and 10.

Appendix
1
USDA Plant Hardiness Zone Map

European Plant Hardiness Zone Map

Appendix
2

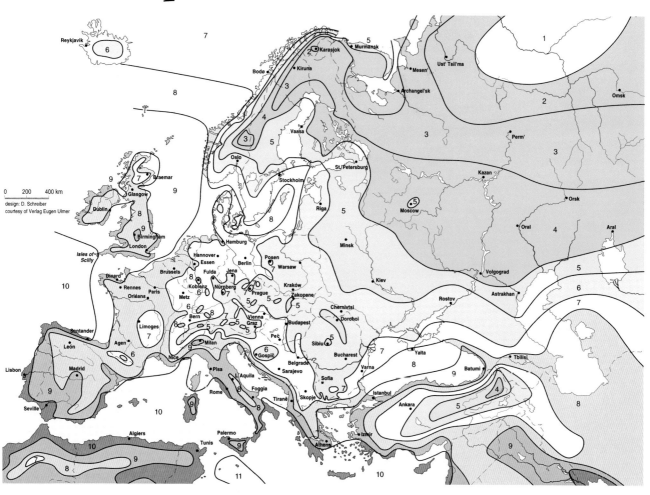

design: D. Schreiber
courtesy of Verlag Eugen Ulmer

0   200   400 km

Appendix 3

Award-Winning Ferns

Britain's Royal Horticultural Society Award of Garden Merit Program selects plants that are recommended as excellent for garden use based on a number of criteria including decorative value, pest resistance and ease of cultivation. The ferns that have passed their testing program as of April 2005 are:

Adiantum aleuticum
Adiantum aleuticum 'Subpumilum'
Adiantum × mairisii
Adiantum pedatum
Adiantum raddianum
Adiantum raddianum 'Brilliantelse'
Adiantum raddianum 'Fritz Luth'
Adiantum raddianum 'Kensington Gem'
Adiantum tenerum 'Farleyense'
Adiantum venustum
Asplenium bulbiferum
Asplenium nidus
Asplenium trichomanes
Athyrium filix-femina
Athyrium filix-femina 'Frizelliae'
Athyrium filix-femina 'Vernoniae'
Athyrium niponicum 'Pictum'
Athyrium otophorum
Blechnum braziliense
Blechnum chilense
Blechnum penna-marina
Blechnum spicant
Cyrtomium falcatum
Cyrtomium fortunei
Dicksonia antarctica
Dicksonia fibrosa
Dicksonia squarrosa
Dryopteris affinis
Dryopteris affinis 'Crispa Gracilis'
Dryopteris affinis 'Cristata' (The King)
Dryopteris affinis 'Cristata Angustata'
Dryopteris affinis 'Polydactyla Mapplebeck'
Dryopteris cycadina
Dryopteris dilatata 'Crispa Whiteside'
Dryopteris dilatata 'Lepidota Cristata'
Dryopteris erythrosora
Dryopteris erythrosora 'Prolifica'
Dryopteris filix-mas

Dryopteris filix-mas 'Cristata'
Dryopteris filix-mas 'Grandiceps Wills'
Dryopteris wallichiana
Gymnocarpium dryopteris
Gymnocarpium dryopteris 'Plumosum'
Matteuccia struthiopteris
Osmunda cinnamomea
Osmunda claytoniana
Osmunda regalis
Osmunda regalis 'Cristata'
Pellaea rotundifolia
Phyllitis scolopendrium
Phyllitis scolopendrium 'Crispa Bolton's Nobile'
Phyllitis scolopendrium 'Kaye's Lacerate'
Polypodium cambricum 'Cambricum'
Polypodium cambricum (Cristatum Group) 'Grandiceps Fox'
Polypodium cambricum 'Wilharris'
Polypodium glycyrrhiza 'Longicaudatum'
Polypodium interjectum 'Cornubiense'
Polystichum aculeatum
Polystichum munitum
Polystichum polyblepharum
Polystichum setiferum
Polystichum setiferum 'Divisilobum Densum'
Polystichum setiferum 'Iveryanum'
Polystichum setiferum 'Pulcherrimum Bevis'
Polystichum tsus-simense
Rumohra adiantiformis
Selaginella kraussiana
Selaginella kraussiana 'Brownii'
Selaginella martensii
Selaginella uncinata
Woodsia polystichoides
Woodwardia radicans

The Elisabeth C. Miller Botanical Garden in Seattle, Washington, recommends outstanding plants for gardeners in the Pacific Northwest via its popular Great Plant Picks educational program. The following ferns merit the "Great Plant" designation:

Adiantum aleuticum
Adiantum venustum
Asplenium trichomanes
Athyrium filix-femina 'Frizelliae'
Athyrium 'Ghost'
Athyrium niponicum 'Pictum'
Athyrium otophorum
Blechnum penna-marina
Blechnum spicant
Cyrtomium caryotideum
Cyrtomium falcatum
Cyrtomium falcatum 'Rochfordianum'
Cyrtomium fortunei
Cyrtomium macrophyllum
Dryopteris crassirhizoma
Dryopteris cycadina

Dryopteris erythrosora
Dryopteris wallichiana
Gymnocarpium dryopteris
Osmunda regalis
Osmunda regalis 'Cristata'
Osmunda regalis 'Purpurascens'
Osmunda regalis 'Undulatifolia'
Phyllitis scolopendrium
Polystichum makinoi
Polystichum munitum
Polystichum neolobatum
Polystichum polyblepharum
Polystichum setiferum Divisilobum Group
Polystichum setiferum Plumosum Group
Polystichum tsus-simense
Woodsia polystichoides

Appendix 4

Favorite Ferns for Sites Around the World

The following ferns have been selected by specialists as appropriate and recommended choices for gardens in their areas.

Zone 4/5
Catharine Guiles, New Gloucester, Maine
  Adiantum aleuticum
  Adiantum pedatum
  Athyrium filix-femina 'Victoriae'
  Athyrium niponicum 'Pictum'
  Dryopteris affinis 'Revolvens'
  Dryopteris ×*australis*
  Dryopteris ×*complexa*
  Dryopteris crassirhizoma
  Dryopteris filix-mas
  Dryopteris goldiana
  Dryopteris intermedia
  Dryopteris marginalis
  Dryopteris remota
  Matteuccia struthiopteris
  Osmunda cinnamomea
  Osmunda regalis
  Polystichum acrostichoides
  Polystichum braunii
  Polystichum retroso-paleaceum
  Polystichum setiferum 'Plumosum Bevis'

Zone 5
Jean and Scott Lundberg, Niles, Michigan
  Adiantum pedatum
  Adiantum venustum
  Asplenium trichomanes
  Athyrium filix-femina
  Athyrium otophorum
  Dryopteris affinis
  Dryopteris championii
  Dryopteris erythrosora
  Dryopteris filix-mas 'Barnesii'
  Dryopteris goldiana
  Dryopteris marginalis
  Dryopteris oreades
  Dryopteris tokyoensis
  Phyllitis scolopendrium
  Phyllitis scolopendrium (ruffled)

  Polystichum braunii
  Polystichum makinoi
  Polystichum neolobatum
  Polystichum setiferum 'Divisilobum'
  Woodsia polystichoides

Zone 5
James Horrocks, Salt Lake City, Utah
  Adiantum aleuticum
  Adiantum venustum
  Cyrtomium fortunei var. *clivicola*
  Cyrtomium macrophyllum
  Dryopteris caucasica
  Dryopteris ×*complexa*
  Dryopteris crassirhizoma
  Dryopteris filix-mas
  Dryopteris filix-mas 'Barnesii'
  Dryopteris marginalis
  Dryopteris sublacera
  Dryopteris uniformis
  Polystichum aculeatum
  Polystichum braunii
  Polystichum makinoi
  Polystichum mayebarae
  Polystichum neolobatum
  Polystichum polyblepharum
  Polystichum setiferum
  Polystichum xiphophyllum

Zone 5/6
Sue Hollis, Kansas City, Missouri
  Adiantum capillus-veneris
  Adiantum pedatum
  Asplenium platyneuron
  Athyrium filix-femina subsp. *asplenioides*
  Cheilanthes lanosa
  Cystopteris bulbifera
  Cystopteris protrusa
  Deparia acrostichoides
  Diplazium pycnocarpon
  Dryopteris ×*complexa* 'Robust'

Dryopteris goldiana
Dryopteris marginalis
Equisetum hyemale
Matteuccia struthiopteris
Osmunda cinnamomea
Osmunda regalis
Phegopteris hexagonoptera
*Polystichum acrostich*oides
Woodsia obtusa

Zone 6
Ralph Archer, Louisville, Kentucky
Adiantum pedatum
Athyrium filix-femina subsp. *angustum* f. *rubellum*
    'Lady in Red'
Athyrium 'Ghost'
Athyrium niponicum 'Pictum'
Athyrium otophorum
Cystopteris bulbifera
Deparia acrostichoides
Dryopteris ×*australis*
Dryopteris crassirhizoma
Dryopteris erythrosora
Dryopteris filix-mas 'Barnesii'
Dryopteris filix-mas 'Grandiceps'
Dryopteris goldiana
Dryopteris intermedia
Dryopteris marginalis
Dryopteris oreades
Dryopteris pseudofilix-mas
Phyllitis scolopendrium (any crested, crisped, or
    undulate form)
Polypodium vulgare
Polystichum polyblepharum

Zone 6
Joan Eiger Gottlieb, Pittsburgh, Pennsylvania
Adiantum aleuticum
Adiantum venustum
Arachniodes standishii
Asplenium trichomanes
Athyrium filix-femina subsp. *angustum* f. *rubellum*
Athyrium niponicum 'Silver Falls'
Athyrium otophorum
Blechnum spicant
Cyrtomium lonchitoides
Cystopteris tennesseensis
Dryopteris goldiana
Dryopteris sieboldii
Osmunda regalis 'Gracilis'
Phegopteris connectilis
Phegopteris decursive-pinnata
Phyllitis scolopendrium
Polystichum acrostichoides
Polystichum braunii
Polystichum setiferum 'Plumosum Bevis'
Woodsia polystichoides

Zone 6
Christian Kohout, Dresden, Germany
Arachniodes standishii
Araiostegia hymenophylloides
Blechnum magellanicum
Blechnum spicant 'Cristatum'
Dennstaedtia wilfordii
Dryopteris championii
Dryopteris crispifolia
Dryopteris sieboldii
Dryopteris wallichiana subsp. *coriacea*
Matteuccia ×*intermedia*
Matteuccia orientalis
Osmunda japonica
Phyllitis scolopendrium 'Crispa'
Polypodium scouleri × *P. glycyrrhiza*
Polystichum aculeatum 'Cristatum'
Polystichum aculeatum 'Zillertal'
Polystichum braunii
Polystichum multifidum
Polystichum neolobatum
Polystichum setiferum 'Plumosum Bevis'
Polystichum ×*wirtgenii*

Zone 6b
Jack Schieber, Otto Heck, and John DeMarrais,
    Mid Atlantic States
Adiantum pedatum
Adiantum venustum
Arachniodes standishii
Athyrium filix-femina 'Minutissimum'
Athyrium niponicum 'Pictum'
Diplazium pycnocarpon
Dryopteris ×*australis*
Dryopteris championii
Dryopteris ×*complexa*
Dryopteris erythrosora
Dryopteris filix-mas
Dryopteris goldiana
Dryopteris intermedia
Dryopteris marginalis
Dryopteris tokyoensis
Osmunda claytoniana
Phegopteris decursive-pinnata
Phegopteris hexagonoptera
Polystichum braunii
Polystichum polyblepharum

Zone 7
Berndt Peters, Süderbrarup, Germany
Arachniodes standishii
Athyrium atkinsonii
Athyrium vidalii
Coniogramme intermedia
Cornopteris decurrenti-alata
Cyrtomium fortunei var. *clivicola*
Diplazium pycnocarpon

Dryopteris pycnopteroides
Dryopteris remota
Dryopteris stewartii
Dryopteris tokyoensis
Matteuccia orientalis
Osmunda cinnamomea
Polypodium cambricum with its varieties
Polystichum hancockii
Polystichum lonchitis
Polystichum neolobatum
Polystichum setiferum with its varieties
Polystichum vestitum
Woodwardia areolata

Zone 7b

Tony Avent, Raleigh, North Carolina
Adiantum capillus-veneris
Adiantum thalictroides
Adiantum venustum
Arachniodes standishii
Astrolepis integerrima
Athyrium filix-femina 'Victoriae'
Athyrium 'Ghost'
Cheilanthes bonariensis
Davallia mariesii 'Korea Rocks'
Dryopteris ×*australis*
Dryopteris crassirhizoma
Dryopteris cystolepidota
Dryopteris erythrosora
Dryopteris ludoviciana
Pellaea ovata
Polystichum acrostichoides
Polystichum polyblepharum
Pteris vittata 'Benzilan'
Pyrrosia polydactyla
Thelypteris kunthii
Thelypteris ovata var. *lindheimeri*
Woodwardia orientalis

Zone 7b

Karen and Dan Jones, Birmingham, Alabama
Adiantum capillus-veneris
Adiantum pedatum
Arachniodes standishii
Dryopteris championii
Dryopteris ×*complexa*
Dryopteris decipiens
Dryopteris erythrosora
Dryopteris formosana
Dryopteris goldiana
Dryopteris marginalis
Dryopteris polylepis
Dryopteris sacrosancta
Dryopteris stewartii
Dryopteris uniformis 'Cristata'
Microlepia strigosa
Osmunda cinnamomea
Phyllitis scolopendrium 'Kaye's Lacerate'

Polystichum makinoi
Polystichum polyblepharum
Polystichum xiphophyllum

Zone 7/8

Naud Burnett, Dallas, Texas
Adiantum capillus-veneris
Arachniodes simplicior
Athyrium filix-femina
Athyrium 'Ghost'
Athyrium niponicum 'Pictum'
Cyrtomium falcatum 'Rochfordianum'
Dryopteris ×*australis*
Dryopteris cycadina
Dryopteris erythrosora 'Brilliance'
Dryopteris ludoviciana
Dryopteris pseudofilix-mas
Dryopteris remota
Matteuccia struthiopteris
Microlepia strigosa
Osmunda cinnamomea
Osmunda regalis
Phegopteris decursive-pinnata
Polystichum acrostichoides
Polystichum polyblepharum
Polystichum tsus-simense

Zone 8

Alan Ogden, Alvechurch, England
Adiantum venustum
Athyrium filix-femina 'Cristata'
Athyrium 'Ghost'
Athyrium vidalii
Ceterach officinarum
Dryopteris affinis 'Polydactyla Mapplebeck'
Dryopteris crassirhizoma
Dryopteris remota
Dryopteris sieboldii
Dryopteris wallichiana
Gymnocarpium dryopteris
Matteuccia struthiopteris
Onoclea sensibilis (red-stemmed form)
Ophioglossum vulgatum
Osmunda regalis 'Purpurascens'
Phyllitis scolopendrium 'Crispa Bolton's Nobile'
Polypodium cambricum 'Barrowii'
Polystichum setiferum 'Plumoso-divisilobum'
Polystichum tsus-simense
Woodsia fragilis

Zone 8

Martin Rickard, Tenbury Wells, England
Arachniodes standishii
Athyrium filix-femina 'Clarissima Jones'
Athyrium filix-femina 'Kalothrix'
Athyrium filix-femina 'Plumosum Drueryi'
Athyrium 'Ghost'
Blechnum chilense

Blechnum magellanicum
Dicksonia antarctica
Lophosoria quadripinnata
Osmunda lancea
Polypodium cambricum (Cristatum Group)
    'Grandiceps Fox'
Polypodium cambricum 'Richard Kayse'
Polypodium vulgare 'Elegantissimum'
Polystichum ×*dycei*
Polystichum neolobatum
Polystichum proliferum
Polystichum setiferum 'Green Lace'
Polystichum setiferum 'Plumosum Bevis'
Pyrrosia sheareri
Woodwardia unigemmata

Zone 8

Sue Olsen, Bellevue, Washington
Adiantum aleuticum
Adiantum venustum
Arachniodes standishii
Asplenium trichomanes and varieties
Athyrium otophorum
Blechnum chilense
Blechnum fluviatile
Cheilanthes lindheimeri
Dryopteris crispifolia
Dryopteris erythrosora
Dryopteris lepidopoda
Dryopteris polylepis
Gymnocarpium oyamense
Polypodium scouleri
Polystichum ×*dycei*
Polystichum neolobatum
Polystichum polyblepharum
Polystichum setiferum 'Plumosum'
Pyrrosia sheareri
Woodwardia unigemmata

Zone 9

Alan Smith, Berkeley, California
Adiantum aleuticum
Aspidotis californica
Athyrium filix-femina
Blechnum spicant
Cheilanthes covillei
Cyrtomium falcatum
Dicksonia antarctica
Doodia media
Dryopteris arguta
Equisetum hyemale
Lygodium japonicum
Pellaea andromedifolia
Pellaea mucronata
Pellaea rotundifolia
Pentagramma triangularis
Polypodium calirhiza
Polypodium scouleri

Polystichum californicum
Polystichum munitum
Rumohra adiantiformis
Woodwardia fimbriata

Zone 9b, Xerics

David Schwartz, Bakersfield, California
Actiniopteris semiflabellata
Argyrochosma limitanea
Astrolepis cochisensis
Astrolepis sinuata
Bommeria hispida
Cheilanthes bicolor
Cheilanthes buchtienii
Cheilanthes clevelandii
Cheilanthes lendigera
Cheilanthes lindheimeri
Cheilanthes villosa
Cheilanthes yavapensis
Mildella intramarginalis
Notholaena grayi
Notholaena lemmonii
Notholaena standleyi
Pellaea andromedifolia
Pellaea ovata
Pellaea wrightiana
Pentagramma pallida

Zone 10/11

Robert and Robin Halley, San Diego, California
Adiantum capillus-veneris
Adiantum raddianum (various forms)
Asplenium antiquum 'Victoria'
Athyrium niponicum 'Pictum'
Cyathea cooperi
Cyrtomium falcatum (various forms)
Dicksonia antarctica
Microlepia strigosa
Nephrolepis cordifolia
Nephrolepis exaltata (various forms)
Pellaea rotundifolia
Platycerium bifurcatum
Platycerium superbum
Pteris cretica
Rumohra adiantiformis

Zone 11

Keith Rogers, Australia
Adiantum raddianum 'Fritz Luth'
Asplenium goudeyi
Blechnum brasiliense Red
Cibotium schiedei
Cyathea medullaris
Davallia tyermannii
Platycerium hillii
Platycerium superbum
Platycerium veitchii
Todea barbara

Appendix 5

Ferns for Special Situations

Ferns for dry shade
Plants need to be kept moist until established.

Many dryopteris including *Dryopteris affinis* and cultivars, *D. dilatata* and cultivars, *D. erythrosora*, *D. expansa*, *D. filix-mas* and cultivars, *D. formosana*, *D. lacera*, *D. lepidopoda*, *D. pseudofilix-mas*, *D. remota*
Polystichum acrostichoides
Polystichum munitum

Ferns for wet and boggy areas
Athyrium filix-femina
Dryopteris celsa
Dryopteris clintoniana
Dryopteris cristata
Dryopteris ludoviciana
Matteuccia struthiopteris
Onoclea sensibilis
Osmunda cinnamomea
Osmunda regalis
Thelypteris palustris
Thelypteris simulata
Woodwardia areolata
Woodwardia virginica

Ferns for Rock Gardens
Adiantum aleuticum 'Subpumilum'
Asplenium platyneuron
Asplenium trichomanes and varieties
Astrolepis cochisensis
Astrolepis integerrima
Astrolepis sinuata
Blechnum penna-marina
Ceterach officinarum
Cheilanthes in variety
Cystopteris bulbifera
Dryopteris affinis 'Crispa Gracilis'
Pellaea atropurpurea
Pellaea glabella
Woodsia ilvensis
Woodsia intermedia

Woodsia obtusa
Woodsia polystichoides

Ferns for sunny locations
These tolerate sun within reason; many will not take hot midday sun.

Asplenium trichomanes
Athyrium filix-femina
Blechnum penna-marina
Ceterach officinarum
Cheilanthes in variety
Dennstaedtia punctilobula
Dryopteris affinis and cultivars
Dryopteris filix-mas and cultivars
Dryopteris pseudofilix-mas
Hypolepis millefolium
Nephrolepis cordifolia
Onoclea sensibilis
Osmunda cinnamomea
Osmunda regalis
Thelypteris kunthii
Thelypteris palustris
Woodsia ilvensis
Woodsia polystichoides

Ferns for color
Adiantum hispidulum
Athyrium 'Branford Beauty'
Athyrium 'Ghost'
Athyrium niponicum 'Pictum'
Athyrium otophorum
Athyrium yokoscense
Blechnums in variety, especially *Blechnum appendiculatum*, *B. chilense*, *B. novae-zelandiae*, *B. penna-marina*
Dryopteris erythrosora
Dryopteris lepidopoda
Dryopteris wallichiana
Onoclea sensibilis (red-stemmed form)
Osmunda regalis 'Purpurascens'
Woodwardia orientalis var. *formosana*
Woodwardia unigemmata
Woodwardia virginica

Xeric Ferns

Dryland ferns are not for beginners, but for those who wish to begin, the following are "easier," not to be confused with easy. The list is compiled for Zone 7 and warmer with some entries suitable for Zone 6.

Astrolepis sinuata
Cheilanthes distans
Cheilanthes eatonii
Cheilanthes fendleri
Cheilanthes lanosa
Cheilanthes lindheimeri
Cheilanthes tomentosa
Cheilanthes wootonii

Appendix
6
Fern Societies

The Hardy Fern Foundation

The Hardy Fern Foundation was established to introduce and test the world's temperate ferns for hardiness and ornamental value and to build comprehensive collections for public display, information, and education. The primary study garden is at the Rhododendron Species Botanical Garden in Federal Way, Washington, with research plantings and displays at botanical gardens, arboreta, and related public institutions throughout North America. Members receive the foundation's quarterly, which offers articles of general interest, as well as specifics on cultivation, sites for viewing collections, fern profiles, and evaluations of ferns in the testing program. Special issues include *Directory of Fern Gardens, Nurseries, and Reserves in the United States and Canada*; *Propagation Handbook*; and *Guide to Hardy Garden Ferns*. The Society has an annual Fern Festival in early June. In recent years, in partnership with the British Pteridological Society, members have joined in fern forays to the west and east coasts of the United States as well as Germany. Members participate in a spore exchange and have first access to ferns as they are introduced in an annual distribution. For membership information write to P.O. Box 3797, Federal Way, Washington 98063. The Web address is www.hardyferns.org.

The American Fern Society

The American Fern Society promotes horticultural and scholarly interests in ferns. Their quarterly publication, the *American Fern Journal*, presents scientific papers and recent research. Their bulletin, *Fiddlehead Forum*, presents articles of general interest. They too have a spore exchange. Meetings and field trips are held in different areas of the United States annually. For information contact George Yatskievych, Missouri Botanical Garden, P.O. Box 299, St. Louis, MO 63166. The Web address is www.amerfernsoc.org.

The British Pteridological Society

The British Pteridological Society, the world's oldest fern society, offers members a balance between horticultural interests and the purely botanical. The Society publishes three annual journals: *The Fern Gazette*, which presents scholarly articles; *The Bulletin*, which reports on the annual activities, field excursions, and society business; and *The Pteridologist*, which includes a broad range of articles of general fern interest. In addition special publications are released periodically with the most recent being *Polystichum Cultivars* (Dyce et al. 2005). Regular field meetings and lectures are held throughout the British Isles and at least one overseas excursion is offered annually. Members may also participate in a spore exchange. Contact M. S. Porter, 5 West Avenue, Wigton, Cumbria CA7 9LG, England. The Web address is www.eBPS.org.uk.

In addition to the above there are some active regional societies throughout the United States including Los Angeles, California; San Diego, California; New York City; Delaware Valley, Pennsylvania; Dallas, Texas; Birmingham, Alabama; Miami, Florida; Memphis, Tennessee; and New Orleans, Louisiana. Most have regular meetings and new members are welcome.

Where to See Ferns

Appendix
7

Australia
Adelaide Botanic Garden
North Terrace
Adelaide, South Australia 5000
+61 (8) 8222 9311
www.environment.sa.gov.au/botanicgardens/adelaide.html

Brisbane Botanic Garden
Mount Coot-tha Road
Toowong, Queensland 4006
+61 (07) 3403 2535
www.brisbane.qld.gov.au/BCC:BOTANICG:1212447403:
    pc=PC_1346

Mount Lofty Botanic Garden
Summit Road
Crafers, South Australia 5152
+61 (8) 8370 8370
www.environment.sa.gov.au/botanicgardens/mtlofty.html

Royal Botanic Garden, Melbourne
Private Bag 2000
Birdwood Avenue,
South Yarra, Victoria 3141
+61 (3) 9252 2300
www.rbg.vic.gov.au

Royal Botanic Garden, Sydney
Mrs. MacQuaries Road
New South Wales 2000
+61 (2) 9231 8111
www.rbgsyd.gov.au/sydney_gardens_domain

Canada
Les Jardins de Métis
200, Route 132
Grand-Métis, Québec G0J 1Z0
(418) 775-2222
www.jardinsmetis.com

Van Dusen Botanical Garden
5251 Oak Street
Vancouver, British Columbia V6M 4H1
(604) 878-9274
www.city.vancouver.bc.ca/parks/parks/vandusen/website

England
Cambridge University Botanic Gardens
Cory Lodge
Bateman Street
Cambridge CB2 1JF
www.botanic.cam.ac.uk

Chelsea Physic Garden
66 Royal Hospital Road
London SW3 4HS
+44 (0)20 7352 5646
www.chelseaphysicgarden.co.uk

Greencombe Gardens
Porlock
Somerset TA24 8NU
www.greencombe.org.uk

Harlow Carr Botanic Gardens
(Northern Horticultural Society)
Crag Lane, Harrogate
North Yorkshire HG3 1QB
+44 (0)14 2356 5418
www.rhs.org.uk/WhatsOn/gardens/harlowcarr/index.asp

Lakeland Horticultural Society Gardens
Holehird
Ullswater Road
Windermere
Cumbria LA23 1NP
+44 (0)15 3944 6008
www.holehirdgardens.org.uk

Royal Botanic Gardens Kew
Richmond
Surrey TW9 3AB
+44 (0)20 8332 5655
www.rbgkew.org.uk

Savill Garden (part of Windsor Great Park)
Wick Lane, Englefield Green
Egham
Surrey TW20 0UU
+44 (0)17 5384 7518
www.savillgarden.co.uk

413

Sizergh Castle and (National Trust) Garden
Sizergh, near Kendal
Cumbria LA8 8AE
+44 (0)15 3956 0070
www.visitcumbria.com/sl/sizergh.htm

Tatton Park
Knutsford
Cheshire WA16 6QN
+44 (0)16 2553 4435
www.tattonpark.org.uk

Germany
Botanic Garden and Botanical Museum Berlin-Dahlem
Königen-Luise-Strasse 6–8
14191 Berlin
+49 (30) 8385 0100
www.bgbm.org/BGBM

Flora and Botanical Gardens of Cologne
Amsterdamer Str. 34
Cologne

Planten un Blomen
Jungiusstrasse
Hamburg
www.plantenunblomen.hamburg.dc

New Zealand
Franz Fernery at the Auckland Domain Park
Auckland, 1001
North Island
+64 (0)9 307 7604
http://www.auckland.world-
    guides.com/auckland_parks_gardens.html

Pukeiti Rhododendron Trust Garden
2290 Carrington Road
R.D. 4
New Plymouth
Taranaki
+64 (0)6 752 4141
www.pukeiti.org.nz

Pukekura Park Fernery
New Plymouth
www.newplymouthnz.com/visitors+and+events/fernery.htm

Scotland
Glasgow Botanic Gardens
730 Great Western Road
Glasgow G12 0UE
+44 (0)14 1334 2422
www.clyde-valley.com/glasgow/botanic.htm

Logan Botanic Gardens
Port Logan, Stranraer
Wigtownshir DG9 9ND
+44 (0)17 7686 0231
www.rbge.org.uk/rbge/web/visiting/lbg.jsp#Contact

Royal Botanic Gardens Edinburgh
20A Inverleith Row
Edinburgh EH3 5LR
+44 (0)13 1552 7171
www.rbge.org.uk

United States
Alabama
Birmingham Botanical Garden
2612 Lane Park Road
Birmingham, AL 35223
(205) 414-3900
www.bbgardens.org

Huntsville-Madison County Botanical Garden
4747 Bob Wallace Avenue
Huntsville, AL 35805
(256) 830-5314
www.hsvbg.org

Alaska
Georgeson Botanical Garden
University of Alaska
P.O. Box 757200
117 W. Tanana Drive
Fairbanks, AK 99775
(907) 474-5651
www.uaf.edu/salrm/gbg

California
Balboa Park
1549 El Prado
San Diego, CA 92101
www.balboapark.org

California State University at Sacramento
Department of Biology
6000 J Street
Sacramento, CA 95819
(916) 278-7369
www.csus.edu

Fern Canyon
Prairie Creek Redwoods S.P.
15336 Highway 101
Trinidad, CA 95510
(707) 488-2041
www.terragalleria.com/parks/np.redwood.5.html

Huntington Botanical Gardens
1151 Oxford Road
San Marino, CA 91108
(626) 405-2100
www.huntington.org

Mendocino Coast Botanical Gardens
18220 N. Highway One
Fort Bragg, CA 95437
(707) 964-4352
www.gardenbythesea.org

Quail Botanical Gardens
P.O. Box 23005
230 Quail Gardens Drive
Encinitas, CA 92023
(619) 436-3036
www.qbgardens.com

Rancho Santa Ana Botanic Garden
Claremont Graduate University
1500 N. College Avenue
Claremont, CA 91711
(909) 626-3489
www.rsabg.org

Russian Gulch State Park
P.O. Box 440
Mendocino, CA 95460
(707) 937-5804
www.parks.ca.gov/?page_id=432

San Francisco Botanical Garden at Strybing Arboretum
Golden Gate Park
9th Avenue at Lincoln Way
San Francisco, CA 94122
(415) 661-5817
www.sfbotanicalgarden.org

University of California, Santa Cruz Arboretum
1500 High Street
Santa Cruz, CA 95064
(831) 427-2998
www2.ucsc.edu/arboretum/gardens.html

University of California Botanical Garden at Berkeley
200 Centennial Drive, #5045
Berkeley, CA 94720
(510) 642-3343
www.botanicalgarden.berkeley.edu

Colorado
Denver Botanic Gardens
1005 York Street
Denver, CO 80206
(303) 331-4000
www.botanicgardens.org

University of Northern Colorado
Ross Hall Science Center
Greeley, CO 80631
(303) 351-1890
www.unco.edu

Delaware
Mount Cuba Center
P.O. Box 3570
Greenville, DE 19807
(302) 239-4244
www.mtcubacenter.org

District of Columbia
U.S. National Arboretum
Fern Valley
3501 New York Avenue N.E.
Washington, D.C. 20002
(202) 245-2726
www.usna.usda.gov

Florida
Bok Tower Gardens
1151 Tower Gardens
Lake Wales, FL 33853
(863) 676-1408
www.boksanctuary.org

Fairchild Tropical Gardens
10901 Old Cutler Road
Miami, FL 33156
(305) 667-1651
www.fairchildgarden.org

Harry P. Leu Gardens
1920 N. Forest Avenue
Orlando, FL 32803
(407) 246-2620
www.leugardens.org

Marie Selby Botanical Gardens
811 S. Palm Avenue
Sarasota, FL 34236
(941) 954-1237
www.selby.org

Georgia
Atlanta Botanical Garden
1345 Piedmont Avenue
Atlanta, GA 30309
(404) 876-5859
www.atlantabotanicalgarden.org

Georgia Perimeter College Botanical Garden
Decatur Campus
3251 Panthersville Road
Decatur, GA 30034
(404) 244-5001
www.gpc.edu/~ddonald/botgard/george3.htm

Hawaii
Hawaii Tropical Botanical Garden
P.O. Box 80
27-717 Old Mamalahoa Highway
Papaikov, HI 96781
(808) 964-5233
www.htbg.com

Hawaii Volcanoes National Park
S.W. of Hilo on Hawaii Island
P.O. Box 52
Hawaii National Park, HI 96718
(808) 985-6000
www.hawaii.volcanoes.national-park.com

Honolulu Botanical Gardens
50 N. Vineyard Boulevard
Honolulu, HI 96817
(808) 522-7060
www.co.honolulu.hi.us/parks/hbg

National Tropical Botanical Garden
P.O. Box 340
Lawai
Kauai, HI 96765
(808) 332-7324
www.ntbg.org

Illinois
Chicago Botanic Garden
1000 Lake Cook Road
Glencoe, IL 60022
(847) 835-8221
www.chicagobotanic.org

Kentucky
Whitehall Historic Home and Garden
3110 Lexington Road
Louisville, KY 40206
(502) 897-2944
http://www.historichomes.org/whitehall

Maine
Coastal Maine Botanical Gardens
P.O. Box 234
Barters Island Road
Boothbay, ME 04537
(207) 633-4333
www.mainegardens.org

Wild Gardens of Acadia
Acadia National Park
Sieur de Monts Spring
P.O. Box 896
Bar Harbor, ME 04609
(207) 288-3400
www.acadiamagic.com/wild-gardens.html

Massachusetts
Bartholomew's Cobble
Weatogue Road (off Route 7A)
Ashley Falls, MA 01222
(413) 229-8600
www.berkshireweb.com/trustees/barth.html

Berkshire Botanical Garden,
P.O. Box 826
Intersection of Routes 102 and 183
Stockbridge, MA 01262
(413) 298-3926
www.berkshirebotanical.org

Garden in the Woods
180 Hemenway Road
Framingham, MA 01701
(508) 877-7630
www.newfs.org/garden.htm

Norcross Wildlife Sanctuary
30 Peck Road
Monson, MA 01057
(413) 267-9654
www.norcrossws.org/norcross.htm

Tyringham Cobble
565 Sloan Road
Williamstown, MA 10267
(413) 453-3144
www.thetrustees.org/pages/370_tyringham_cobble.cfm

Michigan
Fernwood Botanic Garden
13988 Range Line Road
Niles, MI 49120
(616) 695-6491
www.fernwoodbotanical.org

Matthaei Botanical Gardens
University of Michigan
1800 N. Dixboro Road
Ann Arbor, MI 48105
(734) 998-7061
www.sitemaker.umich.edu/mbgna

Michigan State University Botany Greenhouses
E. Circle Drive Oval
East Lansing, MI 48824
(517) 355-0229
www.msu.edu/arts/gardens.html

Missouri
Missouri Botanical Garden
4344 Shaw Boulevard
St. Louis, MO 63110
(314) 577-5100
www.mobot.org

New Jersey
Leonard J. Buck Garden
11 Layton Road
Far Hills, NJ 07931
(908) 234-2677
www.njskylands.com/atbuckgar.htm

New Jersey State Botanical Garden at Skyland
1304 Sloatsburg Road
Ringwood, NJ 07456
(973) 962-4353
http://www.njbg.org

New York
Brooklyn Botanic Garden
1000 Washington Avenue
Brooklyn, NY 11225
(718) 623-7200
www.bbg.org

Institute of Ecosystem Studies
P.O. Box R
Route 44A
Millbrook, NY 12545
(845) 677-5359
www.ecostudies.org

Lyndhurst Gardens
635 S. Broadway (Route 9)
Tarrytown, NY 10591
(914) 631-4481
www.lyndhurst.org

New York Botanical Garden
Bronx River Parkway at Fordham Road
Bronx, NY 10458
(718) 817-8700
www.nybg.org

Planting Fields Arboretum
State Historic Park
P.O. Box 58
Oyster Bay, NY 11771
(516) 922-9200
www.plantingfields.org

North Carolina
Sarah P. Duke Gardens
Duke University
426 Anderson Street
Durham, NC 27708
(919) 684-3698
www.hr.duke.edu/dukegardens/dukegardens.html

University of North Carolina at Charlotte Botanical Gardens
9201 University City Boulevard
Charlotte, NC 28223
(704) 687-2364
http://gardens.uncc.edu

Ohio
Hocking Hills State Park
20160 State Route 664
Logan, OH 43138
(614) 385-6841
www.dnr.state.oh.us/parks/parks/hocking.htm

Holden Arboretum
9500 Sperry Road
Kirtland, OH 44094
(440) 256-1110
www.holdenarb.org

Inniswood Metro Gardens
940 S. Hempstead Road
Westerville, OH 43081
(614) 895-6216
www.inniswood.org

Oregon
Berry Botanic Garden
11505 S.W. Sommerville Avenue
Portland, OR 97219
(503) 636-4112
www.berrybot.org

Leach Botanical Garden
6704 S.E. 122nd Avenue
Portland, OR 97236
(503) 761-9503
www.leachgarden.org

Mount Pisgah Arboretum
33735 Seavey Loop Road
Eugene, OR 97405
(541) 741-4110
www.efn.org/~mtpisgah

Pennsylvania

Barnes Foundation Arboretum
300 N. Latch's Lane
Merion, PA 19066
(610) 667-7917
www.barnesfoundation.org/ed_a_main.html

Bowman's Hill Wildflower Preserve
Washington Crossing Historic Park
P.O. Box 103
Washington Crossing, PA 18977
(215) 862-2924
www.bhwp.org

Chanticleer
786 Church Road
Wayne, PA 19087
(610) 687-4163
www.chanticleergarden.org

Longwood Gardens
P.O. Box 501
Kennett Square, PA 19348
(610) 388-1000
www.longwoodgardens.org

Morris Arboretum
University of Pennsylvania
9414 Meadowbrook Avenue
Philadelphia, PA 19118
(215) 247-5777
www.upenn.edu/arboretum

Nescopeck State Park
1137 Honey Hole Road
Drums, PA 18222
(570) 443-0400
www.dcnr.state.pa.us/stateparks/parks/nescopeck.aspx

Phipps Conservatory & Botanical Gardens
One Schenley Park
Pittsburg, PA 15213
(412) 622-6914
www.phipps.conservatory.org

Texas

Dallas Arboretum
8617 Garland Road
Dallas, TX 76107
(214) 327-8263
www.dallasarboretum.org

Fort Worth Botanic Garden
3220 Botanic Garden Boulevard
Fort Worth, TX 76107
(817) 871-7686
www.fwbg.org

Stephen F. Austin State University Arboretum
Box 13000
Wilson Drive
Nacogdoches, TX 75962
(409) 468-4343
www.arboretum.sfasu.edu/

Virginia

Lewis Ginter Botanical Garden
1800 Lakeside Avenue
Richmond, VA 23228
(804) 262-9887
www.lewisginter.org

Washington

Bainbridge Public Library
1270 Madison Avenue N.
Bainbridge Island, WA 98110
(206) 842-4162
www.krl.org/Use%20Library%20Services/bi.htm

Bellevue Botanical Garden
12001 Main Street
Bellevue, WA 98005
(425) 452-2750
www.bellevuebotanical.org

Bloedel Reserve
7571 N.E. Dolphin Drive
Bainbridge Island, WA 98110
(206) 842-7631
www.bloedelreserve.org

Elandan Gardens
3050 W. State Highway 16
Bremerton, WA 98312
(360) 373-8260
www.elandangardens.com

Elisabeth C. Miller Botanical Garden
The Highlands
Olympic Drive
Seattle, WA 98177
(206) 362-8612
www.millergarden.org

Homestead Park
3715 Bridgeport Way W.
University Place, WA 98466
(253) 566-5656

Kruckeberg Botanic Garden
20312 15th Avenue NW
Shoreline, WA 98177
(206) 542-4777
www.kruckeberg.org

Lakewold Gardens
12317 Gravelly Lake Drive S.W.
Lakewood, WA 98499
(253) 584-4106
www.lakewold.org

Perry Creek Trail
Mount Baker
Snoqualmie National Forest
Forest Service Rd #4063
off Mt. Loop Highway east of Granite Falls, WA
(425) 775-9702
www.fs.fed.us/r6/mbs/recreation/activities/trails

Rhododendron Species Botanical Garden
2525 S. 336th Street
Federal Way, WA 98003
(253) 838-4646
www.rhodygarden.org

West Virginia
Blackwater Falls State Park
P.O. Box 490
Davis, WV 26260
(304) 259-5216
www.blackwaterfalls.com

Wisconsin
Olbrich Botanical Garden
3330 Atwood Avenue
Madison, WI 53704
(608) 246-4550
www.ci.madison.wi.us/olbrich

Rotary Gardens
Parker Education Center
1455 Palmer Drive
Janesville, WI 53545
(608) 752-3885
www.rotarygardens.org

Appendix
8
Where to Buy Ferns

Canada
Pacific Rim Native Plants
P.O. Box 413
Chilliwack, British Columbia V2P 6J7
(604) 792-9279
www.hillkeep.ca
(The nursery, nature reserve, and display garden are open by appointment from April to October.)

United Kingdom
Fibrex Nurseries
Honeybourne Road
Pebworth
Stratford-upon-Avon
Warwickshire CV37 8XP
+44 (0)17 8972 0788
www.fibrex.co.uk/index.html

Rickard's Hardy Ferns
Carreg-y-Fedwen
Sling, Tregarth nr Bangor
Gwynedd LL57 4RP
+44 (0)12 4860 0385
www.rickardshardyferns.co.uk

Spinners Garden
Lymington
Hampshire SO41 5QE
+44 (0)15 9067 3347

United States
California
California Ferns
792 Weeks Street
East Palo Alto, CA 94303
(650) 323-0332
www.californiaferns.com
(Wholesale only.)

Rainforest Flora
19121 Hawthorne Boulevard
Torrance, CA 90503
(310) 370-8044
www.rainforestflora.com
(Has a wide selection of platyceriums. Wholesale.)

Santa Rosa Tropicals
P.O. Box 6183
Santa Rosa, CA 95406
(707) 528-3244
www.srtrop.com
(Wholesale only.)

Yerba Buena Nursery
19500 Skyline Boulevard
Woodside, CA 94062
(650) 851-1668
www.yerbabuenanursery.com

Florida
Charles Alford Plants
Vero Beach, FL 32962
(772) 770-9119
www.rareferns.com
(Mail-order only. Specializing in tropical ferns.)

Georgia
Eco-Gardens
P.O. Box 1227
Decatur, GA 30031
(404) 294-6468
(Price list $2.00. Visitors by appointment.)

Michigan
Lundberg Nursery
1069 Carberry Road
Niles, MI 49120
(269) 683-8068
(Wholesale only.)

North Carolina
Meadowbrook Nursery
2055 Polly Sprout Road
Marion, NC 28752
(828) 738-8300
www.we-du.com
(Catalog $2.00.)

Plant Delight's Nursery
9241 Sauls Road
Raleigh, NC 27603
(919) 772-4794
www.plantdelights.com
(Catalog 10 stamps or a box of chocolates. Visitors by
    appointment.)

Ohio
Glasshouse Works
Church Street
P.O. Box 97
Stewart, OH 45778
(740) 662-2142
www.rareplants.com

Oregon
Forest Farm
990 Tethrow Road
Williams, OR 97544
(503) 846-6963
www.forestfarm.com
(Catalog $4.00.)

Siskiyou Rare Plant Nursery
2115 Talent Ave.
Talent, OR 97540
(541) 535-7103
www.siskiyourareplantnursery.com

Squirrel Heights Gardens
6934 S.E. 45th Avenue
Portland, OR 97206
(503) 771-6945
(Visitors by appointment.)

Pennsylvania
Appalachian Wildflower Nursery
723 Honey Creek Road
Reedsville, PA 17084
(717) 667-6998

Asiatica Nursery
P.O. Box 270
Lewisberry, PA 17339
(717) 938-8677
www.asiaticanursery.com
(Catalog $5.00.)

Texas
Casa Flora
P.O. Box 41140
Dallas, TX 75241
(972) 225-6111
www.casaflora.com
(Wholesale only.)

Virginia
Lazy S'S Farm Nursery
2360 Spotswood Trail
Barboursville, VA 22923
www.lazyssfarm.com/index.html

Washington
Collector's Nursery
16804 N.E. 102nd Avenue
Battle Ground, WA 98604
(360) 574-3832
www.collectorsnursery.com
(Catalog $2.00.)

Fancy Fronds Nursery
P.O. Box 1090
Gold Bar, WA 98251
(360) 793-1472
www.fancyfronds.com
(Catalog $2.00. Visitors by appointment.)

Foliage Gardens
2003 128th Avenue S.E.
Bellevue, WA 98005
(425) 747-2998
www.foliagegardens.com
(Catalog $2.00. Visitors by appointment.)

Henry's Plant Farm
4522 132nd Street S.E.
Snohomish, WA 98290
(425) 337-8120
www.henrysplantfarm.com
(Wholesale only.)

Rhododendron Species Botanical Garden
2525 S. 336th Street
Federal Way, WA 98003
(253) 838-4646
www.rhodygarden.org

Sundquist Nursery
3809 N.E. Sawdust Hill Road
Poulsbo, WA 98370
(360) 779-6343
www.sqnursery.com

Glossary

abaxial the under side of a frond or pinnae, facing away from an axis

acicular needlelike, pointed

acroscopic pointed towards the apex of the frond

acrostichoid a solid covering of sori on the underside of the frond

acuminate gradually tapering to a long point

adaxial the upper surface of a frond or pinnae, facing an axis

adnate fused with or broadly attached to an unlike part, for example, a pinna united with a rachis

allelopathy the release of a chemical by one plant to inhibit the growth of nearby plants

alternate not opposite

anadromous with the first branch of a pinna aimed towards the frond's apex

anastomosing with veins joining in a network rather than freely branching

antheridium the sperm-producing male organ, found on the underside of the prothallus

apogamous producing a sporophyte directly from a prothallus without sexual fertilization

appressed pressed flat together

archegonium the egg-producing female organ on a prothallus

areole the space enclosed between veins

articulate jointed, a natural breaking point usually on a stipe

auricle an earlike lobe, frequently on a pinnae adjacent to its juncture with the rachis

axis the main structural support of a frond or its subdivisions

basiscopic pointing towards the base, frequently as on a lower pinnule

biauriculate with two earlike lobes usually at the pinnae attachment to the rachis

bipinnate twice divided

blade the expanded leafy part of a frond above the stipe

bulbil, bulblet a small bulblike growth on a frond that reproduces vegetatively

calcareous type of soil or rocks containing lime

ciliate bearing hairs (cilia)

circinate coiled with the apex of the emerging frond at the center of the coil

cone modified leaves that carry sporangia

cordate heart-shaped as in the base of a blade

costa the midvein of a pinna

crenate with scalloped margins, rounded teeth

crested with frond, pinnae, or pinnule tips forking

crisped with wavy margins

crosier the curled unfurling frond, also called the fiddlehead (sometimes spelled crozier)

crown the growing point of a stem, producing fronds usually in a circle

cultivar a cultivated variety of a species

deciduous with fronds that die back at maturity, usually in the late fall or winter

dentate with teeth along the margins

dimorphic having two types of fronds, sterile and fertile, different in form

discombobulated "the feeling an uninitiated fern amateur might have when encountering technical terms" (Palmer 2003)

disjunct from a different geographical area

elliptic oval, widest in the middle and rounded at the ends

endemic native to a particular country or region

entire undivided, with smooth margins

epiphyte growing on another plant, usually a tree, but not parasitic

evergreen carrying fronds throughout the winter

falcate sickle-shaped

false indusia with frond margins rolled over the sori

farina waxy powder, usually white or yellow, found on the undersides of blades

fastigiate narrowly erect

fertile bearing spores

fiddlehead crosier, the unfurling curled frond

free not united, usually in reference to veins

frond the leaf of a fern including the stipe and blade

gametophyte the sexual plant produced from spores, the prothallus bearing both sperms and an egg, which after fertilization will produce the sporophyte.

gemma (plural, **gemmae**) an asexual bud that can reproduce the parent plant

glabrous smooth

glaucous dull bluish-green with a very thin, white waxlike coating

hair composed of a single cell or row of cells only one cell thick

hastate shaped like an arrowhead

heterosporous having two types of spores usually differing in size

imbricate overlapping of similar parts

incised deeply cut

indusium (plural, **indusia**) a small membrane or tissue covering the sori

jointed breaking at certain points

lacerate torn

lamina the blade of a frond

lanceolate lance-shaped

leaflet a small division of a frond

linear narrow and parallel-sided

lobe a rounded but not separate segment

medial midway between the midrib and margin, usually in reference to the sori

midrib, midvein the central vein of a blade or its subdivisions

monomorphic having one type of frond

node the point on a stem where new growth is attached

nothospecies a species derived from existing species, usually originating following hybridization between species.

palmate like a hand

peltate circular, centrally attached, usually in reference to indusia

petiole a stalk, the stipe

pinna (plural, **pinnae**) a primary division of a fern blade

pinnate having pinnae in rows on both sides of an axis, once divided

pinnate-pinnatifid once divided with deeply lobed pinnae, but not cut to the midrib

pinnatifid deeply lobed but not cut to the axis

pinnule the secondary division of a twice-divided blade

proliferous having propagable buds or plantlets

propagule a structure capable of forming new plants

prothallus (plural, **prothalli**) the gametophyte, a small fertile plant bearing sperms and an egg

pteridophyte a fern

quadripinnate four times divided

rachis the midrib of the blade, a continuation of the stipe

reniform kidney-shaped

rhizome a stem from which fronds are produced, can be erect to short- or long-creeping

scale a multicellular flat growth, usually only one cell thick

segment a small division of a divided frond

serpentine soil or rocks high in magnesium and low in phosphorous and calcium supporting limited plant life

serrate with teeth as on a saw blade

sessile without a stalk

simple undivided

sinus a space between two lobes or segments

sorus (plural, **sori**) a group of sporangia

spinulose having spines along a margin

sporangiaster a structure, usually consisting of a short stalk terminated by a cluster of bulbous and/or glandular cells and interspersed among sporangia in a sorus

sporangium (plural, **sporangia**) the fern's spore-bearing structure

spore a one-celled reproductive unit formed in the sporangium, produces a prothallus

sporeling a very young fern, name given to one just developing from a prothallus

sporophyte the familiar fern, the generation that produces spores

stalk a supporting structure

stalked attached with a stalk

stellate branching in a starlike fashion, often referring to hairs

sterile not producing spores

stipe the stalk connecting the blade to the rhizome, petiole

stolon a runner, capable of rooting at the tips and forming new plants

strobilus (plural, **strobili**) a conelike reproductive structure at the tip of a fertile branch

subevergreen evergreen in mild winters

symbiotic two mutually supportive organisms growing together

tripinnate three times divided

truncate ending abruptly, perpendicular to an axis

undulate wavy

vascular bundles the internal conduction system carrying water and nutrients

vegetative frond lacking fertile material

vein strands of vascular tissue in the foliage, may be netted or free

whorled three or more leaves growing at the same level around a stem

wing frond blade tissue along a stipe or rachis

References

Abbe, Elfriede. 1981. *The Fern Herbal*. Ithaca, New York: Cornell University Press.

Ackers, Graham. 2005. *Polystichum richardii* split at last. *Pteridologist* 4 (1): 106–108. London: The British Pteridological Society.

Ackers, Graham, et al. 1997. Fern hardiness symposium. *Pteridologist* 3 (2): 54–78. London: The British Pteridological Society.

Allen, David E. 1969. *The Victorian Fern Craze*. London: Hutchinson.

Archer, Ralph C. 2000. The effect of heat and drought stress on native ferns during the growth cycle of the following year. *Hardy Fern Foundation Quarterly* 10 (3): 56–60. Seattle, Washington.

Archer, Ralph C. 2002. A report on the emergence of fern species in the United States during the spring of 2001, and general comments and recommendations regarding the study. *Hardy Fern Foundation Quarterly* 12 (1): 10–17, 20–27. Seattle, Washington.

Archer, Ralph C. 2003. A report of the emergence of fern species in the United States during the spring of 2002. *Hardy Fern Foundation Quarterly* 13 (1): 8–20. Seattle, Washington.

Archer, Ralph C. 2005. Propagation of ferns by division with special emphasis on *Athyrium niponicum* 'Pictum'. *Hardy Fern Foundation Quarterly* 15 (1): 6–10. Seattle, Washington.

Archer, Ralph C., and Betty Hamilton. 2000. Observations on the effect of heat and drought on native mid-western ferns and response of native ferns in the garden to heat and drought stress. *Hardy Fern Foundation Quarterly* 10 (1): 15–20. Seattle, Washington.

Beddome, Colonel R. H. 1883. *Ferns of British India*. Calcutta: Thacker, Spink.

Benham, Dale. 1992. Additional taxa in *Astrolepis*. *American Fern Journal* 82 (2): 59–62.

Benham, Dale, and Michael Windham. 1992. Generic affinities of the star-scaled cloak ferns. *American Fern Journal* 82 (2): 47–58.

Bennert, H. Wilfried. 1999. *Die seltenen und gefährdeten Farnpflanzen Deutschlands*. Bonn, Germany: Bundesamt für Naturschutz.

Britten, James. 1881. *European Ferns*. London: Cassell, Petter, Galpin.

Brownsey, Patrick J., and John C. Smith-Dodsworth. 2000. *New Zealand Ferns and Allied Plants*. Auckland: David Bateman.

Burrows, John E. 1990. *South African Ferns and Fern Allies*. Sandton, South Africa: Franden Publishers.

Busby, A. R. 1996. Ferns for the alpine gardener. *Pteridologist* 3 (2): 13–18. London: The British Pteridological Society.

Cabot, Frank. 1984. As it was in the beginning—the origins and roots of rock gardening in North America. *Bulletin of the American Rock Garden Society* 42 (5).

Ching, Ren-chang. 1930–1958. *Icones Filicum Sinicarum*. 5 vols. Beijing, China: The Fan Memorial Institute of Biology.

Ching, Ren-chang. 1964. *Acta Phytotaxonomica Sinica* 9: 63.

Clute, Willard N. 1901. *Our Ferns in Their Haunts*. New York: Frederick A. Stokes.

Cobb, Boughton. 1956. *A Field Guide to the Ferns*. Boston: Houghton Mifflin.

Cobb, Boughton, Elizabeth Farnsworth, and Cheryl Lowe. 2005. *Ferns of Northeastern and Central North America*. 2nd ed. Boston: Houghton Mifflin.

Cody, William J., and Donald M. Britton. 1989. *Ferns and Fern Allies of Canada*. Ottawa: Research Branch Agriculture Canada.

Cranfill, Ray. 1980. *Ferns and Fern Allies of Kentucky*. Kentucky Nature Preserves Commission Scientific and Technical Series, No. 1. Frankfurt, Kentucky.

Crowe, Andrew. 1994. *Which Native Fern? A Simple Guide to the Identification of New Zealand Native Ferns*. Auckland: Viking.

Cullina, William. 2002. Tales of Lady in Red. *Hardy Fern Foundation Quarterly* 12 (3): 68–70. Seattle, Washington.

Davies, Hugh. 1813. *Welsh Botanology*. London

Descloux, Joyce. 2003. Drought-tolerant evergreen ferns. *Hardy Fern Foundation Quarterly* 13 (4): 100–103. Seattle, Washington.

Druery, Charles. 1910. *British Ferns and Their Varieties*. London: George Routledge and Sons.

Dunbar, Lin. 1989. *Ferns of the Coastal Plain*. Columbia, South Carolina: University of South Carolina Press.

Duncan, Betty D., and Golda Isaac. 1986. *Ferns and Allied Plants of Victoria, Tasmania, and South Australia*. Melbourne: Melbourne University Press.

Dyce, James W. 1988. *Fern Names and Their Meanings*. London: The British Pteridological Society.

Dyce, James W. 1991. *The Cultivation and Propagation of British Ferns*. London: The British Pteridological Society.

Dyce, James W., Robert Sykes, and Martin Rickard. 2005. *Polystichum Cultivars: Variation in the British Shield Ferns.* Special publication No. 7. London: The British Pteridological Society.

Eaton, Daniel C. 1979. *The Ferns of North America.* 2 vols. Salem, Massachusetts: S. E. Cassino.

Firth, Susan, Martyn Firth, and Elizabeth Firth. 1986. *Ferns of New Zealand.* Auckland: Hodder and Stoughton.

Fisher, Muriel, and L. Ward. 1976. *New Zealand Ferns in Your Garden.* Auckland: Collins.

Flora of North America Editorial Committee. 1993. *Flora of North America North of Mexico.* Vol. 2. Oxford: Oxford University Press.

Fraser-Jenkins, Christopher R. 1989. *A Monograph of Dryopteris in the Indian Subcontinent.* Botany Series 18 (5). London: British History Museum.

Fraser-Jenkins, Christopher R. 1997a. *New Species Syndrome in Indian Pteridology and the Ferns of Nepal.* Dehra Dun, India: International Book Distributors.

Fraser-Jenkins, Christopher R. 1997b. *Himalayan Ferns (A Guide to Polystichum).* Dehra Dun, India: International Book Distributors.

Frye, Theodore C. 1934. *Ferns of the Northwest.* Portland, Oregon: Binsford and Mort.

Gaddis, Iris. 1994. Ferning around the world in 34 acres. *Hardy Fern Foundation Newsletter* 4 (3): 3–11. Seattle, Washington.

Garrett, Michael. 1996. *The Ferns of Tasmania.* Hobart, Tasmania: Tasmanian Forest Research Council.

Gledhill, David. 2002. *The Names of Plants.* Cambridge: Cambridge University Press.

Gottlieb, Joan E. 1995. Hybrid hi-jinks. *Hardy Fern Foundation Newsletter* 5 (1): 3–8. Seattle, Washington.

Gottlieb, Joan E. 2001. *Dryopteris filix-mas*—a fern find in Pennsylvania. *Hardy Fern Foundation Quarterly* 11 (2): 38–41. Seattle, Washington.

Gottlieb, Joan E. 2003. Perplexing pellaeas. *Hardy Fern Foundation Quarterly* 13 (2): 42–45. Seattle, Washington.

Gottlieb, Joan E. 2004a. Ferns in research—1. The gametophyte. *Hardy Fern Foundation Quarterly* 14 (2): 49–55.

Gottlieb, Joan E. 2004b. Ferns in research—2. The sporophyte. *Hardy Fern Foundation Quarterly* 14 (3): 85–92. Seattle, Washington.

Gottlieb, Joan E. 2005a. Further reflections on apogamy and alternation of generations—1. *Hardy Fern Foundation Quarterly* 15 (3): 29–33. Seattle, Washington.

Gottlieb, Joan E. 2005b. Further reflections on apogamy and alternation of generations—2. *Hardy Fern Foundation Quarterly* 15 (4): 44–47. Seattle, Washington.

Gottlieb, Joan E., and Sara J. Gottlieb. 2000. Directory of fern gardens, nurseries, and reserves in the United States and Canada. *Hardy Fern Foundation Quarterly* 10 (3): 1–30. Seattle, Washington.

Goudey, Christopher J. 1985. *Maidenhair Ferns in Cultivation.* Melbourne: Lothian.

Grantham, Martin. 1998. Xerophytic ferns at U.C. Berkeley Botanical Garden. *Hardy Fern Foundation Quarterly* 8 (3): 60–65. Seattle, Washington.

Grillos, Steve J. 1966. *Ferns and Fern Allies of California.* Berkeley, California: University of California Press.

Guiles, Catharine. 1993. Bartholomew's Cobble and the Norcross Wildlife Sanctuary, Massachusetts. *Hardy Fern Foundation Newsletter* 3 (3): 10–11. Seattle, Washington.

Guiles, Catharine W. 2001. The role of the alpine house in the hardy fern garden. *Hardy Fern Foundation Quarterly* 11 (1): 4–9. Seattle, Washington.

Haines, Arthur. 2003. *The Families Huperziaceae and Lycopodiaceae of New England.* Bowdoin, Maine: V. F. Thomas.

Halley, Robin. 1996. Cheilanthoids. *Hardy Fern Foundation Newsletter* 6 (3): 34–37. Seattle, Washington.

Hallowell, Anne C., and Barbara G. Hallowell. 2001. *Fern Finder.* Rochester, New York: Nature Study Guild Publishers.

Hassler, Michael, and Brian Swale. 2002. *World Ferns on CD-ROM.* Christchurch, New Zealand.

Haufler, Christopher, Michael Windham, and Eric Rabe. 1995. Reticulate evolution in the *Polypodium vulgare* complex. *Systematic Botany* 20: 89–109.

Heath, Eric, and R. J. Chinnock. 1974. *Ferns and Fern Allies of New Zealand.* Wellington: A. H. and A. W. Reed.

Hegi, Gustav. 1984. *Illustrierte Flora von Mittel-Europa.* Vol. 1, *Pteridophyta.* Berlin: Paul Parey.

Horrocks, James R. 1990–2005. Fern profile series in *Hardy Fern Foundation Newsletter* and *Quarterly.* Seattle, Washington.

Hoshizaki, Barbara Joe, and Robbin C. Moran. 2001. *Fern Grower's Manual.* Portland, Oregon: Timber Press.

Hutchinson, George, and Barry Thomas. 1996. *Welsh Ferns.* Cardiff, Wales: National Museums and Galleries of Wales.

Ide, Jennifer. 1998. Blechnums in New Zealand. *Pteridologist* 3 (3): 44–47. London: The British Pteridological Society.

Ide, Jennifer, et al., eds. 1992. *Fern Horticulture: Past, Present and Future Perspectives.* The Proceedings of the International Symposium on the Cultivation and Propagation of Pteridophytes. Andover, England: Intercept.

Iwatsuki, Kunio, ed. 1992. *Ferns and Fern Allies of Japan.* Tokyo: Heibonsha.

Iwatsuki, Kunio, et al., eds. 1995. *Flora of Japan.* Vol. 1. Tokyo: Kodansha.

Jermy, Clive, and Josephine Camus. 1991. *The Illustrated Field Guide to Ferns and Allied Plants of the British Isles.* London: Natural History Museum Publications.

Jiao, Yu, and Cheng-Sen Li. 2001. *Yunnan Ferns of China.* China: Science Press.

Jones, David L. 1987. *Encyclopaedia of Ferns.* Portland, Oregon: Timber Press.

Kato, M., T. Suzuki, and N. Nakato. 1991. The systematic status of *Matteuccia* ×*intermedia. The Fern Gazette* 14 (1). London: The British Pteridological Society.

Kaye, Reginald, 1968. *Hardy Ferns.* London: Faber and Faber.

Khullar, S. P. 1994, 2000. *An Illustrated Fern Flora of the West Himalaya.* 2 vols. Dehra Dun, India: International Book Distributors.

Knobloch, Irving W., and Donovan S. Correll. 1962. *Ferns and Fern Allies of Chihuahua, Mexico.* Renner, Texas: Texas Research Foundation.

Kruckeberg, A. R. 1993. Lady fern and male fern—what's in a name. *Hardy Fern Foundation Newsletter* 3 (4): 14. Seattle, Washington.

Kruckeberg, Arthur R., and Mary Robson. 1999. A gardener's lexicon. *Washington Park Arboretum Bulletin* 60: 4. Seattle, Washington.

Large, Mark F., and John E. Braggins. 2004. *Tree Ferns.* Portland, Oregon: Timber Press.

Lellinger, David B. 1985. *A Field Manual of the Ferns and Fern Allies of the United States and Canada.* Washington, D.C.: Smithsonian Institute Press.

Li, Hui-lin, et. al., eds. 1975. *Flora of Taiwan.* Vol. 1. Taipei, Taiwan: Epoch Publishing.

Lowe, Edward J. 1908. *British Ferns and Where Found.* London: Swan Sonnenschein.

Maatsch, Richard. 1980. *Das Buch der Freilandfarne.* Berlin: Paul Parey.

Marticorena, Clodomiro, and Roberto Rodríguez, eds. 1995. *Flora de Chile.* Vol. 1. Concepción, Chile: University of Concepción.

Mattei, Lisa, ed. 2002. Ferns. *Conservation Notes of the New England Wild Flower Society.* Framingham, Massachusetts.

Mehltreter, Klaus, et al. 2003. Moth-damaged giant leather-fern, *Acrostichum danaeifolium,* as host for secondary colonization by ants. *American Fern Journal* 93 (2): 49–55. Oxford, Ohio.

Merryweather, James, ed. 1996. *Pteridologist* 3 (1). London: The British Pteridological Society.

Metcalf, Lawrie. 1993. *The Cultivation of New Zealand Plants.* Auckland: Godwit Press.

Mickel, John T. 1979. *How to Know the Ferns and Fern Allies.* Pictured Key Nature Series. Dubuque, Iowa: William C. Brown.

Mickel, John T. 1994. *Ferns for American Gardens.* New York: Macmillan.

Mickel, John T., and Joseph M. Beitel. 1988. *Pteridophyte Flora of Oaxaca, Mexico.* Bronx, New York: The New York Botanical Garden.

Mickel, John T., and Alan R. Smith. 2004. *The Pteridophytes of Mexico.* Bronx, New York: The New York Botanical Garden.

Montgomery, James D. 1981. *Dryopteris* in North America. *Fiddlehead Forum* 8 (4): 25–31.

Montgomery, James D. 1982. *Dryopteris* in North America. Part 2: the hybrids. *Fiddlehead Forum* 9 (4): 23–30.

Montgomery, James D., and David E. Fairbrothers. 1992. *New Jersey Ferns and Fern Allies.* New Brunswick, New Jersey: Rutgers University Press.

Moore, Thomas. 1869? *British Ferns and Their Allies.* London: George Routledge and Sons.

Moran, Robbin C. 2004. *A Natural History of Ferns.* Portland, Oregon: Timber Press.

Ogden, Alan. 2006. On the beauty of ferns: the psychology of pteridophilia. *Hardy Fern Foundation Quarterly* 16 (2). Seattle, Washington.

Ohwi, Jisaburo. 1965. *Flora of Japan.* Washington, D.C.: Smithsonian Institute Press.

Øllgaard, Benjamin, and Kirsten Tind. 1993. *Scandinavia Ferns.* Copenhagen: Rhodos.

Olsen, Sue, ed. 1998. Special publication on propagation. *Hardy Fern Foundation Newsletter* 8 (2). Seattle, Washington.

Olsen, Sue, ed. 2005. Special publication on hardy garden ferns. *Hardy Fern Foundation Quarterly* 15 (2). Seattle, Washington.

Olson, Wilbur. 1977. *The Fern Dictionary.* Los Angeles: Los Angeles International Fern Society.

Page, Christopher N. 1982. *The Ferns of Britain and Ireland.* Cambridge: Cambridge University Press.

Page, Christopher N. 1988. *Ferns: Their Habitats in the British and Irish Landscape.* London: William Collins.

Palmer, Daniel D. 2003. *Hawai'i's Ferns and Fern Allies.* Honolulu: University of Hawai'i Press.

Parsons, Frances Theodora. 1899. *How to Know the Ferns.* Toronto: The Publishers' Syndicate.

Perrie, L. R., et al. 2003. Evidence for an allopolyploid complex in New Zealand *Polystichum* (Dryopteridaceae). *New Zealand Journal of Botany* 41: 189–215. The Royal Society of New Zealand.

Piggott, A. G., and C. J. Piggott. 1988. *Ferns of Malaysia in Colour.* Kuala Lumpur, Malaysia: Tropical Press.

Plummer, William. 1998. Deer-resistant ferns. *Hardy Fern Foundation Newsletter* 7 (1): 2. Seattle, Washington.

Prelli, Rémy. 2001. *Les Fougères et Plantes Alliées de France et d'Europe Occidentale.* Paris: Belin.

Rickard, Martin. 1997. Cultivation of tree ferns in cold climates. *Hardy Fern Foundation Newsletter* 7 (2): 15. Seattle, Washington.

Rickard, Martin. 2000. *The Plantfinder's Guide to Garden Ferns.* Devon, England: David and Charles; Portland, Oregon: Timber Press.

Roux, J. P. 2000. The genus *Polystichum* in Africa. *Bulletin of the Natural History Museum (Botany)* 30 (2): 33–79. London.

Roux, J. P. 2003. *Swaziland Ferns and Fern Allies.* Southern African Botanical Diversity Network (SABONET) Report No. 19. Pretoria, South Africa: Capture Press.

Rush, Richard. 1984. *A Guide to Hardy Ferns.* London: The British Pteridological Society.

Schenk, George W. 1984. *The Complete Shade Gardener.* Boston: Houghton Mifflin.

Schneider, George. 1890–1894. *The Book of Choice Ferns.* 3 vols. London: L. Upcott Gill.

Schneider, H., K. M. Pryor, R. Cranfill, A. R. Smith, and P. G. Wolf. 2002. Evolution of vascular plant body plans: a phylogenetic perspective. In Q. C. B. Cronk, R. M. Bateman, and J. A. Hawkins, eds., *Developmental Genetics and Plant Evolution*. London: Taylor and Francis. 330–364.

Schwartz, David. 2000. Hunting for xeric ferns in northern California. *Hardy Fern Foundation Quarterly* 10 (2): 30–37. Seattle, Washington.

Scott, John D. 2001. List of state fern floras. *Hardy Fern Foundation Quarterly* 11 (2): 28–37. Seattle, Washington.

Scott, John D. 2003a. Forms of the American Christmas fern—part 1. *Hardy Fern Foundation Quarterly* 13 (1): 25–33. Seattle, Washington.

Scott, John D. 2003b. Forms of the American Christmas fern—part 2. *Hardy Fern Foundation Quarterly* 13 (2): 54–60. Seattle, Washington.

Scott, John D. 2003c. Forms of the American Christmas fern—part 3. *Hardy Fern Foundation Quarterly* 13 (3): 86–96. Seattle, Washington.

Singh, Sarnam, and G. Panigrahi. 2005. *Ferns and Fern Allies of Arunachal Pradesh*. 2 vols. Dehra Dun, India: Bishen Singh Mahendra Pal Singh.

Sleep, Anne. 1998. *Polystichum* ×*dycei*: A new ornamental fern hybrid for the garden. *Pteridologist* 3 (3): 49–55. London: The British Pteridological Society.

Smith, Alan R. 2002. Horsetails and whisk ferns re-examined: when a "fern ally" is really a fern. *Hardy Fern Foundation Quarterly* 12 (1): 4–7. Seattle, Washington.

Sowerby, John E., and Charles Johnson. 1855. *The Ferns of Great Britain*. London: John E. Sowerby.

Stansfield, Abraham. 1858. *Fern Nursery Catalog*. England.

Stoll, Heather M. 2006. The Arctic tells its story. *Nature Magazine* 441 (7093): 579–581.

Stuart, Thomas W. 2002. *Hardy Fern Library*. www.hardyfernlibrary.com.

Stuart, Thomas W. 2005. Apogamous ferns. *Hardy Fern Foundation Quarterly* 15 (3). Seattle, Washington.

Tagawa, Motozi. 1977. *Coloured Illustrations of the Japanese Pteridophyta*. Osaka, Japan: Hoikusha.

Taylor, Thomas M. C. 1970. *Pacific Northwest Ferns and Their Allies*. Toronto: University of Toronto Press in association with the University of British Columbia.

Thorne, Frank, and Libby Thorne. 1989. *Henry Potter's Field Guide to the Hybrid Ferns of the Northeast*. Woodstock, Vermont: Vermont Institute of Natural Science.

Tryon, Alice F., and Robbin C. Moran. 1997. *The Ferns and Allied Plants of New England*. Natural History of New England Series. Lincoln, Massachusetts: Massachusetts Audubon Society.

Wagner, W. Herb. 1998. Producing fern hybrids for hardy garden cultivation. *Hardy Fern Foundation Quarterly* 8 (3): 50–56. Seattle, Washington.

Wang, Peishan, and Xiaoying Wang. 2001. *Pteridophyte Flora of Guizhou*. Guiyang, China: Guizhou Science and Technology.

Wardlaw, Alastair. 2000. Protecting tree ferns in winter. *Hardy Fern Foundation Quarterly* 10 (3): 71–72. Seattle, Washington.

Wherry, Edgar T. 1961. *The Fern Guide*. New York: Doubleday.

Windham, Michael. 1987. *Argyrochosma*, a new genus of cheilanthoid ferns. *American Fern Journal* 77: 37–41.

Two of the many useful Web sites are Integrated Taxonomic Information System (www.itis.usda.gov) and USDA Plant Database (http://plants.usda.gov).

Index of Plant Names

Boldface numbers refer to pages with main entries. *Italic* numbers refer to pages with photographs that are not part of the main entries.

Schizaea, 264, 376
Schizaea pusilla, 55, 376
Scott's spleenwort, see *Asplenium ebenoides*
scouring rush, see *Equisetum hyemale*
sea anemone fern, see *Pteris actiniopteris*
sea spleenwort, see *Asplenium marinum*
Selaginella, 205, 260, 262, 264, 376–383
Selaginella apoda, 377
Selaginella bigelovii, 381
Selaginella borealis, 377–378
Selaginella braunii, 378
Selaginella caulescens, see *S. involvens*
Selaginella convoluta, 377
Selaginella densa, 381
Selaginella douglasii, 378
Selaginella erythropus, 381
Selaginella helvetica, 381, 382
Selaginella involvens, 378
Selaginella kraussiana, 377, 378–379
　'Aurea', 379
　'Brownii', 379
　'Gold Tips', 379
Selaginella martensii, 381
　f. *albovariegata*, 381, *382*
Selaginella moellendorffii, 379
Selaginella nipponica, 382
Selaginella oregana, 379–381
Selaginella pallescens, 382
Selaginella rupestris, 382
Selaginella sanguinolenta, 382
　var. *compressa*, 378, 382
Selaginella siberica, 382
Selaginella stauntoniana, 382
Selaginella tamariscina, 382–383
Selaginella uncinata, 380, 381
Selaginella wallacei, 381
Selaginella wallichii, 382, 383
Selaginella watsonii, 383
Selaginella willdenovii, 383
sensitive fern, see *Onoclea sensibilis*
shaggy shield fern, see *Dryopteris cycadina*
shaggy wood fern, see *Dryopteris cycadina*
Shasta fern, see *Polystichum lemmonii*
shining spleenwort, see *Asplenium oblongifolium*
shore spleenwort, see *Asplenium obtusatum*
Siebold's wood fern, see *Dryopteris sieboldii*
sierra cliff brake, see *Pellaea brachyptera*
sierra water fern, see *Thelypteris nevadensis*
silver cloak fern, see *Cheilanthes argentea*
silver dollar fern, see *Adiantum peruvianum*
silver fern, see *Cyathea dealbata, Pityrogramma calomelanos*
silver lady, see *Blechnum gibbum*
silver staghorn, see *Platycerium veitchii*
silvery glade fern, see *Deparia acrostichoides*
silvery spleenwort, see *Deparia acrostichoides*
single sorus spleenwort, see *Asplenium monanthes*
Sitka clubmoss, see *Diphasiastrum sitchense*

slender fragile fern, see *Cystopteris tenuis*
slender lip fern, see *Cheilanthes feei*
slender rock brake, see *Cryptogramma stelleri*
smooth cliff brake, see *Pellaea glabella*
smooth cliff fern, see *Woodsia glabella*
smooth rock spleenwort, see *Asplenium fontanum*
smooth scouring rush, see *Equisetum laevigatum*
soft shield fern, see *Polystichum setiferum*
soft tree fern, see *Cyathea smithii*
southern adder's tongue fern, see *Ophioglossum vulgatum*
southern beech fern, see *Phegopteris hexagonoptera*
southern brittle fern, see *Cystopteris protrusa*
southern lady fern, see *Athyrium filix-femina* subsp.
　asplenioides
southern maiden fern, see *Thelypteris kunthii*
southern maidenhair, see *Adiantum capillus-veneris*
southern polypody, see *Polypodium cambricum*
southern running pine, see *Diphasiastrum digitatum*
southern wood fern, see *Dryopteris ludoviciana*
southwestern brittle fern, see *Cystopteris reevesiana*
Sphaeropteris cooperi, see *Cyathea cooperi*
Sphaeropteris horrida, see *Cyathea princeps*
Sphaeropteris medullaris, see *Cyathea medullaris*
Sphenomeris, 384
Sphenomeris retusa, 384
spider brake, see *Pteris multifida*
spikemoss, see *Selaginella*
spinulose lady fern, see *Athyrium spinulosum*
spinulose wood fern, see *Dryopteris carthusiana*
staghorn fern, see *Platycerium*
star-scaled cloak fern, see *Astrolepis*
strap water fern, see *Blechnum patersonii*
Struthiopteris pensylvanica, see *Matteuccia struthiopteris*
sunset fern, see *Dryopteris lepidopoda*
Syngonium hoffmanii, 384

Tagawa's holly fern, see *Polystichum tagawanum*
tapering fern, see *Thelypteris noveboracensis*
Tasmanian tree fern, see *Dicksonia antarctica*
tassel fern, see *Polystichum polyblepharum*
tatting fern, see *Athyrium filix-femina* 'Frizelliae'
Tennessee bladder fern, see *Cystopteris tennesseensis*
Thelypteris, 55, 65, 77, 262, 296, 385–389
Thelypteris beddomei, **388–389**
Thelypteris decursive-pinnata, see *Phegopteris decursive-pinnata*
Thelypteris hexagonoptera, see *Phegopteris hexagonoptera*
Thelypteris kunthii, 385, **386**
Thelypteris limbosperma, see *T. quelpaertensis*
Thelypteris nevadensis, **386**, 387
Thelypteris normalis, see *T. kunthii*
Thelypteris noveboracensis, **386–387**, 389
Thelypteris oreopteris, see *T. quelpaertensis*
Thelypteris ovata, **389**
　var. *lindheimeri*, **389**
Thelypteris palustris, 387, 388, 401
　var. *pubescens*, **387**